Gabriel Fauré: a musical life

GABRIEL FAURÉ
a musical life

Jean-Michel Nectoux

translated by Roger Nichols

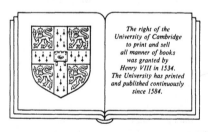

The right of the
University of Cambridge
to print and sell
all manner of books
was granted by
Henry VIII in 1534.
The University has printed
and published continuously
since 1584.

CAMBRIDGE UNIVERSITY PRESS

CAMBRIDGE
NEW YORK   PORT CHESTER
MELBOURNE   SYDNEY

PUBLISHED BY THE PRESS SYNDICATE OF THE UNIVERSITY OF CAMBRIDGE
The Pitt Building, Trumpington Street, Cambridge, United Kingdom

CAMBRIDGE UNIVERSITY PRESS
The Edinburgh Building, Cambridge CB2 2RU, UK
40 West 20th Street, New York NY 10011–4211, USA
477 Williamstown Road, Port Melbourne, VIC 3207, Australia
Ruiz de Alarcón 13, 28014 Madrid, Spain
Dock House, The Waterfront, Cape Town 8001, South Africa

http://www.cambridge.org

First published 1991
First paperback edition 2004

A catalogue record for this book is available from the British Library

Library of Congress cataloguing in publication data
Nectoux, Jean-Michel.
Gabriel Fauré: a musical life/Jean-Michel Nectoux; translated
by Roger Nichols.
    p. cm.
Includes bibliographical references.
ISBN 0 521 23524 3 hardback
1. Fauré, Gabriel, 1845–1924. 2. Composers – France – Biography.
I. Title.
ML410.F7N43   1990
780′.92 – dc20   90–1530   CIP   MN
[B]

ISBN 0 521 23524 3 hardback
ISBN 0 521 61695 6 paperback

The French original version is published by Flammarion, 26 rue
Racine, 75006 Paris, 1990, with the title Gabriel *Fauré: les voix du
clair-obscur*

For Colette Ledran
and to the memory of
Vladimir Jankélévitch
in token of my gratitude

Tanta dolcezza avea
più l'aere e'l vento

Petrarch, Sonnet 123

Contents

x   Contents

Illustrations

xi

Plates 1, 3, 7, 10, 11, 18, 26, 33, 51, 53, 54, 63 come from the archives of Gabriel Fauré given to the Bibliothèque Nationale, Music Department, by the Fauré-Fremiet family.

Prelude

I have often been asked, during the many years I have spent in research on Fauré, the basic question: why Fauré? The way this question was asked often contained, as well as curiosity, a touch of astonishment, even of regret, that I should have devoted so much time and effort to a man still often considered as a marginal or minor composer . . .

On reflection, I would say that I did not choose to work on Fauré, but rather that his music slowly took me over and caught me in its toils.

The first book on music that I bought was Vladimir Jankélévitch's *Ravel* and I have to admit that since that time my fascination with Ravel, the man and the composer, has remained intact. But I did not dare to begin researching on him: the timidity of youth dissuaded me from trying to continue the labours of Jankélévitch and Roland-Manuel, who at that time stood as the *nec plus ultra* of Ravel scholarship, and I did not envisage the possibility of adopting another point of view, another way of tackling such a lofty subject. I will not hide the fact that I still feel Ravel's sensibility as being close to mine – and not only close, but familiar: an exhibition (Paris, 1975), radio interviews, notably with Pierre Boulez (1985), various articles and an album of historic records (1987) are witnesses to my enthusiasm – and sometimes I regret this lack of daring.

Even so, some works of Fauré had for years been exercising their charms on me, and the impression they made was all the more powerful for their being inaccessibly lodged in long distant memory; it needed only a new encounter for all these old impressions to be revived with a force I had thought exhausted. Thus the *Cantique de Jean Racine* speaks to me of childhood: 'Les Berceaux' and 'Automne' bring back the one-time adolescent so wisely and enthusiatically guided by Colette Ledran, who was in charge of a 'music option' for the students of the Lycée in Montgeron and introduced them to Mozart (*Le nozze di Figaro*), Beethoven (*An die ferne Geliebte*), Debussy (*Pelléas*), Fauré . . .

I must confess that it was some years before I fully appreciated Fauré's songs, kept at a distance probably by the old-fashioned look of some of the poems and by the extreme sophistication of the French *mélodie* itself. I found it easier to come to terms with the Requiem, the incidental music and the piano works, and the chamber music especially, which I discovered at the same time as Brahms's, joined with reading Proust as the main enthusiasms of my twentieth year. I decided to make Fauré's chamber music the subject of a study which would give for each work a clear historical background, a formal, thematic analysis – inspired by Claude Rostand's fine book on Brahms – and an anthology of critical writings.

The historical part of my project soon came up against the vague and often contradictory nature of the information relayed in the ten or so monographs devoted to the composer. Large grey areas remained in the catalogue of works marshalled by Fauré's younger son, Philippe Fauré-Fremiet, as an appendix to the second (1957) edition of the book which he had written on his father in 1929. He had also published in 1954 an invaluable collection of Fauré's letters to his wife, under the title *Lettres intimes*. This well documented book was proof that only by returning to the original sources – to letters, but also to musical manuscripts – could one escape from the narrow circle of the composer's bibliography which had been based, over a period of nearly a century, on the information given by Fauré to his earliest biographers, mistakes and all.

I began my research, at that time restricted to the letters and manuscripts relevant to the chamber music, and this brought me into contact with Mme Philippe Fauré-Fremiet, the composer's daughter-in-law. She was still living in the apartment on the rue des Vignes where the composer had spent his final years, and she welcomed this timid student with a warmth and a sympathy which at the time seemed to me perfectly natural. Today I am better placed to appreciate my good fortune.

This lucky meeting combined with the march of History to expedite my first attempts. The events of May 1968 left the energies which I had been harnessing towards my final law examinations at a loose end and opened up a vista of unoccupied time which would end who knew when. The general assemblies broke up in disorder, so, keeping an anxious ear open to the latest manifestations, I pursued my study of Fauré's chamber music. Paris was soon deserted, with no *métro*, no petrol and no pump attendants, and I used up my last precious litres of fuel crossing the spectral city to go and work in the rue des Vignes.

During the many hours I spent in the large studio, Blanche Fauré-Fremiet tirelessly made available to me the archive which she had inherited directly from the composer; several hundred letters, sixty or so musical manuscripts, documents and original iconography, not to mention souvenirs and portraits which filled the apartment and whose history she was able to tell me.

Her constant encouragement, her approachability and her friendly solicitude were an enormous help in getting my research under way, and I was all the keener to pursue it because it fitted in with my parallel interest in the work of Marcel Proust; the Paris society dreamed of by Proust before he came to know it was the very one in which Fauré himself developed. The only letter from Proust to Fauré preserved in the composer's archive symbolised the union of the two areas of my research and I traced the relationship between the two in an article 'Proust et Fauré' in 1970.

Meanwhile my work on the chamber music had progressed some way, but I put it to one side for good when I was commissioned to write the volume on Fauré for the 'Solfège' series of paperbacks produced by Editions du Seuil. This, as well as being an opportunity, was also a challenge for a totally inexperienced author of twenty-three, whose first book was to appear in the very same collection as Jankélévitch's *Ravel*.

At the start of my research, Blanche Fauré had been kind and thoughtful enough to introduce me to Vladimir Jankélévitch and now, when I look back on those early years, it is this meeting which seems to me to have been the crucial event. Despite his unparalleled knowledge of Fauré, he never imposed his own point of view but, on the contrary, wanted to know mine; and even though he disapproved of certain aspects of my research methods, which were aimed at establishing precise facts and attaining a measure of historical truth – difficult as that may be – he never tried to turn me from them. Instead, he welcomed me with a generosity, a warmth, an enquiring spirit and an accuracy of speech which made my visits to him unforgettable, chatting over a cup of Russian tea in the famous study with books up to the ceiling, leaving only the window free through which the apse of Notre-Dame could be spied in the dusk.

Jankélévitch was a profound influence on the development of my approach from one that was strictly analytical or historical to one that allowed ample room for sociology and above all for aesthetics. This influence is obvious in the little 'Solfège' monograph, published in 1972, but is to be found on a still deeper level in the thesis 'Gabriel Fauré et le théâtre', which I wrote under his guidance and presented in 1980, and in the present book.

The publication of the initial monograph made clear the need for work on a broader basis, encompassing the whole of his output and involving systematic research on original documents; they alone could form a solid basis for future efforts. In the course of twenty years' research in public and private collections in Europe and North America, I have studied about a hundred and twenty of Fauré's musical manuscripts and more than three thousand of his autograph letters.

Not all this correspondence is of equal interest: the telephone was still a rarity and the contents of the *pneumatiques*, which fulfilled a parallel function, are often dull or incomprehensible. I chose four hundred of the letters for publication. On the advice of Yves Gérard, to whom I owe a large part of my strictly musicological training, I began by publishing the complete correspondence between Saint-Saëns and his pupil Fauré, covering a period of sixty years, and in a number of articles I brought out letters between Fauré and such major creative artists as Ravel, Debussy, Albéniz and Flaubert. In 1980, I published an anthology of more than two hundred letters (G. Fauré: *Correspondance*) forming a kind of autobiography of the composer built up through his contacts with friends. It was in fact translated into English in 1984 as *Gabriel Fauré, His Life through his Letters*. My other work in the field of Fauré studies has included a discography in 1979, listing all the recordings of his works made between 1900 and 1977; an album of historical records and a small travelling exhibition in 1974; some twenty articles, lectures and an edition of the Requiem in both its versions.

One reason for the extent of this involvement was that there was a battle to be fought on behalf of a composer who was unjustly looked down on. Nothing stirs the energies of youth like the notion of defending a noble cause . . . With hindsight, I realise that all this activity had in it an element of unreality: there is value in making a composer's works known, but it is the music and only the music that bears within it its own destiny, depending on the workings of chance and on changes in tastes and fashions. Our contemporaries will only ever adopt the music which speaks to them and which fulfils their needs.

The French always like attaching labels to things, and my sustained interest in music soon led to my being regarded as a 'Fauré specialist'. So I should like to say that, both through choice and through my jobs at the Bibliothèque Nationale and now at the Musée d'Orsay, I have worked not only on Proust and Ravel, as I have mentioned, but also on Debussy, Stravinsky, Falla, Honegger, Mallarmé, the Ballets russes and Mahler. These studies which, being directed towards the setting up of exhibitions, tended to be angled towards iconography, allowed me to put my work on Fauré into some kind of perspective and to avoid the dangers of a narrow monomania! I have to admit that nowadays I no longer have any great desire to hear Fauré's music, no doubt because I know it too thoroughly, but I also have to confess that when I hear it, on the radio or in the concert hall, I find that its emotional power remains unaltered.

In the present book I have tried to present a summary of my ideas and to make a synthesis of the somewhat piecemeal labours of these twenty years. The initial proposal for the volume came from Michael Black, then editor at the Cambridge University Press, who first suggested the idea in principle and then, in 1976, gave me a firm commission. Basically it is a biography, but I wanted to avoid the division into 'life' and 'works' which, apart from being unsubtle and artificial, makes it almost impossible to avoid tedious repetitions. I have therefore proceeded along chronological lines, but with frequent breaks where it was natural to pursue some particular topic. So I have not followed the composer step by step, as in the classic biographies, but I have chosen to vary my approach, which may be either analytical, historical or aesthetic or may even, briefly, turn towards the essay form.

The basic facts of Fauré's life will be found in linear, chronological layout at the end of the book (p. 501).

As for the catalogue of works, since the one drawn up by Philippe Fauré-Fremiet followed the order of opus numbers, and the one I published in 1980 in *The New Grove Dictionary* was organised by types of work, I have chosen this time to observe the chronological order of composition. This order will undoubtedly be revised as a result of future research, because the dating of Fauré's works during the first fifteen or twenty years of his composing life is hard to establish. Few letters of his survive from the period between 1860 and 1875 and he did not date his letters until his last years. His musical manuscripts, on the other hand, often carry dates, but few of them survive from these years because Fauré was in the habit of giving them away to interpreters, friends or relations, usually without bothering to keep a copy. In a letter written late in life to Roger Ducasse, Fauré admitted that for years he paid no attention to maintaining an archive of his own music. His characteristic casualness and the lukewarm opinion he had of himself combined to lay many a trap for his biographers.

With the chronology of Fauré research now more or less established, it remains to study the music in depth. In this book, which deals with the whole of Fauré's output, I have had to discuss most of his works only briefly, including information on form and thematic treatment that will, I hope, help readers to appreciate pieces some of which are little known. A start is at last being made to publish the critical editions that are indispensable. Some idea of the discoveries yet to be made in the field of Fauré autographs in private collections can be gained from the fact that we have still not found the manuscripts of such well-known works as the Ballade (the version for piano solo), *Thème et variations*, 'Clair de lune', 'Après un rêve', 'Les Berceaux' and the Trio. Fauré research is only at its beginning.

Acknowledgments

I should like to thank the individuals and the institutions who have responded so kindly and who have been invaluable in helping my research. First of all, my thanks go to the Fauré-Fremiet, Risler, Ceillier and Maspéro families who, since I began my studies, have bequeathed their valuable archives to the Music Department of the Bibliothèque Nationale. As a result, between 1978 and 1985 the state collections received autographs of around two-thirds of Fauré's output, as well as more than a thousand letters to and from the composer.

I am grateful to the Fondation Singer Polignac and its president, M. Etienne Wolf, who gave me a grant to help with my research in the United States. I also thank particularly the families who gave me access to their unpublished archives: Albéniz-Ciganer, Baugnies de Saint-Marceaux, Blacque Belair, N. Boulanger, Castelbon de Beauxhostes, Clerc, Cortot, Delaquerrière, Dumora-Messager, Emmanuel, Fauchois, Fraysse-Hasselmans, Gentil, Gounod, M. Grey, Julia (Chausson), M. Kahn, Koechlin, Krettly, de Labeau (R. Lortat), Laloy, Lerolle, Lecesne (Viardot), Mouquet Derville (Samain), Nussy Saint-Saëns, Ollivier (Polignac), de Pengüern, Réglade (R. Ducasse), Roulleaux-Dugage, Samaran (Taffanel), Trélat, Viardot, Ysaÿe.

Among the many people who gave me help and advice, I should like to thank: Mr Otto Edwin Albrecht (Philadelphia), M. Pierre Auclert, M. Olivier Bernard, M. D. Buffeteau, M. Thierry Bodin, Mme G. Thibaut de Chambure, Mr H. Robert Cohen (University of Maryland), Mr Herbert Cohen (Westport), Mimi S. Daitz (New York), M. Roger Delage, M. Jean-Jacques Eigeldinger (Geneva), M. Joël-Marie Fauquet, M. Vladimir Fédorov, Mme Jacqueline Gachet, M. Yves Gérard, Mme H. Gouin, Dr Gumbacher (Basle), M. Joachim Havard de la Montagne, Mr Kern Holoman (Davis), M. Jean-Claude Honegger (Geneva), Mr Charles Jacob (North Bergen), M. Stefan Jarocínsky (Warsaw), M. Vladimir Jankélévitch, Miss Ellen Knight (Arlington), Pr Louis Krasner (Brookline, Bos-

François Lesure, Mr Ralph P. Locke (Rochester), Mr David Mackibbin
(Boston), M. Jean-Marie Martin (Hollogne-aux-Pierres, Belgium), Mr
Hans Moldenauer (Spokane), Mr Roger Nichols (Leominster), Mr Arbie
Orenstein (New York), Mr Robert Orledge (Liverpool), Mr Richard
Ormond (London), M. Peyrotte, M. Max Reis (Zurich), M. Ludovic de
San (Brussels), Mr Lionel Sawkins (Beckenham), M. Jean de Solliers, M.
Alexandre Siguitov (Moscow), M. Gérard Souzay, Mr Robin C. Tait
(North Humberside), M. Jean Touzelet, M. Alex van Amerongen (Rotter-
dam), M. Robert J. Van Nuffel (Brussels), M. Alexandre Zviguilsky.

The publishers Durand, Hamelle, Heugel, Schirmer. The manuscript
dealers 'Les Argonautes', H. Baron, Th. Bodin, Coulet et Faure, M. Loliée,
R. Macnutt, Guido Morssen, Albi Rosenthal.

I thank my wife Isabelle for the long hours of uninterrupted work she
was able to ensure for me and for her excellent advice, my translator and
friend Roger Nichols who has patiently followed the long gestation of this
book, and the staff of Cambridge University Press: Rosemary Dooley,
Penny Souster, Linda Matthews and Rachel Neaman.

Finally, I should like to express my gratitude to the librarians and staff of
the institutions who have allowed me access to their archives and valuable
collections and, for the most part, made it easy for me:

BELGIUM
Brussels: Académie des Beaux-Arts; Bibliothèque royale Albert Ier;
    Bibliothèque du Conservatoire
Liège: Bibliothèque du Conservatoire
Ghent: Fondation M. Maeterlinck

CANADA
Montreal: McGill University Libraries

DENMARK
Copenhagen: Mekanisk Museum

FRANCE
Carcasonne: Bibliothèque Municipale
Chantilly: Bibliothèque Spoelberch de Lovenjoul
Dieppe: Musée (Archives Saint-Saëns)
Muret: Archives municipales
Paris: Archives Nationales; Archives de la Seine; Bibliothèque et Archives
    de l'Institut de France; Bibliothèque Nationale; Bibliothèque de la

Société des Auteurs et Compositeurs Dramatiques; Archives de la Société des Auteurs, Compositeurs et Editeurs de Musique

GERMAN DEMOCRATIC REPUBLIC
Berlin: Deutsche Staatsbibliothek

GREAT BRITAIN
Brentford: Musical Museum
London: The British Institute of Recorded Sound; The British Library; J. B. Cramer and Co; Delius Trust; Theatre Museum (Victoria and Albert)
Oxford: Bodleian Library

MONACO: Théâtre de Monte-Carlo (Archives de la Société des Bains de Mer)

SPAIN
Barcelona: Biblioteca central de Cataluña

SWEDEN
Stockholm: Stiftelsen Framjande Musikkulturens

SWITZERLAND
Geneva: Bibliothèque du Conservatoire
Lausanne: Bibliothèque cantonale et universitaire

UNITED STATES
Austin: Humanities Research Center, The University of Texas
Boston: Isabella Stewart Gardner Museum
Cambridge, Mass.: The Houghton Library, Harvard University
Chicago: University Library
New Haven: Yale University Library
New York: Pierpont Morgan Library; New York Public Library at the Lincoln Center
Rochester: Eastman School of Music
Washington: The Library of Congress

The music examples were prepared on computer by M. Christian Roy (Versailles)

1 Gradus ad Parnassum

In 1845 France was entering a period of industrial and colonial development that was to make her, with Britain, one of the richest and most
powerful nations in the world. The previous half-century had been the
most disturbed of her entire political history. Even if Louis-Philippe's reign
was shortly to come to an end, the lesson of 1789 was not to be completely
grasped and assimilated until 1871 when defeat in the Franco–Prussian
War finally put paid to dreams of returning to the monarchy or the
Empire.

The desire for power shown by the bourgeoisie in 1789 had been no
more than a flash in the pan. Those institutions which had been brought
into being by the Revolution evolved towards a gradual reconcentration of
power, and Napoleon's vision of a France that could hold its own on the
European stage had done no more than mask this process. Louis XVIII had
wanted to fashion a constitutional monarchy on the English model, but the
idea did not survive his restoration which, though rejecting absolutism,
made no secret about giving power back to the land-owning aristocracy.
The 1848 Revolution, and the deceptively grandiose façade of the Second
Empire, were the harbingers of the bourgeoisie's final achievement of a
power that would last. It was a power carefully graded according to merit,
from the village schoolteacher at one end of the scale to the government
minister at the other, and work was its new religion, closely allied with the
idea of progress – whether collective progress in the sense of the nation's
material possessions and influence, or individual progress measured in
terms of social advancement. This opening-out of French society, so
accurately captured by Balzac, is well illustrated by the history of Fauré's
family.

The name 'Fauré', pronounced 'Faoure' in the Provençal dialect, belongs to a very old family in the Pyrenean district of the Midi, appearing as
early as the thirteenth century in the list of the parishes in the Toulouse
area. The composer was descended from the branch that settled at

Varilhes, near Foix, in the middle of the fifteenth century. Its members were bourgeois land-owners of considerable means. A number of birth certificates dating from the seventeenth century show the noble 'de' before the 'Fauré', but this prefix died out gradually as the family became poorer, probably owing to the repeated division of land with each new generation.[1]

The composer's paternal grandfather, already bearing the name Gabriel Fauré, was following his own father's trade as a butcher in Foix when Toussaint-Honoré, the composer's father, was born there on 8 October 1810. The composer's maternal grandfather, Germain Lalène, born and buried at Gailhac-Toulza in the district of Toulouse, had reached the rank of captain in the course of his service with Napoleon's army. With the Restoration of 1815 he went back to using his full name, Germain de Lalène-Laprade. His daughter Marie-Antoinette-Hélène (born 9 January 1809) did not let this title of the minor nobility prevent her from marrying Toussaint Fauré in 1829; he had broken with his family's business tradition and was beginning his professional life as a schoolmaster at Gailhac-Toulza.

Beneath his side-whiskers Toussaint Fauré was a strict and dignified man, the archetypal dedicated government servant. He was formal in his manners and conscientious in performing his duty, all the more so since his schoolmaster's post was what gave him his place in society. Being an energetic conformist, he could look forward to a fine career as a man of standing in the area, a pillar of the Establishment from the time of the Restoration to that of the Second Empire. He became assistant inspector of primary education at Pamiers in 1839, inspector in 1847, and in 1849 he was appointed director of the Teachers' Training School at Montgauzy, on the way to Foix. He was in Corsica for a short time and ended his career at Tarbes.

Toussaint was the first of the family to graduate to government employment, and he set a powerful example:[2] his five sons and his brother-in-law all saw government service at one time or another. Amand (1834–1918) was the eldest of his sons and his career was both successful and varied. At twenty-one he became a tax official, but left the world of finance in 1863 to study law. He soon came to the notice of the Imperial regime due to his militantly republican opinions which brought him into the ranks of reforming journalists. From 1865 to 1877 he was political correspondent for several newspapers, both in Paris and in the provinces, even acquiring a printing works in 1877. His independence and his political attitudes led to all kinds of problems and worries, both under the Empire and in the years after the defeat of 1870. In Constantine he founded *Le Progrès de l'Algé-rie*, only to see the paper banned by General MacMahon at the end of 1869.

He returned to Paris, worked on *Le Réveil* and collaborated with Pierre Larousse in editing the law articles in the *Grand dictionnaire universel du XIXe siècle*. When the Republic was finally established, his fidelity to its principles and his talents as a publicist earned him entry into the prefecto-rial system in 1877. He was sub-prefect at Murat, Louhans and Tournon, and was appointed prefect of the Ardèche in 1883. He was married and had two children, but led an openly riotous life, drinking heavily, acquir-ing a succession of mistresses, accumulating large debts with tradesmen, to the point that in 1885 he asked to be released from his duties. He was dismissed the following year.

He returned to journalism and managed to satisfy his creditors, but by the time his dismissal was revoked by President Carnot in 1890 he was ill and could not take up any administrative post. He retired to Toulouse.

His brother Paul's life was as adventurous as it was brief. Born in 1835 or 1836, he joined Napoleon III's army, went through the Italian cam-paign and was made an officer; then he took part in an expeditionary force to China and died in Algiers of yellow fever at the age of thirty.

Fernand (1837–1918) followed, on the other hand, the moderate, worthy lifestyle of his father. He was a brilliant pupil at the Ecole normale supérieure and was appointed as a teacher of mathematics at the Lycée in Tarbes. He then became a school inspector successively at Gap, Perpignan and Pau, where he retired in 1902.

Albert (1840–1908) became an officer in the Marines. He too took part in expeditions to China and the fever he caught there was responsible for his early retirement. Rose-Elodie-Gabrielle (1830–95), known as Vic-toire, was the eldest of the six children and the only girl and her husband, Casimir Fontes, succeeded his father-in-law as head of the Ecole normale in Montgauzy. Gabriel was fifteen years younger than her, the Benjamin of the family. His career may have followed quite different paths from the rest, but even so he too spent long years as a government employee – the material benefits of which have to be set against the consumption of time that might have been spent in composition.

According to his mother, Gabriel's arrival was unplanned but he was brought up in the same way as the others. He was born at 4 o'clock in the morning on 12 May 1845 at Pamiers (Ariège) and was called Gabriel after his father's father, and Urbain after an uncle on his mother's side. Gabriel-Urbain Fauré was registered at the *mairie* and baptised in the church of Notre-Dame du Camp, close to the house where he was born, at 17 rue

Major. The baby was sent out to a wet-nurse at Verniolle, near Varilhe, which had been the family base since the end of the Middle Ages. In 1849 the whole family moved to the Ecole normale in Montgauzy, a vast building, recently put up on the road out of Foix on the ruins of an old convent, and backed on to by a chapel which was a place of pilgrimage for the local inhabitants. Gabriel spent many hours there as a boy and found his way towards music by improvising on the harmonium. He was later to remember[3] that 'an old blind lady' had given him some basic instruction. His brothers spent the school terms at the lycée, but then Gabriel had the forty boarders of the Ecole normale as companions in the large house. Even so, as Fauré later confided to his wife:[4] 'already as a child . . . I tended, so my parents said, to be preoccupied and silent'.

'He would be sent to spend the summer at Verniolle with his nurse', wrote Philippe Fauré-Fremiet.[5] 'The old *curé* of the neighbouring village of Rieucros was a friend of the family and he used to come and fetch my father in a pony and trap to spend two or three days with him. The boy was free to do what he liked, was given the run of the church and had the old man at his beck and call . . . It looked then as though Gabriel Fauré might become a priest.' The whole of his early childhood was steeped in this solitary, clerical atmosphere.

It is more than likely that the young men who were training to be teachers at Montgauzy received some musical instruction. We know, from a letter of Toussaint Fauré published by his grandson,[6] that the Ecole normale did have a piano, and it is reasonable to imagine that someone there showed him how to put his fingers on the keyboard – perhaps one Bernard Delgay, who later claimed the honour of being his first teacher during the years in question.[7] At all events, by the summer of 1853 Gabriel, then aged eight, had made enough progress for his father to ask him to play for a visitor, Simon-Lucien Dufaur de Saubiac, a senior civil servant in the Chamber of Deputies[8] (or *Palais législatif*, as it was known in the Second Empire). So far the young Gabriel's musical gifts had not been taken seriously. He went to primary school like all children of his age and the piano, or the harmonium, was just a harmless diversion. 'My father', he said in 1922,

... was surprised to discover my leanings towards music as there was no musician in my family. My talent showed itself before I was ten, and at such an early stage no one worried about any possible effect on my future. A little later on there were perhaps doubts about my adopting music as a career. Anyway my father was undecided – I was the sixth child in the family and he couldn't afford to take risks.

(*Excelsior*, 12 June 1922)

The boy's career was determined by M. Dufaur de Saubiac, who advised
that he should be entered for the new school of religious music which was
then being founded by Louis Niedermeyer. Toussaint-Honoré, after a
year's reflection, decided to accept his advice. The curriculum included the
'humanities' as well as musical instruction, and boarders were supported
by the Ministry of Fine Arts and Religious Culture to the tune of thirty-six
bursaries of 500 francs each – the annual boarding fees were 1,000 francs
for each child. Because of Toussaint-Honoré's family commitments he had
to pay only a quarter of the boarding fees.

Louis Niedermeyer (1802–61), Swiss by birth, had received an exten-
sive European musical education. In Vienna he sat at the feet of the great
virtuoso Ignaz Moscheles, and made the acquaintance of ancient polyphonic music in Rome, where the tradition lived on (after a fashion),[9] by
working with Valentino Fioraventi, the choirmaster of the Papal Chapel.
Finally, he spent time in Naples studying operatic technique with Rossini.
Their friendship developed to the point where Rossini entrusted him with
the arrangement of some of his earlier operas to satisfy the incessant
demands of the Neapolitan theatres. Back in France Niedermeyer first
made a name as a composer. But his various attempts at opera were
unsuccessful and his reputation was built on fashionable romances and
ballads. They may seem very dated nowadays but Niedermeyer shows
himself to have been a man of literary taste: his choice of texts by outstanding contemporary poets like Hugo and Lamartine was to have an influence
on Gounod.

Nonetheless the name 'Niedermeyer' is indissolubly linked with the
renaissance of religious music in France. Church choirs had almost entirely
disappeared during the 1789 Revolution. Their subsequent revival had
been hampered by the confiscation of clerical property and that of the
emigré nobility who had supported them in the past. Services in the Chapel
Royal itself did not survive the Revolution of 1830, and the Royal School
of Religious Music, founded by Alexandre Choron in 1817, was dis-
banded at his death in 1834. Despite these unfavourable circumstances,
Louis Niedermeyer founded a 'Society of Vocal and Religious Music' in
1840, with the help of his 'pupil' Prince de la Moskowa. This Society
performed sixteenth- and seventeenth-century works, and from 1843
these were published in an eleven-volume anthology.

The details of these performances did not, understandably, conform all
that closely to modern musicological practice, containing as they did
tempo indications (generally slow), dynamic markings and so-called 'corrections' of the harmony. Even so we must acknowledge Niedermeyer as a

pioneer in the rediscovery of polyphonic music in France, fifty years before the famous performances of the Chanteurs de St-Gervais, conducted by Charles Bordes and so much admired by Debussy. To appreciate Niedermeyer's boldness we only have to hear the ridiculously naïve and banal stuff churned out at that same period by Alfred Lefébure-Wély on the organ of the Madeleine; his repertoire shows the depths to which religious music had fallen by succumbing to the infectious influence of the theatre. We can nowadays hardly imagine the extent to which the theatre dominated musical life, nor was it always the best theatre music that found its way into the churches.

If these degenerate practices were to be rooted out, reforms had to take place in the training of organists and choirmasters – a necessity already identified by Choron. In 1853 Niedermeyer persuaded Napoleon III to recognise the small boarding-school he had just founded, under the official title 'School of Classical and Religious Music'. It became better known under its later name, the Niedermeyer School. Its aim was to train organists and choirmasters who could then be employed by the bishops of each diocese. Gabriel Fauré was admitted in 1854, at the age of nine, as a scholar under the patronage of the Bishop of Pamiers. A report written by the director in that very year gives details of the curriculum.[10] Apart from the traditional subjects (*solfège*, harmony, counterpoint) the emphasis was on instrumental performance (organ and piano). Alfred Bruneau, in his tribute to Fauré (Paris, 1925), mentioned the fifteen pianos congregated in a single classroom. We learn also from Niedermeyer that students had access to a pedal piano and an organ with twelve stops. The organ repertoire included works by Bach, Mendelssohn and the Belgian composer Lemmens – who had been hailed somewhat prematurely as the Bach of the nineteenth century; the piano teaching was based on Bach, Mozart and Beethoven. Fauré's organ teachers were Xavier Wackenthaler and particularly Clément Loret but, as we shall see, the young student does not seem to have been greatly inspired by the instrument. The best exam result he achieved on it was a lowly 'accessit' in 1863.

On the piano, however, he proved to be a pupil of exceptional talent. Under Wackenthaler and Niedermeyer himself he won a first prize in 1860, followed by another first prize the next year and by a prize with distinction in 1862; by this time he was a pupil of that great virtuoso Saint-Saëns. In 1864 he was even refused permission to compete.[11] He was equally successful on the technical side, winning a prize for *solfège* (1857) and for harmony (1860) in spite of the sour disposition of his teacher Louis Dietsch (Dietsch was choirmaster at the Madeleine and a conductor at the

Opera – he conducted the notorious Paris performances of *Tannhäuser* and wrote an opera on the libretto for *The Flying Dutchman* which Wagner had discarded). Fauré left the school in 1865 with a first prize in counterpoint and fugue, gained under the supervision of the young Eugène Gigout.

Apart from its methods of harmony teaching, which will be discussed later, the Niedermeyer School is notable for the time it gave to choral singing. Three times a week all the students came together under Louis Dietsch to sing Josquin, Palestrina, Bach and Vittoria, usually unaccompanied. The secular repertoire was sung only on student walks. Niedermeyer himself wrote a considerable amount for his school choir which regularly sang services at the church of St-Louis d'Antin, in the 9th *arrondissement*. His *Pater noster* was for a long time in the church repertoire and his *Grande messe solennelle* in B minor was praised by none other than Berlioz in an article in the *Journal des débats* (27 December 1849).

Another noteworthy feature of the Niedermeyer School was that pupils taught each other, the more senior ones helping out with *solfège* and piano courses, and so acquainted themselves with the pedagogical tasks that were to be a necessary part of their future jobs as choirmasters. It was open to the most brilliant pupils to be appointed to the staff as soon as they had left, as happened to Eugène Gigout who wrote in an autobiographical article:[12]

Fauré and I never left . . . and we never left each other either! I was a year older than he was and had to keep an eye on him as well as teaching him *solfège* and plainsong. I'm embarrassed to think that I corrected the counterpoint exercises of our greatest composer. In those days he used to draw cartoons for me, done with great facility and considerable wit.

Fauré himself taught composition at the Niedermeyer School for several months in 1871, as we shall see.[13] In 1873 he was appointed a member of the Board of Studies responsible for awarding the outstanding students their choirmaster's and organist's diplomas. Gigout was a prize-winner, unlike his friend Fauré, it seems, who perhaps paid the penalty of some mediocre results in such important courses as organ-playing ('accessit' in 1863) and plainsong (2nd prize in 1864).

As well as courses in music, the School also provided 'some sort of general education', as Fauré describes it.[14] Niedermeyer's report, from which I have already quoted, gives the weekly *corpus* of instruction for 1854: 'three French language lessons, two Latin, one arithmetic, one geography, one history and literature', to which were later added some smatterings of Italian. These subjects, together with religious instruction, were taught by the clergy of St-Louis d'Antin and Ste-Elisabeth. A report by Niedermeyer for 1857 states:[15] 'The students listen to a religious reading every evening and they go to Mass on Thursdays and Sundays.' The teaching of the old priest at Rieucros was not forgotten – in 1857 Fauré won a prize for religious knowledge.

Fauré remained at the school for eleven years and seems to have weathered the intensive regime without very much difficulty. He was a pleasant, outgoing boy and was generally popular. Several of his fellow students were to be lifelong friends, including Eugène Gigout, Albert Périlhou and Julien Koszul, the grandfather of the composer Henri Dutilleux. The school schedule was fairly strict but, as Fauré later reported,[16] this did not prevent them from getting into mischief. Gigout recalls, in the article already quoted, the memorable evening when they went to hear Gounod's *Faust* for the first time (in 1859 it was the very latest of operatic productions).

We wanted to hear this masterpiece which everyone was discussing so passionately. But, being boarders, we weren't allowed out at night. What was to be done? The work was being played at the Théâtre Lyrique on the evening of Shrove Tuesday. We were careful to inform the staff that we would be dining and staying the night with our 'boarding-parents', who stood *in loco parentis* during termtime. We'd been saving up and by pooling our resources managed to find places up in 'the gods'. We had no dinner that evening and after the performance of this masterpiece – which made the same impression on us as *Pelléas* did on the young of 1902 – we found ourselves on the streets of Paris in the middle of the night . . . We had a few sous left, enough for a bock. We went into a café, half-a-dozen of us including Fauré and Périlhou.

At two o'clock in the morning the waiter threw us out because we weren't eating or drinking . . . for one very good reason! And we had to spend the night out in the open, walking along the boulevards till we were exhausted, then having a rest on benches here and there; when the doors of the Madeleine opened we waited inside until a reasonable hour for returning to school. The authorities took a lenient view.

Niedermeyer himself was very fond of Fauré who had come to his new school at such a tender age. 'He was the apple of Niedermeyer's eye', Gigout goes on.

The Director would ask the boy to his parties where he met the most elevated members of the aristocracy and the official world. Gabriel used to sing them songs from his own area of France, and these *dilettanti* would find his mid-southern accent and his innate musicianship quite charming and delightful. That was Fauré's début in the polite society which he was never to abandon. Niedermeyer used to give him jam as a reward – just as Victor Hugo did to his grand-daughter when she deserved to be punished! – Gabriel's healthy appetite never forgot dear Niedermeyer's indulgence.

Because Fauré was so young and nice he was treated differently from the others. Even so he was scatterbrained and one day, when he'd committed some misdemeanour or other, Niedermeyer shut him up in his dressing-room and forgot about him . . . He discovered him in the evening, fast asleep.

In Niedermeyer the young Fauré found a teacher and a father, who could be tender even while being severe. The notebook bequeathed to the Bibliothèque Nationale by Niedermeyer's grand-daughter Marie-Louise Boëllmann-Gigout reveals that the work of Fauré, Gabriel,[17] had its ups and downs. But Niedermeyer understood the boy's character – his wit, his warmth of heart, his dreaminess, his budding originality and his taste for literature, marked by two prizes in 1858 and 1862. Fauré was always to remember with gratitude the lessons he had from his first teacher. Niedermeyer's sudden death on 14 March 1861 distressed him greatly and all the more so because his place was taken by Louis Dietsch, the most despised of all the teachers, who took over as Director until the arrival in 1865 of Gustave Lefèvre, Niedermeyer's son-in-law.

Camille Saint-Saëns took over the senior piano class and in him Fauré discovered more than a teacher – he became a friend and guide. Saint-Saëns was the older of the two by ten years, already an established master and at this time beginning to make a name for himself as an organist and especially as a dazzling pianist. He turned his class into a veritable musical seminar devoted to tackling those 'modern' composers who did not find a place in the school's official list of studies: Liszt, Schumann and Wagner, with the last of whom Saint-Saëns maintained a close relationship. In the years that followed, Fauré never lost an opportunity to proclaim that he 'owed everything' to this young teacher he met in the formative years of adolescence. Their friendship was unclouded until Saint-Saëns' death in 1921, as I have indicated in my introduction to their published correspondence.[18]

Under Saint-Saëns' friendly and conscientious eye Fauré began to compose. Only some of these juvenilia have survived, such as his opus 1 no. 1, a romance on a rather insipid poem by Victor Hugo 'Le Papillon et la fleur', probably written at the period of Saint-Saëns' arrival (1861) to judge by what Fauré said of it:[19] 'it was in fact my very first song, written in the school refectory surrounded by smells from the kitchen . . . and my first interpreter was Saint-Saëns'. Not that this little work, strophic in form, has much that could be termed individuality, recalling as it does the rather faded charms of the *opéra-comique* or even of the operetta, which were all the rage under the Second Empire. In this same year of 1861 Fauré was allowed to compete for the first time in the annual *concours* of the composition class, and obtained an 'accessit'. The works he submitted were a four-part fugue on a given subject, a fugue on a subject of his own composition and a 'piece of religious vocal music with instrumental accompaniment'.[20] In 1862 his name did not figure in the prize list but the following year he received a mention, according to an enigmatic report in *Le Ménestrel* (9 August 1863, p. 228): 'As he had not strictly complied with the rules laid down for the *concours* he could not be awarded a prize; but Gabriel Fauré and Adam Laussel both received a highly honourable mention . . . for their outstanding entries.' Fauré's 'piece of religious vocal music with instrumental accompaniment' has come down to us: a setting of Psalm 126, *Super flumina Babylonis*, the autograph orchestral score bearing the date 14 July 1863. This tuneful work, opening with a gentle evocation of the Euphrates, is scored for 5-voice mixed choir (SATBB) and large symphony orchestra (triple woodwind, three trombones, three trumpets). Although it was carefully preserved by the composer it has remained unpublished and has never appeared in any catalogue of his works.

In 1864 Fauré won a second prize for composition. It is most unfortunate that his entry has not survived because *Le Ménestrel* comments (7 August 1864, p. 286): 'this *concours* was quite exceptional'. He finally won a first prize for composition in 1865, very probably with the *Cantique de Jean Racine*, op. 11. In spite of a number of rather routine melodic and contrapuntal formulae there is character and originality in the serenity of mood, in the flow of chordal harmony and in the delicate but substantial choral writing. It recalls the most seductive and melodious passages of Mendelssohn or Gounod. The jury were so taken by its inner intensity and by its fervour, which matched Racine's text, that they did not hold Fauré to the letter of the rules. Perhaps because he had run short of time he had submitted his score with organ accompaniment instead of the instrumental accompaniment that was specified.

There exist two orchestral versions of the *Cantique de Jean Racine*. The first, for organ (or harmonium) and string quintet, was performed on 4 August 1866 at Rennes where Fauré was employed as an organist, as we shall see. This is probably the version conducted by César Franck – to whom the work is dedicated – in an orchestral concert given by the Société nationale de musique on 15 May 1875. The score and parts were once available for hire from Hamelle but unfortunately they can no longer be found. A fuller orchestration, with duple woodwind, two horns and string quintet but without organ, was made (by Fauré?) in 1906 for the Société des concerts du Conservatoire, if we are to go by the programme note for the 'first performance' (28 January 1906), contributed by Maurice Emmanuel. Like the earlier orchestration, this one has remained unpublished.

It was in all probability during his years at the Niedermeyer School that Fauré composed his three *Romances sans paroles*, op. 17 for piano, in self-evident homage to a composer whose works and style he admired all his life: Felix Mendelssohn. The same period (1862–3) saw Fauré continuing with the production of his early songs. We find a list of these in correspondence between Victor Hugo and Paul Meurice in May 1864, over the question of royalties to be paid to the poet. The songs mentioned are 'Le Papillon et la fleur' (op. 1 no. 1), 'Mai' (op. 1 no. 2), 'S'il est un charmant gazon' (op. 5 no. 2, published with the ridiculous title 'Rêve d'amour'), 'Puisqu'ici-bas toute âme' (op. 10 no. 1, which Fauré turned ten years later into a duet for sopranos and piano), and finally two songs, 'L'Aube naît' and 'Puisque j'ai mis ma lèvre', neither of which was ever published and only the second of which survives. Fauré set little store by these early works. He went as far as to say in 1910:[21] 'I have never managed to set Victor Hugo's poetry successfully', even though he chose ten of his poems for this purpose between 1860 and 1875!

2   Scenes from provincial life

Fauré left the Niedermeyer School on 28 July 1865. He was twenty and this long immersion in ancient polyphonic music and in modal usage was to have a profound and increasing influence on his composing language. His musical development consisted of an ever-increasing reliance on counterpoint, combined with an ever-increasing absorption of modal techniques and the foundation of a tonal–modal system based on bitonality. But for the moment his early works showed hardly any break with the rather strict, classical harmonic usage he had been taught in the Niedermeyer School. In an interview[1] he remarked: 'My early musical education was extremely narrow. We were not allowed to play Schumann or Chopin. Niedermeyer reckoned it was not fit music for the young.' We can see from this that Niedermeyer's teaching had its limitations; for a musician born in 1802, Schumann and Chopin (and Berlioz and Gounod in France) were modern composers. Even so the permitted musical territory had been enlarged unofficially thanks to Saint-Saëns and his highly progressive teaching.

During the autumn of 1865 the director of the School, Gustave Lefèvre, obtained a job for Fauré as organist at the church of St-Sauveur in Rennes. He took up the appointment in January 1866. The years Fauré spent in Rennes remained until recently some of the most obscure in his career. The documents I have collected, together with cuttings from the local press,[2] shed new light on these four years.

In a lecture given in 1908,[3] the general secretary of the Conservatoire, Fernand Bourgeat, included some details which he had probably got from Fauré himself: 'He was lodging with some excellent people, very pious, who made him go to bed at 8 o'clock and condemned him to a truly monastic existence.' It seems that the young *maître de chapelle* did not put up with this way of life for very long. The 1868 directory for Ille et Vilaine shows that he was living by then at 4 rue de Nemours as a friend of the Leyritz family. Musical life in the Breton capital was, alas, fairly dull. The programmes put on by the various local societies – the Concert populaire, the Société musicale or the Société philharmonique – were full of caprices and fantasies on popular tunes, ending up with extracts from Meyerbeer and Donizetti. The visit of a star like Adelina Patti or the violinist Henry Vieuxtemps was something sensational. In the theatre there was a short winter season of operas, operettas or *opéras-comiques* by Bellini, Offenbach, Meyerbeer and particularly Adolphe Adam. During the 1868–9 season the success of *Faust* was front-page news, and the management had to take the unheard-of step of mounting eight consecutive performances! Fauré took part in one of them, no doubt much to the outrage of his landlord, as a replacement for the organist needed to accompany the church scene.[4] He liked to tell the story of how, as there was only a harmonium at his disposal, at one crucial moment he had to recruit the fireman on duty to play a note on the pedals!

Britanny being a Catholic stronghold, musical life in the churches was of a quite different order. Each year at Easter you could hear a Vittoria Passion in the cathedral and at various times during the rest of the year there were large-scale concerts: a Mass by Gounod (12 March 1866) or the famous *Ode Symphonie* by Félicien David, *Le Désert* (29 June 1869). Nearly every one of the eight parishes boasted an organ and a choir to which instrumentalists would be added on festival days. Fauré therefore had an opportunity to perform some of the repertoire that he had sung at the Niedermeyer School, especially on Sundays when he had to provide music for High Mass at 10 a.m., for Vespers at 3 p.m., as well as for the Adoration and Benediction of the Holy Sacrament, followed by a meeting of the 'Brotherhood of the Sacred Heart of Mary' which always included a very full programme of music.

The *Semaine religieuse du diocèse de Rennes* gives some idea of the very wide-ranging repertoire introduced by the new organist: choruses from Haydn and Handel oratorios, motets by Weber, Lambillotte (1796–1855), Arcadelt and Edouard Silas (1827–1909). The young musician's arrival did not go unnoticed; according to Fernand Bourgeat his organ improvisations and the quality of his choral performances drew an ever-increasing number of churchgoers. He had various opportunities to bring himself to public notice. On 23 June 1867 the 'procession générale', with the bishop at its head, culminated in a service at St-Sauveur where they heard an *O Salutaris* by Mozart[5] and various organ pieces in which the soloist 'showed the skill that we have all come to expect from him since his arrival', to quote from the *Semaine religieuse*.[6] But the outstanding occasion, on 4 August 1866, was the blessing of the organ of St-Sauveur, reconstructed by the organ-maker Merklin-Schutze in the beautiful seventeenth-century case. The abbot Massabiau wrote a long article[7] deploring the fact that this two-manual organ was hardly more than a 'magnificent accompanying instrument' and not a recital organ, because of its lack of power and attack. A virtuoso organist had been specially invited from Paris: Renaud de Wilbach, a past winner of the Prix de Rome and organist at the Paris church of St-Eugène. The programme included organ pieces and a number of songs, including Gounod's *Ave Maria* which was all the rage at that time, and a 'quartet with orchestra, composed by Monsieur G. Fauré' – most probably the *Cantique de Jean Racine* sung by four voices, accompanied by organ and string quintet as already mentioned. Fauré also played some solo organ pieces including a fanfare by Lemmens (1823–81) and one of the Mendelssohn sonatas.

He began to acquire a reputation among the middle-class citizens of Rennes as a piano and harmony teacher, providing a very necessary addition to his small organist's salary. To begin with, Fauré's youth and good looks led to problems, but very soon he began to make friends. Most notable among these were the Leyritz family. The two daughters, Valentine and Laure, retained not only fond memories of their teacher but also some of his compositions, including several autograph manuscripts: a Gavotte in C sharp for solo piano, a fugue in A minor and a prelude and fugue in E minor. It is highly likely that all these works, and the fugues especially, were products of his student years. Laure de Leyritz was the dedicatee of the second of the three *Romances sans paroles*. As for Valentine, who hated trills, Fauré made her work at them by including some in the short cadenza he wrote for her to Beethoven's C minor concerto.[8]

Fauré found Rennes extremely boring and came to feel more and more like an exile, but there were interesting moments. On 9 February 1866 he took part in a charity concert given by the Société musicale for the poor of the city in the Théâtre de Rennes. He played a fantasy on Gounod's *Faust* by Saint-Saëns and accompanied a local violinist called Hy (!) in a duet by Brisson and Guichard on Donizetti's *La Favorita*.[9] In August 1866 Fauré went with Saint-Saëns and a group of painters (Georges Clairin, Henri Regnault, Emmanuel Jadin and Ulysse Butin) to the 'pardon' at Sainte-Anne-la-Palud in the Gulf of Morbihan, a brief, enjoyable holiday during which Saint-Saëns sketched his *Trois Rhapsodies sur des cantiques bretons* for organ, dedicated to his favourite pupil. On 8 February 1868 a concert at the Hôtel de Ville in Rennes included an Intermezzo for orchestra by the organist of St-Sauveur, in all probability the piece he transcribed the following year for the Leyritz sisters under the title of *Intermède symphonique.*[10]

In August 1868 Fauré took Saint-Saëns' place as accompanist for Caroline Miolan-Carvalho, who had created the rôle of Marguerite in Gounod's *Faust* and was the wife of Léon Carvalho, the influential director of the Théâtre Lyrique in Paris. The singer Hermann Léon also took part in the concert, which was given at the Casino de Saint-Malo. Between songs, arias and duets by Gounod, Bizet, Boïeldieu and Mozart, Fauré played Liszt's version of the March from *Tannhäuser*, an Impromptu by Chopin (we are not told which), *Le Chant du braconnier* by Théodore Ritter, a virtuoso piece of some contemporary appeal, as well as the Waltz from *Faust* in Saint-Saëns' concert transcription. By way of thanks Madame Carvalho sang 'Le Papillon et la fleur', and Fauré dedicated it to her.[11]

Nonetheless, on the whole he found life in Rennes fairly monotonous and, freed from the strict discipline of the Niedermeyer School, he relapsed into his innate listlessness. In a letter of 28 September 1896 Fauré outlined to his wife the following psychological portrait of himself in those years: 'My head was empty. I had no great opinion of myself, indeed I regarded everything with complete indifference except for manifestations of beauty and high intelligence. But I hadn't the shadow of an ambition. What a strange character!' he concluded. In 1922 he declared in an interview,[12] 'It was Saint-Saëns who encouraged me continuously and rescued me from stagnation. He kept me working and saw to it that I sent him my earliest efforts as and when I wrote them.' It is all the more regrettable that Fauré kept only a small proportion of the letters Saint-Saëns sent him during this period, as they might have helped us to rectify the rather tentative chronology of his early works and must have contained references to works which have since been lost. A solitary letter of 1867[13] informs us that the young musician was thinking of writing a motet on a text which he had already set to music once. The *Semaine religieuse du diocèse de Rennes*[14] announced that on 19 July 1868 a *Cantique à St-Vincent de Paul* was performed at St-Sauveur, it being the saint's feast-day. This work has not survived, whereas we do know something of the famous *Tantum ergo*, which he probably never completed: he 'gave' it to Saint-Saëns in the spring of 1868 and it found a place as the principal theme of the first movement of his G minor Piano Concerto.[15]

The Catholic community in Rennes did not in the least approve of the fact that their choirmaster was to be seen in cafés with teachers from the *lycée*, but even this companionship could not make up for his boredom: in

Rennes he felt cut off from the musical world of Paris. It did not take him long to get the measure of the town's *salons* and the taste for good music which he had acquired as a student earned him the reputation of being a severe musician.[16] His impatience broke out in the form of a brilliant fantasy based on a comic song associated with the popular singer Thérésa: 'Rien n'est sacré pour un sapeur' ('Nothing's sacred for a sapper'). This love of musical mystification was part of the playful side of his nature which showed itself when he was among friends, balancing the dreamy, almost tortured workings of his inner creative self.

After four years he began to think of escape. 'In vain', recalled Alfred Bruneau,[17] 'did the vicar preach the virtues of austerity, admonishing him for going out into the church porch for a smoke during the sermon. One morning the organist came straight from the municipal ball and entered the organ loft in white tie and tails. He was discreetly dismissed.' Fauré takes up the story in the interview of 1922 (see n. 12): 'The vicar found in me an incorrigible religious defaulter. When his hostility came out into the open it was once again Saint-Saëns who rescued me and found me something in Paris.' His tenure, then, came to an end and he left Rennes at the very beginning of 1870.[18] 'I became organist at Clignancourt,' Fauré went on, 'but there too I had clashes with my superiors and my departure was hastened by a premeditated act of absenteeism. I left Clignancourt because I had been to hear *Les Huguenots*!'

He had been deprived of good music for a long time and on his return to Paris he drank deep. He went to hear *Faust* with Mme Miolan-Carvalho, and Jean-Baptiste Faure, his famous near-namesake, in the rôle of Mephisto; was at the first performance of Saint-Saëns' Third Piano Concerto with the composer as soloist; and above all went regularly to Saint-Saëns' celebrated Monday receptions at 168, rue du Faubourg St-Honoré, where composers and performers congregated in a cheerful, relaxed atmosphere. It was here that Fauré had the memorable experience of meeting Anton Rubinstein. Unfortunately, all his friends from the Niedermeyer School had left Paris with the exception of Eugène Gigout who, at the age of nineteen in 1863, had been made organist of the new church of St-Augustin.

The Franco-Prussian War put an end to his Parisian rediscoveries. He was enlisted on 16 August 1870 in the 1st Regiment of the Imperial Light Infantry and was posted to the 28th Infantry Regiment on 10 September. He took part in the fighting at Champigny in October and at Le Bourget and Créteil in November and December. As in other walks of life, he made many friends. Between actions he regaled his comrades with improvised recitals in the abandoned villas on the outskirts of Paris – a warmonger after the fashion of Stendhal (one of his favourite authors, according to M.-L. Boëllmann). But he was under fire at Champigny and was awarded a *croix de guerre*. Alfred Bruneau gave details of the end to this adventure:[19]

He was a liaison officer involved in a secret mission to Vincennes, and it was there he learned that the armistice had been agreed (28 January 1871). He ran home, shaking and panting, and scattering his military papers as he went. When he got there he slept solidly for 24 hours.

He was officially demobilised on 9 March 1871 and became organist at St-Honoré d'Eylau, a rich parish church in what is now the place Victor-Hugo in the 16th *arrondissement*. It was a short appointment because a large proportion of the inhabitants of Paris condemned the surrender to the Germans and formed themselves into a Commune to fight the Establishment, which had taken refuge at Versailles. Fauré avoided enlistment, feeling no doubt that he had done his duty and that he was not cut out for street fighting. Violence of any sort was against his nature and his experience of war had given him a horror of it. Like many artists he decided to escape from Paris. With the help of a false passport he crossed the lines of troops and walked to Rambouillet to join one of his brothers.[20] In the course of the summer he accepted an invitation from Gustave Lefèvre to go and teach composition on Niedermeyer's old estate at Cours-sous-Lausanne in Switzerland.

The defeat of 1870 was a great national disaster for France and one that affected Fauré deeply. In his music at this time we find a quite new seriousness which nothing in his previous compositions has led us to expect. But (characteristically) he keeps this feeling of tragedy buried deep below the surface and expresses it with a reticence born of his natural sense of delicacy. His first instinct was always to rise above the material world and although in this one instance mundane events did have some effect on his work, he normally found no difficulty in resisting the lure of patriotic tub-thumping. For this particular occasion César Franck composed an ode called *Paris*; Gounod, who like many French artists had fled to England, wrote a 'biblical elegy' called *Gallia*; and Saint-Saëns dedicated his *Marche héroïque* to the memory of his friend, the painter Henri Regnault, and proceeded to play it (in the uniform of the National Guard) with Albert Lavignac at a charity concert at the Grand Hôtel. As for Gabriel Fauré, his contribution was an uncomplicated song called *L'Absent*, to words by Victor Hugo, which he finished on 3 April 1871. Its profound, even sober, tone reflects in the only way available to him the shattering discoveries he had made about irrationality, violence and death. Two other songs to words by Gautier – 'Seule!' (1871) and 'La Chanson du pêcheur' (on the poem *Lamento* which Berlioz and Gounod, among others, had also set) – tapped these profound experiences still further.

While he was in Switzerland, Fauré wrote an *Ave Maria* (for the pupils of the Niedermeyer School), for three-part male voices and organ, to celebrate the pupils' ascent of Mont-St-Bernard on 20 August 1871. It was not published until 1957 and bears little indication of its authorship. Its chromaticism and austerity bring it close to the late religious works of Liszt; its musical quality does not.

Fauré returned to Paris in the autumn of 1871 and this time he stayed there for good. All through his long years as a bachelor frequent financial problems led to regular changes of domicile.[21] For the moment he was at 19, rue Taranne (now 167, Boulevard St-Germain, opposite the Café de Flore), only a couple of steps from St-Germain-des-Prés and, more importantly, close to the church of St-Sulpice where he became second organist in October 1871. His duties, it must be said, were not particularly arduous. The main organ, a marvellous instrument of one hundred stops which Cavaillé-Coll had just completed, was in the hands of Charles-Marie Widor. Fauré had to content himself with the little organ intended for accompanying the choir, who were often supplemented by the choir of the Seminary of the place St-Sulpice. Widor recalls[22] that during the services the two organists would engage in complementary improvisations, sending themes from one to the other and each doing his best to engineer some daring modulation at the moment of the 'takeover'. Needless to say, this musical jousting passed over the heads of congregation and clergy in more senses than one.

His job as accompanist led Fauré to write several motets and canticles, some of which have no doubt been lost. Widor, in the article already quoted, remembers the great impact made by Fauré's *Tu es Petrus* for baritone solo, mixed choir and organ when performed beneath the dome of St-Sulpice by the large choir from the Seminary. Maybe the acoustic conditions were responsible . . . The truth is that the work's inflated style, while ensuring its popularity in any number of churches, makes it one of his least interesting compositions. A catalogue from the publishers Hamelle also mentions a *Cantique pour la fête d'un supérieur* (perhaps the Abbot of the Seminary of St-Sulpice?), but it does not seem to have appeared in print and does not survive; it is unlikely to have been a major loss.

More than ever, Saint-Saëns was the guardian angel watching over

Fauré's career. He never lost an opportunity of recommending him to influential friends or to celebrated performers, like the pianist Caroline de Serres. With increasing frequency he asked Fauré to deputise for him on the main organ of the Madeleine when his dual career of composer and piano virtuoso took him to the provinces or abroad. Secretly Saint-Saëns was hoping to make him his successor at the Madeleine and by way of preparation for this he advised Fauré to leave St-Sulpice and become his deputy, though still on an unofficial basis. So in January 1874 Fauré was replaced as second organist by his friend André Messager, who had been his first composition pupil at the Niedermeyer School in Cours-sous-Lausanne. In July 1874 he moved to a small apartment on the fifth storey of 7, rue de Parme in the 9th *arrondissement*, nearer his new church; and moved again in April 1877 to 13, rue Mosnier (now rue de Berne, 8th), overlooking the cutting through which the trains pass to the Gare St-Lazare.

Saint-Saëns was also quick to put Fauré in touch with the best musicians of the time: César Franck, Edouard Lalo, Vincent d'Indy, Henri Duparc, Jules Massenet and so on. He joined them, on 25 February 1871, in founding the Société nationale de musique. Under the joint presidency of Saint-Saëns and the singing teacher Romain Bussine, the 'Nationale', as it soon came to be called, aimed to make known the body of 'serious' French contemporary music which existing organisations almost entirely ignored.

For half a century public taste had in general favoured the opera and the ballet; they had enjoyed a veritable golden age under the Restoration and the July Monarchy. Rossini, Bellini and Donizetti at the Théâtre Italien; Verdi, Halévy and especially Meyerbeer at the Académie royale (or, later, impériale) de musique – the Opéra; Adolphe Adam, Auber and Hérold at the Opéra-Comique: all these composers catered for a public that relished grand spectacle or neatly turned lyrics and was always ready to admire a pretty voice or a shapely ankle. It was only the initiative of Léon Carvalho that gave one the chance to hear Mozart, early Gounod, Berlioz or Bizet at the Théâtre Lyrique – which was continually in difficulties. The concert platform was given over to the worst excesses of virtuosity. Violinists and particularly pianists drew the crowds by their technical prowess, polishing off works rather like circus performers, greatly to the detriment of music. The repertoire consisted entirely of caprices and brilliant fantasies on popular Italian arias, 'bravura' variations and sundry 'galops' and 'grand concert studies'. The vogue for descriptive music was unabated, pursuing the most tiresome precedents of the late eighteenth century.

Popular audiences provided handsome profits for the *café concerts* which thrived under the Second Empire. Here they could enjoy ditties on historical or sentimental topics, comic recitations in decidedly broad vein, watch a cross-section of society and all sorts of 'novelties'; they came to have fun and, for the price of a few drinks, to buy an evening's respite from the harsh injustices of their everyday lives.

The 'connoisseurs' came from the intellectual fringe of the bourgeoisie and from the artistic world which had become, since the beginnings of the Romantic movement, a real community based on a complex network of friendships and varied interests. Gautier loved the opera and the ballet; Baudelaire was a devotee of contemporary music; Gérard de Nerval collaborated on opera librettos; Delacroix valued his long conversations with Chopin; Balzac and even Victor Hugo were seen at concerts; Liszt (possibly with the help of Marie d'Agoult) published a number of books; while it must be remembered that Hugo was also a fine draughtsman, just as Stephen Heller and Berlioz were born writers. Many of these celebrities found their way to George Sand's salon, either in Nohant or in Paris. This summary list must also include the chamber music evenings (we shall come back to these later), usually held in private houses, at which large numbers of amateur instrumentalists played what they could from the classical and post-classical repertoire. As for concert societies, they sprang up in quantity only to die quick deaths from lack of money, like the Société Ste-Cécile, founded by François Seghers in 1848. The only permanent institution was the Société des Concerts du Conservatoire founded in 1828 by François-Antoine Habeneck, a violinist of German origins (his father was born at Mannheim). But in accordance with the tastes of its founder the 'Société des concerts', as it came to be called, was a temple dedicated to the god Beethoven. Haydn and Mozart were allowed in as precursors, Bach as a historical curiosity, while so-called 'contemporary' music on rare occasions came as far up to date as Mendelssohn.

The founding of the Société nationale de musique in 1871 undoubtedly introduced new blood into a near-moribund system. The social and political climate after the Franco–Prussian War led to the new society being not only progressive but openly nationalistic and, most of all, anti-German, as we can see from the modest jingoism of its slogan *Ars Gallica*. Each member made a financial contribution to cover the cost of the concerts. The programmes were arrived at in wholly democratic fashion: works submitted to the organising committee were played on the piano and were then voted on in secret according to a graded scale of appreciation. Successful composers like Franck, Lalo and Saint-Saëns were quite happy to submit to this procedure.

Fauré was one of the Society's founder members and was made secretary on 22 November 1874. He did, however, have to accept a vote of censure on 1 March 1875 for 'deplorable unpunctuality'![23] The Society certainly had its problems and its limitations. Orchestral concerts were so expensive that only two or three could be given each season; the audiences were drawn from a small inner circle of devotees, though snobbery gradually attracted a richer and more cosmopolitan clientele; the old-fashioned musical press looked on their concerts with condescension, *Le Ménestrel* accusing the group of being a 'mutual admiration society'. In spite of all this, the Society worked through fire and flood for more than twenty years to provide a kind of permanent exhibition of contemporary French music: Franck, Lalo and Saint-Saëns were heard together with early works by Duparc, Fauré and Debussy. The admission in 1886 of modern works from abroad and of works from the classical repertoire led Saint-Saëns to resign. This, and the move after Franck's death towards works of a 'd'Indyste' persuasion, meant that Fauré too became less involved with the Society, as we shall see.

In the early 1870s Fauré's songs were often sung at the Society's concerts by semi-professional singers. This was a regular procedure at a time when there was no clear dividing line between the salon and the concert hall, and among such singers we might mention Mme Edouard Lalo, Marie Trélat who was equally popular as a hostess and as a teacher, Henriette Fuchs, the founder of the choral society called La Concordia, which had Widor and Debussy among its accompanists, and plain amateurs like Léonce Valdec and Félix Lévy. Fauré himself, as a gesture of friendship and to help save money, played the works of his colleagues, engaging in four-handed piano recitals with Pauline Viardot, René Lenormand, André Messager, Vincent d'Indy and most frequently of all with Saint-Saëns, in arrangements of *Le Rouet d'Omphale* or *Phaéton*, or in the *Variations sur un thème de Beethoven*. Following the example of Saint-Saëns, Duparc and d'Indy, Fauré decided to bring together various pieces he had jotted down at Rennes or during his student days under the heading of Symphony in F. On 8 February 1873 Saint-Saëns and Fauré played an arrangement for two pianos of the first three movements: Allegro, Andante and Gavotte (the one he had written at Rennes, transposed into F). He added a Finale for the first orchestral performance, given at the Société nationale by Edouard Colonne on 16 May 1874.

Fauré's first substantial work did not satisfy either the critics, who were fairly lukewarm, or the composer; we shall see later what became of it. This relative lack of success was no great blow in fact because Fauré's reputation did not extend beyond a small circle of professional musicians and enlightened amateurs. His output consisted of a few religious pieces, some short unpublished works for piano and chiefly of some twenty songs, in which publishers were beginning to show some interest. On 6 March 1869 he signed a contract with Antoine Choudens whose flair for business and lack of generosity were to make him a rich man. It was at this time that Choudens also signed up, whether through intuition or sheer luck, the two composers who were to be the mainstay of his publishing house, Bizet and Gounod. It must be admitted that he was not attracted to Fauré's songs wholly by their musical quality – it would have been a clever man indeed who could divine the composer's future from looking at 'Le Papillon et la fleur' – but rather by the patronage of Madame Carvalho. This song was a success and was even published by Choudens in Italian! It encouraged him to go ahead with the publication of Fauré's other vocal works, though he tried the composer's patience by taking several years to honour signed contracts and by arbitrarily giving new, eye-catching titles to the most innocuous romances. 'I'll send you the Gavotte one of these days,' Fauré wrote to his friend Julien Koszul in June 1870,[24] '... and I'll include a copy of my romance 'S'il est un charmant gazon' which is due to be published soon. Choudens, who appears to have a sense of humour, has renamed it 'Rêve d'amour'! Not a title *I'd* have thought of.' In making this start in the musical world Fauré could look to two families, the Viardots and the Clercs, for their encouragement and support.

3 Friends and lovers

From 1872 Fauré found in the Clercs a sympathetic family of the kind that had been almost entirely lacking during his long stay at the Niedermeyer School. Camille Clerc (1828–82) was a graduate of the Ecole polytechnique, and was employed as an engineer in the Department of Roads and Bridges. He came from a well-off industrial family in Le Havre and his enthusiasm for music almost matched that of his second wife Marie, née Depret. During the summer they used to organise frequent private concerts both in Paris and Normandy, with artists of the calibre of the 'cellist Joseph Hollmann and the violinists Hubert Léonard and Gustav Friedrich. Fauré and his friends Messager and Bussine often stayed at their house at Sainte-Adresse, near Le Havre, and later at Villerville,[1] among a large number of artists who used to spend the summer in this village on the cliffs between Deauville and Honfleur. Among Fauré's hosts were painters like Roger Jourdain, the half-brother of his friend Marguerite Baugnies; the Chilean-born Errazuris; and Ernest Duez, Duez's wife, Amélie, was an amateur singer and used to perform Fauré's early songs ('Aubade' is dedicated to her). It was in the milieu of these music-loving artists that the eighteen-year-old Winnaretta Singer, the future Princess Edmond de Polignac, heard Fauré playing Schumann incomparably well and was introduced to him.[2] Fauré also found in the area some of the piano and harmony pupils he taught in Paris. Thanks to the Clerc family and to recommendations from Saint-Saëns and Pauline Viardot, he was frequently invited to musical evenings in the huge, verandahed villas that the middle classes were building on the Normandy coast.

All this activity was valuable experience and encouragement for Fauré. He was profoundly lacking in confidence over the value of his compositions and their warm reception was a great comfort to him. The Clercs were won over by him from the start and lost no opportunity of giving him a chance to shine – a piece of clairvoyance that deserves to be remembered. Camille Clerc also helped out on the business side, handling in masterly

23

fashion the difficult negotiations over the publication of the First Violin Sonata which Fauré had written almost entirely under his roof at Sainte-Adresse in 1875. To persuade the famous firm of Breitkopf and Härtel in Leipzig to accept a long and ambitious sonata by an unknown composer was absolutely amazing; Pauline Viardot was astonished, having been 'convinced that Germans would not be willing to give young French composers any help in making a name for themselves'. The terms of the contract were certainly harsh – Fauré got no financial return whatever. But after consulting Saint-Saëns and the violinist Hubert Léonard he accepted gladly 'for the honour of appearing in the most prestigious catalogue of all'.[3] The sonata was published in 1877 and was a great and instant success, of which we shall have more to say later.

The year 1877 was an uneventful one for Fauré. In April he was appointed *maître de chapelle* at the Madeleine, in July he became engaged to Marianne Viardot and in December he paid his first visit to Liszt.

Saint-Saëns now gave up his job as organist at the Madeleine. Théodore Dubois succeeded him, thereby creating a vacancy in the post of *maître de chapelle*. The position was much sought after and Saint-Saëns naturally urged his pupil's claims, while Camille Clerc arranged for his friend Father Monsabré to go and see the vicar of the Madeleine, Almire le Rebour. Fauré's own efforts were directed towards Gounod, whom he had met at the Viardots and who carried considerable weight in clerical circles: 'I've just been to see Gounod', Fauré wrote to Clerc (unpublished letter of around 8 April 1877); 'he called on the vicar this morning but didn't find him at home. He's agreed to see me at half-past three at Notre Dame where he's going to be conducting a rehearsal of his Mass, and he'll introduce me to one of the bishops who's a friend of the vicar. Gounod is being very helpful in the whole business.' Fauré was appointed the following week, as could reasonably be expected from Théodore Dubois' appointment as first organist, announced in *Le Ménestrel* on 15 April 1877.

For nearly twenty years (1877–96) Fauré was known to the Parisian musical world as '*maître de chapelle* at the Madeleine'. The post was not particularly well-paid but it did carry a certain prestige, because the church of Ste-Madeleine (usually called just 'the Madeleine') was the parish church of the Elysée and so one of the most important Paris churches after the Cathedral of Notre-Dame, the seat of the archbishop. The Madeleine received large subsidies from the State to cover the arrangements for ceremonial occasions (receptions of sovereigns or heads of state, state funerals and so on) and it could be said to have become something of a specialist in such matters. It also received support from the aristocracy and the richer bourgeoisie of the Faubourg St-Honoré: important weddings and funerals of the famous assumed the air of public spectacles. High Mass on Sunday was the occasion for a fashion display and the departure from the church took place before an admiring crowd.[4] The Madeleine was, therefore, a kind of 'church de luxe', chiefly concerned with the sumptuous ordering of ceremonies. Anyone looking at the church accounts may well be amazed by the number of clergy (twenty-seven priests) and still more by the 'life-style' of the church as revealed by the size of its permanent staff and the considerable amounts of money spent on its daily upkeep (repair of vestments and fresh flowers in particular).

Music had a large part to play in this wholly formal despatch of the holy offices which more or less reduced religion to its most superficial, social elements. Pierre Vignon's neo-antique building, dating from 1806, measures thirty metres from the dome to the floor and the acoustics are wretched; nonetheless, music was an indispensable ingredient of the ritual performances. The major festivals (Christmas, Easter, the Assumption . . .), important weddings and high-class funerals necessitated additions to the number of singers and musicians, just as they did to the amount of flowers, candles and embroidered linen.

In Fauré's time the 'personnel attached to the choir' numbered about twenty people. At the head of the hierarchy was the first organist. He played the main organ, a fine Cavaillé-Coll (fifty stops, dated 1845) situated in the high gallery over the porch, and for the most part he was heard on his own during the entry of the priests, the communion and for the recessional. After him came the *maître de chapelle*. His duties were far more onerous since it was he who was really in charge of the musical organisation: he had to decide with the clergy what music was to be performed and then rehearse both the choir and the accompanying band of instruments. Following ecclesiastical tradition, the choir of the Madeleine did not contain women. The soprano and alto parts were taken by a group of some thirty boys – the 'Maîtrise' – and the church was entirely responsible for their general and musical education. In return they sang frequently for services and occasionally received some financial reward. The best of them sang the solos, and they were given a regular salary.

The job of choirmaster was time-consuming, taking up practically the whole of every morning. In the course of rehearsals for the second performance of Gounod's *Requiem*, to mark the first anniversary of the composer's death, Fauré wrote to Saint-Saëns on 15 October 1894:[5] 'Gounod's *Requiem* and those cruel boys of the *Maîtrise* are killing me with exhaustion.' In a letter of 1895 to Marguerite Baugnies he referred to them as 'my geese'.

The men's voices were not numerous – normally four tenors and five basses – but they were professional singers, some of them taking minor rôles in the city's opera houses. The choir was accompanied by its own organ, another Cavaillé-Coll of 1843 with ten stops; it had a separate organist and was usually supported by two double-basses.

For festivals and ceremonial occasions the men's choir was augmented, as were the accompanying forces which sometimes reached the size of a veritable orchestra, with some twenty strings, one or two harps, timpani and assorted brass (horns, trumpets and trombones). The choir organ, the choir itself and the instrumentalists were all together behind the main altar and the large monument above this, carved by Marochetti and depicting the Assumption of Ste-Madeleine, hid them from the congregation. Rehearsals were held in the chapels on the ground floor and were accompanied by a harmonium and a double-bass (see pl. 9, pp. 125–6).[6]

Fauré's job demanded much of his time and skill but gave him no satisfaction whatever. Apart from the constant worry about recruiting singers and the labour of rehearsing the boys, he had to cope with the opinions and the obstinacy of the clergy. Their chief concern was to keep the congregation happy, and the congregation was appalled by any sort of innovation; the kind of music they preferred was nearer to *opéra-comique* than to Palestrina. A few examples will show what the situation was like. Saint-Saëns on one occasion played his transcription of Liszt's *St Francis preaching to the birds* and afterwards one of the clergy voiced to the organist his astonishment that he should tune the organ during a service! To requests that he should play something simpler, Saint-Saëns replied that he would play Offenbach when Labiche[7] was declaimed from the pulpit. Fauré also had to put up with the clergy's curious taste in music. A violent article by Pierre Lalo in *Le Temps* (11 June 1902) makes interesting reading in this respect: Lalo records that the repertoire included extracts from *Faust* dressed up with Latin words and mentions a performance of the 'Meditation' from Massenet's *Thaïs*!

These 'mercenary tasks', as Fauré described them in a letter to his wife, only brought him in the modest sum of 3,000 francs a year, the same salary as a curate's. It was not enough for him to live in comfort. His music was bringing in almost nothing and Choudens was giving him on average sixty francs for the total rights of each song. When he took Choudens his C minor Piano Quartet in 1879 the publisher refused it so rudely that he went instead to Durand – who refused it politely. It was finally accepted by a publisher in a smaller way of business, Julien Hamelle, who had a shop not far from the Madeleine at 22, Boulevard Malesherbes; the first contract between the two was signed on 16 November 1879.[8] Hamelle had great faith in Fauré's work and bought from Choudens the rights of the first volume of twenty songs which had just come out that year. He went on to publish nearly all Fauré's works until 1905.

In order to survive, Fauré had to spend a large portion of his time not composing but giving private piano lessons, which meant travelling all over Paris and the suburbs and spending hours in trains and trams. He also gave theory lessons to groups of middle-class young girls in the drawing-room of a friend's house. Singing classes for young 'society ladies' were very popular in the 1880s and Fauré often acted as their accompanist. For the one run by Pauline Roger he wrote a piece for two female voices and piano (*Le Ruisseau*, op. 22): its smooth melodic lines are easy to sing – the sutbleties lie in the many unusual progressions in the piano part. Fauré also gave his services to Marie Trélat, Henriette Fuchs and Gabrielle Kraus, and in the late 1880s he directed a small group of amateur singers, La Lyre, organised by Marguerite Baugnies. With them he prepared the first performance in Paris of Gounod's *Redemption*, conducted by the composer. In 1882 he was commissioned to write a more ambitious choral work, *La Naissance de Vénus*, for the amateur choral society founded by Antonin Guillot de Sainbris (see page 107). He did so not without difficulty, thanks to the extraordinary emptiness of the text provided.

He toyed briefly with the idea of a career as solo pianist, encouraged by his successes in this field at the Niedermeyer School and by Saint-Saëns' urgings. An unpublished letter survives from around 1878 in which he suggests to an unnamed conductor (probably Edouard Colonne) that he might play one of Mozart's concertos. Unfortunately Fauré fell ill and the project came to nothing. The taste for brilliance and the unremitting hard labour demanded for success as a soloist were in any case hardly compatible with Fauré's own rather passive, introspective nature. He must have found far greater pleasure in playing piano duets or being an accompanist (that is to say, sharing a musical experience) than basking in the limelight. Even so his technique was superb and he was able to play the Ballade and the piano parts of his chamber works even as an old man.

Fauré's situation, like that of numerous less gifted fellow musicians, was not, in short, particularly dazzling. There was only one way to escape this humdrum existence. Gounod had unerringly identified it thirty years before in his *Mémoires d'un artiste*:[9]

The 1848 Revolution had just broken out when I left my job as musical director at the Eglise des Missions étrangères. I had done it for four and a half years and I had learnt a lot from it, but as far as my future career was concerned it had left me vegetating without any prospects. There's only one place where a composer can make a name for himself: the theatre.

It was Pauline Viardot who naturally encouraged Fauré to try the same successful path. She had retired from the stage years before, after a brief but brilliant career, but she was still one of the legendary musical personalities of Europe – the daughter of the great Manuel Garcia, the sister of la Malibran, and a friend of the most distinguished figures of the Romantic era. She had studied composition with Reicha, the piano with Liszt, and had been on intimate terms with George Sand, Clara Schumann and with Brahms, who had recently dedicated to her his *Rhapsody* for contralto and male chorus.

In 1872, when Fauré was introduced to her by Saint-Saëns, Pauline Viardot had only just returned to Paris. For some years she had been living in Baden Baden, where she had gone to get away from the political restrictions of the Second Empire. Her *salon* at 50, rue de Douai, in the 'Europe' quarter of Paris, was the meeting place for friends from every walk of life. In the interview in *Excelsior* from which we have already quoted, Fauré recalls playing charades there with Turgenev and Saint-Saëns before a distinguished audience: George Sand, Ernest Renan, Louis Blanc the revolutionary, and Gustave Flaubert. The evening's entertainment was not in the least highbrow: apart from charades there were playlets, games of verse-capping and 'consequences'. Fauré was very much at home in all this. He had always appreciated this sort of gentle nonsense and was ever happy to drown his latent melancholia in high party spirits. When it came to making up doggerel he was an incomparable virtuoso. On more intimate occasions manuscripts were brought out to be admired: of a Bach cantata (authentic, one wonders?) and above all the autograph of *Don Giovanni* which, through Mme Viardot's generosity, was later to find its way to the Conservatoire Library.[10]

Fauré soon became close friends with the Viardot children. Not surprisingly, they were all musical: Louise (Mme Ernest Héritte) was a composer, Claudie (Mme Georges Chamerot) and Marianne were singers and Paul played the violin. Pauline kept a critical eye on her family's incessant musical activity and busied herself with vocal transcriptions, such as the well-known one of Chopin's Mazurkas which she had often heard the composer play. She also wrote songs, a singing method and even some miniature operas which were produced in her *salon*. Fauré was obviously much in demand. He rewrote his song 'Puisqu'ici bas toute âme' as a duet for Claudie and Marianne and also dedicated to them another duet, the sparkling 'Tarentelle', which they sang at the Société Nationale on 10 April 1875. A year later, on 22 April 1876, Pauline Viardot herself sang

'La Chanson du pêcheur' which is dedicated to her and the same concert included *Les Djinns* for mixed chorus and piano (the last text by Victor Hugo that Fauré was to set) which he intended to dedicate to Louise. Finally Paul was the dedicatee of the First Violin Sonata.

Pauline Viardot was very happy to be Fauré's adviser and took a real interest in his career. She herself gave a great many music lessons and she knew what teaching was like. In an unpublished letter to one of her friends she painted this portrait of the composer:[11]

I'd like to introduce to you a young friend of ours, M. Fauré: a fine musician, an excellent pianist and a charming young man. He's organist at St-Sulpice and he's going to spend a month or so at le Havre where he's been invited to stay by some of his pupils. I'd be so glad if he could come and see you and I'm sure you would be delighted to make his acquaintance. He's a pupil of Saint-Saëns – in itself a considerable recommendation because Saint-Saëns is very fussy about whom he teaches. M. Fauré is an admirable accompanist and, after what I've told him about you, will be looking forward to hearing you sing. He's an excellent composer and what's more he has a good sense of humour and he's mad about dancing. We're very fond of him. I'm sure you'll get to be so too, because he's really a delightful young man.

Be that as it may, Mme Viardot began to point out to the 'delightful young man' that writing songs, motets and chamber music was not the way to make a wide reputation, especially as his musical language was becoming more and more individual. Even trained musicians were finding it strange and disturbing. In a letter to Marie Clerc,[12] Fauré mentioned that the first performance of his Romance in B flat op. 28 for violin and piano at the Viardot's house in Bougival had 'succeeded to the accompaniment of grinding teeth' and that it had had to be repeated, and then repeated again. Fauré's lack of application was a particular target in the household, being quite at odds with the working habits of the Garcias. 'A composer must be able to work fast' Pauline would remark. 'But what about taking trouble?' Fauré would reply. At which point Louis Viardot, Pauline's husband, said sharply: 'You must take less trouble and get on with it!' – which upset Fauré more than somewhat.[13] Louis, who was the French translator of *Don Quixote*, also found the First Violin Sonata 'involved and meaningless'. Soon Fauré's only idea was to write an opera. To do that he had first to find a libretto, and he began to go round the current purveyors of such things. He approached Louis Gallet for one and pestered him with his requests, even getting Gounod to intercede on his behalf. For twenty years Fauré was to pursue the phantom of a theatrical success which would bring him fame and deliver him from the 'mercenary tasks'. We shall come later to the many ideas that were projected.

Louis and Pauline Viardot's close interest in Fauré's career was connected with the strong possibility that he would marry their youngest daughter Marianne. In 1877 she was twenty-three and for four years Fauré had been deeply in love with her. Her response was no more than lukewarm and their shyness of each other did nothing to clarify a state of affairs that was gradually becoming more and more embarrassing, Fauré being a frequent visitor, both in Paris and at Bougival (the house 'les Frênes') during the summer. Marianne was very fond of him – he was intelligent, funny and good-looking – but was she really in love with him? She did not know and her doubts and anxieties about it grew increasingly stubborn.

During the summer of 1877 Fauré's normally easy-going temperament began to show signs of his exasperation. He engaged the help of Claudie and Georges Chamerot and of Ivan Turgenev, a close friend of the family who had taken Fauré under his wing. Together they got Marianne to make a decision, an affirmative one, by the middle of July. Fauré's friend Romain Bussine wrote to Mme Clerc, who was keeping a close eye on events, 'He's normally so taciturn, but now he's become extrovert, gossiping, running and jumping around – gentleness and affection simply shine out of his face.'

The emotional strain told on Marianne's health. She went to stay at Cabourg while her fiancé was packed off to the Pyrenees, ostensibly to take the cure at Cauterets for his hoarseness. It was a testing time for a young man in love. Cauterets bored him stiff and there was no sign of Marianne returning from Normandy. The letter he received during this exile from his future mother-in-law was full of real affection[14] but urged him strongly to be calm and patient. The truth was that Marianne was still not sure of her feelings. It would indeed be interesting to read the letters (if they have survived) which she wrote in reply to Fauré's; his demonstrate an almost childish liveliness surprising in a man of thirty-two, as well as a deep affection, and an anxiety that he has a job to hide.[15] Marianne's apprehension comes across in a letter to Marie Clerc of 2 August:[16]

the date of the great event is fixed for the end of September ... To begin with there was talk of 1 November, which brought *groans* from M. Gabriel. Now that it's been brought forward by a month he's apparently still not satisfied! You must *scold* him for his impatience; I have no wish to *drain* his emotions, which is the phrase he uses! I just ask for time to prepare myself – materially, and beyond that *psychologically* – before taking this *vital* step. It's an important moment in a woman's life and it's bound to be emotionally taxing for a girl who has never been away from home for a moment! May I count on you to tell him how things stand if he complains to you how cruel I'm being?! I give you permission to deal with him as you like, as his *dominion* over me is not yet ratified. He'll have the time to make up any losses he incurs when he's my Lord and Master . . . I tremble at the thought!

On her return to Paris in September Marianne postponed the wedding date. Even so preparations went ahead. Gounod agreed to be Marianne's witness at the ceremony and an apartment was found for the newly-weds in the rue de Vintimille. But this further procrastination on Marianne's part was more than Fauré could stand and, apparently, he gave vent to violent complaints. Marianne took these as an excuse to break off the engagement. The intensity of his love frightened her and in a letter of 30 November 1877 Pauline Viardot wrote to her friend Charlotte Valentin,[17]

Perhaps it's a good thing for both of them. If Fauré had gone back to being his old self their feelings would never have had any balance or stability. He would have burned her up with his love. She in return could only have offered a gentle but shallow affection. Let's hope it's all for the best.

The sudden breaking off of the engagement left Fauré prostrated. The blow was all the greater because he felt it was entirely his own fault. 'It took him months, perhaps years, to get over it' wrote his son Philippe.[18] He turned more than ever to his close friends, Romain Bussine, André Messager, Camille Saint-Saëns, Marie and Camille Clerc, and to his parents now in retirement in Toulouse, with whom he had rather lost touch. He went on with the planning of theatrical projects and continued to write about them to Pauline Viardot,[19] but he also came back to his favourite forms: songs, piano pieces and chamber music. He finished two extended works, the First Piano Quartet in C minor and the Ballade op. 19. He also produced a series of compositions notable for a new strength and depth of expression. We should not be too insistent in involving his private with his creative life, but the influence of his psychological disturbance is fairly plain. The all-too-celebrated 'Après un rêve' is a direct transposition of his feelings and he must surely have put some of his own bitterness into setting Bussine's rather trite adaptation from the Italian: 'Je rêvais le bonheur . . . ardent mirage'. The popularity of this song, in C minor, comes from its excess of feeling. It has been rendered by generations of 'artistes' and transcribed for all kinds of forces from light orchestras to bands in res-taurants. The ultimate accolade was awarded by Pablo Casals who arranged it in 1910 for 'cello, thus providing a companion for Saint-Saëns' everlasting *Swan*.

The pieces that followed were likewise in minor keys. The 'Sérénade toscane' (C minor), also on an Italian text, is shot through with passionate chromaticisms, being delivered to an uncaring beauty who shows no sign of responding to the poet's call. The equivocal major/minor tonality of the coda conjures up his hopes of eternal rest: a final solution to the torments of love which Fauré may have considered, at least in passing.

The 'desolate horizons' of 'Automne' (summer 1878, in B minor) are echoed by the 'beckoning horizons' of 'Les Berceaux' (summer 1879, in B flat minor) and by the black, violent despair of 'Le Voyageur' (?1878, in A minor), while the sombre threnody of the Elégie for 'cello (1880, in C minor) unfolds over the rhythm of a funeral march. But we may detect in Fauré a will to free himself from sorrow – a 'cathartic phase', to use psychoanalytical terminology – in the way he then moved from taking a morbid joy and masochistic pleasure in his love for Marianne to making a summary of his experience. With sharp psychological insight he brought together three, individually rather dull, poems by Charles Grandmougin under the overall title 'Poème d'un jour'. The first song, 'Rencontre', delicately expresses the emotion stirred by the appearance of the 'un-looked for mistress', in lyrical, tender tones that hint at abandon. The second, 'Toujours', throbs with the fury of thwarted passion:

> You bid me keep a silent tongue
> And go for ever far from you.

Its authenticity of feeling and vehement declamatory style make this one of the most powerful things Fauré ever wrote. But the jewel of the triptych is without a doubt 'Adieu', bitter sweet, clothed in a kind of ironic veil and achieving an extraordinary 'truth'. Poème d'un jour was probably written in 1878[20] and through it Fauré was able, if not to forget, at least to overcome the despair he had felt in the autumn of 1877. With 'Nell' he reached unsurpassed heights in expressing, beneath the voluptuous surface, his profound and unfulfilled capacity for tenderness.

This serious emotional crisis was probably responsible for turning Fauré into something of a Don Juan. All accounts of Fauré the man agree about his extraordinary charm. He was of medium height, rather rotund, with regular features: he had a short, strong nose and his mother's obstinate chin. His hair was thick and black, but began to go grey in his forties, when it made striking contrast with his olive complexion and with the dreamy, almost oriental expression in his dark, gold-flecked eyes. He was clean-shaven until he came back to Paris from Rennes, when he began to sport a moustache and a little tuft of a beard, a reduced version of a Napoleon III goatee. They can both be seen in the two best portraits of him which are roughly contemporary: the one by Paul Mathey done in dark ochre, and Sargent's oil portrait of 1889(?) worked in delicate greys. From 1900 till his death he wore just the moustache, of the white, flowing variety like Nietzsche's or Clemenceau's, which gradually turned yellowish from the smoke of innumerable cigarettes.

To this characterful appearance was added the unforced, almost casual nature of his movements and the impression of not being wholly in the world, which came partly from modesty and partly from habits of deep introspection. The overall effect was of almost feline elegance, of almost feminine charm. He was called 'The Cat' or 'The Odalisque', and Georges Servières, who knew him, writes perceptively that Fauré was 'a feminine type without being in the least effeminate'.[21] His clothes were always formal and correct – black jacket, striped trousers, a white shirt with detachable collar. When he was at Rennes he wore a loosely tied bow but by the 1890s he had followed fashion and changed over to a tie with a broad knot. In the early years of this century his frock coat with satin lining was matched either by a top hat or by a black bowler, depending on the occasion; and after the First World War he always appeared in a suit. White tie and tails remained regulation wear for the evenings.

He never quite lost the rolled 'r's of his birthplace which were softened by the warm, veiled, youthful timbre of his voice. All in all his personality exercised a magnetic attraction: women did not merely find him charming, they literally fell into his arms! The moral code of the Third Republic was strict on the surface. Divorce was rare and socially unacceptable. But under this surface it is fair to say that morality was extremely flexible, as a result both of the rampant anti-clericalism of the times and of reaction to the restrictive codes of conduct established under the preceding regimes. A President of the Republic, Félix Faure, as good as died in the arms of a lady of easy virtue. Women now began to use their power to make or break careers, and many an aristocratic male fortified his line with a middle-class fortune.

'Woman' became the central artistic symbol in the years around 1900, with Sarah Bernhardt as a possible archetype. Not without hypocrisy, the naked feminine figure found its way into salons and into the statuary of official buildings, fountains and public gardens. The decorative arts blossomed with a profusion of water-nymphs, sirens and Oceanides. These were well-rounded figures in conformity with the taste of the time and their long tresses flowed freely round their shoulders. We find the same erotic image of 'woman' in the paintings of Fernand Khnopff and Lévy-Dhurmer, in the poetry of Baudelaire, Pierre Louÿs and Mallarmé – the 'femme fatale' of Aubrey Beardsley and Félicien Rops, the omnipresent 'Salomé' . . .[22]

It is no surprise then to discover this image of 'woman' at the very centre of Fauré's work, as Proust accurately observed when including the composer in *A la recherche du temps perdu*.[23] The image colours Fauré's songs and theatre music, even his religious compositions, of which motets to the Virgin form a large part. Debussy somewhat ironically drew a likeness between Fauré's Ballade for piano and a pretty woman adjusting her shoulder-strap,[24] and through much of his work there breathes that *odor di femmina* which had such a powerful effect on Don Juan. This is not the place to play Leporello and draw up a catalogue of Fauré's conquests. Some are well documented and a historian must take note of them. The majority, while possibly falling short of 1,003, have been obliterated by the sands of time.

Of more interest is the fact that with Fauré this image of 'woman' is a dual one. Certainly, the beloved is a key figure in the world of his imagination and perhaps the subject of a mild obsession, worked out in his numerous love-songs, but 'woman' is also a refuge, a confidante for his cares and troubles, the substitute for that 'mother' whom he had so sorely lacked as a child. During the 1870s this rôle was taken by Marie Clerc, and taken with great understanding; then, in the 1880s, Fauré turned to Marguerite Baugnies, to whom he dedicated 'Après un rêve' and the First Nocturne, and who is better known under the name of her second husband, the sculptor René de Saint-Marceaux. The most important figures in the artistic world of Paris attended her Friday *salons*. At the beginning of the 1890s Fauré also formed close friendships with two 'leading ladies' of the Parisian aristocracy who became both his confidantes and his patrons: Winnaretta Singer, whom he had already met at Villerville, and Elisabeth de Caraman Chimay, Countess Greffulhe, who dominated Parisian high society by her startling beauty, her intelligence and her extravagant life-style. It was for her that Fauré wrote his *Pavane* to words by her cousin, Count Robert de Montesquiou. While he was at work on it he wrote to Marguerite Baugnies, on 12 September 1887, referring to the Countess as his 'King of Bavaria' – she, like all of the 'upper crust', was a passionate Wagnerian. The world in which Fauré moved was, in fact, precisely the one that the young Marcel Proust for years dreamt of entering and many of the composer's friends left their mark on characters in Proust's novel: Montesquiou on the Baron de Charlus and the Countess Greffuhle on the haughty Duchess de Guermantes, while Marguerite Baugnies was a Mme Verdurin who had the taste and insight to choose as 'regulars' of her salon the finest musicians of the period. The principal model for Mme Verdurin was Madeleine Lemaire. She and her daughter painted terrible pictures of flowers which some buyers actually liked but which others bought merely out of politeness. At all events it was at one of the crowded, enthusiastic gatherings in her tiny house on the rue de Monceau that one of the first public performances took place of one of Fauré's major song cycles, *La Bonne chanson*, to poems by Verlaine. Fauré had been guided to Verlaine's poetry by the Count de Montesquiou. Another cycle based on his poems owed its birth to Winnaretta Singer, who was to become the Princess Edmond de Polignac in 1893: the five songs op.58, written in the spring of 1891 under the spell of Venice where he was staying in her 'palazzo'. As for the Countess Greffulhe, she commissioned not only the stately *Pavane* but also numerous theatrical projects which we shall discuss later (see pp. 172–3).[25]

Fauré was often to be seen in the Parisian *salons*. This fact has been held against him and has even led some people to consider his whole output as being 'salon music'. In 1922 a journalist made the loaded remark, 'You've had a lot of success in the salons', to which Fauré replied, 'I was very much involved in making a living. I had some good friends, and when you're an unknown to the musical public at large it's nice to find people who understand you.'[26] From this reply and from other examples of his behaviour, it is clear that he was no snob. He patronised equally the luxurious apartments and *châteaux* of the high aristocracy and the salons held in middle-class dining-rooms, provided that there was good music to be found and in particular that he should be given a chance to promote his own. Added to which there is the point that going out nearly every evening is one way of forgetting a narrow, joyless private life.

Fauré married in 1883, not so much for love as out of cool calculation: he was approaching his fortieth birthday, the age when, according to late nineteenth-century custom, you had to put your young bachelor days behind you. This advice was constantly on the lips of Marguerite Baugnies who, sentimentalist that she was, loved arranging marriages. She herself had in 1870 thought of marrying Saint-Saëns but her parents were opposed to the idea because of the 'delicate health' of the gentleman in question, who lived on into his late eighties. In 1894 she was to arrange the, shortlived, engagement of Debussy with Thérèse Roger. But twelve years before that her mind was concentrated on marrying off her dear Fauré.

The composer Georges Migot who, as a young man, used to attend Mme Baugnies' salon, has passed on the following story. Fauré had finally decided to put an end to his bachelorhood but he was faced with a difficult choice. Marguerite Baugnies suggested three 'possibles' from the artistic fraternity of her acquaintance – three young girls whose names all began with F: the daughters of Octave Feuillet and Georges Feydeau, two writers popular at the time, and the daughter of the animal sculptor Emmanuel Fremiet. The three names were placed in a hat and Fauré drew out that of Marie Fremiet. Mme Baugnies and her mother paid several visits to the Fremiets to present the intending fiancé and he was soon accepted. This sequence of events could be said to constitute one of the arranged marriages which were common at that period and after a brief engagement the wedding took place in Paris on 27 March 1883 at the Mairie of the 16th *arrondissement* and again in church the following day.

The young couple made their home at 93, avenue Niel in the 17th *arrondissement*, and their eldest son Emmanuel was born there towards the end of the year. In 1886 they moved to a six-room apartment on the fifth floor of a solid, old-fashioned building at 154, boulevard Malesherbes. They stayed there till 1911 when they left the Plaine Monceau for newly built 'luxury flats' in Passy, at 32, rue des Vignes in the 16th *arrondissement*.

A second son, Philippe, was born on 28 July 1889 at Bougival, in a part of the Seine valley much frequented by the Impressionist painters and often chosen by the Faurés as a place to spend the summer months. They generally moved out of Paris during the hot weather and rented a house in the country, taking a large part of their belongings with them. In the 1870s Fauré's parents-in-law bought a small house at Prunay, not far from Bougival, and here Fauré wrote some of his finest music, the Sixth Nocturne, the Fifth Barcarolle and *La Bonne chanson*. This song cycle was inspired by his very close friendship with Emma Moyse, who lived nearby. She was married to the banker Sigismond Bardac and had two children by him: Raoul, who became one of Fauré's favourite pupils, and Hélène, called Dolly, for whom Fauré wrote his suite for piano duet. Mme Bardac led a highly independent existence (see p. 181), but in 1908 her husband gave her a divorce so that she could marry Debussy, by whom she had already had a daughter, Chouchou.

Fauré's affair with Mme Bardac was a desperate, and perhaps inevitable, escape from his own marriage which had proved a disappointment. The problem stemmed from his initial decision to marry as if playing roulette. An arranged marriage might have been all very well for some steady, materially minded man, but not for someone of Fauré's sensual, passionate nature, and his feelings at the beginning of 1883 were very far from what they had been six years earlier when his love for his 'adored Marianne' had turned him into an extrovert – when, as he wrote to Marie Clerc, he lived 'surrounded by blue sky'. Writing to Marguerite Baugnies about Marie Fremiet, he found it hard to quell his doubts: 'Don't you think she is really kind and charming?' And we may sense some auto-suggestion in his claim that 'I have reached a high pitch, I assure you; and I revel in this sense of well-being.'

Unfortunately Marie Fremiet was without beauty, or wit, or a fortune. In an unpublished letter to Marie Clerc (Bibliothèque Nationale, Music Dept), Romain Bussine, who five years earlier had been a close observer of Fauré's engagement to Marianne Viardot, wrote about his marriage: 'I'm unable to tell you what he could have been hoping for in the way of collaboration from his wife . . . to begin with . . . I thought he'd got engaged to his mother's chambermaid, and I could not persuade myself I was wrong . . . her extremely modest appearance seemed to me to have a mean look, something narrow and cold; she has no taste in clothes and is impossibly silent.' But there was something touching about this young girl who had a talent for painting flowers on panels and fans which found a market among Fauré's female relations. Her energies above all were channelled into motherhood and in this task her devotion reached self-sacrifice and beyond. Sadly, her determination to guard the health of her two sons was combined with an unswerving and excessive belief in the virtues of hygiene. As a result she coddled them so that they had no resistance to infection and fell ill, either in turn or together. This vicious circle operated for years. She refused to send them to school because of the likelihood of unhealthy contacts and instead gave them lessons at home, a curious upbringing which came close to having a serious effect on their future. Emmanuel told me that when eventually he began his secondary education he was far behind and caught up only by means of intense hard work. He was of a scientific bent and survived this handicap to become a biologist of international repute and a member of the Institut, keeping his laboratory at the Collège de France until the end of his life. Philippe was more literary in his interests. He started by being involved with the theatre and several of his plays were put on in Paris. Then he turned to philosophy, as well as writing biographies of his father and grandfather. He was less independent than Emmanuel and came more under his mother's influence. It is significant that he married in 1926, at the age of 37, after her death. When they finally moved to Passy, it was to an apartment on the fifth floor consisting of a huge *atelier*, accommodating Marie's desire to return to her sculpture. She spent long hours there alone but all that resulted from her labours were the shapeless lumps of abandoned projects. She could not fulfil herself on the artistic level any more than on the personal one and she seems to have been inhibited by living too close to the works of her father and her husband. She admired them both to the extent of signing herself Marie Gabriel Fauré and giving her children the surname Fauré-Fremiet.

Understandably such a domestic situation held few charms for Fauré. He liked to go out in the evenings but Marie was a stay-at-home and nearly always refused to go with him – her absence from the first performance of *Prométhée* at Béziers upset him deeply. To prevent him going out at night she 'forgot' to do the necessary laundry and he spent a fortune on new shirts . . . As Emmanuel said to me, she was such a reluctant wife that it was tantamount to abandoning the rôle. There grew up between her and Fauré a barrier of silence, full of unspoken reproaches. After Fauré's death Marie admitted to M.-L. Boëllmann that she missed him but she wrote also, 'He crucified me by his silence.' They communicated by letter, even when they were both in Paris, because they spent less and less time together in the same house. These letters, published by their son Philippe, are of prime importance. Fauré's love for his wife had soon died and in its place we find an expression of his thoughts and precise information about how his works are going. In spite of everything, he still felt a tenderness towards her as well as guilt and profound pity for her unhappiness.

In Emmanuel Fremiet, on the other hand, Fauré found not just a father-in-law but a real friend and adviser. Their mutual affection and esteem grew to such an extent that it was sometimes said Fauré had 'married his father-in-law'. Fremiet's career was an example of modest endeavour and integrity. There were, it is true, some important commissions from official quarters: the Joan of Arc in the place des Pyramides, four groups above the columns of the Pont Alexandre III and above all the fine horses of the Observatoire fountain. But even so the Fremiets had to live frugally since sculpture was totally dependent on patronage. When Fauré and Marie were first married they spent much of their time with the Fremiets and Fauré did not find the narrow parsimony and austerity easy to bear, being used to a much freer life with less emphasis on correct conduct and respectability. Gone were the days when he could travel to Cologne or Munich or London to see an opera from *The Ring, Lohengrin, Die Meistersinger, Tannhaüser* or *Tristan,* as he had done between 1879 and 1882.[27] He had a job to escape for a few days in the August of 1885 when he went (alone, of course) to Anvers, where his recent Symphony in D minor was to be played – and even then the performance was postponed . . . He spent four days in 1887 staying with the Countess Greffulhe at her large villa la Case, looking out over the cliffs at Dieppe, and in 1888 Octave Maus invited him to take part in one of the concerts given by the group 'les XX' in Brussels. On 3 March he played the piano part in his First Piano Quartet and accompanied Ysaÿe in the First Violin Sonata. He went back to Brussels on 25 February 1889 to play the Second Piano Quartet with the Ysaÿe Quartet and to hear d'Indy conducting the *Madrigal* for four voices, *Le Ruisseau* and the choruses from Act V of *Caligula*; but these journeys did not please his parents-in-law and they accused him of wasting his family's money. A passage from a letter of d'Indy to Maus of 22 January 1889 puts the matter plainly enough:

Fauré begs you, when you have a minute, to write him a short, urgent letter – *extravagantly urgent* – saying that his presence is vital etc., and recommending a *very cheap* hotel (real or fictitious). The reason is that his wife and especially his parents-in-law are very tight with the money and when he wants to go on journeys, which always mean spending some, then they bully him so much about his presence not being necessary that he ends up by washing his hands of the whole business. All this between ourselves, naturally, but he would be very grateful for a brief note of support as he has really been looking forward to this short stay in Brussels.[28]

Octave Maus finally put Fauré up in his own house, an act of kindness which caused Fauré considerable embarrassment.

Marguerite Baugnies was aware of Fauré's financial problems and in 1888 she and the guests of her salon organised a tombola, the profit from which was to send Fauré and his friend Messager to Bayreuth. There they heard *Die Meistersinger* and, especially, *Parsifal* for the first time, with Ernest van Dyck in the title rôle. They found several acquaintances there: Pierre de Bréville and his friend Maurice Bagès, Claude Debussy and Winnaretta Singer who 'is three parts mad!!! I'm the one looking after her', as Fauré wrote to his patroness.[29] He was to return to Bayreuth at the Princess de Polignac's invitation for the revival of the *Ring* in 1896.

The French musical world of the 1890s was submerged by the Wagnerian flood. Fauré admired Wagner greatly and was familiar with the smallest details of his music, but he was one of the few musicians who managed to keep a cool head. He fundamentally disapproved of d'Indy's intention of producing a French *Parsifal* in *Fervaal* and, like Debussy, thought that in *Le Roi Arthus* Chausson had succumbed to the magic potion of *Tristan*.

In the introduction to the third chapter of Fauré's *Correspondance*, I have discussed the various facets of his language and orchestration which seem to owe something to Wagner, but it has to be admitted that they need looking for. Fauré agreed with Debussy that direct imitation of Wagner was necessarily useless. For all his modesty he knew that his aesthetic world lay elsewhere and that his most important task was to explore it and to achieve an individual musical language through emulation, however ineffectual, of the masters he had so long admired: Mendelssohn, Liszt, Chopin and Schumann.

4 'En blanc et noir'

From his student days Fauré was far more interested in the piano than in the organ. He seems to have preferred the almost monochrome timbre of the piano to the organ's complex, semi-orchestral possibilities. We should perhaps note here that in 1860 French organ music had fallen into some disrepute through the strange effusions of Edouard Baptiste and Lefébure-Wély, for which Alexandre Boëly's correct neo-classicism was no real compensation. While the art of organ-building was at its height, the instrument's function was still, by and large, decorative: to impress and astonish the faithful with music equally compounded of the dextrous, the descriptive and the grotesque. This state of affairs had lasted since the end of the eighteenth century and Benoist's teaching at the Conservatoire seems to have done little to change it. Deliverance came from Belgium in the persons of Lemmens and then Franck, who were to found the great French organ school of the late nineteenth century. Even so Lemmens' organ method, which they used at the Niedermeyer School, hardly stressed the emotive side of the instrument. Lemmens set his face against the spectacular registrations used by popular organists and opted for an unexceptionable neutrality bordering on austerity: in old music, especially Bach, he deadened the colour by an overwhelming reliance on foundation stops.[1] This approach could still be heard almost up to the middle of the twentieth century. It must be said that it was greatly encouraged by the skills of organ-builders like the Cavaillé-Colls who made their foundation stops marvellously full and rounded, and it is typical of this school of thought that when Fauré used to come and improvise at Notre-Dame he always asked Louis Vierne, the organist, to pull out just the eight foot Bourdons![2]

But, as Saint-Saëns confirmed, Fauré was 'a first-class organist when he wanted to be'[3] – the compliment cannot be ignored, coming from such a great virtuoso, but the qualification is interesting too. He had not the energy to pursue a career as a solo pianist, and in the same way he never

made great efforts to keep up his organ technique. He much preferred
to improvise, giving rein to his many original harmonic ideas, rather
than stun the complaisant congregation with some pompous, noisy vol-
untary. F. de Ménil gives this rather flowery description of Fauré the
organist:

An airy, fluid line extends itself without contrapuntal interruptions above strangely attractive harmonies, its undulating lines coloured by a delicate play of sonorities . . . The only notes he reads are written on his artistic soul and here, incessantly,
he discovers untold wonders. He prefers to play these ideas on quiet stops, with
exquisite harmonic reminiscences of *La Bonne chanson* or *Prométhée*. In these
restless songs sometimes the severe sorrow of the Requiem combines with the
tender melancholy of the *Elégie* and all these ideas are scattered in echoes between
the four manuals, in sounds that are both noble and gently poetic. M. Gabriel
Fauré is the poet of the organ.   (*Musica*, January 1903)

At the same period Emilie Girette, the future wife of Edouard Risler,
recorded in her diary[4] that Fauré had played for her an improvisation on a
theme from his *Prométhée* ('Ne pleure pas, O Prométhée' from the chorus
of the Oceanides); this was on the main organ of the Madeleine, to which
Fauré had been appointed in 1896. When, on 1 October 1905, he finally
left the Madeleine, he thumbed his nose at the 'employers' who had so
often made difficulties for him by introducing into the service a, no doubt
discreet, improvisation on the popular song 'Il était une bergère . . . et ron,
et ron, petit patapon'![5]

Jokes like this and a more or less exclusive taste for improvisation did
not prevent Fauré from being an 'ardent admirer' of Bach's organ music, as
the Princess Edmond de Polignac recalls in her memoirs,[6] but she adds that
he admitted finding certain fugues 'utterly boring'. For him as for many of
his French contemporaries, Bach was an historical reference point. Where
he differed from those contemporaries was in knowing the music thoroughly, thanks to the years he had spent studying with Niedermeyer. He
belonged to what was then thought of as the great school of Bach playing,
his teacher, Clément Loret, having learnt from Nicolas Lemmens (1823–
81) who in turn had been a pupil of the celebrated Adolf Friedrich Hesse
(1809–63); it was Hesse who had so upset the Parisians in 1844 when he
came to play Bach fugues on the new organ in St-Eustache.

In addition, the 48 and the *Inventions* formed the basis of Niedermeyer's piano teaching. The cantor of Leipzig thus lay at the centre of
Fauré's musical upbringing and it is understandable if in later years he
somewhat abandoned him. Nonetheless, in 1915 he wrote the preface for

a Durand edition of the 48, and here he justly condemned the intrusive revisions of the nineteenth century and joined Schumann in insisting how valuable the work was as teaching material. Around the same time Durand asked him to revise the whole of Bach's organ works, which he did with unofficial help from Joseph Bonnet and from his friend Gigout.

In a brief preface, Fauré (and no doubt Gigout as well) takes sides in the current dispute about how to play old organ music. He does not see that he ought to 'deprive himself of the advantages possessed by modern organs, thanks to a long series of technical improvements' and suggests to the player that he should 'bring these works alive again, instead of emphasising what is dated about them'. He finishes by saying 'the main problem with masterpieces is that they are surrounded by excessive respect and this ends up by making them boring'.[7]

All in all, Fauré respected the organ as an instrument possessing a classical repertoire, but he had no great love for it. For him it was something he had to play every day, not from choice but from the necessity imposed by his job at the Madeleine. It is easy to see why, in spite of commissions from Abbot Henri Hazé and from Saint-Saëns,[8] he never wrote a piece for organ solo. He preferred the piano as being the instrument with the most advanced repertoire, including above all the music of Schumann: the Princess Edmond de Polignac goes on to recall, 'he was particularly fond of Schumann and used to play most of his works better than any other pianist I've ever heard, including the great names of the keyboard'.

Various descriptions of Fauré's piano playing have come down to us. 'His style was so individual', wrote his son Philippe,[9]

that there is no pianist alive today who can approach his way of playing his own works. His hands were strong and looked heavy;[10] in fact they were supple and light. He hardly raised them above the keys but was still able to obtain any effect he wanted. He had a horror of virtuosity, of *rubato* and effects aimed at making the audience swoon. He followed the printed notes meticulously, keeping strict time. What was so overpowering about his playing lay below the surface, in the areas of thought and emotion where teaching is helpless to guide you. There's no doubt he could have had a brilliant career as a virtuoso if he'd been more ambitious and more concerned with the plaudits of the crowd.

Fauré's piano playing was in fact a synthesis of what he had been taught. His two principal teachers were Niedermeyer and Saint-Saëns and through them he inherited the traditions of Ignaz Moscheles and Camille Stamaty (a pupil of Kalkbrenner). The emphasis lay on a high degree of virtuosity and on a clear, brilliant, almost dry sound, obtained by a crisp articulation of the fingers. Less importance was attached to the suppleness of the wrist demanded by Chopin or to Liszt's development of strength in the arm. The extreme clarity of Fauré's playing owed a lot to Saint-Saëns. Mme Pochet de Tinan, a mutual friend, remarked on this when writing to Saint-Saëns on 2 September 1874 (the letter is now in the Dieppe Museum):

Here's a style you can't disown! The clarity, the simplicity, the gentleness, the charm, it's your playing to the life. He places his small hands on the keyboard just as you do and, give him your 'fire', in another ten years he'll be a Saint-Saëns. But you have to goad him on all the time.

Even so Fauré's piano playing came to resemble his teacher's less and less. He developed a style of his own and it seems as if, in his case, pianistic habits were quite quickly modified in the light of what Fauré the composer was writing and thinking. His keyboard style was less sparkling, less nervous than Saint-Saëns'. Increasingly it took on an overall gentleness, with a legato produced by keeping the fingers close to the keys as Chopin did[11] or, to go further back in time, as Bach did, according to J. N. Forkel.[12] He was helped in this by the lessons he had learnt from Clément Loret, his organ teacher at the Niedermeyer School, in sliding the fingers from key to key and in changing them on the same note.[13] In Niedermeyer's own report of 1854, which I have already quoted from, he makes this relevant comment about his piano teaching: 'the course for beginners is designed to prepare them for learning the organ'. If, in spite of this, Niedermeyer intended his own advanced piano class to give pupils a firm technique on that instrument, it was only because he knew that the future *maîtres de chapelle* he had in his care would be forced to give piano lessons to make a living. Fauré, for example, was giving piano lessons at least up until 1900 and seems to have been much sought after as a teacher.[14]

Marguerite Long knew Fauré's playing well and described it in her book on the composer:[15]

It lacked the impact and brilliance Fauré himself used to demand from his interpreters. He had a wholly personal way of striking the keys, heavy but at the same time supple, which gave his playing that precise accentuation and wonderfully tender strength his music needs. His hand was rather heavy and it produced a beautifully rounded sonority – that's what pianists must aim for.

Georges Servières agrees with her and says[16] that Fauré's playing certainly did not lack 'impact in loud passages, thanks to his strong hands and short fingers'.

Fauré made piano rolls for various companies between 1905 and 1913 and the most trustworthy of them bear out what these witnesses say.[17] These perforated paper rolls obviously cannot give such a reliable indication of a performing style as records do. But if they are played back on a good player-piano that is working properly (an important proviso), then they do provide evidence about tempo, which was precisely notated at the time of recording, and about articulation and phrasing. The best of them (the Welte Mignon rolls of 1913) even reproduce nuances and pedalling quite faithfully, whereas earlier systems indicated such things by a kind of notation and the delicate task of interpreting this was left to the 'pianolist'.

'There were two sayings', Marguerite Long goes on, 'which Fauré was fond of and which he used to come out with every ten minutes or so: *Nuances without changing speed*, and *Let's hear the bass!*' In 1913 in Paris Fauré made a recording of his First Barcarolle for the German firm Welte Mignon, a performance that has often been transferred on to LPs. It shows most strikingly how even, regular, and yet supple his playing was, and what an individual way he had of bringing out the top and bottom lines of the texture. In other hands this piece might be no more than charming. Played by the composer, the return of the opening achieves a measure of real grandeur.

Many professional pianists never really came to terms with the particular pianism Fauré's work demands. The composer himself confessed as much to Emilie Girette in 1902,[18] at a time when the greatest French pianists such as Alfred Cortot, Edouard Risler, Ricardo Viñes and Raoul Pugno were playing his pieces fairly regularly. So we should treat their observations, and those of Marguerite Long, with some caution. In the passage quoted above, Mme Long suggests that Fauré's playing lacked brilliance, the quality that she herself brought to his works as no one else did. Another of the great teachers of the time was Louis Diémer, who favoured absolutely clear playing in which expression was secondary, and Philippe Fauré-Fremiet in his biography (p. 156) notes that in Diémer's circle Fauré was thought to play his own works 'coldly'. As for Cortot, he declared to Bernard Gavoty in 1955:[19]

I was amazed that this sensitive poet could be such a dry pianist. His playing was percussive, without much body to it, and he never used the pedals. It must have been the teaching at the Niedermeyer School that inculcated such an inflexible style which, by the end of the nineteenth century was already somewhat archaic.

Surrounded by these conflicting opinions, let us state a fact: that Fauré was ambidextrous. That is why his figurations, themes and countermelodies so often have to be passed smoothly and imperceptibly from one hand to the other, and why he likes to place his tunes in the resonant centre of the keyboard.

The beginning of the First Barcarolle (Ex. 1) provides a good example of Fauré's ambidextrous piano writing, while the F sharp major *cantabile* section of the Third Barcarolle (Ex. 2) demonstrates his use of textural layers.

Ex. 1 Barcarolle no. 1

Example 2 shows how complex his writing can be, although the actual sound is extremely clear. His thorough education in counterpoint led him to complicate his scores, to add extra parts, to fill in the gaps, as it were. The result was an imaginative recreation of the Baroque style, and of Bach's keyboard writing in particular. Fauré seems to take a fiendish delight in weaving the most subtle arabesques, just as he is fond of surprising the ear by sudden excursions into distant keys. His early works may remind us of Schumann and Brahms in these respects; indeed in complexity he may even outdo them, achieving a kind of mosaic writing which the eye sees as learned but which strikes the ear as being quite spontaneous.

This is undoubtedly one of the reasons why Fauré's piano works are not played that often, at least in public recitals. A great pianist like Horowitz will declare that he knows and admires the whole of Fauré's piano output, but cannot easily bring himself to put any of it in his programme; Giese-king had the same problem. Virtuosi nearly always prefer playing Chopin

Ex. 2 Barcarolle no. 3

or Liszt rather than Brahms or Schumann, because their music 'lies under the fingers better'. Fauré's music suffers similarly.

One possible explanation of this is that Fauré always composed at the table before trying each page over on his favourite Erard. On a more general front it could be argued that despite Fauré's great love for the piano he was primarily a composer, and one who was far more concerned with quality and originality than with making his music comfortable to play, still less with creating sensational effects. His piano music demands the highest virtuosity but, unlike Liszt or Ravel, he did not take it as a compositional premiss.

Virtuosity for Fauré was not something to be striven after. It was secondary to his chief aim – expression. All his life he shunned picturesque titles, as he did descriptive or programme music in general. He did imitate the titles used by the Romantic composers, but in fact he would, as his son Philippe recorded,[20] 'far rather have given his Nocturnes, Impromptus and even his Barcarolles the simple title Piano Piece no. so-and-so', following the example of Schumann (*Klavierstücke*). His son further comments (p. 138) that 'the thirteen piano pieces called Nocturnes are not necessarily based on rêveries or on emotions inspired by the night. They are lyrical, generally impassioned pieces, sometimes anguished or wholly elegiac, like the Eleventh Nocturne, dedicated to the memory of Noémi Lalo.' When a lady asked him in what sunny climes he had written his Sixth Nocturne, he replied 'The Simplon tunnel'.

So in writing for his favourite instrument Fauré did not want just to write 'piano music' which would give him the chance to demonstrate his keyboard technique. His aim was rather to write 'music for the piano' regardless of other factors.

Fauré's piano music consists of some sixty pieces or more. They are varied in length and date from every period of his creative life, and they record perhaps more clearly than any other genre the evolution of his language; as he wrote to his wife,[21] 'when you're writing piano music you have to pay in cash and keep up the level of inspiration all the time. If you try, as I do, to give continual satisfaction then it's possibly the most difficult medium of all.'

Somewhat strangely, at the time when he was most often appearing as a solo pianist, in the salons of Pauline Viardot, Saint-Saëns, the Clercs or at numerous concerts of the Société nationale de musique, he wrote very little for the instrument. The chronology of his earliest piano works is, admittedly, very hard to establish as the manuscripts have been lost. The *Trois Romances sans paroles* would seem to date from his time at the Niedermeyer School, but there is doubt about the 'morceau de piano' he mentions in one of his letters to Marianne Viardot in the summer of 1877.[22] This might refer to his single Marzurka, a long-winded piece in which his admiration for Chopin takes the form of pastiche. Equally it could be the First Nocturne in E flat minor. This was published as op. 33 no. 1 in 1883 but its highly romantic style puts it considerably earlier than that, and in fact the lovely final phrase is found among the sketches for the First Violin Sonata, dating from 1875–6. This First Nocturne is one of the best of Fauré's early works. It established an individual voice and a keyboard style that were to be developed in the numerous works of the 1880s.

Chopin was one influence on the young composer that we can hardly mistake, and we may surely agree that he could have made a worse choice of presiding genius. On the technical level this influence can be seen in the chromatic counter-melody in the Fourth Barcarolle (bars 18 and 20), in the light-footed episode in alternating fifths and sixths from the Second Nocturne and in its extremely delicate passagework, and in his habit of introducing pieces with bars of discreetly atmospheric accompaniment, as in the First Impromptu and the Fourth Barcarolle. But Fauré was chiefly influenced by one of Chopin's most original contributions to piano writing: his pliable, decorative melodic line. The Third and Fourth Nocturnes begin with 'accompanied singing' like the early Nocturnes of Chopin, and elsewhere there are beautiful lyrical passages where the melodic phrases escape from rigid bar-lines and expand in the pure, free flow of *bel canto*, and where the two hands, after being subtly set against each other, come together in triplets and brilliant demi-semiquavers. The B minor *dolce espressivo* section on the third page of the Second Nocturne and the G flat *cantando* from the Fourth Nocturne are two notable examples.

Something else that Fauré took over from Chopin and then developed was the arpeggio formula. He was ingenious at finding variations of it and, having a large left hand, extended the pattern to cover as much of the keyboard as he could. The resulting fluidity and poise are typical of his early work and contribute greatly to the charm of pieces like the Third and Fourth Barcarolles and the Ballade. He also followed Chopin's example (as offered by the B major Nocturne op. 62 no. 1) in inserting long trills into the melody and the accompaniment, to produce a sort of sound-pedal (see the end of the Second Barcarolle and the reprise of the Second Nocturne).

Nonetheless these detailed borrowings from Chopin were gradually to disappear from Fauré's work. His debt to the older master was probably greater on a general aesthetic level and I would say the important areas of agreement between the two lay in their desire to be expressive, in their distaste for anything flashy, in their determination to make every page perfect, however short it might be, and finally in their way of introducing the most daring flights with a discretion that marks the 'classical' composer.

As far as technique goes, Fauré seems to have been more profoundly influenced by Saint-Saëns and Liszt. The brilliance and lightness that are Saint-Saëns' hallmark can be heard in the sparkling tarantella rhythms of the Second Impromptu, in the toccata passage (*Allegro ma non troppo*) of the Second Nocturne and, in the Allegro of the Fifth Nocturne, in the high passage-work. What Saint-Saëns could not have written are the superb melodies which thread their way through these virtuoso pages; with Fauré, tunes go hand in hand with his most imaginative technical discoveries. Saint-Saëns' influence is also to be found in the very manipulation of linguistic elements. Fauré got from his teacher the very French ability to take a phrase of just a few notes and with it write whole pages of music: for example, the echo motif of the First Nocturne (bars 39 foll.), which is built up of five notes from the C major scale, or the opening theme of the First Impromptu, whose four notes go blandly on to fill two entire pages. A valid comparison can be made with the four-note idea that opens Saint-Saëns' First Violin Sonata, dating from the same period (1875). Even so this is another field in which the pupil surpasses his master. Whereas this motivic technique is an essential part of Saint-Saëns' language, with Fauré it is only sporadic and secondary. Right from his earliest piano works we find an abundance of tunes, a harmonic inventiveness and a kind of tender warmth which override any debts he may owe to others and proclaim a distinct personality.

Saint-Saëns was also responsible for Fauré's meeting with Liszt. In December 1877 the young composer went with Camille Clerc to Weimar for the première of *Samson et Dalila*. It was a memorable visit, and nearly forty years later Fauré wrote in *Le Figaro* (20 June 1913): 'being at that first performance was one of the greatest pleasures and one of the most moving experiences of my life'. He met Liszt again in July 1882, when he went to a music festival in Zürich and heard Liszt's *Légende de Ste Elizabeth* and Saint-Saëns' *La Lyre et la harpe*. On 9 July 1882 Fauré wrote to Marie Clerc:[23] 'First of all, I saw Liszt – an emotional occasion! Saint-Saëns claims I went green when he presented me to the master, and words cannot describe the welcome Liszt extended to me.' Fauré must have seen Liszt a second time on that visit because in his letter, after describing his welcome, he says that Liszt played them one of his transcriptions and adds 'Tomorrow it's my turn on the piano stool.' Probably this was the famous occasion when he played Liszt his Ballade. Fauré tells the story in the already quoted interview in *Excelsior*. 'I was worried about its length', he said to Marguerite Long,[24] 'and I admitted as much to Liszt. His reply was splendid. "Too long, young man? That's a meaningless phrase. A composer conceives something, then writes it down." ' Liszt sat down at the piano and began to sight-read it 'but after five or six pages he said to me "I've run out of fingers" and, to my terror, asked me to continue.' This is a first-hand account of an episode which might otherwise seem suspect and it is worth noting also that Fauré's version of Liszt's remark ('I've run out of fingers') is different from the 'It's too difficult' which is normally quoted.

Whether Liszt's eyes were not up to it, or whether he wanted to listen in judgment to what a young artist could do, it seems he was acting absolutely in character. The great pianist Francis Planté (1839–1934) describes in a letter his meeting with Liszt at a Paris salon on 28 March 1886:

Just as I was going to sit down at the piano with Liszt next to me – he'd asked if he could turn the pages for me – I saw him put several pages of musical manuscript *on the music-rest* ... He announced to the audience that it was something he'd written specially for his young friend the 'cellist Brandoukoff. The manuscript was some way from being easily legible and realising this he hesitated for a moment ... 'Yes' he said *loudly*, 'there are too many flats and I can't see very well. You', he said (*turning to me*), 'your eyes are young; you can read it for us!' I didn't dare refuse this invitation and in fact I got through my accompaniment quite well. Liszt turned to Gounod, who was on his right, and said 'You see? Not a *single* flat fell under the rest'; a reminiscence of Mozart's remark to his Sovereign about the overture to *Don Giovanni*.[25]

Alfred Cortot recounted in a lecture what Fauré had told him about Liszt and the Ballade: that 'Liszt had simply suggested adding a few touches on the orchestra to the original piano version, so as to highlight certain details and give the whole texture a more characteristic colour.'[26] Saint-Saëns' young pupil seems to have made a great impression on Liszt, who gave him a photograph of himself with the dedication 'F. Liszt to Gabriel Fauré as a mark of my high esteem and sympathetic understanding'. His library, housed in the Academy Franz Liszt in Budapest, contains a surprisingly large collection of Fauré's early printed works.[27]

This contact with one of Europe's greatest musicians seems to have had a considerable effect on Fauré. Through Saint-Saëns, he came as a very young man to know and love Liszt's finest compositions, which is not necessarily to say his most spectacular ones. The pianistic language, at its best, fascinated him by its bold manipulation of form and by its profound poetry, as found in the great B minor Sonata, the *Harmonies poétiques et religieuses* and the *Années de Pèlerinage*. The undulating outline and the almost improvisatory, questioning character of the opening of Fauré's Fifth Nocturne probably owe something to the central theme of *Sur le 123ᵉ*

Sonnet de Pétrarque, and the delightful beginning of the Second *Valse-Caprice* reminds us of *Au bord d'une source*; while the massive, broadly declaimed chords of the First Nocturne's second paragraph have something in common with the great chorale theme of the Sonata.

Fauré's predilection for the middle part of the keyboard did not prevent him following Liszt's example and also exploiting the clarity of its upper registers. At the beginning of the First Nocturne, in the central part of the Sixth Nocturne and at the end of the Ballade, Fauré makes the treble sing with particular delicacy. He tended to reserve this part of the piano for decoration, of which there is plenty in his music of this period: for example, the Third Barcarolle, where the third idea is decorated with sextuplets, like stone tracery on the flying buttress of a cathedral.

In this respect Fauré could be said to have made a link between *Les Jeux d'eau de la Villa d'Este* and the purely French *Jeux d'eau* dedicated to him by his pupil Ravel. The bells of the Fourth Nocturne too, filtered through thick foliage, recall the *Vallée d'Obermann*. Fauré is at times still more adventurous, holding on the pedal for long periods to give a pre-echo of Debussy's delicate sound-world. On the final page of the Fifth Nocturne he punctures this halo of sonority with clear, single notes and in the Sixth Nocturne the wonderful curve of the main theme returns in a harmonic cloud built up over several bars.

The title *Valse-Caprice* is, finally, an inverted reference to Liszt. Suites of waltzes were the fashion around 1880. Even such a 'serious' composer as Henri Duparc was not averse to attempting this unpretentious genre. Massenet's *Valse folle* and the *Valse nonchalante* and *Valse mignonne* of Saint-Saëns are perhaps best forgotten, but Chabrier's *Trois valses romantiques* are masterpieces of their kind; by comparison with them Fauré's four *Valses-Caprices* make a somewhat pale impression. In the first two, for example, pretty music in *salon* style leads straight into clumsy, heavily accentuated themes and the rhythms then get lost in a mêlée of aimless and protracted figuration. Fauré seems to have had a soft spot for these *Valses-Caprices* and in 1908 he recorded them on a DEA player-piano for the German firm Hupfeld. Saint-Saëns liked the second one particularly, though in the end he had to admit to Fauré that he had never been able to play it in public because he could not learn it off by heart.[28]

Despite imperfections and apart from the influences noted above, Fauré's piano music right from the start possesses a feeling and a style of its own. Even in a field so richly worked before him, he was able to produce novel textures, like the runs in thirds and sixths that he almost lazily lets drift across a chord (in the coda of the Fourth Nocturne) or that he makes more involved by using contrary motion (before the reprise of the Second Barcarolle).

The overall result is that from the beginning of the 1880s Fauré's piano music has an individual colour: nonchalance, dreaminess and calm are suddenly shot through with brilliant or lyrical outbursts. His themes are phrased with subtlety and the tone is often reserved, but here and there it is lightened by some flash of humour which could come only from him. French piano music of the time comprised the two triptychs by Franck, prolix and variable offerings from Saint-Saëns and some works of genius by Chabrier; into this world Fauré introduced a new piano sound, and with it a harmonic vocabulary of extreme sensitivity. His influence on Debussy can be judged from the two Arabesques and the D flat Nocturne the younger man wrote around 1890.

For all their peculiar merit and charm, the piano works of Fauré's first period appear at times very dated, and they have been in no small measure responsible for his reputation as an elegant composer rather than a profound one. Their instant attractiveness has led virtuosi to choose them in preference to the works of his maturity or old age, which are less easily appreciated by the public. During the final years of the century a certain equilibrium seems to have been achieved in his piano music between charm and density of musical thought. At the same time as he was finishing his song cycle *La Bonne chanson*, in the summer of 1894, he composed two pieces, both of which stand as major contributions to the piano literature: the Sixth Nocturne and the Fifth Barcarolle.

He worked on these two, very dissimilar works while staying in the country house of his parents-in-law at Prunay, near Bougival. The autographs bear the terminal dates of 3 August and 18 September respectively. Listening to the wonderfully serene melody of the Sixth Nocturne, we may find it hard to imagine how gloomy and depressed Fauré was feeling at the time: 'If I haven't replied to you, that's because I am so immersed in spleen that I'm afraid to write to my friends in case I transmit it to them!' he confided to Winnaretta de Polignac,[29] and he went on: 'Don't you approve of my passion for writing piano music? Don't you think that people will come round to playing it in time, just as they've taken plenty of time to start appreciating my songs! Modern piano music of any slight interest is *very rare*, almost non-existent!'

The Sixth Nocturne op. 70 is in D flat, like so many of Fauré's best pieces, and Chopin's too. The opening theme is one of his finest inspirations in its ample curves, its breadth and grandeur; from the very first bar it gives the impression of floating free, taking us slowly but ineluctably

Ex. 3 Nocturne no. 6

towards another world (see Ex. 3). The lyrical tension of this majestic paragraph is broken by a second motif, light, charming, almost anodyne, with an off-beat accompaniment (*Allegro molto moderato*, in C sharp, the enharmonic equivalent of the principal key). A brief reappearance of the opening theme leads to the central section in which the urgent, impassioned tones of a new theme are heard amid shimmering arpeggios, a sort of musical equivalent to the 'azur' of Mallarmé (*Allegro moderato*, 4/2 in A major). This 'music of the spheres' prefigures fairly closely the finale of Schoenberg's *Verklärte Nacht* (1899) in its mixture of lyricism and rustling animation.

The central development section combines, in a much faster tempo, this new theme with the two preceding ideas. Here Fauré juggles masterfully with contrasts of tonality, nuance, tempo and metre (4/2, 3/4, 3/2), creating an area of disturbance which has as many surprising facets as a kaleidoscope. The second half (or consequent) of the opening theme, which is the true unifying element of the whole work, returns at the height of this climax, in octaves in the left hand. Then, in the echoing void, as the pedal preserves the last embers of a passage of scintillating virtuosity, the opening theme is heard once more, deeper now and softer, evoking the calm of wide, open spaces.

In the Fifth Barcarolle op. 66, in F sharp minor, Fauré reaches the same heights of inspiration, originality and technical skill, but in a quite different, indeed an opposite direction. Where the Sixth Nocturne is all serenity and smooth lyricism, the Fifth Barcarolle consists of drama, passion and jagged rhythms interrupting the musical flow.

The principal motif, heard at the outset, is based on the interval of a descending fourth (F sharp – C sharp) and a dotted rhythm whose firm accentuation is set off by the syncopation of the bass line. The harmony, full of chromaticisms and studded with major seconds and tritones (augmented fourths or diminished fifths), contributes to the bleak, pungent atmosphere (see Ex. 4). The second theme, in G flat major, is more flexible and combines a rising phrase traversed by arpeggios (*cantabile*, bars 16–17) with a scale in octaves, descending by whole tones (*forte*, bars 18–19). The development (bar 32) brings all these elements together with an ease and inventiveness that is astonishing: the rhythm of A with the whole tones of B (bars 36–40); the rhythm of A softened by the undulating arpeggios of B (*tranquillamente*, bars 44–6). As in the central section of the Sixth Nocturne, metres, tonalities and moods follow hard upon each other: almost warlike outbursts (bar 51) melt into a catlike agility (bar 85) and lights and colours mingle and answer each other in a sort of musical pointillism (Georges Seurat's *Le Cirque* dates from 1891).

Ex. 4 Barcarolle no. 5

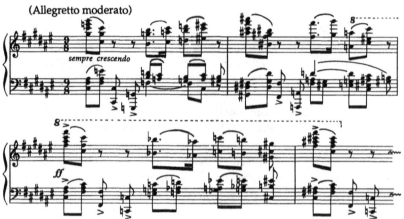

In the final section the two thematic constituents of the Barcarolle are repeated with their order and tonalities inverted (B in F sharp minor, bar 89; A in the same key, bar 104, then in F sharp major, bar 110). Finally the coda restores calm and a relaxed atmosphere. Altogether the boldness and spontaneity of this fine piece recall the wildest transports of *La Bonne chanson*.

Little is known of the Sixth Barcarolle op. 70, in E flat, except that it was first printed in London by Fauré's new publisher, Metzler & Co., in March 1896, then early that summer by Hamelle in Paris. To judge by the style, one would guess that it was sketched, if not actually written out, some ten years earlier, in the wake of the Fourth Barcarolle (1886) whose flowing charm and facility it recalls in a more refined fashion. The second theme especially, in the key of B major, could be regarded as an archetype of the '1880 style', omnipresent in Fauré's early piano music. The piece is agreeable and goes down well at concerts but it is, as Fauré said about his *Pavane*, 'of no particular importance'. It has nonetheless been favoured by pianists who want to show off their dexterity – Marguerite Long, for one, who championed it with all her usual brilliance and panache.

At the time of its conception, the summer of 1895, Fauré was gloomily putting the finishing touches to one of the most ambitious and successful works in his piano output: the *Thème et variations* op. 73, in C sharp minor. During that summer Fauré was forced to remain in Paris by his application for the post of music critic on *Le Figaro* (unfortunately, the job went to Alfred Bruneau). As he wrote in September to his friend, Eugène d'Eichthal, in whose house he had begun the Sixth Nocturne a year earlier and to whom the work is dedicated, 'I'm not best pleased to have been kept here like this for such an outcome', going on to say 'I'm in the throes of writing the last variation, a "variation–conclusion", of a theme and variations for piano. I don't know whether it's a good piece but I don't imagine I'll surprise you if I say it's very difficult!'[30] The score is dedicated to Thérèse Roger, a pupil and friend of the composer.[31] It was published in 1897 in London by Metzler and in Paris by Hamelle, who had announced it in 1896 as opus 71.[32] It has been claimed, not unreasonably, that Fauré took Schumann's *Etudes symphoniques* as a model, but that suggestion does nothing to diminish the success of the work nor its radical originality; it stands clearly on a level with the Sixth Nocturne and, especially, with the Fifth Barcarolle, with which it shares a predilection for writing in the bass register, often in octaves, for dotted rhythms and off-beat accompaniment figures.

The theme has the simplicity of a frieze carved in marble. It is no more than a simple scale of C sharp minor, rising to the tonic and falling again by stages over a total of four bars. It is answered discreetly but logically by another phrase (or consequent) of twice two bars, hovering between tonic and dominant (see Ex. 5).

Variation I, *Lo stesso tempo* (= *Quasi adagio*) is in 4/4. The theme and its consequent, in the bass, are decorated with a continuous pattern of semi-quavers in the treble. Variation II, *Più mosso* in 4/4, presents the first eight notes of the theme (the rising scale), *leggiero e staccato*, in close imitation, in the manner of a toccata. The consequent now undergoes an interesting displacement effect, brought about by the syncopations in the top line. Variation III, *Un poco più mosso* in 3/4, follows on from its predecessor and continues its light, rapid texture. It draws its interest from the contradiction between the very strong outline of the theme and its presentation in triple time, in the rhythm ♩♩♩ . In the consequent (bars 9–16) this rhythm is given in a varied form ♩♩♩ with the main theme recalled in the bass (D, E, F, G, A).

Variation IV, *Lo stesso tempo* in 3/4, brings to an end the first, virtuoso section of the work, comprising variations II to IV. The theme is declaimed *fortissimo*, passing from the left hand to the right and occupying the centre of the keyboard while tumultuous figuration surrounds it. The consequent (bars 9–24) is barely recognisable beneath the ornamental complexities.

Ex. 5 *Thème et variations*

Variation V, *Un poco più mosso* in 3/4, now opts openly for triple metre and presents the noble, spacious theme unexpectedly as a kind of waltz decorated with appoggiaturas. The style is similar to that of the childlike movements of *Dolly*, which we shall consider at the end of this chapter.

Variation VI, *Molto adagio* in 4/4, is again a dance, a kind of slow pavane whose stately steps, by turns smooth and abrupt, mark the notes of the theme in the bass; the pattern of the consequent (bars 2–3) is inverted. Counterpoint returns in Variation VII, *Allegretto moderato* in 4/4. Here

the theme, treated in strict imitation like an invention, is barely recognisable, while the consequent, also in imitation, indulges in polyphony briefly
but obviously (bars 5–8).

The two variations that follow, VIII and IX, *Andante molto moderato*
and *Quasi adagio* in 4/4, plunge us suddenly and completely into a dream
world. The theme here becomes the pretext for a moonlit reverie, with the
sounds of slow bells and of thirds descending a veritable Jacob's ladder
over a range of five octaves. The gentle gloom and refined harmonies of the
ninth variation approach the limits of what the ear can stand and we can
understand what Poulenc meant when he said, of *La Bonne chanson*, that
some of Fauré's modulations 'made him feel ill' (Ex. 6).

Ex. 6 *Thème et variations*

Variation X, *Allegro vivo* in 3/8, is the most fully developed of them, the
theme taking the form of a staccato *perpetuum mobile* in the left hand with
syncopated chords in the right. The open texture is remarkably effective.
Beginning *pianissimo*, this virtuoso movement works steadily up to a
magnificently powerful climax.

Many composers might have ended the work on this apotheosis, but not
Fauré. His eschewal of the over-dramatic gesture and his desire to avoid
the usual type of finale are too typical of him for us to be surprised by now,
even if concert pianists greedy for immediate applause have some reason
for regrets. Instead, Fauré preferred to end on a note of meditative calm
(*Andante molto moderato* in 3/4, in C sharp major). The theme (*un poco*

marcato) is in the bass, but discreetly reduced to the function of a modest bass line in a passage of four-part counterpoint. After a slightly solemn repeat of the beginning of the variation, the work ends in the simplest possible manner, as it began: with the first five notes of the theme. Despite the apparent austerity of these two final pages of polyphony, there is something masterly in this 'variation–conclusion', as Fauré called it. In many respects it foreshadows the richness of his late style.

The fervent Fauré enthusiast, the conductor Désiré–Emile Inghelbrecht, had the unusual idea of orchestrating the *Thème et variations* for a ballet, with the dancer Carina Ari, produced at the Paris Opéra in 1928 under the title *Rayon de lune* (!). To judge by the radio recording made by this same conductor, it was not a successful experiment and has sensibly been forgotten.

There is no stylistic break between the *Thème et variations* and the Seventh Nocturne op. 74 which Fauré finished in the summer of 1898. The key (C sharp minor) is the same, as is the chromatic, polyphonic texture. The sombre, doleful theme with which the piece opens evokes the organ in its three-part writing: a chorale theme in long notes (in 18/8!), a chromatic, contrapuntal line and left-hand octaves low down in the bass (bars 1–6) (see Ex. 7). The smooth, rapid second theme (*un poco più mosso*)

Ex. 7 Nocturne no. 7

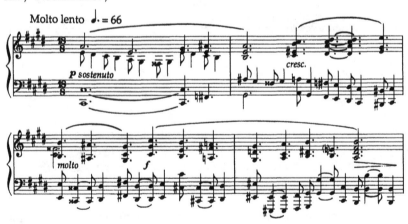

modulates quickly through a succession of arpeggios (bars 11–18). A third section (bars 19–38) develops the first theme and the concluding motif of the second with considerable invention.

The central section (*Allegro* in 4/4, in C sharp major, bars 39–104) offers a striking contrast with the first. It contains three themes which could easily find a place in the collection of Barcarolles. The first (bar 42) deals playfully with consonances and dissonances (major seconds), like the start of the Second Nocturne or the Fourth Barcarolle; the second (bar 55) is more heroic, with more than a hint of Wagner about it (*forte*, bars 59–61). We may perhaps see it as a 'souvenir of Bayreuth', being contemporary with Fauré's second visit there in August 1896. The third theme is a delicate, bell-like motif.

The final section (bars 104–21) repeats the end of the first, the chorale theme now being violently harmonised with chords made up of sextuple appoggiaturas. The resulting pathos is an emotion which Fauré tended in general to avoid out of a desire for elegance and an innate *pudeur* (see Ex. 8).

Ex. 8 Nocturne no. 7

The coda, in the enharmonic key of D flat, cites the first theme of the central section, surrounded by scales, and the piece ends with the barcarolle-like arpeggios.

The success of the Seventh Nocturne is paradoxical. Its thematic constituents are extremely diverse, so much so that one might reasonably suppose them to have been taken from sketchbooks stretching over a decade. Nevertheless, the mastery and easy continuity of the writing exert a charm that holds the listener throughout.

The last piano work to be considered in this chapter is the suite *Dolly* op. 56 for piano duet, which Fauré wrote between 1893 and 1896 for Emma

Bardac's daughter Hélène, known as Dolly. The well-known 'Berceuse' is in fact an extremely early piece. It was written initially for the young Suzanne Garnier, the daughter of a family friend who was prefect of Tarbes; this information comes from a recently discovered manuscript bearing the date 12 January 1864 and the title 'La Chanson dans le jardin'. This tender little piece had to wait thirty years before being published with some tiny corrections. The pieces that follow allude poetically to the world of the growing girl. 'Mi-a-ou', written for her second birthday on 20 June 1894, has nothing to do with feline antics as has often been supposed: the original manuscript has a quite different title, 'Messieu Aoul!' – Dolly's version of Monsieur Raoul, her elder brother Raoul Bardac. 'Le Jardin de Dolly', a present for New Year's Day 1895, is perhaps the jewel of the suite with its lovely tune, moving harmonies and limpid, subtle counterpoint: in bars 7 and 8 there is a clear reference to the finale of the First Violin Sonata, written twenty years earlier. 'Kitty valse' was a present for Dolly's fourth birthday and is a kind of whirling portrait of the family dog, Ketty. The last two pieces were written in 1896. 'Tendresse' returns to the lyricism of 'Le Jardin de Dolly', but the style is more abstruse and the chromaticism of the opening theme in D flat looks forward to the broader inspirations of the Seventh Nocturne and of *Pelléas et Mélisande*. The suite ends with 'Le Pas espagnol', a brilliant tribute to *España* by Fauré's friend Chabrier.[33] It is one of the few 'genre' compositions in Fauré's output and its success gives cause for regret that he did not pursue this vein of brilliantly coloured, rhythmic effervescence. According to Marguerite Long, 'Le Pas espagnol' was inspired by a bronze equestrian statue by Emmanuel Fremiet[34] that Dolly was fond of.

Although the language of the *Dolly* suite is relatively simple, the work is not very easy for young amateur pianists. It was first performed in public on 30 April 1898 by Alfred Cortot and Edouard Risler and soon became popular. Fauré himself used to enjoy playing it, often with children like Mlle Lombard, the daughter of his host on Lake Lugano (as seen in a delightful photograph) or with Charles Oulmont or Jean Wiéner.

The suite was published in London and Paris in 1897. It was orchestrated by the young composer Henri Rabaud (1873–1949), who won the Prix de Rome in 1894 and was to succeed Fauré as director of the Conservatoire in 1920. The work was first given in this form in Monte Carlo on 6 December 1906, under the direction of Léon Jehin. It was later staged, in 1913, at the Théâtre des Arts, when it was under Jacques Rouché's outstanding direction. Debussy's friend Louis Laloy wrote a jolly scenario for the occasion including, as well as Dolly (the 'spoilt child') her Governess, two Clowns, the Musician, the Dancer, the Handsome Spanish Pirate (who goes off with Dolly at the end) and some 'wild female dancers'. The choreographer, Léo Staats, was helped by Miss Eva Reid (who played Dolly) and two real clowns, the Footit brothers, and the ballet, programmed together with Chabrier's *Une éducation manquée* and the prologue to Lully's *Thésée*, was a great success. Maurice Ravel, in his review,[35] praised Henri Rabaud for having orchestrated these pieces 'with the most ingenious tact and subtlety' and enthused over Miss Lloyd's décor, 'an amusingly stylised country scene ... with pretty, multicoloured birds perched on unlikely-looking flowers'. He was touched too by the sight of the stage 'being crossed by M. Marcel Héronville as a large, plush rabbit, pushing a cart full of red balloons'. A tiresome little girl, a dancer, acrobatic clowns ... one wonders whether it was from this version of *Dolly* that Jean Cocteau took these characters for the famous ballet on which he was soon to collaborate with Picasso and Satie: *Parade*.

5   Roses for *Des Esseintes*: from the *romance* to the *mélodie*

It is hardly fortuitous that Fauré's first published work, his opus 1 no. 1, should have been a vocal one – 'Le Papillon et la fleur'. His song output, stretching over sixty years, consists of over a hundred pieces and was largely responsible for getting him known as a composer. Indeed, they were perhaps too popular for his own good. As he himself said, 'Yes ... they've been sung a lot. Not enough to make my fortune, but too much even so. My colleagues in the profession reckoned that as I'd done so well in the medium I ought to stick to it all the time!' (*Le Petit Parisien*, 28 April 1922).

The sixteen-year-old Fauré's decision to write a romance was influenced by the examples of his first teacher Louis Niedermeyer. It was probably he, or else Saint-Saëns, who prompted Fauré to set words by Victor Hugo and, a little later, Théophile Gautier, rather than by some obscure versifier. Hugo and Gautier seem to have remained his favourite poets over a long period. In Niedermeyer's hands the romance had moved closer to the dramatic *scena*, with alternating passages of recitative and *arioso* – in fact had become the long, romantic ballad, replete with the histrionics of the age. Fauré turned aside from this and chose instead to follow the path of the new French *mélodie*. His mentor was not so much Berlioz, whose importance in this field was yet to be appreciated, as Gounod. He seems to have discovered Gounod's songs very early on and while 'Le Papillon et la fleur' is rather pale by comparison with *Venise*, nevertheless it shows the influence of Gounod's song in its strophic form and in the importance given to the piano *ritornelli*.

The songs that followed ('Mai', 'Rêve d'amour') remained faithful to Hugo, without being of any greater interest. As we have seen earlier (p. 11), Fauré attached little importance to them. The chronology of these early romances is hard to establish. They were published by Choudens between 1869 and 1879, some time after they were written; the opus numbers were added in 1896 when Fauré asked his new publisher Hamelle to draw up a catalogue of his works, to be sent with his first application to the Institut. Hamelle distributed the eight lowest available opus numbers among the twenty *mélodies* in the first Fauré volume which Choudens had brought out in 1879 and which Hamelle had then taken over in 1887. The order of the opus numbers follows neither that of composition nor of publication, but simply follows the order in which the songs were printed in the collection.[1] For my article on Fauré in *The New Grove Dictionary* and for the complete EMI recording of the songs in 1974 I attempted to establish their chronology on a sounder footing, using evidence from manuscripts (often lost or undated), editions, first performances, allusions in letters[2] and from stylistic comparisons with other music of the period.[3]

Further research will, I hope, unearth more details. In the meantime the chronology we do possess shows this early period of Fauré's composing life as one of continual and highly coherent change. But it is marked too by hesitations. His *mélodies* tend to come in groups, each group defining a particular style, showing a possible way forward. Then, as soon as he has explored it, he abandons it. Right from his youth we find this constant desire to renew himself, and this openness of attitude, this determination to avoid stereotypes recalls Schubert, as do his almost infallible melodic instinct and his treatment of words.

Nothing at Rennes seems to have encouraged him to write *mélodies*. No inspiring interpreter was to be found in musical circles which, at best, boasted impassioned lovers of Donizetti. Even so one strophic *mélodie* on a rather grandiloquent text of Gautier could well date from the very end of his stay there. The unchanging formula of the accompaniment in 'Les Matelots' keeps it close to being a romance, but the chromatic nature of its harmonic progressions show that Fauré was searching for a new style. It was written for the low voice of Edouard Lalo's wife Marie, probably around the time of Fauré's return to Paris at the beginning of 1870; it thus brings to a close the period of the early romances and coincides with his movement towards the *mélodie*. The distinction between the two was made by the composer himself in a letter to Julien Koszul in June 1870,[4] announcing the publication of his *romance* 'Rêve d'amour' and promising to send him 'a short *mélodie*' – quite possibly 'Lydia'. The romances of the 1860s were long, fairly extrovert pieces. But in 'Lydia' we are struck by a totally new concentration, both in the inner intensity of its expression and in its structure. After writing ten or so romances, Fauré was becoming more scrupulous in his choice of poems. He realised that, even with cuts, Hugo's grandiose and sporadically inspired verses did not suit him nearly so well as four strophes by Leconte de Lisle.

However, the change in Fauré's aesthetic outlook that occurred around

1870 cannot be explained merely by a broadening of his literary tastes. The song 'l'Aurore', a posthumously published setting of Hugo, is a successful attempt to do something different which leads straight on to 'Lydia'. These two short songs are true *mélodies*. In both of them the second quatrain introduces a new motif, breaking the strict mould of strophic repetition, and their unity derives from a new conception of the rôle of the piano, which supports the voice and at the same time engages it in dialogue. In 'Lydia' it is the piano which preserves the melodic continuity between the two parts of the first strophe; it also offers a bold solution to the difficult run-on between verses 2 and 3 ('et plus blanc/Que le lait') by taking over the voice part.

In general, the piano doubles the melodic line. As in the case of 'Lydia', this doubling is sometimes very close, but the piano also occupies itself with the poem's content: in the second strophe of 'l'Aurore' the delicate dissonances are dictated by the sense of the words: 'Everything sings and murmurs, Everything speaks with one accord.' Finally, the bass line often fulfils a double function as a harmonic basis and as a line moving in counterpoint with the voice. 'Lydia' shows signs of all these characteristic traits which were then developed into a more or less organised system, serving Fauré fairly consistently up to the song cycles of the 1890s. This change of style can probably be attributed to a single, direct influence. When Fauré returned to Paris in 1870 he was struck forcibly by Duparc's *L'Invitation au voyage*, published in that same year. It not only introduced him to Baudelaire, but demonstrated that the *mélodie* could successfully adopt the grand manner and that it was time to put the romance behind him.

This evolution of one genre into another marks an important stage in Fauré's life. From here on he was to be guided more by true, inner necessity and to channel his enthusiasm into the innovatory paths forged by some of the finest composers of the age.

In 1870 the French *mélodie* was still emerging. It would appear to have been born in the years 1835–40 as a reaction against 'the miserable products of the romance industry which not only makes us the laughing-stock of the rest of the world but also stands more firmly in the way of our artistic progress than all the other daily obstacles that abound' (Berlioz, *Gazette musicale*, 1835, p. 351). It was at this time that Adolphe Nourrit and Franz Liszt began to promote Schubert's songs, soon published in French by Richault, that Berlioz wrote his *Mélodies irlandaises* and above all his wonderful *Nuits d'été*, and that Gounod composed his earliest songs – *Venise* dates from 1842.

Schubert's *lieder* conquered the French public by their originality and expressive power. Indirectly, they also stimulated the development of the French *mélodie*, less through imitation than through a spirit of emulation. Whereas the *lied*, in the hands of Schubert, Schumann and Brahms, transports the listener into a Germanic cultural world, full of landscapes, supernatural beings and popular legends, the French *mélodie* is a 'scholarly' creation, not in any sense drawing its sustenance from the collective unconscious, which is made up of customs and traditions and 'everything that is not in books' and which defines a Nation. Schumann's *Der Nussbaum* and Schubert's *Die Forelle* have, what is more, entered the repertory of the oral tradition as practised in taverns, at parties and banquets, whereas in France there is no question of a chorus striking up with Berlioz's *Villanelle*, Gounod's *Sérénade* or Fauré's 'Après un rêve'; and if sometimes 'Les Berceaux' is sung at a school prizegiving, that is only to adorn the ceremony with a little high culture.

'In my view we lack a historical sociology of the French *mélodie*,' wrote Roland Barthes, 'of that particular musical form which developed from Gounod to Poulenc, by and large, but whose heroes are Fauré, Duparc and Debussy ... The ecology, if I can call it that, of the French *mélodie* is different: its birth, development and appreciation owe nothing to the populace and it is a national (French) art only because other cultures ignore it: its milieu is the bourgeois salon.'[5]

A historical sociology of Fauré's mélodies would show that, until around 1914, his vocal works were cultivated in the uninterruptedly homogeneous atmosphere of the artistic, cultivated salon of the upper bourgeoisie. It was the done thing to be able to draw accurately, play the piano and sing. The talented amateur had no hesitation in appearing in private or semi-public concerts and Fauré's earliest interpreters in this field were the hosts and hostesses who received him every week on their appointed day: Marie Trélat, the wife of Napoleon III's surgeon, Mme Edouard Lalo, the wife of the composer, Henriette Fuchs, Marguerite Baugnies, whose brother and husband were both painters, Emmanuel Jadin, himself a painter, Félix Lévy, Amélie Duez, married to a painter and later Emma Bardac, married to a banker ...

They may not have had exceptional voices, but Fauré discovered in these highly gifted amateurs a real enthusiasm and a certain sense of style. Instinctively, he shied away from what he called 'big theatre bellowers', singers used to performing Meyerbeer who knew nothing of subtle nuance. Fauré realised that his music could be appreciated only in a restricted circle where intimacy and a gentle *mezza voce* would tell.

These singers, who soon became friends, were often as much interested in the visual arts and literature as they were in music, and would draw the composer's attention to a little book of poems or to a poetry review that might interest him. In 1870, under the impact of the appearance of *Les Fleurs du mal*, Fauré composed 'Hymne' to a poem by Baudelaire, producing a vigorous song but one smacking rather of grandiloquence than of power, owing probably to the lack of discretion or variety in the accentuation of the words. With the development of the *mélodie*, the text was no longer a secondary support, with little or no effect on the music. To achieve success, a composer had to effect a marriage between the melodic line and the poetry. Once again, Roland Barthes touches on this in one of his best-known essays ('Le Grain de la voix', in: *L'Obvie et l'Obtus*, 1982, p. 242):

The historical sense of the French *mélodie* resides in a certain cultivation of the French language. As we know, the Romantic poetry of France is more oratorical than textual, but what our poetry has been unable to do on its own has been done, at times, by the *mélodie* in combination with it; it has worked on the language through the poem. This work (in the specific sense in which it is applied here) is not to be seen in the general run of song production which accommodates itself all too readily to minor poets, to the format of the *petit-bourgeois* romance and to the customs of the salon. But it is indisputably present in certain works among which we may include, somewhat haphazardly, some of the songs of Fauré and Duparc, practically all the late Fauré songs (where prosody is of the essence) and in Debussy's vocal works (even if, from the dramatic point of view, *Pelléas* is often sung badly). The point at issue in these works is far more than a musical style, it is (to coin a phrase) a practical reflection on the language; and progressively the language is assumed into the poem, the poem into the song and the song into its performance.

After the Franco–Prussian War, Fauré began to move in quite new directions. 'Seule!' (Théophile Gautier), 'L'Absent' (Hugo), 'La Rançon' and 'Chant d'automne' (Baudelaire) form a group very different from what had gone before and could justifiably be labelled 'experimental'. All four are marked *Andante*, are sombre in tone, and are written in a medium or low tessitura and, of course, in minor keys. They are also contrapuntal in texture and the piano parts have none of the seductive brilliance found in earlier *mélodies*. This is Fauré in severe mood. The whole of 'Seule!' (in E minor) is based on a kind of passacaglia of three notes punctuated by octaves. An even more radical simplicity informs 'La Rançon' (in C minor, and dedicated to Duparc), where the first two strophes are reduced to a sort of minimalist texture; in contrast, the second half moves to C major and is decked out with expressive appoggiaturas. From the formal point of view 'Seule!' is monothematic: each strophe presents the same tune, with some variations to accommodate the text, deliberately aimed at creating a kind of stupefied monotony. However in 'Chant d'automne' (in A minor, and not to be confused with 'Automne') Fauré follows closely the emotional shape of the poem. Vocal line and accompaniment change with every verse and, for the new atmosphere in the last one, abruptly so.

This final barcarolle of 'Chant d'automne' made a great impression on the young Marcel Proust.[7] Even so it can hardly be said to match 'L'Absent' (in A minor), an outstandingly successful song written just after the end of the Franco–Prussian War. Here Fauré sets a dramatic dialogue and, by the simplest of means and without histrionics, brings it off completely. In the last verse, the descending melodic line, the increasing pauses in the voice part and the gradual solidifying of the accompaniment are particularly moving and impressive.

The texture in these four songs is often complex. This, together with frequent octave doublings and a preference for the low registers of both voice and piano, suggests to me a German influence such as we find in Saint-Saëns' works at the same period (his splendid First Cello Sonata, in particular). The defeat of 1870 seems to have stirred the younger French composers to action. They began to write songs, piano pieces and chamber music that strove for the power and depth achieved by their German counterparts in these fields. There are traces of Schumann in the appoggiaturas of 'La Rançon' and particularly of *Der Nussbaum*[8] in the lovely descending figure which punctuates the final section of 'Chant d'automne'. Likewise the postlude to Duparc's *Phydilé* looks back to *Frauenliebe und -leben*. As for the long piano introduction to 'Chant d'automne', it looks forward an amazing twenty years to the style of Brahms's *Intermezzi*.

The seriousness of Fauré's music was not a quality calculated to bring him resounding success. Songs like 'Seule!' and 'L'Absent' were more likely to send an audience away with shivers down its spine than captivate it with charm. Contact with the Viardot circle was gradually to change Fauré's musical attitudes, but for the moment he was happy to stay as he was. A mixture of modesty and melancholy led him to think that his compositions were not worth the attention some people were pleased to pay them. In Saint-Saëns' words, he 'lacked a fault which, in an artist, is a virtue: ambition'.[9] His next two songs, 'Tristesse' and 'La Chanson du pêcheur' (sub-titled 'Lamento'), are both on texts by Théophile Gautier and tap the same melancholy, romantic vein as the four that precede them.

Fauré's early songs are often marred by over-accentuation and here the recurring emphasis on the first beat, and sometimes the third as well, is wearisome. The 'merry drinkers' and the young ladies swooning in the arbours are entitled to their slow waltz rhythm but it leads to painful melodrama in the refrain: 'Hélas! j'ai dans le cœur/Une tristesse affreuse.' (Alas! I have a fearful sadness in my heart.) 'La Chanson du pêcheur', on the other hand, is one of the best of Fauré's early works. The form of this extended *mélodie* is fairly complex: A – Refrain – A' – Refrain – B – Refrain. At the same time the vocal writing develops from recitative at the beginning into the sweeping curves of the last verse. The style of the song and its intensity of expression bring it close to being a French operatic aria and it was entirely logical for Fauré to orchestrate it (not something he normally did and indeed in this case he was probably encouraged by the song's dedicatee – Pauline Viardot).

The *mélodies* that followed are not on the same expansive scale. Instead they demand a voice of brilliant virtuosity and, in the case of 'Au bord de l'eau' and 'Après un rêve', of wide range (an 11th from middle C to top F). Only rarely did Fauré exceed this. His reasons were both practical and aesthetic: at that time there were practically no singers specialising in *lied* or *mélodie* and he had to bear in mind the limited technique of his interpreters who were mostly semi-amateurs; also high notes too often became the focus of undue attention for singers and audience alike and, more important, made the words hard to understand. In addition, there was Fauré's personal preference for timbres that were warm and on the low side. A large proportion of his song output was written for either mezzo-soprano or baritone. Mme Edouard Lalo, who gave the first performances of so many of his earlier songs at the Société nationale, was a contralto, as was Pauline Viardot by the time Fauré got to know her. His friend Romain Bussine (the dedicatee of 'L'Absent') was a baritone and Emilie Girette recorded in her diary how Fauré appreciated her low mezzo tones. In the 1890s there was a break in this pattern, brought about by the appearance of other interpreters in Fauré's circle, like Maurice Bagès or Emma Bardac, but it was to be no more than temporary.

From 1872 to 1878 Fauré followed the dictates of Pauline Viardot both in the style of his writing for the voice and in his, fairly disastrous, choice of poems. The songs of this period are identifiable by the formula of a rising sixth or octave followed by a descent through conjunct steps, the prototype appearing in the accompaniment to 'Barcarolle'. This fairly slow tenor *mélodie* in the style of a gondolier's song dates from 1873 and offers some subtle colouring, despite Marc Monnier's rather heavy, sentimental text. Fauré, like Musset, Mendelssohn, Wagner and others before him, was alive to the melancholy of the gondoliers' songs heard echoing across the lagoon. The song is, of course, dedicated to Mme Viardot and the 'Viardot motif', already outlined in 'La Chanson du pêcheur' (on the words 'je chante ma romance'), occurs again in the duet 'Puisqu'ici bas toute âme', written around 1873 for Claudie and Marianne; in 'Au bord de l'eau' of 1875, dedicated to Claudie – Mme Georges Chamerot, as she then was; in the 'Sérénade toscane', in 'Adieu', in *Poème d'un jour* and finally in 'Le Voyageur' (?1878) (see Ex. 9).

Ex. 9 'Barcarolle'

'Puisqu'ici bas'

'Au bord de l'eau'

'Sérénade toscane'

'Adieu' (*Poème d'un jour*, III)

'Le Voyageur'

For a time Fauré renounced formal subtlety and contrapuntal ingenuity. He turned instead (or else was turned) to Italian *bel canto*. The piano now began to play a slightly less important rôle and the grammar of the new style was made up of vocal leaps and ornaments and (in 'Barcarolle') of appoggiaturas. With this new emphasis went, unfortunately, a slackening in attention to the text and to the prosody in particular. We find several passages like the following which Fauré's literary taste would certainly not have permitted two years earlier:

la– bri - se em - porté - e   *(Sérénade toscane)*

The edition of this 'Sérénade', like that of 'Après un rêve', prints the original Tuscan text with a few variants as well as Romain Bussine's very free adaptation which Fauré used for his setting. The idea came to him from the *Poésies toscanes* that Pauline Viardot had published in 1880. But the most Italian of all his songs is the 'Tarentelle' for two sopranos and piano,[10] written for Claudie and Marianne, who used to love singing this lively song. The text is fairly bold – we don't need to dig deeply to find an erotic interpretation – and the two voice parts unfurl with an easy, almost faultless assurance. No one listening to this completely convincing demonstration of virtuosity could accuse Fauré of lacking wit or sparkle. But he simply knew that that was not the direction his music should take. The breaking off of his engagement to Marianne brought this exploration of the Italian style to an abrupt end. Much later Fauré commented,[11] 'Perhaps this separation was not such a bad thing for me. With the best will in the world the Viardots would have deflected me from my true course.'

The truth of this can be seen from the indisputable fact that in 1878 Fauré found himself artistically stranded. The interesting experiments of 1871 might never have taken place and when he decided to abandon the Italian style he relapsed into that of the romances of his adolescence. 'Aubade' is on a level with its text by Louis Pomey (or Pommey, in Fauré's orthography), 1831–91, a painter friend of the Viardots. 'Ici-bas!' is a sentimental romance with a rather laboured melodic line. As for 'Sylvie', Fauré wrote it as an essay in tact: the words are by Paul Choudens and the composer hoped thereby to encourage Choudens' father to bring out at long last the first volume containing twenty of his songs. In a letter to Marie Clerc[12] of 3 October 1878 Fauré jokingly refers to it as a 'labour of Hercules'. *Poème d'un jour* appears as a healthy reaction to all this. Its underlying violence is more directly expressed in 'Le Voyageur' (containing, as we have seen, the last references to the 'Viardot motif'). Here it is indeed the despair of thwarted love which provokes the traveller to march so furiously to an accompaniment of off-beat chords. In this song Fauré renews his debt to the Romantic era – we need only think of what the 'wanderer' idea meant to Schubert. He rounds off this strange period in his song-writing activity as he began it, with a work of the most intense lyricism: 'Automne'. In fact it forms a parallel with 'La Chanson du pêcheur' in the quality of its declamation and in what one may term the composer's commitment in entering fully into the meaning of the text. The opening motif of 'Automne', with its chromaticism and its leaps in the bass, is nothing less than an inspiration (see Ex. 10), punctuating each

Ex. 10 'Automne'

phrase of the text with a dramatic effect like the ebb and flow of the sea. The bass octaves, heard here and in many of the finest of his early songs ('Chant d'automne', 'Au bord de l'eau', 'Après un rêve') and deriving perhaps from the pedal parts in three-part organ writing, disappear almost entirely from now on. For all 'Automne''s qualities, I see Fauré's future more truly outlined in 'Nell' (op. 18 no. 1), which opens the second collection and marks the composer's move to the house of Hamelle.

'Nell', a setting of a poem by Leconte de Lisle, is a striking demonstration that Fauré had at last found his own style of song writing. Gone is the approximate prosody of his Italian period. Instead he adopts a style of word setting that mirrors the emotion of the poem, allowing for the expressive lengthening of key words such as 'enivrée', 'plainte amoureuse' and 'charmé'. The word 'cœur' symbolically grows from a crotchet in the first verse to a dotted crotchet in the second and a dotted minim in the third. There is in 'Nell' a masterly rightness of phrasing, a flow and a melodic suppleness through which the constraints of the bar line are barely felt. The form is ABA, with the second of the four strophes being a varied repetition of the first (A A', in G flat major; B, rapid modulation through C minor; A", return to G flat major). The piano part is as important as the vocal line, surrounding it with a network of regular semiquavers, following its lead, doubling it and from time to time entering into a dialogue with it, as in the canon at bar 20. The whole is supported by a superb, singing bass line, as in the typically Faurean descent through seven conjunct steps which underpins the arch of the opening phrase (see Ex. 11).

Ex. 11 'Nell'

'Nell' is the archetype of Fauré's songs during the 1880s, celebrating the pleasures of love in a voluptuous style that sometimes verges on the sentimental. This was the period when he discovered the dreamy indolence of Armand Silvestre's poetry. Silvestre was far from being a genius but he gave Fauré what he needed. Among their collaborations 'Notre amour', op. 23 no. 2, seems to have been intended for singers with superior vocal equipment. It needs an agile, rather light voice which can pass easily from a low D sharp (bars 5, 17) to the high B of the coda. It is surprising that this brilliant song is not better known and the same could be said of 'La Fée aux chansons', op. 39 no. 2, a light-footed scherzo dating from the summer of 1882. The central section of this song (*molto meno mosso*) is striking in its long held notes and its mysterious, almost meditative atmosphere, evoking autumn in the deserted forest. These fourteen bars conjure up with amazing prescience the sound world of Debussy in their sombre colouring, their silences and even in the setting of the text – one thinks in particular of *Colloque sentimental*, published in the second volume of *Fêtes galantes* in 1904 (see Ex. 12).

Ex. 12 'La Fée aux chansons'

'Aurore', op. 39 no. 1, dating from 1884, is a setting of a fairly insipid poem by Silvestre and leans dangerously close to Fauré's early romances. 'Chanson d'amour', op. 27 no. 1, dating from 1882, is merely a pretty serenade in the less demanding manner of Gounod, or even of Reynaldo Hahn. In the famous 'Roses d'Ispahan', op. 39 no. 4, written in 1884, we find a nonchalance that borders on languor. Amidst the roses of the harem, death comes either from passion or from boredom and this vision of Ispahan owes less to Leconte de Lisle, who wrote the text, than to Pierre Loti. Truly this is decadent music for a decadent epoch!

Such preciosity is transcended in 'Le Pays des rêves', op. 39 no. 4, a subtle barcarolle also dating from 1884. Sentimentality is not wholly lacking but the second part in particular explores a highly ingenious harmonic world. The bass *ostinato* oscillates round the tonic while the modal inflections of the curious melodic line take it through the most distant keys before finishing up on the dominant, E flat. This is the real tonal centre, from which the music constantly departs and to which it always returns through harmonic byways of which Fauré alone possessed the secret (see Ex. 13).

Into this oasis of static languor represented by op. 39 'Fleur jetée', written in 1884, breaks like a tornado with its terrifying repeated chords and its angrily roaring scales. The influence of Schubert's *Erl König* is unmistakable. 'Fleur jetée', like 'Le Voyageur', *Poème d'un jour* and above all the *tragédie lyrique Prométhée*, testifies that under Fauré's gentle exterior lay energy and even violence; it is simplistic to regard his works of this period as being merely the self-indulgent musings of a *fin-de-siècle* voluptuary. In July 1879[13] we find him confiding to Mme Clerc, 'I've been going through a crisis for some time but I don't know what lies behind it! ... I bleed and I can't find the wound.' It cannot have been pure coincidence that one of his finest and most sombre songs dates from this time: 'Les Berceaux', op. 23 no. 1, on a poem by Sully-Prudhomme. Marie-Claire Beltrando remarks in her thesis on Fauré's songs that the vocal range in 'Les Berceaux' is the largest of all: a 13th, from a low A flat to a high F. I do not feel it is an exaggeration to see in this 'lullaby of death' a foreshadowing of the Requiem. It is certainly true that Fauré's propensity for tragic expression found an outlet in the passionate cries and tears of 'Toujours' and 'Le Voyageur', but 'Les Berceaux' marks his first attempt since 'L'Absent' to affect us still more deeply by adopting a tone of gentle poignancy. Fauré has learnt from Mozart, Schubert and Chopin how to make a *pianissimo* eloquent and convincing.

'Les Berceaux' is indisputably successful, but for all its human feeling I find it inferior to 'Le Secret', written in 1880 or 1881 to a text by Armand

Ex. 13 'Le Pays des rêves'

Silvestre – a mere two pages of moving simplicity and concentration. This is the first of Fauré's songs in D flat major, a key which he was particularly fond of. He chose it for those works where his intimate lyricism is most in evidence and where he evokes the calm and peacefulness of night: the Sixth Nocturne, 'Soir' and the first of the Nine Preludes. The motif of four chords punctuating the vocal line is almost liturgical in its utter simplicity, bringing with it a rare quality of silence.

In my view these two pages point ahead to Fauré's greatest achievements. Here is the seed of that discreet, meditative lyricism which informs such works as 'Soir', 'Le Parfum impérissable', 'O Mort, poussière d'étoiles', 'Dans la nymphée' and 'Diane Séléné', all central to his aesthetic. 'Le Secret' prefigures as early as 1880 the simplicity and sobriety of his late style. It also asks the question that has exercised every creative artist and which Fauré was to find no less absorbing: what is music?

6   Sotto voce: chamber music I

When Fauré entered the Parisian musical world in the spring of 1870 it was dominated, as we can see from reading *Le Ménestrel, La Revue et gazette musicale* or *La France musicale*, by the stars and successes of the operatic stage. Meyerbeer had died in 1864 and Berlioz in 1869. While Berlioz's stage works met only with misfortune, intrigue or, worse still, indifference, those of Meyerbeer were still be staged regularly. The conception of 'grand opéra' that he shared with Halévy was overwhelmingly popular, containing as it did the most spectacular elements the stage could offer in the shape of scenery, ballet and elaborate production.

By comparison chamber music drew little attention to itself and was not much heard in public concerts. But it was extremely popular with a wide circle of amateurs who played it regularly in private, often with a stiffening of professional players. In fact such gatherings could accommodate a large number of people if held, say, in one of the Princess Mathilde's vast salons. Obviously such private performances were more appropriate to the intimate nature of the music and to its social origins. But times had changed in that it was no longer heard surrounded by the gilded panelling of the eighteenth-century aristocracy, but in the salons of the bourgeoisie, stuffed with carpets, tapestries and Indian draperies. This assumption by the bourgeoisie of the musical mores of a declining aristocracy can be analysed in sociological terms as a way of fixing its own class image. It confirmed the bourgeoisie's respectability in a convenient, if sometimes slightly austere, manner. In any event it was rich compensation for the prosaic way in which they earned their living. Those who were involved in chamber music were the most discerning devotees of music in Paris, made up of enlightened industrialists, men from the liberal professions, senior civil servants and the sizeable group of professional musicians – instrumentalists, publishers and instrument makers. Bankers and businessmen went to be seen at the Opéra; shopkeepers and junior officials patronised operetta at the Opéra-Comique; and workers and domestic servants spent what little free time they had at the *café-concerts*.

This institutionalising of chamber music as an activity of the upper and middle bourgeoisie entailed a certain degree of conservatism. The repertoire included classical and post-classical composers, among whom Mozart and Haydn held first place. Onslow, Boccherini and Mendelssohn offered worthwhile music for various instrumental combinations and early Beethoven works, too, were played. But the music of Beethoven's middle and last years had yet to find a home in this milieu. Its difficulty meant that only professional groups would play it, like the quartet founded by Pierre Baillot at the beginning of the nineteenth century or the Society formed in 1851 to play his last quartets.

Brahms's early chamber music, as well as Schumann's, was played much more frequently than we might suppose. This contemporary repertoire and the French works that were more or less directly inspired by it (by composers like Lalo, Saint-Saëns, Reber and Castillon) were taken up by various new professional quartets. These included one founded in 1860 by Charles Lamoureux with the support of Edouard Colonne and another founded in 1855 by Jules Armingaud, in which Edouard Lalo played the viola.

The foundation of the Société nationale de musique in 1871 brought a timely change to this static situation. For young composers like Fauré or, ten years later, Debussy, 'La Nationale', as it was popularly known, marked an important breach in the 'old repertoire'. Fauré admitted as much to a journalist on the *Petit parisien* (28 April 1922):

The truth is, before 1870 I would never have dreamt of composing a sonata or a quartet. At that period there was no chance of a composer getting a hearing with works like that. I was given the incentive when Saint-Saëns founded the Société nationale de musique in 1871 with the primary aim of putting on works by young composers.

Fauré's Violin Sonata op. 13, his first great masterpiece, probably stems from his meeting with the great Belgian violinist Hubert Léonard and from Saint-Saëns' example in writing his own First Violin Sonata. Fauré was thirty in 1875, but even so the success of his work and its far-reaching implications seem like something of a miracle when we consider its apparent independence from anything that had preceded it in this difficult genre of chamber music.

All the evidence suggests that Fauré was discovering the violin's expressive possibilities. He had had the opportunity several times of hearing the famous virtuoso Pablo de Sarasate, for whom Saint-Saëns had written his first concerto (1867), and presumably he had also gone to hear Henri

Vieuxtemps when he gave concerts in Rennes. On a more modest level he had no doubt played duets with his friend Paul Viardot, in particular a Sonatine that Pauline had had published in 1874. The dedicatee was Hubert Léonard (1819–90), a pupil of Vieuxtemps and a professor at the Brussels Conservatoire. Léonard watched closely over the composition of Fauré's sonata during a long visit Fauré made to the Clercs' house at Sainte-Adresse, near Le Havre, and gave the young composer advice on how to make it more playable and effective. When Fauré left them in October to go and see his parents, he wrote from Bagnères-de-Bigorre: 'My Sonata's getting on but it's not finished yet. I'm surrounded by nephews and nieces and [Offenbach's] *La Jolie parfumeuse* is more to their taste! Still, I hope to finish it before I get back to Paris on the 31st.'[1] In fact the sonata does not seem to have been completed until the following summer (1876).

The opening *allegro* in 2/2 at once makes it clear that this sonata is a real duo, each instrument being treated in a broad, concerto style. The piano writing is reminiscent of that in the best of Fauré's early songs, with its powerful basses in octaves and its patterns of arpeggios and broken chords. But all these elements are now handled with a sweep and a violence which lend this first movement an almost symphonic intensity.

The piano, in its energetic introduction in A major, presents the two ideas making up theme A. The violin immediately asserts its independence by playing a variant of this motif and develops it before turning to the second motif (A') (bars 37–8). The second main theme (B, *piano ed espressivo*), modulating to the dominant E major, is given to the violin and is more discreet in character. After a complete reprise of this exposition comes the development, in which Fauré gives us striking proof of his compositional skill. Developments are never easy to write and we might have expected him to show some uncertainty or clumsiness at this point: instead we find a wholly remarkable inventiveness and assurance, bearing witness to the value of his formal training. His song-writing efforts too, quite apart from their success or failure and the fact that they were conceived only on a small scale, helped him in his early struggles with form by forcing him to confront the basic problem of integrating the different strophes of the poem in a coherent and continuous musical whole. In writing the twenty or so songs that preceded the sonata, Fauré had acquired an ability to make episodes flow into each other and, above all, to construct harmonic and melodic variations on a given theme.

The second section of this Allegro molto movement begins with a clearcut development of the first five notes of the initial motif, first in F major, then in A major, then in its relative F sharp minor. The motif A′ is then developed in the course of an episode in F sharp minor (*piano e leggiero*, starting in bars 159–60), which becomes G flat major enharmonically before making a particularly happy modulation to D flat major. The importance given to this motif almost suggests Fauré was structuring his sonata form with three subjects, as Brahms was also doing at this period.

This first part of the development section is almost entirely gentle in character and marks an area of tranquillity in a movement that is otherwise impetuous in its virtuosity and in its melodic lines. A much briefer development of theme B leads to the recapitulation. Here the harmonic scheme deviates almost at once so that the motif A′ is heard in F sharp minor. The second theme, now transposed up a fourth from its original E major, rises to a *fortissimo* and then in the coda the opening theme reappears in a high *pianissimo* – an irresistably touching moment.

The first movement is based on the opposition of the two players. The Andante and the Scherzo (*Allegro vivo*) require them to combine, sometimes so intimately that violin and piano seem to become just one imaginary instrument. The Andante is a 9/8 barcarolle in D minor which sighs languorously above the heartbeat of its repeated chords. In the second theme the rhythmic distribution is changed around, widely arpeggiated melodic curves mounting the scale step by step. The modulatory, wilfully chromatic character of this episode is an astonishing anticipation of César Franck's Violin Sonata, published ten years later. The structure of this Andante is unorthodox. After a repetition of the rocking theme a new barcarolle idea is heard on the piano and is then developed to fine lyrical effect in the very centre of the movement. The reprise reverses the initial layout of the instruments, the barcarolle now being heard on the violin and the accompanying idea on the piano. The second theme is transposed a third lower and leads to a final cadence in D major.

The third movement is a 2/8 Allegro vivo in A major. Its brittle piano writing, its *pizzicati*, its cross-rhythms and its air of stylish wit make it undoubtedly the most original of the four movements and in the astonishing 3/4 section in D flat major, where the initial notes of the theme appear in augmentation, the atmosphere of abandon even threatens to get out of control. The melodic lines of the trio, in F sharp minor, unfold in the simple, uncluttered manner of Schumann's Romances for oboe, with an increase in speed to carry us into the reprise. When the work was given its first public performance at the Société nationale the audience insisted on this movement being repeated and we can legitimately regard it as the model for the sprightly serenades that Debussy and later Ravel put into their String Quartets.

The last movement, Allegro quasi presto, is remarkable both for its ideas and for the way in which they are handled. There are two main subjects and the form is tripartite with a central development section. Beyond that, the numerous melodic and rhythmic elements combine in such a long lyrical flow that minute analysis of individual sections seems pointless. It is hard indeed to know which to admire more: the melodic fertility, the variety of rhythm, or the harmonic progressions which are at once supple, unexpected and totally convincing. In the finales of his later chamber music, Fauré rarely matched this movement's easy assurance.

Some slight mystery attaches to the sonata's first performance. It was dedicated not to Hubert Léonard, who had contributed so much to its creation, but to Paul Viardot, perhaps in fulfilment of an earlier promise. By 1877 Viardot, then aged twenty, had become a very close friend of Fauré and seemed likely, moreover, to become his brother-in-law. Neither of these violinists, however, was granted the honour of playing the sonata in public for the first time. A cloud of some sort seems to have passed over relations between the Société nationale and the Viardot family, Pauline resigning her membership on 26 November 1876. On 31 December of that year the committee of the Société nationale unanimously accepted the sonata for performance, and it was given for the first time on 27 January 1877, to a rapturous welcome. Fauré played the piano part and the violinist was Marie Tayau, a young player who had founded a female quartet. Fauré wrote to Mme Clerc:[2]

The sonata had more of a success this evening than I could ever have hoped for ... Saint-Saëns said he felt that *sadness* that mothers feel *when they see their children are too grown-up to need them any more!* ... All the Viardots were there, sporting red trousers! I pretended to be short-sighted! Finally I must say, not without pride, that I played better than yesterday. Mlle Tayau's performance was impeccable.

An enthusiastic article by Saint-Saëns greeted the arrival of this 'new champion, perhaps the most sterling of them all'.[3]

There remained the awkward matter of finding a publisher. Choudens, who was bringing out Fauré's early songs piecemeal, could not possibly print a work that stretched to over fifty pages, and a chamber work at that. So Camille Clerc brought into play his experience as a businessman. He had bought quantities of music from the famous Leipzig firm Breitkopf und Härtel and as a result was on excellent terms with them. He offered them the Fauré sonata, quoting the highly favourable opinions of 'Saint-Saëns and Lalo in their capacity as composers, and of Léonard and Sarasate as violinists'.[4]

Negotiations began in the middle of October 1876 and ended a month later in an agreement under which Breitkopf und Härtel would pay for the printing and publishing of the sonata but Fauré had to renounce a fee of any kind. As they explained, 'M. Fauré is not known in Germany and the market is overflowing with works of this sort, even though they're often inferior to the one we're discussing.'[5]

Fauré sensibly accepted these terms and the sonata was soon taken up by a number of violinists. He himself gave countless performances of it with the finest contemporary players such as Eugène Ysaÿe or, later on, Jacques Thibaud and Georges Enesco.

Fauré was encouraged by the Clercs' interest and enthusiasm, and while staying with them at Sainte-Adresse in the summer of 1876 he began a new chamber work, the Piano Quartet in C minor, going on with it when he went to stay with his parents in Tarbes. As with the sonata, progress was so swift that Fauré had hopes of finishing it, or nearly so, by the time he returned to Paris in mid-November, but several things conspired to prevent it: the first performance of the sonata, serious money problems which meant Fauré having to ask the Clercs for a loan as well as moving house (from 7, rue de Parme to 13, rue Mosnier), his application for a job at the Madeleine, the Viardots' insistence on his settling down to an opera and particularly the whole unhappy episode of his engagement. The Quartet was not to be finished for another three years, in the summer of 1879, and even after that there were to be revisions.

During these troubled years Fauré seems to have tried to follow up the success of the Violin Sonata. The Romance in B flat for violin and piano was written during his miserable exile at Cauterets in the summer of 1877. Its opening theme is really too blatantly decorated in '1880s style', conjuring up visions of windows surrounded by lace and of the extravagant bustles that all the ladies of the time were wearing. But the second, G minor episode suddenly breaks out of this suffocating languor, and its purposeful sweep and Schumannesque colouring recall the fine lyricism of the Violin Sonata's last movement.

In a letter of 17 September 1877,[6] Fauré wrote jokingly to Marie Clerc that the contorted line of his Romance reflected that of the mountain ridge round Cauterets, and goes on to give an account of its performance with his friend Paul Viardot at 'les Frênes', the family's house in Bougival: 'The first time round we were greeted with applause through clenched teeth. At the second performance a little light began to dawn and after the third they were comparing it to the limpid stream that runs through the green meadow! What a shame the third performance can't always come first!'

It is interesting to read this detailed observation of how the Viardots, a highly cultivated musical audience, reacted to a new work of Fauré's which strikes us now as fairly lacklustre and traditional. It calls into question Saint-Saëns' views on the Violin Sonata when he writes (in the article from which I have already quoted): 'Over it and around it all hovers a charm which persuades the mass of ordinary listeners to accept the most violent novelties as being entirely natural.' We may well ask ourselves exactly what 'ordinary listeners' Saint-Saëns had in mind.

Some mystery surrounds the orchestral version of this Romance. Hamelle's original edition of 1883 carries the title: '*Romance* (in B flat) for violin with piano (or orchestral) accompaniment'. Even though no record has been found of a performance with orchestra at this period, Fauré would definitely seem to have produced a score. It figures in the worklist printed by Hamelle in 1896, while in the publisher's general catalogue, brought out in 1906, the orchestral version is said to be 'available on hire'. 'Père Hamelle' being a man of economical ways, both score and parts probably existed only in a single manuscript copy. Was this score lost?[7] It seems likely because when Camille Chevillard wanted to put on the *Romance* at one of the Lamoureux concerts after the First World War, he had to get a new orchestration done. Fauré was probably responsible for suggesting Philippe Gaubert, the chief conductor of the Conservatoire Concert Society. His orchestration was played at a Lamoureux concert on 11 January 1920 and was billed as a 'first performance'. Gaubert was born in 1879, so could not have been the orchestrator of the version referred to in 1883 and 1896. The likelihood that Fauré did the job himself is increased by the fact that at this same period (1878–9) he was working on a Violin Concerto (played but left unfinished, as we shall see) and that he also orchestrated his *Berceuse* for violin and piano.

The *Berceuse* probably dates from 1879. Sad to say, it played a large part in getting Fauré dubbed for years as a 'salon composer'. The melodic ideas are weak and although the rhythmic structure of the accompaniment is certainly quite ingenious, it is too insistently presented. Fauré attached no importance to this conventional little piece but it was taken up by violinists of every kind, from international soloists to café serenaders, with an enthusiasm that bordered on mania. I have found over sixty recordings of it, ranging from Ysaÿe in 1912 to Menuhin in 1971. The violinist at the first performance, on 14 February 1880 at the Société nationale, was Ovide Musin and he also gave there the first performance of the orchestral version on 24 April 1880, with Edouard Colonne conducting.

Julien Hamelle was far-sighted enough to hear the *Berceuse* and on that evidence decided he wanted to publish Fauré's music. He bought the

Berceuse and the three songs of op. 18 ('Nell', 'Le Voyageur', 'Automne') for fifty francs each[8] and, in the same contract of 16 November 1879, agreed to publish the C minor Piano Quartet on the same conditions that Breitkopf insisted on over the First Violin Sonata – that is to say without payment of royalties. Hamelle found the arrangement highly profitable and became Fauré's regular publisher between 1880 and 1906, though there were frustrations on both sides. Fauré set a precedent for both Debussy and Ravel in having his early works brought out by a rather small publishing house, before being accepted by the top flight of Parisian publishers, first Heugel and later Durand. Hamelle had taken over from J. Maho in 1878 and was now on the lookout for new talent. Certainly Fauré must have been slightly encouraged to find any editor showing sustained interest in his work after the rude rebuffs he had received from Choudens, as recorded in his letters to Mme Clerc during the summer of 1879. Not that his new editor was without his faults. Fauré, like many composers, was a careless proof-reader and Hamelle failed to notice many of his mistakes – the piano works, in particular, are full of errors. The layout, too, is unattractive, and Hamelle managed to lose numerous autographs and complete sets of parts. Worst of all was the absence of printed orchestral scores for some of Fauré's works which made it hard for them to get known. The composer, not being ambitious, cared little for such matters and put up with this treatment for a long time. He felt, with some justice, that his music was of such an individual cast that he would be hard put at that time to find another publisher of Hamelle's unshakable good-will. Choudens and Durand had both refused his C minor Piano Quartet; Hamelle's terms might be miserly but at least he agreed to publish it.

The choice of an unusual medium like the piano quartet showed Fauré's desire to break new ground and be his own man. Debussy and Ravel might launch into writing string quartets but Fauré was less rash (or more modest) and did not dare to attempt this supreme form of chamber music until the very end of his working life, being afraid, as he admitted, of the shadow cast over the medium by Beethoven. The piano quartet, on the other hand, offered an area in which masterpieces were thin on the ground. Apart from Mozart – and especially his G minor Quartet K.478 – the examples of the medium in the works of Beethoven, Schumann and Saint-Saëns, though they are far from valueless, do not count among the very best of their composers' chamber music.

It is quite possible that Fauré knew the first two of Brahms's Piano Quartets, written in 1861–2, because they were among the scores which Brahms had sent to Hamelle's predecessor, Jacques Maho, and which Hamelle then distributed. Even so, he would probably not have paid very much attention to them, as Brahms's music was so much looked down on in Paris. In his book *Les Sociétés de musique de chambre à Paris, de la Restauration à 1870*, Joël-Marie Fauquet quotes a review of the Piano Quintet which appeared in *La Revue et Gazette musicale* in February 1870: 'We should be sorry for Brahms if he had to be judged by this work alone; it is tortured, laboured, and the exaggerated sonorities seem to demand an orchestra; the work does not breathe, except perhaps in the scherzo.' Fauré himself played the brilliant piano part when his work was given its first performance at the Société nationale on 11 February 1880, with Ovide Musin (violin), Louis van Waefelghem (viola) and Ermanno Mariotti (cello). It was received almost as warmly as the First Violin Sonata, but after the concert some of his musical friends expressed reservations about the last movement. Disconcerted by this, Fauré allowed only the first three movements to be sent off to the printer and after three years' cogitation ended up by rewriting the finale entirely. He finished it in November 1883 and the whole quartet was performed in the revised version at the Société nationale on 5 April 1884 by Lefort, Bernis, Jules Loeb and Fauré.

In fact, Fauré's early works achieved success only within narrow, society circles. The attitude of players to his new compositions speaks volumes about the general standing of this modest young man. Robert Lortat, in the number of *Conférencia* dated 20 August 1919, remembered that

with regard to the first performance of the Quartet, Fauré told me how carelessly and casually the music had been played by artists who were then fashionable. And how, when summoned to a rehearsal on the eve of the first performance, he had dared to make some timid observations about tempi and had asked them to put in some dynamic nuances. The 'cellist of the quartet immediately interrupted him: 'My dear fellow, we're in a hurry, it's all we can do to get the notes right: we haven't got time to worry about nuances.'

Like the Sonata, the C minor Quartet is a work of breadth and eloquence. The opening Allegro (molto moderato in C minor) is, formally, in strict sonata form, but the affirmation of the first theme on unison strings is unusually strong and the way the theme develops, too, is surprising. After the square rhythms of the exposition, the development section (bar 73) begins with a tenderly nostalgic barcarolle. Development in fact takes place throughout the movement. The instrumental balance is hard for the players to achieve but through it Fauré creates a marvellously full sound with a strong underlying pulse.

The second movement (Allegro vivo in E flat) returns to the light-hearted, acrobatic style of the scherzo from the Violin Sonata, with an even greater rhythmic assurance. The piano theme, the alternations of duple and triple time and the delicate *pizzicati* are combined in an ensemble of ideas that is continuous but never aimless. In the central Trio, Fauré shows a skill worthy of Saint-Saëns (and of Ravel in years to come) by combining the piano's *perpetuum mobile* with a richly harmonised melody on the strings.

The slow movement in C minor establishes straight away a mood of tragedy with an accompanied theme based on a rising octave and a major second, a motif which was to recur frequently in his work. The poignancy of the writing and the marking *Adagio* are exceptional for Fauré; so much so that attempts have been made to see in this movement a reference to the abortive engagement with Marianne Viardot. This kind of approach is particularly fruitless when dealing with Fauré, since he always tried to keep his work and his life wholly distinct. Anyway, in this case it has to be remembered that the basic ideas for the quartet go back to 1876, before the engagement was even contracted.

Fauré probably destroyed the original version of the Finale. The new version (Allegro molto in C minor) successfully returns to the broad conception of the opening Allegro and the surging arpeggios which run through it may make us think of Brahms's third Piano Trio. This is not, I feel, just a passing resemblance. Even if the young Fauré and the aging Brahms knew practically nothing of each other, their chamber music in particular seems to me to contain many similarities: in the length of melodic lines that sometimes reaches an almost symphonic dimension, in the emphasis on the bass, in the wealth of themes that stretches the confines of sonata form, and in mood – reserved, passionate, intimate and deliberately elegiac.

The success of two chamber works one after the other must have convinced Fauré that, whatever the dictates of fashion, this was a genre which suited him and that he ought to pursue it further. As soon as he had completed the first version of the quartet he began to think about a 'cello sonata. Here again, perhaps, he was following the example of Saint-Saëns whose C minor Cello Sonata, performed in 1872, had proved to be one of his best works. Fauré began his sonata in this same key (the key too of his recent quartet) starting, as he often did, with the slow movement. This is probably the piece that was played on 21 June 1880 at Saint-Saëns' salon where it was enthusiastically received;[9] but, as often happened, it remained 'in progress' for years and was never finished. In January 1883 Fauré had this single movement published under the title *Elégie*.

In its sombre, reflective mood and accompaniment of repeated chords the *Elégie* recalls the Adagio of the C minor Quartet. 1880 was the last year in which Fauré permitted himself such a direct expression of pathos, and we might well regard this fine work as one of the last manifestations of French musical Romanticism. From now on Fauré's music was to be more introverted and discreet, following Verlaine's advice in *L'Art poétique*: 'Take eloquence and wring its neck.'

Just as the Adagio of the Quartet was brightened by the appearance of a tender barcarolle (bar 27), so the central section of the *Elégie* is a kind of relaxation, openly presenting a highly decorated theme of the sort we find in other works of the period, like the Ballade and the Fourth Nocturne. The funereal opening melody then surges back with a passion worthy of Liszt and sweeps it away, but it returns in the coda like a half-forgotten memory or a landscape seen from afar. Finally Fauré resolves the opposing forces – nuances, rhythms, timbres and moods – into an atmosphere of calm. We shall have reason to note this predilection quite often in the works that follow: Fauré had been a reader of Baudelaire since 1870 and like the poet he was determined to move beyond the garish excitements of the Romantic era: 'Sorrow, be still and take your rest' ...

The Elégie was a great success as soon as it appeared and Hamelle soon asked Fauré for another virtuoso cello piece to complement it. The composer complied but without much enthusiasm – virtuosity for its own sake left him cold. He wrote the brilliant scherzos of the First Violin Sonata and the First Piano Quartet only because he felt they were necessary to preserve an overall balance within the works concerned. A commission to write a virtuoso work had, in his view, no musical justification, and the results were always uninspired. *Papillon* is a case in point. Fauré also had arguments with Hamelle about the title: the composer wanted to call it *Pièce pour violoncelle*, the publisher, with an eye on sales, preferred *Libellules* (Dragonflies), which appears on the contract dated 14 September 1884. Hamelle had to wait fourteen years before Fauré would agree to it being published as *Papillon*, and even then the composer was angry: 'Butterfly or dungfly', he declared in exasperation, 'call it whatever you like.' Once again, Hamelle's instinct was right. As *Papillon*, the piece was played by 'cellists the length and breadth of France, though such is the inventive poverty behind all the agitation that I find this success hard to understand.

Fauré's life between the years 1882 and 1887 is difficult to trace because so little of his correspondence for this period has survived. In 1886 he moved to 154, Boulevard Malesherbes, one of the newly-built, freestone 'middle-class apartments' then going up in the fashionable Plaine Monceau, which had the further advantage for Fauré of being near the Madeleine. The apartment (on the fifth floor, on the left) is spacious, with four rooms in addition to the usual drawing room-cum-dining room facing the street, but not exceptional for a middle-class family of the time, any more than their having a maid and a cook. As Louis Aguettant recorded,[10] 'His study, where he welcomed me, had nothing personal about it – an Erard grand piano, a glass-fronted bookcase full of scores, a table piled high with papers.' The panelled walls were decorated with a large number of his father-in-law's sculptures, including a bust of Marie and some of the watercolour animal studies he specialised in. The most imposing picture, however, was the fine portrait of Fauré painted in about 1887 by Paul Mathey. His worktable was lit by two medium-sized candlesticks and by an enormous oil lamp with frills round the base. Fauré and his family lived in this apartment from October 1886 to April 1911; a memorial plaque was put on the house in 1974.

His mornings were spent at the Madeleine, teaching and rehearsing the choirboys (see pp. 25–6). In the afternoon he composed, unless he had to give lessons or take a rehearsal in the Salle Pleyel or the Salle Erard or in some friend's house, where he might be going to spend a musical evening. Often he might have dinner in one house, then hurry off to take part in a public concert, and finish the evening around 11.00 p.m. or midnight in one salon or another in order to keep the promise obtained from him by an all-too-charming hostess to play some of his piano music, or to accompany a selection of his songs or his violin sonata.

This giddy whirl of activity served to allay the spleen – his own word – which so often beset him, but through it all he found time to write a host of songs and piano pieces and to start thinking about a new chamber work.

A second piano quartet had probably been in his mind right from the time the first one was published in 1884, and its composition seems to have occupied him for most of 1885 and 1886, during which time he produced little else. Since the manuscript is undated and there is no allusion to the work in any of the surviving correspondence, we know nothing about the process of its composition. The first date we can put to the G minor Quartet, a key work in Fauré's output, is that of its first performance at the Société nationale on 22 January 1887, with Guillaume Rémy (violin), Louis van Waefelghem (viola), Jules Delsart (cello) and Fauré himself playing the piano part. It was published a year later and the composer wrote to Hans von Bülow to tell him that he was the dedicatee; this was probably a way of thanking him for a kind mention in an open letter he had written to the conductor Colonne and which had appeared in the Paris press.[11] Bülow seems to have been rather surprised by the gesture to judge by his letter of acknowledgment, written from Hamburg on 30 January 1888: 'Dear Fauré, I have been away and so have only just received your letter of the 21st. Please accept my heartfelt thanks for your kind wishes and for the honour you have done me in making me the dedicatee of your new quartet. I will do my best to value the music at its true worth'!

A general view of the G minor Quartet could lead us to conclude straight away that it bears a close resemblance to its predecessor in the powerful but clear part-writing, in the layout of the movements and even in the nature of its thematic material. In the first movement, Allegro molto moderato, we find the same, almost symphonic, breadth and the contrast between the two main themes; in the scherzo a delicate dexterity with the piano unfolding a *perpetuum mobile* underneath string *pizzicati*; a meditative Adagio, even if more serene than tragic, and a finale, Allegro molto, which returns to the same Brahmsian *élan*, interrupted by an energetic chordal theme on the piano. In spite of these striking resemblances the G minor Quartet has individual qualities and, by comparison, the lively but slightly easy charm of the C minor Quartet seems somewhat pale. The interplay between the instruments is now of a quite different kind, with piano and strings frequently in opposition; indeed, at times the two blocks of sound drive each other to a fury.

The opening theme of the first movement (see Ex. 14) sounds like the product of considerable labour. Its tortuous chromaticism, its structure of small cells repeated and modified, and its explosive force all bring it close to the world of César Franck. In fact the whole quartet shows Fauré moving in this direction, both in its aesthetic stance and in its cyclic procedures. The opening theme, for example, gives rise to two separate motifs: the first is relaxed and song-like, played by the viola as a kind of intermezzo between the two themes of the movement; the second is developed at length in the scherzo, alternating with the piano theme in a ternary structure (bars 50–5 and 68–72). It is then heard again over the *perpetuum mobile* in the central 2/4 section – a marvellously deft and scintillating passage. Where the scherzo of the C minor Quartet offered charm, that of the G minor casts a spell, in its headlong career through a night illuminated by occasional flashes: we are reminded of Schubert's *Erl King*, Berlioz's *Faust* and Franck's *Le Chasseur maudit*. The febrile, almost fantastic colours of this movement make it exceptional among Fauré's output. The same might be said of the third movement, Adagio non troppo which, if not exactly descriptive, is completely successful in evoking an atmosphere. In general Fauré was not greatly concerned with timbre, but here it becomes one of his prime considerations. The bell-motif on the piano and the long viola phrase which unfolds in the ensuing silence together conjure up most powerfully a twilight calm, in which we hear the Aeolian harp caressed by a gentle breeze, as imagined by Berlioz in his *Lélio*.

'The slow movement of my second Quartet', Fauré wrote to his wife on 11 September 1906, 'is one of the few places where I realise that, without really meaning to, I recalled a peal of bells we used to hear of an evening, drifting over to Montgauzy from a village called Cadirac whenever the wind blew from the West. Their sound gives rise to a vague reverie, which, like all vague reveries, is not translatable into words. It often happens, doesn't it, that some external thing plunges us into thoughts that are so imprecise, they're not really thoughts at all, though the mind certainly finds them pleasurable. Perhaps it's a desire for something beyond what actually exists; and there music is very much at home' – an important and almost unique declaration among the Fauré letters that survive, constituting an artistic credo which we shall consider later.

He recalled those distant bells from his childhood round Ariège, as he said, 'without really meaning to', and they can be heard again in the opening of the Second Nocturne, in the central sections of the Fourth and Seventh Nocturnes and of the First and Seventh Preludes and, in a more general sense, in the resonant piano-writing of the Barcarolles.

We might even go further and suggest that perhaps the chordal accompaniments to such deeply contemplative songs as 'Le Secret', 'Le Parfum impérissable' and 'Diane Séléné' also derive from this secret source, this 'enclosed garden' in which impressions of night, reveries, and memories of childhood are indissolubly intertwined. Apart from his love of the *perpetuum mobile*, and even a certain casual chattiness in his writing, Fauré's music is constantly verging on immobility. This tendency may even overcome his technical purism, as in the consecutive 7ths he allows himself in 'Prison' to illustrate the lines: 'La cloche dans le ciel qu'on voit/Doucement tinte' 'I see the sky, wherein the bell/Is softly ringing'. No other work of his can match this Adagio's sense of repose, unless it is the brief but superb eighth variation from the *Thème et variations* for piano which he wrote ten years later. The sense of space it creates, rapt and profound within a narrow range of notes, marks it out as being truly the music of silence.

Compared with the preceding three movements, the Finale (Allegro molto) is less successful and one suspects that, like its companion in the First Quartet, it was the result of re-writing. The introduction (G) is splendidly energetic but the second motif (H) (bars 68–73), all in chords, is rather on the heavy side; more than that, the following development of it is, unusually for Fauré, lacking in imagination. There is more inspiration to be found when variants of it occur in the reprise (bar 283) but here the development goes on too long. Even so this movement is worth examining in more detail because it shows how interested Fauré was in the principles of cyclic composition. We have already noted that the opening theme of the work (A) returns in the scherzo (D). The second theme of the first movement (B) (bars 59–64) also seems to be recalled in the brief rhythmical idea which punctuates the scherzo (E) (bars 86–91; 175–85) and again in the chordal theme of the finale (H). The insistent tone of this could therefore be explained by formal necessity, with Fauré being its servant instead of its master.

Ex. 14 Second Piano Quartet

The links between the Adagio and the other movements are subtle – so much so that I had not noticed them until now! Like the Scherzo, it opens with the notes E♭, G low on the piano, and the descending curve of its single theme (F), played by the viola, takes as many as six of its notes from the opening theme of the whole work; this would then qualify according to d'Indy's classification as a 'generating theme'.[12] The quartet's interlocking structure is therefore fairly complex:

Movements   I   II   III   IV

AB   CDE   F   GH

This homage to Franck was probably inspired not so much by the older composer's Violin Sonata, which was played in Paris three months after the first performance of Fauré's Second Quartet, as by his Piano Quintet which was a resounding success when heard for the first time at the Société nationale on 17 January 1880. Franck's genius as a harmonist seems to have impressed Fauré quite early on in his life and he was undoubtedly attracted by Franck's penchant for surprising modulations. The foundation too of the Société nationale meant that the two men met every week at the sessions of the organising committee. Fauré's admiration is attested by the dedication 'To Monsieur César Franck' on the *Cantique de Jean Racine*, published in 1876; and Franck must have liked the work because he conducted the first performance of it with orchestra at the Société nationale on 15 May 1875. Technical reasons aside, Franck provided the young Fauré with a model of artistic integrity and true humility. Twenty-five years later Fauré mused on Franck's lack of worldly success and we can detect in his words an echo of the soul-searching he entered into on his own account:

Did he really mind the world's neglect? Or did it merely lead him, serene and warm-hearted as he was, to derive still greater pleasure from his own compositions and from the fervent enthusiasm of his pupils and faithful admirers? Those who had the honour of knowing him can testify how happy he used to look when the slightest approbation came his way, however humble the source! But, search as you might in his music or in his conversation, you would never find the slightest hint of antagonism or bitterness. He worked and waited.[13]

In spite of these links, Fauré and Franck are very different composers. There is a world of difference between Franck's determinist structures, the interdependence of his forms and modulations and, it must be admitted, his slightly heavy touch, and Fauré's essential suppleness; the attribute of a composer who is so confident in matters of form that he can allow his harmonic inspiration to wander as the fancy takes it, and then can return it to the home key for the reprise, if need be by the most unexpected paths. Franck's example was certainly valuable support for Fauré's belief that when it came to modulation all things were possible; and while he gave up using cyclic principles from now on in his chamber music he soon found a place for them in his songs.

Hardly had he finished the Second Piano Quartet than he found himself haunted by an idea for another work for piano and strings, as he wrote to Marguerite Baugnies in September 1887.[14] A sketchbook dating from that summer contains what was to be the theme of the work's Finale, noted down in F major. The project soon expanded to become a piano quintet and it could be that the transformation had something to do with the friendship between Fauré and Ysaÿe, formed during the concerts they gave together in Brussels in 1888 and 1889; the programmes contained the Violin Sonata and both the Piano Quartets. Most of the Quintet was sketched out at the end of 1890. 'The Allegro and the Andante', recalled Fauré's son Philippe,[15] 'were sketched more or less simultaneously, but only the exposition [of the Allegro] was written out in full. Written and rewritten: the arpeggios were too heavy.'

Ysaÿe tried over the opening during a visit to Paris. He was enthusiastic and Fauré promised to dedicate the work to him. But Fauré had trouble developing the ideas to his satisfaction and he abandoned the work in favour of two song cycles: the Cinq mélodies 'de Venise' op. 58 (1891) and La Bonne chanson (1892–4). After that he came back to the Quintet 'with the firm intention not to leave it until it's finished', as he wrote in June 1894 to the Princesse de Polignac.[16] Hamelle announced the work as 'to appear shortly' in the spring of 1896 and allotted to it the opus number 60 ... which was never used because once again the Quintet was put on one side. It eventually needed three summer holidays of intense and arduous work in Switzerland from 1903 to 1905 before Fauré could pronounce it finished.

The opening of Fauré's Quintet is perhaps the most beautiful passage in the whole of his chamber music; the strings ascend and descend a modal scale underneath a halo of piano arpeggios, and the result is at the same time memorable and disturbing. The regular rhythm and the incantatory string theme, almost like a litany, recall the freedom and gentleness of the 'In Paradisum' from his Requiem. Fauré's elder son Emmanuel told me how delighted he was as a boy, listening through the drawing-room door in the house on the Boulevard Malesherbes while Fauré tried out this opening with the Ysaÿe Quartet. 'But I only heard it that once', he went on.[17] 'One day I plucked up courage and timidly sang to my father the first bars of this 'vanished' tune. I'll never forget how he threw his arms around me and embraced me, then sat down at the piano and played me the whole of the opening paragraph.'

The strings present the strong, compact second theme while the piano is entrusted with a third idea which bears a marked resemblance to the cyclic theme from the 'Venice' songs, written in the summer of 1891. The same idea can be seen in one of the rare Fauré sketches to survive (a rough draft of the Quintet) see Ex. 15. This can be dated fairly precisely because on the

Ex. 15 First Piano Quintet

same sheet is a drawing by Fauré of Verlaine in his hospital bed, which the composer included in a letter of 30 January 1891 to the Princesse de Polignac.[18] Taken all together, this evidence suggests that the modifications Fauré made thirteen years later were not so much to the thematic material as to its development. However the hard labour of that summer of 1904 did produce one melodic idea of the first water. Here we can see Fauré the technician at work and anyone who cares to follow in detail the way he juggles with inversions, abbreviations and derivatives of the three main themes will marvel at his skill. At Figure 11 in the score, for example, the lovely phrase that begins on the 'cello and in the left hand of the piano and is then heard to its full effect on the first violin is made up of the opening notes of the first theme followed by the first five notes of the second one. The result is a new and perfectly balanced melody, worked in canon to boot. This leads to a concentrated, contrapuntal and rhythmically complex development of the third theme (at four bars before figure 12) (Ex. 16). Fauré wrote to his wife on 31 August 1904,[19] 'I've rewritten the first movement; the proportions are right and in general it's much better. But it was extremely hard work. When I look through the movement now and hear the music in my head it all sounds spontaneous, which is very, very far from the truth.'

He had briefly thought of making it a four-movement work but soon settled on three movements without a scherzo; 'like the marvellous Quintet by César Franck', as he himself wrote.[20] We may regret the absence of a

Ex. 16 First Piano Quintet (I)

scherzo because the limpid first movement (*molto moderato*) with its gentle, dreamy coda seems to demand a change of atmosphere, and this the beginning of the Adagio does not provide. The berceuse theme, prominently displayed at the start by the violin over a soothing piano accompaniment, has something rather indefinite about it. When Fauré first sketched this passage he intended it to be the opening of a violin sonata; it was only five days later that he discovered it was really 'the second movement of the Quintet, to go with the first movement which ground to a halt years ago!'.[21]

The second theme brings an increase of speed. This first appearance is decked out in the most subtle, crystalline piano writing but in the course of its development, as the mood of lyricism grows, the theme returns unexpectedly as a powerful bass line. The final movement, an Allegretto moderato in D major, is the first example in Fauré's output of a sonata rondo, a form he was to use often in the chamber music of his old age. The main theme, which he had jotted down in 1887, is simple and unassuming but the process of variation and amplification it then undergoes makes one think of Beethoven. Fauré's son Philippe recorded[22] how his father was worried that people would find a similarity between this movement and the Finale of the Ninth Symphony, which also ends in D major.

The formal strength of this last movement suggests that Fauré had inherited from his teacher Saint-Saëns his sense of proportion and shape. Everything is in its rightful place and the logic of the argument is unshakable. The overall form is of one long crescendo and inside that there are moments when the texture is almost symphonic in feeling, though without any hint of bombast: nor, on the other hand, does his mastery of the craft of composition lead to dryness, still less to academicism. The effect is rather that of a game well played; there is liveliness and fun which we may well interpret as the pleasure of a creative mind in at last reaching the end of a laborious task – that 'joy of Vulcan' which Marcel Proust was disturbed to find in, of all places, the third act of *Tristan*.[23]

On the day of the Quintet's first performance, 23 March 1906 in Brussels, Fauré wrote to his wife: 'Ysaÿe finds the style of the Quintet broader and loftier than that of my Quartets: he says it is absolute music, free of all attempts at effect ... [Roger] Ducasse may not like it as being a work which stands only on its own two feet, but I couldn't care less. I've come to the firm conclusion that the way I write music is not within the capabilities of *everybody*!'[24]

1 Gabriel Fauré in the uniform of the Ecole
Niedermeyer, *c.* 1864

2 Fauré *c.* 1866

3 Fauré with three of his brothers; 1878?, from left to right: Albert, Gabriel, Amand and Fernand Fauré

4 Pauline Viardot with her daughters, Marianne (right) and
Claudie (left), Baden Baden, 1870

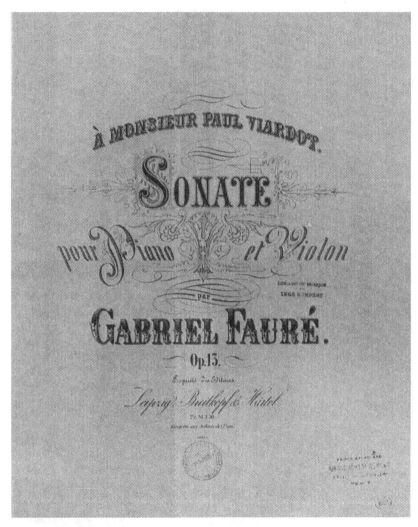

5 Title page of the Sonata op. 13 for violin and piano, first edition, Breitkopf, 1877

6 *Dans les ruines d'une abbaye*, lithograph by A. Jannin for the first edition, Choudens, 1869

7 Second Impromptu for piano, autograph manuscript

7   Choral Music

Choral singing was one of the essential elements in Fauré's musical education. At the Niedermeyer School the pupils all assembled three times a week for 'simultaneous singing', as Niedermeyer called it in his 1854 report. Naturally these sessions were devoted to the religious repertoire and the vast collection published as a supplement to the magazine *La Maîtrise* gives a good idea of the composers they got to know: Lassus, Palestrina, Vittoria, Andrea Gabrieli, Michael Haydn and Mozart, as well as contemporary composers like Gounod and Niedermeyer himself.

This repertoire was practised more assiduously than might otherwise have been the case because the choir performed regularly for services at the church of St-Louis d'Antin, and was involved in the concerts organised by Gustave Lefèvre, with Niedermeyer's help, for the Société du progrès artistique. The pupils also used to sing works by Costeley and Janequin on their Sunday walks.

There is little need to underline the extraordinary opportunity afforded a young composer by this thorough immersion in Renaissance polyphony. The more general discovery of this music was not to take place until the very end of the century, with the performances by Charles Bordes and the Chanteurs de St-Gervais which made such an impact on Debussy. Fauré was surrounded by this music for ten years. Not only was it a good preparation for the study of counterpoint, it also opened up for him a historical perspective and gave him from his earliest years a feeling for the relative position of the classical tonal system within the development of musical language as a whole – and it was to prove an important liberating influence.

It is well known how Debussy had to fight against the rigid, normative harmony teaching at the Conservatoire; Fauré was able to find his own path without any acts of iconoclasm. Where Debussy was forced to break with the tonal system, Fauré rearranged it from the inside using all the possibilities offered by modality. It was here that Louis Niedermeyer's extremely broad-minded teaching bore fruit: it was directly responsible for the ease, the clarity and the balance of Fauré's choral technique, for example in the four- and six-part writing of the *Cantique de Jean Racine* as well as in the whole of his later work, both religious and secular.

Even so, in his secular choral works any influence of the polyphonic French chanson is overshadowed by that of Schumann. This is especially noticeable in *Les Djinns* op. 12, written around 1875 for mixed choir with orchestral or piano accompaniment. In choosing one of the most famous of the poems from Victor Hugo's *Orientales*, Fauré was not exactly out to make life easy for himself: the poet here indulges in a splendid display of verbal virtuosity by first of all lengthening the lines progressively from two to eight syllables and then, in the second half, shortening them in the same manner. Fauré follows the implications of Hugo's scheme with a crescendo followed by a decrescendo, though in rhythm he marks only the extreme brevity of the first and last strophes. Otherwise he treats the text in an almost uniform way and in a decidedly brisk tempo. *Les Djinns* reveals to us a composer susceptible to the ghosts and apparitions of the Romantic era, a fervent admirer of Mendelssohn's *Midsummer Night's Dream* and of Schumann's *Scenes from Faust* and *The Pilgrimage to the Rose*. Fauré blends choir and orchestra into an indissoluble whole which goes far beyond the simplistic format of 'choir and accompaniment'. Even if the result is not highly individual, it does offer some real musical interest and for my part I prefer it to *Le Ruisseau*, a piece for chorus and piano which Fauré wrote around 1881 for a female choir run by Pauline Roger. He seems here to be trying to go one better than he did in the early Barcarolles and the piano Ballade in exploring a style of undulating languor, and so blatantly does it flourish in these pages that even the subtle harmonies of the accompaniment cannot save the day. This is living up to his reputation as a composer doted on by those well-bred music classes he spent so much time accompanying at this period. No doubt financial necessity played a part, but he was also known to admit to enjoying it. With his affectionate, passionate nature he was strongly drawn to the charms of delightful young girls – and the attraction was mutual. At the time he was writing *Le Ruisseau* he confided to Mme Clerc his feelings for one of the pupils in his harmony class. In a letter dating from the summer of 1878 he mentions only her surname: 'the spring rose of the month of May' who, he says, was the inspiration for his song 'Automne'.[1] It would seem she can be identified as Alice Boissonnet, to whom Fauré dedicated 'Automne' and two other songs of the same period, 'Les Berceaux' and 'Le Secret'. The idyll was short-lived as in 1881 'the spring rose' married Henri de Lassus, to whom she was to bear seven sons.[2]

We come closer to Fauré's true creative self with another work of these same years, *La Naissance de Vénus* op. 29. This 'mythological scene' was commissioned by the Société chorale d'amateurs, founded after the war of 1870 by Antonin Guillot de Sainbris. His previous commission was César Franck's biblical *scena Rebecca*. The librettist for this was Paul Collin, a rich man of letters whose love of music led him to write numerous librettos for 'scènes lyriques' and cantatas and to publish a collection of them in 1886. Fauré probably had his Collin text imposed on him; certainly he does not seem to have been inspired by its wealth of platitudes.

Even so the prelude to *La Naissance de Vénus* and the Nereids' chorus which follows it are quite nicely done. The Nereids are represented by a theme of alternating thirds and this is developed, with Fauré's characteristically lazy gracefulness, on low flutes, clarinets and oboes over a suitable accompaniment of broken chords. The ensuing symphonic interlude contains ingenious variations on a new, convoluted theme representing Venus and is undoubtedly one of Fauré's finest orchestral passages. But the level of inspiration falls sharply with the appearance of Neptune who, by words alone, provokes the birth of Venus from the spray, and the banality of his bass monologue is unfortunately surpassed in the interminable final chorus 'Salut à toi, déesse blonde'. The empty, repetitive text moved Fauré to write some utterly academic pages which may fairly be seen as a musical transposition of the large mythological pictures produced by the more celebrated 'establishment' painters – Cabanel's *La Naissance de Vénus* or Bouguereau's *l'Océanide*.

The presence of such an academic work in Fauré's output is surprising when we consider how unacademic he was in his attitudes and how outspoken he was later to be in his opposition to the Prix de Rome cantata.[3] Its turgid style may in part be due to the text, but also to his intention to keep things simple and not risk upsetting the amateurs brought together by the instigator of the project. Perhaps the most surprising thing of all is that he never repudiated this occasional work. The original version with piano was published and he had it played not just by the Société chorale d'amateurs (7 March 1883) but also at the Société nationale de musique (3 April 1886). He orchestrated it in 1895 and this version was given by Edouard Colonne (1 December 1895) and then – the final accolade – at the Société des concerts du Conservatoire (5 February 1899).[4] He himself conducted it on 8 October 1898 with a choir of 400 at the Leeds Festival in an English version by his pupil Adela Maddison[5] and, furthermore, he chose this minor work to represent him at the festival of French music which opened the Théâtre des Champs-Elysées (2 April 1913), a month before the Paris première of *Pénélope*!

All in all, I find far more in the *Madrigal* for four voices op. 35: it may stick too closely to Armand Silvestre's poem, but the resulting sentimentality is not without its attractions. Fauré wrote it in 1883 with piano accompaniment and orchestrated it a year later. He dedicated it to Messager and this, together with the date of composition (that is to say, after Fauré's marriage and shortly before Messager's), explains the knowing allusion it contains. Charles Koechlin was the first to point out, in his excellent biography,[6] that the opening theme is in fact taken from the introduction to Bach's Cantata 38, 'Aus tiefer Noth', which Bach also used in Fugue no. 8 from the first book of the *48* (see Ex. 17).

Ex. 17

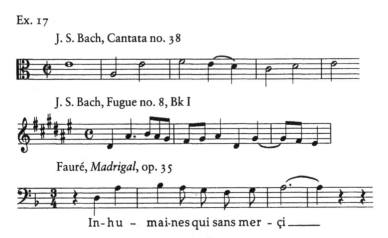

J. S. Bach, Cantata no. 38

J. S. Bach, Fugue no. 8, Bk I

Fauré, *Madrigal*, op. 35

In-hu – mai-nes qui sans mer - çi ____

This deliberate use of a borrowed theme is practically unique among Fauré's works. It probably refers back to the year 1871 when the eighteen-year-old Messager was in Lausanne studying with Fauré, who was himself barely any older – the beginning of a long friendship.

The *Pavane* in F sharp minor op. 50 has done much in forwarding Fauré's reputation, and there will be few to deny that it is one of the most attractive of his lesser works: the flute theme, once heard, is not easily forgotten. It was written at Le Vésinet during the summer of 1887 for one of the concerts run by Jules Danbé, the conductor of the Opéra-Comique, but the dedication was offered to the Countess Greffulhe, the undisputed queen of Parisian society, who had agreed to realise Fauré's dream of seeing the *Pavane* danced to the accompaniment of an invisible choir and orchestra. In the choral version the pre-existing music is overlaid with a mannered text written anonymously by the Countess's cousin, Robert de Montesquiou, in the style of Verlaine; hence the lack of character or autonomy in the vocal writing. In general the addition of voices seems to me rather to weigh down the pure line of this work which Fauré with justice described as 'elegant ... but otherwise not important'.[7]

A performance of the *Pavane* including miming and dancing was given in the course of a nocturnal party held by the Countess in the Bois de Boulogne on 21 July 1891, and after that it formed part of a display of 'ancient dances' given at the Paris Opéra on 29 December 1895. But its most prestigious presentations took place from 1917 when it entered the repertoire of the Ballets Russes, under the title first of *Las Meninas* and later *Les Jardins d'Aranjuez*, with choreography by Massine and décors by José Maria Sert. This stage version to some extent replaced the score that Diaghilev asked Fauré for in July 1909. The composer had accepted in principle but the project was postponed for a long time owing to his work finishing *Pénélope* and then because of the outbreak of war.[8] Quite a number of Fauré's works have been danced to,[9] but he was never to write music specifically as a ballet.

The *Pavane* was soon well known and two of Fauré's younger contemporaries took it as a model: Debussy in the *Passepied* (also in F sharp) of his *Suite bergamasque* of around 1890, which was moreover initially announced as *Pavane*, and of course Ravel who wrote his equally famous *Pavane pour une infante défunte* while he was a pupil in Fauré's class.

Fauré's secular choral music (and in this we must include the incidental music for *Caligula* and especially the very important choral sections of *Prométhée*) is, despite individual pages of real charm, on a far lower level of interest and originality than his motets and his two masses. He was a church musician for forty years (1865–1905). He had therefore plenty of opportunities for writing religious music, either prompted by some special occasion like finding a new interpreter or a friend's wedding, or else because he felt the need to introduce some new blood into a repertoire that he knew all too well. 'I've had them up to here', he complained in 1902, talking about his Requiem (*Paris-Comoedia*, 3–9 March 1954). Even so, for all their functional and occasional nature, Fauré's religious works are a very direct reflection of his personal attitudes.

He felt, and with some justice, that once the Church had abandoned its authentic repertoire of Gregorian chants and turned to music by named, individual composers, the so-called 'problem' of musical style was not really a problem at all. He had the chance to express his point of view with the publication in 1904 of Pope Pius X's edict reminding church musicians and clergy of the need to remove from their repertoire all music of secular, and especially theatrical, origins and to concentrate on the plainsong tradition and the products of Renaissance polyphony. In reply to a questionnaire in *Le Monde musical* (15 February 1904), Fauré stated:

The edict you mention will do nothing to change established habits, at least not in the churches of Paris. Firstly because, with the best will and the worst taste in the world, the clergy is convinced it was doing the right thing even before this edict was published. And secondly because there's an unconscious understanding between the congregation and the clergy which leads them to see everything as being just as it should be. And also because it's really rather difficult to demarcate between what is a truly religious style and what isn't: it's purely a matter of personal judgment.

Gounod's religious faith is quite different from Franck's or Bach's. Gounod is all heart and Franck is all spirit. Take the case of Saint Teresa of Avila: her faith is expressed in words whose ardour and passion sometimes spill over into licentiousness. But she was still a saint and you would not dream of banning her from the Church.

The truth is, this edict isn't radical enough. The only music we should have in church is plainsong and it should be sung in unison, given that it dates back to a time when polyphony hadn't been discovered. To set up religious music of the sixteenth century as an unalterable model is an impossibility. At the period when it was written this music represented an art of extreme luxury and if it seems simple to us today that's only because of what's happened to music in the meantime.

With that independence which characterises Fauré's creative self, he wrote his religious works in the style he wanted to and they reflect as clearly as can be his character as man and artist. To those who professed themselves surprised to find in his Requiem more gentleness and tenderness than terror he replied: 'Gounod too has been criticised for making his religious music too human and sympathetic. But it was in his nature to feel that way; that's how his religious impulses manifested themselves. Surely an artist's nature is something that just has to be accepted?'[10]

This determination to go his own way placed Fauré at one remove from the basic tastes of the clergy and their congregations. They were set on confusing vapid, simplistic, sentimental music with the expression of religious feeling. But Fauré equally stood apart from the 'neo-Palestrinian' movement of d'Indy, Charles Bordes and Alexandre Guilmant, the three apostles of the Schola Cantorum which they had founded in 1894. Writing in June 1894, Fauré refers to this movement which was directly inspired by the Vatican's recommendations: 'I've also written four short religious pieces, but (I'm sorry to say) not in the spirit of the new Society for Sacred Music! Maybe they're not music of importance, but I've endowed them with human feeling according to my taste!'[11]

His religious output contains very little that is conventional. As in the rest of his works, compassion and tenderness are the dominant emotions and throughout we are made aware of his personal philosophy based on the possible, if not probable, existence of a better world.

Like so many church musicians faced with the routine and the petty observances of the liturgy, Fauré very soon ceased to be a practising Catholic. Already at St-Sauveur in Rennes the clergy were casting aspersions on his lack of piety. But it would, even so, be quite wrong to regard him as an atheist. His letters to his wife show him to have been appreciative of natural beauty and especially of the various effects of light. He was a contemplative who preferred above all else to lose himself in reverie. The calm grandeur of the Swiss lakes especially appealed to him. Painting might not interest him much but it is worth knowing that he did try and capture some of the beauty in the world by means of photography.[12]

At heart, however, he was a doubter and the resulting mixture of pessimism and resignation set him apart from the 'despair' of the Romantics. Fauré's attitude was much closer to the 'spleen' of Verlaine. 'Yesterday I copied M. de Lamartine', he wrote from Zürich on 1 October 1904.[13] 'I went and confided my lack of interest in things to Mother Nature, who replied, as far as I could judge, that she couldn't give a damn. Towards M. de Lamartine she was more maternal!'

In a more serious vein, meditating on the sources of inspiration for the Andante of his second Piano Quartet led him to ponder on the meaning of that inspiration: 'the desire for things that don't exist, perhaps'. The human condition in his view deserved chiefly compassion and charity. He wrote to his wife on 6 April 1922:[14]

You were speaking in one of your last letters of your admiration for the Creation and of your distrust of created humanity. Is that fair? The universe is order, man is disorder. But is that his fault? He's been thrown on to this earth, where everything appears to be in harmony, and he walks about on it staggering and stumbling from the day of his birth to the day of his death, weighed down with such a burden of physical and spiritual infirmities (so much so that someone had to invent 'original sin' to explain the situation!) ... And the clearest indication of the misery in which we find ourselves is this promise, the best that man can be offered: the obliteration of *everything*, the Hindu nirvana, or the Catholic *Requiem aeternam*.

Fauré's religious beliefs are, as we can see, hardly orthodox for someone who spent half his life in churches. We could describe them as amounting, if not to agnosticism, at least to an aspiration towards that ideal which was an essential basis of his art. Questioning his 'desire for things that don't exist, perhaps', he added, 'and that is very much the domain of music'. There is much truth also in what his son Philippe Fauré-Fremiet wrote:[15] 'Certainly there are pages of Bach – pages upon pages – or of César Franck in which a more decided optimism shines through. For Bach and for Franck the kingdom of God is a certainty; the only doubt lies in us, as to whether we reach it or fall short of it. For Fauré the appearance of the choir of angels coming to greet the tormented soul is no more than *probable*.' But we need at this point to quote the little-known testimony of Eugène Berteaux:[16] 'For him – and I have it from his own lips – the word "God" was merely the imposing synonym for the word "Love". The all-embracing nature of this belief was bound in the end to demolish the charges of slack, Epicurean indifference and of a lack of religion which various musical cliques were pleased to tax him with. Party spirit led them to claim that "such an attitude of philosophical neutrality was unworthy of an ex-organist of the Madeleine ..." "Poor people!" was Fauré's only reply, accompanied by his most charming and indulgent smile.'

I would add that in Fauré's opinion divine love and human love were just facets of a single reality; furthermore, finite man can come no closer to the infinite than when he fulfils himself in the human sphere. There is nothing fortuitous about Fauré mentioning the mystical exaltations of St Teresa of Avila and defending Gounod's religious views. He saw musical asceticism as an aberration. On one occasion a journalist asked him about the Requiem and the often-expressed opinion that it was more pagan than religious. Fauré replied: 'But pagan doesn't necessarily mean irreligious! In any case I can't deny, pagan antiquity has always held an enormous attraction for me.'[17]

Fauré's religious output consists of two masses and about sixteen motets. Apart from the *Messe basse*, almost all these works were composed for services at the Madeleine and, as he wrote to his publisher Edgard Hamelle who was preparing a collection of the motets: 'for that reason they are in manageable keys, not too high and not too low'.[18] This collection appeared in 1911 and includes the *Cantique de Jean Racine* and most of the Latin motets which had already appeared separately. It is worth mentioning that the indications on these various editions do not always correspond with what Fauré originally intended. The two motets for three voices op. 65 *Ave verum* and *Tantum ergo*, published 'for female voices', were written for the choirboys of the Madeleine; while the duet *Maria*

Mater gratiae op. 47 no. 2 and the trio *Ecce fidelis servus* op. 54 were for
the choir's male soloists. These changes were prompted simply by commercial motives. The wave of anticlericalism in the early years of the
century led to the separation of the Church and the State and made
religious music hard to sell. After signing a contract with Heugel, Fauré
more or less apologised for sending him an *Ave Maria* for two sopranos
and organ:[19] 'This *Ave Maria* is by its nature destined more for the chapel
or the salon than for a large church. I see its future lying especially in the
choral classes for young ladies and I'm counting on Mme Trélat's fair
pupils to launch it.' I find very little of interest in this rather long motet; it is
based on an earlier piece performed at the Madeleine by Claudie and
Marianne Viardot in May 1877.[20] Conventionality is also the hallmark of
the *O Salutaris* op. 47 no. 1 for baritone solo written at the request of his
well-known near-namesake Jean-Baptiste Faure in 1887.[21] Its total lack of
originality makes it unlikely that it was in fact written at the same time as
the Requiem and this occasional work more probably derives from the *O
Salutaris* 'composed at the Hippodrome and sung at the church of Arromanches', which Fauré mentions in a letter of 1878 to Mme Clerc.[22] The
motets for mixed choir and soloists – *Tu es Petrus, Tantum ergo* op. 55 in
A major (with organ and harp), *Tantum ergo* without opus no. in G flat
major – are more ambitious but do not call for prolonged scrutiny.

It would be unfair, however, to write off his motets altogether. The more
intimate of them, like the ones composed in 1894–5 (op. 65 and 67) are
small masterpieces of harmonic refinement. If they are a little too easy on
the ear – and finding the right performing style is a delicate matter – then
they do reflect an almost passionate feeling as well as that tenderness and
gentleness characteristic of all his music for the church. When sung by
children or young girls they can be ravishing, or sickly, depending on your
taste. One of the best is the *Salve Regina* op. 67. This was written for
Emma Bardac, who inspired *La Bonne chanson*, and contains 'human
emotions' that Fauré was happy to express under cover of a prayer to the
Virgin. As often, he concentrated on the overall sense of these texts rather
than on the detail and this explains the rather slack Latin prosody together
with his habit, a general one among composers of the time, of fitting new
words to pre-existing music.[23]

We must realise that for a musician of Fauré's gifts his duties at the
Madeleine were a real penance. The decorative, worldly atmosphere of the
ritual and the clergy's innocently execrable taste when it came to music
were hardly encouraging and further reinforced his philosophical scepticism. With this in mind we can see that his apparent casualness in writing

an O *Salutaris* in the Hippodrome at Arromanches masked a profound sadness. This comes through also in a letter he wrote to Henriette Fuchs in September 1882 about his *Messe basse*:[24]

I've just spent a long and very pleasant holiday at Villerville with my friends the Clercs. There were some excellent musicians there and some nice voices, and this willing company prompted a performance of a little *Mass* of mine, accompanied by a small orchestra. Despite the jollity of the rehearsals, or perhaps because of it, the performance was splendid. And this *ad hoc* choir was as good to look at as to listen to – something of a rest from the severities of the Madeleine!

What Fauré fails to mention is that this mass for women's voices was written in collaboration with André Messager and had already been performed at Villerville the previous year. Marie Clerc described the occasion in a letter of 4 September 1881 to her mother-in-law Alexandrine Clerc:[25]

Yesterday Adelbert [one of M. Clerc's sons] took the collection at high mass with General Donay's daughter, they made a charming couple. The mass and the collection were in aid of the local fishermen's benevolent fund. A deputation of fishermen, with flag and 'collector' at their head, went to find the collector's female counterpart and then processed through the village, it was a lovely sight. Our visiting musicians, MM. Fauré and Messager, had written a mass which we sang very well, if I may be immodest for a moment. The collection raised 560 francs which for a little spot like Villerville is good going.

The *Messe des pêcheurs de Villerville* was given in 1881 by a choir of thirteen women's voices, with a simple accompaniment on the harmonium and a solo violin for the O Salutaris, in the church of Villerville on the cliffs between Trouville and Fécamp, where the Clercs used to spend the summer. For its second performance on 10 September the following year it was decided to adorn it with a modest orchestration, though getting the players together proved to be a major problem: the forces were a flute, an oboe, a clarinet, a double string quintet and a harmonium. The autograph score of this version was written out by Messager apart from the Agnus Dei, which was orchestrated by Fauré.

After these two performances at Villerville, the *Messe des pêcheurs* remained in the Clerc family's archives until Fauré came to sign a contract with his new editor Heugel and thought of publishing these pages written twenty-five years before. So in 1907 they appeared under the title of *Messe basse* in the version for female voices (solos and chorus) with organ or harmonium accompaniment. A comparison of the two versions shows that Fauré made some important changes. The two movements by Messager (Kyrie and O Salutaris) were taken out – a pity, because the O Salutaris is touching and graceful in a Mozartian manner. Fauré's replacement for the Kyrie is in antiphonal style, with solo and unison choir in alternation. He probably took it from an earlier work as the undulating vocal lines and the melting harmonies seem much closer to his musical language of the 1880s than to that of the *Chanson d'Eve*, the great song-cycle on which he embarked in 1906.[26]

The rather noisy Gloria was for the most part suppressed, though the gentle, A flat lullaby for the Qui tollis reappears as the Benedictus, with major changes from bar 10 onwards. The whole movement is reworked in the antiphonal style of the Kyrie. The Sanctus remains very much the same, though with six extra bars and major alterations in the fitting of words to music. The only movement to remain unchanged apart from the prosody, is the Agnus Dei. Here the three-part writing is not only sonorous but forms an entity with the accompaniment, producing a solid texture and a logical development of ideas. Its more ambitious character naturally led Fauré to insist on orchestrating it himself.

Messe des pêcheurs de Villerville	*Messe basse*
Fauré/Messager (1881–2)	Fauré (1906)
Messager: Kyrie (3/4, E flat)	Fauré: Kyrie (3/4, A flat)
Fauré: Gloria (2/4, E flat) ('Qui tollis', 9/8, A flat)	
Fauré: Sanctus (4/4, G)	Fauré: Sanctus (4/4, G)
	Fauré: Benedictus (9/8, A flat) based on the 'Qui tollis' from the Gloria)
Messager: O Salutaris (2/4, G)	
Fauré: Agnus Dei (2/4, G)	Fauré: Agnus Dei (2/4, G)

The complete version of the *Messe des pêcheurs*, in Messager's excellent orchestration, certainly deserves to be known.[27] In Fauré's published revision the *Messe basse* offers subtler harmonic progressions and a simplicity and transparency which compensate for any excessive softness. Fauré was determined to follow the dictates of his own heart.

This religious work of the *fin-de-siècle* may employ a somewhat ambivalent language but over and above that, it seems to me, it recaptures the simplicity and the direct fervour of Racine's 'cantiques', admirably caught by Fauré fifteen years earlier. When we hear the *Messe basse* performed, as it often is by choirs in France and England, we may well think of the girls of the royal school at Saint-Cyr singing Clérambault's short motets, or choruses from Jean-Baptiste Moreau's *Esther*.[28]

REQUIEM MASS op. 48

That's how I see death: as a joyful deliverance, an aspiration towards a happiness beyond the grave, rather than as a painful experience.

(Fauré to Louis Aguettant in 1902)

Most of Fauré's biographers have noted that he composed his Messe de Requiem between the death of his father on 25 July 1885 and that of his mother on 31 December 1887. But a letter from the composer to Maurice Emmanuel[29] provides evidence which, yet again, breaks the link one might otherwise establish between his daily life and his creative one: 'My Requiem wasn't written *for* anything . . . for pleasure, if I may call it that!' and in his interview with Louis Aguettant in 1902 he added: 'Perhaps my instinct led me to stray from the established path after all those years accompanying funerals! I'd had them up to here. I wanted to do something different.'

Composition and early performances

The few Fauré sketchbooks we possess contain various ideas for the Pie Jesu, the 'Te decet' from the Introit and Kyrie and the baritone solo 'Hostias' from the Offertory. From these it would seem that before settling on an overall tonality of D minor Fauré thought of employing the traditional key of C minor. The sketches for the Requiem are found with those for 'Clair de lune', for the baritone solo *O Salutaris* and for a third Piano Quartet, so they can be dated around the end of the summer and the early autumn of 1887 which Fauré spent with his family in a rented house at le Vésinet. An early, incomplete version of the Requiem was finished in à few months, rehearsals began on 9 January 1888 and it was performed at the Madeleine on 16 January under the composer's direction 'for the funeral of some parishioner or other', as Fauré put it in the letter to Maurice Emmanuel I have already quoted. It has been possible to establish from the Madeleine archives that it was a 'first class' funeral, that is to say with choir and orchestra, for a well-known architect, M. Lesoufaché.

'Immediately the ceremony was over', wrote Armand Vivet, once choirmaster at St-Augustin,[30] 'the vicar called Fauré into the sacristy and questioned him as follows: "What was that mass for the dead you've just conducted?" "It was a Requiem of my own composition." "Monsieur Fauré, we don't need all these novelties; the Madeleine's repertoire is quite rich enough, just content yourself with that."'

At that time the work consisted only of five of the seven movements we now know: 1, Introit and Kyrie; 3, Sanctus (manuscript dated 9 January

1888); 4, Pie Jesu (manuscript lost); 5, Agnus Dei (manuscript dated 6 January 1888); and 7, In Paradisum. The score of this original version gives us a provisional orchestration, made for the performance on 16 January 1888; the forces are a solo violin, divided violas and 'cellos, basses, a harp, timpani and organ. The latter was soon reinforced by brass because by the time of the public performance at the Madeleine on 4 May 1888 the critic Camille Benoit was able to mention in his notice[31] the 'short fanfare for horn and trumpet' in the Agnus Dei. The autograph includes later sketches for four brass parts: two trumpets and two horns in F.

Fauré further added two whole movements: 2 the Offertory, and 6 the Libera me. Both are movements with baritone solo and the second one was probably written for Louis Ballard, a singer from the Paris Opéra whom Fauré brought into the Madeleine choir in January 1890. The Libera me probably goes back to pages Fauré played to his friend, the singer Romain Bussine, at the time of his engagement to Marianne Viardot.[32] In its final version for solo, choir and orchestra (including three trombones) it was heard separately in a concert given under the auspices of the Société nationale in the church of St-Gervais on 28 January 1892, with Louis Ballard as soloist. In all probability, despite the claims made on the programme that this was a first performance, the Libera me had already been heard at the Madeleine as the parts were copied there.

The Offertory was composed in several stages. The baritone solo 'Hostias' was sketched in the autumn of 1887 but seems not to have been completed until the spring of 1889,[33] while the chorus that surrounds it, 'O Domine', is probably later still.[34]

In 1890 Fauré considered his Requiem was more or less finished and offered it to his current editor, Julien Hamelle. A contract of 16 September 1890 includes it but publication did not take place for another ten years. This delay was partly due to Fauré's negligence. He had used his 1888 manuscript as a basis on which to draft changes in the orchestration and as a result it was quite unusable as a fair copy for the printer. Also, as he had written it directly into full score, a reduction had to be made for choir and piano. For this the choice fell on Léon Boëllmann. His qualifications were impeccable – organist of St-Eugène in Paris, a friend of Fauré's and Niedermeyer's son-in-law – but in 1897 he died, and Fauré handed the task over to his pupil Roger Ducasse. The vocal score appeared in 1900 and the orchestral score in the autumn of 1901.

During these ten years there seems to have been some debate between Fauré and his publisher as to the orchestral forces to be used. The absence of violins, apart from a solo violin in the Sanctus, and the even more unusual absence of woodwind was not going to recommend the work to concert-giving bodies. It is not clear what Fauré meant in a letter to Hamelle when he promised to have it 'in a fit state to be published' by 1 December 1898. At all events the score published in 1901 is very different from the original orchestration, played several times under the composer's direction. The published version expands Fauré's specifically chosen forces into those of a conventional large symphony orchestra: two flutes, two clarinets, two bassoons, four horns, two trumpets, three trombones, timpani, two harps, strings and organ. The chorus and solo parts remain almost unchanged.

Without going into great detail, a general comparison of the two orchestral versions does nonetheless throw up some interesting points. By adding a large body of first violins (there are no seconds) to the most tuneful sections of the work Fauré underlines the undulating contours – in passages like the solo in the Sanctus, which is the same as in the original version but now played by all the violins an octave lower, or the long line of the Agnus Dei. The addition of two further horns completely alters the function of these instruments from being melodic to being harmonic, while the added strings and the wind are confined almost entirely to doubling other parts. The bassoons reinforce the basses in the tuttis and flutes and clarinets have precisely twelve bars to play (in the Pie Jesu)! The individual character of the Madeleine version is thus considerably changed and the overall effect is heavier. Numerous touches of colour on the horns have been quite suppressed, as have various timpani entries (at the 'Christe' and the end of the Kyrie, in the 'Dies Irae' from the Libera me) and the highly appropriate harp entry at the 'Lux aeterna' in the Agnus Dei. The string parts have been almost entirely rewritten and in particular dynamic markings have been increased from *pp* to *p* and from *f* to *ff*.

The revised score certainly achieves a more decisive effect, but it is sad to lose the choral accents on the word 'Christe' and the breathtaking *pianissimo subito* at the end of the 'Dies Irae'. Furthermore there are numerous printing mistakes and signs of carelessness in the handling of the Latin text, faults for which Fauré's antipathy to correcting proofs must be held largely responsible.

This published version of the Requiem, which we may call the 'symphonic' version, is extremely practicable for performances in large concert halls with large choirs. In my opinion, however, it will always sound better in a specifically religious setting. The material and its orchestration both seem to have been destined for a highly reverberant acoustic like that of the Madeleine in which they can expand without sounding confused – though it is only fair to add that Hamelle's acumen paid off in terms of performances: from 1900 onwards the work was taken up by a large number of concert societies. The symphonic version was heard in Lille on 6 May 1900 (170 performers), in Paris on 12 July 1900 at the Trocadéro as part of the Universal Exhibition (250 performers), and on 6 April 1901 at a Conservatoire concert where it made a strong impression. Fauré himself was surprised at this instant success and wrote to Willy in October 1900: 'My Requiem's being played in Brussels, Nancy, Marseilles and at the Paris Conservatoire! You wait, I'll soon be a celebrated composer!'

A century after its first performance, Fauré's Requiem remains the most often played and recorded of his works the world over and increasingly it is being heard in churches. It is therefore high time the original orchestration was restored, especially since it is the only one that in the present state of our knowledge can be considered as entirely authentic.

After some fifteen years of researching the question, I can still not state with any grounds for confidence that Fauré is the sole author of the symphonic version in the form in which it has been played since its publication. Fauré certainly began his new orchestration by working yet again from the 1888 autographs, sketching on the blank staves parts for bassoons, third and fourth horns and so on. But these changes are very far from corresponding with what we find in the published score. A new manuscript version must have been completed in 1898–9 for use by the printer.[35] Unfortunately, despite my researches, no trace of this manuscript has been found and this lacuna is all the more to be regretted because almost all the autographs of Fauré's other orchestral scores have been preserved, either in his family archives (now in the Bibliothèque Nationale) or in those of Hamelle, and because the Requiem is a key work in his output.

It is not unwarrantably daring to suppose that Fauré might have taken his publisher's advice and got a collaborator to prepare a new score from manuscripts and suggestions supplied by himself. This would explain why there are so many differences between the manuscripts, even those bearing Fauré's revisions, and the printed score. One might, with due caution, put forward the name of Roger-Ducasse whose name appears on the vocal score. In 1914 Fauré was to ask him to make an orchestral version of *Prométhée* in similar circumstances.

However authentic or inauthentic the symphonic version of the Requiem may be, there can be no question of condemning it, still less of taking it out of circulation. Its practicability is undeniable and, after all, Fauré not only accepted responsibility for it but seems even to have been pleased with certain aspects of it. In a letter of October 1900 to Ysaÿe who was preparing the first Brussels performance he wrote: 'You'll see how angelic the violins are in the Sanctus after all those violas!!!' But in an earlier letter[36] he clearly remains faithful to his initial conception: 'The orchestration is based on violas and 'cellos, each in two parts. There's no second violin part and the firsts only come in from the Sanctus (no. 3) onwards ... Also the brass and woodwind have very little to do as the organ is always there to fill in the harmony', and he offers Ysaÿe this rather curious piece of advice: 'To give the violas more body (and the more there are of them the better) you could ask the better violins to play the viola just for the occasion. Also, if you could possibly have two more 'cellos than usual that would be perfect.' We may note too that during rehearsals for the first official performance at the Trocadero ten extra viola parts were copied in a hurry.[37]

It seemed to me highly desirable to restore Fauré's original orchestration, which corresponds to his musical thinking and his aesthetic preoccupations at the time he penned this masterpiece (c. 1893), and before the general revision of 1898–9. The original manuscript had been used as a conducting score for ten years and, unfortunately, could not be used as a source: apart from the absence of three of the solo sections (Offertory, Pie Jesu, Libera me), the various versions from 1888 to 1899, established according to the circumstances and particularly the forces at Fauré's disposal, found themselves superimposed in layers on the manuscript. In 1969, thanks to the kind offices of M. Joachim Havard de la Montagne, the choirmaster at the Madeleine, I was lucky enough to discover the original orchestral parts used by Fauré at the Madeleine.[38] This is the only source which allows us to decipher and interpret the autographs and so to arrive at a definitive score.

These instrumental parts were made by Manier, a bass and the copyist for the Madeleine choir until June 1889, relying on Fauré's autographs. The composer himself later copied complete parts for trumpets and horns and revised his copyist's work with some care. The Offertory appears in its original form as a baritone solo. The choral parts barely figure among this material but what does exist shows that the choral writing was changed only in a few small details.[39]

Musical commentary

The movements may be scattered in date but, as is often the case with Fauré, they form a recognisable ensemble. The structure of the Requiem is organised around the central point of the soprano solo, the Pie Jesu (no. 4, B flat). Everything radiates from this, which is present in the earliest sketches and forms in some sense the nucleus for the development of the whole work.

On either side are placed two groups of three movements, alternating chorus alone and chorus with baritone solo: no. 1, Introit and Kyrie (D minor); no. 2, Offertory (B minor) with baritone solo; no. 3, Sanctus (E flat) – then, after the Pie Jesu, no. 5 Agnus Dei (F major and D minor); no. 6, Libera me (D minor) with baritone solo; no. 7, In Paradisum (D major).

The homogeneity of the work is further assisted by a number of thematic references, though we cannot speak here of any system of cyclic organisation or of leitmotifs. The 'Te decet' in the Introit (bar 42) reappears at the words 'fac eas' in the Offertory (bar 57), and the second theme of the Sanctus ('Pleni sunt caeli', bars 27–8) is an anticipation of the Pie Jesu; while the beginning of the work ('Requiem aeternam, dona eis Domine'), on the ascending notes A, C (D), F is repeated exactly at the end of the Agnus Dei and in the same key of D minor. The same melodic idea also lies behind the brief 'Dies irae' in the Libera me (bars 54–8).

The choral parts are well-balanced against the instrumental ones, even though the texture is very varied. Vertical, homophonic writing for four, five or six voices (with men's parts doubled) is used for the moments of direct prayer where Fauré obviously wanted to make the words absolutely clear. Words like 'Requiem aeternam' (in the Introit, Agnus Dei, Libera me, In Paradisum) and 'Kyrie' are placed in a kind of halo of light. The same clarity of word-setting is to be found in passages of great emotional intensity, where Fauré brings together choir and orchestra in massive ensembles that are all the more effective for being short and sudden: the 'Hosanna' in the Sanctus (bars 42–53), the 'Dies irae', and the unison repeat of the Libera me (bars 52–122). The gentleness and intimacy of Fauré's music in general here give way to an impressive dignity.

Overall the vocal writing shows the discreet influence of Gregorian chant, to be taken up again in Maurice Duruflé's beautiful Requiem of 1947 which is very close to Fauré's in spirit. With Fauré the curves of the vocal line are not far from those of the Gregorian archetypes taught by the monks of Solesmes in their simplicity and meandering expansiveness: in the strange immobility of the Hostias, for example, or the psalm-like character of the Sanctus, the Agnus Dei and the In Paradisum. Often, as we have seen in the *Messe basse*, the choir sings antiphonally: tenors/sopranos in the Introit (bars 20–49); sopranos/tenors + first basses in unison throughout the Sanctus; tenors/choir in the Agnus Dei, and so on.

On the other hand polyphony, too, is an important ingredient, as in the remarkable 'lux aeterna' in the Agnus Dei (bars 45–69) or the canon at the

octave between altos and tenors in the Offertory, which is then transformed into a large polyphonic chorus in four parts. But perhaps nothing
displays such a combination of ingenuity and beauty as the rising vocalise
which crowns the Offertory: this 'Amen' in B major has a radiance, a
poignancy and a serenity worthy of Josquin at his best.

The Libera me is set apart from the other movements by its clearcut
ostinato rhythms, its angular vocal writing – with leaps of an octave – its
dynamic contrasts (*pp* to *ff*), its harmonic progressions and the repeat of
the whole by the choir in unison. The resulting dramatic intensity is
certainly justified by the text but we may also suspect that it bears some
relation to the attempts Fauré was making, at the time he wrote this solo,
to compose for the stage.

Some idea of how the Libera me should be sung comes from a letter the
composer wrote to Ysaÿe[40] about the kind of soloists who should be
employed: 'a soprano and a soothing bass–baritone with something of the
precentor in him. When Torrès sang the Pie Jesu at the Trocadéro, it was
encored ... The bass, Vallier, came from the Théâtre de la Monnaie in
Brussels but he was appalling – a real operatic singer who had no conception of the *calm* and gravity the part requires.' The choice of a singer for the
Pie Jesu poses problems because, as Fauré wrote to Claire Croiza on 1
August 1922, 'it was written for a *boy's voice*. Its first interpreter (at the
Madeleine) is now a gentleman with a large moustache: Louis Aubert,
who is a talented composer too.'[41] A desire for authenticity leads people to
give this difficult solo to a young boy, but we should bear in mind that this
was the only option available to the composer since the clergy of the
Madeleine, in traditional fashion, excluded any female presence from the
choir. It seems, on the other hand, that in all the concert performances
given during his lifetime, Fauré entrusted the Pie Jesu to a female soprano;
when, that is, he could escape the jurisdiction of the Madeleine clergy. It is
therefore an act of misplaced authenticity to give this solo to a boy treble.
In any case the long, undulating phrases place a severe strain on any boy's
technique and especially on his breath control. One of Fauré's favourite
interpreters was his pupil Thérèse Roger.

The Pie Jesu is a profoundly touching prayer despite the rather dated
style of the music. Its simplicity, gentleness and candour transcend the
'odour of sanctity' to reach some kind of expressive truth. In the first half
of the movement the soloist alternates with an orchestral motif which
creates an echo effect. Saint-Saëns was particularly fond of this – there is a
good example in the Hostias of his own Requiem, written ten years before
Fauré's – and indeed his pupil's Pie Jesu as a whole drew from him

wholehearted admiration: 'Your Pie Jesu is the *only* Pie Jesu, just as Mozart's *Ave verum* is the *only Ave verum*', he wrote to him in a letter of 2 November 1916.

Fauré's choice of this text, which only rarely appears as a separate movement in a Requiem Mass, leads us to consider this aspect of the work.

The text: philosophy and aesthetics

Fauré's attitude towards the Missa pro defunctis, as presented in the Roman Catholic rite, was not neutral; his views about how to treat it came not only from the composer in him but also, more profoundly, from his feelings as a man. To begin with he permitted himself to make several changes in the liturgical text. For example, he suppressed certain repetitions which would have interrupted the logical development of the musical form, leaving out the 'Cum sanctis tuis . . .' from the end of the communion as well as the 'Dum veneris . . .' from the Libera me. On the other hand this movement contains a repetition of the words 'dies illa' before 'dies magna et amara valde', made for reasons of metrical balance. Fauré's boldest strokes come in the Offertory which, from the musical point of view, is the best organised of all the movements. He cuts two important words, 'omnium fidelium', after the plea 'libera animas', and omits all reference to St Michael, finding that the opening polyphonic section comes to rest naturally on the word 'obscurum' and that from here there is an easy lead-in to the baritone solo ('Hostias'). This solo, as we have seen, was written before the surrounding chorus, but Fauré lengthened the rather abrupt ending found in the original version so that it brings us back logically to the opening polyphony. We can see at this point how carefully he managed the verbal underlay to allow the melodic curves to unfold.[42]

In the choice of the texts themselves we may note that Fauré left out the Dies irae and the Benedictus and added two prayers which do not belong to the Missa pro defunctis, properly speaking, but to the Office for the Dead: Libera me and In Paradisum.

His omission of the Dies irae has been explained as a function of the gentle aesthetic propounded by the work as a whole, which, as it were, forbade the inclusion of the famous sequence describing the anger of the God of Abraham and Jacob. This is a somewhat simplistic view. The composer's real attitude, it seems to me, is rather more complex. Certainly he set to music the most tranquil part of the sequence, the Pie Jesu, and emphasised it by making it a separate movement. But it is not true to say that Fauré refused – still less that he was unable – to set the introductory

'Dies irae, dies illa' since he dealt with this passage in the Libera me with a totally convincing sweep and grandeur. All in all, the text of the Libera me is no less dramatic or terrifying than that of the sequence. Even if the exclusion of the Dies Irae was due in some measure to Fauré's philosophical beliefs, I feel the more important reasons were musical ones. We may remember he declared that his instinct had 'led [him] to stray from the established path' and that he had 'wanted to do something different'. The Dies Irae is a kind of resumé of the traditional Requiem. Ever since Lully's version composers have treated it as a set piece in the grand manner, demanding mass effects. Fauré may have felt with good reason, that it was impossible to outdo Berlioz and Verdi. In any case he had little affinity for large musical gestures and the very length of the text might well have caused him problems.

The function of the Libera me is entirely liturgical: it is the prayer for absolution which follows the Mass for the Dead. The In Paradisum is the logical continuation of this but it marks really the moment of burial, that is to say outside the church. Such a choice shows how determined Fauré was to get away from tradition (settings of it are, in fact, quite rare) and also makes clear his philosophical attitude. This angelic chorus is the musical expression of the 'joyful deliverance', the 'aspiration towards a happiness beyond the grave' which, for him, was the meaning of death. For this final movement he chose a style close to that of a litany in which finely judged harmonies gravitate slowly round a central D major, whether stated or only implicit. The vocal tessituras are higher than before and in the original version he leaves out the double-basses. This texture, together with the absolute rhythmic regularity and the long held chords on the strings, creates a kind of weightless music outside time. 'I ascend, and all is white', D'Annunzio's St Sebastian was later to exclaim. Fauré's In Paradisum and the Le Martyre de St-Sébastien are based on the same paradoxical mixture of the chaste and the voluptuous. Here, beneath the surface, is felt the genius of the seventeen-year-old who boasted how at mass he had played 'the most vulgar ditties that the most refined brain could invent'.[43] The lover of beautiful harmonies is revealed, delighting in an inversion of a dominant 7th (bars 17–20) which, while giving the listener a sudden jolt, has no other purpose than the composer's own musical pleasure – unless he found a perverse satisfaction in introducing the interval of the tritone (alias *diabolus in musica*) into the courts of the new Jerusalem ...

8 Church of the Madeleine, Paris, view of the choir; high altar carved by Charles Marochetti 'the apotheosis of St Madeleine'; mosaics by Charles Lameire, photo c. 1900

LA MAITRISE DE LA MADELEINE

9 The choir school of the Madeleine in 1902, reproduced from *Musica*,
January 1903

10 'Sanctus' from the Requiem, autograph (1888), bearing various revisions to the orchestration, not carried out in the edition of 1901: bassoons (at the top), violins (4th stave), 2 then 4 horns and 2 trumpets
(below)

11 Gabriel Fauré, *c.* 1885

12 Pierre-Georges Jeanniot, *La Chanson*, 1891. From left to right: G. Fauré, J.-L. Forain (standing), Mme Jacques Normand, Amélie Duez, Louis Ganderax, Jacques Normand, the song-writer Gibert, Ernest Duez, Mme L. Ganderax, Henriette Roger-Jourdain, Roger-Jourdain, Suzette Lemaire, Madeleine Lemaire, Jacques-Emile Blanche, Mme Jeanniot, Paul Hervieu.

13 Marguerite Baugnies (Mme de Saint-Marceaux), pencil, anon.
c. 1891

14 Elisabeth de Caraman Chimay, Comtesse Greffulhe, *c.* 1890

15 'Les donneurs de sérénade': G. Fauré with Winnaretta and Edmond de Polignac, *c.* 1895

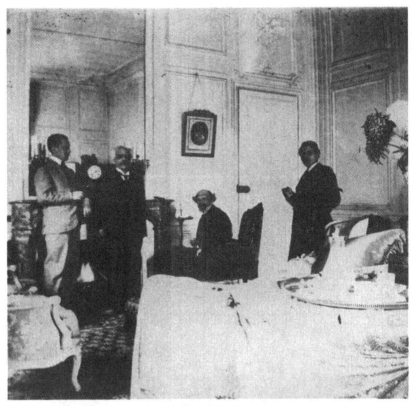

16 Fauré in the company of Prince Edmond de Polignac, c. 1895

17 At the Polignac's: Gabriel Fauré kneeling in front of Armande de Chabannes, c. 1895

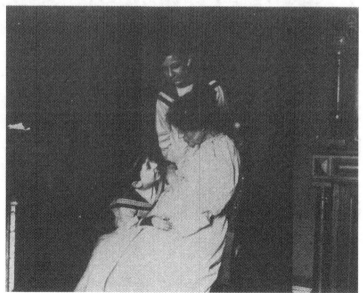

18 Marie Fauré and her sons: Emmanuel (right) and Philippe (left), c. 1895

19 Fauré, *c.* 1898

8   The theatre I: operatic projects and incidental music

THE SEARCH FOR A LIBRETTO

Although nineteenth-century French music was dominated by the stage, it must be emphasised that nothing in Fauré's education had prepared him for working in this genre. The aim of the Niedermeyer School was strictly to produce organists and choirmasters, and their mission was precisely to revive a repertoire into which theatre music had made damaging inroads. Even so Niedermeyer and his successors were free from bias against the stage and Fauré records (*Revue musicale*, October 1922) that pupils were free to consult the scores of operas by Gluck, Méhul, Weber and Mozart. We also know that on winning his composition prize in 1865 he was given the full scores of *Don Giovanni* and *The Magic Flute*, a fact worth noting at a time when *La Juive* was more often performed than *Così fan tutte*.

For all the Niedermeyer School's pure aesthetic intentions, neither it nor its pupils could escape theatre music altogether. The worthy founder himself had, after all, followed Rossini's advice and tried his hand at historical operas in the manner of the times: *Stradella* (1837), *Marie Stuart* (1844), *La Fronde* (1853). Louis Dietsch, the formidable professor of harmony and composition, was also chief conductor at the Opéra. His name is remembered above all in connection with the notorious Paris performance of *Tannhäuser* in 1861, echoes of which probably reached the classrooms of the boarding school. Newspapers, of course, were not allowed there but the boarders had the opportunity of hearing the Paris news in full when they went to have their weekly meal with their 'correspondents': in Fauré's case, with Saint-Saëns' mother.

Saint-Saëns, who took up his teaching post at the school in 1861, was at this period mad about Wagner, spending hours with him during his long stay in Paris and playing from memory large sections of his works. His extra-curricular championing of this 'music of the future', sneered at by the public and the critics, was a revelation to his young pupils. We may recall that a passion for *Faust* led Fauré to break bounds and later, at Rennes, to forfeit his popularity with his superiors; and he himself admitted that he gave up his post as organist at Clignancourt to go and see *Les Huguenots*.[1]

His job as accompanist for various vocal groups, like those of Marie Trélat and Gabrielle Krauss, gave him a thorough acquaintance with the operatic repertoire, especially Italian opera – Marie Trélat's mother, Mme Molinos, had been one of Rossini's favourite pupils. His regular attendance at Mme Viardot's salon from 1872 to 1877 increased his knowledge not only of the Italian repertoire but also of the German, as she had made friends with Brahms and Robert and Clara Schumann.

Twenty-five years earlier Mme Viardot had played fairy godmother to Gounod in commissioning him to write *Sapho* and now she dreamt of repeating the role and seeing Fauré in turn make his debut as an opera composer. With Gounod's support in 1877 Fauré set about obtaining a libretto from one of the main purveyors of the epoch, Louis Gallet, who had worked with Saint-Saëns, Massenet, Gounod, Bizet and other lesser mortals. Fauré, being aware of the difficulties, wanted to begin by setting a one-act libretto, but Gallet, as a writer who was very much in fashion, found this proposal far too modest.

Fauré then had the idea of entering for the composition prize which the Paris city authorities were offering in 1877. Gallet suggested a 'legendary scene' which Bizet had left unused at his death – probably *Geneviève de Paris* – but nothing seems to have come of this. Fauré, undaunted, continued to ask, indeed to pester, Gallet for a libretto that would suit him. In spite of the broken engagement with Marianne, Mme Viardot remained his operatic consultant at least until 1879,[2] and it was at this time that Fauré tried to convince Gallet to make a libretto out of a play by Louis Bouilhet, *Faustine*, a sombre drama full of politics and passion set in the bloodthirsty Rome of Marcus Aurelius. Flaubert, who was a close friend of Bouilhet, took considerable interest in this project and gave it his approval, but his sudden death in 1880 deprived Fauré of a valuable ally. One last attempt to persuade Gallet in 1883 came to nothing and he gave it as his opinion that *Faustine* was not a good subject 'because the directors and the public don't seem to be attracted by stories of Ancient Rome'.[3]

After considering *Manon Lescaut*, five years before the première of Massenet's opera, Fauré fell back on a one-act *opéra-comique* libretto by Jules Moineau, the father of Georges Courteline.[4] In an unpublished letter of September 1879 to Mme Clerc he gives an outline of the plot, feeble and idiotic and spiced with doubtful jokes. It is a matter for surprise and amazement that he should ever have started on such a text, which was probably called *Barnabé* after its hero. I have found in the Fauré family archives a sextet with piano accompaniment which, almost certainly, was intended as the opera's finale.

In 1879 Fauré went twice to Wagner's *Ring*, at Cologne in April and at Munich in September, and no doubt these performances added to his desperation in the search for a libretto: 'I accept in advance anything you care to offer me', he wrote to Gallet in July 1880,[5] 'but for Heaven's sake send me something.' It was not to be, and Fauré turned instead to Armand Silvestre, the Parnassian poet whom he had already set successfully several times in the realm of song ('Automne', 'Le Secret', 'Le Pays des rêves' . . . .). In 1881 the two collaborators persuaded Léon Carvalho to accept an *opéra-comique* in three acts called *Lizarda*; it was announced that spring as being on the point of completion and as a definite production for the following season at the Opéra-Comique.[6] Perhaps this was the 'almost finished opera' which, according to Maurice Imbert,[7] Fauré destroyed in manuscript, because *Lizarda* was never performed and no trace of it remains, so far as I know.

A few years later, Debussy was similarly to give up his *Rodrigue et Chimène* on a text by Catulle Mendès, even if he did not go as far as destroying the manuscript; it has therefore been possible to perform parts of it, although the results are more interesting than convincing.

In 1885 Fauré became enthusiastic about a *Mazeppa* based on Pushkin, having read a series of articles by the Count de Voguë, an expert on the Russian novel, in the *Revue des deux mondes*. During the summer he enlisted the help of the critic and essayist Ernest Dupuy. But then news came that Tchaikovsky had had an opera performed on the same subject (15 February 1884). The abandoned project at least provides us with an important letter in which Fauré delivers a kind of profession of musical faith: 'Tchaikovsky's *Mazeppa* cannot help but be a remarkable work', he wrote to his friend Poujaud on 3 September 1885,[8]

but I don't think there's any need for a French composer not to set the same subject after him since he's so essentially Russian. It's not that I myself have ideas about turning *Mazeppa* into an essentially French opera: I will even admit to you that in general I don't hold with such subtleties in dealing with this art called music, whose primary quality is to be a universal language, or rather the language of a country so far above all others that it lowers itself when it treats of the feelings or the traits of character proper to any particular nation. It's a theory too easily accepted, that

French music should be light and spruce and that German music should be heavy, compact or unintelligible in its search for depth. I believe, on the contrary, that a really gifted composer writes music without a nationalist mask. This is not the case (and that is what I was getting at) with the Russian school and Tchaikovsky in particular. Anxiety about not being sufficiently Russian leads him generally to use popular tunes, which he develops more or less skilfully. I feel the same about Brahms and his exploitation of Hungarian tunes and about Grieg who has built himself a fine reputation by using the songs of his native country. But don't you find that, for the most part, the works of these composers are no more than piquant curiosities, interesting in the same way as a pretty Hungarian costume or a gilded Russian Orthodox picture of Christ?

So if, by the grace of Dupuy and God, I write a *Mazeppa*, I can promise you it won't sound intentionally French or German. I shall do my best to translate human emotions using accents that go beyond what is human, if that's possible. That sounds arrogant but if I was able to explain what I mean properly, then it would seem extremely humble.

Despite this proud declaration of aesthetic independence (which one could well discuss at length), *Mazeppa* never progressed beyond the project stage. Probably Fauré was unable to persuade his librettist to pursue it.

Fauré's whole approach to writing operas was rather paradoxical and reveals a certain lack of artistic maturity in the range of subjects he was willing to consider; ancient Rome, medieval Spain, eighteenth-century France ... and Denmark! ... legendary Russia ... In this way he was following the tastes of the time and Saint-Saëns showed the way by writing a *Jota aragonaise*, a *Suite algérienne* and an 'Egyptian' concerto, not to mention the Salon painters who were devoted to representations of history, mythology and foreign parts.

Fauré knew he was ignorant of the ways of the theatre and entrusted himself blindly to his librettist's supposedly superior abilities in this direction, expecting him to sort out all the problems and at the same time trying to force him to find a subject congenial to Fauré. Louis Gallet's evasive behaviour and his resistance to the persuasive powers of Saint-Saëns, Gounod and Flaubert, suggests, to me at least, that this 'old pro' of the opera house sensed Fauré's lack of dramatic skill. The young man's wild enthusiasm for *Faustine* proves the point. Reading Bouilhet's play, we may find it hard to imagine what sort of opera it might have become; not devoid of merit, but certainly contradictory and fairly confused.

Although these various operatic projects came to nothing, they do reveal Fauré as a man of passion beneath his nonchalant, reserved exterior: 'I've been waiting desperately', he wrote to Gallet in 1880, 'for your reply about

Faustine and I won't hide from you the fact that for all my calm appearance I've been churned up inside for the last three months! Take this suffering of mine into account.' The commission in the autumn of 1888 of some incidental music at last enabled him to fulfil his theatrical ambitions, and in complete harmony with his artistic principles. In an article which has never before been quoted,[9] Fauré gives us a good idea of the reasons which brought him to write half a dozen pieces of incidental music in the space of fourteen years (1888–1902):

In this genre music does not, as in opera, draw itself up to its full height, matching every turn of the drama. Instead it is content to comment on the action, to recall the characters' feelings and amplify their expression, to extend into another sphere the charm of the scenery and bring to life the forces of nature which surround the characters and act so powerfully upon them. I myself have more than once shown my own predilection for this kind of musical support for the drama, imbuing a literary work with a lyricism and a musical atmosphere.

INCIDENTAL MUSIC

Caligula, incidental music op. 52 for the tragedy by Alexandre Dumas *père*

In the summer of 1888 Fauré received a commission to write incidental music for Dumas' *Caligula*, which Paul Porel had decided to revive at the Théâtre de l'Odéon at the end of the year. This tragedy in alexandrines was first performed in 1837 at the Théâtre Français and contains some good scenes and a lot of rather ordinary verse. In his preface Dumas claimed to be illustrating 'the struggle of dying paganism against a growing faith'. This idea is embodied in Stella, a young Christian girl used by Messalina to engineer the murder of the emperor Caligula. The text offered several opportunities for music to be inserted and developed 'in the grand manner', on the lines of the Odéon's current policy. In the event *Caligula* contains two musical additions; at the end of the prologue and in the middle of Act V.

Prologue: Fanfare, March, Choruses

At the end of the prologue the stage is set for Caligula's triumphal progress. The emperor's arrival is announced by five fanfares on six trumpets, each one nearer than the last. Unfortunately there is no hiding the fact that these fanfares are banal in the extreme. A march theme is superimposed on the trumpet motif and this in turn gives way to a phrase whose supple chromaticism marks it as typical of its decade.

Caligula finally appears 'on a chariot of ivory and gold, drawn by four white horses led by the Hours of Day and Night'. The chorus of the Hours of the Day is written in a disjointed style with an accompaniment off the beat, while that of the Hours of the Night unfolds a languid melody over modulating arpeggios. The Andante that follows is for orchestra only and depicts a funeral procession, included in the imperial progress out of that 'Shakespearian' love of contrast which affected the whole romantic theatre. As the emperor passes across the stage he is met by the funeral procession of Lepidus, put to death for taking the imperial name in vain. This Andante in B flat, in the rhythm of a slow march, is close in style to a German hymn and would not be out of place in a work by Brahms. Its repeat, *fortissimo*, after a large Wagnerian phrase on the violins, is the signal for the end of the prologue.

Such success as this score has had in the concert halls has been due to the choruses in Act V. During the first four acts the plot revolves around Stella, Caligula's foster-sister, who has returned to Rome accompanied by her fiancé, the Gaul Aquila. Caligula lusts after the young girl and has her kidnapped. Messalina, Claudius's wife and Caligula's mistress, arms Aquila and smuggles him into the palace. At the end of the fifth Act, Caligula is strangled by Aquila during his sleep; Messalina denounces the culprit and has Claudius proclaimed as emperor.

Act V: Chorus. Air de danse. *Chorus. Melodrama and chorus*

The scene is a banqueting hall in Caligula's palace. The first chorus 'L'Hiver s'enfuit', and the one in scene 3, 'De roses vermeilles', are stylistically close to that of the 'Hours of the Night'. The extremely refined, voluptuous atmosphere of this portrait of a decadent Rome is depicted in music whose sole aim seems to be to give pleasure. The sensuality of Fauré's harmonies here reaches its apogee and is not far from the borders of bad taste. At the words 'l'été brûlant a ses grasses moissons' it hovers between G major and D major; at 'noir hiver' B natural undergoes an enharmonic change to C flat, followed by a delicate, floating phrase passing through G minor on its way to the final D major tonic.

The second chorus, 'De roses vermeilles', preceded by a duet for solo violin and 'cello, is less successful. Perhaps the composer tried to follow too faithfully the suggestions of the words which are spoken above this passage : 'cradle our passion in the gentle Ionian cadences of your singing'. The curiously banal 9/8 rhythm in the brief introduction to the chorus, has however, nothing to do with Ionian metre! In the chorus itself sopranos and altos are heard in strict canon one beat apart, with the result that the words are very hard to hear. Fauré, in a letter to d'Indy, asked for the sopranos and altos to be separated 'so that the contrast in the dialogue between the various voices should be very clear and obvious.'[10] In spite of this attempt at stereophony the chorus is long and too redolent of its period.

Between these two choral passages comes a charming 'Air de danse' for flute and orchestra which Fauré develops at some length. It's one of his most delicate inspirations, beautifully orchestrated, and shows that his stated admiration for some of Delibes' music was perfectly sincere.[11]

The last chorus (scene 5) comes immediately before the murder of Caligula. As in the best of his songs Fauré intuitively grasps what the poet meant but was unable to express, and unleashes at this point the full emotional force of which his music was capable. The gentle lullaby of the 'Coryphée at the head of the emperor's bed' becomes, in his hands, a moment of extraordinary tension as we wait for the violence that is to come. The introduction is profoundly mysterious; a B flat pedal runs beneath a funeral motif in which A flat major and E flat major (the tonic) are combined. The melody gently murmured by the sopranos is wonderfully moulded. It conquers all the conventions of theatre music in evoking, by its line and its harmonic progression, the real spirit of antiquity (Ex. 18).

The revival of *Caligula* at the Odéon lasted for thirty-four performances, from 8 November 1888 to the beginning of 1889. Fauré produced a concert version of his score, increasing the forces to the usual full orchestral complement (duple woodwind, four horns, two trumpets, three trombones and strings), in all some thirty players, from the more modest resources available in the theatre pit (single woodwind, horn and trombone backed up by a harmonium!). The concert version was the only one to be published and in this form the work was conducted by Gabriel Marie at the Société nationale on 6 April 1889. The chorus 'L'Hiver s'enfuit' and the 'Air de danse' were encored. Fauré produced and published a version with piano (the orchestral portions for piano duet) and this was performed frequently under his direction.

Ex. 18 *Caligula*, final chorus

Shylock, incidental music op. 57, for the comedy by Edmond Haraucourt, based on Shakespeare

Some months after the production of *Caligula* Fauré received a new commission from Porel for his Théâtre de l'Odéon. 'At first sight it looks tempting enough and as though there might be something in it', Fauré wrote to the painter Jacques-Emile Blanche in September 1889, 'but when you've been through the mill with the Odéon orchestra, then things don't look so rosy!'

In the 1880s Shakespeare was never given in faithful French translations and even to put on adaptations, as Porel did, was considered daring. Edmond Haraucourt's *Shylock* is a verse drama 'based on' *The Merchant of Venice* and without question closer to the French comedy of manners of its own decade than to Shakespeare's blend of fine language and social criticism.

It may be as well to recall that the play contains three interconnecting plots: the elopement by night of Jessica, the daughter of the rich Jewish merchant Shylock, with her fiancé Lorenzo (Act I); the marriage of Portia who has, by her father's will, been promised to the suitor who can choose from three caskets – of gold, silver and lead – the one that contains her portrait (Act II); and finally the bizarre lawsuit heard before the Doge and his council between Shylock and the merchant Antonio, a friend of Bassanio, who is in love with Portia (Act III). The three plots finally reach a harmonious conclusion with the help of *travesti* and various dramatic twists.

The music in *Shylock* is much more closely wedded to the action than it was in *Caligula*. Shakespeare himself, who was a great lover of music, indicates several places where it would be suitable but Fauré goes some way beyond these indications; in this he was following the demands of Porel who wanted to underline certain moments in the story and, quite simply, to provide agreeable cover for the changes of scenery!

The incidental music begins with a serenade to Jessica from an unseen singer: 'O les filles! ...' The responsibility for the text of this lies firmly with Haraucourt. There is no basis for it in Shakespeare and one feels for Fauré having to set to music the worst verse in the play! This Chanson is near in style to the choruses in *Caligula* but Fauré excels in such 'galant' situations and he reinforces its charm with a delicate orchestration on flute, harp, clarinets and muted strings.

The whole of the second Act takes place in Portia's house at Belmont, on the very day when the choice of caskets is to decide her future. She is sighing for Bassanio and is impatient with the eulogies offered by her noble suitors. During the first scene the Prince of Aragon comes and sings an *aubade* under her window: 'Celle que j'aime a de beauté . . .', which has the title Madrigal in the score. Another insipid text calling for another display of the 'galant' style . . . This time Fauré is less successful: the melodic lines droop and the accompaniment, with its predictable harp entries, is banal. Its trochaic rhythm is similar to that of the other *Madrigal* for four voices op. 35 already discussed. These two vocal pieces from *Shylock* are best known in the piano versions which appear in the third Hamelle volume of the songs. The orchestral versions are, in my view, superior – the piano writing sounds thin and inadequate compared to that in most of his other accompaniments.

The hour of decision at Belmont is at hand and in the hall a brilliant throng assembles. Each of the suitors (Bassanio included) comes forward with his retinue, to the sound of horn and trumpet fanfares. These form the opening of the substantial orchestral piece published (no. 2 of the orchestral suite) under the misleading title of Entracte. It is doubtful whether this title was Fauré's; it does not appear on the autograph and the programme for the first concert performance bears the more explicit one of 'Scene of the caskets'. This is no mere archival quibble. The dramatic function of the music determines the way it is written and organised. It is not a piece to go between the acts but 'background music', played *pianissimo* almost throughout (letters A, B and C in the score) so as not to drown the dialogue.

The woodwind underline the march rhythm as Portia's suitors make their grand entrance. Fauré here adopts a decorative style in the manner of Saint-Saëns and it fits the situation perfectly, becoming, as it were, part of the spectacle. Its structure would seem to be based on the action of the play: two *fortissimo* statements of the march theme accompanying, almost ironically, the entrance of the foreign suitors, the Bey of Morocco and the Prince of Aragon, and then a tender violin solo, probably representing Bassanio. He has managed to choose the casket (the lead one) containing Portia's portrait and the act ends with the blessing of their nuptials. During this brief scene we hear a lyrical fragment on the strings which Fauré was later to expand into the Epithalame in the *Shylock* orchestral suite. It is one of the composer's most beautiful pages. The development of the theme over a moving chordal texture, its increasing passion and then the return of the theme in the woodwind over broken chords in the strings, all combine to give this movement a symphonic breadth and weight in spite of its relative brevity. The influence of Wagner is certainly audible but beyond that we can hear foreshadowed the calm lyricism of *Pelléas et Mélisande*. I would add that the marking *Adagio non troppo* on the autograph seems to me better than the *Adagio* which appears on the printed score.

The second tableau of Act III takes place in Portia's garden by moonlight. During the famous love scene between Jessica and Lorenzo we hear on muted strings the lovely Nocturne, as it is called in the score. The violin melody soaring above divided string chords is one of Fauré's most moving inspirations and it haunted him for years, recurring in the *Romance* op. 69 for 'cello and piano and at the beginning of his song 'Soir'. 'I had to find for *Shylock* a musical phrase with a certain penetration, like Venetian moonlight', he wrote to Elisabeth Greffulhe at the end of October 1889, 'and now I've got it! It was the air I breathed in your park which gave it to me; yet another reason to express my gratitude!'[12]

The last scene of *Shylock* sees the reunion of all the lovers, and it is as effervescent as the previous scene is serious and intimate. 'All's well that ends well' and the extended movement that Fauré provides here could again be classed as 'musique d'ameublement', to use Satie's term. In the theatre the whole of this Finale was in fact played beneath the spoken dialogue. This is why rhythm for once plays a larger part in the music than melody. To convey the right cheerful spirit for the denouement, Fauré has exercised all his adroitness and lightness of touch in manipulating *pizzicato*, *staccato* and *spiccato* effects. The second theme (letter C) and its development are rather weak but interest is continually kept alive by the rhythm and the brilliant orchestration, to which we will refer again in due course.

Shylock received its first performance at the Odéon on 17 December 1889 and was played fifty-six times altogether. The critics praised the beauty of the décor, directly inspired by the palaces of Venice, but for the most part passed over Fauré's music in silence. He conducted the orchestra himself, but had his forebodings: 'For the first three performances', he wrote to Elisabeth Greffulhe,[13] 'I'll have a reasonable little theatre orchestra. But from the fourth night onwards the Odéon's economic cutbacks begin to take effect: several of the good players are being dropped and instead they're hiring all the useless, feeble and superannuated hacks they can scrape together from the Luxembourg quarter. I can see there's a bumpy ride ahead!'

As he'd done with *Caligula*, Fauré extracted from this incidental music an orchestral suite, but in this case the transformation was a good deal more radical. The order of the movements was changed; the Chanson was given a brief orchestral introduction and transposed from C to B flat; the Madrigal too was transposed from F to E flat and the Epithalame, considerably extended, from B flat to C, while some of the short interludes were omitted. The orchestration, especially of the two larger movements (Entracte and Finale), was almost entirely reworked; flute, oboe, bassoon, trumpet and harp were doubled and the single horn was increased to the usual four.

This expanded version is the only one to have been published and was first played on 17 May 1890 at the Société nationale, conducted by Gabriel Marie. The balance that Fauré achieves between intimate lyricism and extrovert excitement makes it a cause for regret that this score should so rarely be heard in public. Conceivably the two tenor serenades militate against its acceptance as a symphonic work as well as discouraging concert promoters for financial reasons, although the conductor D. E. Inghelbrecht was always one of its champions.

Three unknown pieces of incidental music: *La Passion, Le Bourgeois gentilhomme, Le Voile du bonheur*

The collaboration between Fauré and Haraucourt continued during 1890. Haraucourt was put on his mettle by Sarah Bernhardt's commission to write a Passion for her in a matter of weeks and he responded with a long 'mystery' in verse, for which he asked Fauré to write some music. The stage representation of the Passion was forbidden by officials of the Académie des Beaux-Arts, who were afraid of public reaction, so Haraucourt's work was simply read aloud in the course of a religious concert given by Charles Lamoureux at the Cirque d'Hiver on 4 April 1890. Despite Sarah's participation, this long reading was very badly received by the music-loving audience and had to be abandoned. As for Fauré's music, this was not to be heard on that occasion; always a slow, painstaking worker, Fauré had only got as far as writing a Prelude with mixed chorus, depicting suffering Humanity, and had not even had time to finish the orchestration of that.[14]

It is quite possible that the success of the Requiem had led Fauré to think of writing a Passion on his own account, as we find him during July and August 1890 in Oberammergau at a performance of the famous Passion play given in this Bavarian village every ten years. At all events only the Prelude was ever finished, and was first played at the Société nationale on 21 April 1890 conducted by d'Indy. Julien Tiersot, writing in *Le Ménestrel*, praised its 'fine religious atmosphere, its strict forms, its conservative tonality and its strong, well-articulated bass lines in the manner of Bach'.

Fauré must have intended for some time to complete the Passion as he kept the orchestral parts carefully among his personal effects, though not the autograph full score which must have been destroyed or lost.

Paul Porel resigned as manager of the Odéon in 1892 and took over instead the Eden, previously known as the Grand-Théâtre. In keeping with his policy of putting on plays with music he asked Saint-Saëns to 'restore' Marc-Antoine Charpentier's original score for Molière's *Le Malade imaginaire* and at the same time commissioned Fauré to write some music for a comedy by Georges de Porto-Riche: *Manon Lescaut* – a curious way to be involved with a work he had thought of setting thirteen years earlier!

Porel also asked Saint-Saëns for some new music to accompany *Le Bourgeois gentilhomme*, which he was due to revive on 3 April 1893. Saint-Saëns, hard at work on his opera *Phryné*, asked his favourite pupil to take on this latest commission. 'I like the idea, but can I manage it??' Fauré replied on 19 September 1892, 'It won't be easy. At the same time I'll be pegging away at minuets and gavottes for Porel's *Manon*!'[15] In an unpublished letter to Marcel Girette he gives reasons for his apprehension: 'Comedy is not my thing and I'm terrified of the Turkish ceremony ... I'm not happy with turbanised music!' Even so, on 27 February 1893 he was putting the final touches to the serenade which, in Molière's play, is composed for Dorimène by one of the music master's pupils at M. Jourdain's request (Act I scene 2). It was published by Heugel in 1957.

The Serenade's 9/8 accompaniment figure, in F minor, foreshadows the 'invisible flute' of the song 'Arpège', which Fauré was to write four years later to a text by Albert Samain. Two other pieces undoubtedly belong with it, both short works for chamber orchestra: an F major *Menuet* in 3/4 which, in the play, precedes the F minor Serenade and is still unpublished, and the famous *Sicilienne* which he was later to insert into *Pelléas et Mélisande*. An early orchestral draft of this piece is dated March 1893 and has been partially realised by Fauré in the form of a brief interlude (Letters A and D in the published score), perhaps as an accompaniment to one of the ballet *entrées* which, in Molière, separate each act. It is to be noted that the orchestration of this first version of the *Sicilienne* differs from the final version in *Pelléas et Mélisande* (the main theme, for instance, is given to the oboe, not the flute).

Fauré was in the middle of his work on the score when, on 30 March 1893, the Eden-Théâtre went bankrupt.

The incidental music for *Le Voile du bonheur* by Georges Clemenceau dates from shortly after *Pelléas et Mélisande* and *Prométhée*, but I deal with it here because of its small forces and because it is unpublished. It consists of six short interludes written very rapidly at the end of the summer of 1901 and performed the following 4 November at the Théâtre Firmin Gémier. The play was no more than a form of relaxation on Clemenceau's part; the plot deals with a philosophical subject in a Chinese setting and is briefly outlined in Emile Vuillermoz's biography of the composer.[16] The small pit orchestra assembled for the occasion is rather interesting: flute, clarinet, harp, violin, viola, 'cello, gong, tubophone, trumpet. *Le Voile du bonheur* is undoubtedly Fauré's strangest work and his only adventure into the world of exoticism. Unlike Saint-Saëns, Debussy or Ravel, Fauré lent no more than a passing ear to the strange sounds of the Javanese gamelan orchestras at the Paris Exhibition of 1889 and 1900 and his creative progress took no account of them whatever. So it is rather curious to see him faced with a commission for 'oriental' music. The gong and the 'tubophone' (or tubular bells, as we should call them) are obviously there for Chinese effects, as are the pentatonic scale and various rhythms on repeated notes.

These stereotypes aside, we can see in these interludes certain methods of thematic development and certain uses of counterpoint which belong to Fauré alone. In this sense the music corresponds to Clemenceau's pseudo-philosophical text and to the exotic décor by Amable. The only interest in this score lies, in fact, in the virtuosity with which the composer exploits all the possibilities offered by the heterogeneous nature of the orchestra, provoking a comparison with Schönberg's pointillist orchestration of his *Klangfarbenmelodie* in the *Five Orchestral Pieces* op. 10 (1910).

Unfortunately there are reasons for suspecting that this avant-garde orchestration is not in fact the work of Fauré. Certainly the orchestral score is in his hand but this is a fair copy and not a true composer's autograph. Furthermore, Bernard Gavoty told me that he had it on Vuillermoz's authority that Vuillermoz orchestrated *Le Voile du bonheur* at Fauré's request. As Vuillermoz had been one of Fauré's composition pupils at the Conservatoire he could well have been approached by him, as Koechlin and Roger Ducasse were in similar circumstances. According to Gavoty's testimony, Vuillermoz showed him a copy of his book *Musiques d'aujourd'hui* with his dedication from Fauré (who had also written the preface): 'To my collaborator on *Le Voile du bonheur*'.

In his biography of Fauré, Vuillermoz says that he simply conducted the orchestra. But he showed considerable interest in this music and went to the trouble of trying to find the score in the archives of the Théâtre de la Porte-St-Martin where the work had been revived for four performances on 8 December 1910. There was no chance of his finding it as Fauré had carefully kept all the orchestral material with a view to getting it published. He signed a contract on 15 September 1902 with Hamelle and the opus number 88 was set aside for it, but then he had second thoughts, probably realising that these interludes would seem rather unusual divorced from the text which inspired them. Coming after the publication of his music for *Pelléas et Mélisande*, that for *Le Voile du bonheur* might well have made an unfortunate impression.

Pelléas et Mélisande, incidental music op. 80 for the play by Maurice Maeterlinck in the English version by Jack W. Mackail

We know that Debussy was present at the only Paris performance of *Pelléas et Mélisande* given on 17 May 1893 by Lugné Poe's company at the Théâtre des Bouffes parisiens; the music consisted merely of one brief song 'Les Trois sœurs aveugles' which Mélisande sings at her window at the beginning of the tower scene (Act III scene 2), and which had been set to music by an obscure composer who was a friend of Georgette Leblanc[17] and Maeterlinck, called Gabriel Fabre (and not Gabriel Fauré, as one sometimes finds even in well-informed circles).

Lugné Poe's company produced Maeterlinck's work in the original French text while on tour in London in March 1895 at the Prince of Wales' Theatre.[18] The English actress Mrs Patrick Campbell got to know the work at this time through an English translation made for her by one of her friends, Jack W. Mackail,[19] the brother-in-law of the painter Burne-Jones. *Pelléas* was one of the great emotional experiences of her life. She devotes a whole chapter to it in her memoirs, which appeared in the 1920s:[20] 'I *knew* Mélisande as though she had been part of me before my eyes were open. I *knew* I could put the beauty of the written word into colour, shape and sound.' She confided her project to another great actor of the period, Sir Johnston Forbes Robertson and managed, not without difficulty, to convince him to put on the play, the condition being that she should also partner him in a number of others presented in turn, including *Hamlet* and *Macbeth*.[21] Martin Harvey took the role of Pelléas and Forbes Robertson that of Golaud. 'The incidental music needed was a most important element', wrote Mrs Patrick Campbell, who went on 'I felt sure M. Gabriel Fauré was the composer needed.'[22]

It is well known that the actress was aware of Debussy's opera on the subject, which he had finished in 1895, and that she had asked him to

extract incidental music from it for the London performances. Pierre
Louÿs, in a letter to Debussy of 27 November 1895, wrote:[23]

Why do you refuse to make a symphonic suite out of *Pelléas* for London? It's none
of my business, but do you think it's such a bad idea? Obviously, if you insist, you
can stop anybody else doing it instead but in your shoes I wouldn't bother insisting!
... You can rest assured that none of your fellow-composers is going to stick his
neck out and try and out-Debussy you on this one.

Debussy's opinion is expressed in a letter to his publisher Georges Hartmann, who had taken him to task for turning down the London offer:

The impact of this [Fauré's] music seems to me hardly likely to survive the current
production and, if I may boast, I don't see there can be any confusion between the
two scores, at least not in the matter of intellectual weight. In any case Fauré is the
mouthpiece of a group of snobs and imbeciles who will have nothing whatever to
do with the other *Pelléas*.[24]

Faced with this cold refusal Mrs Patrick Campbell turned to Fauré who
had been introduced to London musical circles around 1894 through his
friends the Maddisons and Leo Frank Schuster. His meeting with Mrs
Patrick Campbell was set up by Schuster, almost certainly during Fauré's
stay in London during March and April 1898. 'I had not spoken French
since my visit to Paris seventeen years before,' writes the actress, 'but I
stumbled through somehow, reading those parts of the play to M. Fauré
which to me called most for music. Dear M. Fauré, how sympathetically he
listened, and how humbly he said he would do his best!'[25] From this it is
clear that it was the actress herself who decided the main places where the
incidental music should come.

Fauré returned to Paris at the beginning of April 1898, but a fortnight
later had to leave again to go on one of his detailed inspections of the
provincial conservatoires which were his responsibility. He wrote to his
wife, around 25 April: 'All I know is that I'll really have to get down to
Mélisande as soon as I get back. The whole score has to be written in a
month and a half, though it's true some of it is already lying around in this
old head of mine!'[26]

In fact he worked even faster than he expected and the whole of the
incidental music was written in the space of one month (May 1898): on the
early orchestral draft the 'Prélude' has the date 'May 1898' and the
'Chanson de Mélisande' '31 May 1898' – and this with the London
première fixed for 21 June! Fauré was, as usual, snowed under with his

Conservatoire composition class (see chapter 12). He also received an urgent commission for two flute pieces for the Conservatoire flute examination in July and these had, without fail, to be finished before he left for London. He therefore decided to delegate the orchestration of *Pelléas* to his pupil Charles Koechlin. The orchestral sketches and notebooks that Koechlin kept, together with some of Fauré's letters, allow us to follow the two musicians' collaboration in some detail.[27] Koechlin submitted his work for approval before making a fair copy, as we can see from various corrections on the sketches and from the note he received from Fauré on 26 May, about a point in his orchestration of the 'Fileuse' (no. 2 in the Hamelle orchestral score): 'I meant to drop you a line yesterday and ask you to *leave* this passage

Ex. 19 *Pelléas et Mélisande*

as you originally scored it with the horns in the *low* register. You were a hundred per cent right. I didn't *see* because of the row the students were making! Your help is being invaluable. Yours with affection and gratitude!'

A fortnight later Fauré expressed his satisfaction to Koechlin and asked him to come with him to London on 16 June:

My dear friend, I can't hope to pay you back for your time or for your excellent ideas! But please allow me to subscribe a little towards the cost of your rail ticket. I'm looking forward to our journey together and it is a pleasure for me, as a really *senior* composer, to offer this small contribution. Many thanks once again. Without you I'd never have made it!

On 21 June 1898 Fauré himself conducted the orchestra of the Prince of Wales' Theatre, Piccadilly (Coventry Street) for the première of the English version of *Pelléas et Mélisande*. In the audience were Maeterlinck, Charles van Lerberghe, Reynaldo Hahn, the Princess Edmond de Polignac (who was to be the dedicatee of the orchestral suite), the painter John Singer Sargent and all Fauré's London friends. The production was a great success with the public and the critics. Maeterlinck himself wrote an enthusiastic letter to Mrs Patrick Campbell which finished: 'In a few words, you ... filled me with an emotion of beauty the most complete, the most harmonious, the sweetest that I have ever felt to this day ...'[28]

The Symbolist poet Charles van Lerberghe, a friend and compatriot of Maeterlinck who was to inspire Fauré to write two of his finest song cycles, wrote from London to Albert Mockel on 23 June:

I've just been with Maeterlinck to see the first performance of the English version of *Pelléas et Mélisande*. The production put on in Paris and Brussels gives no idea of what we've just seen. The Mélisande is pure Burne-Jones and the Pelléas is an actor of genius. Maeterlinck was bowled over. His little masterpiece, with actors like that and ravishing scenery, has been a real triumph. I heard it with a beating heart and tears in my eyes. It was so beautiful! – All the critics are congratulating Maeterlinck. One newspaper has the headline 'Enchantment and Poetry at the Prince of Wales Theatre'. It's a verbal recreation of Burne-Jones, with Gustave Moreau and Memling added. A marvellous dream![29]

The programme of the performance preserved in the Theatre Museum of the Victoria and Albert Museum does not unfortunately mention the names of the producer or the designer, and it is equally a cause for regret that no reproduction of the scenery or costumes is to be found in any of the illustrated papers of the time.[30] A letter from van Lerberghe written to Fernand Séverin on 22 January 1900 about the Berlin production of *Pelléas* gives us some idea of what the London one looked like:

it's all a long way from those aristocratic English actors who were able to make *Pelléas et Mélisande* such a marvellous experience. I was thinking yesterday of the Pelléas, as handsome as Lord Wharton, and of the wonderful Miss Campbell, both of them in costumes designed by Burne-Jones himself and surrounded by a décor of golds and liquid greens, so distant from us, immersed in legend, murmuring their sublime, childish words of love, almost without gestures, immobile, like figures in a primitive painting[31]

Koechlin, in the unpublished diary of his visit to London, gives this description of the occasion:

I went back on Thursday to see *Pelléas et Mélisande*. The ensemble – play, production, costume, music, acting, decoration of the theatre – was superb and quite exceptional in being so closely unified. The costumes and the gestures were very 'English Pre-Raphaelite', with Mélisande especially charming delicate and graceful, and Fauré's vague, supple music went well with the English translation. The small orchestra was excellent (especially at this second performance) and was heard sometimes between the acts and sometimes under the words, as in *L'Arlésienne*. The whole impression was exquisite and, if Colonne does play the music at the Châtelet this winter, I'm not sure he'll be able to reproduce its effect. As for the play itself, Maeterlinck's ploys, though they're no longer new, are not always easy to understand. But apart from that there are some profoundly poignant moments and from the beginning right through to the death of Pelléas the grading of emotion is admirably done. I met Hahn on the way out and he said: 'What an ensemble! What a performance! Why don't we have anything like that in Paris?' And I'm bound to say I agree with him.

Indeed all the critics agreed about the work's powerful, poetic impact and the success of the ensemble, and most of them were enthusiastic about Fauré's music, saying how close he had come to the feeling of the play.[32] Only the anonymous critic of *The Times* delivered himself of a notice as detailed as it was disagreeable, comparing the music with the gauze and the stylised attitudes adopted by the actors in Lugné Poe's production! This opinion was flatly contradicted by the *Athenaeum* review: 'Mr Gabriel Fauré's music was responsible for much of our delight.'[33] The play was given nine times between 21 June and 1 July, and was then revived at the Lyceum on 29 October for several performances.

The London conducting score has luckily been preserved and from it we can learn a number of interesting details about this original production. For a long time it was in the possession of Alfred Cortot (who probably had it from Fauré himself) and was then bought by the collector Robert Lehman who in 1967 gave it to Nadia Boulanger on her eightieth birthday. I am grateful to her for putting this precious document into my care in 1973; until then it had never been closely examined.

This score is Koechlin's manuscript fair copy, based on his sketches and Fauré's corrections. It is strange that for many years it was regarded as a Fauré autograph, both in the book by Claude Rostand, in which two pages are reproduced in facsimile,[34] and after its acquisition by Robert Lehman. It has since been given to the Bibliothèque Nationale by Nadia Boulanger.

It is a collection of nineteen numbers, the ordering of which was apparently established later, for Martin Harvey's revival in the summer of 1900. The score contains a lot of cuts and insertions and various performing indications for the conductor, some in English (in blue pencil), some in French for the performances with Sarah Bernhardt (see below) whose name appears on one of the added interludes (no. 6 *bis*). Working out the exact details of the various versions during the years 1898–1905 is a difficult task because of the mass of often contradictory markings. It is highly probable that the order of the interludes originally intended by Fauré was decided only during the rehearsals in June 1898. The instructions Mrs Patrick Campbell had given the previous March referred only to the principal movements: Prélude (1) 'Sicilienne' (5), 'Fileuse' (10), 'Chanson de Mélisande' (11), and 'Mort de Mélisande' (17). The brief interludes, in general taken from the thematic material of the entractes (nos. 2,4,8,9,14,16,18), are all marked 'to be put in order' in Fauré's hand.

As I have already given a detailed description of the London performance in the *Revue de Musicologie* (1981, no. 2), I will discuss here only the parts of the score that were later published. The Prelude to Act I is of symphonic breadth and is certainly one of the composer's most profound and moving inspirations. The opening phrase, whispered by the strings, expresses Mélisande's evasive gentleness in dreamlike tones that seem to emerge from silence. A fine contrapuntal development leads to the second theme (figure 5 in the Hamelle orchestral score), heard on flute, bassoon and 'cellos in unison over repeated string chords. Its lofty, almost desolate air suggests that it is the theme of destiny, one of the main characters in Maeterlinck's drama. The violent way it is answered is very near to the style of *Prométhée*, the lyric tragedy which I shall discuss shortly. The development of these two ideas is one of the best moments in the score; the oboe and clarinet solos are superbly effective, making us think back to the perfection of Mozart's orchestration in his last symphonies. The movement ends in a grand climax (figure 8) which discharges the tension, *fortissimo e allargando*, in a long chromatic descent which Fauré laboured hard to achieve. The ensuing coda presents a horn call on a single E flat which personifies Golaud the hunter.

Those who have wondered why *Pelléas et Mélisande* should include a spinning song ('Fileuse') forget that in Act III scene 1, cut by Debussy, Mélisande is working at her spinning wheel while she talks to Pelléas and Yniold. In this entracte the oboe sings a long delicate cantilena, a kind of song without words. There is a controlled naivety about it, a cheerful tenderness very characteristic of the composer. The seventeen-bar theme flows with a naturalness and ease that speak of no ordinary melodic invention and it can hardly be overstressed that to write such an original spinning song, after it had been done so well so often, was a real *tour de force*.

When Fauré came to write a spinning chorus for his opera *Pénélope* he was, in my opinion, not so successful. In presenting this glimpse of the homely Mélisande, Fauré comes close to Maeterlinck who always liked to contrast symbolism, 'metaphysics' if you like, with the simple, everyday actions he portrayed. Even so, from the strictly musical point of view, this spinning song is very far from being just another one of its type, even if that is how the public regarded it – it reached popularity in Cortot's piano transcription. There are subtle but basic links between it and the rest of the incidental music; its key of G major is also that of the Prelude, while the

'Sicilienne' is in G minor and the 'Mort de Mélisande' in D minor. But beyond that nobody has so far noticed the essential thematic affinity between the oboe theme in the spinning song and Mélisande's theme in the Prelude (see Ex. 20).

Ex. 20 *Pelléas et Mélisande*

The similarity lies not merely in the melodic curve, but also in the articulation (held notes at the beginning and end of the phrases).

As for the second, more stately G minor theme of the 'Fileuse' (figure 2. in the score), it looks forward to the theme of the 'Chanson de Mélisande', which is also that of the final Molto adagio (Ex. 21).

Ex. 21 *Pelléas et Mélisande*

We can see that beneath its seemingly peaceful and uninvolved surface the *Fileuse* heralds the heroine's tragic destiny. This use of a musical portent corresponds exactly to the profoundest intentions in Maeterlinck's dramaturgy, based on his admittedly sometimes childish devotion to Symbolism.

Fauré has sometimes been criticised for inserting into *Pelléas et Mélisande* the 'Sicilienne' from *Le Bourgeois gentilhomme*. Its lightheartedness, its rhythmic animation and its bright colours all mark it out very noticeably from the brooding, distant atmosphere of the Prelude. But if one did not know where the 'Sicilienne' originally came from, very few people would guess that it did not belong to *Pelléas*. In any case it is important to note the precise place in which it comes: the beginning of the second act, that is to say the scene of the well and the ring. A minute's thought will reveal that this piece is absolutely right for introducing one of the few playful scenes in the drama in which, for one brief instant, Pelléas and Mélisande seem to escape their destiny and enjoy a few moments of unclouded happiness. Compared with the lovely prelude that opens the same scene in Debussy's opera, Fauré's 'Sicilienne' is not, in essence, all that different. The orchestral forces certainly are very similar, with the light clear sound of flute and harp against a discreet string background.

It is at the end of this first scene in Act III that Mélisande gently sings the words 'Saint-Daniel et Saint-Michel, Saint-Michel et Saint-Raphaël' which look forward to her song from the tower in the next scene. There are in fact several different texts for this song, which Dr G. Hermans has studied in a detailed article.[35] The original edition of Maeterlinck's play (1892) gives the version set by Debussy: 'Mes longs cheveux descendent jusqu'au seuil de la tour ...'. Maeterlinck then wrote several other texts for this song and left the choice to the actress who played Mélisande in Paris (Mlle Meuris). She chose a different version: 'Les trois sœurs aveugles ont leurs lampes d'or ...' which from then on appeared in the printed text of the play. This was the text set by Gabriel Fabre for the Paris performance on 17 May 1893; it was also the basis of Mackail's fairly free translation, set by Fauré: 'The King's three blind daughters'. But for the London production this number, 'Mélisande's song' was moved back from the tower scene (Act III scene 2) to the end of the preceding one (in which Mélisande is sitting at her spinning wheel) and replaced the two verses murmured by Mélisande ('Saint-Daniel et Saint-Michel') which I quoted above. For the song from the tower, Mackail decided to translate the text of the original edition, 'Mes longs cheveux ...', and not without reason, as the highly Symbolist text of the 'Trois sœurs aveugles' obviously has nothing whatever to do with the scene where Mélisande sits at her window, combing her long tresses. All the evidence suggests that for the London performances the text of this song ('Mes longs cheveux ...') was simply recited and not sung.

This is the source of Koechlin's misleading statement[36] that the 'Chanson de Mélisande' was not sung in London, while Hahn goes further and claims this was because Mrs Patrick Campbell found it too difficult![37] If the 'Chanson de Mélisande' had indeed been omitted, that part of the conducting score would have been removed, crossed out or marked 'not used', like one of the interludes that was cut; and there would have been no point in adding the indication (in French this time) with reference to Pelléas for the 1904 production: 'He is sleepy, he fights against sleep and his eyes close.' Koechlin's recollections must be viewed with some suspicion – they were written, be it said, some thirty years after the performance he attended – and it is little short of amazing to read what he told Reynaldo Hahn on the occasion of the 1939 revival at the Odéon: that the original incidental music consisted only of 'four pieces, no more ... The theatre version was exactly the same as the concert version, just the four movements ... I see that at the Odéon someone has borrowed bits out of these and re-used them here and there, which could work quite well. But this arrangement was not Fauré's idea, or mine'![38]

The extended orchestral movement that precedes Mélisande's death (Molto adagio) appears in the conducting score (no. 17) as an entracte before Act V. In its gravity and poignancy it recaptures the high level of inspiration we find in the Prélude. It is based on a single motif, an arpeggio D–A–B flat–D. The opening funeral march on low woodwind looks forward to the noble, meditative *Chant funéraire* of 1921. The motif is in fact that of the 'Chanson de Mélisande', already foreshadowed by the second theme of the 'Fileuse', and now it takes on its true significance, lending its previous appearances the sense of forebodings of death. This theme is heard plainly on the strings as the march continues on its way and reappears in the coda surrounded by a halo of divided strings, before the simple rising phrase on the flute which concludes this wonderful movement.

As with his earlier incidental music, Fauré collected the main entractes of *Pelléas et Mélisande* in the form of an orchestral suite and this version is the only one that has been published. It does not, as has often been stated, reproduce Koechlin's orchestration note for note. The Fauré-Fremiet family donated to the Bibliothèque Nationale the autographs of the three pieces which made up the first version of the suite op. 80: Prélude, 'Fileuse' and Molto adagio. Certainly, Fauré based his orchestration closely on his pupil's but he made numerous modifications in scoring it for a larger orchestra. The 'chamber' forces available in London were: two flutes, one oboe, two clarinets, one bassoon, two horns, two trumpets, timpani, two harps and strings. Fauré expanded this to: duple woodwind, four horns, two trumpets, timpani, two harps and a larger string section – the whole of this orchestra is heard in the Prélude and the Molto adagio.

If we compare the two orchestrations at the point where the development section of the Prélude reaches its climax, before the horn calls announcing Golaud,[39] we find that in the first bar Fauré uses two oboes a third apart instead of Koechlin's oboe and clarinet and in bars 5 and 6 he doubles the bassoon part. His most important changes affect the powerful descending passage on woodwind and strings (bar 7) which is the expressive climax of the movement (figure 8 in the Hamelle score). His dissatisfaction with Koechlin's version had already led him to upgrade the dynamic markings and now he added two horns and completely reworked the upper woodwind writing. This now underlines the poignant descent of the violins, while the timpani part is made simpler and more effective.

We should note that Fauré's corrections are to be studied not only on the manuscript of the orchestral suite but also on the London conducting score; the numerous changes Koechlin made on this stem, at least in part, from Fauré's own suggestions. As for the last movement (Molto adagio), the composer's letters written to Koechlin in June 1898 contain a request to revise yet again the orchestration of the coda which had been extended by two bars. This ending is worth study: the London conducting score shows substantial corrections and Fauré, in revising the coda for the Suite op. 80, adds one further bar to the last chord. From this we can see what care and attention Fauré lavished on the more expressive passages in the score.

Overall the composer's reworking of Koechlin's version was in the direction of a greater breadth in the sound. The addition of an oboe, a bassoon and two horns on to the original forces allowed him to double both melodic lines and their harmonic support, and to achieve his own brand of orchestral colour. He deliberately toned down Koechlin's clear outlines, aiming for a more indistinct atmosphere and a thicker texture in keeping with the other-worldliness and desolation of Maeterlinck's play.

One of the strangest parts of the story is that Koechlin himself did not realise what changes had been made to his work and registered his orchestration with the Société des Auteurs as being that of Fauré's Suite op. 80, at the same time bringing forward as evidence the sketches he made in 1898! This mistake can be explained by the fact that Fauré's modifications, though numerous and interesting, are not of a radical nature; also Koechlin had had time to forget the finer points of a task which had been done in a hurry and which Fauré had overseen and corrected right from the start. In fact Fauré probably worked on the Suite during 1898–9 and in the autumn of 1900 (that is to say, before and after *Prométhée*), as the first performance was given at the Lamoureux concerts on 3 February 1901, conducted by Camille Chevillard.[40]

It was well received and the 'Fileuse' was encored. Even so Fauré was not entirely happy with Chevillard's interpretation and he wrote to his wife on 2 October 1906:[41] 'the wretched man, for all his talent, has never really got the idea of the first movement: he plays it much too fast. But I shall write to him and draw his attention to it – in the most polite and tactful manner!'

Koechlin's diary tells us he was present at this first performance, though he says nothing about the orchestration. In his book (p. 86) his only comment is about the 'Fileuse': 'When performed by a full symphony orchestra it loses something of its lightness because there are too many violins.'[42] The full score was published by Hamelle at the end of 1901 and two important movements from the incidental music were omitted: the 'Sicilienne' and the 'Chanson de Mélisande'. Some years later Fauré decided to publish the orchestral version of the 'Sicilienne' which had already appeared in 1898 in arrangements for 'cello and piano and for piano solo. The full score of the 'Sicilienne' was engraved by Hamelle in 1909 and, although Fauré had always thought of it as forming part of the *Pelléas et Mélisande* suite, it was only later formally incorporated in accordance with his express wishes.[43] He must have been happy in this case with Koechlin's orchestration as he published it unaltered. As for the 'Chanson de Mélisande', Koechlin made a second orchestration of it in 1936 and Hamelle published the version for voice and piano the following year. From this we can see that Fauré used this music again in 1906 in the song 'Crépuscule' from the cycle *La Chanson d'Eve*.

The publication of the orchestral suite did not, however, lead to the disappearance of the music in its original form. *Pelléas* has been seen on the stage in numerous revivals almost up to the present day. According to Robert Orledge[44] it was put on in Mackail's translation at the Royalty Theatre in London between 28 June and 14 July 1900, with Martin Harvey again playing Pelléas. Later, and somewhat strangely, the rôle was taken over by Sarah Bernhardt. She had been enthusiastic about the London performances and eventually persuaded Mrs Patrick Campbell that they should act in the play together, this time in French. These performances, at the Vaudeville Theatre in London in July 1904, were followed a year later by a tour of England, Scotland and Ireland. In the meantime Mrs Patrick Campbell had put the play on in Boston (Boston Theatre, 12 April 1902) and taken it on tour round several American cities. If we are to judge from the various annotations to the conducting score, in English and French, then it looks as though Fauré's incidental music was used throughout, prolonging as it does the dreamlike atmosphere of the text and affording a practical way of covering Maeterlinck's many scene changes.

What exactly Maeterlinck thought of Fauré's incidental music is not known; though, bearing in mind his low opinion of music in general, we may imagine that its chief virtue in his eyes was discretion. True, van Lerberghe wrote, in the letter quoted above: 'Maeterlinck was bowled over', but here he was referring only to the actors, the costumes and the scenery.[45] The playwright was probably content to follow the opinion of his mistress, Georgette Leblanc, who was active both as an actress and a singer. In an interview she gave some years later she came down firmly in Fauré's favour: 'Some of the scenes will be completed, supported, prolonged or preceded by Fauré's music with its wonderful, other-worldly atmosphere.'[46] Certainly Maeterlinck and Leblanc must have been moved to appreciate Fauré's music even more in those early years of the century because of the playwright's violent opposition to Debussy: Georgette Leblanc had hoped to play the part of Mélisande in the première of his opera at the Opéra-Comique in 1902, but the rôle went to Mary Garden.

Georgette Leblanc was even more indignant because she had already played the rôle in the theatre – in Brussels in 1901 and in the United States the following year. She gave the interview quoted above in 1910, before the lavish production put on at the abbey of Saint-Wandrille (this was where Maeterlinck was living at the time and some of *Pelléas* had actually been written there). It was given in aid of charity and the twenty-five privileged spectators moved through the scenery provided by the gardens, cloisters and ruins of the abbey. Beginning at sunset, it finished by moonlight and Fauré's music, played by an invisible orchestra, conducted by Albert Wolff, reached the audience through a curtain of foliage.

This production of 29 August 1910 was revived on 22 August 1915, together with *Macbeth* (in Maeterlinck's translation), on behalf of L'Oeuvre fraternelle des artistes [Artists' Benevolent Fund]. Published photographs[47] of the occasion show that it took the form of a masquerade in costumes from the Middle Ages, with helmets, suits of armour and a horse. Gustave Labruyère made a film of it for the Eclair film company and this was shown on 29 November 1915 in Robert de Montesquiou's Pavillon des Muses at Neuilly.[48]

Fauré's incidental music underwent various transformations to accommodate different productions. The material for the one put on by Martin Harvey at the London Lyceum in July 1911 contains a score based closely on Fauré's but with changes and additions by the English composer W. H. Hudson.[49] Fauré himself revised his score for the performances at the Odéon in 1918. The poster for the première (10 February 1918) states that his music will be played by the orchestra of the Association des concerts Monteux, conducted by Armand Ferté. Fauré had a new conducting score copied for the occasion, almost certainly from the London score, and this ignores practically all the additions and modifications made in the course of successive revivals. Although this score is in the hand of a copyist, its authenticity was verified by Armand Ferté who, according to Reynaldo Hahn, recalled that 'Fauré asked him to come one day to the Conservatoire so that he could hand it over duly copied and absolutely in order, before the first rehearsal.'[50] The only major difference between this and the original London version is that the four principal entractes (Prélude, 'Fileuse', 'Sicilienne', Molto adagio) now appear in the revised, expanded form we know from the published score.

We have seen earlier how Debussy expressed forthright opinions on Fauré's music before he ever heard it. When he did, he referred sarcastically to the 'Fileuse' as 'fit for seaside casinos'. The remark is relayed at second hand by Koechlin, who adds: 'not that there's anything surprising about it, considering his own treatment of Mélisande's character overall – rather different from Fauré's playful, almost coquettish charmer in the style of the *Rouet d'Omphale*; and in the scene by the well, when she is playing with the ring, she is no longer the mysterious alien child, feeding on her memories; it is a mistake to see this as being her complete, unalterable personality'.[51] As André Schaeffner has perceptively commented, Debussy interpreted Mélisande rather in the light of Poe's sinister sacrificial heroines[52] and the human face which Fauré gave her was bound to offend him.

Mary Garden, the Mélisande in the première of Debussy's opera, recalls how he came with her to one of the performances of the play with Fauré's music in London in July 1904:

We went back to London to hear Sarah Bernhardt as Pelléas and Mrs Patrick Campbell as Mélisande. But neither Sarah nor any of the other actors on that occasion seemed to have the slightest understanding of the text. Debussy and I sat there dumbfounded. He began to fidget and I whispered to him 'She's impersonating Robin Hood.' By the third act things were, frankly, becoming painful. We left and caught a train.[53]

As I have already mentioned, Maeterlinck and van Lerberghe were among those who were delighted with the London performance in 1898. If, in 1904 Debussy and Mary Garden felt just the opposite, this was in effect bound to be their reaction. Having spent ten years of his life setting this text to music Debussy was not apt to be content hearing it in its spoken form. Any admirer of his opera tends to feel the same way — it is almost impossible not to hear Debussy's music under the words, as though once steeped in it they must always retain its flavour. Over the years Fauré's music has moved in the opposite direction, away from the text with which its links were in any case more fragile, and now it has taken its place as his orchestral masterpiece.

20 Philippe Chaperon, design sketches for *Caligula* by A. Dumas, *père*, Act I, Théâtre de l'Odéon; ink and gouache, 1888

21 A. Vignola: Shylock and Antonio, costume designs for *Shylock* by E. Haraucourt, Théâtre de l'Odéon, 1889

22 George Dobson, design for *Pelléas et Mélisande* by Maurice Maeterlinck. Act II, sc. 1: 'A fountain in the park'. Taken at the Lyceum Theatre, London, July 1911

23 Adolph De Meyer: Mrs Patrick Campbell as Mélisande (costume by Burne-Jones), reproduced from *The Sketch*, 27 November 1901

24 J. Canvall Smith: Martin Harvey in the role of Pelléas (costume by Burne-Jones)

25 John Singer Sargent: Gabriel Fauré and Mrs Patrick Campbell, inscribed: 'The Hut. June 98'

The Verlaine years: song cycles and
further operatic projects

During the twelve years between the Requiem and the end of the century, the extent of Fauré's musical development surprised even those who had so far followed it with sympathy. The works of this period, in which he came to artistic maturity, are marked by boldness, innovation and originality. It was a time of several important encounters: with Joachim, Ysaÿe, Cortot, Risler, Jean Lorrain, the young Marcel Proust, Robert de Montesquiou, Paul Verlaine, Albert Samain, Henry James and John S. Sargent.

I have already discussed in chapters 4 and 8 respectively, the piano and stage works dating from these years. But, as in all Fauré's periods of change and experiment, the central productions of the years 1887–97 were songs. In particular he pursued the idea of the song-cycle, possibly in response to a feeling that his vocal output was too fragmented. This formal preoccupation was also linked to his propensity for motivic working in his chamber and orchestral music.

There is reason, furthermore, to see the songs of this period as the counterparts of the operatic projects which he abandoned of his own free will. This led to the fading of his relationships with two poets, Paul Verlaine and Albert Samain, who had suggested and even written complete librettos for him, aided by the generosity of Elisabeth Greffulhe and Winnaretta de Polignac.

Winnaretta had been an enthusiastic friend of Fauré's from her youth (see p. 23). Although the relationship was platonic, her domineering intensity at once fascinated the composer and, in his heart of hearts, terrified him.[1] Winnie, as she was known to her friends, had inherited a vast fortune from her father Isaac Singer, the sewing-machine manufacturer, and in the early 1890s she decided to build a music-room in the rue Cortambert, where it joins the Avenue Henri Martin. It was to contain an organ and here she would entertain all that Paris had to offer in the way of writers, painters, musicians and representatives of high society. She planned to mark the opening of her 'hall', as Proust later called it, with a work specially written for the occasion by Fauré, on a text of his choice. For this she offered him the tidy sum of 25,000 francs (that is, a hundred times his monthly salary as choirmaster at the Madeleine). He agreed most willingly and suggested a collaboration with Verlaine. Negotiations began in January 1891 and then dragged on for months while the poet relapsed into alcoholism, to the point where he only left his house to go into hospital. By the spring still nothing had been decided, despite the 'long siege' conducted by Fauré who periodically went to see him.[2] Finally Verlaine suggested his play *Les Uns et les autres* might be suitable if adapted, but Fauré was not at all happy with the idea. Then Verlaine announced that he had found a new idea, entitled *L'Hôpital Watteau*. Winnie recalls in her Memoirs:

The subject chosen was the end of the *Comédie italienne* and the scene was a ward in a hospital in which from one bed to another Pierrot, Columbine, Harlequin and others discoursed on the various aspects of life and love. Verlaine's letter to Fauré, which I have kept, seemed to me promising, and I am sure his libretto would have been wonderful, but I am sorry to say that Fauré refused to write the music, although it would have been a delightful theme that he could have treated marvellously.[3]

Her view cannot be expected to convince everyone. It is hard to see what operatic material resided in this Watteau scene taking place inside a hospital. Verlaine, his genius now wearing thin, had simply imposed his own situation on the subject. Fauré must be given due credit for invariably refusing to write just to please others; he openly stated that he was incapable of setting a text to music unless he was convinced of its quality and its musical possibilities. He managed to persuade the Princess to give Verlaine an advance on the money promised to him and, spurred on by this, the poet does seem to have written part of the text. But so far these lines have not been discovered.[4] Fauré, for his part, retired into a sulky silence.

The Princess then suggested a stage work on the subject of Buddha in collaboration with Maurice Bouchor, who had provided the text for Chausson's *Poème de l'amour et de la mer*. Orientalism was all the fashion and Buddha had been considered as a subject by none other than Wagner. At the time Bouchor was working at a play on the same topic for a marionette theatre, so he refused the Princess's offer and suggested instead his friend Albert Samain.[5] Samain started work in 1892 and produced 750 lines of verse, according to Georges Jean-Aubry who read them. All that has survived[6] of the project is a detailed plan of scenes 3 to 7, the autograph text of scene 1 and fragments of scene 3. From these it is clear that Samain had no idea what was required for a stage work; he wrote as a poet, without troubling himself over what would or would not work in the theatre. His *Tentation* (or *Vocation*) *de Bouddha* is full of blazing visions in the true Symbolist manner, impossible to stage. In scene 3, for example, he describes the boat journey of Siddharta and Gopa:

Now they enter the forest, and in the blackness we hear the manifold rustlings of the night. Moonbeams rain down upon them through the interstices of the foliage … And the boat, starting from a broad bend in the river, reaches a clearing lit with a bluish light and as though dusted over with stars.

The literary quality of what does survive is fairly poor, and we can sense that it was written at speed and to order. During the summer of 1892 Fauré admitted to the Princess that

Faced with Samain's verses I've dried up: whenever I do write something, it turns out to be *malformed* and has to be crossed out again. The miseries of mankind leave me cold, perhaps because of my own! But a true artist has to learn to escape from *self* and I shall have a go! … Forgive me. When you return, I hope to be able to show you a beginning! It upsets me not to be able to get to grips with it![7]

The project was still in the doldrums two years later, by which time Fauré was in the full flood of his passion for Emma Bardac, to whom he had just dedicated *La Bonne chanson*. Winnie, meanwhile, was out of humour and in a long, gloomy letter recalled the promises he had made and his expressions of gratitude and enthusiasm. 'I'm a simple human being', was his reply

and I don't claim to be better or worse than anyone else. Even so I'm fairly certain I'm better than you seem to think! I have not kept my promise but I am still most anxious to do so. Whatever this work turns out to be, I should like it to be acceptable both to you and to me. I could not offer you my last songs [*La Bonne chanson*] as you were kind enough to accept the five previous ones [the 'Venice' songs, op. 58]. Otherwise all I have written are two piano pieces [Sixth Nocturne and Fifth Barcarolle] which would not have interested you [!] and some church music [the motets op. 65]. I promise you most earnestly that the first major work I write will be sent to you.[8]

This time Fauré kept his promise, dedicating to the Princess his suite *Pelléas et Mélisande*. He kept faith with the two poets too. Some of his finest songs were on texts by Verlaine – 'Clair de lune' (1887), 'Spleen' (1888), *Cinq mélodies 'de Venise'* (1891), *La Bonne chanson* (1892–4) and 'Prison' (1894) – and when in 1896 the poet died, Fauré played the organ at his funeral. The same year Mme Bardac made him read Samain's *Au jardin de l'Infante* which was one of her favourites and from it he took four poems. He wrote his song 'Soir' and the duet *Pleurs d'or* in 1896, 'Arpège' the following year and 'Accompagnement' in 1902, all of them among his best. On 8 March 1896, Fauré, Samain and Mme Bardac spent the evening together for a private rendering of 'Soir'. Samain wrote to his sister Alicia

I found the said Mme Bardac at Fauré's, a young woman of about thirty. She's pretty, elegant, a woman of the world, her husband's a banker. After dinner she sang. Fauré said to me 'You'll never hear it sung better.' And in fact she has a real feeling for nuance and an unusual purity of style.

Winnie almost certainly did not realise that at the same time that Fauré was engaged on projects for her he was also enlisting the support of the Countess Greffulhe.

Her cousin, the Count Robert de Montesquiou was her *arbiter elegantiae* and on his advice she lavished on Fauré both admiration and support. This was done without thought of any gain for herself and in general she showed herself less demanding than the Princess de Polignac, and more worldly. She acted as a kind of fairy-godmother to the struggling composer's family. She would send Mme Fauré a watch, or some sea-shells for the children, or some pheasants shot on her estate at Bois-Boudran in Seine-et-Marne. Fauré was often a guest there and in 1887 she asked him to organise concerts in her imposing Paris mansion in the rue d'Astorg. Every other Wednesday he was to put on musical programmes that were 'short, not too heavy but even so highly artistic!!', as he wrote;[9] 'a few instrumentalists and two singers, one male, one female'. During the summer of that year she entertained him for several days at her villa, La Case, at Dieppe. In gratitude he dedicated to her his *Pavane* op. 50 (see chapter 7) and it was in her beautiful park at Bois-Boudran, in September 1889, that Fauré found the theme for the wonderful Nocturne from *Shylock*. In 1893, when he had given up Samain's libretto, he persuaded Elisabeth Greffulhe to commission a libretto from Catulle Mendès: she was the high priestess of Wagnerism in France and Mendès was another of its supporters.

Among his librettos were those for Chabrier's *Gwendoline* (no great recommendation) and for the *Rodrigue et Chimène* that had until the previous year been causing Debussy such soul-searching.[10]

In April 1893 Mendès suggested to Fauré a libretto on the historical subject *Lavallière*.[11] The composer was both enthusiastic and puzzled: 'this idea of *Lavallière* is very tempting when he's actually talking about it: but as soon as I get to thinking about it *on my own*, then I'm full of misgivings'.[12] Mendès lost interest, and it was through Theodore de Wyzewa, one of the founders of the *Revue wagnérienne*[13], that Fauré made the acquaintance of Raymond Bouthor, alias Jean Thorel. Thorel was the translator of the plays by Gerhart Hauptmann that Antoine[14] and Lugné Poe[15] had put on in Paris, and was at this time translating the well-known fantasy tale *Ondine*, written in 1813 by Lamotte Fouqué. At the Countess Greffulhe's request he made an operatic adaptation of it with the help of the great Swiss stage theorist Adolphe Appia[16]; the surviving manuscript of the adaptation is in Appia's hand and appeared recently among his Complete Works. Fauré met Thorel at a concert in Geneva on 14 November 1894[17] and the libretto reached him shortly afterwards. In spite of Appia's prominent position in the history of the stage, there is no getting round the fact that his *Ondine* is on the mediocre, not to say regrettable, level of so many of the librettos of the period in which the aim seems to have been to imitate the doggerel turned out by the main purveyors, such as Louis Gallet or Barbier and Carré. We may presume that Fauré was not content with the Thorel–Appia *Ondine* since another operatic version of the same subject is to be found in the Greffulhe archives. This adaptation, in ten scenes, is the work of Charles Grandmougin whose poetry Fauré had set fifteen years earlier in his song 'Poème d'un jour'.

'What are we to do with Mr. Thorel?' Fauré wrote to the Countess on 27 April 1893[18] when the subject of *Lavallière* was rearing its head again; and Fauré goes on to answer his own question somewhat cynically: 'Somebody else we'll have to handle with kid gloves.'

Fauré's encounter with Verlaine and Samain marked a turning-point in his literary development. As a young man he had been keen on the Romantic poetry of Hugo and Gautier and then, after 1875, had been caught up in the Parnassian movement of Leconte de Lisle, Sully Prudhomme, Charles Grandmougin and, most of all, Armand Silvestre, who was his favoured poet in the 1880s. The sudden appearance of Villiers de l'Isle Adam and Verlaine in this company was certainly due to Fauré's contact with Des

Esseintes, the celebrated figure at the centre of J. K. Huysmans' novel *A Rebours*, published in 1884. The novel became the breviary of the decadent youth of the time and Des Esseintes was based on the real Count de Montesquiou Fezensac. An aesthete, an occasional poet and a social personage of the highest class, Montesquiou was later to be immortalised by Proust as the rather disturbing Baron de Charlus. Fauré probably met him in 1886, when he began to frequent the salon of Montesquiou's relative, Elisabeth Greffulhe.[19] I do not intend here to describe Fauré's relationship with the Count, as I have done so at some length elsewhere.[20] But it is important at least to discuss his role as Fauré's literary adviser. Letters from the composer preserved in the Montesquiou papers in the Bibliothèque Nationale[21] often refer to books he has borrowed: Victor Hugo, Marcelline Desbordes-Valmore and particularly Verlaine, of whom Montesquiou was a passionate supporter.

In gratitude for his help and sympathy, Fauré dedicated to the Count one of his most subtle songs, 'Les Présents', based on a poem in the appendix to Villiers de l'Isle Adam's *Contes cruels*. He took from the same volume the text for 'Nocturne' (1886), a song of calm, dignified beauty, all too rarely sung. It seems to me to belong to what one might call an 'incantatory aesthetic', which Erik Satie exemplified in several of the piano pieces he wrote in this same decade: his *Sarabandes*, *Ogives*, *Gnossiennes* and particularly his three *Gymnopédies*.

Fauré's 'Nocturne' conjures up an atmosphere of its own, poetic, shadowy, secret and intense. We may note also that it dates from the very year of Jean Moreas's 'Manifesto of Symbolism'. The calm, majestic simplicity of this song sounds a new note in Fauré's work, which the more contemplative passages in the Requiem were soon to confirm. The feeling of continuity in these two Villiers settings is carried through into 'Clair de lune,' Fauré's first Verlaine setting, made in the autumn of 1887.

The independence between voice and accompaniment, the piano's clear predominance and the dance rhythm which runs through the whole song suggest as a model the ninth of Schumann's *Dichterliebe*, which Fauré obviously knew well. But whereas Schumann deals with tragedy and anger, Fauré elicits a mood of irony mixed with tenderness, wholly appropriate to the masks and bergamasks of Verlaine's world.

Verlaine's aesthetic, like Fauré's, can be defined in terms of its musicality, its feeling for line, its mingling of discretion and audacity and its gently probing 'spleen'. The famous precepts outlined in Verlaine's *L'Art poétique*, published in 1882, seem like a very exact description of Fauré's art:

Fuis du plus loin la Pointe assassine,
L'esprit cruel et le Rire impur,
Qui font pleurer les yeux de l'azur,
Et tout cet ail de basse cuisine!
Prends l'éloquence et tords-lui son cou!

(Shun absolutely the murderous epigram,
The spirit of cruelty and indecent laughter,
Which makes the heavens weep,
And all that garlic of low-class cooking!
Take eloquence and wring its neck!)

Fauré's music is indeed the sort Verlaine described as being 'sans rien qui pèse ou qui pose' ('without anything heavy or pretentious'):

Car nous voulons la Nuance encor,
Pas la Couleur, rien que la nuance!
Oh! la nuance seule fiance
Le rêve au rêve et la flûte au cor!

(For we want still more Nuance,
Not colour, nothing but nuance!
Nuance alone joins
The dream to the dream and the flute to the horn!)

Montesquiou could with reason congratulate himself, in his memoirs, on having lent Fauré a copy of Verlaine's *Fêtes galantes*: 'I can boast of being the first to put into the great composer's hands the slim volume that was to be the seed of such a successful collaboration.'[22] In fact, in the space of seven years, Fauré set to music eighteen Verlaine poems, which he chose freely and well. 'Verlaine is a marvellous poet to set', Fauré declared.[23] 'In his short poem, "Green", there's a vivid, melancholy country scene, but it's entirely atmosphere, ambiance. And the harmony must try and *underline* the deeper meaning which the words do no more than *hint* at. It's the same in "Il pleure dans mon cœur comme il pleut sur la ville . . .", the sound of the drops of water is only a secondary factor. The important thing is the sense of unease in the lover's lament.'

'Il pleure dans mon cœur', from *Romances sans paroles*, was the second Verlaine poem Fauré chose. He gave the piece the title 'Spleen', taken from another poem in the same collection,[24] no doubt because he liked the word – he uses it in his letters to describe a mood he was familiar with. This brief song (in D minor, like the Requiem written at exactly the same time) is completely successful in the evocation of atmosphere. Using the simplest of means, a pattern of quavers out of phase between the two hands, Fauré pictures the leaden monotony of the rain pattering 'on the ground and on the roofs'. Debussy was to use the same syncopated texture in *Children's Corner* in 1908 to depict snow ('The snow is dancing'); and the two composers are still more closely linked around this song, since Debussy published a song on the same poem in that same year 1888, in the collection *Ariettes oubliées*. Debussy's song, written for the agile voice of Mme Vasnier, has a certain charm, but of the two composers Fauré is the more restrained and faithful to the text, both in overall attitude and in the details of the declamation. By a curious paradox, this exactitude in the treatment of the words foreshadows that in Debussy's *Pelléas*!

Fauré's 'Spleen' forms part of his op. 51 together with two other songs in minor keys. The composer announced his completion of the trilogy in a letter to the Countess Greffulhe of 23 November 1888:

I've written three very cheerful songs!!! They're called: 1 'Au cimetière' 2 'Larmes' (both to words by Richepin) 3 'Spleen' (Verlaine). For one of them [no. 1] I tried to write a very simple accompaniment just for the right hand. But after ten bars I had to bring the left hand to its aid and after twenty bars the going gets difficult for both hands! Another paving-stone on the road to Hell![25]

'Larmes', published eventually as the first of the set, is one of the composer's most violent outpourings. This is a fierce C minor, vehement and aggressive. Richepin's text is rendered by chromatic harmony, the phrases separated by the refrain 'Pleurons nos chagrins, chacun le nôtre'. Stylistically it looks back to 'Le Voyageur' (1878?), 'Rencontre' (1878) and 'Fleur jetée' (1884). 'Au cimetière', on the other hand, prefigures the peacefulness of late Fauré.[26] In this Andante in E minor we find once more the successions of chords, the linear writing and the melodic tension which, in his work, are regular indicators of profound emotion. One thinks of 'Le Secret', the *Elégie* for 'cello or, to turn to an exactly contemporary work, Brahms' song *Auf dem Kirchhof* op. 105 no. 4 (1886).

> Heureux qui meurent ici
> Ainsi que les oiseaux des champs
>
> (Happy are those who die here
> Like the birds of the fields.)

Within the narrow range of a fourth, rising to and descending from the tonic by step, Fauré writes one of those melodic lines that are impossible to forget. He marks the voice part *dolce e sereno*, a phrase to be noted because it is unique in his output. The atmosphere of religious meditation is suggested by modal inflections, like the beautiful B minor passage in the first strophe, before the return to the tonic. We may be reminded of the confident opening to the 'Agnus Dei' from the Requiem, written in the same year.

The central section of 'Au cimetière' provides a violent contrast with this serenity. Marked *declamato*, with heavy accents on the beat, it builds up to a slightly self-satisfied fortissimo evocation of the bodies of sailors drowned at sea. Richepin has none of Verlaine's discretion, and when Fauré is required to raise his voice he falls rather readily into bombast. The same applies to the end of 'La Rose', an anacreontic ode in the Parnassian manner by Leconte de Lisle which was tacked on somewhat arbitrarily to the three songs I've been discussing. This airy barcarolle comes from the slightly frivolous Fauré, the lover of melting harmonies and female visions; delightful tonal diversions exploit the tritone (B natural in F major) and carry us with the speed of quicksilver through the flat keys, glimpsed but never arrived at. The second section, with its Botticellian depiction of the birth of Venus, appears less inspired, its last stanza sounding rather over-elaborate and settling heavily on the tonic. Altogether it recalls the mediocre music Fauré had written to order nearly ten years earlier for *La Naissance de Vénus*. It seems likely that 'La Rose' remained for some time unfinished, to judge from the date 'August 1890' on the manuscript, that is to say two years after the composition of the other three songs of op. 51 for which it stands as an awkward companion. After 1878–9, perhaps following his publisher's advice, Fauré took to writing songs in groups of two, three or four, in which the ordering is carefully planned. In the three songs op. 23, the D flat major of the last one ('Le Secret') relates to the relative B flat minor of the first ('Les Berceaux') – two powerful songs enclosing a tender, more lighthearted one in E major ('Notre amour'). The two songs op. 27 ('Chanson d'amour' and 'La Fée aux chansons') are in F major, while the first song of op. 39 ('Aurore'), in G, stands at the interval of a fifth below no. 4 ('Les Roses d'Ispahan') in D and nos. 2 and 3 ('Fleur jetée' and 'Le Pays des rêves') are in F minor and its relative A flat major. The first three songs of op. 51 are set in a narrow range of minor keys (C, E and D) and 'La Rose', the fourth one, is in F major, the relative of no. 3 ('Spleen'). Needless to say, the transpositions made by his publisher for commercial reasons often destroy these carefully laid plans.

But right from the time of writing *Poème d'un jour* in 1878, Fauré had been searching for more complex means of organisation and had explored the possibilities of coherence on three levels: of tonality, of themes and of poetic content. Nos. 2 and 3 are enharmonically related (F sharp minor, G

flat major),[27] nos. 1 and 3 are constructed on a descending motive related
to the 'Viardot theme' (see chapter 5), and the whole triptych consists of a
highly condensed account of a love affair: 'Rencontre' – 'Toujours' –
'Adieu'.

Fauré's reading of Verlaine was to lead him to explore the possibilities of
the cycle more closely.

THE VENETIAN SONGS

In May and June 1891, Fauré stayed in Venice together with his painter
friends Ernest Duez and Roger Jourdain, at the invitation of Winnaretta
Singer. 'What a country!' he wrote to Marguerite Baugnies, in one of
several ecstatic letters on this holiday;[28] 'and what a life we're leading!
Divine is too feeble a word: I don't think there is one that would do! Still
less to describe the admiration and a little bit more (alas) our delightful
hostess inspires in me!' He goes on modestly: 'The tranquillity I need for
working in is certainly not to be found here and the tiny scrap I've sketched
out, on a poem by Verlaine, could perhaps turn into something when I get
back to my Paris den.' When he did get back, on 20 June, after stopping off
briefly in Florence and Genoa, 'the tiny scrap' called 'Mandoline' was
finished, and it was performed the next day at Mme Baugnies' salon. The
idea of writing a group of songs followed soon after and on 26 June Mme
Baugnies gave the first, private performance of 'En sourdine'. In July he
sent the third song, 'Green', to Winnaretta, deciding at that point to make
her the forthcoming cycle's dedicatee. 'Have I succeeded', he wrote to
her,[29] 'in transposing this wonderful canticle of adoration? I don't know.
"Don't destroy it with your two white hands",[30] and if you don't like it at
first sight, will you promise me not to lose heart, but read it through again?
It's difficult to interpret: slow moving but agitated in feeling, happy and
miserable, eager and discouraged! What a lot in thirty bars! And maybe
you'll think I've been making a fuss over nothing?'

Writing to Marguerite Baugnies,[31] he gives her too the following advice:
'Bréville tells me you sang "En sourdine" admirably. In "Green", I can't
insist too strongly that it mustn't be sung *slowly*: it has to be *lively*,
passionate, almost *out of breath*! And above all, sing it as if to yourself. I've
no desire to intrude *my personal accents* into other people's reveries.'

In August 1891 Fauré and his family installed themselves at Chatou for
the summer. 'I'm going on with the group of songs', he wrote to
Winnaretta.[32] 'The fourth one, "A Clymène", came fairly easily but the
fifth one, "C'est l'extase", is being recalcitrant. I showed the fourth one to

Benoît and I have to confess he told me, with a gloomy, severe expression, that I was becoming too *incoherent* and *nebulous*! Which left me very worried, as I've always thought I was too classical!' Winnaretta received the manuscript of the fifth song in September, with this commentary.[33]

You'll see that, as in 'Clymène', I've tried out a form which I think is new, at least I don't know anything like it; trying something new is the least I can do when I'm writing for you, the one person in this world who is least like anybody else! After the opening theme, which doesn't recur, I introduce for the second stanza a return of 'Green', now calm, and restful,[34] and for the third one a return of 'En sourdine',[35] now a cry of frustration, ever deeper and more intense right up to the end. It forms a kind of conclusion and makes these five songs into a sort of *Suite*, a story.

These commentaries by the composer on one of his works are all the more quotable for being rare, unfortunately. They reveal clearly the emergence of the idea of a cycle and the twofold organisation, both musical and literary, which the composer associated with it. To make up this 'suite', or 'story', he chose five poems from the two Verlaine volumes which had already inspired him: 'Mandoline', 'En sourdine' and 'A Clymène' from *Fêtes galantes* (as was 'Clair de lune'); 'Green' and 'C'est l'extase' from *Romances sans paroles* (as was 'Spleen'). The stages in the story are as follows: 'Mandoline' sets the atmosphere, of Watteau or Walter Pater, evoking the dreamlike, shadowy, rather vague scenery against which the four love-poems are to be played out. 'En sourdine' is the incontestable masterpiece of the cycle, a song of intense and tender lyricism, mirroring the spiritual and carnal link which unites the lovers. 'Green' is mischievous, high-spirited, a passionate but playful declaration of feeling. 'A Clymène' offers a kind of portrait of the beloved, based on a sensuous but mystic mode whose ambiguity no doubt had a great appeal for Fauré, that 'gregorianising voluptuary', as Reynaldo Hahn called him. 'C'est l'extase' brings all these themes together in a magnificent whole, a pantheist expression of human love.

In the letter to Winnaretta quoted above (n. 33) Fauré emphasised the strong coherence between 'Green', 'En sourdine' and 'C'est l'extase', nos. 1 and 4 remaining relatively isolated. This analysis is confirmed by the critic Louis Aguettant: 'Fauré told me that the Venetian songs were conceived as a cycle with the exception of the first one ('Mandoline') and 'A Clymène'.[36] These two, even so, are integrated on one level since the *Cinq mélodies* contain a repeated motif which Vladimir Jankélévitch was the first to identify.[37]

This descending motif runs through the whole cycle, possibly without Fauré having been aware of it, and it was one that haunted his imagination. We find the earliest signs of it in the Fourth Nocturne of 1884, further developments in an 1891 sketch for the First Quintet and in the Venetian Songs of that summer, sporadic appearances in *La Bonne chanson*[38] before its final form as a secondary idea in the Molto moderato movement of the same Quintet, in the definitive 1903 version (see Ex. 15, p. 96).

From another point of view, the Venetian songs can be seen as a sort of suite in five movements:

1 Prelude (G major) 'Mandoline'. (Allegretto moderato).
2 1st slow movement (E flat major). 'En sourdine'. (Andante moderato).
3 Scherzo (G flat major). 'Green'. (Allegretto con moto).
4 2nd slow movement (E minor). 'A Clymène'. (Andantino).
5 Finale (D flat major). 'C'est l'extase'. (Adagio non troppo).

In addition to alternating fast and slow songs, Fauré deploys two kinds of piano texture: *staccato* in nos. 1, 3 and 5 and smooth arpeggios in the intermediate ones. The most extraordinary thing is that the meticulous organisation on all musical and literary fronts can be appreciated only by careful study. In performance one is struck only by the diversity and rightness of Fauré's invention.

LA BONNE CHANSON

In finishing the Venetian songs Fauré reckoned that he had 'exhausted the musical possibilities of Verlaine', as he wrote to Mme Baugnies, but the next year he embarked on a cycle of nine songs taken from *La Bonne chanson*. In the meantime the tender but rather ill-defined feelings he nursed for Winnaretta Singer made way for a passionate devotion to a neighbour of his summer holidays in Bougival: Emma Moyse.

She was not so much pretty as distinctive. Her charm lay in her wit, taste, elegance and her musical gifts. She sang beautifully, in an easy soprano voice, and was an excellent sightreader. She preferred performing in private and was happy, indeed enthusiastic, about putting her talent at the service of contemporary composers. Her husband, Sigismund Bardac, was a banker: 'still a young man', wrote the poet Albert Samain, in an unpublished letter to his sister of 7 December 1897; 'thirty-five to forty years old, dark, with terribly thick eyebrows. Charming, absolutely charming, to me at any rate.' The two Bardacs led lives of unusual freedom, as is evidenced by a letter on the subject from Pierre Louÿs to his brother Georges in October 1904, shortly after Emma had run off with Debussy: 'He's quite used to his wife running away and when people ask about her he smiles and says: "She's just treating herself to the latest fashion in composers; but I'm the one with the money. She'll be back."'[39]

In the 1890s Fauré was a regular visitor to the Bardac's house in the rue de Berri, near the Champs-Elysées, and used to introduce into this 'progressive' salon his most promising composition pupils, like Koechlin and Ravel. Madame Bardac seems to have taken a fancy to the latter, though the sentiments were not reciprocated, if we are to believe Tristan Klingsor[40] and to judge by Ravel's dedication to her of the song *L'Indifférent* in 1902. Fauré had for some years been teaching the Bardacs' son, Raoul, who after his mother's remarriage to Debussy in 1908 became that composer's pupil and seems to have been highly regarded as a composer himself. Ravel wrote of him: 'he's an accomplished musician; but also one of the earliest pupils of Fauré who was very fond of him. If he's not very well known it's because of his character. He may not be too modest exactly, but at any rate he's very distant.'[41]

Raoul's sister, Hélène, was born on 20 June 1892. She was so tiny that she was called Dolly – it was a time of Anglomania – and she proudly kept the name all her life, recalling as it did the suite of pieces for piano duet which Fauré wrote for her between 1893 and 1896, some of them for 1 January, some of them for her birthday (see end of chapter 4). It has been rumoured occasionally that Dolly was Fauré's daughter. But this is highly unlikely as Fauré's infatuation with Emma dates more probably from the summer of 1892 when he was starting to write *La Bonne chanson* for her. The manuscript of the first song to be completed ('Donc ce sera par un clair jour d'été') bears the date 9 August 1892 ...

From many points of view *La Bonne chanson* appears as the natural successor to the Venetian songs. It contains the same compositional elements but presented more boldly and on a broader scale. The cycle's expressive incandescence and formal complexity lend it a colour unique among Fauré's works. 'I've never written anything as spontaneously as I did *La Bonne chanson*', he wrote thirty years later.[42] 'I may say, indeed I must, that I was helped by a similar degree of comprehension on the part of the singer who was to remain its most moving interpreter. The pleasure of feeling those little sheets of paper come alive as I brought them to her was one I have never experienced since.' The composer's son Emmanuel, at the end of his life, used to recall to me with emotion the private performances Emma gave of *La Bonne chanson* during the warm summer evenings at Bougival, with his father at the piano.

Roger Ducasse tells us that Emma was far more than the inspiration and the first interpreter of the cycle. On many occasions Fauré was the recipient of her advice: 'Every evening Fauré used to go to the "château" to show her what he had written that day. And frequently, quite frequently, she used to send him back to make corrections. I possess the first version of "La Lune blanche" ...; she was absolutely right! She made him rewrite whole bars.'[43]

A close study of the manuscript sources[44] reveals clearly that the remarkable tonal and thematic organisation of *La Bonne chanson* was the fruit of continuous reflection right through the very act of composing. The order of the nine songs occupied Fauré's thoughts for a long time and the one he finally adopted is very different from that in which they were composed (see Table 1).

Table 1 *Development of* La Bonne chanson *(from manuscript sources)*

Title	Final order	Original Order	Key	Date
'Une sainte en son auréole'	1		A flat	17 September 1892
'Puisque l'aube grandit'	2	2	G	[1893]
'La lune blanche'	3	4*	F sharp	20 July [1893]
'J'allais par des chemins perfides'	4	3	F sharp minor	[Autumn 1892]
'J'ai presque peur, en vérité'	5	[7?]	E minor	4 December 1893
'Avant que tu ne t'en ailles'	6	4*	D flat	Autumn 1892
'Donc ce sera par un clair jour d'été'	7	5	B flat	9 August 1892
'N'est-ce pas?'	8	6	G	25 May 1893
'L'Hiver a cessé'	9		B flat	February 1894

* The number 4 appears clearly in the Royaumont manuscript on each of the two songs finally published at nos. 3 and 6.

This table calls for a number of comments. We can deduce the dates of nos. 2, 3, 4 and 6 from a study of the handwriting in the Royaumont manuscript: the writing is small in the manuscripts of summer 1892 and nos. 4 and 6 present a similar appearance to no. 1, dated 17 September 1892 on Fauré's own copy; on the other hand, no. 2 is written in a much larger hand, similar to nos. 5 and 9 which date from December 1893 and February 1894 respectively.

The preliminary numbering, like the final one, is not autograph with the exception of no. 2. We may suppose that the definitive numbering was set down by Julien Hamelle acting on the composer's verbal instructions. This would have been at the beginning of August 1893, when the songs Fauré had then finished were sent to the engraver. A fortnight earlier, he was still working on no. 3, 'La Lune blanche', the second version of which he finished on 20 July, and probably also on no. 5, "J'ai presque peur', since he wrote to Paul Poujaud on 9 July: 'I promise you *some* new songs.'

The proofs reached Fauré in September. On 2 October he wrote to Saint-Saëns, being nervous about his reaction: 'I'm keeping the proofs of my latest extravagant songs to show you!'[45] These last two references are the only ones to *La Bonne chanson* that I have been able to find in the whole of his correspondence. But the publisher's ledger (*cahier de cotage*), in which he wrote down the works he was going to publish in the order in which the plates were engraved, gives us some further information. At the beginning of August 1893, when the work was entered in the ledger, Fauré thought his labours were almost over, but at that stage the cycle contained only eight numbers. No. 9 was added only on 10 March 1894 (the manuscript is dated in fact a month earlier), which meant that another work entered by the publisher in the meantime had to be moved. As for nos. 7 and 8, Fauré seems to have had doubts about them, as they are written into the ledger in pencil.

The order he finally adopted reveals an unusual tonal plan, the first six songs being situated within the range of a fifth (A flat to D flat), moving downwards in each case. The penultimate song forms a symmetrical balance to no. 2 and is in the same key of G major, with the central song in the relative minor, and indeed both the songs that are in the minor mode (nos. 4 and 5) are centrally placed.

Text

As he had done for the five Venetian songs, Fauré chose nine of the twenty-one poems Verlaine wrote for his fiancée, Mathilde Mauté, whose mother, a few years later in the early 1870s, was to give piano lessons to the young Debussy. Again he organised them to form 'a suite, a story', in which a portrait of the beloved is built up from a series of episodes: No. 1 'Une sainte en son auréole', an evocation of the poet's enthusiasm and heartache; no. 2 'Puisque l'aube grandit' and no. 4 'J'allais par des chemins perfides', leading to the declaration of love at the end of no. 5, 'J'ai presque peur, en vérité', the musical and expressive centre of the cycle. The wedding and the confirmation of the lovers' spiritual union are the subject of no. 7, 'Donc ce sera', and no. 8 'N'est-ce pas?' while songs no. 3 'La Lune blanche', no. 6 'Avant que tu ne t'en ailles' and no. 9 'L'Hiver a cessé', are pantheistically inspired landscapes – they thus form interludes and a postlude to the chapters of the story, each of which consists of two songs (1, 2; 4, 5; 7, 8).

Even if Fauré does not change any of the words here as he usually does (see chapter 15), he allows himself the liberty of shortening some of the poems by leaving out entire stanzas: no less than four of them in 'Puisque l'aube grandit', three in 'N'est-ce pas?' and one in 'L'Hiver a cessé'. The tonal and textual coherence of the cycle is further reinforced by a sytematic use of recurring themes (see Ex. 22).

Ex. 22 *La Bonne chanson*

Cyclical themes

Three motives dominate the score. The descending curve of A, clearly presented in the piano part in the opening bars, is easily recognisable in a number of the keyboard interludes, such as the 'vaste et tendre apaisement' of no. 2, the breathless accompaniment and the *un poco più mosso* section in no. 4, the brief interjections between each stanza of no. 5 and, at the very end of the work, the explicit recall of the opening. Theme B, climbing stepwise and using the tritone as a modulating interval is none other than a new version of the 'Lydia' theme. It appears in the vocal line of no. 2 ('puisque voici l'aurore', 'les lenteurs de la route') but is more prominent still in the piano part of no. 3 ('sous la ramée' and 'que l'astre irise'), in no. 5 ('de vous aimer et de vous plaire') and in the vocal line of the last song ('ainsi qu'une flamme entoure une flamme'). Finally theme C is a rising arpeggio that responds to the deeper emotions: in the powerful 'je vous aime' that closes 'J'ai presque peur' as well as in the calmer endings of 'Donc ce sera' and 'N'est-ce pas?' (*marcato* in the bass).

Two other themes are of secondary importance, being purely descriptive and not being heard until late on in the cycle: D, the bird theme in no. 6, 'Avant que tu ne t'en ailles' and E, the sun theme in no. 7, 'Donc ce sera', recur only in the final gathering of the threads in the last song where they answer each other in a truly symphonic spirit.

Texture

Fauré offers an amazing variety, from the four-voice polyphony of nos. 1 and 4, to the tune over rich arpeggios of nos. 2, 7 and 9, the expressive use of *staccato* (as in 'Green') in no. 5 and Fauré's favourite splitting of themes between the hands in nos. 3 and 8.

Harmonic instability in *La Bonne chanson* reaches a pitch rarely equalled in Fauré's output. Tonality is undermined by tortuous chromaticism so that at times (in 'J'allais par des chemins perfides', for example) a sense of key is almost obliterated. The rhythm too, normally in Fauré continuous and unified, is here diversified and there are moments of extreme fluctuation in metre and tempo: in the third song 9/8, 3/4 and 4/4 alternate, while the sixth one is built on rapid tempo contrasts between *quasi adagio* and *allegro moderato* – six different metronome marks in three short pages.

Variety and flexibility are the cycle's outstanding characteristics. It seems to me that apart from the many descriptive figurations in the music, such as the upward curve denoting the sunrise at the end of no. 6, a whole thesis could be devoted[46] to the symbolism of light and darkness, which constantly alternate both in the words and in the music, giving this sunny work an undercurrent of shimmering moonlight. Whatever else one says about the cycle, one must emphasise the surging, lyrical flow that carries it forward. Textual subtleties and harmonic ingenuities aside, it radiates energy, love and an overpowering happiness.

Fauré's passion for Emma Bardac not only disrupted the even, bourgeois tenor of his life but, unusually for him, had the effect of completely reorientating his compositional activity. In *La Bonne chanson* he made a deliberate break with his habitual blandness; he cast off from the moorings of what was reasonable, what was respectable, what 'sounded well', and at a stroke achieved the sovereign liberty that marks the great creative artists.

La Bonne chanson is far more, then, than just a volume of songs. It reaches the proportions almost of a vocal symphony in which voice and piano are an entity. Such a concept is supported by the fact that two attempts have been made to orchestrate it. In 1933, after his death, one of his pupils, Maurice le Boucher, made a version for voice and full orchestra which was even recorded in 1934–5 under Piero Coppola. It is a conscientious piece of work but not really worth more than a passing mention – songs for voice and orchestra were all the rage between the wars. Much more interesting is Fauré's own transcription of the piano part for piano and string quintet (and not quartet, as is often stated). This version was sung at a private concert in London on 1 April 1898, with Fauré playing the piano. He wrote to his wife just before it:[47] 'After the first rehearsal I was fairly happy with it. Yesterday evening it seemed horrible and *pointless!*' The next day he wrote again: 'Everything went splendidly, both the Franck Quintet and *La Bonne chanson*. Bagès sang admirably and it was an extraordinary success ... but, personally, I still find this version of the accompaniment unnecessary and I prefer it just on the piano.'

For my own part I agree with this categorical opinion. The essentially polyphonic texture of some passages (especially 'Une sainte' and the very end) certainly comes over wonderfully on strings, and they often serve to clarify the somewhat dense piano writing; even so the general effect of the transcription is far from being as convincing as that of the Ballade, where the same intentions were brought to bear. In the moments of the most exultant lyricism (nos. 2, 7 and 9), although the piano is still the leader of the ensemble, it sounds impoverished and in general the sweep and passion of the work are weakened and softened.

In producing this transcription, Fauré made a couple of changes in the cycle's key scheme, transposing the first two songs from A flat and G major up into B flat and A major. This reinforces the cycle's coherence, with the first and last songs now being in the same key and no. 4 (in F sharp minor) in the relative key of no. 2.

The single London performance of this version was given by Maurice Bagès de Trigny. He was a gifted amateur who was introduced into the circle of the Société nationale by his close friend, the composer Pierre de

Bréville. His light tenor voice must have been possessed of a certain charm and style, as he was asked to give a number of first performances: of Fauré's 'Clair de lune' with orchestra (28 April 1888), 'La Fée aux chansons' (12 May 1888), 'Au cimetière' (2 February 1889) and the five 'Venetian songs' (2 April 1892); and of two of Debussy's *Ariettes*, accompanied by the composer.

Bagès was often invited to perform in the most progressive salons of the city and sang, apart from contemporary works, music by Mozart and Wagner. He was the soloist in the first two performances of *La Bonne chanson* that we know of in Parisian salons: on 25 April 1894 for the Countess de Saussine and on 26 March 1895 for the flower artist Madeleine Lemaire. The official first performance at the Société nationale, on 20 April 1895, was given by Jeanne Remacle.

Fauré's new cycle caused a sensation. The young Marcel Proust, who was an enthusiastic follower of the development of one of his favourite composers, wrote to his friend Pierre Lavallée at the end of September 1894:

Bagès left me all his Fauré. But half of it is in Fauré's own *manuscript* and the other half, though printed, has dedications on, so I was terrified of spoiling them and sent them all back. All the young musicians are pretty well unanimous in not liking Fauré's *La Bonne chanson*. Apparently it's needlessly complicated etc., very inferior to the rest. This is the view of Bréville and Debussy (who everyone says is a great genius, far superior to Fauré.) Personally, I couldn't care less – I adore this collection and the songs I don't like are the early ones which they claim to prefer. 'Au Cimetière' is truly awful and 'Après un rêve' really dud. I didn't like 'Les Présents' to begin with, but it holds up much better than some of the others.[48]

Saint-Saëns was nonplussed by the cycle's technical licence and initially declared that his pupil had gone 'completely mad'. The complexity of *La Bonne chanson* does indeed make it a hard work to approach but, as with many true masterpieces, each reading and each performance of it reveals new aspects. Its power and originality place it outside time.

Composers frequently tend to be more interested in the works they are currently engaged on or planning for the future than the ones they have finished. Fauré showed a similar tendency when questioned about *La Bonne chanson* by an excellent young critic, Louis Aguettant, who was preparing an article on his songs for *Le Courrier musical* (1 February 1903): 'I asked him about his intentions at certain points and on the meaning of certain themes', Aguettant wrote.[49] 'He denied having thought of most of them, saying "Composers are often saddled with intentions they have never had."' Aguettant went on:

I was particularly keen to ask him about *La Bonne chanson*. Do the basic themes of the 'cycle' have some literary connotations? Are they just musical arabesques? At this point Fauré answered disconcertingly: 'Themes? But there's really only one theme in the various songs of *La Bonne chanson*: it comes from my song 'Lydia' and refers to a singer' [Mme Bardac? or Mlle Boissonnet, to whom 'Lydia' is dedicated?][50] This is the theme in question:

Ex. 23

That is how it appears in 'La Lune blanche'... on the 'é' of 'ramée'. It is in fact the opening theme of 'Lydia' and the symmetry continues for two bars. But to call it the only theme in *La B. Ch*! I couldn't accept that. At my suggestion Fauré put the volume on the piano. 'And this theme', I said, 'and this other one? Are the resemblances purely coincidental?' Gradually he 'admitted' to two or three other themes (the 'Carlovingian' theme recalled in the major epilogue to no. 4, the 'quail' theme, the accompaniment figure in 'Donc ce sera par un clair jour d'été' borrowed from the end of no. 5, which develops so curiously later on; and finally the gathering of all the themes in the final song). But I had to put my finger on each one of these similarities and force him to recognise one by one all these brothers whose resemblance he seemed to have forgotten. Sometimes he would play the passage over again to fix it in his memory. 'It's a collection I wrote ten years ago...' Naturally, I apologised for inflicting this vivisection on him. But I don't in the least regret it.

In 1894, the year in which *La Bonne chanson* was finished, Fauré also made his last Verlaine setting, 'Prison'. The intensity of this song is exceptional in his output. As in the cycle, Fauré shook off the dull hand of his spleen and gave full vent to Verlaine's cry:

> Dis, qu'as tu fait, toi que voilà,
> De ta jeunesse?
>
> (Say, you there, what have you done
> With your youth?)

This poem, from the collection *Sagesse*, spoke to him not only as an artist but as a man: a few months later, in May 1895, Fauré was to celebrate his fiftieth birthday ...

The gradation of feeling in 'Prison' is treated with a masterly hand. It begins with the slow, resigned repeated chords which Fauré so often used to display introverted lyricism. The suffocating heat and the endless immobility of time are suggested by the soft, regular pulsations and by the simplicity of the harmonic movement, from tonic to dominant and back again. Any comparison with 'Au cimetière' serves only to measure the ground covered in six years: the earlier song, to words by Richepin, is a conventional set piece, whereas the Verlaine song looks forward unmistakably to the twentieth century in its conciseness and understated tone. Even the details of the musical language are affected by this radical evolution: the scene in verses 5 and 6,

> La cloche, dans le ciel qu'on voit,
> Doucement tinte

> (The bell, in what sky one can see,
> Tolls softly)

is depicted discreetly by a succession of parallel sevenths which (see chapter 11) Fauré claimed to be a novelty in a letter to René Lenormand,[51] adding: 'The young woman who first read this song from the manuscript, an excellent musician, has since become Mme Claude Debussy! Even in those days she was unflustered by successions of sevenths!' The young woman was, of course, Emma Bardac.

In early March 1896 a grand dinner was given by Fauré and his wife for Emma, her mother and son, and Albert Samain, whose libretto for *La Tentation de Bouddha* Fauré had unkindly relegated to the bottom of a drawer. The purpose of the evening was to let Samain hear a song called 'Soir' which Fauré had composed on a poem from his best-known collection *Au Jardin de l'Infante* (1893). On 8 March Samain wrote to his sister,[52]

At the Fauré's I found the said Mme Bardac, a young woman of about thirty ... She's a pretty, society type, her husband's a banker. She was very nice to me and not in any ordinary way either. She showed me a copy of *Au Jardin de l'Infante* beautifully bound in a kind of mauve silk with her monogram embroidered on it. It was a present from a friend who knew she liked the work. After dinner she sang. Fauré said, 'You'll never hear it sung better.' In fact she has a feeling for nuances and especially a purity of expression which are extremely rare.

'Soir' is one of Fauré's finest lyrical creations. It is not the existential cry of 'Prison', but a recreation of the calm of a fine summer evening in a large, shady park in which a Beloved is dreaming dreams. There is passionate ardour too, as in the Sixth Nocturne, also in D flat and finished in the same year, 1894. The whole-tone phrases in the voice part induce a mood of exaltation above the calm, regular motion of the accompaniment in which arpeggios and staccato notes, as in *La Bonne chanson*, form a continuous flow. Just as the 'Lydia' theme made an appearance in that cycle, so in

'Soir' we find the string theme which accompanied the sweet words between Jessica and Lorenzo in *Shylock* (see Ex. 54, p. 251).

The end of 'Soir' (which Claire Croiza used to sing with such heart-breaking tenderness) is shaped by a simple return to the dominant through the flattened mediant (F flat major). But its success was the fruit of a long search on Fauré's part. The only manuscript of 'Soir' that has survived reveals a quite different and certainly less satisfying conclusion, published by Robert Orledge in a short article in 1979.[53] Hesitations over endings were frequent with Fauré, and in this case it probably explains why a song finished in essence in December 1894 was not published until the spring of 1896 together with 'Prison'. Curiously it was the firm of Fromont who brought it out, the publishers of some of Debussy's early work including *Pelléas*.

This masterpiece left Samain perplexed. At a second dinner, this time at the Bardacs' on 18 July 1898, the company included several notables (Robert de Montesquiou, Pierre de Bréville...) and, as Samain wrote to his sister, were regaled with 'several songs from *Le Jardin de l'Infante* including a repetition of 'Soir' which Montesquiou is enthusiastic about. As for me, I have my reservations.'[54] The performers were Emma Bardac, Maurice Bagès and Fauré, who had in the meantime set two more of Samain's poems, 'Arpège' and the duet 'Pleurs d'or'. He finished 'Pleurs d'or' in the spring of 1896. Harmonically, it is one of Fauré's boldest works, with unexpected juxtapositions and interrupted cadences which reach heights of refinement – or of perversion!

'Arpège', op. 76 no. 2, written in 1897, is a light song based on a flute-like theme: not dissimilar in outline, even if it is in sentiment, from the one which Fauré was using at the same period for his *Thème et variations* for piano. Like 'Clair de lune', 'Arpège' is an essentially in-strumental work to the extent that the flute motif, which introduces the first verse, is then heard as a refrain. But the jewel of op. 76 is the other song of the set, 'Le Parfum impérissable', on a famous poem by Leconte de Lisle. Here once more is the passionate, revolutionary composer of 'Prison', with the same slowly pulsing chords and a texture in which harmony and melody fuse into a single whole, so simply and totally that one has difficulty in believing it to be the result of a human hand at work on a plain sheet of manuscript paper, one day in September 1897.

Fauré, as always, hides his greatest audacities under a cover of regula-rity. The power of the music derives from the furtive and repeated escapes of the principal key, E major, towards a more exotic ground (Ex. 24). The whole-tone scale, still dormant in early works like 'Lydia', is now in the 1890s coming to haunt Fauré's harmonic imagination.

Ex. 24

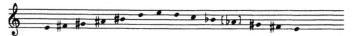

Never again, perhaps, was Fauré to give this feeling of traversing vast spaces, unknown territory in which Modality and Tonality meet. He takes us with him gently but inflexibly – the marks of this character – and with the relaxed assurance of the mature artist.

10   The theatre II: *Prométhée*

PROMÉTHÉE, LYRIC TRAGEDY OP. 82, TEXT BY JEAN
LORRAIN AND ANDRÉ-FERDINAND HÉROLD

Towards the end of the nineteenth century, the wine-growing area of
central France entered a period of unprecedented prosperity. This wealth
led to considerable activity in the life of the district, and in this music had a
part to play. Saint-Saëns, on the way to Béziers in 1897 to give an organ
recital, made the acquaintance of a rich proprietor with the splendidly
resonant name of Fernand Castelbon de Beauxhostes. He was an amateur
composer and the founder of a wind band, La Lyre biterroise. Castelbon,
as he was popularly known, was a man of considerable public spirit, full of
grand ideas about putting on festivals to resemble those of antiquity. He
had conducted La Lyre biterroise in the arena at Valencia, in Spain, and
this prompted him to think of mounting performances in the one at
Béziers; it had been damaged in a fire in 1896 and although reconstruction
had begun it was then abandoned for lack of money.

Saint-Saëns was fascinated by the theatre's exceptional acoustics. He
was interested in open-air theatre and, at his own expense, he had conducted experiments in resonance during the various attempts to make
artistic use of the theatre at Orange. Within a few months he and his friend
Louis Gallet had taken the first steps towards producing a tragedy called
Déjanire, including several pieces of incidental music. It was performed in
the arena at Béziers on 28 and 29 August 1898 to an enthusiastic reception.

Gallet and Saint-Saëns went along, some way at least, with Castelbon's
original idea, which was to return to ancient tragedy. Thus the Béziers
festivals, to begin with anyway, conform to that 'return to antiquity'
championed by the Parnassians. From the musical point of view this return
had a certain relevance as the excavations by the French School at Athens

had brought to light some important lyrical fragments bearing musical notation. Fauré himself had been closely involved – Théodore Reinach had discovered and deciphered the *Hymne à Apollon* in 1893 and asked Fauré to harmonise it.[1] Historical considerations duly had their effect on *Déjanire*, as on *Prométhée*, in the alternation of spoken and sung texts, in the choice of a story from ancient legend and in the importance placed on the choruses, headed by soloists. But any scheme to revive the spectacles of antiquity, however vaguely, came up against impossible obstacles: the amount of sound required to fill the huge arena, the popular character of the enterprise and the need to use local musicians. Hence the choice of wind bands, which produced the necessary volume and of which there was a large number at that period. In addition there was a huge orchestra of about 100 strings and, above them all, a 'curtain' of harps, recalling the lyres of ancient tragedy. This last was Saint-Saëns' idea – they were placed high up so that their evanescent sound would not be lost. A large mixed chorus, solo singers, actors and a female *corps de ballet* completed the Béziers forces. The whole vast enterprise recalled not only the festivals of antiquity but those of revolutionary France, as well as Berlioz's 'Babylonian' visions; while some critics, in rather chauvinistic vein, were bold enough to invoke the *Gesamtkunstwerk* and began talking of Béziers as a French Bayreuth.

This was not at all what Gallet and Saint-Saëns had intended. They saw it as following in the steps of the *comédie-ballet*: 'If you look at Molière's preface to *Les Amants magnifiques*', Gallet wrote to Castelbon on 26 November 1897, 'you'll find the clue to what we're after: a *divertissement* made up of all the theatre has to offer.'[2]

In spite of these references to the theatre of antiquity and to the *comédie-ballet* of Lully and Molière, we should not lose sight of the fact that these performances at Béziers were part of a larger movement in favour of popular theatre. This had first been established on any solid basis by the Théâtre du peuple founded in 1895 by Maurice Pottecher, at Bussang in the Vosges. This movement, based on socialist principles, had the support of Octave Mirbeau, Anatole France and especially Romain Rolland.

Perhaps the deeper meaning of these spectacles escaped the mass of the audience; perhaps the ancient myths appeared to them as no more than anecdotes, and sometimes rather confusing ones. Nonetheless the local population felt itself to be deeply involved with the success of these performances and followed them in reverential silence. The members of La Lyre biterroise and, mostly, of the male choruses came from among the wine-growers and workmen of the region who were put through numerous rehearsals, starting in the spring. The scenery, too, needed an army of stagehands recruited for the occasion.

The visual impact of these performances was undoubtedly one of the main reasons for their success. The scenery designed by Marcel Jambon, from the Paris Opéra, was gigantic and entirely naturalistic. It was set up in the part of the arena that caught the sun most continuously and the portions furthest away from the spectators were seen against a backdrop of blue sky. The performances began in late afternoon and ended as the sun was setting. For *Déjanire* the décor consisted of a life-sized ancient city; for *Prométhée* a massive pile of rocks, inspired by the scenery of the Pyrenees, representing the heights of the Caucasus. The choir of Océanides moved around on a carpet of rushes and sagittarias to the murmur of real cascades rushing down from on high.

The atmosphere of these occasions is preserved in numerous photographs (see pl. 26–9) and we can well understand that their panoramic, 'pre-Hollywood' style was an enormous success with a public as yet untouched by the 'realism' of the cinema. Béziers acquired its legendary moments: the arrival of Déjanire in a horse-drawn chariot; Cora Laparcerie as Pandore in a flimsy, partly transparent tunic; the 'sublime' roars of Edouard de Max as Prométhée chained to his rock, naked but for his scarlet cloak.

After the decided success of *Déjanire* in 1898, Castelbon de Beauxhostes made up his mind to continue along the same lines. He turned again to Saint-Saëns, but the composer refused and instead suggested Fauré who, for all his reticence, had dreamt for twenty years of taking on a large-scale work for the theatre. Saint-Saëns introduced him into the Béziers circle in 1899 by getting him to conduct the revival of *Déjanire* in his place and strongly urged Castelbon to get Fauré to write something for the following summer. Indeed Saint-Saëns' whole object in participating in these enterprises was not so much personal aggrandizement as the chance to allow the younger generation some theatrical experience at a safe distance from Parisian intrigue. This is worth stressing because it flies in the face of the legend of Saint-Saëns as an egoist holding grimly on to his academic laurels. After Fauré, other composers such as Max d'Ollone, Déodat de Séverac and Henri Rabaud,[3] benefited from Castelbon's generosity.

Fauré now had to find a librettist as Louis Gallet, Saint-Saëns' friend and collaborator, had died shortly after finishing *Déjanire*. A libretto on *Les Bacchantes* by André-Ferdinand Hérold, an enthusiastic supporter of the Greek theatre and a regular attender at the Béziers performances, was offered and rejected. Lionel des Rieux submitted one on *Prométhée*, a popular theme at the time, but this too was unsuccessful except in suggest-

ing a subject. It was the actress Cora Laparcerie's idea to commission both
Hérold and Jean Lorrain: Hérold, the gentle poet of Hellenistic inclinations – Lorrain, fat as a butcher's boy, covered in jewels and make-up and
smelling of ether. However, his personal notoriety should not blind us to
his real merits as a writer. *Monsieur de Phocas*, published in 1901, may be
compared with *The Portrait of Dorian Gray* written by Oscar Wilde ten
years earlier; both men may be regarded as among the most talented
figures of that period of fervent decadence, in which refinement mingled
with vice and delicacy was tainted with the odour of putrefaction.

The hesitations in choosing a text and the inevitable difficulties of
literary collaboration meant that Fauré's work was held up for some time.
He received the first part of the text in mid-November 1899 and so began
work without knowing what the end was like. Lorrain and Hérold did not
finish their labours until the beginning of April 1900, with the first
performance already announced for the following August.

Fauré worked at the score in fits and starts right through the winter and
the spring of 1900, in between all his other regular activities – the
Madeleine, his composition class at the Conservatoire and his tours of
inspection in the provinces. We can follow his slow progress by reading the
letters he wrote to Castelbon and Hérold. He did not follow the exact
order of scenes because he had to take account of choral rehearsals and, for
example, the demands of the designers who wanted to relate the size of the
scenery to the duration of Pandore's grand procession in Act II. Fauré was
nervous also about the extended interruptions from the avenging gods, all
of which had to be set to music; in an unpublished letter of 5 March 1900
to Hérold[4] he asks the two librettists for a drastic shortening of this
overlong passage. By 16 June, as he admitted to Castelbon, he still had to
write all the choruses of Act III ...

As luck would have it, in July 1900 Paris was hit by a heat-wave, with
the temperature ranging between 30° and 40° centigrade. Fauré's younger
son later remembered his father 'wearing a flannel waistcoat and pacing
up and down the apartment, with all the shutters closed and the doors
banging. He'd write one or two notes at his worktable and then leave
again, glowering and swearing that *never again* would he write a commissioned work to a deadline.'[5]

An examination of the original manuscript (in the Paris Opera Library)
shows that the composer's first concern was to complete the vocal score,
which had to be engraved and printed in time for the solo and chorus
rehearsals. As for the orchestration, the sections for wind band were
entrusted to Charles Eustace, the conductor of the military band at Mont-

pellier. Saint-Saëns had used him for a similar task in *Déjanire*, being no more willing than Fauré to try his hand at such a particular and demanding skill, but it would be a mistake to imagine that Fauré relied wholly on Eustace for the instrumentation. Fauré himself orchestrated all the passages where the texture thins out to strings, harps and a few woodwind (Aenoë's solo in the second Act, the chorus of Océanides and the beginning of the final chorus in the third). Where the texture demanded mainly, but not wholly, woodwind, he would sketch the layout on several staves accompanied by indications of instruments to be used; these became more and more precise as the work progressed. Eustace then submitted to Fauré his rough drafts of each movement, or later, as time was pressing, his complete orchestrations. Scores were travelling constantly in the post between Paris and Montpellier, as Fauré corrected these preliminary versions and sent them back to Eustace. Eustace then had the job of preparing two fair copies of the enormous orchestral score, which was never engraved.

Reading Lorrain and Hérold's libretto[6], we can see that they relied heavily on their Aeschylean model; Hérold had translated the *Persae* and was obviously familiar with Aeschylus' work. *Prometheus vinctus* was first performed at some time between 467 and 458 BC and is more or less all that is left to us of a trilogy based on the Prometheus legend. The almost complete absence of any action in *Prometheus vinctus* prompted Hérold and Lorrain to include in their drama the events the trilogy is known to have contained. Act I deals with the theft of the fire and the appearance of the avenging gods Power and Force, under their original Greek names of Kratos and Bia, together with Hephaistos the blacksmith; Act II shows Prometheus in chains, and Act III presents the Océanides, nymphs from the depths of the sea, and prepares for Prometheus' coming deliverance by Herakles.

In order to bring some action to Act I, the librettists introduced the character of Gaia, Prometheus' mother, who receives a passing mention in Aeschylus' original. But their main addition was the myth of Pandora: this carries the, indispensable, love-interest right up to the end. In this sense, the Béziers *Prométhée* is really the work of Lorrain and Hérold – Aeschylus' name does not appear either on the score or on the published libretto. Indeed the additions are the most interesting part, making this very much a 1900 view of the Prometheus story.

On a deeper level, a certain Manicheeism manifests itself in such contrasts as Prométhée/Pandore, Masculine/Feminine, Day/Night, Water/

Fire, Height/Depth and so on. The style of the writing and the images it uses come directly from Symbolism: a wide, rather precious vocabulary, a baleful atmosphere, noxious vapours, the attraction of stagnant water, the looming presence of death ...

All in all we are here not far from Gustave Moreau's sulphurous visions, and in Pandora's long tirades we find the central motifs of *fin-de-siècle* decorative art: flowers, hair and woman. This is the Hellenistic, even decadent, manner of treating ancient Greek myth beloved of Vielé Griffin.[7] It has its virtues and it could be argued that they outweigh any weaknesses. But although the authors should be treated as such, rather than as more or less faithful adaptors of Aeschylus, Hérold did at times stay quite close to the original Greek text, especially in the portrayal of Prometheus in chains.

The drama was written in only a few months and certainly does not qualify as one of the best literary works of its time. But even though it is patchy, and for the most part mediocre, it is not wholly devoid of interest: in the declamatory monologues of the two main spoken roles, Prométhée and Pandore, there are many fine lines. Perhaps the best approach is to think of the text as a canvas which needs music to fill it and bring it to life. The work is, after all, always spoken of as Fauré's *Prométhée*.

From the start it had been agreed that the music and speech were to be distributed according to fixed principles: the two main roles, Prométhée and Pandore, and the very short one of Hermes were to be entirely spoken, while those of Gaia, the avenging gods and the human element were to be sung. Once the text had arrived, Fauré was faced with the crucial question of what musico-dramatic system to adopt. He had already shown in his music for *Pelléas et Mélisande* that he was happy to follow Wagner's scheme of leading motives: it was part of the equipment of all the younger French composers of the time, right down to the youngest – Claude Debussy. Like Debussy, Fauré aimed at clarity by reducing the number of his themes: three for the main characters (Prométhée, Pandore, the gods on Olympus) and three as inanimate symbols (Fire, Punishment, the Hope of Mankind). Fauré's use of these six themes is entirely personal. He rejects the rather rigid Wagnerian approach and instead subjects them to a thorough-going variation technique that embraces melody, harmony and rhythm; as with the Punishment theme,[8] for example, given in Ex. 25.

Fauré follows Wagner in subordinating the voice to the richly thematic texture of the orchestra, but the vocal lines nonetheless remain vocal and any of Wagner's 'continuous melody' is incidental. In any case, the

Ex. 25 Prométhée (punishment theme)

alternation of words and music in these productions meant that the music was inevitably shaped as separate numbers, bringing it closer to classical opera than to Wagner's music drama. *Prométhée* can be seen, therefore, as a synthesis of Italian opera (with arias), music drama (leading motifs, thick orchestral polyphony, continuous melody) and incidental music (alternation of words and music). In it Fauré realised the wishes of Saint-Saëns and Gallet and returned to the French dramatic traditions of the eighteenth century in which acting, dancing and music were combined.

Analysis: Act I

Prélude

The work opens with an orchestral movement in C major called *Prélude*, according to the conventions of the lyrical drama. It is built on four of the principal themes:

Prométhée's theme (A), which is heard at the start on low clarinets, saxophones and 'cellos, presents a musical portrait of the intrepid hero and his tragic destiny in its firm, rising outline followed by an abrupt leap of a ninth. This basic motif is immediately succeeded by a blazing fanfare depicting the gods (B) (Ex. 26).

Ex. 26 Prométhée (I, Prélude)

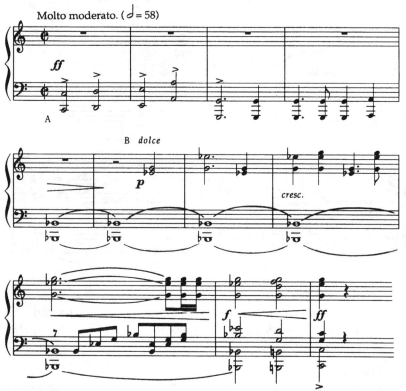

After a long silence we hear, *dolce espressivo*, the modulating theme of the Hope of Mankind (C), over Prométhée's theme (A) in the bass. A short development concerned increasingly with (A) leads to the theme of Fire (D), a simple motif made up of a rising major second and a sixth, a shape which Fauré was to return to again and again (Ex. 27).

Once more, under the chromatic harmonies of (D) in the upper woodwind, we hear the brass playing (A), with which the *Prélude* concludes.

Ex. 27 Prométhée (I, Prélude)

Act I scene 1: 'Among savage mountain scenery ... men and women are running from every side in jubilation.' – Allegro, 2/2, C major; pp. 9–40

This huge choral scene shows us primitive mankind and his joy at the news of the gift of Fire, as promised by Prométhée. It is broad, almost rough-hewn, and must be regarded as one of Fauré's finest and most original inspirations, far as it is from his usual aesthetic concerns. This first scene breaks down into five connected episodes. First, a male chorus is punctuated by Wagnerian calls of 'Eia, Eia' over a syncopated bass derived from an inversion of (A); from the harmonic point of view, we find that Fauré often makes expressive use of the tritone (C–F sharp) and underlines its ruggedness by dissonances (F sharp/E, F sharp/G). The vocal line frequently includes melismas belonging to the whole-tone scale. A beautiful chromatic modulation rises to introduce the solo of the male-chorus

leader, Andros, who praises both Fire and the hero who is bringing it to
mankind:

> C'est l'oiseau feu! Dans l'ombre épouvantée
> Il va jaillir comme à l'horizon clair
> Le clair archer qu'aime et retient la mer
> Il va jaillir et c'est toi Prométhée!

(It is the bird of fire! In the scattered darkness he will shine as, on the clear horizon,
dazzling Apollo, loved and guarded by the sea. He will shine, and it is thou,
Prométhée!)

A brief fanfare reintroduces the male chorus who chant the text in a
rhythm close to that of the spoken word (Ex. 28), a passage which seems to

Ex. 28 Prométhée (I)

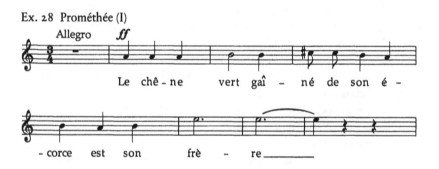

have been in Honegger's mind twenty years later when he came to write
King David. The men sing 'Prométhée est la force' ('Prometheus is
strength') and are answered by the women singing 'Prométhée est la joie'
(Prometheus is joy'), followed by a passage for six-part mixed chorus
introducing a parallel solo for the female chorus leader, Aenoë. Here
(p. 34) the arioso style gives way to more melodic writing, with a lovely
accompaniment in canon, heard low in clarinets and saxophones, and
based on an idea derived from the Fire theme (pp. 36–7). Finally a short
six-part mixed chorus brings this expressive and finely constructed scene
to a powerful conclusion.

After an initial monologue in which Prométhée praises the benefits that
fire will bring, Pandore appears and declares her opposition to his plans.
Her entry is accompanied by a brief interlude, added at the request of the
actress Cora Laparcerie. These ten bars (p. 41) present for the first time
the heroine's motif of descending fifths, depicting her weakness and her
doomed love.

Her rather stormy dialogue with Prométhée is followed by the entrance of another character: 'From one of the caves in the mountain appears an austere-looking woman, enveloped in long veils. She holds out her hand to stop Prométhée.' It is Gaia and her appearance is, from a dramatic point of view, rather a feeble stroke as it is an exact repeat of the pattern in the previous scene. In spite of this, it inspired Fauré to write an aria which is one of the most beautiful things in the score. The title 'aria' in fact is barely relevant to this passage, written in the dark 'religious' key of C minor. Aria it may be in its function and in its superficial design, but it is not a classical aria as far as its structure is concerned. Fauré was truly inspired here by the strength and nobility of the language. The extremely flexible musical style follows closely the nuances of the text. It underlines the continuation of the sense between the two three-line groups in the second strophe, and it emphasises key words in the third strophe with large intervals which reflect the visual impact of the text. Thus the words 'cimes' ('heights'), 'foudre' ('thunderbolt'), and 'réduire en poudre' ('reduce to powder') in the fourth strophe are accompanied by octave leaps, while in the accompaniment wide leaps in the bass depict 'les abîmes' ('abysses'), and 'les gouffres' ('chasms').

This aria also includes a new leading motif: that of Prométhée's punishment, foretold by Gaia (p. 44: 'take care lest you destroy yourself', and the whole of p. 46; cf. Ex. 25).

Gaia's entrance has sometimes been compared with that of Erda in the third Act of *Siegfried*. The likeness exists more in the matter of the character (Mother Earth) than of the music. Although the chromatic progressions, the fidelity to the text and especially the size of the orchestra suggest Wagner, I do not think we can speak of a direct Wagnerian influence. Fauré was simply following the spirit of the times and, in my opinion, he comes far closer to the style of Gluck in his 'tragédies lyriques'. This powerful aria is chiefly notable for its purity of construction, its effective use of simple means and in particular Fauré's feeling for the balance of his text. His corrections, though few and minor, were all in the direction of lightness, ease of delivery and hence of comprehensibility. In the second strophe, for instance:

> 'Quel Fléau peut sortir
> De la nuit dont tu veux écarter les nuées!
> Au milieu des sanglots, des cris et des huées
> *Fauré* (*A travers les* sanglots, *les* cris et *les* huées)
> Crains de t'anéantir!'

Fauré seems to have been happy with this aria, which he wrote free from pressure in the winter of 1899–1900, because he chose it to form a supplement in *Le Figaro*[9] and in 1919 offered it to Madeleine Grey, who gave the first performance of the song-cycle *Mirages* and asked him to write for her an aria with orchestral accompaniment.[10]

The crucial scene in which the fire is stolen is somewhat confused on the dramatic level, as it is made up of a rapid succession of dialogues and monologues, broken up by brief musical interludes: a chorus, a melodrama (p. 57), and a very short solo for Aenoë (p. 58). The appearance of the fire is treated curiously as a melodrama with murmuring tremolos on strings and woodwind trills under the spoken text (pp. 59–61):

> *Prométhée*: Hommes, hommes, riez, chantez, soyez heureux,
> Voici le don que j'ai promis, voici le feu!

Prométhée is struck down and the chorus of Humanity cries: 'Horreur! Horreur!' at the appearance of the three avenging gods.

The librettists' idea of having some of this very rapid text set to music posed a difficult problem for the composer and his interpreters: the various fragments change tempo, key and metre and demand considerable virtuosity from the singers and players and a cool head from the conductor. It would have been more effective to have a spoken chorus at this point rather than break the scene's momentum by alternating speaking with singing.

The act ends with a trio for the gods Bia, Hephaistos and Kratos, divided in two by a short interlude for Pandore (p. 68). Neither the D minor recitatives for Bia and Kratos in the first part, nor the angry trio in the second seem to me particularly inspired. All Fauré's talents are concentrated on the brief solo for Hephaistos: 'Je t'aime encore, ô Prométhée' (p. 66), an intense expression of the pity he feels for his brother whom Zeus has ordered him to punish. Unusually, the theme of Punishment is here given to the voice on the words: 'Dans la forge tous deux nous chantions autrefois' (p. 66).

The accompaniment is rich in themes: of Prométhée and the Gods, of Fire (pp. 70–2) and of Punishment (p. 73), all presented in new guises. Even so, I feel this trio brings the act to a noisy conclusion rather than an exciting one. Fauré is perfectly capable of depicting the Titan's size or Humanity's joy, but the violence of Kratos and Bia leave him cold. Try as he might, hate was not an emotion he was familiar with; instead it came out as conventional padding or even as bombast.

Act II

Prélude and Pandore's cortège

Pandore, who fell 'as though dead' at the end of the Act I, is now the
subject of a long dirge sung by her companions, who bear her body on a
bier of leafy branches:

> Larmes coulez
> Lourdes et lentes!
> Pleurs ruisselez!
> Nos mains tremblantes ne vous essuieront plus!
>
> (Tears, flow
> Heavily and slowly!
> Drop, tears!
> Our trembling hands can no longer wipe you away!)

The Prelude which introduces this chorus is a funereal fanfare on Pandore's motif in fifths. The rhythm and the melody (unison on the tonic,
subdominant and dominant only) are both so simple that it is natural to
search for reasons. A look at the full orchestral score (pp. 93–6) reveals
that this passage was played by four trumpets placed at the top of the
theatre; the distance from the stage and the resonance both justify Fauré in
being cautious. This fanfare in B flat minor (a key chosen with B flat
trumpets in mind) takes on a lighter air as flutes and clarinets pick out a
motif in alternating thirds and sixths, accompanied by gently arpeggiated
chords on the harps. Under this delicate tracery the principal theme of the
cortège appears over a tonic pedal – a beautiful rising phrase in the style of
a chorale, which has some affinity with the beginning of the song 'Au
cimetière', written twelve years earlier on a poem by Jean Richepin:

Ex. 29

Heu - reux qui meurt i - ci, Ain-si que les oi-seaux des champs

Cortège de Pandore
    (Prométhée, II)

This choral dialogue for female choir has a certain languid charm. Despite its serious tone it is very much a 1900 vision of antiquity: white, graceful, feminine and highly decorated. There is an unaffected plaintiveness about its atmosphere, but there is no denying that after the opening section the composer found it hard to deal with the irregularity of the metre and the repetition of words (this part of the text was probably written by Hérold). All Fauré's efforts could not entirely disguise the laboriousness of the text, and too often it jars against the natural flow of the melodic line; indeed, the fourth strophe is a clear example of Fauré distorting this to fit the words. Aenoë's solo that follows, 'Tu passais royale et sacrée' (pp. 90–7), is worthy of *La Bonne chanson* in its rich lyricism. Fauré himself regarded it as the finest, 'the most musical', passage in the score.[11] It is more than possible that it had been composed earlier as a separate piece because the transition (p. 97) between the end of the solo (in 3/4) and the return of the chorus (in 4/4) needs careful handling in performance.

The final strophes of the chorus, describing Pandore in the kingdom of the dead, are on the same high level. Her theme of descending fifths blends effortlessly with the rest of the texture, while the two-part choral writing and the increasingly sombre accompaniment tap an exceedingly rich harmonic vein, leading to a powerful modulation into F major at the words 'Elle qui possédait l'Amour!' The calm, serene coda is mysterious and dignified, like the best of Monteverdi's madrigals.

Despite one or two weaknesses, Fauré was almost entirely successful in welding the patchy, laborious and confused text of this long chorus into a harmonious whole.

The scene of the binding of Prométhée is to some extent the logical sequence to the final trio of Act I. The recitatives for Bia and Kratos are not particularly outstanding but Hephaistos' noble E flat minor aria, 'Ô sublime et bon Titanide' (pp. 106–9), certainly deserves a mention: it is one of the most daring numbers of the score, with its chromaticism and startling atonal countermelodies (end of p. 109: Ex. 30).

The point at which Prométhée is committed to his chains is accompanied by a short rhythmic motif (Ex. 31), rather hard in outline, which is a kind of contraction of the Punishment theme.

Underneath this chromatic chords are directed by a brief dotted motif, describing the rise and fall of the hammer; and here Fauré's incessant modulations give an utterly appropriate sense of movement. Although he might not seem a suitable composer for such a scene, he in fact succeeds admirably by treating it symphonically, as he had some of the awkward

Ex. 30 Prométhée (II, 2)

sections of Pandore's cortège. Once he had found his rhythmic basis and set it in motion, it was enough to allow the conversation between the three characters to unfold over the orchestral texture without troubling to observe the nuances of the text, which, in any case, he felt free to change and abbreviate. These verbose deities take their leave at last and Prométhée, in chains, delivers his elaborated monologue.

The librettists wanted to make the rôle of Pandore as important as that of Prométhée, and so they were forced at this point to revive her, whatever the damage to verisimilitude and to the lasting impact of the funeral cortège at the beginning of the act. True, the libretto tells us that she falls 'as though dead', but such subtlety is inevitably lost in performance.

Ex. 31 Prométhée (II, 2)

Pandore's reawakening is illustrated by an effective orchestral interlude (4/4 in D flat major), including the descending fifths motif over an accompaniment of harps and murmuring strings.

This scene, which follows on immediately, consists of a stirring 3/4 aria for Bia in E flat minor, 'Pandore arrière', balancing Gaia's aria in Act I, but shorter and not so successful. There is little original about it, built as it is in ABA form and reworking various of the leading motifs (the gods, Punishment, Prométhée) as the text demands. Bia's 'Apostrophe' was obviously written just to give this ungrateful rôle an aria and has absolutely no justification from the dramatic point of view. Violence is expressed in octave leaps and a high tessitura almost throughout, ending on an impressive high B flat. During this aria Prométhée is hidden from Pandore's sight by a fall of boulders.

The act ends with a long monologue for Pandore. The opening verses of this are played as melodrama, with a short orchestral passage in D flat which expounds Pandore's theme in the grand Wagnerian manner.

Act III

The final act begins with a long female chorus, balancing Pandore's cortège, but of a rather different cast. Compassion for the dead girl is, certainly, expressed in tones of gravity, but the overall impression is of a transparent tenderness, blending reticence with sensuality. Depicting the slightly risqué chorus of the Océanides no doubt had its attractions for Fauré who, as we know, was susceptible to such things ... This chorus, together with the one that begins the work, is in my opinion one of the most bewitching in the whole of French music.

In the orchestral prelude Fauré presents a marked contrast between two textures. The opening bars are gloomy, with the themes of the gods and Punishment appearing like some nightmare on the lowest instruments of the orchestra (horns, saxhorns, double basses). Suddenly the atmosphere clears and flute, strings and harps combine to seduce the listener with sweet harmonies. There is a particular intensity in the scoring for flute and clarinet of the Punishment theme (Ex. 32).

In a shortened form it becomes the central motif of the chorus, the true musical symbol of the message of peace brought by the Océanides. This chorus is another Requiem, a pagan Requiem which renews the promise of eternal rest found in the In Paradisum. Here too all is clarity and gentleness, in which we can 'bathe ourselves', to use Fauré's own expression.[12] Anyone scrutinising the score in quest of the magician's secrets will be

Ex. 32 Prométhée (III, Prélude)

surprised to find that the spell is cast, for the most part, within the confines of C major or F minor!

The chorus is a musical unity, though divided into three sections by two interruptions from Prométhée and Pandore. In the central section, an *allegro* in A flat, we hear another transformation of the Punishment theme over an accompaniment of repeated chords (p. 145). Here Fauré has refashioned the text fairly freely to achieve a logical expression not found in the librettists' own efforts. This uneasy berceuse is followed by the reappearance of the 'Lydia' theme, as in the more contemplative pages of *La Bonne chanson*, its whole-tone outline being easily absorbed into harmonic progressions that foreshadow the wonderful end to the first act of *Pénélope* (Ex. 33).

The Océanides' charm has failed to deflect Prométhée's purpose as he lies chained on his rock. After a bitter dialogue with Pandore, the drama returns inevitably to the realm of tragedy. Kratos and Bia reappear, obedient to the claims of formal symmetry but without any real dramatic justification, and threaten Prométhée with a divine thunderbolt: 'Ta douleur est-elle complice du geste enflammé d'autrefois?' ('Your misery is the outcome of your headstrong deed.')

Thunder. Zeus and the Olympians appear on the topmost peaks of the mountains. Among them is Hermes, holding a casket. Men come running at the noise.

Ex. 33 'Lydia'

'La Lune blanche' (*La Bonne chanson*, III)

Prométhée (III, no. 4)

Pénélope (I, end)

'Cygne sur l'eau' (*Mirages*, I)

Over a mighty roll on all the timpani (p. 161) the theme of the gods is heard in canon, scored for both orchestras together. The chorus-leader Andros has a solo leading to a mixed chorus in unison. This chorus serves as a form of musical punctuation before the great monologue in which Hermes announces the hero's future deliverance; although its monumental style and C major tonality recall the opening chorus of the whole work, in my view it is too short to be completely satisfactory.

Pandore takes the casket and, to the accompaniment of gently arpeggiated chords, descends slowly towards assembled Mankind. The tragedy reaches its conclusion in a beautiful final chorus. The opening strophe, for sopranos and tenors in unison over a string accompaniment marked by chords on the harps, is the only part of the work where one might detect the influence of Greek music (pp. 167–9). In the last two strophes Fauré uses the complete chorus in up to eight parts, with the theme of the gods dominating the orchestral texture up to the final *fortissimo*.

There is more of serenity in this chorus than of the joy of grateful mankind, while in the first strophe the moderate tempo and the scattered silence evoke (deliberately?) the sense of unease which the real contents of Pandore's casket might well inspire. Here the music matches the ambiguity of the libretto: Mankind celebrates the benefits of the gods now that Pandore has promised to cure all their ills. Meanwhile Prométhée denounces their impending treachery:

> Contemplez en riant ma chair ensanglantée
> Dieux lâches! Vous tuez l'oeuvre de Prométhée!
>
> (Look on my bloody flesh and laugh, foul gods!
> Thus Prométhée's designs are set at nought!)

The original orchestration relied heavily on the wind bands. The posters announced a total complement of 450 instrumentalists and of these 100 were strings, 13 harps (18 for the 1901 revival) while the three wind bands together included more than 300 players. One of these bands, placed among the scenery, was used exclusively to accompany the solo gods when they made their appearance on the highest level of the stage. The other two bands were for the most part heard singly, joining together only for the main climaxes. The scoring of Charles Eustace and Fauré made a strong impression on the professional musicians who heard it, including Saint-Saëns, Koechlin and Henri Büsser.[13] Its expressivity and the real sense of the dramatic, testify both to Fauré's care in indicating his wishes and to Eustace's skill in realising them. The impressive mass effects are reserved for crucial moments in the drama: the prelude to Act I, appearances of the gods and the finale, complete with stereophony from two orchestras. These Berliozian passages are complemented by the delicate female choruses and the interludes which Fauré insisted on orchestrating himself. 'You can't imagine how charming the Océanides' chorus is in performance', Saint-Saëns wrote to Charles Lecocq on 30 August 1900,[14] and the combination of harp, woodwind and strings does certainly display a wonderful ear for sound.

The première was arranged for 26 August, but it had to be postponed because, just as the performance was about to start before an audience of nine thousand people, an amazing storm broke over Béziers. Everybody was drenched, musicians, dancers, actors ... The theatre was evacuated, according to Jean Lorrain,[15] 'amid scenes of crush and panic; women fainted from heat and terror and the scenery was left in tatters'. Jules Véran wrote in Comoedia:[16] 'A journalist went up to Fauré, who was still on the podium in a trance, and led him, soaked to the skin, into the "wings", improvised out of a section of the gallery. Sympathetic hands began to wipe him down, when a torrent of water suddenly came rushing off the gallery roof and he got another drenching.'

So the première took place the next day. It more than made up for this unfortunate start. Fauré wrote to his wife back in Paris: 'Everything went splendidly. They gave me an ovation and I had to make an appearance on the stage between two of the actors! The weather had cleared up at last and it was sunny, though there was rather too much wind ... The actors are extremely kind and full of my success as well as their own.'

Although Fauré had deliberately aimed at keeping the music simple it seems, at this first performance, rather to have overtaxed the performers' abilities. The solo singers acquitted themselves 'honourably', according to Pierre Lalo in *Le Temps* (30 October). The singer engaged to sing Kratos, Valentin Duc, was upset at not having a single 'grand aria' – a late addition he had asked for – and refused to take part. His place was taken at very short notice by a singer called Fonteix 'from the Grand Théâtre in Marseilles'; Mme Fiérens-Peters 'of the Paris Opéra' sang Bia, and Vallier 'of the Théâtre de la Monnaie in Brussels' played Hephaistos: 'three imbeciles' wrote Fauré,[17] 'real screamers in the good old tradition of France and elsewhere, and generous with their mistakes'. The wind bands too provided their share of problems. Fauré was impressed by the band from Montpellier, directed by Eustace, but had terrible difficulties with the infantry band, used to accompany the singing of the gods from a position high up among the scenery. 'That poor little infantry band', he wrote to his wife on 10 August, 'after a lifetime of playing polkas, marches and fantasias on *Robert le Diable*, it had a fearful time coming to grips with its task. And as things turned out its task was the most onerous and difficult of all, because it had to accompany the dramatic roles whose music is the most detailed and complicated in the entire work.' As for the female chorus recruited with so much labour, they sang with languor and lassitude, according to the reviewer in *La Revue blanche* (15 September 1900). There seem, too, to have been problems of ensemble between the choirs and orchestras directed by Fauré himself, despite (or maybe because of) the network of sub-conductors it had been thought necessary to employ. But, as Fauré wrote to Ravel on 27 August 1901, when *Prométhée* was revived at Béziers 'the imperfections, many as they were, evaporated in the open-air – the sun simply soaked them up'.[18]

Real as these faults undoubtedly were, we should not lose sight of the fact that the work made an enormous impression. The critics were there in force and, by and large, their reports were highly favourable, while the public was wildly enthusiastic. Thanks to Castelbon's tireless organisation 17,000 people in all attended the two performances on 27 and 28 August

1900 and elsewhere in the town there was a host of popular entertainments: torchlight processions, free concerts of military music from the bandstand on the Citadelle, illuminations, a concert in the theatre involving both Fauré and Saint-Saëns, and a banquet for the main participants in *Prométhée*. Under the vast plane-trees of the allée Paul Riquet a crowd from the whole of the Languedoc area gathered. 'The cafés are overflowing right out into the middle of the roadway' wrote Pierre Lalo, the critic of *Le Temps*, his austere character not untouched by the happy-go-lucky atmosphere. 'Everyone is wandering around waiting for the performance to begin, greeting each other and the celebrities who are taking part in it. Everywhere there is sunshine, dust and noise.'

Charles Koechlin later recalled:[19]

The air and the music made us feel fit and strong. Fauré, on his home territory, conducted with assurance and precision and, when he gave the down-beat for the opening bar, the brass filled the immense bowl of the theatre. The open-air sonority came as a revelation! ... And we marvelled at the combined effect of draperies rustling in the wind, the play of clouds over the auditorium, the sunlit processions of women on stage and the magic light of the Midi! I remember still the reciter's words, 'it is the bird of fire' and the triumphal choruses. No one who was not there can imagine the splendid effect of the sounds blending so perfectly with the musical argument, with the scenery, the gusts of wind, the gentle warmth and the immense, azure dome of the sky. Paris gives you no idea of what Greek theatre was like; at Béziers the realisation overwhelmed you, borne on a rising tide of emotion.

Prométhée is a key work in Fauré's output, not only for the originality and beauty of the music but also because it is perfectly adapted to its intended surroundings. It is proof that Fauré was not just the miniaturist of his current reputation – he was also capable of composing on a broad canvas. He took account of the size of the theatre and of the open-air acoustic in not modulating too often and in choosing well-defined themes and simple rhythms. In an unpublished letter to A.-F. Hérold, Fauré speaks of the 'absolute necessity of remaining extremely clear and simple, without any fast detail. In a word, the music must be visible at a distance. I might almost say it should be written in block capitals!' Hence the rather impoverished summary appearance of the vocal score, which is little more than a skeleton. As Saint-Saëns pointed out, only in the orchestra does the beauty of Fauré's score reveal itself.

Unfortunately the very particular demands it makes have not helped it to be performed widely. The 1901 revival at Béziers drew a smaller audience and the idea of annual performances, mooted after the success of the première, was abandoned. There were, however, offers from several theatres to include it in their repertoire, including the Société des grandes auditions in Paris which, in 1902, had organised some widely publicised performances of Wagner; it was run by Alfred Cortot who at that time was trying to make a name for himself as a conductor. But, to get *Prométhée* put on, it had first to be reorchestrated for the traditional symphony orchestra. Fauré began work on this in 1902 but then Cortot changed his mind and the reorchestration was left incomplete.[20]

On 5 December 1907 there was an attempt to recreate the conditions of Béziers at the Paris Hippodrome, but the acoustics proved to be so terrible that the second performance on 12 December had to be moved swiftly to the Opéra. Eventually the work was reorchestrated at the request of the Opera director Jacques Rouché during the First World War. Fauré was then anxious, after his unfortunate experience with *Pénélope*, to get back to writing songs and chamber music, so he handed the task over to his pupil Roger Ducasse. Although this version is perhaps closer to Wagner than to Fauré, it made its mark and after its first performance at the Paris Opéra on 17 May 1917 was heard some forty times, mostly in the concert hall.

When *Prométhée* was revived in Paris in 1907 the critics took up the central question of the division between sung and spoken text. Clearly this did not conform to the established categories of the period, although it prefigured similar usage in Debussy and D'Annunzio's *Le Martyre de St-Sébastien* (1911), Stravinsky and Cocteau's *Oedipus Rex* (1927) and Stravinsky and Gide's *Perséphone* (1934), as well as in Honegger's semi-staged oratorios. Nowadays, when 'musical theatre' takes such a variety of forms, we no longer have the problem of finding a category for *Prométhée*. Instead we have to find a solution to the mis-match between a relatively fragmented musical contribution and a text that is too long and uneven in quality. There have been attempts to perform Fauré's music shorn of the surrounding drama, but that is to remove its dramatic significance. Similarly, substituting an entirely new text, far from solving the dichotomy, actually makes it worse. The only way for *Prométhée* to shine in its true glory is for it to be given in the conditions of its première: in a large open-air theatre, with the original orchestration for strings, harps and wind bands and with a very large choir; it could be performed in a semi-staged version in which two reciters could limit their interventions to the essential moments, as in *Œdipus Rex*. This would be to fulfil the dreams of Monsieur Croche who wrote, through the persona of Debussy:[21]

We may imagine a large orchestra enriched through the support of the human voice ... and music specially made to be heard in the open air, new vocal and instrumental sounds in long phrases, floating and dancing above the tops of the trees, unrestricted. Harmonic progressions which might sound curious in the confines of a concert hall could there be judged at their true value ... We must be clear that it is a question of composing not 'grand' music but 'great' music; and it is certainly not intended that the open-air resonance should provoke noisy trumpet-calls, but that the composer should use the echoes to encourage the souls of the multitude to indulge the dreams his harmonies call up within them.

26 Devienny: illustrated cover for the official programme of *Prométhée*
at Béziers, August 1900; centre: Cora Laparcerie (Pandore)

27 Charles Koechlin: a rehearsal of *Prométhée*, Act III, arena at Béziers, August 1901

28 *Prométhée*, Act III (Pandore and the Océanides), production of August 1901, conducted by Fauré

29 At Béziers, August 1902 (Première of *Parysatis* by Saint-Saëns), from left to right, Marguerite Hasselmans, Gabriel Fauré, Fernand Castelbon de Beauxhostes, Alphonse Hasselmans

30 At the Catulle Mendès' house, 1905: Gabriel Fauré, Reynaldo Hahn and the actress Berthe Bady

31 Marie Trélat at the piano, *c.* 1900

32 At the *fête* in Marne-la-Coquette, *c.* 1895, from left to right: Henri Duparc, Pierre de Bréville, Maurice Bagès

33 Sightreading at Jeanne Raunay's house, November 1903, from left to right: Paul Daraux, J. Raunay, René Lenormand, Gabriel Fauré, G. Mauguière

34 Marguerite Long and her husband, Joseph de Marliave, Challes-les-Eaux, 1911

222

35   Two interpreters of Fauré: Edouard Risler (left) and Jacques Thibaud,
1920

11 Works and days

The last decade of the nineteenth century and the years immediately following were perhaps the fullest and most intense of Fauré's life. He underwent a profound renewal both in style and in musical language, while his personality began really to assert itself; maturity may have been slow to arrive, but there was no doubting it when it came. In 1890 Fauré was still an obscure choirmaster, in 1905 he was appointed (and not by his own efforts) to one of the most highly regarded posts in French musical life, the directorship of the Paris Conservatoire.

The climb in social status was a gradual one and attended with considerable difficulties. In fact the decade began badly for him and his family. His second son Philippe, born in 1889, turned out to be even more prone to illness than his brother Emmanuel, six years his senior. The whole decade and beyond was a history of crises, remissions and anguished medical consultations in search of a miracle cure. Questions of health and hygiene assumed the same obsessional proportions in Fauré's household as they did in Proust's during these same years, and his wife Marie devoted herself unstintingly to her rôle as nurse and martyr. To these problems was joined an ever-increasing lack of money, and the combination began to affect Fauré's peace of mind and even his own health. He wrote to Marcel Girette in an unpublished letter of 1890: 'My only excuse for not writing to you is that for the last three months my health has been appalling. I've had a terrible summer, ill and unable to work, living a quiet, retiring life like a real old man!' The migraines, which were to plague him all his days, attacked him mercilessly and it was with a yellowish complexion and glassy eyes that he used to drag himself off to his 'mournful Madeleine'. 'He had terrible attacks of giddiness', wrote his son Philippe,[1] and sometimes, in the street, he had to lean against the wall of a house to stop himself falling over.'

It is hard not to see in these frequent outbreaks of illness a protest against the stale mediocrity of his life, just as Mallarmé was depressed in the days when he was a teacher in Tournon or Besançon and mocked by his pupils. In a heartfelt letter to Marguerite Baugnies, Fauré complained of the endless round of music lessons and, now that summer had arrived, of having to follow his pupils to their residences in the country to the west of Paris: 'On average, I spend three hours every day in the train . . . I really feel the need, just for ten days or so, to have a break from it all, see other parts of the country than the Gare Saint-Lazare and meet new people, with no sonatas to be heard and different air to breathe and airs to listen to!' As he wrote to the Countess Greffulhe, 'If my family enjoyed good health I should give eternal thanks! As it is, that side of things is a continual worry and I hardly ever feel free of it!'[2]

Even so, it was from 1890 onwards that signs of public recognition began to come his way. On 12 July that year he was made a Chevalier of the Legion of Honour – though this could have been due more to his friendship with Marcel Girette[3] than to his standing as a creative artist, if we remember that only five years earlier César Franck had received the same distinction, not as a composer but as 'organ professor at the Conservatoire'!

In 1892 the death of Ernest Guiraud meant that a post became vacant for a composition teacher at the Conservatoire. Saint-Saëns encouraged his pupil to apply, but it was soon made clear that Fauré was *persona non grata*. 'Fauré? Never! If he's appointed, I resign', declared the venerable Ambroise Thomas who was then the director – and we have it from Charles Koechlin[4] that this remark was confirmed to him by unimpeachable sources. Instead Fauré applied for another of Guiraud's posts, that of inspector of musical education. Chabrier too put in for the post and when Fauré heard of his friend's candidature he wrote to Marcel Girette a hitherto unpublished letter[5] which, from a man who was reserve and modesty incarnate, gives an amazingly frank description of what a wretched life he was leading:

My dear Monsieur Girette,

Thank you for being so open about your support for Chabrier's application, which I quite understand. I would not trouble you further had you not seemed anxious to know to which of us two candidates the post in question would be more useful. I may say quite bluntly that from the material point of view (which, alas, one cannot ignore!) I am the more *interesting* party! Chabrier has some small private means which allow him to devote himself entirely to composition and to spend ten months of the year in Indre et Loire,[6] far from the hubbub of Paris. As for me, I have no capital behind me and the only way I can live and support my wife and children is by training the choir of the Madeleine and giving private lessons, thereby spending a great deal of time which, people are always telling me, I could use to better effect.

In writing this I do not feel that I am being disloyal to Chabrier and the friendship between us, as he has expressed to me any number of times how sorry he is to see my days spent in this way merely on making a living! Please accept my apologies for thus advertising my hardship, and rest assured that it gives me no pleasure to do so.

On 1 June 1892 Fauré was appointed 'Inspector of musical education in the branches of the Conservatoire national, in the national schools of music and choir schools'. With this post he became a government functionary and acquired a standing in Paris musical life. He could also now give up most of his private lessons. On the other hand, for the next thirteen years he was obliged to make journeys of inspection which allowed him to sample the variable charms of provincial towns: their dull, restricted social life, uncomfortable hotels and gloomy railway stations, seen in the course of incessant changing of trains. When he got back to Paris, Fauré, tired, bored and covered with dust, then had to undergo the miseries of writing the hallowed 'inspector's report' – a real torment for a man who much preferred writing music!

In between these journeys he would immerse himself, not with total enthusiasm, in the whirlpool of public and private concerts. Thanks to the far-sighted support of the Princess Edmond de Polignac (Winnaretta Singer), of Count Robert de Montesquiou and the Countess Elisabeth Greffulhe, this quiet bourgeois man found himself, around 1887, launched into the most rarefied atmosphere of Parisian high life. This entry, so earnestly sought after by the young Proust, took Fauré to the aristocratic environs of the Faubourg St-Germain and to the bourgeois salons of the 'plaine Monceau'. Those who received him included the Princess de Cystria, the Countess d'Haussonville, the Count de Saussine, the Countess de Chevigné, the Countess de Gauville and the Princess Potocka, as well as Madeleine Lemaire, Marguerite de Saint-Marceaux, Marie Trélat, Henriette Fuchs and Pauline Roger. In particular Fauré spent time with artists who were personal friends of his, musicians, painters and writers whose gatherings provided a marvellous opportunity to exchange ideas: Ernest Chausson, the Lalos, Jules Griset, Paul Taffanel, Louis Diémer; the painters Roger-Jourdain, Ernest Duez, Emmanuel Jadin, Eugène Baugnies, Jacques-Emile Blanche, the sculptor la Heudrie, the architect Jean Girette; and the writers Edmond Haraucourt, André Beaunier, Eugène d'Eichthal, not to mention Fauré's friendly relationship with Albert Samain, Marcel Proust, Henry de Régnier and Paul Verlaine ... In all these circles music played an important part, and Fauré's compositions found a place between those of Benjamin Godard or Théodore Lack,[7] surrounded by a short play and recitations of more, or less, inspired poems.

To say that the Mme Verdurins of the age desired Fauré's presence would be to understate matters – they practically kidnapped him. 'I'm exhausted with pointless efforts', he wrote in February 1897 to Mme M. Girette, 'I dream of peace and tranquillity but they don't seem greatly interested. There's *too much* of my music being played this winter and too many people want me actually to be there, no doubt to make sure I'm aware of all this flattering activity.' The critic Louis Aguettant, who was one of the first to recognise Fauré's true worth, describes in a letter of 1902 the 'Fauré of the salons, moving at his ease among the milling crowds, with a blissful smile on his face like some ancient Olympian deity who has had his fill of incense.'[8]

Open as Fauré was to the slightest manifestation of sympathy and always unsure of the real value of his works, he could never refuse his support to anyone sincerely interested in his music and the smallest token of approbation was a comfort to him. I do not think it is going too far to suggest that he attended these soirées not merely to forget his otherwise mundane existence but also to keep up the courage he needed to go on composing. This indisputably weak side of his character contrasts with the apparently flawless certainty and energy he admired so much in d'Indy, the effortlessly regular output of his teacher Saint-Saëns and, even more sharply, with Debussy's lofty isolation, born of his belief in his own superior genius. 'One must remain alone ... without stain', wrote Debussy in the *Revue blanche*'[9]; 'when an artist's milieu begins to wax enthusiastic about him I become suspicious, fearing he may eventually become no more than the expression of that milieu.' This conception of the artist's social situation does, I think, explain quite straightforwardly Debussy's severe judgment on Fauré's socialising tendencies, at the time when the latter had got in first with his music of *Pelléas*: 'Fauré is the mouthpiece of a group of snobs and imbeciles who will have nothing whatever to do with the other *Pelléas*.'[10]

The vanity of the social round certainly did not escape Fauré's notice, but it had become an indispensable drug and in the excitement of making new acquaintances he tended, quite unintentionally, to lose sight of his real friends. Marguerite Baugnies and Winnaretta Singer both regretted this inconstancy of his in their memoirs, even though they forgave him. For all his modesty, Fauré was well aware that his social success outshone that of contemporaries like Théodore Dubois and Widor whose career and reputation were far in advance of his own; while he particularly objected to the hullabaloo surrounding Massenet's least considerable compositions, reckoning that Massenet's rapid rise to fame was based on a generally cynical view of art, dangerously bolstered up by facility and technical competence. A disinterested devotion to the cause of Music lay at the root of Fauré's creative philosophy. He may have appeared 'worldly' to some people, but there was never any question of his compromising his art by pandering to the often appalling taste of the circles in which he moved.

More than that, at the very time when his music – and his vocal music especially – was beginning to reach a wide audience, his style underwent a radical change. The extreme chromaticism of *La Bonne chanson* must have nearly choked those who heard it in Madeleine Lemaire's salon in 1895, and three years later the splendid but austere Seventh Nocturne perplexed an audience more used to the sweet nothings of Chaminade, the 'rêveries' of Francis Thomé or Massenet's *Valse Folle*. Fauré now began to renounce the slightly overwritten, prettily decorative language of the 1880s and, in the final years of the century, moved towards the creation of a truly masterly style.

The various aspects of Fauré's musical language certainly merit profound analytical study. So far attention has understandably been focused for the most part on his harmony. In her 1954 thesis on Debussy and Fauré's harmonic practice,[11] Françoise Gervais drew up a long and well-researched catalogue of the characteristic harmonic habits to be found in Fauré's music. She also usefully drew attention to Gustave Lefèvre's *Traité d'harmonie*, a resumé of the musical theory taught at the Ecole Niedermeyer. Lefèvre refers in his introduction to the teaching he received from Pierre de Maleden, who passed on to him, as to Saint-Saëns, a very flexible conception of harmony deriving from the Abbé Vogler, from whom it had spread to influence a whole galaxy of composers including Weber and Meyerbeer. In fact Lefèvre explicitly adopts Vogler's system of figuring, which is concerned not with the intervals as related to the bass notes but with the degree of the scale on which the chord is placed; this at once introduces a conception of harmony that is linear and modal in spirit. He took his examples from Bach, Handel and Mozart, but also from Palestrina and Gesualdo, so that he was able to get across the point that the rules of classical harmony were relative and could bring to them all the nuances of an open and highly cultivated mind.

Right from the start he confronted his students with the variety of resources available in tonality. One of the first exercises he set them was to draw up a table of perfect triads (figured as 'I' throughout) on each degree of the scale and in all the keys. From here they passed on to various other kinds of chord including, in chapter 4, that of the 9th – which, on the part of a man who in 1855 had founded a Society for Artistic Progress and made Wagner an honorary member, should perhaps not surprise us – and when he wrote (p. 51), 'Every consonant or dissonant chord can be modified by alterations to the notes that compose it', he was instructing his pupils in a dynamic view of musical language far removed from the 'steady-state' view found in so many textbooks. Thanks to the eight 'figures of exceptional resolution' he taught them, these budding composers could allow themselves a fair number of harmonic audacities. As far as Fauré's harmony is concerned, chapter 14 of Lefèvre's book is particularly relevant. One of the essential aspects of Fauré's musical language, the fluctuating nature of his tonality, finds its source in Lefèvre's extraordinarily broad-minded attitude to the subject (p. 145):

Modulation can be either real or passing. It is real when, by its character especially and by its duration, it destroys the main key. It is passing when it depends on the main key and lasts only a short time.

Further on in the book Lefèvre sums up 'modulatory procedures' under four headings: chords held in common, chordal progressions, which 'lead to a great number of passing modulations' (p. 152), chromatic chords and 'foreign' chords. In this last category

you must explore the directions in which each note of the chord can move, either diatonically, chromatically or enharmonically, so as to form a new aggregation. You can then assign this to a certain key depending on how you designate the notes that compose it.

For example, in a C major chord the E can be considered as itself, the G as an F double sharp, an appogiatura of G sharp, and the C as an appogiatura of B natural. From here the chord can move either to B major, E major or G sharp major. According to this principle every chord can be thought of as consisting both of 'true' notes and of 'artificial' notes 'capable of assuming the harmonic interpretation of one's choice and of moving towards a resolution that conforms to it' (p. 159).

We can well imagine the Conservatoire purists regarding such an attitude as the depths of laxity. It is in direct opposition to the rigid system, widely taught in French and stemming from Rameau, according to which every alteration implies a change of tonality and every aggregation of notes is treated as an entity. Perhaps the most remarkable aspect of the Niedermeyer School's harmonic practice was its pragmatism. It was based on the notion of key feeling and its permanence at the perceptual, auditory level; it was in no way an abstract, *a priori* system but an *a posteriori* one based on the evidence of how human beings actually perceived music.

Fauré's personal musical language had its source in this approach and any attempt to analyse his works must take the above principles into account. In particular, his reliance on modality means that any investigation into his harmonic style must look at the horizontal lines that make up his progressions.

TONALITY AND MODALITY

Fauré's use of modality has been widely discussed and it has been generally felt that there is a direct relationship between this aspect of his language and his training as a church musician. Certainly he had in Louis Niedermeyer an expert teacher who insisted on a strictly modal accompaniment for plainchant and deplored the way the ecclesiastical modes were being contaminated by the tonal system;[12] and we may gain, perhaps, a slightly perverse relish from observing that his pupil's work of reform was precisely to open up the tonal system to the contamination of modality ...

It is important to realise that Fauré was not a 'modal composer' in the strict sense of the term. Unlike Koechlin or Messiaen he never wrote a single work that was entirely modal. On the other hand there are a large number that contain 'fragments and sometimes whole passages in a medieval mode', as Françoise Gervais says in her study (p. 25), and she cites one of the most beautiful examples of all, the opening of 'Prima verba', the second song of *Chanson d'Eve*, which is in the Mixolydian mode on G flat (Ex. 34).

Fauré was also fond of modal cadences, especially in the Lydian mode, and writers have often remarked on his preference for the plagal cadence – not so baldly conclusive as the perfect cadence whose tyranny was to attract fire from the young Debussy. In general we find in Fauré a kind of nostalgia for a pre-tonal world. His true precursors are not so much composers like Gounod, as Louis Couperin, Forqueray and his favourites among Renaissance musicians, Costeley, Janequin, Lassus ... The freedom of their harmonic progressions is born again in him, and frequently it is the ineluctable logic of a long melodic paragraph which lies at the root of his most striking harmonic audacities (or, by classical standards, of his solecisms): those items that appear in orthodox treatises under the headings 'false relations' and 'exceptional resolutions' are an integral part of

Ex. 34 *La Chanson d'Eve* (II) 'Prima verba'

Ex. 35 Nocturne no. 6

Fauré's musical grammar, not by any deliberate choice of his but by necessity.

In the marvellous descending progression in the Sixth Nocturne (Ex. 35), Fauré seems to find his way over immense, uncharted wastes with the sovereign ease of a man who has his goal always clearly before him.

From this we may well conclude that Fauré's musical language was essentially melodic rather than harmonic. Where Debussy invents new successions of chords, Fauré is thinking horizontally. Debussy's innovations in the domain of harmony are matched by Fauré's in that of syntax, born of an imaginative but always regulated blending of two areas, the modal and the tonal. Often he will be writing modally and then, at the last minute, slip in a leading note; or else in a clearly tonal passage the leading note will be discreetly blurred, a technique used around this time by Chabrier and later by Ravel. Within this tonal–modal ambience Fauré creates new scales and occasionally Hindu modes, in distant anticipation of Messiaen.[13] A good example of his modal writing is Eumée's beautiful aria in the first act of *Pénélope* (Ex. 36).

Here the scale is the Mixolydian mode with the fourth note sharpened, and we can also observe Fauré's predilection for whole-tone melodic lines. If he never explored this resource as thoroughly as Debussy did, nevertheless it forms the basis of 'Eau vivante' from *La Chanson d'Eve* and of the whole of the Fifth Impromptu. Like Debussy, Fauré was sensitive to the tritone's atonal power and was happy to use the interval as a pivot, escaping the attraction of the dominant and so avoiding any too strenuous affirmation of the tonic. Once again we may note that Fauré's partiality for whole-tone progressions has a melodic basis. The first clear example comes very early in his career in 'Lydia' (1870?) where the B natural of the Lydian mode is in a sense imposed by the song's title. This progression seems to have haunted the composer thereafter and we find it again among the recurring themes of *La Bonne chanson* (1892–4) and in the Océanides' chorus in the third act of *Prométhée* (1900) (see Ex. 33), p. 209.

Pushing still further our observation of this phenomenon of the engendering of one phrase by another, we come to see the notion of *harmonic drifting* as characteristic of Fauré's language; it takes account of the sliding action by which each tonal or modal colouring irresistibly leads to another, then to another, in a game of mirrors comparable to a kaleidoscope. The chorus of the Océanides, already cited, offers a good example of this harmonic drifting.

This is almost certainly the passage referred to by Emilie Girette when she noted in her diary that she had been invited by Fauré to come up to the

Ex. 36 *Pénélope* (I, 4)

organ loft one Sunday in April 1902, and that in response to her request to play 'some echoes of his music' he improvised on the phrase 'ne pleure pas, O Prométhée'.[14]

Ambivalence and flexibility are at the heart of Fauré's harmonic language, and nowhere more so than in his treatment of the third degree of the scale: frequently, in the course of a phrase, it hovers between major and minor, and in the final section of a piece in the minor mode (as at the end of the First Nocturne or the coda to the Concert Prelude to *Pénélope*) Fauré will introduce a brief diversion in the major, as if determined before the

Ex. 37 *Prométhée* (III, 4), Les Océanides

close to show the opposite side of the harmonic landscape. The very end of the Tenth Barcarolle provides the most extreme example of this flexible use of the third degree of the scale, as the composer seems to hesitate interminably between major and minor.

Such techniques as this are far from being arbitrary. By postponing the return of the tonic until the final note, as in the Twelfth Nocturne, Fauré keeps the listener in suspense right to the end, and by prolonging the ambivalence of the harmony he creates an atmosphere of brooding and uneasy mystery. We may recall the surprising opening to the third act of *Prométhée* where the clouds, gathered about the Titan's rock, seem slowly to disperse until Pandore is revealed. Still more ingenious in creating suspense is the prelude to the final chorus in *Caligula* where, over an extended dominant pedal on B flat, Fauré almost mournfully raises and lowers the D, hinting at resolutions in A flat or F minor which never come to anything. The answer to the mystery is provided by the descending phrase sung quietly by the chorus. The D flat has to be seen as a Mixolydian inflection imposed on the overall E flat major tonality. A few bars further on the same D flat is the basis for a modulation to G flat major, changing its function in a manner highly characteristic of the composer from being a flattened leading-note to being the new dominant (see Ex. 18, p. 142).

Fauré's cherished ambiguities often produce a kind of rocking motion which could be regarded as one of the constants in his aesthetic. The opening of the song 'Les Présents', op. 46 no. 1 (1887), is a good example. The mysteriously archaic spell it casts can be explained in terms of a repeated oscillation between the tonic F major and the 'foreign' key of A flat major (with sharpened fourth degree); the pivot note C changes from dominant to mediant. Lefèvre would say the piece is in F major and the chord in the second bar is based on the flattened third.

Fauré himself actually explained his notion of an expanded tonality – of a key coloured by modal inflections – in an analysis he made in 1906 for his son Philippe of the 'Air de danse' from *Caligula*:[15]

The whole piece is composed on a single theme in a mixture of G major and B minor. If you take this scale you find there elements of G major (G, A, B, D, E, F

Ex. 38

sharp) and elements of B minor (B, C sharp, E, E, F sharp, G) that's to say, the notes G, B and D are the tonic, the mediant and the dominant of the first, and the minor sixth, the tonic and the mediant of the second . . . But overall the piece stays entirely in G without any subsidiary theme either in the relative major or the relative minor (in this case E minor). That's how it is because that's how I wanted it to be. You can find a parallel example, also in an 'air de dance', in Berlioz's *Les Troyens*.[16] I wanted the dance to sound antique (something I realised only after I'd written it!) and as earlier composers didn't modulate in the same way we do I wrote it all in the scale I've described. Plainsong is full of similar passages.

In the works of his maturity Fauré was sometimes to push his explorations to the very limits of what tonality could contain. In the scherzo of the Second Quintet or the breathtaking introduction to the finale of the Second 'Cello Sonata, the ear searches in vain for the tonal signposts that Fauré is normally so careful to set up in the course of his wanderings. In *Pénélope* the tragic power of the great dialogue in Act II calls forth – no

Ex. 39 *Pénélope* (II, 2)

doubt justifiably in Fauré's view – tortuous, chromatic passages mixed with no less strange whole-tone progressions (Ex. 39).

Françoise Gervais points out an ultra chromatic, atonal passage in Eumée's part at the beginning of the same act (Ex. 40).

Ex. 40 *Pénélope* (II, 2)

These examples show Fauré contributing, albeit discreetly, to the break-down of a tonality which dates precisely from these years around 1910 when he was finishing his opera, and it is not without interest to compare his general conception of the language of music with Schoenberg's observation[17] that 'a harmonic texture presents itself to me in a more or less melodic fashion, like a succession of broken chords'. The essentially melodic nature of Fauré's language also made a great impression on Milhaud, who wrote of the Fifth Impromptu,[18]

Fauré's use of the whole-tone scale does not depend on the chord of the augmented fifth and does not confine the harmonies to just two chords of three notes each. He remains true to diatonic principles and employs the whole-tone scale to modulate, to escape from the tonic, and to return to it with a wealth of melodic imagination.

In the same memorial article Milhaud singles out among the piano works the fourth of the Nine Préludes op. 103 as a 'masterpiece of harmonic invention and of economy in the means employed'. The incomparable clarity of the first page sums up Fauré's art at its most perfect (Ex. 41).

Ex. 41 *Préludes*, op. 103, no. 4

Here Fauré makes liberal use of the tonal–modal–chromatic palette at his command, alternating F major or the Lydian mode with C major or A major, introducing parallel octaves (bars 15–16) with an insouciance to upset Théodore Dubois quite severely, but balancing the whole around solid perfect cadences – he might well argue that the music is in fact in F major throughout. The beautiful, singing counterpoint between melody and harmony makes us think of Bach. The tenor line spins a delicate, decorative thread and, supporting the melody, the bass twice climbs the F major scale (bars 9–10 and 13–14). The whole page could rightly be described as polyphonic variations around F major.

Fauré's evolution towards such freedom did not please Saint-Saëns. All the friendship and admiration he felt for his pupil could not prevent him admitting confidentially to Charles Lecocq[19] that he was puzzled by *Pénélope*:

I'm making a superhuman effort to get used to *Pénélope*. I'm unable to reach that state which allows one never to come to rest in any key, to gaze without blenching at parallel fifths, at sevenths following each other in conjunct motion, and at chords which wait in vain for a resolution that never arrives ... Fauré has placed himself instantly at the head of the 'young Turks', and a long way above them. It's very clever. But what an example for pupils who see their director constantly breaking the rules they're taught!

And indeed any listener brought up on a diet of classical harmony might write off as 'false' the oddly beautiful progressions of 'Dans la Nymphée', the fifth song of the cycle *Le Jardin clos* (Ex. 42).

Ex. 42 *Le Jardin clos* (V), 'Dans la nymphée'

Of this supremely original music, written immediately after *Pénélope*, Saint-Saëns had in the end to admit to Fauré that he understood nothing.[20] Elsewhere Fauré's dissonances express pathos. At the end of the Eleventh

Nocturne, written in 1913 in memory of Pierre Lalo's[21] wife Noémi, the repeated chords, although bristling with minor seconds, still sing wonderfully; while in the slow movement of the second Violin Sonata (1916) the theme, at its reprise, grates harshly as though the notes were under the influence of some evil spirit (see Exx. 43 and 44).

Ex. 43 Nocturne no. 11

(Molto moderato)

The originality of Fauré's harmonic language is still today a major factor in alienating some listeners, who see its flexibility perhaps as being that much too ingenious, an endless patchwork of keys, the product of an unhealthy obsession with subtlety.

In its more extreme manifestations of the years after 1910, like the passage from *Le Jardin clos* quoted above, Fauré's music could be defined as the art of deviation, in the manner of the convoluted phrases of Proust

Ex. 44 Second Sonata for Violin and Piano (II) – piano part

or the carefully worked arabesques of Hector Guimard.[22] There are times, it must be admitted, when Fauré gets carried away by his own harmonic virtuosity and through excess falls into the trap of a somewhat gratuitous voluptuousness: certain passages in *Caligula*, for instance, or in the Fourth Nocturne must be classed as self-indulgent and they are, it seems to me, a product of that same perverse mentality evident in his remark to Saint-Saëns as a young man:[23] 'I played for Mass and Vespers today on an organ to match the worst you've ever come across: I perpetrated the most outrageous tricks a refined imagination could dream up.'

Some highly sensitive ears have found Fauré's melting harmonies practically impossible to bear. Poulenc, for example, wrote that 'physically his music is, for me, intolerable' and went on to quote the end of 'J'ai presque peur' from *La Bonne chanson* (Ex. 45) and to admit 'the modulation on "que je vous aime" literally gives me pain'.[24]

Fauré himself called *La Bonne chanson* 'extravagant',[25] but this was not necessarily a criticism. After all, in a letter to René Lenormand in 1912 on the subject of his book *Etude sur l'harmonie moderne*,[26] he wrote:

I would have been proud if you'd quoted the two successive sevenths in 'Prison' ('La cloche...doucement tinte'). This quirk is now common enough, but I think at the time I wrote it it was new. And then there are the harmonic progressions (or non-progressions) in 'Le Parfum impérissable'. But I'm not complaining – you've certainly done a good job of turning me into a prize specimen.

Ex. 45 *La Bonne chanson* (V), 'J'ai presque peur, en vérité'

RHYTHM

For those who follow Gaston Bachelard in defining rhythm as 'an irregularity, a temporal disorder',[27] Fauré's rhythm may seem of little interest. The movement of his music is above all regular, to the point where we can speak of an approach to a continuum of sound. Like Nature as seen by the eighteenth-century philosophers, Fauré's music abhors a vacuum. 'It is, first and foremost, continuous, and more so than any music before it', in the words of Vladimir Jankélévich.[28] Olivier Messiaen, in his famous class of analysis at the Paris Conservatoire, took this continuity as a sufficient description of Fauré's place in the historical perspective. Nothing, indeed, could be further removed from Messiaen's abrupt blocks of sound and rhythmic intricacies than Fauré's insistence on a linear flow: one exults with Dionysus, the other sings with Apollo ...

An analysis of Fauré's output shows it to be one long essay on the principle of continuity: from the litanistic effect of the 'In Paradisum' in the Requiem to the slow, contemplative successions of chords in so many of his finest songs – 'Le Secret', 'Le Parfum impérissable', 'Dans la nymphée', 'Diane Séléné'; from the majestic flow of the finale of *Pénélope* to the lyricism of the *Elégie*; from the Mendelssohnian naïvety of the 'Fileuse' in *Pelléas et Mélisande* to the almost hypnotic incantations of 'Les Présents' or 'Nocturne' or the witty variations that make up the finale of the D minor Quintet.

It is worth stressing that the regularity in Fauré's music is one of pulse – this provides the strict framework for his diversification of rhythms and accents. The Fauréan *cantabile* is in no sense amorphous repetition; it is constantly alive with shifting accents and competing rhythms and we might reasonably describe the composer's practice as the art of displacement, especially in his piano music where the style and indeed the technical difficulties recall those found in Schumann and Brahms. This mannerism appears as early on as the reprise of the First Nocturne and is developed particularly in Fauré's late works where it often takes the form of expressive delays in the counterpoint – in the Ninth Prelude, for example, or the Thirteenth Nocturne (see Ex. 46).

Ex. 46 Nocturne no. 13

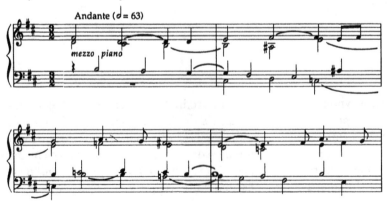

Example 46 shows that in speaking of the 'displacement' of the hands I am referring to something inherent in the music, imagined and written down by the composer, and not of some effect or pseudo-rubato introduced by an interpreter. Such things provoked Fauré's total condemnation. Certain pieces, like the Twelfth Nocturne, the tenth variation from op. 73 or the Fifth Barcarolle are, in effect, based on this principle of displaced writing with the result that, when it is kept up for several pages at a time, it paradoxically creates a feeling of continuity. This leads me to the conclusion that when critics deplore Fauré's 'lack of rhythm', it is not so much any rhythmic poverty that upsets them as the fact that there are no breaks in the texture.

The chief drawback of these regularly displaced accents is undoubtedly that when they continue for too long they make the music sound as though it is limping. But for the most part Fauré uses the technique to produce some telling effects, like the marvellously expressive opening bars of the Ninth Barcarolle (Ex. 47).

Ex. 47 Barcarolle no. 9

One could also quote in this context the Eighth Barcarolle, a celebration of dotted rhythms which last right through to the coda above an arrestingly broken texture. A further aspect of Fauré's art is his habit of sounding the bass on weak beats, either delaying it to create a cross-accent or prolonging it to produce syncopation. Some of his finest pages of piano writing contain delayed bass octaves, and their majestic effect allows us a glimpse

Ex. 48 Nocturne no. 12

of what his organ improvisations must have been like: the Sixth, Seventh and Twelfth Nocturnes all demand to be quoted (see Ex. 48).

In his songs, cross-accents and syncopation tend to take on a particular significance, as expressing intense emotion – for example the wild breathlessness of … 'J'ai presque peur en vérité' from *La Bonne chanson* or the hesitations of an overwhelming reticence in 'Je me poserai sur ton cœur' from *Le Jardin clos*.

By and large triple metre is his favourite. The Barcarolles espouse compound time (6/8 and 9/8) but elsewhere we find less usual time signatures such as 3/2 and 4/2 in the Sixth Nocturne or the Sixth Prélude, 5/4 in the Second Prélude or the even more uncommon 18/8 in the Seventh Nocturne. The most striking aspect, though, of Fauré's rhythmic practice is undoubtedly his characteristic superimposition of binary and ternary, done with a naturalness that reflects his ambidextrous gifts as a pianist. For example, in the central section of the Second Impromptu the melody and the barcarolle-like accompaniment seem to belong to two quite distinct rhythmic worlds (see Ex. 49).

In the Fifth Prélude the opposition of two different metres creates a continuous disturbance which grows more and more furious.

Ex. 49 Impromptu no. 2

From the rhythmic point of view, then, Fauré shows himself a worthy successor to Renaissance composers like Le Jeune and Sermisy and their colleagues who went back to Roman and Greek poetry in an attempt to establish rhythmic variety within a regular metre, producing, in the case of Janequin and Costeley, a veritable jigsaw of interlocking rhythms. Fauré's search for ways of varying the rhythm of a given melodic idea and his concern for bringing about change inside an overall continuity show how deeply he was influenced by his studies of Renaissance music, and the same may be said of his use of polyphony.

POLYPHONY

His fellow composers in France – d'Indy, Saint-Saëns, even César Franck – often seem to have turned to imitative writing as a way out of some compositional difficulty, as a kind of instant repair when their inspiration broke down. With Fauré however, the appearance of *fugato* is so natural that the ear alone sometimes has a job to detect it. In the first movement of the G minor Piano Quartet, for instance, the monolithic exposition is followed by a passage of rhythmic polyphony (bars 44–8) based on the viola motif, then by a *fugato* on the second main theme (bars 119–29): the passionate intensity of this passage takes us a long way from

the academic textbooks. Fauré's acute feeling for polyphony even manifests itself in the accompaniments of his songs, as in the descending bass
line of 'Nell' which sets off the upward thrust of the voice part so splendidly. We often find, in the songs of the second and third Hamelle volumes, a
discreet but effective third part, complementing the bass and the vocal line,
occupying itself with ritornellos when the voice is silent and in the course
of the verses themselves producing a dialogue with it: such a third part
runs right through 'les Roses d'Ispahan' (1884), 'Clair de lune' (1887) and
'Arpège' (1897), while in 'La Rose' (1890) it takes on a *concertante*
character later developed in *La Bonne chanson*. Fauré was to go further
still in *La Chanson d'Eve*, writing a complete song cycle in a strict
polyphonic style.

As he got older, Fauré came to have a marked predilection for canonic
writing. He used it to generate a feeling of immense power at the appearance of the two Olympians at the end of *Prométhée* and again for one of

Ex. 50 *Pénélope* (I, end)

Fin du 1ᵉʳ Acte

the most expressive moments in *Pénélope*, in the first act finale (see Ex. 50).

Fauré thought naturally in canonic fashion and the device usually appears in the earliest sketches. He employed it most frequently in the finales of his chamber works where it is free of any cold, severe, academic inflections. In the two Quintets, the 'Cello Sonatas, the Second Violin Sonata and the Trio the canonic dialogue seems to arise spontaneously, then, after a moment in the limelight, to melt into the flux of some different texture. There is a particularly apt example in the finale of the First 'Cello Sonata (Ex. 51).

Ex. 51 First Sonata for 'Cello and Piano

Fauré's piano works even contain masterly passages of four-part counterpoint; and here I am thinking not just of the two early fugues published
among the *Pièces brèves*, but of the deeply moving final variation of the
Thème et variations and of the last of the Nine Préludes. In the sixth of
these Fauré also takes on the challenge of writing a canon at the octave
from the first note to the last and the result is both expressive and original.
As for the Thirteenth Nocturne, it is a test for the finest pianist to keep the
lines of the counterpoint distinct: each part has its own life and shape in a
melodic polyphony that Fauré shares with Bach.

MELOS

It is only right to emphasise how rich in melody Fauré's music is: not just
his songs, where the details and structure of the texts naturally had to be
taken into account, but his music in general and his instrumental works in
particular. I feel a lot of work remains to be done on Fauré's melodic style.
For the moment I would like simply to suggest some lines of enquiry which
later scholars might care to pursue – or to abandon and strike out on other,
and perhaps more enlightening, paths.

Fauré's chamber music is a particularly rich quarry of melodic ideas and
many of them conform to a specific model. The finale of the Second Violin
Sonata provides a good example (Ex. 52).

A melodic cell begins on the mediant (I A) and is then transposed on to
the tonic (I B). This is followed by the consequent on the supertonic (II A),
then transposed on to the sharpened subdominant (II B). A concluding
motif, returning to the mediant as a starting-point, consists of the first
three notes of the initial cell, first an octave higher (III A), then an octave
lower (III B).

IA	IB	IIA	II B	III A	III B
4 bars	4 bars	2 bars	2 bars	1 bar	1 bar

Ex. 52 Second Sonata for Violin (Finale)

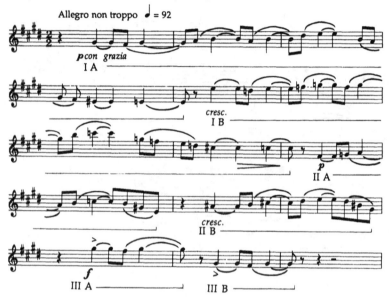

The nonchalant grace of the theme is thus based on a firm structure
which will support the movement's further development.

Paul Dukas used to say, in his class at the Conservatoire, 'When Fauré
begins a sonata movement he has no idea what will be happening on page
five.' To which one might reply, 'Yes and so much the better.' Fauré's gifts
of surprise and continual inventiveness are all the more impressive because, no matter what daring flights of fancy he embarks on, his technique
is equal to the task.

Proust admitted that Fauré's Ballade for piano was one of the inspirations behind the 'little phrase' which torments Swann, and he describes it
as follows:

This time he had clearly distinguished a phrase soaring for a few moments above
the waves of sound. Instantly it had held out to him the promise of delights which
he had never dreamt of before hearing it, to which he felt that phrase alone
possessed the key, and he was filled with a kind of unknown love.

It led him in a slow rhythm first this way, then that, and then away towards a
deep happiness that was at once precise and yet beyond his understanding. And
suddenly, as he was preparing to follow it still further, it paused for a moment and
abruptly changed direction and, faster now, in a mood of gentle, unyielding
melancholy, it bore him away to unknown vistas.

Ex. 53 *Ballade*, first movement

This beautiful theme, the archetype of Fauré's melody as it was around 1880, is made up of four sections (see Ex. 53):

I   basic melodic cell
II condensed form of I, combining the descending fifth with the dotted rhythm
III evocative echo of I, now in the new colouring of A major
IV climax and conclusion of the phrase in a long, semiquaver descent, then floating up again to the treble register 'in a mood of gentle, unyielding melancholy', as Proust so accurately describes it.

One could also think of it in rhetorical terms, with the first and last sections in the affirmative, interrupted by the interrogatives of the third section and ending with a magnificent peroration. It is simultaneously continuous and fragmented, and in the way variations are woven into it and time is given for rhapsodic interpolations it recalls Liszt's Concertos or his *Faust Symphony*. But Fauré's eloquence is his own, without a hint of Lisztian bravura: the theme begins in *chiaroscuro* and ends *pianissimo*.

Generally speaking a fall of a fifth or fourth followed by a rising scale is, with Fauré, a sign of impassioned lyricism. We find it in the 'Nocturne' from *Shylock*, in the song 'Soir', in the *Romance* for 'cello and at the beginning of the First Quintet — a kind of emptying out of the self at a moment of intense emotion (see Ex. 54). Melodic formulae like this seem to have haunted Fauré's unconscious over long periods. We have seen earlier (chapter 5, p. 71) the transformations of the 'Viardot theme'.

Ex. 54 *Shylock* (Nocturne)

'Soir'

Romance in A

First Quintet

In contrast to this suavity, the combination of rising octave and major second is, with Fauré, a sign of tragedy and grandeur. It occurs first in the solemn theme that opens the C minor Quartet (1879) and is then developed in the years 1907–18 with Ulysses' 'royal theme' in *Pénélope* (1907–13), the second theme of the *Fantaisie* for piano and orchestra (1918) and the 'Pastorale' from *Masques et bergamasques* (see ex. 55).

Ex. 55 *Pénélope* (royal theme of Ulysse)

Fantaisie for piano and orchestra

Masques et bergamasques, 'Pastorale'

The evolution of Fauré's melos goes firmly in two directions: an expansion of the intervals, and a tightening and strengthening of the line. The scope of this evolution can be seen simply by comparing the smooth cantilena of the Fourth Nocturne with the spiky, athletic outline of the *Fantaisie* for piano and orchestra (see Exx. 56 and 57).

Ex. 56   Nocturne no. 4

Ex. 57 *Fantaisie* for piano

   In the field of piano music the Barcarolles demonstrate a similar pattern
for development, from the undulating lines of the early ones to the broad
movement of the fifth and the unashamed virtuosity of the Eighth. But it is
never possible to reduce Fauré's work to just a few basic principles. The
continuously rich renewal of his inspiration always breaks free of any
categories the analyst might like to impose on it. The vehement, disruptive
opening of the First 'Cello Sonata (1917) is in fact based on the initial
Allegro of the D minor Symphony (1884); the Twelfth Barcarolle (1915)
returns to the simple *cantabile* style of the very earliest ones and even of the
Romances sans paroles of the 1860s, though in a very different harmonic
language, it is true. The range of Fauré's vocal works in general expanded
until about 1880 (the extreme point is reached with 'Les Berceaux', as
Marie-Claire Beltrando[29] has pointed out) and then contracted again,
especially after 1900, finally reaching the almost parlando style of *Mirages*
(1919).
   As for the strengthening of the lines, we can see this process at work in
the corrections Fauré made to themes from early works when he came to
re-use them later in life. A good example in his work on the two themes of
the Violin Concerto (1878–9) which he put into his String Quartet forty-
five years later (Ex. 58).
   Even if Fauré disowned his two symphonies and his Violin Concerto, it
is significant that he rescued the basic thematic material for use in later
works[30] – it was not so much the melodic style he found fault with as the
orchestration. The only material he kept from the D minor Symphony
were two first violin parts, no doubt because they contained most of the
themes. So, although much has been said on the subject of Fauré's harmo-

Ex. 58 Violin Concerto

String Quartet

Violin Concerto

Allegro

cantabile

String Quartet

cantando

nies, in my opinion his melodic writing is just as important and his whole
evolution is guided by the horizontal concerns of counterpoint.

It has been necessary in this chapter to separate the elements of Fauré's
musical language for analytical purposes, but it must be insisted on that
these elements in fact have an extraordinary coherence. The regular pulse
in the rhythmic field is the counterpart of tonality in the harmonic one: it
permits any number of minor, temporary displacements and irregularities
just as the tonality is widened by harmonic wanderings and false trails.
Fauré's love of accenting weak beats obviously goes hand in hand with his
propensity for modulating to chords built on the so-called weak degrees of
the scale.

As for his rhythmic continuity, it has direct links with his melodic and
harmonic practice. His questing, exploratory harmonic spirit had to exercise itself inside the confines of a regular metre if the structure of his
argument was not to fall apart. No less clear is the link between rhythm
and melody. Fauré was too deeply committed to linear composition to
interrupt the curve in any abrupt or unseemly fashion; like Verlaine, he
'hates the movement that disrupts the lines', and in general his manner
may be compared with that of the friezes that run round the pediments of
Greek temples – the hurly-burly of life contained within a rectilinear
frame.

To finish this chapter I should like to touch on the curious question of Fauré's attitude to the orchestra and to raise the still more delicate one of who was responsible for his orchestrations.

ORCHESTRATION

Some writers have claimed that Fauré's orchestral output was more or less non-existent, to the extent that he was totally uninterested in this form of expression. Such claims need to be seriously qualified. Fauré was indeed interested in the orchestra and tried his hand at it several times during the first twenty years of his creative life. During his time at the Niedermeyer School, he followed the courses in 'instrumentation' given by Gustave Lefèvre, the School's director. The composition prize was awarded, as we know, for a religious work with orchestra. Perhaps it is significant that Fauré won his prize with the *Cantique de Jean Racine* even though he did not have the time to orchestrate it. The work was soon to be given a distinctly modest orchestral garb in the form of a string quintet and a harmonium. During his stay in Rennes, the young organist had played an *Intermezzo* for orchestra (1868), which demonstrated at least some ambitions in this direction. He was encouraged in these by the example of his teacher Saint-Saëns who by then had written no less than four symphonies.[31] Fauré's Symphony in F major or Suite for Orchestra op. 20, which was performed by Edouard Colonne on 16 May 1874 in Paris, was a more or less happy succession of his first orchestral movements, but it had a rather cool reception and Fauré decided not to publish it. The first movement, published later in a piano duet transcription by Léon Boëllmann as the Allegro symphonique op. 68, shows no striking evidence of originality, and only the Gavotte found favour in the eyes of the composer, who used it again half a century later in *Masques et bergamasques*.

The Violin Concerto op. 14, of 1878–9, was likewise withdrawn very soon after its first performances at the Société nationale. Carried along by the extraordinary enthusiasm for symphonies during the following decade, Fauré completed a Symphony in D minor op. 40 in 1884, which was given by Colonne on 15 March 1885. It went the same way as the First Symphony, but this did not prevent the composer from starting a third one, mentioned in a letter of September 1887.[32]

The multiplicity of these unsuccessful ventures is something of a problem, but it testifies at least to Fauré's continuing interest in the idea. This is confirmed by a letter he wrote to his wife on 27 August 1903 at the time he was returning to work on the First Quintet:[33] 'Thank you for your reaction to this new chamber music project; you are right to appreciate the genre as you do. It constitutes, together with symphonic music, what music really is and the most sincere manifestation of a composer's personality.' Among other things, the fact that Fauré left his largest symphonic works unfinished tends to highlight his ambition in this field on the one hand and his ultimate dissatisfaction with it on the other.

He appears to have had some difficulty in thinking of his music in orchestral terms and, as with his pupil Ravel, most of the works he wrote for chorus or instruments with orchestra began life with a piano accompaniment, including the *Berceuse*, the *Elégie*, the *Pavane*, the *Madrigal* for four voices, *Les Djinns*, the *Ballade* and the *Fantaisie*.

As for his purely orchestral works, Fauré often conceived them in the abstract, sketching them out first of all on three or four staves, what is known as a 'particelle'. This is the case with *Pelléas et Mélisande* and with part of *Prométhée*, and it explains why the vocal scores of his two operatic works give only a rough idea of the orchestral version; they were made from the particelle and not from the full score.

Fauré's orchestral writing shows clearly the influence of his double upbringing as a pianist and as an organist. The latter can be heard in the importance given to the bass lines (on 'cellos, often divided, and double basses), taking the place of the pedal, and in the fairly thick wind writing which reminds us of mixtures and of reeds often operating in juxtaposed blocks. Fauré the pianist can be heard in his preference for the strings, which recall the neutrality of the piano in their transparency and homogeneity, as well as in the frequent use of arpeggios in the viola and violin parts and in the use of the harp, one of Fauré's favourite instruments. We should not make too much of this difficulty in breaking free of the two keyboard instruments – it has been true of many other composers, such as Mendelssohn, Schumann, Franck and Liszt – and by the same token we must stand out against affirmations that Fauré loathed the job of orchestration.

The letters he wrote during his work on *Pénélope* show how enthusiastic he could become over this aspect. Not that he was always at ease in writing for the orchestra. He might derive 'enormous pleasure' from orchestrating his opera, as he wrote in 1912,[34] but he also had difficulties:[35] 'I'm already back at work and I have thirty completed pages in front of me. But when I think there'll probably be a *thousand*! Another nine hundred and fifty to go! And they don't run off the pen! I often have to think for hours about four bars!'

Fauré's orchestral manuscripts, which are mostly in the Bibliothèque Nationale, show numerous traces of his indecisiveness in the form of corrections, notes written over other notes, lines added or crossed out and amendments pasted in. The orchestral score of the Requiem, for instance, contains evidence of four or five different stages in the orchestration, even if the musical substance remained practically unchanged.

In addition to these problems in mastering the orchestra, Fauré had to suffer the incomprehension of critics faced with his works in the medium: 'M. Gabriel Fauré's symphony was received rather coldly', wrote Arthur Pougin in *Le Ménestrel*,[36] reviewing the Suite in F, op. 20. 'Personally I found it languid and a little cold, and I did not feel it was particularly inspired; the gavotte which forms the third movement is pleasant, nonetheless, and prettily coloured.' As for the Symphony in D minor, the Andante was generally appreciated, but there was doubt about the Finale, even though it had been hurriedly modified by the composer at Colonne's request.[37] Edmond Stoullig found it 'confused, lacking in clear ideas and with a full, colourless orchestration'.[38] The same reproach was levelled at the opening Allegro of the Violin Concerto, which the anonymous critic of the *Revue et Gazette musicale*[39] judged to be 'dull, monotonous and ineffective'.

These problems explain why Fauré did not make a frontal attack on the field of orchestral music, and he had further difficulties with his deafness which made orchestral sounds particularly painful to listen to. 'The singing voice comes through best', he wrote in 1919. 'But the orchestra is just a painful racket.'[40]

All things considered, it is understandable that Fauré should sometimes have handed over the task of orchestration to pupils or friends, either completely or in part, though he would sometimes revise and correct their preparatory sketches if necessary. Fauré was far from being alone in this practice, which was followed by many well-known composers,[41] but it has thrown suspicion in a totally unwarranted fashion on all his orchestral works. He was indubitably responsible for the orchestration of the considerable amount of orchestral music which he wrote between 1870 and 1895, as we can tell both from the manuscripts and from his letters. There is the further practical point that, until he was appointed as a professor of composition at the Conservatoire in 1896, he had no pupil to hand advanced enough to be entrusted with this kind of work: it was Messager who orchestrated most of the *Messe des pêcheurs de Villerville*, Koechlin who was responsible for the original theatre version of *Pelléas et Mélisande*, Emile Vuillermoz who put the finishing touches to the score of *Le Voile du bonheur* (still unpublished), and Roger Ducasse who transcribed *Prométhée* from its original, giant version into one for ordinary symphony orchestra. In the case of *Pénélope*, Fauré finished the score with the help of the unknown Fernand Pécoud and in his last years he turned to the composer and Prix de Rome winner Marcel Samuel-Rousseau, who orchestrated the *Fantaisie* and two pieces from *Masques et bergarmasques* (the Gavotte and the song 'Le Plus doux chemin') (see table pp. 260–1).

But these works for which Fauré relied on a collaborator are far out-numbered by those which he orchestrated himself: the Ballade, the two symphonies and the Violin Concerto, the choral piece *Les Djinns*, *Madrig-al*, the *Pavane*, the songs 'Clair de lune', 'Les Roses d'Ispahan', 'La Chan-son du pêcheur', 'En prière', the cantata *La Naissance de Vénus*, the Requiem (in its original version at least) and the two sets of incidental music for *Caligula* and *Shylock* ... Altogether this comes to more than a thousand orchestral pages – enough for us to judge his abilities as an orchestrator. We may, and I think with some justice, deplore the excessive sobriety of Fauré's orchestrations, but we cannot call them mediocre. It is not hard to call to mind the profound seductiveness of some of the lighter moments, like the flute solos in the *Pavane*, in *Caligula* and in *Pénélope*. Charles Koechlin was surely right when he observed that the orchestral version of 'Clair de lune' 'cannot match the piano's contribution in these wonderful pages', but the same writer gave it as his opinion also that 'in the Requiem, the deliberately extreme sobriety does not engender monotony in the least' and that 'the orchestral accompaniment in the Ballade sup-ports the piano in a balanced, discreet, even poetic fashion; and there are some charmingly blended sonorities'.[42]

Koechlin's reservations over the orchestration of *Pénélope* (see Chapter 14, p. 333), tactfully expressed, drew from Fauré the humble response that 'I know myself well enough to have taken note of this failing more than once – a failing of nature, obviously and one that I'm afraid I shall not now have the time to put right!'[43] According to Roger Ducasse,[44] Debussy admired the orchestration of *Pénélope* and compared it with that of *Parsifal*. Its transparency and its reliance on string tone brought it very close to the sound he had tried to capture in *Jeux*, first performed at the Théâtre des Champs-Elysées five days after Fauré's opera.[45] But Poulenc went somewhat beyond what one might expect of such a fine composer in describing Fauré's orchestration as a 'leaden overcoat' and as 'in-strumental mud'.[46]

Certainly, by the time of *Pénélope*, Fauré could no longer fully appreci-ate the actual sound of his music, and in a letter to his wife he complained that he had never heard a note of his opera.[47] When *Masques et bergamas-ques* was receiving its first performances at Monte Carlo, he wrote:[48] 'The orchestra here is marvellous and, *apart from myself*, many people have been in their seventh heaven listening to it. All I can be sure of is the *care* taken by the conductor.'

My own feeling is that during the early part of his long creative life Fauré could have become a brilliant orchestrator *if he had really wanted to* – I am thinking in particular of his full-bodied, supple and lively orchestration in the finale of his *Shylock* of 1889, which contains some chromatic descents on the horns that look forward to the poetic sound world of Debussy.[49] It could well be, then, that the sobriety of Fauré's orchestration is not the result so much of any inability as of a definite aesthetic attitude, and we have a right to find fault with this only when we have taken the trouble to analyse it and understand it.

It would in any case be more accurate to speak, not of orchestration, but of instrumentation, since it is obvious that the idea of timbre was not a determining one in Fauré's musical thinking. Fauré viewed the orchestra as a vast, rather complicated instrument, to which music conceived in the abstract had then to be adapted. In the same way that his sources of inspiration exclude exoticism or any literary or philosophical programme, so was he suspicious of the attractions of super-brilliant orchestration. In his article on *Salome*,[50] he wrote of Richard Strauss's orchestral techniques:

This facility, this prodigious dexterity, is not without its drawbacks, and the mobility of the music, the fleeting nature of the orchestral effects – always novel, strange and startling, but barely heard before they are replaced by others – these together end up by producing a continual dazzle that is tiring not only to the mind but – absurd as it may seem – to the eyes.

Fauré's faithful pupil Roger Ducasse gives a clear indication of what line his teacher took in his Conservatoire composition classes:

As for the picturesque, that source of seduction which sometimes lies too readily to hand, I have to say that Fauré did not attach a primary importance to it. It ought to be possible to produce an orchestration, he thought, without resorting to glockenspiels, celestas, xylophones, bells or certain electric instruments.[51]

Fauré's phobia with regard to orchestral effects was all the stronger because such effects seemed to him often to be used by his contemporaries to mask a feebleness of inspiration ... and even by some of his predecessors. In an article in *Le Figaro*[52] he made so bold as to describe Berlioz's Requiem as 'a work marked equally by a taste for grand dramatic effects and by an indifference to religious music – or to any music'; and likewise he deplored the fact that in Gustave Charpentier's *Julien*[53]

Table 2 Fauré's orchestral works[1]

Opus	Title	Date	Fauré[a]	[Fauré][b]	Collaborators
unpub.	Super flumina	1863	*		
4 no. 1	Chanson du pêcheur, 2nd version	1894?	*		
10 no. 2	Tarentelle (orchestration unpub.)	c 1875			A. Messager
11	Cantique de Racine, 2nd version	1866		*	
	Cantique de Racine, 3rd version	1905		*	
12	Les Djinns	1875?	*		
14	Violin concerto	1878–9	*		
16	Berceuse for violin, 2nd version	1880		*	
19	Ballade for piano, 2nd version	1881	*		
20	Symphony (or Suite) in F	1865–73	*		
24	Élégie for 'cello, 2nd version	1895	*		
28	Romance for violin, 2nd version	1919			Philippe Gaubert
unpub.	Messe de Villerville, 2nd version (Fauré et Messager)	1882	* (1/4)		A. Messager (3/4)
29	La Naissance de Vénus	1895	*		
35	Madrigal for four voices, 2nd version	1883	*		
39 no. 4	Les Roses d'Ispahan, 2nd version	1891	*		
40	Symphony in D minor, unpub.	1884		*	
46 no. 2	Clair de lune, 2nd version	1888		*	
	En Prière	1890	*		
unpub.	La Passion	1890		*	
48	Requiem, 1st version	1888–93	*		
	Requiem, 2nd version	1900			Roger-Ducasse?
50	Pavane	1887	*		
52	Caligula	1888	*		

57	*Shylock*, 1st version	1889	*	
	Shylock, 2nd version	1890	*	
80	*Pelléas et Mélisande*, 1st version	1898	*	Ch. Kœchlin
	Pelléas et Mélisande, 2nd version	1900		based on Kœchlin
82	*Prométhée*, 1st version	1900	*	Ch. Eustace et Fauré
	Prométhée, 2nd version	1914–16		Roger-Ducasse
88	*Le Voile du bonheur*, unpub.	1901		E. Vuillermoz
lacks no.	*Jules César* (based on *Caligula*)	1905		?
lacks no.	*Pénélope*	1907–13	*(4/5)	F. collaboration Fernand Pécoud (1/5)
111	*Fantaisie for piano*	1918		Marcel Samuel-Rousseau
112	*Masques et Bergamasques*	1919	*(3/4)	F. collaboration Marcel Samuel-Rousseau

a Definitely Fauré: autograph manuscript preserved.
b Probably Fauré, because of certain documents, but in the absence of the orchestral score in manuscript, the authenticity cannot be confirmed.

1 This table of Fauré's orchestral works, indicating the orchestrator of each work, appeared originally in my article 'Les Orchestrations de Gabriel Fauré: Légende et vérité', *Revue musicale suisse*, September–October 1975, pp. 243–8. I have made one or two corrections. The dates are those of orchestration.

in the pseudo-religious scene of the Temple of Beauty, the music is bound, thanks to the grandiloquence of the libretto, to become solemn and elevated and to reach the heights in its effects: it unquestionably does this but by means that rely less on melodic and harmonic invention than on the choice and accumulation of sounds from an extended orchestra and from a chorus on tiers that stretched up into the flies. This kind of effect has an impact more on the nerves than on the mind or the heart.

Despite such severe strictures, Fauré was able to appreciate the orchestration of some innovative works when he detected in them some richness of expression and originality of thought. In the case of *Salome* he was honest enough to say: 'the above criticisms are aimed not, as I see it, at weaknesses, merely at musical means with which I cannot sympathise, within a work which is vigorously conceived and written with a skill and virtuosity of the first order, and which contains many impressive moments'.[54] Roger-Ducasse may again be quoted: 'even if Fauré enjoyed the regular murmuring of the *Rouet d'Omphale*, the rattle of bones in the *Danse macabre* and the headlong gallop in *Phaéton*, the picturesque for him did no more than add passing colour and did not touch on the real interest of the work – which, sometimes, the picturesque was capable of hiding from him.[55]

We may have our doubts, naturally, about the sort of musical Jansenism that realises in twentieth-century terms the most extreme conceptions of Bach's *Art of Fugue* which the composer imagined without reference to any particular instrument. It could be suggested that in this matter Fauré was influenced by his strict musical education, by the cult of 'music for its own sake' taught by Niedermeyer and Gustave Lefèvre, using examples from Bach or Lassus at a time when Berlioz, Meyerbeer and Wagner were making their orchestral innovations. Even so, André Messager, one of the best orchestrators of the period, had also been a pupil at the school ...

The truth is that Fauré's sober style of orchestration mirrors his artistic aims: to express the most elevated sentiments by the simplest means, so as to reach, in some form, *the naked flesh of emotion*.

12   Pomp and circumstance

The suppleness and freedom that characterise Fauré's own musical language are also the hallmarks of his composition teaching. We have no evidence as to what methods he used in the innumerable piano, solfège and harmony lessons he gave to the well-connected young, either individually or in groups of bourgeois girls who had nothing better to do with their time. Only from his composition classes do we learn the secrets of Fauré the teacher. As for the other lessons, given from necessity not choice, they obviously took up time and energy he might otherwise have devoted to his own creative work.

Fauré did give a few private composition lessons (to François Berthet, for example, and Fernand Alphen) but mostly he did so within the confines of an institution. From 1871 he taught at the Niedermeyer School during its summer retreat at Cours-sous-Lausanne. This first experience worked on his artistic scrupulousness to produce a number of doubts and question-marks about his fitness for the task. When Saint-Saëns began to press him to apply for the composition class at the Conservatoire left vacant by Ernest Guiraud's death in 1892, Fauré replied:

I too have looked carefully at my claims to this post and, apart from certain basic truths, I have not found any sign of a *method*. I've already taught several young pupils and I recall that my teaching has varied to suit their individual natures, not really an appropriate system for a large class where the lips must not pronounce anything that is not objectively verifiable![1]

We have already seen how Fauré finally consented to apply for Guiraud's post and was violently rejected by the Conservatoire's Director, Ambroise Thomas. Four years later Théodore Dubois succeeded him, Massenet resigned and Fauré replaced him. 'What would Massenet say, seeing me sitting in his chair?' Fauré asked his pupil Roger-Ducasse, with a mixture of malice and satisfaction.[2]

Like Messiaen's composition class half a century later, Fauré's has gone

263

down in history as containing the most brilliant composers and musicians of the younger generation: Ravel, Koechlin, Roger-Ducasse, Florent Schmitt and Georges Enesco. Fauré's spell lay as much in his presence as in anything he actually said, and in this respect, as Roland-Manuel points out in his biography of Ravel, his class was comparable with Mallarmé's Tuesday salon. Some of Enesco's reminiscences reach us through the medium of a, no doubt somewhat exaggerated, article by the journalist René Kerdyk:

Fauré used to arrive at the class three quarters of an hour late, with no reason that he could express ... His state of reverie was, curiously enough, respected by his pupils, but eventually he would emerge from it and say, in his veiled tone of voice, rolling his 'r's, 'Ravel, play us your *Jeux d'eau*.' Ravel would sit down and play our favourite piece. With the final note hanging in the atmosphere like a star, Fauré was uninhibited in his enthusiasm for his young pupil. A few moments went by. Fauré looked at his watch, had nothing further to offer. The lesson was over. And Enesco, recalling these lightning sessions, added firmly: 'Those were the days when we really made some progress.'[3]

Another of his most illustrious pupils was Nadia Boulanger, who came into his class by special dispensation at the age of fourteen. 'His influence', she wrote,[4]

was invisible and indefinable, coming not from any substance in the material he taught but simply from the man he was. He inspired in us a kind of veneration. His utter simplicity shielded us from all false pretensions, indeed from any pretensions. He dominated us. Not deliberately because domination in any shape or form was not his goal – he was sufficiently his own master to be uninterested in other people except insofar as he could reach a clearer understanding of them. We for our part were keenly aware of this desire of his to understand us and to offer the verbal guidance that would help us most easily to find our own way.

In his position as a professor of composition, counterpoint and fugue Fauré reckoned, reasonably enough, that those learning to be composers had first of all to possess the basic skills; for which purpose he entrusted them to the capable hands of André Gédalge, leaving himself free to deal with essays in composition proper. Roger-Ducasse later wrote:[5]

Wielding a discreet pencil in his right hand, he would mark errors and excrescences with a small horizontal line and he needed only to change a note or the shape of a phrase or the inflection of a tune to turn a bald school exercise into a work of art. And, what is rare in a teacher who is also a composer of genius, he never opposed ideas that were contrary to his own ... Musical grammar first of all, was learnt through the chorale, to begin with accompanied, then ornamented with free,

decorative part-writing. He recommended Kufferath's *School of the Chorale* ...
The volume of Bach's chorales with harmonised accompaniments led on to the
longer chorales for organ ... Once we had grappled with the difficulties of writing
for double choir through studying Bach's motets for eight voices we went on to
chamber music. Rather unusually, we did not study the different forms in the order
in which they appeared in musical history: the topics were dictated by the pupils'
work, and he would explain the rules governing such and such a form which they
had used, correctly observing or blatantly transgressing them as the case might be.
We covered everything from motets to songs, from movements for string quartet to
fantasies, from symphonic adagios to salon pieces, and in each case he would back
up his teaching with an example from the established masters ... After the symphonic forms came that of opera ... and here he confined his choice of works to the
main masterpieces of the medium ... We read through Monteverdi, Rameau,
Gluck, Mozart, Meyerbeer (yes, Meyerbeer! But with regrets for what he did write,
instead of what he ought always to have written and practically never did),
Wagner, Mussorgsky, Debussy ... Without Fauré, I wonder, would we have
remained indifferent and scornful towards the charms of 'Sombres forêts' from
Rossini's *William Tell*, which he regarded as the model of an authentic melody?
Would we have grasped the fact that without good themes there can be no good
music; that all the clever tricks of developing material, varying rhythms and
creating tonal surprises come after the *idea*, the ultimate reality, a spark of that
divine fire brought down to us by Prometheus?

I shall, I hope, be forgiven for quoting at such length but these first-hand
accounts are not only little known and hard to trace, they are more
evocative than any paraphrase could possibly be. To them may be added
more familiar accounts found in the biographies of Fauré by two other
distinguished pupils, Charles Koechlin and the critic Emile Vuillermoz (see
bibliography).

Among the first and best examples of pupils' work discussed in Fauré's
class were several early pieces by Ravel: the *Deux épigrammes de Clément
Marot*, the *Habanera* for two pianos, *Jeux d'eau* and the *Sonatine*. Fauré
had spotted Ravel's exceptional personality from the start. He found him
highly gifted and the following report on him is extant in the official
Conservatoire files: 'A musical nature. Much taken with the new. Dis-
arming sincerity.'[6] We have already seen how fond he was of *Jeux d'eau*
which Ravel dedicated to him and, although the novel piano writing in this
piece derives ultimately from Liszt, it is not that far from some of the things
Fauré was writing at this same period, notably the clear, limpid second
theme of the Seventh Nocturne of 1898. Even so there were times when the
master was disturbed by his pupil's discoveries. One of Ravel's songs, *Si
morne*, was returned, according to Roland-Manuel,[7] 'with some severe

remarks'. The next lesson, Fauré asked Ravel whether he had brought the offending pages.

'You disliked them so much, I felt we shouldn't speak of them again.' 'I could have been wrong.'

Some years later, in 1907, Fauré was equally shocked by the first performance of the *Histoires naturelles*. As he said to Louis Aubert,[8] 'I'm very fond of Ravel but I'm not in favour of setting stuff like that to music.' This reaction of Fauré's is understandable when we consider that his own output contains practically no examples of musical humour or of the kind of irony that appealed to Ravel so much in Jules Renard's prose poems. The performance did, in fact, provoke a minor scandal. Shortly afterwards Emile Vuillermoz was walking along the street with Fauré and rose to Ravel's defence.

'Fauré listened carefully', he wrote,[9] 'and with the esteem and affection he felt for his young pupil I was quite sure he wanted to be convinced, but his antipathy got the better of him. Nevertheless when I left him at his front door he said to me, "You may be right after all. We should never rely on first impressions. Just in case I'm wrong, tell Ravel to come and see me tomorrow and play me the score again."'

In the brief autobiographical sketch Ravel dictated to Roland-Manuel he declared: 'I am happy to acknowledge that I owe the most vital parts of my technique to André Gédalge. As for Fauré, his encouragement and *artistic* advice were no less valuable.' 'The underlining [conseils d'*artiste*] was enjoined on me by Ravel himself', Roland-Manuel explained.[10] 'For all the respect and loyalty he felt towards his teacher, he felt he owed less to the critical teacher and more to the great composer.'

If Fauré respected his pupils' talent, he could also be demanding. There is considerable firmness in the letter of September 1900 asking Paul Ladmirault not to disappear 'like a little mouse in a hurry as soon as I've finished looking at your exercise' and criticising without reserve mistakes in the word-setting of a choral piece Ladmirault dedicated to him.[11] He could also at times take a harsh view of mediocrity. Louis Aubert, in the interview already quoted, remembered how

One of his pupils whom he couldn't stand won the Prix de Rome. Fauré greeted him smartly with the words, 'You must be honest now and admit you don't deserve it.' Whenever this pupil put one of his compositions on the piano for Fauré to read he would pretend he hadn't noticed it. He'd turn deliberately to one of us and start a conversation which usually had nothing to do with music . . . Then he'd get up, close the lid of the piano, stretch and murmur 'Time I was going' and take his leave.

Around 1900 four of his composition pupils expressed their devotion by jointly writing a string quartet in which the keys of the four movements spelt out their teacher's name: F, A, U (G), RÉ (D). This was probably the occasion for which Ravel wrote the first movement of his famous Quartet in F which was to appear in 1904 with the dedication 'To my dear teacher Gabriel Fauré'.[12] The second movement, probably a scherzo, in A major was written by Raoul Bardac, the slow movement, in G major, by Paul Ladmirault and the finale by Roger-Ducasse, who incorporated it some years later into his First Quartet in D minor; not only is this finale in D major, it also takes the four notes F, A, G, D (F.A.U.RÉ) as its basic material, and the whole work is dedicated 'To my dear teacher Gabriel Fauré, in heartfelt homage'.[13] In 1920 an unknown journalist in the Brussels newspaper *L'Eventail* recorded that 'Fauré still speaks of the happiness this surprise gave him; he was moved to tears by it.'[14]

In 1905 Ravel went in for the composition test for the Prix de Rome for the fifth time but was eliminated in the preliminary round. This decision caused considerable amazement among those up-to-date music-lovers and enlightened critics who had seen in *Jeux d'eau*, the *String Quartet* and *Shéhérazade* evidence of a really individual talent, and who were waiting for the distinguished winner of the second Prix de Rome in 1901 to go on to the ultimate triumph. But amazement turned to indignation when it was discovered that the six students allowed through to the final were all from the same composition class at the Conservatoire, the one taken by Charles Lenepveu who was, moreover, on the jury as being a member of the Institut. The music critics Jean Marnold and Pierre Lalo used the uproar caused by the 'affaire Ravel' to move beyond the immediate circumstances and launch an attack on French musical institutions in general, and on the Paris Conservatoire in particular. The director, Théodore Dubois, had in March already announced his intention of resigning and someone of Lenepveu's standing was expected to replace him. But when the decree was issued on 15 June 1905 it named ... Gabriel Fauré.[15]

This unlooked-for sequel to the 'affaire Ravel' did not, however, do much to calm the turmoil. Although Fauré was a professor at the Conservatoire he was not really a member of the inner circle: he was an old pupil of the Ecole Niedermeyer, he was not even a member of the Institut like Dubois, Massenet or Lenepveu and, above all, in his teaching as in his compositions he had given proof of being an independent spirit, unshackled by academic constraints.

Le Figaro on 14 June 1905 carried a declaration of intent from the new director:

I should like to take a line that is both classical and modern, sacrificing neither contemporary practice to hallowed traditions nor traditions to the fashion of the moment. Above all, I favour liberalism: I would not wish to exclude anything that has a serious contribution to make. I'm not biased in favour of any school and there is no type of music I'm inclined to ban, provided it is the outcome of a sincere and well-founded point of view.

Fauré took up his post on 1 October 1905, the Conservatoire then being situated in the rue de Faubourg-Poissonière behind the porte St-Martin. He pushed 'the awful bureaucratic desk into a corner', replacing it with a table, and as his first task in office wrote a letter of friendly gratitude to Saint-Saëns.[16] He had spent the summer pondering on the reforms that were needed in the teaching of the establishment, now that it was entering its second hundred years. His zeal was directed especially at the privileged position of the operatic repertoire which was the focus both of the singing classes, where the programme of study was limited to works performed at the Paris Opéra, and of the composition classes, which were seen almost exclusively as training grounds for the sacrosanct Prix de Rome cantata.

The first group of Fauré's reforms came in the shape of a decree (8 October 1905) followed by a series of ministerial orders. They stipulated among other things:

1 the creation of two posts for professors of counterpoint and fugue, thereby setting these studies apart from that of composition
2 that first-year singing students should concentrate on exercises and vocalises and that later on in the course they should no longer be obliged to choose pieces in the repertoire of the Opéra or the Opéra-Comique
3 that Bourgault-Ducoudray's music history classes should become obligatory for all composition and harmony students
4 that more importance should be given to collective music-making in the vocal, orchestral and chamber ensemble classes.[17]

The most radical change was in the entrance examinations. From now on titular professors of Conservatoire classes were not allowed to serve on the juries of these – a measure aimed at the suspect practice of 'private' lessons which entrance candidates felt themselves more or less forced to take with members of the teaching staff to ensure their support in the entrance examination.

This might seem an obviously right and proper measure, but among the professors it raised a general outcry (in their defence it may be said that they were very poorly paid). Two of them resigned in a blaze of publicity, there were delegations to the Ministry,[18] all to no avail. The reforms had the full support of the necessary committee and of the Secretariat of Fine Arts which at that time took its orders from the Minister of Education. Saint-Saëns himself, as he explained to Fauré many years later,[19] resigned from the Conservatoire's governing body 'because it was *expanded* and stuffed with journalists, theatre directors and women, and because it was no longer composed of people who knew their job and now found itself wide open to the intrigues of the outside world'. Théodore Dubois also resigned, so as not to have to sit next to Pierre Lalo, the music critic of *Le Temps* who had publicly attacked his directorship. The storm subsided eventually, at least to the superficial eye, and the new director was able to put his programme of reforms into effect. There remained, however, apart from the outright protesters, the mighty force of inertia mobilised by the mediocrities and those of a timorous spirit.

Fauré's chief purpose was to give Conservatoire students not just a firm technical basis but also a real education in musical understanding. He was determined to spread the appreciation of good music through every level of teaching and through every discipline. As we have seen, he instituted new chamber music classes and took particular pains over the teaching of singing. He refused to allow first-year singing students to go in for examinations and enlarged the repertoire: where Auber, Halévy and especially Meyerbeer had reigned supreme, trailing clouds of somewhat tarnished glory from the Opéra, it was now possible to sing an aria by Rameau or even some Wagner – up to this moment a forbidden name within the Conservatoire's walls! Late eighteenth-century *opéra-comique* was also encouraged, together with the older Italian repertory of Monteverdi, Caccini, Alessandro Scarlatti and Pergolesi, while German *lied* (Schumann, Schubert) and French song at last achieved respectability.

Fauré gave a completely new look, and a new repertoire, to the students' public 'exercises', that is the concerts they gave once or twice a year during their studies. Instead of a disparate group of pieces presented in the manner of student auditions, these public exercises became properly structured concerts and the repertoire they embraced was enormous, ranging from Renaissance polyphony to the works of Debussy. 'There are no more second-rank composers', wrote Pierre Lalo of an exercise in 1909, 'no more of the mediocre works which would have lain heavy upon it ten years ago. Instead we find Monteverdi, Bach, Händel, Leclair, Mozart, Beethoven, Schubert and Schumann. It's an amazing transformation and it is a pleasure to see that the Conservatoire has turned away entirely from the worship of false gods' (*Le Temps*, 25 May 1909).

As for the new works required for the end-of-year instrumental examinations, Fauré commissioned many of them from leading composers of the day, such as Dukas (*Villanelle* for horn, 1906), Ravel (*Prélude* for piano, 1913) and Debussy (*Petite pièce* and *Rhapsodie* for clarinet, 1910). Fauré himself wrote a large number of sight-reading pieces for the singing examinations. Throughout his time at the Conservatoire he was concerned to attract professors of the highest quality and reputation and among those who taught under him were Dukas and d'Indy in the conducting class; Alfred Cortot and Edouard Risler for piano; Eugène Gigout for organ; and Lucien Capet for violin. At the piano examinations Fauré might preside over a jury consisting of Ricardo Viñes, Alfred Cortot, Moritz Moszkowski and Albéniz, while the Conservatoire's governing body came to include Dukas, Messager (then the Director of the Opéra), the organist Alexandre Guilmant, Rose Caron, the great dramatic soprano and, in 1909, Debussy.

Fauré's letters show how dedicated he was to his task and how firm he was in demanding money from the politicians who controlled its supply.[20] In 1911 he oversaw the institution's move to a new site in the rue de Madrid. During all this time he had the unstinting support of his general secretary Fernand Bourgeat whose administrative responsibilities had been expanded in order to lessen Fauré's own. Even so, it has sadly to be admitted that Fauré's remaining duties took their toll on his creative work and he could never really get down to composing except at holiday time. The entrance and end-of-year examinations were particularly exhausting for him. As Director he had to preside over the juries and he wrote to his wife, from Vitznau on 8 August 1906, 'Every night I dream about examinations and prizes.'[21]

As soon as the working year was over, in the last days of July, Fauré would leave Paris and spend the two months until early October in one of the spacious foreign hotels which had been built to accommodate the first wave of tourists at the turn of the century. One of his favourite spots was the Swiss lakes. He finished the D minor Piano Quintet near Zürich in the summer of 1905; at Vitznau, a charming town on the Lake of the Four Cantons, he wrote in 1906 one of his most beautiful songs, 'Le Don silencieux'; and *Pénélope* was begun at Lausanne in 1907 and 1908, continued and completed at Lugano in 1909, 1911 and 1912.

Fauré loved the peace and serenity he found by these lakes and was fond of photographing them (see plates 52–3). The effects of light on water especially appealed to the contemplative side of his nature and the Mediterranean atmosphere of Lugano reminded him, as he said, of the landscapes of Ariège which he had known as a child and which now sometimes came back to him with the full force of nostalgia (see *Lettres intimes*, p. 181). Above all Fauré found there the calm, the space and the anonymity he needed for his work, to which end he usually had installed in his room an Erard grand sent from Paris. Marie meanwhile stayed in France with the children and his letters to her give a fascinating account of his hard musical labours (they were later published, with some cuts, by Philippe Fauré-Fremiet under the rather misleading title of *Lettres intimes*.) Although Fauré spent these summer months working, excursions and friendly reunions were not excluded. In Zürich in 1905 Fauré met Albéniz and his family, and a warm friendship developed.[22]

Albéniz and Fauré – a curious conjunction! On the face of it their aesthetic attitudes might seem as opposed as fire and water, but they had in common their Mediterranean character with its mixture of gaiety, warmth and melancholy, as well as their delight in the good things of life. Albéniz was at the time writing *Ibéria*, his masterpiece whose dissonant clusters may well have had an influence on Fauré's later piano writing. Fauré tried without success to get his publisher Hamelle interested in Albéniz's work, just as he tried to revive the interest once shown in his comic opera *Pepita Jiménez* by Albert Carré, the director of the Opéra-Comique. From 1905 to 1907 Albéniz was often to be found on the jury for the Conservatoire's piano competitions, and when his health became a matter for concern, he received a letter unique in Fauré's correspondence for the depth of feeling it portrays:

My dear friend, thinking of the future I've often felt you ought to come and live permanently in Paris where you would be surrounded by close friends. It is possible here to *shut one's door*, lock oneself away and work every bit as calmly as one can elsewhere. Those of us whose heads and hearts have something to offer the world, we need to be in frequent contact with each other, to rekindle our ideas, to talk, discuss and express our mutual admiration and friendship – there are not many of us. Paris then, my dear Albéniz, that's where you should finally bring your caravan to rest. The whole family would find it a healthy place to be, more so than anywhere. One feels so much better surrounded by friends, and you must know how completely you have won us over, and that you all have a place in our hearts.[23]

At the end of that same year (1908) Albéniz arranged for Fauré to be awarded the Order of Isabella the Catholic. He also introduced him to the musical circles of Barcelona. In 1909 the town's musical association was celebrating its bicentenary and that spring Fauré was invited to participate. On 11 March he conducted the Requiem, *Shylock* and *Caligula* and three days later he gave another performance of the Requiem, accompanied the singer Joana Aleu in some of his songs and conducted the Ballade with Marguerite Long as soloist. 'Like many great composers', she wrote in her memories of Fauré (pp. 91–2), 'he was an appalling conductor'; and, with specific reference to the rehearsal on 13 March, she added:

His usual lack of expertise was made worse on that occasion because it was the very day he was being proposed as a member of the Institut ... The rehearsal began at 8 o'clock in the evening. My husband stayed in the hotel to wait for the telegram so that he could then bring it round to us straight away. All through the rehearsal Fauré kept looking at me, not because of anything in the Ballade but out of desperation to know the result. In that huge auditorium of the Liceo, holding seven thousand people, I kept my eyes glued to the door. The rehearsal finished at midnight and still there was no news so Fauré went off to find out what he could. At the post office we discovered there was a postal strike and nothing was getting through ... Then, around dawn, just as we were all having some much-needed sleep, Fauré banged on our door, waving the telegram ... he'd been elected.

His election had, in fact, met with some resistance, but it was duly celebrated the next day with a grand banquet given by the famous choral society Orfeó Catalá and by a concert at the Catalan music Palais.

Albéniz by now was seriously ill. While he was staying at Passy at 55, rue de Boulainvilliers, Dukas and Fauré came to see him often and the day before he left for Cambo, where he died on 18 May, he asked Marguerite Long to come and play for the last time one of his favourite pieces, Fauré's Second *Valse-Caprice*.[24] His body was taken to Barcelona and there Orfeó Catalá sang extracts from the Requiem during his funeral procession.

According to Henri Collet,[25] it was Albéniz who brought Fauré and Dukas together. They met on holiday at Lausanne in August 1907. Fauré wrote to Albéniz the following month, 'At Lausanne I got to know Paul Dukas and I hardly need add what a pleasure that has been. He's a man of intelligence and goodness, to use those words in their fullest sense, apart from having a delightful sense of humour!' Dukas had in fact been joining in with Fauré and Marguerite Hasselmans in writing ludicrous pastiches of Maeterlinck and van Lerberghe which were then sent on to the Albéniz family.[26] This appears rather as self-mockery when we realise that at the time Fauré was working on the song-cycle *La Chanson d'Eve* to words by van Lerberghe, and Dukas had just had his opera *Ariane et Barbe-bleue* produced on a text by Maeterlinck. Joking apart, Fauré must surely have discussed with Dukas the problems of writing a post-Wagnerian opera, given that those problems were currently exercising him in composing *Pénélope*. Dukas' solution, consisting of a varied treatment of leitmotifs within a richly textured symphonic web, was a useful model for Fauré, though he adapted it to his own purposes.[27] In other respects, however, such as the vocal writing, the construction of ensembles, the use of the orchestra and the general aesthetic approach, the two works are markedly dissimilar.

Dukas left Lausanne at the beginning of September 1907. 'Dukas continues to improve on acquaintance', Fauré wrote to his wife (*Lettres intimes*, p. 150). 'He's serious-minded, with a real bent for philosophy and very well-read, though not exactly agreeable to begin with. You'd like him; but there'll be no smoothing his rough surface!' The two composers' meeting is preserved in a photo taken by Mme Hasselmans: Fauré and Dukas are on the bridge of one of those majestic, white paddle-boats you find on the Swiss lakes.[28] It was on another of these, on Lake Maggiore, that Fauré met the Italian composer Umberto Giordano on 30 August 1906. 'When the Italian opera was on last year', Fauré wrote to his wife next day (*Lettres intimes*, p. 125),

he was the only composer I could be polite about in my *Le Figaro* article. It seems he'd been encountering considerable opposition back home and my article brought about a volte-face . . . Everyone had been treating him like an idiot and all it needed was one article in *Le Figaro* and suddenly he was a great man. People!

Fauré's visit to Italy in September 1906 was one of the most enjoyable of them all. He was overwhelmed by the beautiful view of Stresa, the luxuriant gardens of the Grand Hôtel des Iles Boromées and the Neapolitan serenaders with their mandolins and guitars. 'It's beautiful enough to make you weep', he wrote to his wife on 4 September, 'and so calm and peaceful! I only hope I can produce something worthy of the surroundings' (*Lettres intimes*, p. 128). In fact four days later he finished 'Paradis', the first song of the cycle *La Chanson d'Eve* which was to occupy him until 1910. Unfortunately a 'severe stomach upset' meant he had to leave and put himself in the hands of Dr Combe in Lausanne.

Very occasionally in these parts there was a concert containing some of his music. He went to one concert of French music in Zürich on 26 August 1904 and wrote to his wife next day (*Lettres intimes*, p. 87): 'This concert, like the previous ones . . . included not one note from the Hamelle repertoire!'

For many years Fauré's relations with his official editor Julien Hamelle had been subject to frequent crises. If Fauré was reluctant to write *finis* to his compositions, Hamelle for his part was dilatory, always concerned with the money side of things and had no real respect for Fauré's genius. In one of his well-known rages, in 1896, Fauré wrote down a list of complaints – the letter was found among his papers:

I am simply unable to tolerate any longer your indifference to the fate of my compositions. I am fifty-one, I am a professor of composition at the Conservatoire, organist of the Madeleine; but you treat me as though I was some student just out of school. All this time my colleagues (some of them a good deal younger than me, some mere beginners) are played far and wide, and their music is circulated far and wide too, because their publishers *take trouble over them*. If I were to make a list of all my disappointments on this front I'd never get to the end. *I've had enough*. I'm eaten up with impatience and useless regrets and I want an end of it.

(Bibliothèque Nationale, Music Dept.)

This crisis, like others before it, was probably dealt with by 'père Hamelle' by means of definite promises which, like others before them, he promptly forgot. Without painting Hamelle too black it has to be admitted that his lack of commercial dynamism and his strong mean streak hampered the popularisation of Fauré's music. Fauré was well enough known in Paris but in the provinces he was still confused with his namesake, the singer Jean-Baptiste Faure, while abroad he was almost completely unknown.

He did at least have the pleasure of conducting a 'perfect performance' of his *Pelléas* suite at the Kursaal in Lucerne on 14 August 1908. The following year, in Lugano, he met a rich music-lover, M. Lombard, who organised private concerts in his luxurious villa at Trevano, and he was able to relax from his work on *Pénélope* with dinners, car rides, orchestral concerts conducted by his host and piano duet sessions with the eldest daughter of the family. From time to time he had to put *Pénélope* aside in order to honour the terms of his new contract. This was signed on 11 July 1905 with Henri Heugel, the heir to the famous house which published *Le Ménestrel*. Under it Fauré was obliged to complete thirty compositions between 1 January 1906 and 1 January 1909: this explains the reappearance, with the title *Messe basse*, of some of the movements from the *Messe des pêcheurs de Villerville*, written in collaboration with Messager some twenty-five years earlier (see chapter 7) as well as his reworking of an early motet sung by the Viardots in 1877[29] – *Ave Maria*, op. 93 for two sopranos and organ. Fauré also decided to follow up the cycle *La Bonne chanson* with one of a quite different character, *La Chanson d'Eve* (see chapter 15), and returned to the writing of piano works, which he had been neglecting somewhat, with the Fourth and Fifth Impromptus, nos 7–10 of the Barcarolles, nos 9–11 of the Nocturnes and the group of Préludes (see chapter 16).

This firm contract not only provided a regular supplement to his annual salary of 12,000F. from the Conservatoire, it also stimulated his over-scrupulous and somewhat indolent nature. Heugel was, what is more, the ideal publisher for *Pénélope*. He handled Massenet and brought to his dealings all the care, the influence and the resources of a prestigious publishing house, the very things Fauré had always been denied. The ageing Hamelle seems to have let Fauré go without undue regret – an ironical state of affairs, since it was his association with Fauré that was to make his name well known. Roger Ducasse used to tell the story of how he had met Hamelle around this time and had asked him whether he was not upset at Fauré's departure. 'Père' Hamelle tapped his pocket and replied: 'No skin off my nose. I've got what sells!'

The terms of the first treaty with Heugel proved a strain on Fauré's creativity so when, on 1 January 1909, it was renewed for a further three years he gave up his monthly salary (500 F.) and instead agreed to sell Heugel each work (600 F.) as it was written, up to a maximum of ten a year. After *Pénélope*, for reasons that have never been explained, he went over to Jacques Durand. Durand had inherited the business founded by his father Auguste in 1870 and made it into the foremost music publishing house of the early part of the century, including among his composers Saint-Saëns, Dukas, Debussy, Ravel, Roussel and various others.

The years leading up to the First World War were some of the busiest and most intense of Fauré's career. His reputation began at last to extend beyond the circles of enthusiasts and amateurs and reach a larger, more varied public. This development was not hindered, at least, by his appointment as director of the Conservatoire, followed by his election to the Institut: the *Figaro illustré* of Christmas 1905 reproduced the complete manuscript of the Seventh Barcarolle, and in February 1909 the review *Musica* devoted a complete number to his music. Newspapers and reviews regularly noticed each of his new works, journalists began to ask for interviews and editors for forewords. His orchestral and choral works appeared frequently in the Colonne and Lamoureux concerts and in those of the Société des concerts du Conservatoire of which he was the *de facto* president. In 1912 Messager and Broussan of the Opéra, Albert Carré of the Opéra-Comique and Gabriel Astruc, the founder of the new Théâtre des Champs-Elysées, fought among themselves for the honour of giving the première of *Pénélope*, and even the President of the Republic asked for some 'music by the Conservatoire director': so it was that the conductor of the Garde Républicaine found himself detailed to transcribe for wind band extracts from *Caligula* and *Shylock*, not to mention the *Pavane*!

Fauré turned a slightly jaundiced eye on all this celebrity, feeling it had come somewhat late in the day – he was, after all, sixty-eight when

Pénélope had its triumph on the Parisian stage. Even so he was happy for his family's sake and could not help feeling, deep down, some satisfaction at his revenge on those old rivals who had tasted official honours long since, like Théodore Dubois, Widor, Massenet and the now-forgotten Lenepveu, elected to the Institut in preference to Fauré in 1896.

Most important of all, though, was the interest shown in his music by a new generation of performers: the pianists Alfred Cortot, Marguerite Long, Edouard Risler, Raoul Pugno, Ricardo Viñes and later on Robert Lortat and Robert Casadesus; the singers Rose Féart, Jeanne Raunay, Jane Bathori, Claire Croiza, Félia Litvinne and Lucienne Bréval; the violinists Lucien Capet, Jacques Thibaud, Georges Enesco, Johannes Wolff and Jules Boucherit; and among the 'cellists Joseph Hollmann, for whom Fauré transcribed his well-known *Sicilienne* in 1898, and the prodigious Pablo Casals, for whom in 1908 he wrote his lovely *Sérénade* op. 98. Nonetheless few of these first-rate performers seem to have satisfied the composer. Writing to his wife, he complains that neither Edouard Colonne nor his fellow-conductor Camille Chevillard really understands the *Pelléas* suite. 'For composers', he wrote, 'interpreters are the dark side of the picture',[30] and in a letter of 1902 to the Countess Greffulhe he writes bluntly about his songs: 'I would love you to hear them sung by perfect interpreters. But I don't know of any in the professional ranks. The amateurs are the ones who understand me and interpret me best.'[31] Understandably, therefore, he spared no pains in appearing as a performer of his own works. As he wrote to his wife on 25 September 1906 about his recent D minor Piano Quintet, 'It's best if I play the piano part myself for the time being. It's the most effective way of getting it into people's skulls, pianists' skulls included. Capet [the violinist] is an admirable Beethoven player, but he hadn't got the measure of the Quintet at the Salle Erard performance.' For the same reason he agreed to record some of his music on piano rolls from around 1906 to 1913 (see Discography). Only a small proportion of these vital recordings has been transferred on to LP.

Fauré's wish to have personal control over concerts of his works meant travelling both in France itself and abroad. Belgium was the first foreign country to welcome him: the D minor Symphony was played at Anvers on 14 October 1885 with d'Indy conducting. Brussels was the most receptive city of all to Fauré's music[32] thanks to the twin influences of the ever-faithful Ysaÿe and of d'Indy who had been one of the first to make contact with the circles of the Libre esthétique and the Groupe des XX directed by Octave Maus, one of the founders of European Art Nouveau.

From 1888 to 1906 Fauré was a regular visitor to these avant-garde milieux in Brussels, playing the A major Sonata or the Piano Quartets with Ysaÿe, or accompanying his songs. It was Ysaÿe too who gave one of the first concert performances of the Requiem, in Brussels on 28 October 1900, and who on 23 March 1906, with Fauré at the piano, led the first performance of the D minor Quintet, written especially for him. Octave Maus introduced Fauré to the works of two Belgian poets: Marie Closset (alias Jean Dominique), the author of the poem *Le Don silencieux*, Fauré's setting of which was sung by Jane Bathori at the Libre esthétique on 12 March 1907; and, more importantly, Charles van Lerberghe. Maus also acted as intermediary between Fauré and Maeterlinck when the composer was thinking of starting work on *Sœur Béatrice* (see chapter 13). Fauré's popularity in Brussels was further shown by the fact that the Théâtre de la Monnaie was the first foreign opera house to put on *Pénélope*, on 1 December 1913, with Claire Croiza in the title rôle.

Elisabeth, the Queen of the Belgians, was one of Fauré's warmest admirers. She was herself a violinist and played the second violin part in the D minor Quintet at a private performance. On 8 May 1912 Fauré conducted his *Pelléas* suite in her presence at the Théâtre de la Monnaie at a concert in honour of Maeterlinck, and four years later she accepted the dedication of his Second Violin Sonata.

Fauré gives a detailed account of these musical journeys in his letters to his wife. In January 1905 he went to Cologne, Frankfurt and Strasbourg (which was at that period in Germany). He played in the A major Violin Sonata, and the First Piano Quartet 'because that's the work I play least badly!' as he wrote to Edouard Risler.[33] He was warmly welcomed in Germany but he was not really at home there and felt he was not generally understood. In a letter from Frankfurt on 16 January he wrote:

The criticisms of my music have been that it's a bit cold and too well brought up! There's no question about it, French and German are two different things. The advice of Mme de Rothschild is as follows (I quote): make a return visit to Frankfurt with a singer who is glamorous, well dressed and sings my songs well. Then I'll make some money. Everyone here sings my 'chansons', as they call them!

He took advantage of his visit to renew, in a sense, the pilgrimage he had made with his friend Messager in 1879 to the tomb of Schumann by calling on the composer's daughter Mme Somanhof. He noted briefly, 'She lives miles from anywhere in a superb villa on the banks of the Rhine. Very interesting visit.' Joseph Joachim sent him not only an engraving after

Bendemann's portrait of Schumann, dated 'Berlin, 20 April 1905', but a dedicated photo of himself, suggesting that he and Fauré had already met in Paris on 30 January 1887. Both the engraving and the photo are now in the Music Department of the Bibliothèque Nationale.

The concerts Fauré gave three years later in Berlin (21–7 November 1908) were much better received. He took the risk of playing his Second Quartet and accompanied Mme de Mendelssohn, a descendant of the composer. 'Not much voice', he confided to his wife on 25 November, 'but a *first-class* interpreter ... I owe my success to the fact that the audience had spent nearly a week listening to my music played by myself and to the numerous receptions I've been to' (*Lettres intimes*, pp. 171–3). In the end all this musical and social activity exhausted him: 'I ought to have brought my cross of the Legion of Honour with me. Here it's the done thing in the evenings to bring out the ironmongery!' Three days earlier he had admitted, 'It's all just as pointless here in Berlin as it is in London or Paris! But it's a charade one has to go through with!'

Fauré's longest journey was in November 1910, when he went to Russia at the invitation of one of his greatest admirers in St Petersburg, Alexander Siloti.[34] His music was not unknown there or in Moscow – it had been played by artists such as Raoul Pugno and Ysaÿe, Lucien Capet, Leopold Auer, Enesco and Casals. Through Saint-Saëns and Anton Rubinstein links had been established around 1880 between the Société nationale de musique and the Society for Russian Music. We have already seen that Turgenev wanted to translate Saint-Saëns' article on Fauré's A major Violin Sonata 'for a Russian newspaper', and when Taneyev came to Paris in the autumn of 1876 Turgenev introduced the two composers. Taneyev wrote to Tchaikovsky of the 'astonishing beauty' of the sonata, to which Fauré was just putting the finishing touches. Tchaikovsky himself appeared twice at the Société nationale, in 1886 and 1889, and on his first visit he wrote to Taneyev in a letter of 18 June 'I've met several musicians including your friend Fauré. I very much approve of him, both as a man and as a musician ... I've heard an excellent Quartet by him.'[35]

In March 1888 Tchaikovsky conducted two concerts of his works at the Concerts Colonne. Fauré had just published his Second Piano Quartet and gave Tchaikovsky a copy with the inscription: 'To my honoured friend P. Tchaikovsky, with all my affection and respect, Gabriel Fauré, 15 March 1888'.[36] The following year Tchaikovsky was present at the first concert performance of *Caligula*, which formed part of a programme given by the Société nationale (6 April 1889). This was followed by dinner at the Café de Paris with just Tchaikovsky, Fauré and d'Indy. Tchaikovsky entered his impressions of the evening in his diary: 'Concert of *Jeune France*. Rubbish (it's charlatanism to believe one thing and publicly state something else. D'Indy and co ...) But Fauré is delightful!'

A few months later Rimsky-Korsakov was invited to conduct in Paris as part of the Universal Exhibition and, given Fauré's Russian connections, he must surely have gone to listen. On 24 June he wrote to the Countess Greffulhe;[37] 'There's a very, very talented young Russian composer in Paris, recommended to me by Tchaikovsky': this was Alexander Glazunov who had come, like his teacher Rimsky, to conduct his own music. Fauré invited Paul Poujaud (in a letter hitherto unpublished) to come to Bougival, where he was spending the summer, with Messager and Glazunov whom he describes as an 'amazing young Slav'. His last link with Russia was with César Cui, the least known member of the Five, who was a passionate admirer of Fauré's work, the songs and piano music especially.[38] It is interesting to note in passing a close resemblance between Fauré's early piano works and those of Cui.

When Fauré arrived in St Petersburg on 11 November 1910 he was, therefore, already well-known in influential musical circles. The public too gave him an enthusiastic welcome. On 12 November he conducted *Shylock* and *Pelléas*, and the *Berceuse* and *Romance* for violin (with Lucien Capet as soloist), and the day after he played the piano part in his Second Quartet and the First Quintet, with the Capet Quartet, as well as accompanying Maria Kouznetsova in some of his songs. That same day the St Petersburg Conservatory and its director, Glazunov, gave Fauré a resounding reception. As he wrote home to his wife, 'All the students were shouting "Fauré! Fauré!" loud enough to bring down the building. What a pity Dubois and Widor didn't have a bird's eye view of it all! I've no doubt they'd have found the whole thing "greatly exaggerated"!'

After a chamber music concert at Helsingfors (now Helsinki) on 14 November, Fauré finished his tour with two concerts in Moscow on 18 and 19 November. The artists were all excellent – the Capet Quartet, Ysaÿe, Pugno, Siloti and the cellist Anatole Brandoukov – but the Moscow critics were more reserved than those in St Petersburg. In the avant-garde review *Apollo* Fauré is described as 'a profound disappointment ... both in his flabby, awkward conducting and in his dull piano playing'. Elsewhere in the review the *Pelléas* suite is condemned as 'utterly unremarkable'. But the more advanced circles of Russian music found Fauré's works much to their taste – as is proved by the visit he received in July 1909 from Diaghilev in person, to commission a score for the Ballets russes.

But of all foreign countries it was Britain that gave Fauré's music the warmest and most lasting welcome. This success was due partly to his frequent stays there and the many friends he made, and partly to the English taste for music that dealt in nuance and understatement.

Once again it was Ysaÿe who had been the pioneer, playing the A major Sonata in London on 28 May 1891. At the St James' Hall on 22 November 1894 Fauré himself accompanied the sonata and also played in his First Quartet and accompanied Jeanne Remacle in some of his songs, including extracts from the recently finished *La Bonne chanson*; unfortunately on this occasion he had to share the programme with the vapid Francis Thomé, then at the height of his popularity. While he was in London, Fauré tried to find a publisher who would be more active than Hamelle in getting his work known in England, but without success. 'I tried to sell the English my wares (I've got enough of them) but they weren't interested. They've got a surfeit of their own', he wrote, half-jokingly, to the Countess Greffulhe.

In Paris Fauré was lucky enough to get to know the American-born painter John Singer Sargent, famous chiefly for his brilliant portraits of the Anglo-American gentry. The oil-portrait he painted of Fauré, probably in 1889, with its subtle grey-blue tones, corresponds perfectly with the character and music of the sitter – after all, when Fauré invited the Countess Greffulhe in 1899 to come and hear *La Naissance de Vénus* he described it to her as an 'essay in pearly grey'. Sargent was one of those responsible for introducing Fauré into London musical society, together with Frank Leo Schuster, 'the son of a family of Jewish bankers from Frankfurt who had chosen to devote himself to art rather than to business', in the words of Robert Orledge.[39] Schuster soon became one of Fauré's English champions and often acted as Fauré's host, either at his London home, 22 Old Queen Street, Westminster, or at his misleadingly named property 'The Hut', at Bray-on-Thames. Fauré also made the acquaintance of the Maddisons who were to take a continuing and devoted interest in the progress of his music in England. Frederick Brunning Maddison was a lawyer and also one of the directors of a small music publishing firm, Metzler and Co. Fauré signed a contract with them on 15 January 1896, by which he promised to give them first refusal on each of his forthcoming compositions and handed over to them the rights both for England and for its colonies. This is why the Sixth Barcarolle came out in London in February 1896, four months before Hamelle's French edition. Some twenty of Fauré's works were published in this way between 1896 and 1899, including sixteen songs with English words. Hamelle seems not to have been very pleased with this arrangement and on 8 April 1896 he came to an agreement with Metzler about distributing the songs and piano works published by him.

From this time onwards Fauré was a frequent visitor to London. He even arranged for some first performances to take place there, as of the duet *Pleurs d'or*, to words by Albert Samain, given on 1 May 1896 by its dedicatees, the soprano Camille Landi and the baritone David Bispham. On 10 December of that same year two thousand people filled the St James Hall for a Fauré festival at which the composer played the piano part in his Second Quartet and the Second and Fourth *Valses-Caprices*, transcribed for two pianos by Léon Delafosse who also played the *Thème et variations*. Fauré wrote to the work's dedicatee,[40] Thérèse Roger, 'The public didn't seem to find it any more boring than the other music in the programme, in spite of the notice proclaiming that it was a first performance.' Nine days later he made his last appearance accompanying the Dutch violinist Johannes Wolff, once more in the St James Hall ... and in the A major Sonata.

Philippe Fauré-Fremiet, on p. 24 of his edition of his father's letters, mentions a visit to London in December 1897 but so far no corroborating evidence has been found. In late March and early April 1898 *La Naissance de Vénus* was sung at the Maddison's house, 11 St George's Place, Hyde Park Corner and on that occasion Fauré brought with him from Paris a new version of *La Bonne chanson* for voice, piano and string quintet. The first performance was given at the Schusters on 1 April 1898 and the tenor was Maurice Bagès (see chapter 9). Three months later Fauré was in London again, to conduct the first performances of the incidental music Mrs Patrick Campbell had commissioned from him for Maeterlinck's *Pelléas et Mélisande* (see chapter 8). On 26 June Schuster gave a party at 'The Hut' in the course of which Sargent made two fine charcoal sketches of the composer: one of him in profile, deep in rêverie (now in the collection of R. A. Cecil in London), the other full face with Mrs Patrick Campbell in the background (the whereabouts of this portrait are unknown – but see plate 25). Sargent had also made a pencil drawing of Fauré when he came to London in 1896. This was for many years in the possession of his pupil and passionate admirer Adela Maddison and is now in the Fogg Art Museum, Cambridge, Massachusetts.

Like Gounod twenty years earlier, Fauré fell under the spell of a guardian angel, the wife of his contact at Metzler and Co. Katherine Mary Adela Maddison, née Tindal, was of Irish descent, a sensuous and amusing brunette (see plate 38) who played the piano quite well and devoted her leisure hours to composition. In September 1896 Fauré spent several happy days with the Maddisons at St-Lunaire in Brittany (see chapter 3 of

Lettres intimes) and after that Adela put all her heart and energy into getting his music better known, taking the initiative in persuading him to come to London and present his works in person. She made English translations of some of his songs, duly published by Metzler, as well as of Paul Collin's feeble text for *La Naissance de Vénus*. Fauré himself conducted this version at the Leeds Festival on 8 October 1898, with a 'magnificent orchestra' and an 'excellent, 400-strong choir of a calibre I'd never dreamt of. I'm still astonished at the accuracy and expressive detail in their performance.'[41]

In August 1898 Fauré enjoyed a magical holiday at Llandough Castle, the home in Cowbridge, South Wales of Mr and Mrs George Swinton. He seems to have been particularly appreciated by Mrs Swinton, a lively young woman of imperious manners who asked him for a master-class on his early song 'Dans les ruines d'une abbaye'. In return Fauré asked for the stunning full-length portrait of her in gleaming satin – the work, needless to say, of John Sargent (see plate 39).

Le Figaro devoted its musical supplement of 1 October 1898 to one of Adela Maddison's songs, 'Rien qu'un moment', on a poem by Dante Gabriel Rossetti. The beautiful and (in Fauré's opinion) 'highly gifted' Adela had a penchant for song-writing. A collection was published by Metzler in 1895 and six songs to French texts were brought out two years later by Fauré's first publisher Choudens. Following the dictates of her muse and her heart Adela Maddison left her husband and two children and came to live in Paris. Mme de Saint-Marceaux had her and Fauré to stay at her country house, Cuy-Saint-Fiacre, in September 1899, and noted in her unpublished diary: 'The triumph of love. She's abandoned everything to follow the man she adores. She's charming, rather childlike, but her courage and determination are heroic. Fauré has brought with him a marvellous new Nocturne.' This was the Seventh in C sharp minor, written during the blissful summer of 1898 and dedicated to Adela Maddison, who also received the manuscript as a gift.

Mme de Saint-Marceaux went to a concert of Adela's works on 23 April 1904 and noted: 'She played her own works and also persuaded Enesco and Viñes to take part. Her music is a pot-pourri of Debussy and Fauré, but the overall effect is pretty enough.' The quality of Adela's work was good enough, at least, for the director of the Leipzig Opera to put on eight performances of her opera *The Talisman* in November 1910.

Fauré made further visits to stay with Frank Schuster in London in the summers of 1906 and 1907, according to Sir Adrian Boult.[42] In March 1908 he was joined by the singer Jeanne Raunay, the pianist Edouard Risler and the Capet Quartet in a concert at the Bechstein (now the

Wigmore) Hall. It included some twenty of his songs, among them *La Bonne chanson*, and the Ballade in Isidore Philipp's arrangement for two pianos in which Fauré liked to play the orchestral part. The next day, 20 March, he accompanied Jeanne Raunay in a private concert before the Prince and Princess of Wales, and two days later Schuster gave an evening reception at which Risler played some of the Nocturnes and Fauré played the piano part in the Second Quartet. Fauré's last appearance was at another private concert on 23 May, this time before Queen Alexandra and the Empress of Russia at Buckingham Palace. He played the accompaniments in some of his best-known songs sung by Susan Metcalf, 'an American singer. Her father's American, her mother's Swiss, she was born in Florence and looks like a Japanese!' To this cocktail, served up in a letter to his wife, we might add a further ingredient – that she was to marry Pablo Casals, the Spaniard from Paris ...

In November of the same year Fauré came to London again, direct from Berlin. The Buckingham Palace concert had opened many doors. He dined with Lady de Grey, the high priestess of London society, and with Admiral Lord Beresford. He also gave two concerts, in Manchester on 30 November and in London on 5 December and, although he sent his usual letters to his wife giving some of the details, he did not mention the name of the singer whose contralto voice he found 'delightful' ... Mrs George Swinton. Fauré's next visit to London was in June 1914 for a complete cycle of his piano works, a bold undertaking on the part of the young Robert Lortat, a pupil of Diémer's at the Conservatoire, who played them at the Aeolian Hall on 16, 19 and 22 June. Fauré and his enthusiastic young interpreter were to become close friends and the following year Fauré dedicated his Twelfth Nocturne to him (see pp. 386–9).

Although Adela Maddison was now living permanently in Paris, her contact with the man for whom she had given up everything became rarer and rarer. We may imagine that Fauré found somewhat embarrassing the attentions of this 'pupil' who was prepared to brave the heat and discomfort of the Midi to attend the first performance of *Prométhée* at Béziers, in the company of Winnaretta Singer and Jack Mackail, the English translator of *Pelléas*. This occasion (see chapter 8) was to bring a new development to Fauré's already somewhat complicated love-life.

The 'wall of harps' which Saint-Saëns envisaged in 1898 to fill the vast arena at Béziers meant that an unusually large number of harpists had to be found, so Fauré thought of the pupils of his Conservatoire colleague Alphonse Hasselmans (1845–1912). This well-known virtuoso had been appointed harpist to the Théâtre de la Monnaie in Brussels at the age of twenty. He then came to Paris as a soloist at the Théâtre lyrique, then at the

Opéra-Comique, and finally became professor of harp at the Conservatoire in 1884. The whole Hasselmans family was musical. Alphonse had been a pupil of his father, Joseph Hasselmans, the director of the Strasbourg Conservatory and the conductor of the theatre orchestra there, and Alphonse's son Louis, who was born in Paris in 1878, won a first prize for 'cello at the Conservatoire at the age of fifteen. He was the 'cellist of the Capet Quartet when it was founded in 1904 and he went on, like his grandfather, to become a conductor. With Arthur Dandelot he founded the Société des concerts Hasselmans in 1909, and in the Salle Gaveau gave Parisians their first chance to hear such works as Bruckner's symphonies and Albéniz's *Catalonia*. Albert Carré signed him up for the Opéra-Comique and during the First World War he toured America with the Society of Ancient Instruments. In 1917 he was appointed principal conductor of the Chicago Opera, followed by a similar post at the Metropolitan in New York from 1922 to 1936. Here he was responsible for the American premières of such works as Debussy's *Pelléas*, Ravel's *L'Heure espagnole* (in 1925) and Charpentier's *Louise*. Then he was appointed professor of chamber music at the University of Baton Rouge in 1936 and conducted the New Orleans Symphony Orchestra. He retired to Puerto Rico and died there in December 1957. I give all these details of his career because the musical dictionaries pass him by in almost complete silence and because Fauré held him in the highest regard. He entrusted the Paris première of *Pénélope* to him in 1913 and four years later dedicated to him his First 'Cello Sonata. Louis' sister, Marguerite, occupied a very special place in the composer's life.

She was born on 29 May 1876 and studied as a pianist. She was never a great virtuoso, but she did appear in public, often with her father and brother. An article in the review *Comoedia* of 28 March 1926 praised her 'sensible, delicate' gifts and her 'colourful, expressive and particularly well-balanced playing'. The story of her unconsummated marriage with the luckless André Tracol, a violinist in the orchestra of the Société des concerts du Conservatoire, provided much material for the less charitable tongues on the Parisian musical scene.

She was twenty-four when she went to Béziers with her father in August 1900 for the première of *Prométhée*. She was rather tall, well made in the manner of late nineteenth-century beauties, with a round face, a small mouth and large, clear eyes beneath long, well-marked eyebrows (see plate 40). She wore jewellery and lace. The impact of her youth and beauty on Fauré was immediate and total even if he was, to the year, the same age as her father. He installed her in a luxurious apartment at 23, avenue de Wagram, on the Plaine Monceau, and they were seen everywhere together, even on his long, working summer holidays in Italy and Switzerland. There was no secret about their liaison which lasted almost a quarter of a century, up until Fauré's death, and it may be seen as a second marriage which was prevented only by the mores of the time, divorce at this period being regarded as a severe social stigma.

In her fine apartment, complete with telephone, Mme H. (as Fauré used to call her to his friends) used to give piano lessons from under the shade of one of the enormous hats then in vogue. Her discretion and her complete lack of careerism did nothing to dim the attraction that this friend of the Conservatoire director held for a host of budding pianists, much to the fury of her rival (in pianistic ability, if not in beauty), the 'other' Marguerite, Marguerite Long – who, having laid claim to Fauré, was to harbour the lifelong dream of being his one, chosen, incomparable interpreter.

If Fauré never dedicated any of his works to Marguerite Hasselmans it was because he felt, at least, a duty and respect to his wife and because his mistress shared so fully in all his activities. In 1906 she received the flattering dedication of Albéniz's third book of *Ibéria* which Fauré had first marvelled at being played by her 'pretty fingers', as he wrote to the composer. She also spoke Russian, taught her by her mother, read Nietzsche in the original and held her own in philosophical conversations with Paul Dukas. She was, moreover, a 'modern' young woman, using make-up and daring to smoke in public, and it was she who introduced Fauré to photography.

But with Fauré's death, those who had courted and lavished praise on her were quick to show their ingratitude and lack of real concern. At forty-eight she suddenly found life difficult. Pupils began to leave her and she had to abandon the comfortable life-style she had always known. According to Vladimir Jankélévitch, who knew her at the end of the 1930s, she would have been destitute without the discreet financial aid afforded her by Fauré's two sons who knew how utterly disinterested her devotion to their father had been.

After his death she did homage to him in a number of chamber music concerts and in 1938 she was the moving spirit behind the Société fauréenne de musique de chambre, founded by Philippe Fauré-Fremiet and E. de Stoecklin. During the Second World War she went down to Nîmes to stay with Mme Felon, whose daughter Blanche (1895–1983) had in 1926 married Fauré's younger son Philippe. He and Marguerite never, unfortunately, completed their project of a book on the interpretation of Fauré's piano music, to which she would have brought unrivalled knowledge. As it is, only a few scattered remnants of this knowledge have come down to us: the 'Notes on Interpretation' to be found as an appendix to the second edition of Philippe Fauré-Fremiet's book, an article on the Ballade by her pupil Pierre Auclert,[43] probably some annotations on printed scores, and notes made by another of her pupils, Vladimir Jankélévitch's sister Ida.

Marie Fauré, resigned to her solitary life, lived increasingly the life of a recluse. When, in May 1911, the Fauré's moved to 32, rue des Vignes in Passy, she chose an apartment on the fifth floor including a large studio. There she began to try her hand at sculpture – a pious but not particularly fruitful attempt to follow in the footsteps of her father, who had died on 11 September of the previous year. Fauré himself lived in the salon, a homely room with red wallpaper, black wooden panelling with gold fittings, a small Erard grand, a white marble Louis XVI mantelpiece and a bow window opening out on to the greenery which decorated the studio where he worked and slept. Philippe had a room looking out on the courtyard, but he preferred to get out of the sepulchral atmosphere of the apartment and used to go and work in a café on the corner of the rue de Boulainvilliers. Finally, Emmanuel had a small apartment on the upper storeys which were really intended for servants (a staircase and an external passage-way connected this to the studio at fifth floor level), but he saw little of the apartment as in 1913 he married Jeanne Henneguy, the daughter of his biology professor.

Marie Fauré survived her husband by only eighteen months, dying on 13 March 1926 at the age of seventy. Adela Maddison died three years later, on 10 September 1929, in Ealing, Middlesex, after spending her last years in Geneva with a friend from Königsberg in Prussia, Martha Gertrud Mundt, who inherited all her manuscripts and her Bechstein grand.[44] Marguerite Hasselmans, much the youngest of the three women in Fauré's life, died in Paris on 13 September 1947 at the age of seventy-one. Vladimir Jankélévitch, in his book on Fauré, has left this description of her final years:[45]

Modesty, reflectiveness, delicacy, taste in literature and ideas ... Marguerite Hasselmans possessed all these qualities from birth. Her conversation was fascinating. By a tactfully probing remark, by a caustic anecdote or a memory she could recreate the atmosphere in which a work came to be written, whether it was *Pénélope* or *Pepita Jiménez*, the Sixth Nocturne or *El Albaicín*. She could make you feel the power of Dukas' formidable intelligence, Albéniz's amazing virtuosity, his kindness and creative flair, Fauré's genius; all these she would bring to life for a few moments, sitting at the modest Erard upright on which lay these composers' annotated scores. In that humble ground-floor apartment on the rue du Bouquet-de-Longchamp, she was able to conjure up the presence of those wonderful years.

36 Gabriel Fauré at the Bardac's house, rue de Berri, Paris, *c.* 1900

37 Emma Bardac and her children: Raoul and Hélène (Dolly), *c.* 1895

288

38 Adela Maddison, photo from *The Sketch*, 16 November 1910

40 Marguerite, Louis and Alphonse Hasselmans (from bottom to top), c. 1895

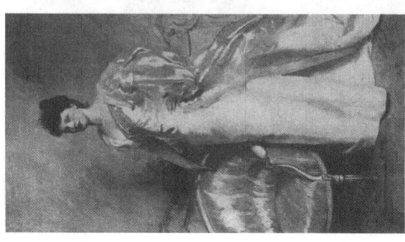

39 John Singer Sargent: Mrs George Swinton, 1897

41 Gabriel Fauré, caricature by A. Barrère

42 The jury of the theatre class at the Conservatoire de Paris, caricature by Emmanuel Barcet, *L'Assiette au beurre*, 20 July 1908

13   Towards the twentieth century

The years leading up to the 1914–18 war seem to have been particularly rich ones for Fauré in the sense that they brought him tardy but widespread recognition, on the social front as well as the musical one. But appearances are deceptive. The first decade of the century was for him, in fact, a period of profound turmoil and great change, both creatively and in his private life. From 1902 onwards, the migraines and attacks of dizziness and vagueness from which he had been suffering for some time were exacerbated by hearing difficulties of the most worrying kind. Fauré mentions it for the first time in his letters to his wife during the summer of 1903:

The problems with my hearing remain as fearful and depressing as ever! ... Every moment of the day I have occasion to feel the extent to which music is passing me by, and that makes me increasingly miserable! There's no doubt, from this point of view, the deterioration over the past year has been terrible ... I'm knocked sideways by this disease which has attacked the very part of me I needed to keep intact. It's disrespectful or, at least, ill-judged to compare myself with Beethoven. But the second half of his life was nothing but despair! There are passages of music and isolated timbres which I simply can't hear at all! Of mine as well as of other people's. This morning I put some manuscript paper on my table; I wanted to try and work. I feel only this awful cloak of misery and despondency on my shoulders.[1]

Some time later he complains of hearing 'noises that don't exist, sounds of imaginary clocks' and 'sounds that split in two, an appalling din. I feel I'm going mad!'[2]

In July 1910, trying over on his 'splendid Erard' the Préludes he was in the middle of writing, he complains of hearing the middle register faint but in tune, 'while the bass and treble are an incoherent jumble!'[3]

His hearing grew fainter and more distorted as the years passed. After a performance of a Verdi opera in Monte-Carlo, he wrote more specifically to his wife on 1 April 1919: 'The intervals in the bass change the lower they go, those in the treble the higher they go. You can imagine what the result is like – an infernal row. And it's through this *rictus* of sounds that I hear *Pénélope*! The singing voice is the least painful to listen to. But combinations of instruments are pain and torture.'[4]

Fauré's doctors attributed this 'deafness' to sclerosis, but it seems now that it may have been an inherited disease. A docket of information in the administrative file on his elder brother Amand, preserved in the Archives nationales, tells us that at the age of forty-six 'his hearing was not very good'. Perhaps there is some connection between this and the feelings of dullness in the head the composer used to complain of in the mornings. Romain Bussine, who used to share a bedroom with him when they were staying in Normandy, refers to these in an unpublished letter to their hostess Marie Clerc (24 September 1878): 'His first words on waking were unintelligible, the more so because he used to speak in verse, poor fellow ... and what verses! Or should I say, what verse, because one was just about as much as he could manage. The funniest thing about it was that for a good half hour my incoherence was in dialogue with his.'[5]

Fauré took the waters at Bad Ems during the summer of 1910 to try and cure his hearing difficulties – and not for throat problems, as the official news had it so as not to cause alarm at the Conservatoire. But the treatment was unsuccessful. The following summer he had to admit 'my hearing goes from bad to worse. I can't tell you the torment it's causing me. I don't see that I could have been looked after with greater sympathy and attention and, far from getting better, this year the disease has got noticeably worse!'[6] His son recalled that 'he heard bass notes a third higher and treble notes a third lower ... All through the last years of his life Fauré was determined to hide his infirmity, partly out of delicacy (he hated complaining) and partly to keep a hold on his livelihood. For ten years he was the music critic of *Le Figaro*, for fifteen years the director of the Conservatoire ... It needs to be realised that he too knew Schumann's torture and Beethoven's drawn out despair.'[7]

We can imagine what sufferings Fauré had to undergo as he grew older. Even though he composed at his table, he liked to try out what he had just written on the piano; a further torment was the yearly performance examinations at the Conservatoire, which he had to preside over; and he must have needed all his courage, in these conditions, to go on playing the piano parts in his chamber works, and, until 1919 at least, accompanying his songs. Claire Croiza, who often sang with him, especially in the years 1914–15, noted:

Fauré was a metronome incarnate. And more particularly so at the end of his life when he became deaf. Before that he was *galant*, he liked attractive women and used to make concessions. But at the end of his life, when he could no longer hear, he went his own way regardless, not noticing that the singer was sometimes two or three bars behind him ... because she slowed down while he kept strict tempo.[8]

It is only natural to wonder about the influence of Fauré's deafness on his creative evolution. Vladimir Jankélévitch rightly observes that in the vocal works of his last period Fauré sticks to the middle register which, as we have seen, he heard faint but in tune. It has been said, and endlessly repeated, that Beethoven would not have written his last works as we know them if he had been able to hear what they really sounded like and, understandably, comparisons have been made with Fauré's late style. Philippe Fauré-Fremiet makes so bold as to write in his biography: 'When one listens to the first movement of his Second Violin Sonata or the Allegro of his First 'Cello Sonata, one has the feeling that the strings sound somewhat lower than he intended, that they grate and run out of energy.'[9]

Personally I disagree with this viewpoint, and I feel that what Fauré's son attributes to an aural deficiency was the result of a deliberate change of style. The abruptness of the movements he refers to was exactly what the composer intended to convey. As proof we might cite the undeniably seductive orchestration of the two 'airs de danse' from *Pénélope* which Fauré completed at a time when his hearing problems were plainly evident. We might also adduce the rich sounds of the Second Piano Quintet, not to mention the wonderful balance of the String Quartet – which he refused to listen to on his death-bed, exclaiming: 'No! No! I would only hear a terrible noise!'

Many of Fauré's admirers, by attributing the more daring aspects of music to deafness, acknowledge themselves perplexed by his late manner, or what generally passes under that name. This may be the right moment to consider the question of dividing Fauré's work into three periods, following the pattern established by writers on Beethoven. I should say straight away that this tripartite division seems to me entirely valid: the first period (1860–86) being that of his search for a style and the absorption of his Romantic inheritance ('L'Absent', 'Chanson du pêcheur', *Elégie*); the second (1886–1905) being a period of maturation in which Fauré developed a personal style, marked by chromaticism and experiments in counterpoint and harmony which were sometimes overdone (Seventh Nocturne, *La Bonne chanson*, the Prélude to *Pelléas et Mélisande*); and the last (1906–24) being a period of radical self-renewal, involving a lightening of instrumental textures, a stiffening of melodic lines and a still greater harmonic audacity resulting from a more consistent emphasis on counter-point.

This tripartite division has been contested from time to time – in any case it is of only general application. In an article in the *Revue musicale* published in Fauré's lifetime, Florent Schmitt, who was a pupil of his, maintained that in fact Fauré, 'depending on circumstances, made simul-taneous use of these three styles which people try and treat in isolation'. Schmitt reckoned that the third style was already present in the Ballade and *Prométhée*, earlier than *Pénélope*, in *La Bonne chanson*, 'Soir' and 'Le Parfum impérissable' to the same extent as in *L'Horizon chimérique*; 'and if the Second Quintet is undoubtedly a more "third style" work than the First', he goes on, 'the Eleventh Barcarolle, on the other hand, is surely much less of one than the Fifth?'[10]

More recently Yves Gérard has suggested a bi-partite division, 'up to 1894 and from *La Bonne chanson* to 1924'. 'What is remarkable', he writes, 'is the uninterrupted progression in Fauré's development from *La Bonne chanson* (an example of 'private' music-making, 1894) and *Prom-éthée* (an example of public music-making, 1900) to the final pages of the String Quartet of 1924.'[11]

Even if we can agree that Fauré's 'advanced' music, from *La Bonne chanson* to the String Quartet, forms a single stage in his evolution, it seems to me difficult not to introduce distinctions inside the first thirty years of his creative life: there exists between Second Empire romances like 'Dans les ruines d'une abbaye' or even 'Après un rêve' and songs like 'Clair de lune' or 'En sourdine' an abyss just as deep, I feel, as between the *Romances sans paroles* and the Sixth Nocturne.

Whatever the truth about these divisions and the existence or otherwise of a second style, there is general agreement about the considerable change his style underwent in the last twenty or twenty-five years of his life. This 'twentieth-century progress' in Fauré's work is worth examining in more detail.

There is no mistaking the fact that, once the great effort of writing *Prométhée* was over in 1900, Fauré entered on a period of reflection and his output slowed down. The work's enormous success at Béziers was a new experience for him and he was encouraged by it to return to his dreams of writing for the stage – not that he had ever really abandoned them.[12]

In *Pelléas et Mélisande* Fauré, like many other composers, discovered a poetry after his own heart. Debussy had begun work on his masterpiece in 1893 and in the same year Chausson was writing his song-cycle *Serres chaudes* on texts by Maeterlinck. According to Cocteau, Satie had thought of setting *La Princesse Maleine* as early as 1891, while Pierre de Bréville wrote an overture for it the following year and music for *Les Sept princesses* in 1895. Ravel himself toyed with the idea of *Intérieur*, to judge from a single page of sketches for a Prélude, jotted down around 1893.[13]

In 1899 Maeterlinck was writing two operatic librettos, intended to further the career of his mistress Georgette Leblanc: *Ariane et Barbe-Bleue*, the basis of Paul Dukas' operatic masterpiece, produced in 1907, and *Sœur Béatrice*. Of this latter work Maeterlinck wrote to his German translator Friedrich von Oppeln Bronikovski:[14]

The subject is taken from a thirteenth-century Flemish legend. It tells of a young nun who ran away from the convent with her lover and of how the Virgin took her place so that no one knew of her absence, and when she returned it was as though she had never been away. Needless to say, to expand this anecdote so that it fills three acts I've been fairly free in changing and inventing subsidiary details.

He offered the libretto first to a friend of his and of Georgette Leblanc, an obscure composer called Gabriel Fabre (1858–1921)[15], and only then to Fauré in the spring of 1900.[16] This came about through Octave Maus, the leader of the 'Libre esthétique' movement and of the 'groupe des XX' in Brussels, who had organised exhibitions of paintings to go with concerts at which Fauré had appeared.[17] Fauré must have accepted almost at once (he was, at the time, deep in the composition of *Prométhée*), since we learn from an unpublished letter from Maeterlinck to Bronikovski of 31 August 1900: 'If you're talking about my two short plays *Barbe-Bleue* and *Béatrice*, unfortunately I can't let them go to the composer you mention because I've assigned the exclusive rights of the first one to the French composer Paul Dukas and of the second to Gabriel Fauré. The arrangements are formally concluded.'[18] Writing to Bronikovski some time later, on 8 December 1901, Maeterlinck stated that Fauré, 'who is a painstaking artist, has requested a period of three years in which to complete a continuous score [i.e. an opera and not just incidental music]. Since that time only fifteen months have elapsed ... In any case I have given him the exclusive rights to set *Sœur Béatrice* to music.'

Fauré was still thinking about Maeterlinck's play in the spring of 1902, although he was simultaneously looking for some other subject. In a letter to Albert Carré, written in April 1902 at the very time Debussy's *Pelléas* was receiving its first performance, he stated: 'I'm still struggling with *Béatrice* and although I've been looking for something else, and asked all my friends to do the same, I'm afraid I have nothing to offer you.'[19]

So there can be no doubt that Fauré did work on *Sœur Béatrice*, even though no sketches have survived and until now the project has escaped the notice of his biographers. Maybe he 'worked' in his own way – that is to say, in his head without writing anything down. All we know is that at this period he started to reorchestrate *Prométhée*, then abandoned it; and when, in August 1903, he returned to the Piano Quintet, it was after a long blank period, as he himself ruefully admitted.[20]

His collaboration with Maeterlinck seems to have been dropped without any ill will on either side. Fauré for his part had not been the instigator of the project, while Maeterlinck, touchy though he was in general, attached no great importance to *Sœur Béatrice*. He wrote it simply to please Georgette Leblanc and his letters to Bronikovski speak of it in unfailingly disparaging terms.

As no correspondence between Maeterlinck and Fauré has survived, it is difficult to know precisely why Fauré gave the project up. We can only guess at the part played by some kind of creative block after the great intellectual effort of composing *Prométhée*, coinciding with the onset of his hearing problems (see beginning of this chapter); and although the subject must have appealed for him to have signed an exclusive contract, we still do not know how he really felt about it.

The touchingly tender story is based on the same philosophy of divine gentleness as the Requiem. In the words of W. D. Halls:[21] 'Béatrice's soul is as free of guilt as Mélisande's.' If Fauré (the 'gregorianising voluptuary', as Reynaldo Hahn called him) was attracted by the legend's sensuality and mysticism, then we may suppose he was not in tune with the romantic passions unleashed in some of the scenes. Exaltation and even violence are to be found right through the play, even in the religious scenes, and are presented more straightforwardly than in the dreamworld of *Pelléas et Mélisande*. As for giving the Virgin a singing role (in Act III), that must have struck him as a delicate, not to say impossible task.[22] It was to be some years before he found what he regarded as a credible subject and one to which he could devote himself wholeheartedly – the story of Penelope and the return of Ulysses, which was to occupy him for seven years.

During the summer of 1901, when *Prométhée* was revived at Béziers, Fauré wrote some interludes in Oriental style for Georges Clemenceau's play, *Le Voile du bonheur*. This incidental music, which remains unpublished, is no more than a curiosity among his works (see chapter 8) and the two sight-reading pieces he composed for the piano competitions at the Paris Conservatoire do nothing either to fill out his very modest output in this second year of the new century.

Fauré went back to Béziers in the summer of 1902, but this time as a spectator, for the first performance of Saint-Saëns' *Parysatis*, which he found rather disappointing. He also finished the *Huit pièces brèves* for piano op. 84, and immediately ceded the rights to Hamelle. Even if this collection is not as important as the Barcarolles, the Nocturnes or the Préludes, it contains many subtle and interesting pages. Fauré wrote to the dedicatee, Mme Jean-Léonard Koechlin, to say 'they're all fairly new', but in fact they come from various different periods of his life. The oldest pieces are the two fugues (nos 3 and 6) which date from his student days at the Ecole Niedermeyer, almost forty years earlier. The first and fifth pieces (in E flat and C sharp minor respectively) are pieces written for the piano sight-reading tests at the Paris Conservatoire in 1899 and 1901, though the first piece is extended a little beyond its original form. The only really new items were no. 2 (in A flat), no. 4 (in E minor), no. 7 (in C major) and no. 8 (in D flat). These four were the only ones played by Ricardo Viñes at the official first performance on 18 April 1903 at the Société nationale de musique.

The collection as a whole is also interesting for the synthesis it offers of Fauré's different styles of piano writing, past, present and even future. Certain passages display the calm, simple lyricism of Mendelssohn's *Songs without Words* (the second theme of no. 1, the beginning of no. 7) while the fifth piece, with its airy grace and sinuous curves makes one think of Schumann. We may well wonder whether, on this occasion, Fauré has not dipped into some old sketchbook and, finding a number of melodic ideas, has not then worked them up in unmistakeably 1890's fashion. The monothematic seventh piece in C major (a key Fauré used rarely) is fairly characteristic of the contradiction between the Mendelssohnian themes and their treatment; the triplet accompaniment, as well as the delightful and surprising arrival on E major in bar 18, definitely look back to the happiest moments of *La Bonne chanson* of 1892–4, while the concluding idea in C major (bars 34–7) echoes the 'fire' theme from *Prométhée* of 1900 and looks forward directly to the 'royal theme' of Ulysses in *Pénélope* of 1907 and to the second main theme of the *Fantaisie* for piano and orchestra of 1918.

The Schumannesque outlines of the fifth piece are interspersed with a second, chordal theme, in the manner of late Fauré; in contrast the first theme, with its delicate minor thirds and triplet traceries (bars 22 and 24) takes us back to the ecstatic languors à la Chopin which Fauré favoured in the 1880s. The fourth piece is perhaps the most inspired of all. Here we find the dense, severe, concentrated atmosphere of Fauré's last years. Its sharply contoured theme, in the middle register of the keyboard, and the extreme economy of the accompaniment look forward to the sombre rumblings at the beginning of the Ninth Barcarolle of 1909, while the finely worked counterpoint and the chordal progressions of the development in bars 17–24 are clear pointers to the style of the Ninth Prelude of 1910, in the same key of E minor. From many points of view this fourth piece develops the style and technique first apparent in the Seventh Nocturne of 1898. The last piece in the set, in D flat, conjures up in its central section the crystalline sonorities of that Nocturne's second theme. Altogether, therefore, the *Pièces brèves* would seem to support Florent Schmitt's view that all Fauré's styles developed simultaneously, although this medley of attitudes is due to the set's composite character, deriving from Schumann's *Album Leaves*. Not that this variety undermines its quality – on the contrary, it is a factor which should recommend the set for concert performance. The first edition, brought out by Hamelle, bears the general title *Huit pièces brèves* with, in each case, a statement of the key of the piece, as Fauré expressly requested. But when Fauré moved on to another publisher, père Hamelle, sharp businessman that he was, was quick to give the pieces titles in all subsequent editions – hence *Allégresse*, *Adagietto* and other marks of favour. Hamelle's imagination was also responsible for giving the final piece of the set the slightly overweening title of Eighth Nocturne.

The three extended songs of opus 85, written in this same year of 1902, betray the same marks of stylistic indecision. The stormy, marine atmosphere of 'La Fleur qui va sur l'eau' (op. 85 no. 2), on a bombastic text by Catulle Mendès, makes it seem like a remake of Duparc's *La Vague et la cloche*. It follows the pattern of other vehement songs like 'Le Voyageur' (1878), 'Larmes' (1888) and especially 'Fleur jetée' (1884), but without their musical interest. We are reminded, unfortunately, of the violent passages of text in *Prométhée* (the scenes of the avenging gods) which, as we saw, Fauré did not find very inspiring.

'Accompagnement', the third song of the group, stands at the absolute opposite extreme. Here Fauré attempts, not unsuccessfully, to set a text by Albert Samain enveloped in ultra-symbolist nocturnal vapours; he had come across it at the time of his affair with Emma Bardac, who was one of Samain's great admirers. The song was written for Emilie Girette, daughter of a well-known architect and later wife of the pianist Edouard Risler. Her contralto voice, her musicianship – and her great beauty – had stirred Fauré, but to no avail. The young singer's diary[23] relates, sensitively and ingenuously, the story of the song's composition completed, it seems, quite quickly in March 1902. 'From the musical point of view', she notes, 'it will be like 'Soir'; and then, further on, 'in writing it he is thinking of me and my voice ... The poetry, according to him, is entirely *descriptive* – I mustn't let myself be put off at first sight – He's afraid I shan't like it! ... He told me he thought there was a little of me in it and that he'd worked on it heart and soul.'

The piano part in 'Accompagnement' plays an important rôle, as the title suggests it should, taking upon itself the illustration of the images in the text. At the beginning and end of the song, the pattern of off-beat quavers is reminiscent of the breathless writing in 'J'ai presque peur, en vérité' from *La Bonne chanson*: here it suggests the moon's silver reflections flickering on the dark surface of the water. In the succeeding verses this gives way to the regular movement of the oars, underpinning a complex network of rising arpeggios with cross-rhythms in the voice. As in 'Clair de lune', the evocation of moonlit tranquillity is a particularly beautiful moment. Unfortunately, the rather precious, even artificial nature of Samain's text leads, in my view, to a loss of naturalness in the vocal line and to some rather abstruse modulations. The song is only half successful and I value more highly the first of the group, 'Dans la forêt de septembre', a slow song and, like 'Accompagnement', in the key of G flat major.

When Fauré read Mendès' poem in the issue of *Le Figaro* for 21 September 1902, he was no doubt struck by the poignant melancholy of autumn descending on the forest and turning the leaves yellow, just at the time when, in his own life, he was beginning to suffer insistent anxiety at his increasing deafness. Four-part chords in the accompaniment suggest the poet's slow steps alternating with rising arpeggios over a strong bass line, in a manner characteristic of the late song-cycles. The supple, freely flowing vocal line is often chromatic and always expressive. One of the finest lyrical moments (*p dolce*, bars 36–40), depicting the fall of a dead leaf, is a direct anticipation of one of the most beautiful cadences in *Pénélope*.[24]

The success of this extended song was, however, followed by long months of turmoil and inactivity. During the winter of 1902–3 Fauré made a start, at least, on reorchestrating *Prométhée* for a conventional symphony orchestra. Alfred Cortot was proposing to stage it, following the famous Wagner performances he had just put on in Paris, at the Théâtre du Château-d'eau in the place de la République. But the ambitious young conductor soon abandoned the idea without even troubling to let Fauré know.[25]

Emilie Girette noted in her diary that she often found Fauré desperately tired and all too frequently struck down by 'a fearful migraine. His complexion is yellow, his eyes glassy ... quite disturbing, in fact' (February 1903). He was unable to compose and, writing to his wife that summer, he confided to her his anxiety at these long months of creative silence: 'Like you, and just as profoundly, I regret the fact that I've written nothing for almost a year now. I hope a holiday and a rest will restore me to my old self. In any case, I've always aimed for quality rather than quantity and I'm sure the vague ideas that came to me this winter weren't worth bothering with.'[26]

The summer of 1903 saw the beginning of the long series of holidays in Switzerland. During it Fauré began a new work which he thought initially was to be a violin sonata. In fact it became the slow movement of his Piano Quintet in D minor which, as I mentioned earlier (chapter 6) he had abandoned nearly ten years before. The revision of the Quintet took Fauré three summers of unremitting labour, from 1903 to 1905, all of them spent in Zürich. 'God knows, composing's a difficult business', he wrote to his wife on 1 September 1904.[27] 'Happy are those who believe they are geniuses and are satisfied with the least effort! I envy them'; and the following day he complained of having 'really slogged away ... *for absolutely nothing*! A wall of bronze.'

Also in 1904 Fauré wrote two harp pieces for the competitions in Alphonse Hasselmans' class at the Conservatoire: a short sight-reading piece which has remained unpublished and an altogether more interesting test piece, the D flat Impromptu op. 84. In it two ideas are developed alternately. The first(*Allegro moderato molto*) with its imposing chords looks back to Fauré's *Thème et variations* for piano or to the 'Pavane' from Saint-Saëns' opera *Etienne Marcel*; the second, in B flat minor (*meno mosso*), combines a wayward melodic line with a dreamy atmosphere in the manner of Debussy's *Suite bergamasque* – published that same year – together with its descending patterns, its air of indecisiveness and the melting gentleness of its triplets. The second section (*Allegro molto*) brings the two ideas together in virtuoso fashion, the whole being studded with sweeping cadenzas and an effective use of harmonics. The work is excellently written for the instrument and is in every harpist's repertoire. There is reason to think that Alphonse Hasselmans, who received the dedication, had a hand in shaping the more virtuosic passages, as Fauré's writing for the harp in his orchestral works – *Shylock*, the Requiem and *Prométhée* are only three out of many – never went beyond straightforward arpeggios, transcribed from the piano. What is more, the only manuscript fragments that have survived of the Impromptu are not in Fauré's hand but, most probably, in Hasselmans'. They were used by the first pupil in his class to read it through in July 1904, Mlle Charlotte Landrin, who was later to marry Chausson's brother-in-law, Jacques Lerolle.

Finally, in 1904, the Milan firm Il Gramofono commissioned short vocal works from various contemporary composers including Giordano, Leoncavallo, Xavier Leroux, Puccini, d'Indy and Fauré. The idea was to record these works with the composers playing the piano parts. Fauré responded by writing 'Le Ramier', op. 87 no. 2, but unfortunately it seems that Giordano and Leoncavallo were the only ones to record their pieces.[28] Together with 'Le Plus doux chemin' (op. 87 no. 1. 1904), written for Emilie Girette after her marriage to Risler, and 'Chanson' (op. 94, 1907, published separately by Heugel), 'Le Ramier' forms a kind of homogeneous triptych. Certainly the literary inspiration behind these songs remains entirely classical. Armand Silvestre's texts for the two op. 87 songs and Henri de Régnier's for 'Chanson' are delicate expressions of the melancholy of tormented love. They stand in Fauré's work as a sort of cheerful but nostalgic farewell, the last sparks of the galant madrigal which Fauré had practised for so long, from 'Lydia' to the Cinq mélodies 'de Venise', and taking in 'Barcarolle', the 'Sérénade toscane', 'Clair de lune', the two Chansons and Madrigal from Shylock and the Madrigal for four voices ... These works may be seen as the final flowering of a French lyrical tradition, beginning with the troubadours' laments and other songs from the age of chivalry, and passing through the tender preciosity of so many airs de cour by Boesset, Guédron and Michel Lambert.[29]

The three above-mentioned songs also share an almost aphoristic brevity. But it is here, in works which could pass for album leaves of only minor interest that, paradoxically, we find a clear indication of the textures of Fauré's late style. As with the songs of the 1870s, so here the vocal field is the proving-ground for his experiments.

If we open the score of 'Le Plus doux chemin', which for my part I would place among Fauré's most inspired songs, we cannot but be struck by the extraordinary simplification of the writing compared with the complexity of the 1902 songs I have just been discussing. Two minims in the left hand, four quavers in the right, that is the sum of the accompaniment. As for the vocal line, with its light modal inflections, the phrases are perfectly balanced and unroll with a royal simplicity, beginning on the tonic and finishing expressively on the dominant. The accompaniment of 'Le Ramier' is also based on cross accents, with a contrapuntal line in the bass and a very simple motif in the right hand, calmly and boldly distributing syncopations and off-beat accents. The vocal line is more mobile and ends with a descending octave, prefiguring *La Chanson d'Eve* and *Pénélope*. The extreme economy of the texture, the systematic use of cross-accents and syncopation, the generally sober tone and restrained expression, leading to a further interiorisation of the lyrical impulse, the slimming down of the harmonies allied to an ever more obvious attention to intervallic and horizontal elements – all these features are characteristic of Fauré's 'third period'. Indeed in 'Chanson', written in 1906 and still almost unknown, these traits are so firmly in evidence that the song comes over as almost an abstract archetype, an etching, of his late style.

In trying to capture this new manner at its source, we have to acknowledge that it is neither consistent nor continuous in its appearances. Between the madrigals of Silvestre op. 87 of 1904 and the 'Chanson' op. 94 of 1906 we find a group of works extremely diverse in both provenance and style.

During the years 1905–6 Fauré was appointed Director of the Conservatoire and changed his publisher, from Hamelle to Heugel. One almost gets the impression that he was trying to sow confusion, play games with chronology and lose both himself and us! And not without gaining some perverse satisfaction from it all. He at last finished the D minor Piano Quintet, first performed in Brussels on 23 March 1906, and then spent the summer on the less substantial *Ave Maria* for two sopranos and organ op. 93. This had originally been composed for Marianne and Claudie Viardot in 1877: 'It's a duet', he wrote to his wife on 17 August 1906, 'quite long, and as for the bits that are thirty years old, I don't think anyone would guess!'[30] In which, I feel, he rather flattered himself.

A few months later he revised the music he had written in 1881 for the *Messe des pêcheurs de Villerville*, to be brought out by his new publisher. It appeared under the title *Messe basse* (see chapter 7). He also adapted 'Mélisande's song', from the incidental music for the London performance of *Pelléas et Mélisande*, to fit one of the poems from Charles van Lerberghe's *Chanson d'Eve*. It was published on its own as 'Crépuscule' before Fauré had thought of making it the nucleus of a song cycle (see chapter 15). The only really new works of 1906 go a long way towards resolving the stylistic ambiguities characteristic of this crucial turning-point in his development. 'Le Don silencieux', written in five days during the wonderful holiday he spent in August 1906 at Vitznau on the Lac des Quatre Cantons, is one of his most original songs and shares with 'Chanson' op. 94 the fate of being little known because it has never appeared in a collection or a song-cycle. In these wholly inspired pages, Fauré succeeds in combining the intimate lyricism which he had always sought with a form and a technique noticeably different from anything in his previous songs. To judge from two letters he wrote that summer, he himself was well aware of the importance of his achievement: 'Five days ago', he wrote to his wife, 'there were only the opening few notes, and as it is nothing like any of my earlier works, or anything I know, I'm very happy. For one thing, there's not even a principal theme. It develops with a freedom which would upset Théodore Dubois considerably.[31] It follows the words, as they come, it begins, continues and finishes, no more than that; yet at the same time it's a *whole*. But now I'm getting pedantic.'[32]

The original manuscript bears the title *Offrande*. Fauré wrote about this to Octave Maus:[33]

I'm counting on Mme Maus to get the poet to pardon me for giving the title *Offrande* to this poem, which doesn't have one of its own ... If Jean Dominique doesn't like the title, which I've had to think up because of my publisher's insistence, then tell him that the *thirteen-foot* lines with which he has decorated his poetry, nice though they are, have given me more than enough to get my teeth into! Still, I hope my music has allowed them to retain their suppleness: I've done my best, at least.

It may well be that the lovely title he finally adopted was suggested by Jean Dominique, alias Marie Closset, a Belgian Symbolist poetess. The success of 'Le Don silencieux' must have encouraged Fauré to remain in the world of song, the real workshop of his creative forces. After Vitznau he went to Stresa and then, in September 1906, to Lausanne. On the banks of his favourite lakes, he wrote 'Paradis', the striking prelude to his new song-cycle *La Chanson d'Eve*; the poems were by Charles van Lerberghe and, once again, it was Maus who introduced Fauré to them. The composer returned to the concentrated, even severe style we noticed in 'Crépuscule'[34] and continued in it with the second song of the cycle, 'Prima verba', written at this same time. Once again, Fauré's style of vocal writing is in advance of that in his instrumental works, for piano especially. We have only to compare the simplicity of texture in the first few songs of *La Chanson d'Eve* with the profusion and complexity in the Fourth Impromptu op. 91, sketched out during the summer of 1905 and printed a year later as Fauré's first collaborative venture with his new publishers Heugel. This fairly long piece is based on three ideas. The first provides a good example of the rhythmic tortuosities his craftsman's patience led him to indulge in: to the left-hand duplets broken up by brief sighs are added a cross-accented chromatic scale gently undulating between dominant and tonic and above that an irregularly syncopated countermelody. The second motif (bars 15–18), entirely in octaves, is more lyrical and combines with the first one to produce a powerful development of dissonant chords, in the manner of the Fifth Barcarolle. As for the third motif (the central, 3/4 section), its spacious, descending curves over a deep bass go back to the Sixth Nocturne and perhaps even more to the Seventh, in the same key of C sharp minor (enharmonic minor of the Impromptu's D flat major). Fascinating though it is to follow the extraordinary technical skill involved in fashioning this music, one has to admit that this very skill also leads to it being so densely intricate as to be almost indecipherable, hermetic even, at first sight. Pianists have good reason for preferring the Second and Third Impromptus, which are so much more agreeable even if not so intellectually profound.

The Fourth Impromptu is dedicated to Marguerite Long. Her husband, Captain Joseph de Marliave, was at the time one of Fauré's closest and most valued friends. In her brief volume of memoirs *At the Piano with Fauré*, Marguerite Long recalls that she was introduced to Fauré by her piano teacher Antonin Marmontel in the spring of 1903. She played him his Third *Valse-Caprice* and Fauré, delighted to discover such a brilliant and fiery interpreter, at once asked her to work at the Sixth Barcarolle. In her book, Mme Long reproduces in facsimile a flattering letter from the composer: 'May I thank you for your perfect, ideal performances of my pieces. You have left me an exquisite memory which I shall treasure always.'[35]

Marguerite Long devoted herself over many years to rectifying the oblivion with which Fauré's piano music was surrounded. She studied a number of pieces with Fauré himself and, if we are to believe her memoirs, played them in public with great success. On 7 January 1905, for instance, at the Société nationale de musique she played the Third *Valse-Caprice*, the Sixth Barcarolle and the 'Fileuse' from *Pelléas et Mélisande*. 'Père' Hamelle was in the audience and appears suddenly to have realised the stature of the music which he had been publishing for twenty-five years. Mme Long remembered him saying ' "but Fauré's music has such sparkle". He looked absolutely astonished and delighted ... he never got over it.'[36]

In 1908 Fauré asked his latest interpreter to record the *Thème et variations*, the First *Valse-Caprice* and the 'Fileuse' from *Pelléas* for a producer of piano-rolls, M. Stransky. In 1913 she recorded for the German firm Welte Mignon rolls of the Sixth and Ninth Barcarolles, the Third *Valse-Caprice* and the *Thème et variations*. Several of her Fauré interpretations are also to be found on seventy-eight and on long-playing records, notably the Ballade and Piano Quartets.

The composer was at first delighted to have his music played with the éclat of a true virtuoso; 'I'm thrilled', he told her, 'to hear my music played with accents; everybody always plays it muted, trying to aim for unity, just as they think they don't need a voice to sing my songs.'[37] But, in his heart of hearts, did he really approve of her habit of unsynchronised hands and her textual liberties? Like the sudden cascade of chords leading into the coda of the Second Impromptu, an effect of her own devising which, she claimed, he accepted. Doubt must be cast on this when we see that in later printings Fauré had the words 'sans presser' added; they are not to be found in the autograph or in the first edition...

One wonders also what interpretation to give to the laconic phrase he used when thanking her after a performance of the Ballade on 19 January 1908 and again after her Fauré recital at the Salle Erard on 30 March 1909: 'That was an experience for me [Voilà pour moi une chose realisée].'[38]

Mme Long's book of her memories of Fauré would undoubtedly be worth publishing in a critical edition, including corrections of her many errors of dating and other inaccuracies as well as amplifications of her interesting remarks about some of the works she studied with the composer: the Fourth and Sixth Nocturnes, the Second and Third Impromptus, the Ballade and the *Thème et variations*. As we can see, all these come from his first and second periods. She admits in her book (p. 75) that she found his later piano works perplexing, and in fact she played none of them with the exception of the Ninth Barcarolle, the Fifth Impromptu and some of the Préludes.

For all her brilliance and enthusiasm as an interpreter of Fauré, Marguerite Long was also a woman of awkward character and consuming ambition. Historical objectivity forces one to say that she literally annexed Fauré's piano works, claiming from early on that she was the only person who could play them in the 'right style' – that is to say, hers. She used Fauré's name as a banner, considering that the Ballade in particular was her property, like Ravel's G major Concerto whose dedication, according to Roland-Manuel, she forced out of the composer. The self-satisfied comments in her book are very revealing. She writes, for example, of her appearance at the Société nationale in 1905: 'I had at least the great satisfaction of seeing myself designated as Fauré's "official" interpreter by the musicians who literally hurled themselves upon me as though I was responsible for this music ... A Fauré tradition had been born.'[39]

This famous 'Fauré tradition' in which Marguerite Long draped herself all through her life has come in for varied comment. One must at least quote the remarks of Philippe Fauré-Fremiet, the composer's younger son and biographer:[40] 'I insist on saying loudly and clearly: there is *no Fauré tradition* and what people teach our young pianists under that heading is in general *what ought not to be done*' (Fauré-Fremiet's own italics). Despite the almost laughable impudence of some of her claims, it is clear that Fauré did have great esteem for Joseph de Marliave, who married Marguerite Long in 1906. After giving up a career as a professional soldier, Marliave used his musical perspicacity to become a notable critic. His remarkable book on the Beethoven string quartets, with a preface by Fauré, has been reissued many times. His articles on musical history, published in *La Nouvelle Revue* under the pseudonym of J. Saint-Jean, testify to the breadth of his knowledge and to an open mind which allowed him to appreciate such different musical styles as those of Albéniz, who was a close friend, the Russian Five, Elgar, Strauss, Bruckner and Mahler, all at that time more or less unknown in France.[41]

'My husband was a Fauré enthusiast from his earliest years', Mme Long wrote. 'He could accompany all his songs from memory and knew every detail of the piano pieces' (*At the piano with Fauré*, p. 39); and further on: 'They had total confidence in each other. Fauré frequently asked for his help. He would arrive at our house in the morning, asking him to write an article or help him in some other task' (p. 111). Mme Long says, on p. 50, that during the summer of 1909 Marliave copied out some of Fauré's manuscripts of *Pénélope* while they were staying together at Lugano.

Unfortunately this friendship was affected by the problems of Mme Long's career at the Conservatoire. In 1906, at the age of thirty-two, she had taken over a preparatory piano class. Then, less than a year later, she set her sights on the senior class left vacant by the death of her teacher Marmontel. Fauré wrote to her in the summer of 1907 – a long, straight-forward, friendly but firm letter (published here for the first time):[42]

You know how unwilling I am to play the dogmatic apostle like d'Indy. But even if it's true that when Dubois was running the Conservatoire I didn't mind what happened to it, now that I'm in charge and can see the good one can do there, its future takes priority for me over all other considerations. So, in my view it is vital for the Conservatoire that Cortot takes over the class and, together with Risler, Chevillard,[43] Capet[44] and yourself, makes his contribution to the strengthening and rejuvenation of our teaching.

Writing to his wife on 31 July 1907, Fauré expressed himself more clearly still on the subject of Cortot's candidature:

It would be the most brilliant addition possible to the list Chevillard, Risler, Lucien Capet. It would serve the Conservatoire's needs admirably and be an honour for me too. It ought to go through on the nod as he's infinitely superior to the other candidates. But I know them, unfortunately, and I shall have a fierce battle on my hands.[45]

In his letter to Marguerite Long, Fauré continues:

You make a touching allusion when you say that no one could carry on the methods of Marmontel's teaching as well as you could. I liked Marmontel and admired the passionate commitment he brought to his teaching – the sort that is not likely to be found again. But I was far from agreeing with all his methods; and, while I'm on the subject, you should think carefully before continuing with them, if I'm to judge by the progress of your young pupils.

It would seem that Fauré was shocked by this premature candidacy. He read the impetuous Marguerite a lesson: 'You know how important your career is to me, you know how much I should like to give you a chance to display your gifts, but you also know – and I think my life as an artist is a good example of this – that I prefer things to happen in due time. That way one avoids the onslaughts of envy!' Unfortunately Fauré was unwise enough in this letter to promise her, for some future occasion, his 'warm, devoted, *enthusiastic*' support. He must soon have wished that unwritten because, from 1913 to 1919, the question of a woman taking over a senior class at the Conservatoire (in the end it was indeed Mme Long) was to become a real bone of contention in an establishment which was certainly not short of such things.

In her book she attributes her 'tardy' nomination – she was then forty-five – to Fauré's 'fierce hostility', urged on him, she thought, by his advisers. After 1913 connections between Fauré and the Marliaves were severed. The composer must surely have been sad to lose such a good friend as the husband, who was killed at the front on 24 August 1914. As for the wife, her ambition and above all her oft-proclaimed pretensions to possess 'patented rights' on Fauré's compositions finally exhausted his indulgence: one day, in the presence of the young violinist Robert Krettly, he referred to her as 'a shameless woman who uses my name in order to get on'. Even so, on his death-bed he wanted to heal this twelve-year-old quarrel. Roger-Ducasse passed the message on, but when she reached Fauré's house he had just died.

All this is very characteristic of Parisian musical life. Whatever the facts, whatever one's view of them, and even if one feels that both sides bore some responsibility for the rift (as they probably did), by piecing together the evidence one can certainly detect that Fauré was surrounded by a battle between females. Not another 'War of the Roses' maybe, but at least a 'War of the Marguerites' ...

Marguerite Long seems to have been possessed of a burning jealousy towards Marguerite Hasselmans. Fauré's mistress had the unpardonable effrontery to be a pianist like herself, to give lessons, to know Fauré's music even better than she did and, the crowning insult, to be beautiful and attractive. When, in her book, Mme Long recounts his meeting with her rival at the performance of *Prométhée* in 1900, the finger of jealousy may be seen to point:

One's attention was drawn to the composer, with his white boater tilted rakishly over one ear, much taken up by a young woman, very pretty be it said, who was his latest muse. She was a pianist ... and ambitious, and had just begun to occupy the place left vacant in Fauré's somewhat volatile affections.[46]

Much later, in the spring of 1918, Mme Long found herself in San Salvador in the Var district; she was in the ballroom of the Grand Hôtel, practising Ravel's *Le Tombeau de Couperin*.

The piano was in this enormous room in which I felt a little lost ... But I was not alone. When I got up from the piano, someone said to me: 'Do you know who was listening to you? ... Gabriel Fauré!' I found out that, at this difficult time, the great man was on a tour of the hotels, playing the *Dolly* suite with his muse, Mme H ..., and accompanying the famous singer Félia Litvinne, then past her best. It was sad. No-one was any longer where they should have been.[47]

None of this, though, affects her qualities as an interpreter. Her recording of Fauré's G minor Piano Quartet, made in 1940 with Jacques Thibaud, Maurice Vieux and Pierre Fournier, remains unsurpassed, even if her style, like her teaching, is now a historical relic. Drawn as she was to Fauré's more immediately attractive pieces, it would be fair to assume that she had little understanding of the Fourth Impromptu, dedicated to her. She waited nearly three years before giving the 'first public performance' of it, in her Fauré recital of 30 March 1909; and, in the interests of historical accuracy, one has to point out that Edouard Risler had already played it at the Société nationale de musique on 12 January 1907 ...

In the summer of 1905, at the same time as sketching out the Fourth Impromptu, Fauré returned to a genre he had abandoned for ten years and wrote the Seventh Barcarolle. The changes in Fauré's late piano style are now very evident, and particularly so in contrast with the Fourth Impromptu. It is as though the complicated, even overcharged textures of the Impromptu had been slimmed down and had the weight taken off them;

according to Pierre Auclert, Paul Dukas in his composition classes used to speak of Fauré's late style as being 'dephosphatised'. The note-values themselves are simpler: quavers, crotchets, minims, sometimes dotted, are all that Fauré needs. The harmony gathers clearly round the tonic D minor and is decorated with discreet but frequent clashes of major and minor seconds, while the lines move by step and often chromatically. There is, however, nothing dry in this new style: inside the 6/4 metre, unusual for Fauré, suppleness reigns, and the arpeggiated chords of the second motif, their upper notes forming a group of four descending notes, provide an especially beautiful moment (Ex. 59).

After a varied repeat of these two motifs the conclusion, in D major, boldly brings them together (bars 65 to 72).

Far from sounding forced or academic, this combination has a great melodic freshness: the first two notes of the chordal theme fit on to the beginning of the first motif (*marcato*, in the bass) with the naturalness of question and answer. It is an example of Fauré taking his inspiration from the Baroque era in which dialogue, real or imaginary, was a favourite musical constituent.

Ex. 59 Barcarolle no. 7

More generally speaking, the beauty and subtlety of Fauré's handling of motifs is one of the great attractions of his late style. The more carefully hidden they are, the more fascinating the search, so that it is easier to discover them in reading his scores rather than in just listening to the music. From the aesthetic point of view, the simplification of the texture and the resultant emergence of the horizontal lines, the relative restriction of sensuousness in the sound and in the harmonic palette, the introduction of ever sharper dissonances and the increasing linearity of the basses, all these features, characteristic of Fauré's writing in the years 1904 to 1907, are amazingly close to the revolution that was taking place in the plastic arts during these same years. The great Cézanne retrospective exhibition of 1907 revealed the geometric tendencies in the last pictures of this great master, who had died the previous year. Also in 1907, Braque and Picasso were to pursue the new paths of Cubism, renouncing colour – in the full flush of the success of Fauvism – in favour of a reconstruction of space reduced to a few basic forms and marked by firm outlines. Around 1910, the analytical phase of Cubism destroyed volume, reducing it to a synthesis of its lines and renouncing the long obeisance of painters to the laws of perspective. Instead, the modern artists accepted and rejoiced in one, plain fact: a picture is nothing but a flat surface.

It was also the period at which Piet Mondrian, in his trees and sand-dunes, abandoned the hallucinatory expressionism of his early work. He aimed to make his compositions systematic, retaining and developing only their basic lines and their inner structures, and he too, for a time, renounced vivid colours. Throughout the whole of Europe, the oldest and most firmly established laws were reeling under attack. Kandinsky abandoned figurative painting, the hallowed 'subject', and called his pictures 'compositions'. Klee built his pictures on musical ideas and experiences. The move away from perspective found an obvious parallel in the musical field in the jettisoning of tonality, which one can trace both in Debussy (*Préludes*, 1909–13; *Jeux*, 1913) and in Schoenberg (First Chamber Symphony, 1906; Three Piano Pieces op. 11, 1908; *Erwartung*, 1909; *Pierrot Lunaire*, 1912). In 1910 Stravinsky, in the 'Danse infernale de Kastchei' from *The Firebird*, gave warning of the disruption of *Le Sacre du Printemps* (1913), while in the cinema crowds flocked to see the work of Méliès and Griffith, and Gémier was revolutionising the theatre. In Munich, Kandinsky and the *Blaue Reiter* (1912), in Weimar, Gropius and the Bauhaus (1919), in Vienna, Sigmund Freud were all laying the foundations of our modern age.

In each of these different spheres the arrival of the twentieth century took place a little late by the calendar, roughly between 1905 and 1913. Whatever may have been said on the subject, all the post-First World War developments were already in hand before 1914 and it seems to me beyond question that Fauré, acting with his customary discretion and modesty, played his part in this search for new forms. His late style is more abrupt, eschewing prettiness and cascades of ornaments, as well as harmonic voluptuousness. He turned his back too on the slightly double-edged successes of the 1880s and on the sometimes sickly charm which so many modern critics attribute to his work as a whole. The problem is that the instant seductive power of his early music still too often masks the important but more severe creations of his last twenty years. This revolution, which upset – and still upsets – any number of Fauré enthusiasts, happened from within, without manifestos, deliberate suspension of tonality, *Farbenmelodie*, or orchestral or rhythmic innovations. Fauré was unable to deviate from the path he saw as his own. He went along it quite naturally, once he had rounded the difficult headland of these years from 1900 to 1905 – which is why I wanted to look at them in detail. His basic aim was not to become a public figure or get involved in being a revolutionary or a founding father; it was quite simply to develop his gifts and remain faithful to his own deeply held principles.

14   The theatre III: *Pénélope, Masques et bergamasques*

PÉNÉLOPE: DRAME LYRIQUE IN THREE ACTS, TEXT BY
RENÉ FAUCHOIS

The idea of *Pénélope* sprang from a casual meeting with the Wagnerian soprano Lucienne Bréval in Monte Carlo in February 1907. When she admitted her surprise that he had never written an opera, he replied that although he was attracted by remote antiquity he had never found a libretto to his liking. Mme Bréval offered to put him in touch with a young friend of hers called René Fauchois, a playwright who had just written for her a play on the subject of Penelope. Fauré accepted the offer with enthusiasm, the two men were soon on friendly terms and two months later the composer set to work. Fauchois' initial proposal was for a work in five acts but Fauré, at sixty-two and with his duties as Director of the Conservatoire leaving him only limited time for composition, begged for a reprieve, so they decided to eliminate Telemachus as being a secondary character whose activities were not essential to the drama. Fauré's enthusiasm for the subject, which he felt was made for him, can be judged by the fact that he started composing even before Fauchois had delivered the complete libretto. In it he found a straightforward plot, an important female rôle and above all numerous opportunities to express 'human feelings, as far as possible, through music that surpasses plain humanity', to borrow his words of 1885 when he was thinking of Pushkin's *Mazeppa*.

He began *Pénélope* in April 1907 and finally completed it in Lugano on 31 August 1912, his work on it during each of these six years being confined to the summer months. His wife spent these periods in Paris and his letters to her, published by Philippe Fauré-Fremiet in his *Lettres intimes*, give us a detailed account of his progress. Writing from Lausanne on 16 August 1907 he sets out his working methods:

As for the suitors, I've found a theme to represent them which I'm trying out, as I'm still not entirely happy with it ... By 'trying out', I mean exploring all the ways it

313

can be combined with other things to fit particular situations. For example, a servant girl says, speaking of one of the suitors, 'Antinoüs is handsome'; at that point my theme must preen itself . . . like a peacock! I also have to find out whether this theme goes with that of Pénélope. I try all the ways of modifying it and using it to produce different effects, either complete or in sections . . . To put it briefly, I work out the *ingredients* I shall need for the opera or, if you like, I make *studies* as a painter does for a picture.

Vocal and orchestral style

How to write an opera in the aftermath of Wagner? With *Pénélope* Fauré met head on this problem which exercised the ingenuity of several generations of composers. Like Debussy and Dukas, but unlike Saint-Saëns, Fauré considered that the old 'number' opera had had its day. Instead he chose the 'modern' pattern established by Wagner: the lyrical drama, based on the idea of musical and dramatic continuity. He also followed Debussy, Dukas and various lesser composers in adopting the system of leitmotifs to represent the main characters and various important emotional states or philosophical ideas: as he wrote to his wife, again in the letter of 16 August 1907, 'it's the Wagnerian system but there isn't a better one'. Where he differed, however, both from Wagner and from his contemporaries was in the treatment of the voice. He was always a lover of Italian opera and felt that after Wagner there had been too great an emphasis on the orchestra at the expense of the voice: Strauss's *Salome*, for example, he called 'a symphonic poem with voices on top'.[1] Furthermore, his care over declamation and his concern that the words should be understood led him to view with a critical eye the orchestral luxuriance he found in Dukas and Strauss. Of course, Debussy's *Pelléas* was signal proof that an orchestra could be discreet and effective at the same time, but Fauré's love for *bel canto* meant that he found Debussy's vocal minimalism, as it were, not to his taste. He had to look elsewhere and, indeed, find his own operatic style. With some seventy songs behind him, he was not long in coming up with a solution. As he addressed himself to Fauchois' libretto there emerged, right from the first scene, a vocal style that was above all flexible and responsive to both dramatic and expressive needs; it was in fact a kind of synthesis of all the styles, from pure recitative to aria, recalling vividly the early Florentine opera of Caccini or Monteverdi.

In fact there is in *Pénélope* more singing, according to the traditional meaning of the word, than in *Pelléas et Mélisande* or in *Ariane et Barbe-Bleue*. The role of Pénélope herself is particularly beautiful and singable from the first note to the last. Even so there are no arias in the true sense, rather what one might call flights of lyricism, lasting for several pages and blending quite naturally with the accompanied recitative that surrounds them. The styles of declamation are, then, very varied. In the first act, the queen's invocations 'Je l'attends, Minerve le protège' (p. 46)[2] and 'Il reviendra, j'en suis certaine' (p. 49) are the highlights of a rather abrupt dialogue with the suitors Eurymaque and Antinoüs. In the second act her aria 'C'est sur ce banc, devant cette colonne' (p. 126), is of a more classical cast, with unaccompanied recitative merging into arioso and then gradually becoming a real aria, ending on a high note. On the other hand the two arias sung by Ulysse, 'Epouse chérie' (Act I, p. 115) and 'Toute la nuit, sans bruit, comme une ombre' (Act III, p. 184), as well as Antinoüs' charming 'madrigal' 'Qu'il est doux de sentir sa jeunesse' (Act III, p. 202), are all true songs with orchestra, each one given an instrumental introduction posing as a recitative. Recitative, however, indeed an introduction of any sort, is dispensed with in Pénélope's mysterious evocation in Act I, 'Les Dieux ouraniens' (p. 81), and in 'J'ai gardé les bœufs et les chiens', the swineherd Eumée's protestation of fidelity in Act II (p. 132).

The boundaries between passages of accompanied recitative and flights of lyricism are essentially fluid. Occasionally a longish phrase in a dialogue may be the cause of the arioso taking on a melodic character like that of the pages I have just mentioned: for example, Ulysse's arrival in the first act and his opening lines 'Je suis un pauvre de passage', (p. 77), sung over a choral accompaniment; or Eurymaque's stanza 'Depuis qu'en ce travail ta piété s'absorbe' (p. 59); or, near the end of Act I, Pénélope's impassioned phrase 'Ainsi que chaque soir, montons sur la colline' (p. 111). As for strict recitative, it is hardly to be found anywhere. The only place where it operates in any extended fashion is at the beginning of 'O mon hôte, à présent puis-je t'interroger?', the great duet in the second act (pp. 135–42).

If *Pénélope* is of a piece with Fauré's whole output in being highly melodic, there are nonetheless no grounds for thinking that the orchestra is in any sense secondary. In classical French opera the rôle accorded the orchestra was essentially decorative and descriptive. It accompanied the dances in between the action and was useful for recreating storms, battle noises and supernatural interventions, while only a small number of instruments was required for the recitatives. An increase in the expressive and dramatic contributions of the orchestra came with the later works of Lully, the operas of Rameau and especially of Gluck.

Despite such illustrious forerunners (Gluck was a particular favourite of his) Fauré chose for his opera to copy the form and the sumptuous orchestral textures of the Wagnerian music drama – in his view there was no avoiding them. The orchestra in *Pénélope* is a large symphony orchestra with triple woodwind and a full complement of strings. One of its jobs, certainly, is to accompany, but in the density of its texture and the intricate interweaving of leitmotifs it is in every way equal in interest to the vocal lines. Taking the Wagnerian leitmotif as his starting point, Fauré developed his own personal method of manipulating it which was very different from Wagner's. Where Wagner's operas were conceived as dramas, with thematic recurrences standing as so many signposts to the action, Fauré paradoxically based his dramatic style on an essentially symphonic mode of thought. He treats his leitmotifs like the themes of an instrumental work and relies on his powers of melodic invention to supply an endless series of variants and combinations.

As a result, the leitmotif loses much of its signifying force, that is as a direct musical expression of the text. Instead it becomes a quarry for the materials of the accompaniment and its links with the text are often indirect or buried, so that you have actually to look in the orchestral score to discover at various points inversions, retrogrades, compressions – all integrated into counterpoint whose technical expertise is matched by its emotional impact.

At times the orchestra is in the forefront. It is the orchestra and the orchestra alone that shoulders the expressive burden in the moments of deepest feeling. Pénélope's despair (Act I, scene 8) inspires seven bars (p. 108) that are among the most tragic in the whole score, combining the heroine's theme, the final rhythm of the love theme and Ulysse's rising fifths. The masterly end to Act I, Pénélope's exit in Act II (p. 173), the moment in the scene of the bow in Act III when Ulysse picks up his weapon (p. 245) – in all these passages it is the orchestra that surges to the fore, to express emotions whose force the vocal lines can no longer contain.

An analysis

Right from the spacious prelude to Act I (in G minor), Fauré affirms the symphonic dimensions of what is to follow. The prelude is built on the themes of the separated couple. Pénélope's appears straight away, a sad, mournful theme, as much harmonic as melodic over a rhythmic counterpoint whose double-dotted motif will frequently be in evidence. Then comes Ulysse's theme, resplendent, confident and vigorous. Its intervals are simple and striking: an octave, a major second, rising fifths. It is heard first on the trumpet (p. 3) over a shimmering accompaniment of string chords (Ex. 60).

Ex. 60 *Pénélope*

Act I

Scenes 1–3 make up the exposition. The curtain rises to reveal a chorus of servant girls busy at their spinning. The seven-note motif that characterises them is not very clearly defined and depicts the mood of voluptuous nonchalance. 'I can see these spinning maidens are going to cause me problems', Fauré wrote to his wife on 12 August 1907, and this introductory chorus in D flat major does not match the beauty of the orchestral prelude. The vocal line is accompanied by a delicate counterpoint based on the servant girls' motif and beneath them both runs a continuous flow of semiquavers, illustrating the movement of the spinning wheels (Ex. 61).

Ex. 61 Les Servantes

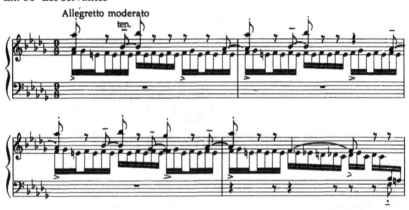

The vague, ambivalent impression of this line, caused by its refusal to define a key, was, it seems, deliberate: 'It's not what they say that matters', he wrote, 'it's the atmosphere and their passivity, as they work in a sort of dream. So it's the orchestra that has got to get all that across and their words must stand out against a background of music that's continually moving.'[3]

Then in scene 2 an incisive, rhythmical motif in D major (Ex. 62)

Ex. 62 Les Prétendants

announces the entry of the suitors. 'I tried to find an idea which described their brutality and total self-satisfaction', he wrote on 16 August 1907.[4]

The suitors insistently demand that the queen join them: 'Nous sommes las de ses dédains.' Ulysse's faithful nurse Euryclée interrupts them in a stormy and effective recitative (scene 3), punctuated by the opening notes of the suitors' motif. To a triumphant statement of her theme Pénélope appears and from this point right through to the end of the Act there is a quickening of interest, while the musical level is maintained almost without a pause. In scene 4, Pénélope's E minor dialogue with the importunate suitors shows Fauré's skill in managing a text in which the rapid to-and-fro of the dialogue seems more suited to spoken theatre than to opera. The clarity, strength and emotional power of Pénélope's solo 'Jadis quand on aimait' make it a model of word-setting and it is a fine example of arioso over a string accompaniment, leading quite naturally to two passages of purely melodic writing, 'Je l'attends, Minerve le protège' and 'Il reviendra, j'en suis certaine': both are deeply felt evocations of the absent hero, whose theme is heard low in the orchestra. It is one of the most moving passages in the score, as Fauré himself realised. When setting the words 'J'ai tant d'amour à lui donner encore' (p. 52) he was pleased, as he told his wife, to have found 'a form of expression which, I hope, conveys all the pathos and emotion, with Pénélope's theme underpinning the accompaniment'. He was particularly successful here in keeping the characterisation going through the suitors' interruption, ending this extended section on Pénélope's impressive high B flat. By purely musical means, and in particular by a judicious use of rhythm, Fauré is able to render the feeling of hope which sustains Pénélope and turns her into a dreamer. She barely seems to hear the suitors, her thoughts are elsewhere; and such is Fauré's intuitive genius that he, far more than his librettist, conjures up the atmosphere of Homer's original.

Relaxation comes in the form of Eurymaque's C minor madrigal, 'Depuis qu'en ce travail ta piété s'absorbe' (p. 59), followed by the brief scene of the presentation of the winding-sheet, still uncompleted. Fauré took advantage of this to introduce a truly memorable musical effect: a vast, silky string chord over an F sharp pedal, creating a moment of calm and mystery. No less masterly is his display of technique at the end of this fourth scene, when he presents first of all an 'air de danse' with the solo flute and then combines it, effortlessly as it seems, with a superb melody at the words 'Ulysse, fier époux.'

Pénélope's hopes are fulfilled. In scene 5 Ulysse reappears but disguised as an old beggar, a piece of subterfuge that allows him to find out what has been going on in his absence. To underline this transformation, Fauré brings in another motif, that of Ulysse's weakness. This is a chorale-like theme (Ex. 63) whose slow, smooth continuum makes the maximum

Ex. 63 Ulysse (begging)

Je suis un   pau-vre de pas - sa-ge Et j'im - plo-re de vous, __

__ sans a-si-le et sans   biens   La pâ - tu - re qu'on donne aux chiens __

contrast with the abrupt energy of what, following Joseph de Marliave, we may call the 'royal' theme. Ulysse's two motifs together make up a lifelike portrait of his double identity.

Then follows a brief septet for the unfaithful servant girls and the suitors, in which Fauré's subtle harmonies go well beyond the rather wooden sensuality of Fauchois' text. This leads to the beautiful sixth scene where Ulysse is recognised by his nurse Euryclée. To introduce it there is heard a discreet reference to the rising fifths of the 'royal' theme and then, over *tremolando* strings, the ecstatic dialogue unfolds between the old nurse and the hero, discovered in spite of all his precautions. For all its beauty, however, this dialogue seems to pass too quickly to be dramatically convincing.

Pénélope has been present throughout, lost in her own thoughts. As soon as she is left alone she begins her nightly task of undoing the day's work and the impressive motif of the winding-sheet (p. 102, now in F minor) is heard once more, while Pénélope's 'work' on it is depicted by a single flute line, winding its way through the held chord like a thread through the cloth (Ex. 64). The suitors enter without being heard and discover the queen's trickery. They insist that tomorrow she choose Ulysse's successor.

Ex. 64 The winding sheet

The last of the principal themes to be heard is the love theme. It has already made a brief appearance in the aria 'Ulysse, fier époux' at the words 'Maître à qui j'ai donné les trésors de ma grâce' (p. 72), but now it is presented plainly for the first time (Ex. 65).

Ex. 65 Love theme

In this eighth scene the love theme is combined with triplets and with the 'royal' theme's rising fifths, and the harmonic progressions that ensue, together with the fleeting implications of the polyphony, produce a passage of true pathos. The scene continues with the powerful evocation of the sea on which Ulysse's ship is riding, and the regular movement of the lower instruments ('cellos, bassoon and horns) induces in the orchestra as a whole a kind of vast, rhythmic breathing.

Ulysse, left alone in the ninth scene, gives vent to his happiness in a tumultuous E major aria in which his ardour carries all before it – the themes of the royal pair and the love theme are mixed in a sort of maelstrom that wonderfully characterises Ulysse's sudden abandonment to joy. In contrast, the final scene is one of gentleness. The actual words spoken by Pénélope, Ulysse and Euryclée are few and of no real importance. It is the orchestra that carries them, and us, in a huge expansion of the love theme leading to a great lyrical climax.

An analysis of the score of this scene tells us only so much: that Fauré uses canon at the octave, that he modulates upward through mediantly related keys, that he dwells on his favourite tritone in both melodic and harmonic contexts and that the VI–I cadence marking the final appearance of Ulysse's theme allows Fauré to reach the haven of E major at the very last moment, as is his wont. But nothing can explain the almost superhuman beauty of these closing bars, except possibly some synthesis of inspiration and learning, of hard work and divine grace.

Act II

The whole of Act II takes place 'on the top of a hill overlooking the sea'. Musically it is an extension of scene 8 in the previous act, opening with an evocation of the sea including, as one might expect, a motif employing the fifth and second and based on the theme of Ulysse. 'I've been searching for ways of creating a nocturnal, countryside atmosphere that is redolent of the sea', Fauré wrote to his wife on 28 August 1908. 'So we have to have the sound of a pipe, but a low, slightly melancholy one.' The opening scene in E minor is almost a symphonic poem joining the orchestral prelude to an aria sung by Eumée, the faithful swineherd, 'Sur l'épaule des monts'. Fauré was often drawn to recreate images of sleep and night-time, and the contemplative side of his genius is beautifully displayed in the feeling of peace that emanates from this passage. The feeling persists through the first part of Pénélope's A minor aria (scene 2), 'C'est sur ce banc, devant cette colonne', with a particularly delicate touch when she sings of the magnificent roses she picks every evening in memory of her absent husband. But soon the tone changes and becomes more passionate as once again she imagines the arrival of Ulysse's ship, and we hear the sea motif in the bass. A second aria for Eumée, 'J'ai gardé les bœufs et les chiens' (p. 132), in F minor with a flattened leading note and accompanied by rich four-part counterpoint, leads to a return of the music for the opening of the act and then to the great duet which makes up the major part of it.

This duet was undoubtedly the part of the opera Fauré worked on the hardest. He laboured at it first in 1909, rewrote it almost completely two years later and then extended it in 1913 between the Monte Carlo and Paris productions. In its final version it consists of two distinct sections, each 127 bars long and constructed along parallel lines of a dramatic *crescendo* cut short by two interruptions from Pénélope, 'Mais toi-même tu pleures, pourquoi, pourquoi?' (p. 149) and 'Comme tu dis cela, comme tu dis cela' (p. 163).

Each of the two halves begins with accompanied recitative and then increases in urgency. While neither reaches the level of an operatic melody, the two dialogues are fine examples of passionate declamation. The thematic working is extremely elaborate, subtly following the suggestions of the text and at the same time playing its part in the construction of the whole. Thus the theme of Ulysse's weakness, already heard at some length in Pénélope's aria 'C'est sur ce banc, devant cette colonne', reappears at the beginning of each half of the dialogue to underline Ulysse's words 'Tu connaîtras jusqu'où mon sort fut misérable', and later 'Toutes tes questions ont rouvert ma blessure'. On the other hand Fauré uses the 'royal' theme to illustrate the 'double manteau de laine pourprée' and the hero's 'tunique étincelante' in the first half of the dialogue as well as the re-membering of his 'triomphes guerriers' in the second; while Ulysse's deeply-felt utterances are made to a condensed but striking combination of Pénélope's theme with the theme of love (pp. 161–2). The truth is that Fauré follows the psychological development of his characters so faithfully as to render analysis futile. In particular the harmonic language changes practically from bar to bar. His continual use of chromaticism loosens the feeling of tonality and leads to a kind of 'disorientation', a rendering in purely musical terms of the emotional upheaval suffered by both hero and heroine.

Euryclée's interruption, 'Il faut rentrer, princesse' (p. 164) and the return of the sea motif announce the end of the duet and lead Pénélope to express her despair. She would rather die than be unfaithful, 'Pour la dernière fois vous me voyez moi-même', and the scene ends with a kind of funeral march based on her theme (p. 173).

The final scene, in D major, resounds with joy and warlike noises. Ulysse reveals himself to his faithful retainers and with their help sets out on the path of vengeance. It is, not surprisingly, the various elements of the royal theme, and especially the rising octave and major second, which form the substance of this brief, hectic scene, dominated by the glowing colours of the brass.

Act III

Ex. 66 Ulysse's rage

The D minor orchestral prelude prolongs the heroic atmosphere of the Act II finale. Here, however, it is no longer Ulysse's joy which signals the unleashing of the orchestra's power, but his anger (Ex. 66). The prelude introduces his aria 'Toute la nuit, comme une ombre' and this is followed by a short dialogue, first with Euryclée (scene 2) and then with Eumée (scene 3), who is enthusiastically at work preparing his master's revenge. Scene 4 presents the Entry of the Suitors. Their life of pleasure, free from cares of hardship, is summed up perfectly by Antinoüs' delightful madrigal 'Qu'il est doux de sentir sa jeunesse' (p. 202), with its relaxed, almost abandoned violin accompaniment. The suitors urge the preparations for the feast that is to mark Pénélope's re-marriage, while the warnings of death become more insistent. The suitor's motif is here varied and developed (p. 209) in combination with the dancing rhythm, punctuated by harp chords, which we have heard already in Act I (p. 67 and pp. 83–4); this is followed by a brief *divertissement*, danced to an almost oriental melody on the flute (pp. 214–19).

In scene 5 the queen makes her entrance, to a repeat in G major of the music heard for her entrance in Act I. Antinoüs is deputed to make the address and reminds her of her stated intention to choose from among the suitors a second husband: 'Reine, dissipe le chagrin qui pâlit ton beau front'. Antinoüs' speech (pp. 220–2) is accompanied by strings alone and has a claim to be considered the most beautiful passage of recitative in the entire score. The setting of the words has the truth and dignity of Rameau or Gluck, supported by a wealth of expressive counterpoint and ending with a particularly fine cadence into A minor.

Pénélope now institutes the archery contest, as suggested by the 'beggar' at the end of their duet. But before it can take place she goes into a kind of visionary trance in which she foresees the outcome of the contest and she describes the suitors' massacre in advance: 'Ah: Malheureux! Un orage affreux vous emporte.' The opening notes of the suitors' theme are now heard to great effect on broken chords in the strings, soon reinforced by the theme of Ulysse's anger, 'La mort est ici'.

The suitors' confidence is shaken, but they get ready for the contest. The musical portrayal of this is supremely appropriate, Ulysse's bow being described by the rising fifths of the 'royal' theme, but with the fifths now diminished, to suggest an insufficient tension in the string. Their resolution in an abrupt, chromatic triplet catches perfectly (indeed almost comically) the aspirants' tame abandonment of their enterprise (see Ex. 67).

Ex. 67 Bow scene

After Eurymaque and Pisandre have exhausted themselves to no avail, Antinoüs refuses even to try. At this point the old beggar demands a turn, 'Autrefois on vantait ma force et mon adresse', in a fine arioso based on the theme of Ulysse's weakness, treated by the strings in counterpoint (pp. 242–3), and the 'royal' theme is heard as he picks up the bow. (Between the Monte Carlo and Paris productions in 1913 Fauré added eight bars at this dramatic highpoint, in addition to the central *allegro* in the duet which I have already mentioned.) The arrow passes straight through the target of twelve rings. Ulysse draws again and aims this time at Eurymaque: 'et cette fois, c'est toi ma cible'. The suitors flee in terror. Ulysse pursues them, helped by his retainers, while amid the orchestral hubbub we hear the 'royal' theme and the theme of Ulysse's anger. The suitors are killed off-stage, following classical precedent, and their theme is now transformed into a funeral march (p. 256). Ulysse reappears (scene 6) and with his cry 'Justice est faite' comes the moment for the majestic finale. Fidelity and ingenuity together have won the day. Acclaimed by the people of Ithaca, the reunited couple look forward to a life of happiness and peace. 'The opera finishes in a mood of serenity', wrote Fauré, as he finally laid down his pen on 31 August 1912. 'Everyone is happy and they sing, without *shouting*, "Gloire à Zeus".'[5] The themes of Ulysse and Pénélope combine with the love theme in the orchestral texture and, after the first moments of exaltation, the tempo begins to relax (p. 259–60) and Ulysse's rising fifths march through the bass of the orchestra with an almost cosmic grandeur; and as in the ancient *tragédies lyriques*, the heavens are revealed.

First and subsequent performances

The sumptuous serenity of this finale was not at all to the taste of Raoul Gunsbourg, the director of the Monte Carlo theatre, who had offered in 1907 to give the work its first performance. Fauré wrote to his wife on 24 February 1913, some days before the première:

I have, whatever else, two good interpreters in Mlle Bréval and Rousselière [as Pénélope and Ulysse], and in some of the smaller rôles. Even so, I'm not expecting anything approaching perfection. As far as Gunsbourg is concerned, I have the feeling my work is totally misunderstood. He keeps saying 'It's classical music, it's a classical opera' in a way which suggests a deep underlying contempt! . . . his most recent idea was to alter the end of *Pénélope* and replace the final calm with a lot of noise and uproar. You may rest assured I shall allow nothing of the sort.[6]

Not content with directing his theatre and working as a producer which directors often did in those days, Gunsbourg also fancied himself as a composer. He wrote both the words and the music of operas which he then got Leon Jehin, the long-suffering conductor of the theatre, to orchestrate. In the middle of *Pénélope* he was entirely preoccupied with the première of his three-act opera *Venise*, which was to take place four days after Fauré's . . . Saint-Saëns wrote to his editor Jacques Durand on 5 March 1913:

Gunsbourg is behaving appallingly, he's doing everything he can to push *Venise* at *Pénélope*'s expense . . . He told Mme Litvinne [the singer Félia Litvinne] that his was the only real music, and before it all other music would vanish. She told him he was mad. She'd been asked to learn the part of Pénélope, as Mlle Bréval could no longer be relied on; but then, when Mlle Bréval let it be known she would be able to sing, Mme Litvinne was no longer wanted. They offered to pay her even so, but she refused.[7]

Alphonse Visconti's neo-Grecian, pre-Hollywood sets (see plate 45, p. 342) were much appreciated, but the production itself had been too hasty to produce satisfactory results in any of the (merely) three performances which had been planned – for 4, 11 and 15 March 1913. Fauré wrote to his wife on 25 February, 'I just hope things will have settled down by the time the opera reaches Paris. Here I get the impression what I've composed is boring, grey and lifeless.'[8] The critic of *Le Journal de Monaco* wrote on 11 March that Lucienne Bréval, who in fact was not very well, 'made praise-worthy efforts to give a moving performance of the rôle of Pénélope'. It seems to have been a static interpretation, more majestic than passionate.

Paris had known for some years that Fauré was at work on the opera and, as he was the director of the Conservatoire and this was his first work for the operatic stage, it was awaited with some impatience. First of all the Paris première was going to be given at the Opéra where Messager was director; then at the Opéra-Comique, under Albert Carré; but it in fact took place at the Théâtre des Champs-Elysées, which had just opened under the guidance of Gabriel Astruc, on 10 May 1913 with an open dress rehearsal the day before. Lucienne Bréval again took the part of Pénélope with a new Ulysse in Lucien Muratore, 'infinitely superior to his predecessor', as Fauré was informed in a letter written on the day of the first performance by Saint-Saëns, the work's dedicatee.[9] Durec's production had brilliant sets by the Nabi painter, Ker-Xavier Roussel, and the costumes were by Ibels (see plates 46–8, pp. 343–5). The only problems were those the conductor, Louis Hasselmanns, had with the orchestra recently formed by the young Inghelbrecht. Fauré wrote to Astruc:

Among the horns, the third horn was playing first, the second was playing third and the fourth's part was deciphered by a musician of sorts. As for the previous performances, *every one* was preceded by *two orchestral rehearsals the same day* and not, need I say, for *Pénélope* ... You can imagine, after so much playing, the brass players' lips began to go and you can't blame them for their mistakes and cracked notes. Only I must say these blemishes were a *very heavy* burden for my opera to bear.[10]

Whatever its imperfections, the Paris première of *Pénélope* was a real triumph. Several reviews hailed it as a masterpiece and Emile Vuillermoz wrote:

It can now be admitted that many of Fauré's supporters were nervous to see the *maître*, after his glorious successes in the field of chamber music, making such a late attempt to conquer the musical stage. The young Suitors smiled to themselves when they saw ranged against them this rival with his white hair, calmly and confidently taking up the mighty bow of opera. And, as in Homer, they suddenly saw the new Ulysse brandish his weapon, draw it with a vigorous arm and let fly an arrow that pierced the audience to the heart. Paris stands amazed at the feat.[11]

Unfortunately, after such a brilliant start, Fauré's opera has suffered unjustifiable neglect. Astruc's opening season of opera and Russian ballet was so extravagant that when the theatre reopened in October it was on the brink of bankruptcy. Its collapse followed hard on the last performances of *Pénélope*, which had become more and more run-of-the-mill, and the sets and costumes had to be sold off, so that there was no question of an immediate revival. 'And so my poor *Pénélope* lies down for a long sleep', Fauré wrote gloomily to Saint-Saëns on 8 November 1913. However, it was put on successfully at the Monnaie in Brussels with Claire Croiza beginning on 1 December, and in Rouen on 17 December. A revival was under way at the Opéra-Comique when war broke out. In the years that followed the impetus of interest in the opera naturally slackened, but in October 1918 Albert Carré asked Fauré if it could be put on at the Opéra-Comique.

It duly appeared on the stage on 20 January 1919, with a new, young Pénélope, Germaine Lubin, and with Charles Rousselière as Ulysse. The sets were by Lucien Jusseaume, the costumes by Marcel Multzer, and Albert Carré was the producer. *Pénélope* was produced quite regularly at the Opéra-Comique between the wars, but always for a short season.

Jacques Rouché was responsible for its première at the Paris Opéra in 1943, with Germaine Lubin and Georges Jouatte, and designs by Georges Lecaron. Twice, therefore, this drama of deliverance had developed further overtones from its staging in a time of national crisis – in 1919 and 1943. However, since 1949 it has not been seen at the Paris Opéra. The provinces have been able to admire Régine Crespin in the title rôle and, perhaps more importantly, the opera has now begun to make its way abroad, with performances in Liège (1951), Buenos Aires (1962) and Lisbon (1966).

Paris found a champion for *Pénélope* in D. E. Inghelbrecht, who used to conduct it on the radio, and Jean Fournet directed it in the course of the 1963 Holland Festival. The BBC performed it for the first time in 1973 (with Josephine Veasey and André Turp) and finally Paul Paray conducted it in Paris in 1974. Whenever *Pénélope* is put on, critics and musicians are enthusiastic about it, but the opera public is disconcerted by a style that makes no concessions and by its uniformity of tone. Despite some two hundred performances it still has not made its way into the world-wide repertory; which, we must remember, did not receive *Pelléas* for sixty years ...

Criticism of the opera has generally been directed at René Fauchois' libretto and at the orchestration, so it will be as well to look at both elements briefly before finishing this discussion.

The libretto and the orchestration

To fit Homer's world to the dramatic style and conventions of early twentieth-century opera was no easy task. The librettist had to reduce the sparkling flexibility of the poem to a regular succession of acts and scenes, turn its quintessentially a-realist, epic declamation into something dramatically plausible and, in short, recreate Homer's myth with two-dimensional, hardboard scenery. Stylistically, the difficulties were no less. Dialogues had to be manufactured from a strong but convoluted poetry whose power stems largely from its incantatory flux, the very opposite of what is needed in the theatre. There was one further problem: as the opera was being written for Lucienne Bréval, the character of Pénélope had to become the focus of the drama. Important as she is in Homer's poem, she is not exactly an arresting figure – her patience contributes far less to the substance of the story than do her husband's wanderings.

When René Fauchois, at the age of twenty-five, addressed himself to these difficulties he was still at the very beginning of his career. But, as well as a wealth of inexperience, he brought to the task a great enthusiasm for opera and a profound knowledge of the *Odyssey*, which had become one of his bedside books. If there is a problem in this respect, it is not that he strayed too far from the original: several passages come straight from Homer, like Pénélope's aria 'Les dieux ouraniens' in Act I scene 5, taken from Book 17, lines 480–7. But if Homer's text was to become an opera of this period some reworking was inevitable and, while Fauchois included in his libretto numerous passages that paraphrase the original, he was unfortunately more faithful to the letter of the *Odyssey* than to its spirit. Taking the story of Ulysse's return home, he treated it in the manner of Edmond Rostand's historical dramas which were very popular at this time – indeed Fauchois' own stage debut was in a supporting role in Rostand's *L'Aiglon*.[12] The ancient tale is thus refurbished with psychological attitudes and a bourgeois morality that belong to twentieth-century France, its surface encrusted with the empty formulae of 'grand theatre' and with liberal helpings of inverted phraseology and poetic cliché. Eumée's aria at the beginning of Act II is a fairly typical example:

On the shoulder of the mountain where the flock used to bleat, the dusk pins its violet mantle ... The passing wind is full of peaceful ecstasy and urges the melancholy pines to song. The moon, emerging from the waters, shines like a silver platter.

Fauchois was later to make his name with the play *Boudu sauvé des eaux* which caused a scandal and provided Jean Renoir with the story for a well-known film. We should therefore, to be fair, point out that in failing as a librettist he was far from being alone. Nineteenth-century operatic history is an unbroken succession of literary betrayals, including famous works by Gounod, Massenet, Verdi ... Any operagoer's memory is a thesaurus of hack-work. The only problem with a libretto in French is that when it is sung in France it runs the risk of being understood by the audience! With a libretto in German or Italian the French public are spared this embarrassment; so that there might be some point in going to the ultimate lengths of absurdity and actually performing *Pénélope* in a German or Flemish translation. Attention could then be directed exclusively to Fauré's music which, it hardly needs to be stressed, operates on an altogether more elevated plane.

Even so, there is no hiding the fact that Fauré found Fauchois' text more than a little tiresome. In his letters to his wife he is moved to complain about 'the blessed poet' who has given him too much text in general and for the spinning chorus in particular:

Fauchois hasn't understood how music prolongs words. A passage may take a couple of minutes to read but when it's sung it takes three times as long, at least. So I have to cut couplets, quatrains and octaves here and there, making sure the sense is still clear. It's not always that easy! Those wretched suitors argue interminably.[13]

(20 September 1907)

Rather strangely, the libretto of *Pénélope*, published by Heugel in 1913, gives not the text set by Fauré but Fauchois' original in full, no doubt in deference to his artistic feelings. A comparison of the two shows quite how active Fauré was in his revisions. Not only did he cut passages, he occasionally improved the sound of certain lines – as he often did in his songs – and sometimes even reshaped whole scenes, moving entire paragraphs (especially in Act III) and altering the distribution of the text between the various characters. This kind of intervention was possible because

Fauchois had written in free verse, but sometimes even the regularity of the rhyme scheme had to give way to the exigencies of the music. Well might he write to Fauchois on 12 October 1907:

I have a very great deal to discuss with you, my dear collaborator. Also a lot to confess, because I've had to sacrifice some of your lines. I wouldn't have done so without consulting you if the holidays hadn't separated us. But the muse was upon me and I wanted to get on![14]

Fauchois must have disapproved because when Fauré tackled the duo in Act II he was careful to ask his collaborator to make the cuts.[15] He also complained that this duo was weighed down by 'the dead hand of the theatre'. When he came to revise it, he confided to his wife (4 August 1911):

The situation is demanded by the theatre, perhaps, but it's quite unbelievable – a wife sings to her husband and doesn't recognise him because he's wearing a false beard! And I have to force myself to feel conviction so that it comes through in her music.[16]

This dialogue between husband and wife is based on Book 19 of the Odyssey and illustrates how difficult it is to adapt this saga to the stage. In Homer, Pénélope does not recognise Ulysse because, thanks to the intervention of Athene, he does really look like an old man (end of Book 13). Fauchois, realising the problem, was careful to make Ulysse arrive at nightfall and to let the dialogue take place, not in the palace of Ithaca, but on a hilltop near the sea at night. In Giacomo Badoaro's libretto *Il ritorno d'Ulisse in patria*, set by Monteverdi, the hero is changed into an old man by Minerva who appears in the guise of a shepherdess. This supernatural element was a more or less indispensable part of seventeenth- and eighteenth-century operas, but was no longer feasible in the more realistic stagings that in general characterised the second half of the nineteenth century.

Still more awkward for the composer was the way Fauchois had split the dialogue into extremely short sentences, so that Fauré had to redistribute the text, particularly among the suitors, and had to suppress various untimely interruptions. Curiously, although Fauré found the libretto in general too prolix, there are places where it seems to stem the natural flow of the music: for example, the scene where Ulysse is recognised by Euryclée, his two arias (end of Act I and beginning of Act III) and the final scene.

But every libretto has its faults and it is simply not reasonable to hold that those of *Pénélope* necessarily make the work a failure. The text possesses one prime quality: it serves the composer's aesthetic purpose. The musical inspiration for the title role owes much, as Fauré recognised, to the fact that 'Pénélope's monologues are well written and free of pathos' (Letter to his wife of 23 September 1907), and two years later, on 1 October 1909, he repeated the compliment: 'I simply allowed myself to be guided by the straightforwardness of the action and by the dignity of the characters.'[17] This clarity of action seems to me a quality all the more remarkable for being absent from most opera librettos.

Contrary to what has often been claimed, Fauré enjoyed orchestrating *Pénélope* enormously. 'When I've finished composing I'll start on the orchestration', he wrote to his wife on 18 August 1912, 'that'll be a pleasantly relaxing task'; and in a letter of 14 September 1912, 'I really enjoy orchestrating. It may be a long job but it's extremely interesting.[18] However, at the end of October 1912 only half the score was orchestrated, with the première announced as taking place in Monte Carlo at the beginning of the following March. Fauré realised that his involvement with the Conservatoire entrance examinations would prevent his finishing the orchestration unless he got someone else to help him. This was quite normal practice for the period: Saint-Saëns, superb orchestrator that he was, had allowed Messager to score an act of his opera *Phryné* and, as is well known, Debussy needed the help of André Caplet to meet the deadline for *Le Martyre de St-Sébastien*.

Much ink has been spilled fruitlessly on the question of the authenticity of the orchestration in *Pénélope*. The truth can only be learnt from the manuscript, donated by Fauré's family to the Opéra library in Paris. Without going into detail, I can confirm that Fauré orchestrated more than two-thirds of the work and kept a close eye on the efforts of his collaborator. This was a young composer called Fernand Pécoud (1879–1940), a pupil of d'Indy and at the time of this collaboration a violinist in the Hasselmans concert society. His name is mentioned by Charles Koechlin in his biography of Fauré[19] and a perusal of the manuscript supports this identification. Pécoud's delicate handwriting takes over in fact in the second act, from the duet 'O mon hôte, à présent puis-je t'interroger' to the end of the act, as well as in some short passages in the final scene of the opera, unfortunately incomplete in the manuscript.

Critics who, in 1913, expressed reserve about the orchestration were few and far between. But Jean Marnold found it was too sober and lacking in impact and variety, though he realised this classicism seemed 'to be the closest possible match for Fauré's inspiration, and it is after all a fact that M. Fauré has never orchestrated in any other way'.[20] This idea was developed by Koechlin, a Fauré admirer and a former pupil: 'As with several other great composers, the work's beauty does not depend on orchestral colours; there is something intimate and profound about it, shining out from pure timbres', and he ends by saying: 'In spite of many a happy detail, I don't find in the opera's orchestration the simplicity, the grandeur, the complete mastery or the charm that reside in the notes. Or rather, it is only in the notes that I find these qualities realised to their fullest extent.'[21] In an unpublished letter of 10 September 1913, Fauré replied to his pupil with his usual simplicity:

You have blunted and cushioned your criticism so that only a professional musician would recognise it as such. Nonetheless, you're right. I know myself well enough to have been aware of this fault (a fault of nature, clearly) on more than one occasion. Alas, at my age I shan't have the time to do anything about it![22]

If such criticisms were rarely expressed in Fauré's lifetime they were more frequently heard when *Pénélope* reached the Paris Opéra, so much so that for the 1949 revival Inghelbrecht, one of the work's staunchest champions, decided to revise the orchestration. In an article on the subject he deplored the monochrome, bass-heavy character of the original and the way in which

the continuity of themes is often broken up as they pass from one instrument to another – notably at the beginning of Act II – because no sound is carried over to link the portions together ... My revision includes marking the bowing throughout; lightening some of the heavier textures by suppressing the doubling of strings by woodwind, or vice versa; reducing the number of desks in the strings at certain points to make it easier to hear the voices; and mending the breaks in continuity I have referred to above.[23]

Reading these judgments and studying the score of *Pénélope*, one is forced to wonder whether the above views have not been distorted by what might be called a fault of perspective. At the time when Fauré's opera was first produced, the orchestral discoveries of Dukas, Strauss, Debussy, Ravel and Stravinsky were still new. So the views relayed to us by Marnold, Koechlin and Inghelbrecht were those of the up-and-coming generation who, in their enthusiasm for orchestral novelty, could not imagine a composer refusing to avail himself of all the latest and best techniques. Hindsight gives a quite different perspective.

When you open the orchestral score of *Pénélope* you are struck by the predominance of strings. The full orchestra, of triple woodwind, two bassoons, four horns, three trumpets, three trombones and tuba, harp and percussion, is used only for the rare climaxes (chiefly the Prelude to Act I, the end of Act II, the beginning of Act III and also the end of Act III). For most of the opera Fauré employs a kind of expanded chamber orchestra: a large string section, much divided, with oboe, horns or solo trumpet picking out the details. At first hearing this economy of means is not at all obvious, but it results in a transparent, discreetly coloured orchestration perfectly suited to the nobility and sobriety of tone the composer was aiming for. At the climaxes the texture becomes thicker, Fauré scoring in instrumental blocks and doubling up his timbres in Wagnerian fashion.

Occasionally, though, when the situation demands it, he allows more arresting colours to intrude, as in the two seductive 'airs de danses' with their flute and oboe solos, harp and pizzicato strings and delicate touches on triangle, tambourine and antique cymbals; or at the point in the second act where a sudden burst of light mysteriously erupts on a harp *glissando* and high woodwind at the mention of 'the most brilliant roses' gathered by Pénélope. In contrast Fauré's depiction of the underworld where, at the end of the duet, Pénélope says she longs to be, makes a tremendous impact through his cunning use of instruments in their low register. As for the technical faults pointed out by Inghelbrecht, we may well ask whether, for all the care he has taken to correct them, such action was in fact necessary. If we compare certain passages in the recordings of the two versions, it becomes clear that Inghelbrecht's suppression of doublings merely brings out primary colours whose sharpness Fauré had been at pains to tone down; and if we actually look at Inghelbrecht's annotated score in the Paris Opéra library we can see that his changes are considerably less far-reaching than he claimed – what is more, in the light of experience he abandoned a good number of the ones he did make and returned to Fauré's original!

The attacks that have been made on the libretto and the orchestration are in my view misguided, since the score is so unified that it must be accepted or rejected as a whole. In particular, to complain about the orchestration is to query the standing of Fauré himself, given that its sober tone is not proof of incompetence but the result (as I see it) of a restrained aesthetic attitude.

Fauré's *Pénélope* can be seen then as the last in the line of 'tragédies lyriques' that stretches from Lully through Rameau, Gluck and Berlioz's *Les Troyens*. Even so it would be nonsense to talk of neoclassicism and still more of academicism. If the general aesthetic, the declamation and the orchestration do display certain classical tendencies, the form, the musical style and above all the harmony are firmly of their time. Saint-Saëns for

one was deeply shocked by his old pupil's 'modernist' bearings and wrote
to his friend Lecocq in March 1913:

> I'm making superhuman efforts to come to terms with *Pénélope*. I simply can't get
> used to never settling down in any key, to consecutive fifths and sevenths and to
> chords demanding a resolution that never comes ... At a stroke Fauré has placed
> himself in a position of authority at the head of the young. A clever piece of work.
> But what an example for students to see their master constantly breaking the rules
> they're being taught! Personally, I look back with nostalgia to *Prométhée*.[24]

Nonetheless the purity and high ideals behind *Pénélope* singled it out in
an era dominated by Strauss's expressionism, Italian *verismo* and the
sumptuous spectacle of Diaghilev's Ballets russes. One can only respect the
artistic honesty of a composer who, all his life, remained true to his own
views and his own aesthetic ideal. Far from courting a stage success, Fauré
wrote his opera without the slightest nod towards the fashion of the times.
The famous pianist Edouard Risler said to him during the rehearsals at
Monte Carlo: 'Your opera will survive but it will take a long time to make
its mark', and Fauré commented in a letter to his wife on 28 February
1913: 'He's very probably right, I'm afraid. In fact there can be no doubt
about it, when you consider the trash the public feeds on, or *is given to feed
on*.'[25]

Pénélope's undoubted place as one of the most beautiful works in the
operatic repertory is due to the unity of its conception and to its profound
originality. Like all his great predecessors Fauré had the ability to turn his
characters into living people. He found a solution to the problem of what
opera should become after Wagner, and *Pénélope* represents, together
with *Pelléas, Ariane et Barbe-bleue* and *Wozzeck*, a viable if inimitable
model of twentieth-century opera. Its stature as a masterpiece must surely
be recognised with the help of recordings and the evident change in the
tastes of the opera-going public: now that the operas of Monteverdi,
Cavalli and Lully hold the stage, Fauré's turn cannot be long in coming.

The undoubted success of *Pénélope* immediately encouraged Fauré to
think of writing another opera and during the summer of 1913 he briefly
considered Fauchois' idea of one on the subject of Antony and
Cleopatra.[26] But the bankruptcy of the Théâtre des Champs-Elysées, the
consequent disappearance of *Pénélope* from the Parisian stage and then
the outbreak of the First World War all served to turn his thoughts away
from the theatre. The collaboration between Fauré and Fauchois was not
renewed until five years later when Prince Albert I of Monaco, acting at

Saint-Saëns' suggestion, commissioned Fauré to write a short work for the Monte Carlo theatre, as we learn from a letter of Fauré's to his editor, Jacques Durand, dated 3 September 1918.[27]

MASQUES ET BERGAMASQUES: DIVERTISSEMENT IN ONE ACT, ON A TEXT BY RENÉ FAUCHOIS

Fauré was not particularly keen to write an entirely new work just for a few performances at Monte Carlo, so he had the idea of reworking and expanding his *Fête galante*, based on some of his earlier pieces. This had been a great success in June 1902 when it was given in the salon of Madeleine Lemaire,[28] whom Proust had used as one of the models for Mme Verdurin. Fauré asked René Fauchois to write a text in the style of Verlaine's *Fêtes galantes* which would link together various songs, instrumental and choral pieces, some of them already in print. The published score of the 'suite symphonique', op. 112, which is how we know the work today, consists of four movements: Ouverture, Menuet, Gavotte and Pastorale. But the Monte Carlo production included eight pieces, including the four of the suite but in a different order.

The title *Masques et bergamasques* was taken from Verlaine and had also been considered by Debussy for a projected ballet in 1911. The stage version begins, naturally, with the Ouverture and its style is remarkably close to that of Mozart – not what one would expect from Fauré at this late stage in his career. The answer to this mystery, I have discovered, is that this movement is among Fauré's earliest orchestral essays, composed when he was around twenty years old: for its basic material the overture draws on an Intermezzo for orchestra, performed on 8 February 1868 at Rennes while Fauré was an organist there, and I have found a piano duet version of it under the title *Intermède symphonique* and dated 1869 (see chapter 2, pp. 14–15). So it is certainly no pastiche, but a mature revision of a piece written by a highly talented student who knew his Haydn and Mozart – which is not to deny that its brand of musical grace also suggest the style of *opéra-comique* as practised by Messager.

The programme for the première, written probably by René Fauchois, states:

The story of *Masques* is very simple. The characters Harlequin, Gilles and Colombine, whose task is usually to amuse the aristocratic audience, take their turn at being spectators at a 'fête galante' on the island of Cythera. The lords and ladies who as a rule applaud their efforts now unwittingly provide them with entertainment by their coquettish behaviour.

It is, in fact, a gently ironical version of the aristocratic, eighteenth-century *divertissements* which had returned to favour so markedly with Robert de Montesquiou's 'Pavillon des Muses'.[29]

The action begins with a conversation between the three *commedia dell'arte* characters and over it we hear the movement published in the suite as the Pastorale. Even though the initial theme of this movement has some affinities with the one at the beginning of the Ouverture, there is no mistaking that the Pastorale is vintage Fauré, as attested by consecutive block harmonies, wide melodic leaps (especially octaves), the juxtaposition of melodic segments to form the exposition and the ease with which the developments unfold. It is reminiscent not only of *Pénélope* but even more of the *Fantaisie* for piano and orchestra of 1918, whose noble character is here somewhat softened.

Among its many beauties is the descending chromatic passage on high strings which betrays a perfect understanding of the subtleties possible within such a texture. Sweetness there may be in the effortless succession of the phrases, but no limpness. The expressive harmonic clashes (p. 31, second system: G–A, G sharp against G natural) become sharper the second time (p. 32, first system: D sharp against E natural, C sharp against D natural),[30] but they are always justified by the four-part writing. Another high point is the return of the Ouverture's initial theme as a countermelody (bottom of p. 32 to p. 33). The Pastorale's control both of technique and of nuances of colour make it beyond doubt the crowning glory of *Masques et bergamasques* and with good reason Fauré placed it as the finale of his orchestral suite. It was also, we may note, his final farewell to the orchestra.

At this point in the action the *commedia dell'arte* characters are scattered by the arrival of an aristocratic company. 'Let's hide', says Harlequin, 'and spy on them. It's time *they* entertained *us* for a change!' There follows the *Madrigal* op. 35, a languid and perhaps too faithful musical setting Fauré made in 1883 of Armand Silvestre's poem (see chapter 7 p. 108).

A brief spoken passage links *Madrigal* with another Silvestre setting, 'Le Plus doux chemin' op. 87 no. 1, originally composed in 1904 for voice and piano. Clitandre 'sitting alone on a bench. He has a guitar slung from his shoulders and sings to his own accompaniment.'

Next comes a Menuet for orchestra alone. In its slightly lazy fashion it reworks certain elements from the Andante of the Suite d'orchestre op. 20 but, like the Pastorale, it is essentially a work of 1918. The rather hesitant nature of its opening theme recalls the secondary idea in the Pastorale

(p. 31) whose outline appears in long notes in the form of a trio. The themes of the Menuet and the Pastorale also have in common conjunct lines broken by wide leaps, but whereas the Pastorale is all light and tenderness, the Menuet smells somewhat of the lamp and is close to pastiche; its most characterful phrase is, strange to say, borrowed note for note from the fourth of the Préludes op. 103 for piano, composed in 1910, and is even in the same key of F major (see Ex. 68).

Ex. 68 Prelude no. 4 bb. 8–10

Masques (Menuet) bb. 13–17

According to the tradition of the orchestral suite, the first minuet is succeeded by a second, this time for voice and orchestra: in fact the celebrated 'Clair de lune' of 1887, which Fauré had orchestrated the following year at the Princess de Polignac's insistence. It was in this form (which I feel detracts from the music's charm) that the song was given by Maurice Bagès at the Société nationale de musique on 28 April 1888.

The sprightly, buoyant rhythms of the Gavotte now break into this nostalgic atmosphere. There is nothing shamefaced or overstudious here, but a wealth of brilliant contrapuntal repartee that reminds one of Fauré's friend Emmanuel Chabrier and also the 'Rigaudon' from *Le Tombeau de Couperin* which Ravel finished during the First World War. The Gavotte, in its quintessential Frenchness, might seem to have been very much of this time; but, if so, it was unintentional because it dates, like the Ouverture, from among Fauré's earliest orchestral compositions. I have discovered a piano transcription exactly contemporary with the *Intermède symphonique* of 1869, but notated in C sharp minor. The Gavotte then appeared in F major in the Suite d'orchestre op. 20 in 1873–4, which has remained unpublished, before its final resuscitation, largely unchanged, in *Masques et bergamasques*.

The *divertissement* ended with the Pavane in F sharp major which has done so much to further Fauré's reputation (see chapter 7, pp. 108–9). The first performance of *Masques et bergamasques* was given in Monte Carlo on 10 April 1919 with scenery inspired by Watteau's *Escarpolette*. It was

such a success that Albert Carré produced it at the Opéra-Comique on 4
March the following year; the scenery was by Lucien Jusseaume who
based it on Lancret's *La Fontaine de Pégase*. Illuminated by the twin stars
of Fauré and Verlaine, this *divertissement* was performed more than a
hundred times between 1920 and 1952 – paradoxically, Fauré's most
frequently performed stage work is also his least ambitious.

Fauré was well aware that in *Pénélope* he had produced something exceptional, so much so that it has never won the hearts of opera-lovers *en
masse*. His letters in the last years of his life show how dear the opera was
to him and, when performances at the Opéra-Comique proved infrequent,
he took the initiative in suggesting it might be staged at the Opéra, then
directed by a superb administrator, Jacques Rouché. Secret negotiations
took place in 1921 through Louis Laloy, but they came to nothing.[31]
Despite this disappointment Fauré, at the age of seventy-six, had thoughts
that same year of writing a new opera, again with Fauchois as his librettist.
Fauchois submitted to him the first few pages of a libretto on *The Liberation of Jerusalem* but, in a letter of 13 April 1921,[32] Fauré admitted a lack
of commitment to the project:

My vocabulary is insufficient to express my total indifference to the fate of
Jerusalem. In these circumstances my music would be bound to lack fire. Such
religious illusions as I ever had went into my Requiem, and even there the dominating sentiment is a human one – confidence in eternal bliss. Quite apart from that, I
suddenly had this terrifying picture of *Parsifal*!

At the height of his creative powers, Fauré closed the doors on his
operatic life and turned again, and with the happiest results, to fields
which he had already conquered: piano music, chamber music and song.

43 Alfons Mucha: poster for the first production of *Pénélope* at Monte Carlo, 1913

44 Prelude from *Pénélope*, orchestral score in Fauré's hand (1912)

45 Alphonse Visconti: set for *Pénélope*, Act 1: 'A hall leading to Pénélope's room'. Opéra de Monte Carlo, March 1913

46 Ker-Xavier Roussel: projected set for *Pénélope*, Act I, first performance in Paris, Théâtre des Champs-Elysées, May 1913

47 Lucienne Bréval (Pénélope) and the shepherds: Act II of *Pénélope* at the Théâtre des Champs-Elysées, set by Ker-Xavier Roussel, costumes by Henri-Gabriel Ibels, reproduced from *Le Théâtre*, June, no. 1, 1913

48 Henri-Gabriel Ibels, costume sketch for Ulysse, Act I, 1913

49 Claire Croiza as Pénélope, Brussels, November 1920

15 Words and music: the van Lerberghe years

The question of the relationship between words and music in Fauré's work, which I should like to take up here, is a particularly delicate one. We have already followed in chapter 9 the development of his literary taste from the Romantics through the Parnassians to the Symbolists. But over and above aesthetic considerations, to which we shall return at the end of the book, we must address the crucial question of the motivations behind Fauré's choice of poems: that is to say, what elements or qualities led him to settle on one poem rather than another?

In looking for an answer we may conveniently start from his extremely explicit declaration published in the review *Musica* in February 1911 in answer to a questionnaire:

The form is very important, but the atmosphere is more so. I've never been able, for example, to set the true Parnassians to music because, despite the elegance and attractive sound of their poetry, it's all in the words and behind the words there are no real ideas ... Indeed the rôle of music is to bring out the deepest feelings in the poet's heart, which words cannot possibly describe with exactitude.

In short, the main thing for a composer is that he should be captivated by the poem's atmosphere and that its overall tone should inspire music. The quality of the writing, too, must be such to allow the flow of the music to adapt itself to the words: 'One must never try and set a mediocre poet', Fauré goes on, 'because it needs only one word too many or a clumsily placed adjective to spoil the finest musical paragraph.'

Such 'words too many' and 'clumsily placed adjectives' probably explain the occasions when he got stuck writing a song, which did happen as he admitted to one of his favourite singers, Emilie Girette. One evening in July 1901 he spoke to her about the poetry of Albert Samain: 'There's a song he's been working on for several years', she wrote; 'he told me he couldn't get beyond the word "Schumann" which was difficult to set.'[1]

347

Later in her diary, the young Emilie copied out the text of 'Soir II', taken from Samain's volume *Au Jardin de l'Infante*, which ends:

> Toute rose au jardin s'incline lente et lasse
> Et l'âme de Schumann errante par l'espace
> Semble dire une peine impossible à guérir.
>
> (All the roses in the garden bow slowly and wearily
> And the soul of Schumann, floating in the air,
> Seems to tell of a pain that cannot be healed.)

And she goes on: 'Fauré told me Samain was overjoyed that he should have set this poem to music.'

The explicit mention of Schumann, one of his favourite composers, seems to have arrested Fauré's creative powers totally. The poem was probably too far oriented towards music in any case and, though the song was begun, he never finished it and so far no sketches have come down to us.

Fauré's references to 'one word too many' and to 'a clumsily placed adjective' also explain why, when he was determined to break through his composing block, he sometimes altered the text – discreetly, but radically enough to cause modern purists some surprise. These alterations, being deliberate, are worth looking at. The most usual kind is to do with the length of the poem. Normally four quatrains were all he needed, sometimes fewer still. We can in fact trace a clear line of development in this respect through Fauré's composing career. He took from his teacher Niedermeyer the narrative romance made up of numerous couplets, and some of his early songs use long poems: twenty-four lines for 'Le Papillon et la fleur', thirty for 'La Chanson du pêcheur', thirty-two for 'Dans les ruines d'une abbaye'. Requirements of musical symmetry led him to lengthen some of his texts by repeating lines, as in 'Dans les ruines d'une abbaye' where the first two strophes reappear as nos. 6 and 7, bringing the total number of lines to forty-four; similarly the second strophe of Richepin's *Au cimetière* and the first of Verlaine's *Mandoline* are repeated to round off the songs. In Silvestre's *Chanson d'amour* Fauré produces a refrain form by repeating the first strophe. These examples are the exception, however. More frequently Fauré shortens the poems rather than lengthening them: he suppresses two strophes in Gautier's *Les Matelots*, in Leconte de Lisle's *Les Roses d'Ispahan* and in van Lerberghe's *Inscription sur le sable*, and three in Baudelaire's *Chant d'automne* and in 'N'est-ce pas?' from Verlaine's *La Bonne chanson*. As we can see, famous writers are not spared! Very occasionally, Fauré takes a few strophes from a very long poem, such as Hugo's *La Tristesse d'Olympio*, with its twenty-eight strophes, or Samain's *Elégie* which occupies three pages of *Au Jardin de l'Infante* and from which Fauré took the last three quatrains for his song 'Soir'.

These changes are hardly perceptible to the listener because Fauré is careful to avoid any sort of hiatus over the join and naturally uses the continuity of the music to supply, in some sense, what is lacking in the words.

The strophes or smaller sections of text which Fauré was unwilling, or unable, to set to music are worth closer attention, since character is defined as much by what one rejects as by what one accepts. He baulked at images which were too solid or well-defined or which in one way or another appeared too realistic and disturbed the elegiac lyricism which he had made his own.

In Gautier's *Les Matelots* he removed these lines belonging to the fourth strophe:

> Le laboureur déchire
> Un sol avare et dur;
> L'éperon du navire
> Ouvre nos champs d'azur.
>
> (The labourer breaks up
> A miserly, hard soil;
> The prow of the ship
> Opens up our fields of blue.)

In Baudelaire's *Chant d'automne*, Fauré suppressed the second, most visionary quatrain:

> Tout l'hiver va rentrer dans mon être: colère,
> Haine, frissons, horreur, labeur dur et forcé
> Et, comme le soleil dans son enfer polaire,
> Mon cœur ne sera plus qu'un bloc rouge et glacé.
>
> (Winter shall spread over my being: anger,
> Hatred, shivering, horror, hard labour,
> And, like the sun in its polar hell,
> My heart will be no more than a red, icy block.)

In general, Fauré avoided figures of speech: 'Epithets grow to enormous proportions when underlined by music', he declared in the issue of *Musica* already quoted: 'For instance, "Helen with her white feet" conjures up a delightful picture when spoken. But if you set that phrase to music and tried to sing it, the feet would seem gigantic, out of all proportion. It would be absurd, ridiculous —you couldn't help laughing.'

This may well explain the omission of Verlaine's second strophe in the last poem of *La Bonne chanson*, 'L'Hiver a cessé':

> Même ce Paris maussade et malade
> Semble faire accueil aux jeunes soleils,
> Et comme pour une immense accolade
> Tendre les mille bras de ses toits vermeils.

> (Even this gloomy, sickly city of Paris
> Seems to offer a welcome to the sun's youthful rays
> And, as though for an immense embrace,
> To hold out the thousand arms of its red roofs.)

The same goes for the fourth strophe in the previous song in the same collection, 'N'est-ce pas?':

> Quant au Monde, qu'il nous soit irascible
> Ou doux, que nous feront ses gestes? Il peut bien,
> S'il veut, nous caresser ou nous prendre pour cible.

> (As for the World, whether it is angry with us
> Or gentle, what are its gestures to us? It can,
> If it wishes, cradle us or treat us as its butt.)

With his refined literary sense, Fauré was implacable in removing anything which seemed to him dissonant or lacking in taste, like Renée de Brimont's unsubtle lines in 'Reflets dans l'eau' from her collection *Mirages*:

> Dans l'ombre molle qui consent
> J'ai parfois sucé votre sang
> Grenades mûres

> (In the soft, consenting shadows
> I have sometimes sucked your blood
> Tasting of ripe pomegranates)

He suppressed likewise the somewhat hysterical 'songs' and 'amorous laughter' with which Charles van Lerberghe's Eve 'waits for a mighty God' (the tenth song of *La Chanson d'Eve*), as well as Gautier's naive lines in *Les Matelots*:

> Les petites étoiles
> Montrent de leurs doigts d'or
> De quel côté les voiles
> Doivent prendre l'essor

(The little stars
Show with their golden fingers
From which direction the sails
Are to receive the wind)

and Hugo's baldly grandiloquent conclusion to *L'Aurore*:

Qu'on pense ou qu'on aime,
Sans cesse agité,
Vers un but suprême,
Tout vole emporté;
L'esquif cherche un môle,
L'abeille un vieux saule,
La boussole un pôle,
Moi, la vérité!

(Whether one is a thinker or a lover,
Everything, continuously in motion,
Towards a final goal
Is borne away;
The boat heads for a pier,
The bee for a willow,
The compass for a pole,
I for the truth!)

But a large number of the changes made by Fauré to his texts show, unsurprisingly, his meticulous preoccupation with their sheer sound. Sometimes a group of phonemes was so rough and rebarbative that alteration was the only possible course, as with Samain's heavy-handed lines at the end of *Pleurs d'or*:

Et toi mon cœur, sois le doux fleuve harmonieux
Qui, riche du trésor tari des urnes vides
Roule un grand rêve triste aux mers des soirs languides

(And you, my heart, be the gentle, harmonious wave
Which, instilled with the tarnished treasure of empty urns,
Sweeps a grand, sad dream down to the seas of languid evenings)

or those in Jean Richepins's *Larmes*:

Le flux de la mer en est grossi
Et d'une salure plus épaisse,
Depuis si longtemps que notre espèce
Y pleure ainsi.

(The flood of the sea has for so long
Been swollen and more thickly salted
That our race weeps from it.)

As soon as the poet starts reaching for his alliterations, Fauré loses interest, knowing that music overemphasises the effect. The only quatrain omitted in his setting of van Lerberghe's *Le Jardin clos* contains nine 's's:

La trace blonde de *s*es pas
*S*e perd parmi les grilles clo*s*es;
Je ne *s*ais pas, je ne *s*ais pas,
Ce *s*ont d'impénétrables cho*s*es.

A similar reason no doubt lay behind the suppression of the third quatrain of Baudelaire's *Hymne*, containing as it does double alliterations in *f* and *ai*:

Sachet toujours *frai*s qui par*fu*me
L'atmos*ph*ère d'un cher réduit
Encensoir oublié qui *fu*me
En secret à travers la nuit.

There are a number of other places in Fauré's song texts[2] where he solves these difficulties by omission. A single line, sometimes, is enough to block the musical flow, like

Et l'eau *vi*ve qui *f*lue a*v*ec sa plainte douce

in Leconte de Lisle's *Les Roses d'Ispahan* (alliteration in *f* and *v*), or in 'N'est-ce pas?' from *La Bonne chanson*:

Et d'ailleurs, possédant l'armure adamantine.

This keen sense of the 'music of poetry' also led Fauré to change just one or two words when these were the only obstacles in his way, and not infrequently his 'corrections' prove him to have been more of a poet than the poet himself. There are a large number of instances, and they show right from the early songs his ear for alliteration, as in the second strophe of 'Dans les ruines d'une abbaye':

Hugo: Dans ces ombres
          Pleines ja*dis de* fronts blancs
Fauré: Dans ces ombres
          Ja*dis* pleines *de* fronts blancs

or in the fourth strophe of 'Chant d'automne':

> *Baudelaire*: J'aime de vos longs yeux la lumière verdâtre
> Douce beauté, mais *tout aujourd'hui* m'est amer
> *Fauré*:   J'aime de vos longs yeux la lumière verdâtre
> Douce beauté, mais *aujourd'hui tout* m'est amer

Frequently Fauré's modifications are directed towards softening dental consonants (*de*, *te*), sibilants (*f*, *s*) and 'ushing' sounds, as well as removing the vowel '*è*' (ϵ), which presents difficulties in the smooth unfolding of the vocal line.

Softening of dentals, in 'Au bord de l'eau':

> *Sully Prudhomme*: S'asseoir tous deux au bord *d'un* flot qui passe
> *Fauré*:   S'asseoir tous deux au bord *du* flot qui passe

Suppression of sibilants (from among numerous examples), in 'La Chanson du pêcheur':

> *Gautier*: Sur moi la nuit immen*s*e
> S'étend comme un lin*c*eul
> *Fauré*:   Sur moi la nuit immen*s*e
> P*l*ane comme un lin*c*eul

in 'Dans un parfum de roses blanches' (*La Chanson d'Eve*):

> *van Lerberghe*: Le *s*oir de*s*cend, le bosquet dort
> Entre *ses* feuilles et *ses* branches
> *Fauré*:   *L'ombre* descend, le bosquet dort
> Entre *ses* feuilles et *les* branches

Suppression of dentals, in 'Chant d'automne':

> *Baudelaire*: J'entends déjà tomber avec *des* chocs funèbres
> *Fauré*:   J'entends déjà tomber avec *un* choc funèbre

Suppression of 'è', as in previous example, in 'Lydia':

> *Leconte de Lisle*: Laisse tes baisers de colombe
> Chanter sur *tes lè*vres en fleur
> *Fauré*:   Chanter sur *ta lè*vre en fleur

in *Les Roses d'Ispahan*:

> *Leconte de Lisle*: Et qu'il parfume encor *les* fleurs de l'oranger
> *Fauré*:   Et qu'il parfume encor *la* fleur de l'oranger

All these changes that Fauré made were aimed at producing a vocal line that was as unified as possible and as favourable as he could make it to clear, sonorous enunciation. He may initially have chosen poems for their meaning and atmosphere but, once the choice was made, he continued to refine them and make them as malleable as possible, even if this meant ironing out some rough patches. In this context we can more easily understand his statement in *Musica*: 'I've never been able to set Victor Hugo either, and only occasionally Leconte de Lisle, because in both of them the poetry is too full, too rich, too self-sufficient for the music to adapt to it successfully.'

Here we may descry the motives behind Fauré's choices of poet. The most suitable poem for setting to music is not necessarily of the highest literary order, and in this respect Fauré was no different from many of his most distinguished predecessors and contemporaries: Schubert, Schumann, Gounod and Debussy wrote any number of wonderful songs to mediocre poems. But we should not deduce from this that only mediocre poems are suitable for musical settings. 'It would be wrong to suppose', Fauré declared, 'that the poetic form does not matter; it's simply that the musical form is a successful complement to it. The important thing is to understand and feel with one's poet' (*Musica*).

Fauré's musical demands explain why the hundred or so poems he set to music are of such unequal literary quality, as carping critics have often pointed out! Knowing of his long struggles with Victor Hugo's grandiloquence, we may understand better his close attachment over a period of six years, from 1878 to 1884, to the more neutral, discreet and frequently less-inspired poetry of Armand Silvestre, which produced some of the best of his early songs such as 'Automne', 'Le Secret' and the four-voice *Madrigal*, even if it was Villiers de l'Isle Adam, Verlaine, van Lerberghe and La Ville de Mirmont who were to inspire his finest pages.

The quest for poetry that touched the heart, that conjured up an atmosphere and was rich in musical possibilities, occupied Fauré constantly throughout his creative life. As the son of a schoolmaster and winner of a first prize for literature at the Ecole Niedermeyer, he came early to the world of books. Niedermeyer himself, conservative as ever, confined literary studies in the school to the great classics – Racine, Corneille, Bossuet, La Fontaine – just as on the musical front he excluded Schumann, according to Fauré, as being 'unsuitable for the young'; and as with music, Fauré's acquaintance with contemporary literature dates from the arrival, on Niedermeyer's death in 1861, of Saint-Saëns who, not content with imparting his love of Schumann and Wagner, introduced (on the quiet, we may suppose) the poetry of his admired Victor Hugo, the great poetry of its time. Fauré's long digression towards Hugo was certainly following in Saint-Saëns' footsteps. He eventually found his own true personality in attempting the poems of Gautier and especially of Leconte de Lisle (in 'Lydia', *c.* 1870), which fitted his search for antique purity through and beyond the *frissons* of Romanticism.

An important step was Fauré's meeting with Henri Duparc at the time of the Franco–Prussian War. At the early meetings of the Société nationale committee, Duparc brought the score of his recently composed song *L'Invitation au voyage*, and Fauré was enthusiastic at this revelation of Baudelaire's poetry. He made two attempts at it and as a mark of gratitude dedicated the second of these, 'La Rançon', to Ellie MacSwiney who was married to Duparc on 9 November 1871. But he never followed them up: the savage splendour of *Les Fleurs du mal* was too strong for his taste. Come to that, few composers after Duparc have really succeeded in transposing into music the richness of this imagery, as Debussy's unequal collection of nearly twenty years later shows.

The years Fauré spent in the Viardot household brought him into contact with some of the writers Pauline knew and admired, like Marc Monnier and the poet and painter Louis Pomey. But from this time on Fauré began to read poetry voraciously. In the 1880s French literature was swept by a great wave of poetic inspiration. The Decadents and Parnassians, who held the stage initially, were thrown into disorder by the appearance of Huysmans' novel *A Rebours* in 1884, then by the founding of the *Revue wagnérienne* in 1885, by the *Manifesto of Symbolism* in 1886 and by the eagerly awaited volumes of the *Revue blanche*, beginning in 1889–90. Lines of poetry were written by the thousand and almost as many found their way into print. Fauré not only bought numerous volumes of poetry, but was an assiduous reader of newspapers and magazines where it appeared in abundance. We have proof of this in the fact that he set some poems to music before they were ever published as part of a collection, like Sully Prudhomme's lines of 'Au bord de l'eau', Armand Silvestre's for the three songs op. 18 and for 'Le Secret', greatly admired by Duparc. So far I have not been able to discover where these poems initially appeared. The small magazines of this period are a veritable jungle and poetry even appeared in political publications. It was in *Le Figaro* in 1902 that Fauré discovered Mendès' text for 'Dans la forêt de septembre'.

We can see from Fauré's letters that he asked a good number of his friends to look out for poetry they thought might be singable. It is well known that Count Robert de Montesquiou introduced him to the work of

Verlaine and probably of Villiers de l'Isle Adam, but he also suggested a number of poems by Hugo and by a poetess he himself had rediscovered, Lucie Delarue Mardrus. Others laid under contribution in the search included the critic and essayist André Beaunier, his wife, the singer Jeanne Raunay, as well as Madeleine and Octave Maus, leaders of the artistic avant-garde in Brussels, who struck lucky in finding for Fauré two Belgian Symbolist poets, Jean Dominique and more important still, Charles van Lerberghe. A letter sent by Fauré some time later to Marguerite Baugnies[3] explains that it was the great actress Julia Bartet who drew his attention to Leconte de Lisle's *Le Parfum impérissable*:

I'm looking (without success) for some good poetry to set to music for Mme de Saint-Marceaux! I've been through countless volumes, but all I find are words, words and very little in the way of ideas. It's all superficial and gives music no purchase whatever. And what sickly twaddle! Mme Bartet came to see me yesterday. After her success in finding *Le Parfum impérissable* she hasn't been able to find anything else.

In some cases Fauré had the opportunity of making friends with his collaborators. Apart from his well-known relationship with Verlaine,[4] he was also in touch at various times with Maurice Bouchor, Louis Gallet, Catulle Mendès, Armand Silvestre, Charles Grandmougin and Albert Samain. His meeting with van Lerberghe has given rise to considerable speculation. It probably took place at a party given by Leo Frank Schuster to mark the première of *Pelléas et Mélisande* in London on 21 June 1898, at which we know van Lerberghe was present with his friend Maeterlinck.[5] But even if it is very likely that they did meet, there was no reason for it to have gone beyond the rapid introduction the occasion demanded. Van Lerberghe does not, after all, mention the music as being among the ingredients in a spectacle which made such an impression on him; as for Fauré, he knew nothing about the poet and was to discover *La Chanson d'Eve* in 1906, one year before van Lerberghe's premature death.

But it is a remarkable fact that from the 1880s onwards Fauré tended to choose poems that were closely contemporary. He set *Les Roses d'Ispahan* the same year it appeared in Leconte de Lisle's *Poèmes tragiques* (1884), and the same applied to 'Chanson' which he took from Henri de Régnier's *La Sandale ailée* in 1906 and to Renée de Brimont's *Mirages* in 1919. In most cases the gap between publication of a poem and Fauré's setting it to music was between two and three years.

Insofar as one can ever get to know Fauré's creative processes, it seems that certain musical elements – thematic motifs, rhythms in the vocal line, harmonies – emerged from repeated readings when once a text had taken his fancy. Emilie Girette mentions in her diary in the spring of 1902 that Fauré was writing a song for her called 'Accompagnement' on a poem by Samain:

> He told me he was composing in his head first of all, *starting with the words*; it's the poetry that inspires him – the melodic line grows gradually within him, maturing even without his conscious application, and then comes the labour of putting everything in order which is very far from being the easiest part.[6]

Still further information comes from a unique document, the copy of Albert Samain's volume *Au Jardin de l'Infante* which Fauré gave to Emma Bardac, with the inscription: 'I beg you to accept this book and choose the poems you would like to sing. Gabriel Fauré. May 1894.'[7] There are pencil marks against three of them: *Elégie*, on p. 29, the last three strophes of which were used for 'Soir' in this same year, 1894; 'Dilection', which Fauré began work on, as we have seen; and 'Arpège', on p. 69, which he set in 1896. There is a cross against 'Ton souvenir est comme un livre aimé', but nothing came of the idea. The most interesting information for our purposes concerns 'Promenade à l'étang', on pp. 20–2. The song was never completed, perhaps never even begun, but Fauré did sketch out a tonal plan for it: G flat, D flat minor, G flat, F sharp minor, A major, E flat minor, G flat, D flat minor.

A document such as this confirms how deeply Fauré thought about his compositions, even if their seductive surface might lead us to believe otherwise. The above volume kept by Emma Bardac is exceptional in that Fauré normally took pains to obliterate all traces of his preparatory workings, and sketches for his songs are likewise very rare. These include two notebooks left among his papers,[8] containing ideas for 'Clair de lune', 'Dans la forêt de septembre', 'La Fleur qui va sur l'eau' and a mysterious work which Fauré never completed, 'Dans le ciel clair'.[9] The evidence of these notebooks suggests that Fauré worked on three elements: the harmonic direction, the prosody and the formulae of the accompaniment. Sometimes he worked on them separately, sometimes simultaneously, but the really striking thing is that of all the ingredients of a song the vocal line seems to have been the hardest for him to get right. This is particularly so in the sketches for 'Clair de lune'. The well-known minuet in the piano part appears in a recognisable if not its final form, whereas his attempts at the vocal line for 'au calme clair de lune' have still a long way to go.

One has the feeling that from time to time an abyss opened up between the music in Fauré's heart and the words which had inspired it – an abyss that could be crossed only by patience and hard work. The sketches confirm this impression. Some parts of a song fall into place as if by magic – prosody, vocal line and accompaniment all together – others after prolonged hesitations and tinkering.

At its best, the flow of words and music seems to exist as an entity. I should like to mention here the last two pages of 'Puisque l'aube grandit' (the second song of *La Bonne chanson*) and a passage from *Le Jardin clos*, 'Il m'est cher, Amour' (Ex. 69).

There are, on the other hand, several places where the music seems to have been composed in the abstract and the words subsequently fitted to it with greater or lesser ease. The setting of *son-on-on-on-ges* and *menson-on-on-on-on-on-ges* in the famous 'Après un rêve', for instance, marks an unhappy approximation to the worst traditions of opera. In 'Tristesse' the underlying slow waltz rhythm leads to the false accentuation of the word (avril ♪ ♪) in the opening phrase, which Fauré certainly did not copy forty years later when he came across the same word at the start of 'La messagère' in *Le Jardin clos*. Some of his best-known songs contain displaced accents which familiarity with the music now makes it hard to hear:

Sully Prudhomme: Le long du quai les grands vaisseaux

Fauré: Le long du quai les grands vaisseaux

In a scholarly article on rhythm in Fauré's songs, Pierre Fortassier points out that the liberties the composer took with the spoken accentuation of his texts derive from his desire to break up the monotony of repeated rhythms – as with the two (∪ ∪ ∪–∪ ∪ ∪–) in the example above. Often he avoided strings of short syllables by lengthening words of secondary importance: articles and prepositions. In this way the flow of the verse is broken up and the musical phrase allowed a breathing space. The first page of *Le Jardin clos* offers a good example, in the incorrect but necessary accentuation of the preposition *en*:

van Lerberghe: Que mon amour en ta pri-è-re

Fauré: Que mon amour en ta pri-è-re

Ex. 69 *Le Jardin clos* (VII, 'Il m'est cher, Amour, le bandeau')

The main agent disturbing regularity of utterance is the expression of emotion. Obviously an exact vocal transposition of what we might call a neutral reading would be almost unbearably monotonous, since music intensifies whatever effects are already in the verse. Satie's famous *Socrate* (1918), with its 'white delivery' is a unique example – a success without any doubt, but one it would be unwise to imitate. In any case Satie was setting prose, not poetry. By accelerating the delivery or, on the other hand, by prolonging syllables inside it, the composer can emphasise what Diderot, in *Le Neveu de Rameau*, called 'impassioned speech' (*diction passionnée*) as opposed to 'calm delivery' (*lecture tranquille*). Monteverdi was one of the earliest and most successful composers to translate impassioned, imitative speech into musical terms.

In *La Bonne chanson* Fauré gives us any number of examples of this, as in the following passage from the seventh song, 'Donc, ce sera':

L'é-mo-ti-on du bon-heur - - - - et l'at-ten- - - -te- - - - - - - - - -

with the contrast between the babbling of 'émotion', accentuated by the diacresis (four syllables in the music to three in the words) and the prolongation of 'bonheur' and 'attente', giving a feeling of eternity. In 'Green', from the *Cinq mélodies* op. 58, this phrase:

lais-sez la s'a-pai-ser de la bon-ne tem-pê-te

produces an extraordinary effect of deceleration, perfectly in keeping with the rhythm and the sense of the poem.

As Pierre Fortassier says, 'the delivery is that of Fauré's own speaking voice', and he goes on to suggest that Fauré's music 'is inseparable from his admirable delivery of the poem, which is undoubtedly one of the reasons why we find it so moving'.[10]

In Fauré's remarkably rich and varied output of songs the relationship between words and music obeys a sort of dialectic, depending on the nature of his inspiration. Some songs are born directly from the poetry and faithfully follow its strophic structure, images and rhythms, as in the fourth song of *La Bonne chanson*, 'J'allais par des chemins perfides', and the sixth, 'Avant que tu ne t'en ailles', or in 'Le Parfum impérissable',

'Accompagnement' or 'L'Absent'. In some songs, on the other hand, the music forms the original basis and the poem is moulded to fit it: la 'Sérénade toscane', for example, and 'Barcarolle' were obviously conceived as 'songs without words' to which a text was added subsequently. Michel Soulard, in his excellent study of *La Bonne chanson*,[11] writes of 'La Lune blanche':

One feels that Fauré's reading of the poem had suggested to him a rhythm based on a pattern (quaver, crotchet, quaver, crotchet) and that having absorbed the rhythm he then reapplied it to the poem, sacrificing the exact spoken accentuation of it to the demands of the melodic line. Here we are at the heart of the antimony between poetry and music. Compromise can be difficult but, in fact, in these borderline cases Fauré refuses to be constrained by the text.

Later on in his study (p. 100) he writes, 'In this instance Fauré translates the unity of the poem into purely musical terms.' Such a procedure brings him into line with composers like Wolf, Schubert and Schumann.

'Compromise can be difficult', certainly, and there are places in his songs which tell us so. Manuscript sources of his early songs, together with varying editions published in his lifetime, reveal as many as three different versions of the prosody in some passages.[12] The attentive listener does feel at times that the musical line has been adapted with some difficulty to the poetic structure, either because the text has something 'missing' or because it is too long. In 'Nell', the musical conclusion of the last two strophes entails lengthening the text with repetitions which are not called for by the sense:

> *Third strophe*: Qui rayonne en mon cœur [en mon cœur] charmé
> *Fourth strophe*: Ne fleurisse plus ton image [Ne fleurisse plus ton image]

In 'Notre amour', the coda drags the last verse out over a whole page. The same uncertainty reigns in the rather laboured ending to 'Ici bas', while the final repetition of the second strophe in 'Au cimetière' is all Fauré's own work. On the same lines, I personally have always found the very end of *La Bonne chanson* unsatisfactory – it sounds incomplete, as though there were lines missing. In 'Lydia' there are one or two curious hiatuses: in the first strophe, Fauré was faced with the difficult enjambement of lines 2 and 3, made worse by a poetic metaphor ('ton col frais et plus blanc / Que le lait') which he found daunting, as we have seen. He finally took the bold step of cutting out the comparison and replacing it by an inserted phrase in the piano part which continues the melodic line:

Leconte de Lisle: Et sur ton col frais et plus blanc
Que le lait, roule étincelant
L'or fluide que tu dénoues

Fauré: Et sur ton col frais et si blanc
. . . . roule étincelant
etc.

Ex. 70 'Lydia'

There are also some passages in *La Bonne chanson* where the chromaticism is so recherché and unnatural that we must suspect the composer of having deliberately complicated the musical discourse in order to accommodate one or two lines which, in fact, he would have done better to dispense with. In 'J'allais par des chemins perfides', for example, he might have omitted the interpolation:

Luisait un faible espoir d'aurore

as he might the harmonic progression in 'J'ai presque peur' which rises at the words 'à penser qu'un mot, qu'un sourire de vous' and then falls at 'pour mettre tout mon être en deuil' for no good musical reason.

Even so, seen in the context of his total song output, such instances are rare. In general, where there is any incompatibility it is the text that gives way. As Michel Soulard rightly observes:[13]

Certainly the phonemes as sung always retain their recognisable identity, but by submitting them to a rhythm, a melodic line, a key, a tempo, the composer in some sense binds them into his music ... the alliance between music and poetry can be made only at the cost of this sacrifice: the word, while retaining its force as a sign (signifier and signified) allows itself to be invaded by the music, which possesses a thousand and one resources for putting her rival in its place; the musical flow submerges the verse and the subtle play of its phonemes.

So in listening to Fauré's songs one must not concentrate on the text alone. One has to try and put oneself into the same position as the composer so as to capture the overall meaning and the general atmosphere of the poem, and not be seduced momentarily by details or attach too much importance to them. Claire Croiza, who gave the first performance of *Le Jardin clos*, had this to say in a masterclass on 'Clair de lune' as set by Fauré and Debussy:[14]

In comparing Fauré and Debussy one is struck by how different they are. Fauré uses the text to stir his creative inspiration; Debussy weds himself to the poetry and follows it step by step. If you read a text that has been set by Debussy, you see that the declamation in Debussy falls rhythmically, which it does not in Fauré. Debussy is rhythmically faithful to the text. Fauré allows himself to be carried away with enthusiasm for the spirit of a poem. His declamation works only when it is sung, whereas one can apply Debussy's declamation to the spoken poem and it is always correct.

Interesting as this view is, it is certainly an over-generalisation. If you follow Fauré's declamation of 'Prison' you discover Verlaine's own rhythm. Similarly, if you compare the two songs Fauré and Debussy wrote on *Il pleure dans mon cœur*, also by Verlaine, there can be no doubt that the more sober and prosodically exact setting is not Debussy's.

To sum up Fauré's attitude to his texts in a metaphor, one could say that he plunges his chosen poem into his music until the music has absorbed it entirely. In this transmutation lies the mystery of the text when clothed in musical finery; at the same time identical and also quite other ... just as it has become in the composer's imagination.

As Fauré's contract with Heugel, made at the time of his appointment as

Director of the Paris Conservatoire, committed him to delivering thirty compositions between 1 January 1906 and 1 January 1909, he had recourse to his files which contained various works long since finished but, for whatever reason, never published. We have already discussed (in chapters 7 and 13) the changes he made to the *Ave Maria* for two sopranos and to the *Messe des pêcheurs de Villerville*, which became the *Messe basse* when published in 1907. He also returned to the music he had written in 1898 for the 'Chanson de Mélisande' in the London production of *Pelléas et Mélisande*, which had remained unpublished because of its English words (see chapter 8). As he had done for several of his motets composed for the Madeleine, Fauré decided to adapt this music to new words. He took these from van Lerberghe's superb cycle of poems *La Chanson d'Eve*, which he had probably been given by Octave Maus at the first performance of his First Quintet, in Brussels on 23 March 1906. Curious as this adaptation may seem, there is no doubting its success; if 'Mélisande's song' had not survived, we should have had no inkling of any earlier version. Fauré, indeed, kept quiet about the transformation and the truth came out only when his sons agreed to publish 'Mélisande's song' in 1937.

The vocal and pianistic style and the hieratic atmosphere of the song do, in fact, give it a special place in Fauré's turn-of-the-century output. In many respects it anticipates his late manner in its sobriety of utterance, sacrificing the tortuous harmonies he had favoured hitherto to the noble beauties of counterpoint. The new song, now called 'Crépuscule', was published separately in August 1906 while Fauré was on holiday on Lake Maggiore. Looking out over the Borromean Islands, he re-read van Lerberghe's poems with a further idea in mind: 'I'm trying to grasp the beginning of the volume', he wrote to his wife on 3 September 1906. 'I intend setting a number of poems to go together and make a companion cycle to *La Bonne chanson*. As the two groups of poems are different in character the music will have to be different too, and that's something that interests me.'[15]

The cycle took a long time to complete and there were many interruptions. The extended song which acts as a prelude, 'Paradis', was written in a few days (27 August–8 September 1906) as was the next one, 'Prima Verba' (25–28 September); but from then on progress was impeded by Fauré's duties at the Conservatoire and by his decision to start on his opera *Pénélope*. Nos. 3 and 5 of *La Chanson d'Eve* were finished in 1908, nos. 4, 6 and 8 in 1909, and the cycle completed with the composition of nos. 7 and 10 in the early days of January 1910. As we can see, Fauré did not work with any fixed framework in mind. Not only were the contents the

Table 2

LA CHANSON D'EVE

Composition	Date of composition	Despatch to the engraver	Publication	No. in the 1907–9 edition	Order in the first, incomplete, performance on 26 May 1909
1 'Paradis', E minor	27 Aug–8 Sept 1906	3 Oct 1906	Jan 1907	1	1
2 'Prima verba', G flat major	25–28 Sept 1906	3 Oct 1906	Jan 1907	2	2
3 'Roses ardentes', E major	June 1908	22 July 1908	Nov 1908	3	3
4 'Comme Dieu rayonne', C minor	before 26 May 1909	5 June 1909	Oct 1909	5	5
5 'L'aube blanche', D flat major	June 1908	22 July 1908	Nov 1908	4	4
6 'Eau vivante', C major	before 26 May 1909	5 June 1909	Oct 1909	7	6
7 'Veilles-tu ma senteur de soleil', D major	Jan 1910	15 Jan 1910	Feb 1910	–	–
8 'Dans un parfum de roses blanches', G major	before 5 June 1909	5 June 1909	Oct 1909	6	–
9 'Crépuscule', D minor	4 June 1906	13 June 1906	Aug 1906	no number	7
10 'O Mort, poussière d'étoiles', D flat major	Jan 1910	15 Jan 1910	Feb 1910	10	–

fruit of long reflection but, as with *La Bonne chanson*, the order of the songs underwent changes and hesitations, as we can see from the variants in the manuscripts and in the original editions, where the songs were published separately.[16] Some idea of the complex development of *La Chanson d'Eve* can be gained from the outline, on the previous page, based on information on the autographs and original editions, in Fauré's letters, in the archives of the publisher (Heugel) and in the programmes for the first performances.

Fauré's new cycle does present a great contrast with *La Bonne chanson*, as he obviously intended. The highly chromatic language, the wide, sweeping lines and the passionate excesses of an almost orchestral lyricism give way to a dreamscape in which the vocal line is modelled on the text, the harmony becomes taut and the texture lighter, denser, more transparently contrapuntal. The lyricism is now introverted and even at times gives the impression of going numb with vertigo. Eve, dreaming and singing in the garden of Eden of the beauties of the world, shares not only its heartbeat but its suffering as well. Fauré's character and artistic inclinations could not help but be engaged by the singular blend of mysticism and sensuality in van Lerberghe's poems, the 'hothouse' of anxiety cultivated to the point of malaise and illuminated and supported by a great nobility of thought.

The publication of van Lerberghe's *La Chanson d'Eve* in 1904 was welcomed by Maeterlinck in a long article in *Le Figaro*. The volume, containing some 200 pages, is in three parts: 'Premières paroles', 'La Tentation' and 'Crépuscule'. As we have seen, Fauré wrote to his wife of 'trying to grasp the beginning of the volume', and in fact seven of the ten songs (no. 1–6 and 8) were taken from the first part, no. 7 ('Veilles-tu') from the second, and the two concluding songs from the last. Selecting the poems was not easy because, as he again wrote to his wife on 9 September 1906, 'it's a large volume containing a lot of poems and one has to make a deliberate choice among them – he often repeats himself'.

In the copy of the book that Fauré used[17] a number of pages are dog-eared, indicating poems that he thought were possible. Some twenty of them attracted his attention. A number of pencilled annotations mark cuts and changes in texts that were sometimes problematic.[18] 'The writing is difficult', he complained to his wife in a letter of 5 September. 'It's descriptive and unsentimental. And then one has to set words for God the Father and for his daughter Eve. It isn't easy dealing with such important persons. Still, I'd be worse off trying to find a musical style for M. and Mme Dubois!'

After the sometimes excessive and barely surpassable complications of

La Bonne chanson, Fauré here returns to a relatively simple style: 'I've worked for seven hours', he wrote, 'and I've resolved the problem of making God sing. When you see what his eloquence consists of, you'll be amazed it took me so long to find. But I'm afraid absolute simplicity, in the current musical climate, is the hardest thing of all to discover.'[19]

Despite – or because of ? – this simplicity, *La Chanson d'Eve* is not an easy work to appreciate. The textual transparency at times approaches a kind of minimalism, for which 'Crépuscule' (the one-time 'Mélisande's song') laid down the pattern and which is to be found in many passages of 'Paradis'. The counterpoint itself is sometimes reduced to two voices – the vocal line and the bass –with a meagre filling of semiquavers, as at the beginning of 'L'aube blanche' and of 'Dans un parfum de roses blanches'. The vocal writing is in a state of constant evolution. Much use is made of recitation – one might almost say recitative at some points – in the form of a kind of psalmody on long held notes, as in 'Paradis' and 'O mort', but Fauré's overall preference is for the broad curves of an arioso style. In the two liveliest songs, 'Veilles-tu' and 'Eau vivante', the diction is modelled on a voluble, almost precipitate style of speaking: the stained-glass atmosphere of the cycle as a whole is shot through, here and there, with flashes of passion which performers are all too liable to damp down. 'L'aube blanche' oscillates constantly between piano and forte; 'Veilles-tu ma senteur de soleil' is full of agitated contrasts; the whole cycle is imbued with an almost uninterrupted sensuality.

This same flexibility, together with the downward leaps of an octave, are to be found in the vocal writing of *Pénélope*, on which Fauré was working simultaneously. In *La Chanson d'Eve* he seems to emphasise the comprehensibility of the text, while at the same time giving the piano a major rôle. Because the piano part is so rich, the vocal line often sounds as though it was added afterwards, with a resulting loss in spontaneity and singability (see 'Comme Dieu rayonne', 'Eau vivante', 'Dans un parfum de roses blanches', 'Crépuscule').

The two generative themes in the work are themselves not particularly melodious. They are heard clearly at the start of the cycle. *A* is no more than the rising arpeggio of E minor taken from 'Crépuscule' and, before that, from the 'Death of Mélisande' in the suite from *Pelléas*. The chromatic outline of *B* is less striking still. It is presented in E major on the second page of 'Paradis' at the words 'Un jardin bleu s'épanouit' (see Ex. 71).

Analysis here is a less complex business than it was in *La Bonne chanson*, where the motifs were also far more numerous. In 'Paradis' *A*, with its slow dotted minims, evokes the uncertain light of 'the first

Ex. 71 *La Chanson d'Eve*

morning of the world'; it reappears, in common time and in diminution, in 'Comme Dieu rayonne' where it sets off a passage of rich counterpoint, developed in the style of an invention; it then returns to its original slow speed in 'Crépuscule', the first song of the cycle to be written, so that it can be regarded as the generative theme of the whole work.

B is heard in the second part of 'Comme Dieu rayonne' and its hesitant curve can be discovered in the moving basses of the eighth song, 'Dans un parfum de roses blanches'. There is therefore nothing systematic in Fauré's use of themes, since a good number of the songs (nos. 2, 3, 5, 6, 7 and 10) are untouched by recurring motifs. The unity of the cycle is nonetheless extremely strong. It comes from Fauré's ability to recreate the atmosphere of the text – strangely pure, at once majestic and intimate and with a mixture of passion and restraint that makes one think of the troubled, hieratic visions of Pre-Raphaelites like Burne-Jones.

In the field of harmony, the emphasis on linear writing produces some harsh clashes. Major and minor seconds and bare fifths are frequent. The overall harmonic instability is due less to a high level of chromaticism, as it was in *La Bonne chanson*, than to Fauré's employment of long sequences descending by whole-tone steps. He uses them to beautiful effect, both in the voice part (in 'L'Aube blanche' and 'Ô mort') and in the piano part (in 'Eau vivante', which is a thorough-going celebration of the whole-tone scale). At the end of the cycle, the harmonic tensions (seconds, passing notes) and the level of chromaticism together bring the music to the borders of atonality. 'Ô mort, poussière d'étoiles' is unique in Fauré's output, and one of his most powerful and expressive songs in its evocation of gloom and total despair. Only a composer who cared nothing for the plaudits of the crowd would have dared to conclude a cycle with such a weighty, funereal song; though it is certainly possible that the end of Schumann's *Frauenliebe und–leben* might have served as a model …

La Chanson d'Eve is dedicated to Jeanne Raunay. According to contemporary accounts, she was a singer in the grand manner and was famous for her interpretations of Gluck and Wagner, especially in Monte Carlo and at the Paris Opéra. She sang in the first two performances of the cycle, both times with the composer at the piano. On 26 May 1909 she gave seven of the ten songs (see outline) and on 20 April 1910 she gave the complete cycle in the course of the opening concert of the Société musicale indépendante, of which Fauré had agreed to be president.[20] Until his death the composer remained on friendly terms with Mme Raunay and her husband, the novelist, essayist and journalist André Beaunier, and contributed a short article on 'Lucienne Bréval and Jeanne Raunay' to the January 1908 issue of the review *Musica*.

Isolated as *La Chanson d'Eve* may appear among Fauré's output, from both literary and musical points of view, it is one of the key works in the development of his later style. It is also a triumphant success in its handling of a bold musical language and in its extreme sobriety of texture. We should not, however, be misled into regarding it as some dark meteorite fallen from nowhere into the Garden of the Hesperides. Some stylistic features, like the whole-tone sequences, were already to be found ten years earlier in the duet 'Pleurs d'or', in 'Soir' and 'Le Parfum impérissable'. A song like 'Prima verba', one of the best of the cycle, belongs plainly with others of the 1890s in its modal atmosphere (G flat major with an F flat) and its beautiful plagal cadence at the end. The phrase 'Depuis que mon souffle a dit leur chanson' even quotes the Agnus Dei from the *Messe de Villerville* of 1881 which Fauré was revising in 1906 for its publication the following year. Both in 'Prima verba' and in 'Ô mort, poussière d'étoiles' the slowly pulsing chords continue the line of lyrical, intimate songs.

In 1906 Fauré composed a long *Vocalise–Etude* in the same limpid style, though certainly not in the same melancholy vein. This was the first in a collection of *vocalises* made by Louis Hettich, the singing professor at the Conservatoire, who was anxious to bring technical exercises up to date, an aim in which he had the support of the institution's director. The fact that the piece, for voice without words and a piano, is of primarily pedagogical intent has led to its neglect – which is a pity, as its calm, transparent logic makes it one of Fauré's finest compositions. The only virtuoso demands it makes are the successions of octaves and the diminutions in the central section and the leap of a tenth at the end, though it needs a solid legato technique and a more than usually firm sense of pitch: the gentle chords of the accompaniment, with a single contrapuntal line lightly touched in, take the fluid vocal line on some fairly distant tonal journeys. The main theme is built around a rising scale of E minor and gives rise to two related motifs in bars 11 and 16. The return of the opening bars in the major is a surprising moment, like an abrupt change of lighting on stage giving the scenery a quite different look. This effect of distance, of an opening up of new harmonic perspectives, is in my view without parallel in the whole of Fauré's work.

Like Ravel's well-known *Vocalise en forme de Habanera,* written the following year for the same collection, Fauré's *Vocalise* is widely known in various instrumental arrangements (for viola, for oboe etc.) under the title *Pièce.* Convenient as these transcriptions may be, they should not distract us from the beauties of the original. This unusual piece is, moreover, only a tiny part of a fairly substantial collection of sight-reading pieces for voice and piano which Fauré provided, almost throughout his period as director, for the Conservatoire singing classes. The rest have remained unpublished.

Even though the authorities kept the promise they had made in 1905 to exempt Fauré from a number of administrative tasks, he still spent the best part of his time at his directoral desk. The progress of his deafness made many aspects of the job difficult for him, paticularly presiding over the numerous examination juries, which he could not escape. His letters to close acquaintances tell of his fatigue, and his patience and politeness were often sorely tested by friends and relations trying to engineer the entry of some pupil into the Conservatoire or, more often still, trying to ensure he did not leave it without the indispensable '1er Prix'. He had also to deal with various machinations – the Marguerite Long affair, already described in chapter 13, is a good example – hold his own against the ultra-conservative 'conseil supérieur' whose job it was to assist him, and do more or less secret battle with the disputatious band of professors. In a letter to Saint-Saëns,[21] Fauré mentions the group who 'make up the opposition in the Conservatoire (the easygoing Duvernoy and that fool Lefèbvre)'. As for the famous Capet Quartet, whose founder Lucien Capet had been appointed to teach one of the chamber music classes created by Fauré, Fauré himself wrote to the pianist Edouard Risler in 1908: 'Even if you're aware of some of their tricks, I'm sure you don't know the *dirtiest* of them.'[22]

In 1910 Capet assumed leadership of a band of rebels. A petition, demanding reforms, was sent to the minister and the newspapers scented a crisis. They even went to the lengths of canvassing Sarah Bernhardt, who had enjoyed a meteoric career as professor of drama at the Conservatoire.

In the review *Comoedia* (issue of 19 July 1910) she raised the whole question of teaching drama inside a conservatory of music: 'As a conservatory of drama the Conservatoire is at the moment in a deplorable state. The self-satisfied contempt of musicians for drama explains the self-satisfied contempt of the Conservatoire's directors.' She concluded in peremptory fashion: 'The "Conservatoire dramatique" ought to be directed by a playwright, a theatre director or a retired actor.'

Bernhardt's outburst led Fauré to write to his wife the following day: 'All very upsetting! Especially when I thought I'd been so considerate towards her! I certainly have every reason to feel contempt for those people ... If only I had the right of reply!'[23]

The campaign was well timed because Fauré's tenure ran out on 1 October 1910, but it was immediately scotched by a ministerial decree of 20 July 1910 renewing his appointment for a further five years; better still, the Minister of Education conferred on him the rank of Commander of the Legion of Honour on 20 December of the same year. From there on his position as a director was secure enough for him to take time off whenever his creative work made it necessary. His forced labour on *Pénélope* led him to extend his spring and winter vacations in 1912, spent at Hyères and Monte Carlo respectively. During the summer after the Paris première of *Pénélope* on 10 May 1913 he went back to Lugano, where he had spent such productive summers in the past. But this time he allowed himself six weeks of almost pure holiday. The only composition he completed was the Eleventh Barcarolle, in a rather dark, anguished G minor, in complete accord with the problems he was having over the future of *Pénélope* and the threatened bankruptcy of the Théâtre des Champs-Elysées.

Fauré enjoyed himself during this summer of 1913 reading Flaubert's letters, as well as a volume of van Lerberghe's poetry sent him by Albert Mockel: *Entrevisions*, published in 1898, six years before *La Chanson d'Eve*. But although Fauré conceived in 1913 the idea of setting some of them to music, he did not settle down to composition until a year later, during the fateful summer of 1914. In July of that year he was at Ems, taking the waters: 'I've started work', he wrote to his wife on the 21st. 'At the moment it's to be a group of three or four songs ... The poems are by the same author who wrote *La Chanson d'Eve*. I can't find anything, I'm afraid, in the contemporary French poets, at least nothing that calls for music.'[24]

His tranquillity did not last long. By early August Europe was at war and Fauré had great difficulty leaving Ems because the Franco-German border was closed. It took him three days to reach Geneva via Saint-Louis and

Basle. But at least in Switzerland he found some old friends and devoted
admirers: Jaques-Dalcroze and his wife and Mme Brunet Lecomte. Work
helped counter his anxiety and the boredom of exile. Setting a Belgian poet
was also a kind of consolation, an outlet for patriotic sentiments which in
his seventieth year he had no better means of expressing. The start of the
academic year was postponed and Fauré went to stay with his brother
Fernand in Pau and slowly went on with his work.

Once back in Paris, Fauré returned to his duties at the Conservatoire,
but every day saw new depletions of its numbers and the new term got off
to a difficult start two and a half months late. Fauré wrote to his old pupil
Charles Koechlin:[25]

On the musical front, I expect the papers tell you what's going on and you can see
to what extent it's dictated by circumstance! Even so, Casella organised a little
concert including two first performances: an excellent Trio for piano, violin and
'cello by Ravel and a Suite of eight songs I wrote recently on songs by van
Lerberghe, a Belgian poet (which is the most up-to-date thing about them) and
called Le Jardin clos.

Fauré had been the accompanist for this performance on 28 January 1915.
The singer was Claire Croiza, one of his most devoted interpreters: she had
sung the role of Pénélope at the Brussels première in 1913 and was to have
undertaken it at the Opéra-Comique in Paris at the very moment when war
was declared.

In the case of La Chanson d'Eve the special nature of the subject has
brought it a measure of celebrity, but Le Jardin clos remains one of Fauré's
least known works. Its brevity and simplicity, together with its appearance
in wartime, seem to have prevented it from reaching a wide audience.
Without ever aspiring to the grand manner or the lofty (and sometimes
uncertain) tone of La Chanson d'Eve, Le Jardin clos seems to me to be an
undeniable success – of importance, too, in that it ushers in the imposing
array of new works which Fauré produced during the war. These thirty
pages of music contain in some extraordinary way all that is best in the
melodic style explored by La Chanson d'Eve. The simplicity of the declamation and the clarity of the piano writing at times reach a sort of
minimum, what Roland Barthes would call 'degree zero', without ever
descending to the aridity of a mere sketch. The accompaniment in many
cases is restricted to a bass line in dialogue with the voice, after the manner
of chamber music, and filled out in the right hand with chords or arpeggiated quavers. Above all, the work displays a new stage in Fauré's development of the cycle, to the extent that the notion of a recurring theme – first

used in 'Poème d'un jour' in 1878 and then expanded in the Venice cycle, *La Bonne chanson* and *La Chanson d'Eve* – is here abandoned altogether. In the letter to Charles Koechlin quoted above Fauré does describe *Le Jardin clos* as a 'suite of eight songs', so that one calls it a 'cycle' only as a matter of convenience. Nevertheless its unity, drawing on that of the poetry and on the homogeneity of musical language and texture, is un-questioned and is even greater than that of *La Chanson d'Eve*, which had suffered from being written over a period of four years.

There is no obvious tonal plan. The keys of the cycle are contained within the range of a perfect fifth (C–G), turning around the mediant E. The speeds are moderate, with two *allegros* (nos. 3 and 7). More remark-ably, all the songs except the last are written in major keys (see Table 3).

Table 3

Title	Key	Tempo
1 Exaucement	C major	*Allegretto*
2 Quand tu plonges tes yeux dans mes yeux	F major	*Andante moderato*
3 La messagère	G major	*Allegro*
4 Je me poserai sur ton cœur	E flat major	*Allegretto moderato*
5 Dans la nymphée	D flat major	*Andante molto moderato*
6 Dans la pénombre	E major	*Allegretto moderato*
7 Il m'est cher, Amour, le bandeau	F major	*Allegro*
8 Inscription sur le sable	E minor	*Andante quasi Adagio*

Each song is dedicated to a female friend, most of whom also sang his music: Mme Albert Mockel (no. 1), Germaine Sanderson (no. 2), Gabrielle Gills (no. 3), Lucy Vuillemin (no. 4), Claire Croiza (no. 5), Mme Houben-Kufferath (no. 6), Nina Faliero-Dalcroze (no. 7), Mme Durand-Texte (no. 8).

The dreamlike quality of the women evoked in van Lerberghe's poems – solemn, evanescent, mysterious – brings them close to the figures in the work of the greatest of the Belgian symbolist painters, Fernand Khnopff. Fauré appropriates the profound melancholy and the gentle eroticism of this *fin-de-siècle* world (explored by Georges Rodenbach in his novel *Bruges la morte* of 1892), though he conveys less of its *morbidezza*. In setting poems from van Lerberghe's *Entrevisions* he retains above all the Symbolist manner of expressing the language of love: often anxious and indirect, simultaneously vague and outspoken. To my way of thinking

Fauré was rarely more in tune with the atmosphere of a poetic text than here. The utterly human tenderness of 'Je me poserai sur ton cœur' is unique in Fauré's work, as is the feeling of mystery that surrounds the female apparition – lover or saint? –in the fifth song, 'Dans la nymphée'. This, perhaps the most beautiful of the set, is characterised by the slowly pulsating chords, the liturgical declamation and the key of D flat major found in many of Fauré's finest songs; while in 'Quand tu plonges tes yeux' he deliberately underlines the boldly erotic imagery with dissonant sevenths and major seconds in the piano part.

The prosody is even more faithful than usual to the natural inflections of the text, mirroring its suppleness and returning to the use of cross rhythms. The harmony (in 'La messagère', for example) is enlivened by discreet chromatic touches, or carried by whole-tone progressions to the point where tonality is endangered (see example 42).

As a conclusion to the cycle, Fauré once again chose a poem about death. But whereas 'O mort, poussière d'étoiles' transmitted a feeling of terror, a truly existentialist anguish, bringing *La Chanson d'Eve* to an end in a mood of total despair, 'Inscription sur le sable' – evoking some princess from Egypt or elsewhere – breathes a spirit of detachment and acceptance, as though death could, at last, be faced with calmness and lucidity. In the austere, meditative nobility of this final song Fauré, after so many vibrant, sensual pages, gives us a great lesson in serenity.

50 Félix Bracquemont: Gabriel Fauré, drawing, 1913

51 Fauré in Switzerland (Lausanne 1907?), photo taken by Marguerite
Hasselmans, sent to Paul Dukas

52–53 Boats on the Swiss lakes, photos taken
by Gabriel Fauré, 1907–8

54 Fauré working in his room in Lugano
(Hôtel Métropole), 1909–12

55 *La Chanson d'Eve* (no. 2), first proof corrected by Fauré, November 1906, annotated by Mimi Risler

16 'Pour le piano'

The piano works Fauré wrote during the last twenty years of his life are a veritable *terra incognita* since, apart from the Thirteenth Nocturne and the Fifth Impromptu, they are hardly ever played. Marguerite Long states quite openly in her memoirs:[1] 'Personally, I prefer the works he wrote before deafness reduced the scope of his hearing ... In the later works, it seems to me, his rhythmic inspiration became weaker and more crystalline and the works overall sparser, more deliberate, without that divine spontaneity.' To speak thus is to cast aside, with a single gesture, almost half of Faurés's piano output. The later works she refers to include Nocturnes nos. 9 to 13, Barcarolles nos. 7 to 13, the volume of Nine Preludes, the *Fantaisie* for piano and orchestra and Impromptus nos. 4 and 5. To be sure, quite a few of the finest pianists of the time took an interest in Fauré's work, apart from Mme Long – for example, Alfred Cortot, Raoul Pugno, Isidore Philipp, Blanche Selva and Edouard Risler – but they included pieces of his in their concert programmes only now and then, usually the same ones and not, unfortunately, always his best. It is worth noting that Cortot recorded only two out of all Fauré's piano works: the 'Berceuse' from *Dolly* (in his own transcription for piano solo!) and the Third of the *Romances sans paroles*.[2]

As for foreign pianists, they simply did not know of the music, partly because it was so inefficiently promoted by Hamelle. Worse still, they despised it on the evidence of appalling performances, such as those of Paderewski, who was even so one of the first pianists to make Debussy's music accepted in concerts or on record.[3] Fauré was very well aware of this indifference and suffered considerably at the thought that he was not understood. His friend and pupil Emilie Girette recorded this declaration in her diary:[4] 'He is depressed that pianists play him badly, saying "The greater they are, the worse they play me."' He also wrote plainly to his wife, on the subject of the Tenth Barcarolle: 'The piece I've started will merely be the fiftieth or so of my piano pieces, which pianists, with rare exceptions, allow to accumulate unplayed. Their turn will come in twenty years' time!'[5]

The obstinacy he showed in continuing to write for the instrument proves how important it was for him. In another letter to his wife[6] he wrote, 'There's no place for padding in piano music, one has to pay in cash and make it consistently interesting. It is perhaps the most difficult genre of all, if one aims to be as good as possible – as I certainly do.'

This unquenchable fidelity to the piano throughout the length of his composing career is all the more astonishing because the disruption of his deafness, during the last twenty years of his life, every day alienated him still further from his favourite instrument. As he was finishing the sixth of the Nine Preludes op. 103, on 27 July 1910, he confided to his wife: 'the worst torture is when I try to work at my lovely Erard. The sounds in the middle of the keyboard sound distant but in tune, whereas the bass and the treble are just an incomprehensible hubbub!'[7]

It is tempting to suggest that this progressive diminution in Fauré's hearing had some effect on the stylistic change noted in chapter 13. One immediately thinks of Beethoven writing his most prophetic works in almost total isolation. But, in fact, it is hard to say with certainty that without the ravages of this disease Fauré's language would have developed quite differently. There existed in him a fundamental instinct towards self-renewal which should not be underestimated.

Certainly it is true that in the works of the 1880s and '90s some of the patterns in his piano music are purely pianistic and indicate a certain pleasure in drawing new sounds out of the instrument. Passages like the beginnings of the Second Nocturne and of the Third and Fourth Barcarolles obviously belong to the tradition of 'French sensuality' as described by Roland-Manuel. Such passages become extremely rare in the works of Fauré's maturity: his piano writing becomes stiffer, more concentrated and more radical as it throws off the languor of the *fin-de-siècle* and reaches out towards a modern idiom.

Personally I see this evolution as a sign of enrichment, because what his work loses in immediate seductiveness, it gains in density. The charming, supple writing of his youth brought with it a certain flabbiness and the indecisive quality of all those exquisite sonorities and perversely changing harmonies was at times in danger of sounding dull and routine.

The end of the century was, for Fauré, a time when dissonance was liberated. The key works in this respect are the Fifth Barcarolle and the Seventh Nocturne and we should note that the quotations in Examples 4 and 8, pp. 56 and 61, date from 1894 and 1898 respectively; that is to say, several years before the onset of his deafness (1902–3).

Those striking chords, encrusted with appoggiaturas, would have been unthinkable at the period of the Ballade (1879). They show that Fauré's attitude to the delights of harmony had been considerably modified and that now he did not hesitate to use the strongest musical spices when he thought them necessary. The works of his contemporaries offer nothing comparable. Those of Debussy (*Suite bergamasque*, 1890; *Images oubliées*, 1894) are promising but generally conventional, while the young Ravel was cultivating a Satie-like modal delicacy (*Menuet antique*, 1895; *Pavane pour une Infante défunte*, 1899). Closer examples of this rhythmic vigour and harmonic sharpness are to be found in Chabrier, in the *Scherzo valse* (1881) and the *Trois valses romantiques* for two pianos (1883), but the nearest parallels to Fauré's innovative ideas are in the last piano works by Brahms, with their full, superbly resonant textures.

Fauré pursued his urge towards self-renewal in the first years of the new century, and especially in the years when he was writing *Pénélope*. The Eighth Barcarolle op. 96, in D flat, written in June 1906, makes no concessions. It is extremely dense and goes on its way without respite, supported by the stirring outburst of intervals of the major second which underpin the harmony in the second episode in C sharp minor (*cantabile*). The work ends abruptly on a *fortissimo* chord, thrown off in the laconic manner so successfully exploited by Albéniz in some of his pieces from *Iberia*, dating from the same period.[8]

Music of this sort may strike us as severe, but it is a severity which can have lasting charms. In order to enjoy a work like the Eighth Barcarolle one must be prepared to follow the rhythmic and, even more, the harmonic development of thematic ideas that are often brief and not particularly singable. The rewards of Fauré's piano music of this period do not lie in the beauty or profusion of his melodic inventiveness. More often than not he is content with two motifs which he then develops with an extraordinary mastery worthy of the greatest composers. The resulting mixture of fantasy and rigour in these works is particularly attractive.

Just occasionally, technique seems to get the better of imagination, for example in the Ninth Nocturne op. 96, in B minor (1908). After the fine exposition of the two themes the development, based on the opening notes of the piece, seems gradually to get lost in abstruse harmonic meanderings which have a minimum of melodic interest (bars 15–25). As if to compensate for such an excess of dryness, Fauré treats us to a richly modulating coda based on a new theme, which is as broad and lyrical as one could wish for, but he then suddenly refuses to develop it or even to repeat its contours. As a result, this brief passage has an incomplete feel to it.

The Tenth Nocturne op. 99, in E minor, was written at Lugano in the summer of 1908, while Fauré was working feverishly on *Pénélope*. He sketched it out in two days, 'to let Heugel have a piano piece' as he said, and finished it at the beginning of November. It is a work of unusual lyrical intensity. The first motif runs smoothly into the second and the development offers for the first time a concertante style of writing, woven out of canonic sequences, which was to figure largely and rewardingly in the late chamber music (bars 19–34). The varied return of the opening theme in E major attains an eloquence that looks forward to the glorious Thirteenth Nocturne. The coda, in E minor, recalling the main theme and softened by triplets, is of an inexpressible melancholy.

A similar atmosphere obtains in the Ninth Barcarolle op. 101, in A minor, written probably at the end of that same year, 1908. It consists of a series of harmonic or polyphonic variations on a strange, sombre, syncopated theme whose monotony recalls some sailor's song. Unlike many of his contemporaries, Fauré was never inspired by popular tunes and always refused to anchor his music to some reference point and so allow real life to enter. Thus the theme of the Ninth Barcarolle belongs undoubtedly to a folklore of the imagination, as does the similar opening of Act II of *Pénélope*, sketched out some months previously, and it partakes of the 'nocturnal, rural, marine' atmosphere and of the 'serious, slightly melancholy' feeling Fauré speaks of in connection with his opera.[9]

The suffocating air of the lagoon is cleared away (bar 32) by a broad gesture in thirds moving down the scale of E. This diversion, repeated in alternating notes, reappears two pages further on (bars 52–5) and on each occasion leads to a return of the principal theme, first in the tenor under scintillating arpeggios (*espressivo*, bars 36–9), then in a succession of chords built on canonic entries (bars 56–61). The modulating ascent of the theme from the dominant (E, F sharp, G sharp) broadens the harmonic perspective in the manner of a long shot in the cinema.

The Fifth Impromptu op. 102, in F sharp minor is, on the other hand, a piece of sheer virtuosity celebrating, not without humour, the beauties of the whole-tone scale. Marguerite Long explained how it came to be written:[10]

At a concert of 'La Trompette' – a very popular chamber music society – we heard a work by Florent Schmitt in which the theme moved by whole tones. Fauré was annoyed by the success of this so-called novelty and said to me, furiously: 'Me too, I'm going to write a piece in whole tones.'

Because it was the result of a self-imposed wager, this Impromptu stands out as an original in Fauré's output. Any thoughts of expressivity or melody are deliberately sacrificed. The brief motif in long notes which, divided between the two hands, serves as its pretext has some difficulty in surviving amidst the incessant figuration. As Darius Milhaud remarked[11] of this piece:

The use of the whole-tone scale does not depend on the augmented triad and does not imprison the harmony in a system of two chords and six notes. Fauré, faithful to the laws of diatonicism, treats it as a way of modulating, of escaping from the original key and then bringing his melodic ideas back to it with the happiest imaginative touch.

Marguerite Long loved the work and in 1933 recorded a sparkling performance which has since been transferred to LP. 'When Saint-Saëns heard me play it for the first time in 1909', she wrote, 'he was astounded by the speed of the figuration and by the descending whole-tone passages which have a dangerously upsetting effect on the fingers, and said to me after a long silence, "Good Heavens, it's difficult." '[12]

A year later (17 May 1910) Marguerite Long gave the first performance, at the Société musicale indépendante, of three Préludes which Fauré had written in the autumn of 1909. They were first of all published separately, then six more preludes were added in the summer of 1910. To begin with Fauré was intending to write a complete volume of preludes, as old editions of the Nine Préludes op. 103 indicate that more are to come (à suivre), but this idea never materialised.

We may remember that the young Fauré had written a Prelude and Fugue in E minor many years before as a student, but after that he had not returned to the genre of the prelude, even though it seems an ideal vehicle for his innate improvisatory gifts. Chopin's success in the field might, it is true, have made him reluctant to try his hand, but this argument does not hold with the other titles Fauré used: Nocturne, Barcarolle, Impromptu, Ballade, Fantasy, all of which were employed by Chopin. I am more inclined to think that it was only with the arrival of maturity that Fauré was able to hone down his natural expansiveness, even prolixity, to writing a three-page Prelude. Debussy published the first volume of his Préludes at exactly the same time, but Fauré's collection does not aspire to Debussy's wide sweep; in its brevity, diversity and expressive qualities it comes nearer to Chopin. In style and texture there are three discernibly separate groupings. First, pieces that concentrate on sonority: no. 1 (D flat), no. 3 (G minor) and no. 7 (A major); then the virtuoso pieces which we might call studies 'in legato' (no. 2, C sharp minor), 'in triplets' (no. 5, D minor) and 'in repeated notes' (no. 8, C minor); and lastly the polyphonic pieces: no. 4 (F major), no. 6 (E flat minor), entirely written in canon at the octave, and no. 9 (E minor). From among these short pieces I would single out three: no. 4, for the harmonic inventiveness and freshness of inspiration which so impressed the young Milhaud (see Ex. 41);[13] no. 7, which achieves a kind of ideal synthesis of Fauré's qualities in its flowing sonorities, the way the lines of the polyphony are made to sing and the complete originality of the harmonies that result at every step; and lastly no. 9, which I would recommend to devotees of Bach's *Das wohltemperierte Klavier* as an example of Fauré's expressive polyphony and what it has to say to us today – thirty-three bars of pure music. The coda appears in Example 72.

Ex. 72 Prélude no. 9 (coda)

It is perhaps legitimate to link the expressive qualities of the final preludes with Fauré's deep sorrow at the death of his father-in-law Emmanuel Fremiet, who was also a close friend.

The years 1911 and 1912 were entirely taken up with his frenzied work on *Pénélope*, but after its première in the spring of 1913 Fauré returned to his favourite domain of piano music and he delivered the Eleventh Noc-

turne and the Tenth Barcarolle to his new publisher, Jacques Durand, in
June 1913. The two pieces appeared as nos. 1 and 2 of op. 104.

The Eleventh Nocturne in F sharp minor was written on the sudden
death of Noémi Lalo, the wife of Pierre Lalo, the music critic of the
newspaper *Le Temps* and the son of the composer Edouard Lalo, and
Fauré dedicated it to her memory. It is a poignant but restrained elegy. A
brief theme of funereal cast, slowly developing over a tolling knell on the
dominant (Ex. 73), returns inescapably all through the piece. The work's

Ex. 73 Nocturne no. 11

profound melancholy makes one think of Chopin's A minor Waltz, op. 34
no. 2, even though the aesthetic context and the musical language are quite
different. It is written almost entirely in four parts and the numerous
dissonances fulfil a decidedly expressive function. Unusually, the second
theme (*cantando*, bar 19) brings nothing in the way of contrast, but the
coda introduces for the first time those successions of modulating chords
(see Ex. 43) which are to be found in the most inspired works of his
old age: the Thirteenth Nocturne, the opening songs of *Mirages* and of
L'Horizon chimérique and the Piano Trio.

The melancholy, nocturne-like character of the theme of the Tenth
Barcarolle is somewhat reminiscent of the *Gondollieder* from Mendelssohn's *Lieder ohne Worte*, but the way this single theme develops points
unmistakably to Fauré's authorship. Tension builds up through increasingly animated rhythms and, at certain points, excessively complex
textures before being released in a succession of descending harmonies
which are as logical as they are unforeseeable (bars 53–9). The Eighth

Barcarolle (bars 54–8), the Ninth Barcarolle (bars 32–5) and the Eleventh Nocturne (bars 54–6) offer further examples of this descending 'harmonic staircase', as Fauré liked to call it,[14] which blurs tonality by means of a modal scale mixed with whole tones. It seems almost as if the composer had recourse to this wholesale 'sweeping out' when the harmonic atmosphere became too intense.

During the summer of 1913, Fauré returned for the last time to Lugano and its Mediterranean light. Between reading Flaubert[15] and van Lerberghe's volume of poetry *Entrevisions*,[16] he drifted back to composition, with a new piece for piano: the Eleventh Barcarolle op. 105, in G minor. This lively, virtuoso piece is dedicated to Laura Albéniz, the daughter of the composer, and Fauré's friend, who died in 1909. The work is constructed on three motifs. The first, slow and sombre, is heard in unison in the lower register of the instrument and leads directly to the second, an essentially rhythmic idea, characterised by chromatically ascending sixths (bars 9–13). After a varied repeat of this material comes a central section based on a modulating idea in octaves[17] (bars 33–6). The succession of harmonies which form the development is rather mechanical (bars 41–51); it leads to a varied repeat of the two initial motifs, which are now joined by the third (bar 69). The solidity and complexity of the writing are, no doubt, grounds for admiration but the overall effect is rather of expertise than of inspiration. The G major coda atones for this impression of dryness, and its calm, meditative polyphony is at one with that of the end of the *Thème et variations*, with the finale of the first Act of *Pénélope* and with the last of the Nine Préludes. Its beautiful theme is in the Mixolydian mode with a flattened leading-note (F natural) and the development of this includes a fairly obvious quotation of the melancholic 'love theme' from *Pénélope*. But the coda still has a surprise in store: on closer analysis, its melodic basis turns out to be a condensed variant of the opening theme (see Ex. 74, second part).

One day in 1912, Fauré received at the Conservatoire a request for a meeting signed by a young pianist whom he vaguely remembered: Robert Lortat-Jacob. Lortat was born on 12 September 1885, won a first prize for piano at the Conservatoire in 1901 and in 1909 was awarded the Prix Louis Diémer, after a competition restricted to those who had already won first prizes at the Conservatoire. In due course, the young pianist presented himself at Fauré's directorial office. As he later remembered:[18]

Ex. 74 Barcarolle no. 11

I was carrying under my arm Fauré's complete piano music, bound in four imposing volumes which I put down on the edge of the piano as I went in. Fauré with the blank look on his face which he used to assume when he was resigned to being deeply bored by something, asked me what I was going to play.

'Whatever you like, *Maître.*'
'No, no, play me what you've been practising for me.'
'But ... everything.'
'What do you mean, everything? I hardly think you play everything I've written!'

'But certainly, *Maître*. I haven't put you to this trouble to play you a few
pieces which everybody plays. No, I know *everything* you've written
for the piano and I can play it for you now, all the way through.'

At that moment, I swear, Fauré's expression changed entirely but I could
still detect some slight scepticism.

'That's a lot of work you've set yourself. Really?'

'Really, *Maître*. What would you like me to start with?'

'Well, how about the Nocturnes?'

He reached for the volume containing the Nocturnes and was about to
put it on the music-rest, when I stopped him:

'No, *Maître*, I can play it all by heart.'

'Ah!'

And for two whole hours I had the rare and exciting experience of seeing the
metamorphosis undergone by Fauré's expression. The twelve Nocturnes were
followed, I think, by the twelve Barcarolles.[19]

Fauré's face took on a look of enthusiasm and tenderness and in that voice of his
which took on a wheedling inflection when he was pleased with something, he
urged me to continue and sometimes to play a piece over again. I asked him why he
should want to hear it twice. And in a voice that trembled with some sadness he
replied: 'No-one has ever played it to me and I'd forgotten having written it!'

A few moments before I had felt a stranger in his office, but now his tone of voice
made me feel I had been there all my life and, when I was leaving, Fauré said:

'Tomorrow, if you like, you can play me the rest, but this time you won't
have the bother of travelling, *I'll* come and see *you*.'

Thus began a friendship which never for a moment faltered and which I count as
the most intense memory of my artistic life.

In 1911 Lortat had given six concerts in which he had played the whole
of Chopin. Now he turned his attention to Fauré. In 1914, with the help of
Claire Croiza and Georges Enesco among others, he devoted four sessions
to his music (29 April, 6, 13 and 20 May) in the series of lecture-concerts
held at the Université des Annales.[20]

The sessions were repeated the following month in London (16, 19 and
22 June) at the Aeolian Hall, interspersed with some of Fauré's songs sung
by Germaine Sanderson and chamber music with the composer at the
piano.[21] He wrote to his one-time editor Hamelle on 7 July, 'In London an
enormous success for Lortat with the piano pieces. A large number of them
were known only to a few connoisseurs.'[22]

According to Lortat:

The sessions were attended by the cream of London society and of the artists and
musicians ... as I was leaving the stage I expressed my disappointment with the
audience which, though enthusiastic, seemed to me rather small. I shall always hear

Fauré's voice replying gently and, I can vouch for it, without a trace of bitterness: 'But, Lortat, I'm not in the habit of attracting crowds!'[23]

And so Lortat became one of Fauré's close friends during the last ten years of his life; in 1915 the composer rewarded his active enthusiasm by dedicating to him the Twelfth Nocturne. When the *Fantaisie* for piano and orchestra was published, Lortat came to stay near Annecy where Fauré was spending the summer of 1919 and studied the new work under Fauré's guidance. He gave its second performance in Paris on 23 November 1919 at the Lamoureux Concerts, with Camille Chevillard conducting.[24] In 1921 Lortat was chosen by Fauré to play the piano part in the first performance of his Second Piano Quintet.

Lortat recorded some of Fauré's works in the composer's lifetime[25] on Duo Art piano rolls, the best of the mechanical systems of that period. From these we are able to judge the clarity, elegance and warmth of his interpretations as well as a style that has not become outmoded. The same qualities are to be found in the records of Chopin (*Preludes*, *Etudes*, *Waltzes*, the Sonata op. 35) which he made for Columbia some ten years later. It is a very French style of playing, perhaps more sinewy than powerful, excelling in the expressive passages and always absolutely straightforward. Lortat owed this style to his teacher Louis Diémer (1843–1919), the senior piano professor at the Conservatoire where he had been teaching since 1888. Diémer was a pioneer in the rediscovery of French baroque music and was fond of playing the harpsichord which he had had built by Gaveau, based on an eighteenth-century original. After the success of the concerts of seventeenth- and eighteenth-century French music which he organised for the Universal Exhibition in 1889, he founded the Société des instruments anciens, and published an anthology of French harpsichord music. At the same time, he had given the first performance of César Franck's *Variations symphoniques*, which the composer dedicated to him.

The records Diémer made in 1905–6 confirm his reputation as a technically impeccable but rather dry pianist. But his pupils formed an impressive list: Alfred Cortot, Edouard Risler, Henri Etlin, Marcel Ciampi, Lazare Lévy, Robert Casadesus ... Fauré, younger than Diémer by two years, had always been close to him and dedicated to him his Twelfth Barcarolle. Diémer gave the first performance on 23 November 1916 (with the Twelfth Nocturne) in the course of a series of concerts organised by Jacques Durand to celebrate the French school of composers, whose most celebrated representatives were published by his firm.

Since at this period commercial relations with the German-speaking countries had been broken off, Jacques Durand took the opportunity to publish the piano works of the great classical composers in editions revised by his house composers, thereby replacing to his own profit the German editions of Peters and Litolff. Durand respected the various elective affinities in making his dispositions: Chopin went to Debussy, Mendelssohn to Ravel, Mozart to Saint-Saëns who, long before the war, had undertaken a large Rameau edition with several collaborators. Beethoven was given to Paul Dukas and Schubert to Roger Ducasse, while Fauré agreed to revise Bach's organ works with the help of the organist Joseph Bonnet. The fourteen volumes of this edition appeared between 1917 and 1920, but Fauré was much more closely involved in the revision of Schumann's piano works, which were published in thirty-seven volumes between 1916 and 1924. None of these editions is in any way comparable to the critical editions of today. The editors contented themselves with reading the texts closely and, where a doubtful passage caused some difficulty, with looking at the original editions and, in very rare instances, at such autograph manuscripts as were to be found in Paris. Despite the appearance since then of numerous critical editions, the Durand volumes are still being sold, surrounded as they are by the halo of the important names who lent themselves to these publications all those years ago ...

With the outbreak of war, Fauré gave up his practice of spending the summer abroad – in Switzerland, especially – as his difficult return from Ems in August 1914 had left painful memories. In 1915 he spent six weeks during August and September at the pension 'le Gui' in Saint-Raphaël, renewing his old and cherished acquaintance with the Midi. 'From my windows, a splendid view over the sea immediately in front of me', he wrote to his wife on 1 August 1915, 'and to the right the Maures mountains which come right down to the shore. It's a superb panorama, only my worries, whether great or small, have not been left behind on the way. What would be powerful enough to set me free from them!' On 9 August he wrote 'I'm working on a Nocturne for piano; apart from which I've brought a volume of Schumann down here with me and I'm getting on with that.' A month later he could say, 'I've got two piano pieces on the go, both at a very advanced stage. But I'm licking them all over, as bears do with their cubs!'[26]

The Twelfth Nocturne op. 107, in E minor, was the first piece Fauré had finished since Lortat's memorable performances of his complete output. This time there is no place left for dreaming: the work's sombre, tumultuous mood, shot through as though with flashes of lightning, mirrors the anxieties of war, beginning with a kind of formal oration over low syncopations in the bass. The dark, epic atmosphere and the monumental texture recall the Brahms of the late piano works, but a Brahms spiced with dissonances which would have given the gruff Hamburger a distinct jolt: in bar 14 the right hand strikes F sharp and B natural while the left hand plays an octave F natural. Harmonic tension increases still further with the second theme, built from two similar motifs: the first, based on intervals of the second repeated with a kind of calm relentlessness, throws out showers of sparks (bars 21–4), the second, lyrical and very rhythmic, recalls the noble outbursts of the Fifth Barcarolle (bar 25).

The second section of the piece (bar 43, *Tempo 1*) varies these thematic ideas in a continuously accelerating tempo – something very rare with Fauré – until it reaches a heroic climax. Bold and complex as the writing may be, this fine piece never loses hold of its logical thread.

The Twelfth Barcarolle op. 106 bis, in E flat, finished in September 1915, offers a direct contrast with the Twelfth Nocturne – its exact contemporary – in its clarity and limpidity. At first sight we may be surprised by this symmetrically arpeggiated accompaniment, taking us back some thirty years to the period of the First Barcarolle. Maybe Fauré was amused to pull the wool over critical eyes by taking this quiet, simple theme from some ancient book of sketches. At the recapitulation we seem to progress in the work's imaginary time-zone, the easygoing harmonies and the straightforward theme in octaves (bars 17–20) reviving memories of 'Le Jardin de Dolly', but the arrival of more acidic harmonies testifies to the composer's late style. The second theme recalls somewhat the Twelfth Nocturne, in the motif in thirds of the first theme combined with the syncopated rhythm of the second, but the expressive context is quite different. The musical argument, it is true, grows more complicated with each episode, but the Barcarolle nature of the piece is not fundamentally altered. Through all the complexities of the polyphonic lines the *cantabile* melody shines out, and neither the presentation of the motif in canon (bars 62–74) nor its transformation into a theme of almost triumphal character (bars 75–83) affect the melodious charm of this original piece, which was one of Saint-Saëns' favourites.[27]

Alongside Fauré's piano works we may conveniently consider the second of his two important pieces for harp, one of his favourite orchestral instruments. Earlier in the century Alphonse Hasselmans had introduced to Fauré one of the outstanding pupils in his class, Micheline Kahn. She had won a first prize for harp in 1904 at the age of fourteen and Fauré entrusted her with the performance of his Impromptu at the Société nationale on 7 January 1905, as did Ravel with his *Introduction et allegro* two years later. At the beginning of 1918 Fauré did her the honour of presenting her with a new piece for her instrument, *Une Châtelaine en sa tour*, op. 110; its title is taken from the first of the poems set in *La Bonne chanson*. This second piece for harp differs notably from the first, following Fauré's persistent policy of self-renewal. The Impromptu was a test piece for the Paris Conservatoire and included a large amount of virtuoso writing, whereas 'La Châtelaine', as harpists generally call it, is a delicate, cloudy, poetic piece bearing the imprint of Verlaine. Over a pattern of arpeggios it develops a kind of song without words (9/8 in A minor) whose outline is faintly reminiscent of the song from which it takes its title: 'Une sainte en son auréole'. It is not impossible that the work has some hidden significance, or that it is a musical (and ironical) portrait of its dedicatee.

A second theme in alternating notes (3/4 in F major) brings with it a certain animation. The canonic repeat of the initial melody, now in 3/4, leads to a brief cadenza in 9/8 based on the second theme (with cross-rhythms between the two themes) which is interrupted by characteristic harp flourishes. The final reprise is in A major, employing the immaterial sound of harmonics.

Micheline Kahn gave the first performance of *Une châtelaine en sa tour* on 30 November 1918 at the Société nationale de musique. Being an enthusiast over Fauré's music, she had in 1913 transcribed and published three pieces for her instrument: the 'Berceuse' of *Dolly* and 'Le Jardin de Dolly', as well as the *Sicilienne*. She and Fauré took part in many concerts in aid of wartime charities. In November 1916 he wrote her the following letter in the form of light verses, for many years one of his specialities:[28]

> Dedans ce grand Palais qu'on appelle 'de Glace'
> Pour guérir votre rhum! venez le mois prochain,
> Sur l'instrument divin dont vous êtes, de face,
> De profil, de trois-quart la Reine, c'est certain,
> Faire courir vos doigts, doux comme ceux des anges.
> Lorsqu'ils bercaient Jésus, qui 'faisait' dans ses langes
> > Tout son bonheur était parfait.
> Oui, venez joindre à un bienfait
> Deux plaisirs infinis: vous voir et vous entendre!
> (Mon Dieu! Mon Dieu! Mon Dieu! que le froid me rend tendre)
> Vous jouerez l'Impromptu, la Berceuse-Dolly
> Et même la *Romance*, et l'on boira du lait!
> Et ce sera je crois le seize de Décembre.

(A l'Opéra-Comique, dans sa petite chambre,
C'est le mois où Werther est seul, tout seul, bien seul!!)
Dans trois ou quinze jours, j'irai franchir le seuil
De votre ravissant mais un peu haut cinquième
   Pour vous fixer sur le quantième
     Du brillant festival
    Dédié a la Bienfaisance
     Où sans penser à mal
    J'ai promis ta présence!
[Inside the great palace known as the one 'of mirrors',
To cure your cold [lit. 'rum']! come next month,
On the divine instrument of which you are, from the front
In profile, and three-quarter-face the Queen, 'tis certain,
Exercise your fingers, like those of the angels.
When they cradled Jesus in his swaddling clothes
     His happiness was complete.
Yes, come and add to your kindness
Two infinite pleasures: to see you and to hear you!
(Goodness! The cold is making me tenderhearted)
You'll play the Impromptu, the 'Berceuse' from *Dolly*
And even the *Romance*, and we'll have some milk!
And that, I think, is on 16 December
(At the Opéra-Comique, in its small hall,
The month when Werther is alone, all, all alone!!)
In three days or a fortnight I shall cross the threshold
Of your delightful but rather elevated apartment on the 5th storey
     To discuss terms
    For the brilliant festival
     Dedicated to charity
   At which, with the best will in the world,
   I have promised your participation.]

[*Note:* The poet begs forgiveness for using the 'tutoyer' at the end. This offence against good manners is authorised by poetic necessity. 'Votre' would make the line one syllable too long!]

A few months before this letter, Mlle Kahn had consulted Fauré over which new pieces he thought could be transcribed for harp. In a letter of 3 August 1916, Fauré suggested she might choose nos. 5, 7, and 8 of the *Pièces brèves*: 'You'll see I've indicated in pencil some outlines of alterations, as examples. Follow them as you wish; *musically*, it's no. 8 which I find the most interesting. Won't it be rather difficult? I defer to your absolute, *complete* artistry!'[29]

Whether these projected transcriptions were in fact realised is not known, as they do not figure in the Hamelle catalogue. Nowadays we may find it hard to imagine how widespread a practice transcription was. In the absence of radio, television or records, music-lovers had a healthy appetite for transcriptions into the most diverse musical combinations.

When a composer signed a contract with a publisher, he gave him the right to publish whatever transcriptions he thought might be useful, on the condition that they were submitted to the composer before publication. The composer could make changes to the new version – which was normally prepared by a specialist in that area or, less often, by a well-known virtuoso – and could even on occasion exercise a right of veto if he thought the transcription was a travesty of the original, although this right existed more in theory than in practice. When agreement had been reached and corrections made, the new version was deposited jointly by the composer and the transcriber with the Société des auteurs, compositeurs et éditeurs de musique (SACEM – French performing rights society).

The imposing list of Fauré's works, published by Julien and then by Edgard Hamelle, contains almost as many transcriptions as original pieces. For the most part these are vocal works transcribed for various instruments or instrumental works adapted for a different grouping. Some have achieved notable success and are still well-known: the 'Fileuse' from *Pelléas*, arranged by Cortot for piano (1902), the three *Romances sans paroles* arranged for 'cello by Jules Delsart (1896) or Casals' version of 'Après un rêve' for 'cello and piano, which is known all over the world.

In addition, very many of his works bore indications for alternative modes of performance right from the start, thanks to the initiative of the publisher acting more or less with the composer's agreement. One frequently finds the designation 'for 'cello or violin' (*Berceuse* op. 16, *Elégie*, *Papillon*, *Sicilienne*), not to mention the orchestral and chamber works which were almost automatically reduced for piano solo (*Pelléas*, *Shylock*), for piano duet (*Pavane*, Allegro symphonique, *Shylock*, Second Quintet), or for two pianos (Ballade and Fourth *Valse–Caprice* by Isidor Philipp, First Quartet, the unpublished 1st Symphony). In his younger days Fauré had made various piano transcriptions for Durand and Co. of works by Saint-Saëns, the most extraordinary of these being the overture to the opéra-comique *La Princesse jaune* for eight hands on two pianos! But he was also prepared to transcribe or reduce some of his own works: he made a piano duet version of *Masques et bergamasques* and of the Andante from his String Quartet and a two-piano version of his *Fantaisie* for piano and orchestra. The *Sicilienne* was written out originally for chamber orchestra (1893) and in 1898 published simultaneously in versions for 'cello and piano and piano solo, before being incorporated that same year in the incidental music for *Pelléas et Mélisande*. The celebrated *Pavane* was published for piano, for chorus and piano, and for orchestra with optional chorus.

There was indeed a sort of mania for publishing the favourite, if not always the best, pieces from the Fauré catalogue in the most curious guises. The pre-eminent example is 'Après un rêve', a song for mezzo-soprano (or baritone) and piano (1879), which appeared in versions for soprano (1895?), for contralto (1908), for 'cello and piano (Casals, 1911), for piano solo (1912), for orchestra (without voice!, 1923), for voice and orchestra (1930), for viola and piano (1932), for piano trio (1934), for organ (1934), and so on ...

The complete list of Fauré's published works runs, therefore, to several hundred items. This commercial exploitation by publishers anxious to get a return on their investments was not peculiar to Fauré, of course. It also reveals the extent to which the piano, the king of nineteenth-century instruments, still held undisputed sway.

Fauré began work on his *Fantaisie* for piano and orchestra op. 111 in the sombre spring of 1918 when Paris was under the threat of German cannon. He finished it at Evian at the beginning of September, at the time of the great offensive which was to lead to the Allies' ultimate victory. The atmosphere of the work is a fairly direct reflection of the hopes and tribulations of those final, apocalyptic months of the war – in itself a sufficiently rare example of Fauré's art imitating life to merit a special mention. The idea of using the *concertante* form came from Fauré's publisher, Jacques Durand. Fauré wrote to him from Evian on 3 September 1918: 'Thank you for suggesting this *Fantaisie*. Works of this kind aren't numerous and, as you say, apart from the Saint-Saëns concertos, modern music for piano and orchestra is fairly hard to find.' In the same letter Fauré gives this description of his new work:

It consists of an initial section, *allegro molto moderato*, interrupted by an *allegro vivace*, and concluded by a return to the opening. The whole work is in a single movement and lasts about twenty minutes, not much more. When I get back I'll give you the manuscript of the solo part with the second piano part over the top. I'd like to wait till Cortot returns to Paris at the end of January before arranging a performance of this little piece and I'm planning to orchestrate it in October. This won't take long.[30]

Fauré's letters to his wife show that work on the *Fantaisie* went exceptionally smoothly: 'I'm working without stopping or getting tired, and to good effect. Alas! it's only when I'm a long way from Paris that I work faster and *well*' (Evian, 16 August 1918), and on 8 September: 'I've almost finished my piece for piano and orchestra. I seem to work more quickly and easily as I grow older . . . I must say the news of the war has cheered me, as I expect it has you'[31] (see plate 57). Even so it took a year to get the two-piano and the full scores ready for publication. Fauré's time was largely taken up with the writing and the first performance of the 'comédie lyrique' *Masques et bergamasques* (Monte Carlo, 10 April 1919) and with the long-awaited revival of *Pénélope* at the Opéra-Comique (20 January 1919). His health was not good, either. Bronchitis and 'flu had weakened him considerably in the early part of 1918, leaving him prostrated for long periods. He confided to his wife, in a letter of 28 March 1919: 'I'm trying to get something started so that I can work on it during the holidays, but my brain is being stubborn. There's nothing there, a void.' His hearing was getting worse too: 'It's appalling', he wrote to his wife on 1 April 1919, 'it's in the middle of this horrible hubbub that I'm hearing *Pénélope*! The singing voice comes through best. But the orchestra is just a painful racket.'[32]

Fauré's decision to ask a young composer to orchestrate the *Fantaisie* under his supervision needs to be seen in this context. From the manuscript score kept by the composer[33] I have been able to ascertain that the composer in question was Marcel Samuel-Rousseau (1882–1955), who had won the second prix de Rome for composition in 1905 and was now teaching harmony at the Conservatoire. The manuscript score of the 'Gavotte' and 'Le Plus doux chemin' in *Masques et bergamasques* are also in his hand.

Alfred Cortot, to whom the *Fantaisie* is dedicated and who had suggested as far back as 1902 that Fauré write a *concertante* work for him, had his own ideas about the piano part which the composer had submitted for his inspection. The proofs of the two-piano score, corrected by both Fauré and Cortot,[34] contain a large number of Cortot's suggestions regarding the layout of his part which the two of them seem to have discussed. We can find an echo of these discussions in a letter from Fauré to Cortot written from Monte Carlo on 22 March 1919:[35]

I've been thinking a lot about the modifications you suggested which, in most cases, would increase the sonority of the texture. But at the beginning I'm a little doubtful about putting in octaves, because of the orchestra's reply which would have to be laid out in the same way. Would you think about it and let me know what you feel? Note that the theme in question is only intended to express a kind of joy, a contentment with everything and everybody. I'm afraid the octaves and *particularly* the low chords in the piano accompaniment may make it too heavy.

It was during this stay at Monte Carlo that Marguerite Hasselmans gave an, unofficial, first performance of the *Fantaisie* on 12 April 1919, with Léon Jehin conducting, in the course of a Fauré festival. Cortot gave the first Paris performance on 14 May 1919 at the Salle Gaveau, during a concert of the Société nationale de musique. The pianist's reservations about the work that Fauré had written for him are expressed clearly, if discreetly, in his rather disappointing article 'La musique pour piano de Gabriel Fauré'.[36] In it Cortot regrets the lack of brilliance in the solo part and the shortage of contrasts between it and the orchestra. Well may he have found the *Fantaisie* a 'light' work, having just returned from the United States where he gave the first American performance of Rachmaninov's Third Piano Concerto in the composer's presence. Cortot was an incurable romantic and the reserved style of Fauré's later work could never be wholly to his taste. He wrote that 'nothing in the layout of this composition exceeds the character of a piece of chamber music in which there are simply rather more players than usual', and this is very true.

What is less well-known is that the idea of a *concertante* work for piano and orchestra came indirectly from Debussy. He had written to Jacques Durand in July 1917 to say that he was thinking of a series of *Concerts* for piano and various instrumental groups. This is a good enough definition of the *Fantaisie* and it is possible that Jacques Durand, who published both men's music, suggested it to Fauré after Debussy's death on 25 March 1918, as well as the idea of a ballet with the characters of the *commedia dell'arte* for which Debussy had prepared a scenario in 1910, intended for Diaghilev and entitled *Masques et bergamasques* (see chapter 14).

The *Fantaisie* op. 111 is indeed written for piano and orchestra, but an orchestra hardly bigger than that of the eighteenth century: duple woodwind, four horns, one trumpet, timpani, harp and strings, in all a grouping Fauré often used. The relationship between the soloist and the orchestra is based on that established thirty years earlier in the Ballade: the soloist takes first place – as a principal, we might say – while the power and colour of the orchestra serve to underline the argument. The strings are used almost throughout to accompany the piano but the woodwind are often treated as soloists. The overall tripartite form, of two *moderato* movements enclosing a central *allegro*, recalls the Ballade quite closely, but the parallels between the two works should not be pushed too far. In matters of expression, language and aesthetic, the *Fantaisie* lies practically at the opposite extreme from the Ballade: instead of *chiaroscuro*, melting chords and sighs of ecstasy and abandon, the melodic lines are now firm, the rhythm dominating to the point of being an ostinato, the harmony tinged with dissonances and polyphony pre-eminent.

The first theme – A – played at once by the soloist, is strongly rhythmical, spanning octaves with an athletic grace and energy; this is the theme Fauré was referring to in the letter to Cortot quoted above, when he said that it was 'only intended to express a kind of joy, a contentment with everything and everybody'. It is repeated immediately on the unusual combination of two clarinets and harp. Variations of it on the piano lead to the second theme (bar 29) on muted violins. This lyrical, almost caressing theme – B – is based on one of Fauré's favourite melodic patterns, a rising octave followed by a major second (see chapter 11), here extended by a rising whole-tone scale (see Example 75).

Despite their different character, these two themes are perfectly complementary, as is shown by the reprise (bar 52) and the developments that follow it, where the themes alternate happily and at times even succeed each other directly (bars 80–5). The musical argument is becoming tauter and the orchestral texture reaching a tutti for the first time, when a large flourish from the piano introduces the abrupt break of the *Allegro vivace*. The introduction to this section is one of Fauré's most astonishing passages: his textures are normally so unified and well organised, but here everything is jagged, disjointed and chaotic, with gusts of whole-tone scales – C – over curious string ostinatos. The main theme – D – is openly stated by the piano over the same string ostinato on a pedal B natural (see Ex. 76).

A motif of two alternating notes leads (bar 211) to a return of the lyrical theme B from the first section. Its upward curve, stretched out in augmented note-values in the higher strings, has a majesty about it that recalls the last scene of *Pénélope*. The calm of this beautiful theme is constantly attacked by reappearances of theme C, and during this heavily contrasted episode the piano is reduced to the rôle of a rhythmic support. The return of the *Allegro vivo* (bar 243) is differently orchestrated, with the ostinato on the timpani or the horn and the lyrical theme on the piano.

The development section (bars 347–84) is richly polyphonic. Fauré combines the noble curve of theme B with the characteristic pattern of theme A on the violins; beneath that he has the motif of two alternating notes on the oboes and then the horns, and the whole ensemble is supported by the ostinato motif in the violas, over the 'rhythm section' of the

Ex. 75 *Fantaisie* for piano and orchestra

Ex. 76 *Fantaisie* for piano and orchestra

piano part – this seems the most appropriate term here, and we shall see in the following chapter what Fauré's chamber music owed to the great musical novelty of the war years – jazz.

All the musical material has now been presented and the scene is set for the third section of the work (bars 389–490). This gives the appearance, certainly, of recapitulating the first, but in repeating its rather few musical ideas it makes of them a splendid synthesis. Where the orchestral texture in the first section was at times rather discontinuous, now it attains an impressive density and fullness. The two themes of the opening section are first of all repeated separately (bar 389 and bar 407), giving rise to new curves in the melody (bars 439–66 in the piano, bars 449–55 in the violins) while the cheerful theme A is heard in canon. These final pages of the *Fantaisie* are some of Fauré's finest. Their power and easy sweep are allied to a technical skill which never militates against the communication of an enthusiasm mirroring that of the forthcoming victory after nearly five years of war.

17   Light and shade: Chamber music II

Fauré's troubles and anxieties persisted during the years of a war which saw 9 million killed, 1,400,000 French and 800,000 British. His letters, relatively few and far between during this period, show him kept in suspense, as so many Frenchmen were, waiting for the next military communiqué whose accuracy, or lack of it, would be revealed all too soon. On 15 February 1915, he wrote from Paris to his pupil Charles Koechlin:[1]

We in Paris, like you there, wait in hope but above all in a state of nerves! Myself, I hardly see anybody and I'm happy not to; all the varying opinions, information usually from unreliable sources and all the rumours, good and bad, end up by demoralising the most hopeful among us.

At the end of the autumn of 1914, Fauré had had to organise the start of a Conservatoire year with most of the male personnel missing, and professors and pupils especially going off to be victims of the war machine. The need to reorganise classes and examinations meant that the term did not in fact start until December. Some months later (20 July 1915) Fauré's post as Director duly came up for renewal and by a decree of 21 September 1915 he was confirmed in the post 'for the duration of the war'. On 26 September 1919, this confirmation was further extended 'for one year'.

All through the war Fauré was in a state of anxiety about the safety of his younger son, Philippe, who was in the 3rd regiment of Zouaves as mobile liaison officer, in which capacity he often found himself in the front-line fighting and, worst of all, in the terrible Allied expedition to the Dardanelles in 1915. His elder brother, Emmanuel, who had in 1913 married Jeanne Henneguy, his professor's daughter, was forced to remain in Paris owing to ill-health. A tubercular infection had meant him being sent to the mountains in 1908, and during the war he suffered from a serious skin condition (anthrax) brought on, it would seem, by working with formol in the biology laboratory of the Collège de France, where he was then an assistant.[2]

Having taken part himself in the Franco–Prussian War of 1870–1, Fauré reacted badly to the stress and doubtful outcome of this new conflict. 'I'd like to be able to offer you moral support', he wrote to his wife on 1 June 1918, 'but I'm in one of those moods, which have been rare till now, when I'm the one who needs it! Whether it's nerves, or exhaustion from too little sleep, my heart and soul are *on edge!*'[3]

Unlike many French composers – particularly Saint-Saëns, and even Debussy – Fauré played no part in the prevailing anti-German attitudes. His patriotism was not of the sort to obscure clarity of judgment or moderation of expression. Like his pupil Ravel, who was now at the front, he refused to participate in the activities of the National League for the Defence of French Music and its noisy insistence on banning performances of German music in France. On the other hand, he was active in the so-called 'sacred union' which was trying to bring together two rival societies: the Société nationale de musique, founded in 1871 after France's defeat, and the Société musicale indépendante, whose breakaway he had supported in 1909. Vincent d'Indy, the uncontested figure-head of 'La Nationale' stood down in favour of his old friend Fauré, who was to be the president of a new Société nationale, on to whose committee were invited Schmitt, Ravel and Vuillermoz, who had been responsible for founding the SMI. A meeting to reconcile the two factions, held on 17 December 1916, served only to exacerbate their differences. 'It didn't work at all', d'Indy wrote to Serieyx,[4] 'Ravel, Koechlin, Grovlez, Casadesus and Co. refused in the name of their "aesthetics"??? "which cannot ever be the same as ours". I must say I thought it was extremely funny and I'm still giggling about it.'

Even so, on 15 March 1917 Fauré issued in *Le Courrier musical* an 'appeal to French composers'[5] inviting them to settle their differences and support the Société nationale 'which one can no longer suspect of being, as once seemed the case, the property of an individual and in which all shades of musical thought will be fully represented'. This appeal was upheld by composers of such diverse characters as Debussy, Alfred Bruneau, Paul Dukas, Henri Duparc, d'Indy and Messager. But d'Indy was disappointed at being rebuffed by the younger element in the SMI. He could not resist rousing old demons and stirring up those 'modernists' who, as he put it, 'can be distinguished by the *stuttering* cut of their uniform, so to speak. They find it impossible to write a phrase, even a two-bar musical syllable, without giving us an immediate repetition of it'. This drew stinging replies from Ravel and Koechlin who adamantly refused to scuttle their beloved SMI.[6]

'Fauré's the only one who's sorry about it; he'd like to escape from this

SMI', d'Indy concluded in his letter to Serieyx. In fact, Fauré's relations with his old pupils and friends in the SMI were excellent. But he was certainly less intransigent than they were, and more anxious to bring about the 'sacred union' which, in wartime, seemed to him to be called for. He therefore remained president, at least nominally, of the SMI as well as of the Société nationale, where he introduced a new openness and harmony of intent.

No record of Fauré's wartime activities would be complete without mentioning the numerous charity concerts he took part in, accompanying his songs or his Violin Sonata. He managed to evade an official commission for a work to celebrate the Allied victory, but he had to agree to set to music a poem which was the winner of a competition in *Le Figaro* on the subject of peace. The reward of a setting by Fauré went to a certain Georgette Debladis for a poem called *C'est la paix*, which she sent in under the anagrammatic pseudonym Gilette Besgador. Writing to his wife on 6 December 1919, Fauré confessed to having to struggle with this 'horrible little poem', the setting of which to music was 'a small *tour de force*'. By 8 December the job was done: 'I've finished the song in honour of the "poilus"', he wrote to his wife that same day. 'Only I've replaced that frightful word by "soldats". If the poetess doesn't like it, too bad! I'm doing her enough of a favour as it is!'[7] The poetess, naturally, was outraged to see her text reduced by half and considerably modified, and when Fauré's music to it was published in *Le Figaro* on 10 October 1920 she insisted on her poem being published separately and in its original form. Fauré manages, in this curious little work, to salvage his self-respect. The poem aside – and it is truly appalling – the heroic sentiment allows the composer to recall Ulysse's music in *Pénélope*; that is all that needs to be said of a piece which is at a far remove from the two last song-cycles, *Mirages* and *L'Horizon chimérique*, which will be discussed in the following chapter.

As for Fauré's private life, he had to weather the many illnesses and deaths that struck both his family and friends. In August 1914 Joseph de Marliave was killed at the front. Even though his friendship with Fauré had been broken by the quarrel between the composer and Marguerite Long, Marliave's wife, this did not alter the fact that he remained one of the most perceptive critics of Fauré's work, especially of the piano pieces and of *Pénélope*.[8] Then, in the spring of 1915, Fauré's mother-in-law, Marie Ernestine Fremiet, died, so her daughter Marie had to spend a lot of time at the house in Châteauroux; in May 1917 Emilie Girette – now Mme Edouard Risler – died from Spanish 'flu;[9] and in February and October 1918 Fauré lost his two elder brothers, Fernand and Amand, the last survivors of his immediate family. During the winter of 1916–17, Marguerite Hasselmans fell ill and had to spend a long time in Pau at the house of their friend Louise Maillot. Typhoid fever was diagnosed at the beginning of 1917, while Fauré himself was very ill with 'flu.[10] He could not travel to Switzerland or Italy as he had done before the war, so the doctors advised him to spend as long as he could in the Midi or on the Alpine lakes. He was at Saint-Raphaël for the summers of 1915 and 1917, at Evian in 1916 and 1918, at Annecy-le-Vieux in 1919 (as he was to be during his last years) (see plates 56–62), at Veyrier-du-lac on Lake Annecy in 1920 and at Ax-les-Thermes, in his favourite Ariège, in 1921, not to mention the long months he spent each winter on the Côte d'Azur: Nice, Menton or Monte Carlo, where the sun was kinder to his lungs than the biting cold of Paris.

In spite of the worries and difficulties of all kinds that assailed him, he was exceptionally prolific during the war years and those immediately after it. His creative efforts were aided by the marked slackening in his social life in Paris and by these periods spent away from excitements. Composing also stopped him becoming gloomy and worried, as well as taking on, in all probability, the aura of a personal duty almost demanded of him by the state of war, as though he felt, for all his innate modesty, that in continuing to compose he was enriching France's cultural heritage.

The quantity and quality of Fauré's output during the last ten years of his life is impressive. In it, chamber music figures largely:

Aug–Sept 1915: Twelfth Barcarolle; Twelfth Nocturne
Aug 1916–Jan 1917: Second Violin Sonata
May–17 Aug 1917: First 'Cello Sonata
Autumn 1917: *Une châtelaine en sa tour* (harp)
March–Sept 1918: *Fantaisie* for piano and orchestra
Feb–March 1919: *Masques et bergamasques* (comédie lyrique)
July–Aug 1919: *Mirages* (cycle of four songs)
Dec 1919: *C'est la Paix* (*Le Figaro* competition)
Dec 1919–Feb 1921: Second Piano Quintet
Feb 1921: Thirteenth Barcarolle
Feb–Nov 1921: Second 'Cello Sonata
Autumn 1921: *L'Horizon chimérique* (cycle of four songs)
Dec 1921: Thirteenth Nocturne
Sept 1922–Feb 1923: Piano Trio
Aug 1923–Sept 1924: String Quartet

Having dealt in the previous chapter with the piano music of the war years and in chapter 14 with *Masques et bergamasques*, in the context of

Fauré's mature music for the stage, I shall discuss here the chamber music he wrote in the period 1916–21, leaving his final two works to be included in my consideration of his very last years.

When Fauré wrote a violin sonata in 1875, he was in a sense paving the way for a number of other composers: in the following ten years his example was followed by Saint-Saëns, Franck, Lekeu, Pierné and d'Indy, among others. His return to chamber music with the Second Violin Sonata came after a long period of neglect, due to the long gestation of *Pénélope* and probably also to the memory of the problems he had had with the First Piano Quintet. But during the intervening ten years the artistic climate had undergone a considerable change. The act of writing a violin sonata in the middle of a war emphasised the links with that specifically French genre so brilliantly exemplified by Francœur and Leclair almost two centuries earlier. It was Fauré's wholly independent way of joining the Movement which, after the war, was to be dubbed 'neo-classicism'. This sympathetic alliance with a certain French aesthetic tradition remains, with Fauré, implicit: in his letters of 1916 he never says why he is writing a violin sonata – at best, we may recall that he was thinking of writing a work for violin and piano in 1903, when he was starting the slow movement of the First Quintet.[11] The same sympathy is far more clearly expressed by Debussy whose Violin Sonata – his last completed work – is an exact contemporary of Fauré's; after which it continued to manifest itself in works by Koechlin, who dedicated his First Sonata of 1916 to his teacher, by Florent Schmitt, whose Violin Sonata dates from 1918–19, and later in the fine sonatas by Roussel (1924) and Ravel (1923–7).

Fauré's Second Violin Sonata was written with remarkable ease during his peaceful stay at Evian in the summer of 1916, when he was the guest of his friends the Maillots who had rented the Villa Saffrettes for the season. The letters Fauré wrote to his wife tell us that in six weeks (mid-August to the end of September) the first movement, the longest of the three, was finished, the finale more than half done and the slow movement sketched out. Then the creative flow was interrupted by the everlasting admission examinations for the Conservatoire which, as director, he had to preside over. The work was finished at the end of the year and the delivery document (in the archives of Editions Durand) is dated 7 January 1917.

Like the Twelfth Nocturne, written a year earlier and in the same key of E minor, the opening Allegro non troppo begins in a sombre atmosphere of agitated rhythms and harmonic tension, with broken octaves on the piano and repeated notes on the violin, which forcibly suggest that tragic year of 1916.

The first theme (A) consists of two motifs of four bars each. The first, essentially a rhythmic idea, is heard first in the chiaroscuro of the piano; the second, shooting out on the violin like flame from among ashes, is based on a descending scale (C). The second main theme (*tranquillo* in G major, bar 44) also has a descending shape, but in its gentle lyricism it forms a contrast with the agitated A. Between these two themes a secondary theme is presented at length, a warm, supple melody, that modulates powerfully upwards over a basis of shifting arpeggios. Paradoxically, it is this secondary idea (B) which offers the composer the most possibilities in the realms of his creative fantasy. The complex plan of this long movement may be presented as in Table 4. The themes A, B and C are indicated in Example 77.

This structural outline shows clearly the freedom with which Fauré approaches his formal models. The hallowed, tripartite division of sonata form is still plainly discernible, but we may note the liberties he takes with the rules in writing the recapitulation in 12/8 time, instead of the original 9/8, and in repeating C, not in the expected E minor, but in E major. A more detailed analysis reveals that each of the three sections in fact varies

Table 4

		Bars	Themes	Keys	Number of bars	Metre
I	Exposition				56	9/8
		1–14	A	E minor	14	
		15–43	B		29	
		44–56	C	G major	13	
II	Development				90	9/8
		57–69	A		13	
		70–103	B		34	
		104–22	C	E major	19	
		123–46	A + C		24	
III	Recapitulation				47	12/8
		147–60	A	E minor	14	
		161–8	B		8	
		169–78	A		10	
		179–93	C	E major	15	
	Coda			E major	34	12/8
		194–205	A		12	
		206–12	B		7	
		213–18	C		6	
		219–27	A		9	

Ex. 77a Second Sonata for Violin

Ex. 77b Second Sonata for Violin

poco a poco cresc.

poco a poco cresc.

Ex. 77c Second Sonata for Violin

Allegro non troppo

Violin

p dolce tranquillo

Piano

p tranquillo

sostenuto

the presentation of themes in harmonic, melodic and rhythmic particulars, to the extent that one could perfectly well regard the entire movement as a succession of variations, exploring the various potentialities of the three basic thematic elements.

Any such bald analytical plan as the above must necessarily omit any mention of the changing textures and atmospheres, or of the violin's powerful, soaring lines above the piano's shimmering arpeggios. The lyrical flow of the movement also admirably conceals extended canonic passages between violin and bass (bars 179 ff.) and between violin and the right hand of the piano (bars 206 ff.). In this context we may note that the codas of Fauré's most recent piano works, like the Eleventh and Twelfth Barcarolles, show a new predilection for canonic procedures following the example of the end of Act I of *Pénélope* – a tendency which was to be still more marked in the late chamber music, bringing a new richness to both texture and musical language.

The Andante, one of Fauré's most affecting movements, is more relaxed, and recalls to some degree the youthful candour of the First Violin Sonata, also in the key of A major. Philippe Fauré-Fremiet, in his book on his father,[12] was the first to point out that the principal theme of this movement is borrowed straight from the A major Andante molto moderato of the Symphony in D minor, op. 40, written more than thirty years earlier and long since withdrawn (see Ex. 78).

Ex. 78 Symphony, op. 40

The thematic material of the symphony, including this exquisite theme, was contained in the violin parts, and these were what Fauré retained.[13] The second theme of the Andante (*espressivo*, bar 24) employs wide intervals and, although lacking definition, it leads to a passage of intense lyricism. The return of the opening theme (bar 64, in C major?) is curiously dissonant – one could almost say spectral – effectively antidoting any excessive or tasteless pathos the violin might be tempted to bring to this chaste and inspired movement.

The violinist Hélène Jourdan-Morhange, who had the privilege of working on the sonata with Fauré at Evian in 1918, liked the Andante the best of the three movements and wrote of it:[14]

I'm thinking of that long continuous melody, suddenly interrupted by an unforeseeable chord (a chord dictated by the senses rather than by logic) and becoming fearfully abrupt: Nature savage and unreclaimed, but giving birth to sweetly scented blooms; a noble phrase of contained passion which has to be played with an intense manner of bowing, very hard to maintain. This passion has nothing to do with romanticism, but rather with an interior turmoil that leaves the surface flat and smooth.

The Finale, Allegro non troppo in E major, is in the form of a sonata rondo – with the first theme forming the refrain – which Fauré was fond of using for the last movements in his late chamber music. The refrain runs like spring water over the fine gravel of a simple piano accompaniment, recalling the finale of the First Sonata in its easy grace. Its remarkable length and its construction out of four-bar units have already been singled out as archetypal characteristics in my chapter on the composer's musical language (see Ex. 52).

After a secondary idea (bar 34, *meno forte espressivo*), the piano announces the second main theme (bar 53, *cantando*). This is unusual in lying outside the boundaries of tonality with its successions of chromatic intervals or of whole-tone scales. Every time, it avoids the leading note and fights shy of any conclusive cadence. This harmonic teasing, together with the elastic rhythm and the melodic grace of the idea, give it rather the feeling of an ancient dance like the famous minuet of 'Clair de lune.' The three themes are then repeated and combined in a shortened recapitulation, at the end of which there comes the surprising return of A, which opened the Sonata, in octaves on the piano (bar 192) followed by C. These two themes are intertwined with luminous appearances of the refrain, the whole so perfectly managed that the sweep of the movement is never for a moment arrested.

No doubt Fauré had intended, when writing the first and last movements together in the summer of 1916, to give the Sonata this circular
form. Some months later Debussy was writing the finale of his Violin
Sonata and he also introduced, in his case at the very start, a repeat of the
initial idea of the first movement. This can have been no more than a
coincidence, naturally. Fauré's model was more probably Schumann's
Violin Sonata no. 1 in A minor, in which the opening theme reappears at
the end of the last movement. In bringing back both the themes of his own
first movement, Fauré was simply taking Schumann's idea a step further.

The work is dedicated 'to Her Majesty Elisabeth Queen of the Belgians'.
The Queen was herself a violinist and a keen admirer of Fauré's music
which she had got to know in the days when she was still known as
Princesse de Bavière and when Fauré was often in Brussels, and through
their common friendship with Eugène Ysaÿe and Elisabeth Greffulhe.

As a result of these ties, Fauré was invited to the château de la Panne in
1917. But he excused himself on grounds of distance (he was at Saint-
Raphaël) from what he considered to be an imposition.[15] Instead he
arranged for Marguerite Hasselmans to take part in private performances
of the Sonata at la Panne and, later on, of the Piano Trio. As for Ysaÿe,
who so often played the First Sonata, either with Fauré or with his usual
partner Raoul Pugno, he never played the Second. In the words of Philippe
Fauré-Fremiet:[16] 'It is infinitely regrettable ... that he did not take to it
when it first appeared, in 1917. He was already old and, to begin with, he
did not understand it. Nevertheless it seemed made for him. He realised the
fact too late.' Whereas the early A major Sonata has been in the repertoire
for many years, players still find the E minor intimidating – that's to say,
when they are not totally ignorant of its existence!

During the spring of 1917, Fauré started work on a sonata for 'cello and
piano, a project that he had had in mind nearly forty years earlier, at the
time of the *Elégie*. The first two movements were completed at the end of
July 1917 when the composer was again peacefully installed at Saint-
Raphaël, as he had been two years earlier, and the finale was written
entirely in the space of three weeks, from 28 July to 18 August. 'I'm glad to
have two more sonatas to my credit', he wrote to his wife. 'Among modern
'cello sonatas, whether French or foreign, there's only one that counts and
that's by Saint-Saëns – one of his best works, too.'[17] Fauré's sonata was
given its first performance by André Hekking and Alfred Cortot at the
opening concert of the Société nationale's 1917 season on 10 November at
which the Second Violin Sonata was also heard for the first time. The First
'Cello Sonata has some similar features – the sombre tone of the first

movement, the intimate lyricism of the second, the grace of the finale – but is distinguished by a greater concision and less complex textures.

The opening Allegro (3/4 in D minor) is of a concentrated force unique in Fauré's output. The first theme is written for the solo instrument in a very unusual manner, with furious accents and down bows disturbed by violent cross-rhythms and syncopations, against a biting piano accompaniment – a far cry from the *legato, cantabile* stereotype so perfectly illustrated by the *Elégie*. We may be reminded of the orchestral prelude to Act III of *Pénélope*, depicting Ulysse's anger. The shaping of the themes is very similar, but there is an earlier model on which they both draw: the *Allegro deciso* which opened Fauré's D minor Symphony, from the *Andante* of which, as we have seen, he rescued material for the similar movement in his Second Violin Sonata, see Example 79.

Ex. 79 Symphony, op. 40

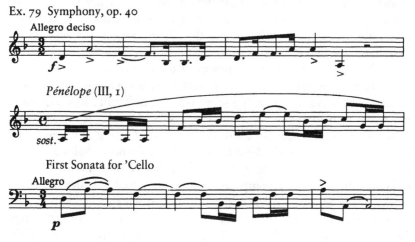

The second theme (bar 36), based on a simple rising arpeggio, brings with it a certain calm, but the frenetic energy takes it over both in the development section and in the varied recapitulation (bar 118). The coda contains some extraordinary 'swung' chords (bars 210–22) which prove, at least, that Fauré in his old age kept up with the latest musical innovations.

After this outbreak of disruptive violence, casting a glance, as it were, at the Fauvist painters, the Andante (3/4 in G minor) comes with the effect of a gentle nocturne. Fauré is inventive in varying a single theme (in ABA form) made up of two linked phrases. He seems content at first to let the music remain imprecise in mood, but then works it up into a passionate crescendo.

The final Allegro commodo (4/4 in D major) goes one better than the recent Violin Sonata in exploiting the *con grazia* atmosphere. Its charm is irresistible, with that mixture of movement and pretended languor, of idleness and energy so well described by Jankélévitch in his words on the Allegretto in Fauré:[18]

A kind of tranquil gaiety rules over such pieces, marked by the characteristic dactylic rhythm of the allegretto bergamasque: a quaver followed by two semi-quavers ... As François de Sales would have said, the Allegretto goes calmly on its way. This balance and equanimity, exemplified by the Allegretto, explain Fauré's aversion both to the sloppy embrace of the Ritardando and to the frenzies of the Accelerando.

But we should not lose sight of the fact that the charm of this music resides in the solidity of its construction. Its two themes possess that firmness, that accuracy of inflection which are the only guarantees of memorability. Amid the vigour and the Mediterranean *morbidezza* of these pages we find (bars 50–70) a strict canon in the long and splendid saltarello which serves as development of the first theme.

The summer of 1919 was the first that Fauré spent in the peaceful village of Annecy-le-Vieux in Savoy. While he was there he began a Piano Quintet and wrote to his habitual confidante, his wife Marie,[19] 'at the moment there are only sketches, so for the time being I'm not saying anything about it to anybody'. As with the First Quintet, the problems of balance in this genre (and the size of the piece) meant a long period of preparatory work and reflection. As always, composition was interrupted by Fauré's Conservatoire duties and then by 'flu and bronchitis, which attacked him during his winter stay in the Midi (Monte Carlo, Tamaris, then Nice) from December 1919 to April 1920. He spent the summer of 1920 with his children and his friends the Maillots, who had rented this time the château de Fésigny at Veyrier-du-lac, on the banks of Lake Annecy. In a letter to his wife of 23 August 1920[20] he said that the scherzo and slow movement of the quintet were now finished, as well as the first half of the first movement.

He finished the first movement in December 1920 and the finale in January and February 1921, while staying in Nice. The work is dedicated to his close friend and neighbour in the rue des Vignes in Paris, Paul Dukas.

In the Second Quintet Fauré adopted for the last time a four-movement form: Allegro, Scherzo, Adagio, Allegro. After using this layout for the First Violin Sonata and the two Piano Quartets, he had abandoned it, omitting a scherzo from the First Quintet.

There are some similarities of form and texture between the initial

Allegro moderato (3/4 in C minor) and in the p: iovement in the
First Quintet: an opening theme presented by successive entries on strings
over a regular piano figuration, a second, rhythmic theme (bar 35) in
strong contrast on strings alone, and finally a sudden interruption by a
secondary idea on the piano (bar 45). But the troubled litany of the First
Quintet is here transformed into a powerful melody which sweeps all
before it like a mighty river. The *élan* of the viola's phrase, spreading
gradually through all the strings over repeated notes on the piano, gives
this exposition a grandeur hard to find elsewhere in Fauré's work. The
same feeling of miraculously organised perfection is certainly evident in
the torrential opening of the Second Piano Quartet, but in that case there
was also a kind of feverishness and something more striven for than
achieved in the melodic writing.

The form of the development section is exceptionally clear, the three
ideas being both constantly varied and always recognisable – and three
ideas there are because the third of them, which was no more than
secondary in the exposition, here rises to a new importance. It is built on
the intervals of the octave and the major second, that characteristic pair
found in such later works as the *Fantaisie* for piano and the 'Pastorale' in
Masques et bergamasques. In the recapitulation (figure 10 of the score) the
themes are combined and superimposed in new ways without in any way
overloading the structure of this splendid movement.

The second movement (as we have seen, the first to be written) is an
Allegro vivo of an astonishingly bold variety. The instrumental texture, to
be sure, recalls that of the scherzos in the Piano Quartets and especially in
no. 2, with rapid piano figuration under a hail of pizzicato chords. But the
musical language is totally new. Right from the first bar the tonality is
obscured, whether because of the continuous scales on the piano in which
E flat major is undermined by whole tones and chromatic intervals, or
because of the interpolations of the strings whose patterns, filled out with
ascending groups of semiquavers, are also tonally indeterminate. A similarity suggests itself with the Fifth Impromptu, but here Fauré goes still
further into that atonal world which Schœnberg was shortly (1925) to
organise according to the principles of serialism (see Ex. 80).

Curiously, these daring feats of harmony alternate with an absolutely
tonal theme (in the dominant B flat major), a measured, relaxed idea on the
violin (bar 41), taken up later by the piano (bar 65, in G flat major) in a sort
of 1900's waltz, rather like the third of the Nine Préludes. But perhaps
Fauré's outstanding achievement is to blend these disparate elements into
a convincing whole.

The slow movement (Andante moderato, 4/4 in G major) stands as one

Ex. 80 Second Piano Quintet (II)

Ex. 81 Second Piano Quintet (III)

of the composer's finest achievements. It is based on three ideas. The first, a questioning, chromatic phrase on the strings, is answered by a tender, modulating theme for strings and piano (Ex. 81) in dialogue that recalls the more expansive passages in *Pénélope*.

The third idea, a kind of slow chorale, is heard on piano alone, then again on the strings, leading to a singularly beautiful polyphonic commentary (bars 35–50; see especially the dialogue between the first violin and the bass line of the piano). In the development section Fauré shows all his customary skill and even a perverse pleasure, it would seem, in twice delaying the true conclusion of the second idea by a false modulation (bars 62–5 and 66–9) (Ex. 81). Further on, at figure 9, this same idea gives rise to a section of chromatic harmony in which the interplay of major and minor raises the tension to a pitch that only the recapitulation can deal with.

In the last movement (Allegro molto, 3/4 in C minor) we find once more the playful spirit and dancing rhythms of the finale of the First Quintet; but, paradoxically, the work of the old master contains more life and joy. The piano leads the dance throughout, emphasising the rhythms and ordering the changes of tempo, and is responsible for imposing unity on the couplet–refrain structure which is once again Fauré's choice. Particularly to be relished is the logical development on the first violin, in the first couplet, of the opening notes of the refrain in cross rhythm against the other strings (seventeen bars after figure 4). As the tempo quickens, alternating octaves on the piano lead to a resounding conclusion in the manner of the G major *Fantaisie*.

The Second Quintet is a monumental work within this difficult genre in which masterpieces such as those by Schumann (1842), Brahms (1864), Dvořák (1887) and Franck (1879) are rare. Fauré's C minor Quintet is something of an isolated example in early twentieth-century music. Even if several composers of every persuasion tried their hand at the medium,[21] few of them succeeded in maintaining the momentum or permanently resolving the problems of balance between piano and strings.

With Fauré, the almost orchestral amplitude of sound is achieved by the use not of massed but of varied textures. The piano writing is noticeably different from that in the two Piano Quartets or even in the First Quintet: light and for the most part in the centre of the keyboard, with few bass octaves but much reliance on arpeggio figuration to support the melodic and contrapuntal outlines of the strings. The string quartet is sometimes treated as such – especially in the first and third movements – but is essentially mobile. Fauré uses various combinations of two or three string instruments with piano, and is especially fond of reinforcing melodic lines with groupings such as first violin, 'cello and piano, or first violin, viola and piano. The viola deserves a special mention since it begins three of the four movements (I, III and IV), and the relative pre-eminence of the first violin and viola forms a further link between this quintet and the second Piano Quartet.

The work was given its first public performance on 21 May 1921 under the aegis of the Société nationale de musique. The players were all young: Robert Lortat, piano; André Tourret and Victor Gentil, violins; Maurice Vieux, viola; and Gérard Hekking, 'cello. It was a notable occasion, as Philippe Fauré-Fremiet recalled:[22]

At the first performance in the old concert hall of the Conservatoire, given by *enthusiastic* players who were themselves transported by the work, the audience were bowled over from the start. They had been expecting a good piece, but not this. Fauré was known to be a fine composer, but no one thought him capable of writing such a masterpiece ... As the work continued, passionate feelings were roused, mixed perhaps with remorse at having underestimated the old man who had such a gift to offer. As the last chord sounded, the audience were on their feet. There were shouts, and hands pointing to the box in which Fauré was sitting (he had heard nothing of the whole occasion). He came to the front row all alone, nodding his head ... and looking so frail, thin and unsteady in his heavy winter coat. He was very pale.

At the beginning of 1921, as he was finishing the Quintet, Fauré received an unusual commission: he was asked by the state to write a work for the ceremony to be held on 5 May at the Invalides to mark the 100th anniversary of the death of Napoleon. For a composer whose preferences lay in private music-making, this was an embarrassing honour. He wrote to his wife from Nice on 22 February 1921:[23] 'I'm busy with *Napoléon* and I find the subject and the occasion thoroughly intimidating!'; but less than two weeks later the work was finished. According to Philippe Fauré-Fremiet,[24] this *Chant funéraire* for Napoleon was written on three staves, as the orchestral accompaniment to *Prométhée* had been. But Fauré in fact had the arrangement for military band made by Guillaume Balay, the conductor of the Garde républicaine. He wrote, again to his wife:[25] 'It's a very special kind of work which I'm not trained for, which would take me a very long time and which I should probably not do very well.' But when the job was over, the funeral march continued to haunt Fauré's imagination – too fine an idea to be hidden away in a military ceremony, even if it was for the Emperor of the French. So, remembering no doubt the success of the *Elégie* all those years ago, he transcribed it for 'cello. But this time the single movement did indeed turn into a sonata: 'I've started on a *second sonata* for 'cello and piano', he wrote on 19 March 1921.[26]

He continued work on it in the studio of his flat at 32, rue des Vignes, and then at Ax-les-Thermes in Ariège, but was held up for a full month by sudden illness: 'I'm suffering from bronchial, stomach, liver and kidney ailments', he wrote to his wife on 19 August 1921. 'I've had to stay in bed and diet, living on drugs and milk.' In his feeble condition the doctors refused to let him do anything strenuous. 'I'm recovering slowly', he went on, 'but I am finally recovering, that's the main thing. I'm reading *Balzac*, which is no bother. But my music? That's asleep!' He also had to give up the idea of joining his friends the Maillots at Annecy-le-Vieux, as he had intended, and in September returned straight to Paris. 'It's annoying, being old!' he wrote. 'But when I get back to work I'll notice it less.'[27]

In a letter of 10 November 1921 he asked his friend, the composer and 'cellist Charles Martin Loeffler,[28] for permission to dedicate to him his Second Sonata op. 117 which he had finished that same day.

The opening Allegro of this sonata (3/4 in G minor) has about it the same quality of inspired necessity that marks the Second Quintet, but also a drive and enthusiasm in the cross rhythms of the accompaniment that hark back to the unrestrained passion of *La Bonne chanson* and of 'J'ai presque peur' in particular. The two sixteen-bar themes on which the movement is based are longer than is usual with Fauré, and the development section opens (seventeen bars after figure 5) with a long passage in canon at a bar's distance (*marcato* in the bass). The recapitulation (twenty-five bars after Figure 7) reverses the instrumental layout (the themes are now on the 'cello), but it is considerably abridged and leads to a new canonic development in G major. Altogether the vigour and gusto of this movement are astonishing, coming from a man of seventy-five in such poor health.

The Andante (4/4 in C minor) is transcribed directly from the *Chant funéraire* (see Ex. 82).

Ex. 82 Second Sonata for 'Cello (II)

If there is less pathos than in the *Elégie*, there is no less nobility. The second theme, in A flat major, gives a good idea of how far Fauré had come since 1880. This beautiful, chorale-like theme centres insistently round the dominant E flat; but its intensity is increased when the piano repeats it and makes a sudden modulation to the distant key of B minor (Ex. 83) – the effect is to strike a note of tragedy rare in the works of a composer who is more usually concerned to express tenderness, contentment or seductiveness. At the height of the climax Fauré superimposes the two themes, introducing a brief recapitulation in the calm of C major.

Ex. 83 Second Sonata for 'Cello (II)

The finale (Allegro vivo, 2/4 in B flat, the relative major of the first movement) is one of the composer's most sparkling scherzos. It begins with three pages of unrestrained fantasy, beside which the flights of *La Bonne chanson* seem almost tame. Fauré almost has a twinkle in his eye as he tells us a story – of a theme that he will never quite get round to finishing. Each time he starts, a modulation intervenes and carries the music off towards new harmonic territory with the aid of strings of scales and whole-tone progressions. After four fruitless attempts, the exposition proper arrives in bar 56 but is swept away by the abrupt appearance of the second theme. The tonal audacity and instability of these pages is reminiscent of the scherzo in the Second Quintet, though without its strangeness. This is the ultimate movement in Fauré's bid to be the 'artful dodger' of music.

The second theme, marked *sans ralentir*, forms the trio. It is in four-part writing and recalls the fourth of the Nine Préludes in its delicate use of delayed harmonies, a feature it shares with Ravel's *Le Tombeau de Couperin* (1914–17). Both works stress the continuing influence of French harpsichord music of the seventeenth and eighteenth centuries.

After a repeat of the scherzando theme comes a development based on its first few notes, a sort of vigorous badinage so individual in character that one could easily mistake it for a third motif (figure 5). The ironic sprightliness of the 'cello makes one think of the 'Sérénade' from De-bussy's 'Cello Sonata, first performed in the spring of 1917. The repeat of this leads to the coda which ends the work in a burst of the highest spirits.

The work was performed for the first time in public on 13 May 1922 (the day after Fauré's seventy-sixth birthday) by Gérard Hekking and Alfred Cortot. Once again, there was surprise at the youthful freshness of Fauré's new composition. The day after the performance, Fauré's old friend Vincent d'Indy wrote to him:[29]

I want to tell you that I'm still under the spell of your beautiful 'Cello Sonata ... The Andante is a masterpiece of sensitivity and expression and I love the finale, so perky and delightful ... How lucky you are to stay young like that! Your old friend is thrilled by your success and especially by the beautiful pieces that are responsible for it. From the bottom of my heart I send my affection to you as my friend and my admiration to you as an artist.

This letter captures well the atmosphere of love and respect that was to surround Fauré in his last years. After a life of modesty and dissatisfaction, fame finally came to him. The enthusiasm and gratitude expressed after the performance of the Second Quintet touched him deeply because they came from the musicians and music-lovers of Paris, the only audience that mattered to him. But on the evening of that triumph, Fauré returned home to say:[30] 'Obviously an evening like that is a pleasure. The *annoying* thing is that after it there's no letting up; one must try and do better still.'

18   Fauré: 'modern style'

During the years following the First World War in which the superiority of rediscovered national characteristics was celebrated as a matter of course, Gabriel Fauré came almost to embody 'French music', with its traditional virtues of moderation, elegance and clarity.[1] The deaths of Massenet in 1912, of Debussy in 1918 and of Saint-Saëns in 1921 not far short of his ninetieth birthday, and d'Indy's relative isolation brought on by the political defeat of the Germanic aesthetic that he espoused, all these factors led to Fauré being singled out as the loved and respected patriarch of a 'French school' of composers going back two generations: those in their forties, made up chiefly of his own pupils and led by Ravel; and those in their twenties, called originally 'Les Nouveaux Jeunes' but rather brutally lumped together by history as the 'Groupe des Six' in 1920, who took Satie as their pope and Jean Cocteau as their prophet.

At the moment these young Turks made their noisy entrance into the Parisian musical arena, Fauré was making a discreet withdrawal from it, on the official front at least. When the administration of the Beaux-Arts renewed his tenure as Director of the Conservatoire 'for one year' (decree of 26 September 1919), it was on the understanding that the time had come for him to leave the institution which he had entered as professor a quarter of a century earlier. This decision, justified by his ever-increasing deafness which was now impossible to ignore, by his worsening health which now meant his spending large parts of the winter in the Midi, and finally by his having reached the age of seventy-four, was notified to him with no excess of tact. 'He suffered deeply but silently', wrote his son Philippe,[2] but he soon came to see the advantages of this return to freedom: 'I spend my time saying: one must make way for the young!' he wrote to his wife on 17 July 1919. 'Provided my brain doesn't immediately degenerate, I must bless the providence which relieves me of a very heavy weight. I've never told you of the daily problems, large and small, which poison that place! Dubois had enough of it after ten years, I'll have stuck it out for fourteen! It's enough.' Six days later he added: 'I can't emphasise enough how much *I'm savouring the idea of my deliverance!*'[3]

The bitterness of this forced departure was further exacerbated by the administrative difficulties that arose when it came to establishing what his pension would be. As he had entered public service on 1 June 1892 – and not in 1890, as he imagined – he could not in theory receive a pension until June 1922 according to the rules then in force which required a minimum of thirty years' service. 'I'm extremely concerned and very upset', he wrote to his wife on 2 March 1920.[4] 'The only thing that's certain is that I stop being Director on 30 September. They think I'm too old ... and they tell me so quite plainly.' It required pressure from the director of the Beaux-Arts, Paul Léon, and the intervention of the Conseil d'Etat before Fauré could, as a favour, obtain financial support from the end of 1920. As devaluation of the franc had substantially eroded civil service pensions, he was granted a supplement under the heading of a substantial 'indemnity for infirmity'![5] If the Republic showed itself relatively generous towards one of its most celebrated citizens, the solutions found by its administration were not outstanding in their delicacy ...

As some slight compensation for this wounding episode he was made Honorary Director of the Conservatoire, and then promoted to the rank of Grand Officer in the Légion d'honneur on 26 April 1920. When Fauré's money worries came to be known among his circle of American admirers, four of them (Miss Fanny Mason, the critic Edward Burlingame Hill, the painter John Singer Sargent and the composer Charles Martin Loeffler) got together more than once and, out of their affection for him, offered him financial help. By way of thanks, Fauré sent Sargent the manuscript of the Second Quintet and Loeffler those of the song 'Dans la forêt de septembre' and of the Second 'Cello Sonata, which is dedicated to him.[6]

During these post-war years, homages and manifestations of friendship multiplied. On the initiative of Fernand Maillot, a national Homage to Fauré was organised on 20 June 1922 in the large amphitheatre of the Sorbonne in the presence of the president of the Republic, Alexandre Millerand. A huge concert of his works brought together the élite of his current interpreters: the singers Claire Croiza, Jeanne Raunay and the young Charles Panzéra, the pianists Alfred Cortot and Robert Lortat, Pablo Casals and the Société des Concerts du Conservatoire Orchestra were conducted in turn by Henri Rabaud (the new director of the Conservatoire) in *Shylock*, by Vincent d'Indy in the *Cantique de Jean Racine*, by Philippe Gaubert in *Pelléas et Mélisande*, by André Messager in the Ballade with Alfred Cortot as soloist, and by Henri Büsser in *Caligula*.

This occasion, organised with the intention of raising money for the composer, was attended by a large and enthusiastic audience, and was an opportunity to measure the continuous curve of Fauré's creative evolution from 'Lydia' to the recent Second Quintet. This national Homage was widely reported by the press, and journalists flocked to the rue des Vignes to extract declarations and memories from a man who had made a principle of being discreet, and who was now at last being touched by fame at the age of seventy-seven.

Fauré, his black evening clothes crowned by his halo of white hair, sat quietly in the box of honour beside President Millerand amid a triumph of which he could hear no more than a few confused and discordant shreds. All this 'fla-fla' (as he called it) had no effect whatever on his ingrained modesty. He had reached the peak of his career and had become, whether he liked it or not, a high dignitary of the republican state, but for all that he remained to some extent a child of Ariège, the quiet, meditative youngest son of Toussaint-Honoré Fauré, director of the Ecole normale at Mont-gauzy, near Foix. 'One day when he had to go and see a minister', recalls Marguerite Long,[7] 'he asked Paul Léon to go with him. When the director of the Beaux-Arts looked surprised, Fauré said, "You know, it's always an occasion for me ... My father was only a schoolmaster."'

'You reproached me once', Fauré wrote to his wife on 24 March 1921,[8]

with trying to set myself up as somebody in your eyes. I was merely hoping that the growth of my reputation –which leaves me personally *absolutely* cold because it's *too late* – would console you and make up for the bitterness and pain my human failings have caused you ... Among so many faults grant me at least one virtue, that I never complain about anything. How many men would have given in to whining when, after what is known as a *good* career, they reached old age with serious infirmities (I've never heard *a single note of Pénélope* other than in my head!) and in a state of poverty, since I haven't in fact got a sou I can call my own!

Deep down, no doubt, Fauré responded more warmly to the homage his old pupils offered him in the form of a special number of *La Revue musicale*, founded by Henri Prunières in 1920. Having dedicated one number to Debussy in 1920, and with the prospect of another to mark Ravel's fiftieth birthday in 1925, Prunières decided in the meantime to honour Fauré with a number which appeared in October 1922, with contributions from Fauré himself ('Souvenirs' on the subject of the Nieder-meyer School), and from Emile Vuillermoz, Maurice Ravel, René Chalupt, Charles Koechlin, Florent Schmitt, Roger Ducasse, Alfred Cortot and Nadia Boulanger. The attached supplement of hitherto unpublished music included piano pieces by Louis Aubert, Georges Enesco, Charles Koechlin, Paul Ladmirault and Florent Schmitt, the delightful *Berceuse* for violin and piano by Ravel and a reduction of the *Poème symphonique* written for the occasion by Roger Ducasse.

When Prunières was first casting around for a theme on which the musical contributions might be based, he asked Ravel to find a theme in Fauré's output to serve as the basis for a set of variations; but when, in September 1921, Fauré himself was let into the secret, he suggested a theme made up of two leitmotifs from *Prométhée*: 'Pandora' and 'Punishment of Prometheus':

Ex. 84 Themes of *Prométhée*

In the end, this theme was tailored to fit the composer's name:

G A B R I E L F A U R É

g a b d b e e   f a g d e

This was a repeat of the musical homage which, twenty years earlier, had brought together Ladmirault, Raoul Bardac, Ravel and Roger-Ducasse in a collective work, a string quartet, the four movements of which were based on the name F A U R É = f a g d.[9]

On 13 December 1922, the Société musicale indépendante gave a Fauré concert in the hall of the Conservatoire including, among other works, *La Bonne chanson*, performed by Jeanne Raunay and Roger Ducasse, the Second Quintet, with Juliette Lampre and the Pascal Quartet, as well as the seven pieces published in *La Revue musicale*, with the pianists Madeleine Grovlez and Daniel Ericourt and with Hélène Jourdan-Morhange playing the violin part in Ravel's *Berceuse sur le nom de Fauré*.

The nine articles published in the review, together with a list of works, made a significant contribution to the corpus of information about the composer which, if we except the large number of newspaper articles, had hitherto been fairly slender. Hugues Imbert's brief study of 1887 had never been widely disseminated and was supplanted only in 1911 by the passage published by Octave Séré (alias Jean Poueigh) in his *Musiciens français d'aujourd'hui*, with a list of works and a bibliography. The first biography of Fauré appeared, thanks to Jacques Durand's initiative, in 1914: *Gabriel Fauré et son œuvre* by Louis Vuillemin, a composer and one of Fauré's old pupils. It is a sympathetic study but very succinct (it runs to no more than fifty-five pages).

Never perhaps had Fauré's music been so often played as in this euphoric period known as 'the silly Twenties'. In the spring of 1919, the society of meetings organised by Mme Brisson, l'Université des Annales, gave four Fauré galas, recalling the ones that had been put on just before the War. The composer himself accompanied two young singers, Madeleine Grey and Germaine Lubin, who had just returned to the rôle of Pénélope at the Opéra-Comique. The Société musicale indépendante repeated the Second Quintet (17 May 1923), while the Société nationale programmed the First Quintet, with Robert Lortat as pianist (4 January 1919), then the Second Violin Sonata with Georges Enesco and Marcel Ciampi (20 March 1920), and *La Bonne Chanson* with Suzanne Balguerie and Roger Ducasse (12 May 1923). The Société des concerts du Conservatoire included the *Pelléas et Mélisande* suite in their programmes almost every year, conducted first by Messager and then by Philippe Gaubert, who gave the first concert performance there of the suite *Masques et bergamasques* (16 November 1919). He also orchestrated the early *Romance* in B flat for violin of 1877, which was played in its new form at the Concerts Lamoureux under Chevillard on 11 January 1920.

Prométhée took on a new lease of life thanks to the reorchestration for large symphony orchestra which Fauré asked his pupil Roger Ducasse to prepare under his direction. This new version was begun in the spring of 1914, finished in September 1916 and given three performances in May 1917, organised by Jacques Rouché at the Opéra. The Comédie-Française lent its support and the work was directed by Camille Chevillard with the utmost care and with a number of excellent artists. The Conservatoire harp classes produced the necessary forces and Maxime Dethomas created original décors, relying largely on lighting effects.

On 3 May 1924, substantial extracts of *Prométhée* were given at the Théâtre des Champs-Elysées as part of the Olympic celebrations with a distinguished cast: Marcelle Demougeot and Charles Panzéra were among the soloists, with François Ruhlmann conducting and Jacques Copeau as the reciter.

The Requiem in particular received numerous performances, under the direction of a new generation of conductors such as Gustave Bret, the founder of the Société J. S. Bach,[10] Paul Paray and Philippe Gaubert, but the most impressive rendition was that given by Willem Mengelberg with the choir and orchestra of the Amsterdam Concertgebouw on 21 May 1924 at the Théâtre des Champs-Elysées. He had a wide reputation as a conductor of Bach, Brahms, Mahler and Schœnberg in particular, but he was now extending his repertory to cover contemporary French music. The idea of Fauré's Requiem was probably suggested to him by Jonkheer J. Loudon, the Dutch Minister in Paris who was married to Lydia Eustis, one of Fauré's favourite interpreters.[11] This concert made a great impression, but by now Fauré was confined to his room and could not attend. The work had previously been given in Amsterdam as part of a French festival, including in particular various works by Ravel given in the composer's presence on 1 October 1922. The soloist was Claire Croiza.[12]

Lastly, *Pénélope* emerged from the shadows into which it had been plunged by Astruc's bankruptcy at the Champs-Elysées in 1913 and then by the outbreak of war, at the very moment when the Isola brothers were preparing a revival at the Opéra-Comique with Claire Croiza. On the eve of the Armistice, Albert Carré came to Fauré asking him to allow *Pénélope* to open his new term as director of the Opéra-Comique. After Lucienne Bréval, Rose Féart and Claire Croiza, the title rôle was given to a young soprano who had won three first prizes at the Conservatoire in 1912, Germaine Lubin. The rôle of Ulysse was again taken by Charles Rousse-lière who had sung it at Monte Carlo in March 1913. This revival, with sets by Jusseaume and (mediocre) costumes by Marcel Multzer, took place on 20 January 1919; now at last, it seemed, justice was being done to a work which, despite the success surrounding the seventeen performances in 1913, was still little known.

From 1920 on, *Pénélope* had a companion in the repertory of the Opéra-Comique in the form of the lyric comedy, *Masques et bergamasques* (première in Paris, 4 March 1920),[13] which again united the names of Fauré and Fauchois. This *divertissement* was danced and sung in a ravishing set by Jusseaume, inspired by Lancret, and was much more to the taste of the regular theatre-going public than the admirable but rather austere *Pénélope*. Carré by now had left the Opéra-Comique and Fauré expended an inordinate amount of energy trying to persuade his successors, the Isola brothers, to keep his opera in the repertory. It was firmly pointed out to him that the work needed two interpreters of considerable stature, not to be found in a troupe who specialised in playing *Manon*, or *Werther*, or Henri Rabaud's light, oriental opéra-comique *Mârouf*.

Germaine Lubin, who had been borrowed from the Opéra, had had to return there and her replacement, Madeleine Mathieu, was possessed of no particular genius. Secret negotiations were set up in 1921 through Louis Laloy which gave hope that *Pénélope* would appear at the Opéra, where Jacques Rouché was the outstanding director, but this did not bear fruit until ... 1943.[14]

Gustave Bret was at one of these mediocre performances in the spring of

1922, sung by Madeleine Mathieu and a new Ulysse, Charles Fontaine, and recalls sitting beside Fauré in one of the stage boxes when he heard the composer whisper in his ear, 'Isn't it boring!'[15] A year later, on 16 April 1923, Lucienne Bréval and Lucien Muratore revived their original rôles for a few performances to mark the tenth anniversary of a work for which they had a particular affection. These seem to have been nostalgic occasions, but perhaps little more.

Fauré at least had the satisfaction of seeing his opera given for the first time in various other opera houses: in Strasbourg (27 February 1923), in Nice (January 1924) and in Anvers (15 March 1924, in a Flemish translation by M. Sabbe). In November 1920 he had visited Brussels to see Claire Croiza in the rôle she had created at the Théâtre de la Monnaie in December 1913; unfortunately, his health did not allow him to attend the single performance of the work given in front of the famous wall of the Roman theatre in Orange on 30 July 1923, before eleven thousand spectators. This was a redoubtable test for Fauré's opera, but in the event it proved to have nothing to fear from such a majestic setting.[16] But most important of all, the performances at the Opéra-Comique in the summer of 1923 had brought forward a new interpreter for the part of Pénélope: Suzanne Balguerie, whose vibrant lyricism and grand manner won the composer over immediately. She was known for her incomparable interpretations in the rôle of Ariane in Dukas' *Ariane et Barbe-Bleue*, of Isolde and of Brünnhilde, and by the time she came to sing Pénélope for the first time she was thirty-five years old. She was to give many more performances of the part up until 1943.

It was also a source of great satisfaction for Fauré to see his music being better understood by the younger generation: among them the violinists Jacques Thibaud, Robert Krettly and Georges Enesco; the 'cellists Pierre Fournier and Maurice Maréchal, the pianists Robert Casadesus, Vlado Perlemuter and Robert Lortat; and the Krettly, Pascal and Pro Arte quartets. It is significant that Fauré entrusted the first performances of his two last song cycles to young singers, to Madeleine Grey for *Mirages* and to Charles Panzéra for *L'Horizon chimérique*; and to ex-prizewinners from the Conservatoire for his two last chamber works, the Piano Trio and the String Quartet.

Although he was now seriously deaf and suffering from sclerosis and had, since the war, become much thinner, he continued to be an attractive figure to both young and old. His drooping moustache, rather yellow due to his heavy smoking, his swarthy colouring under the luxuriant halo of white hair and the far-away expression in his eyes all give him the appearance of a patriarch, but one who was witty and debonair. In summer he was fond of spending his time sitting outside a café, smoking and regaling some old acquaintance with long, entertaining stories about his youth.[17]

He had abandoned the funereal, nineteenth-century frock coat for the lounge suit, shirt sleeves and hard collar which were the fashion in the 1920s. Although he wore a felt hat for preference, on ceremonial occasions he remained faithful to the turn-of-the-century bowler which sat somewhat precariously on his abundant head of hair.

The attraction he exercised until the very end of his life led to his receiving numerous visits, which he accepted with unfailing good nature. 'Whether you were a friend or an inquisitive outsider', wrote Philippe Fauré-Fremiet[18]

he was always in. If he was working, he would put down his pen in front of him, bend his head towards you and listen carefully to catch sentences which often had to be repeated two or three times. Never was a famous old man easier of access. Sometimes we used to urge him to defend himself and not to tire himself unnecessarily. But there was, in determined isolation, something smacking of pride which he was not happy with. And even if he was content with the world inside himself, he had a need still to feel the movement in his direction of a world he was not part of. 'If I close my door', he used to say, 'I shall be all alone.' He had a horror of being alone. He did not seek to surround himself with a band of thurifers, nor even to spend his time exclusively among musicians whom he could dominate by reason of age. He seemed to avoid professionals and performers, especially those driven by ambition, since ambition had never been one of his qualities. More and more, he favoured sincerity, unselfishness and kindness. He chose his friends for their characters and basked happily in their affection.

Among these friends were the banker Fernand Maillot and his wife Louise. Both of them were devoted music-lovers and Fauré regularly attended musical occasions in their large apartment at 4, rue de Talleyrand on the Esplanade des Invalides. It was in this intimate setting that Fauré from here on gave preliminary performances of his chamber music for a few close friends, finding it easier to hear a few, imperfect snatches of his music than he was able to in the concert hall.

The startling increase in performances of Fauré's works during the post-war years goes beyond the usual 'end of career' phenomenon one finds with a composer who has become a household name. By one of those curious reversals so common in the history of artistic taste, his music, from being in some people's opinion 'dépassée' at the time of *Le Sacre du printemps*, came suddenly through its innate qualities to be regarded as up-to-date.

FAURÉ – A 'NOUVEAU JEUNE'?

Fauré's modernity, both discreet and original as it was, had long condemned him in the eyes of Establishment composers like Ambroise Thomas. His ex-pupils, the enthusiasts of the still flourishing SMI, remained, as we have seen, deeply attached to him, but his work was also approved of by the 'nouveaux jeunes': his clear, amiable style of writing provided a model, a reference point for that uproarious band of iconoclasts who, under Jean Cocteau's guidance, were pouring contempt on the fogs of the *fin-de-siècle*.

In *Le Coq et L'Arlequin*, published in March 1918, and then in his articles for *Paris-Midi* in 1919 under the heading 'Carte Blanche', Cocteau launched a formal attack on what was then called 'musical impressionism': Debussy, who died on 25 March 1918, was openly criticised for writing music that was too recherché, too subtle. 'Enough of clouds, of waves, of aquariums, of water-nymphs, of nocturnal perfumes', exclaimed the young poet, 'we need an earthbound music, AN EVERYDAY MUSIC.' In this new aesthetic climate, Debussy's infinitely refined art was suspect, almost as much as Wagner's was, because he was one of those who had succumbed to foreign influences: 'Debussy went astray because, from the German frying pan, he fell into the Russian fire ... Bayreuth's thick fog shot through with lightning becomes a light, snowy Impressionist mist touched with sunlight. Satie speaks with the accent of Ingres; Debussy transposes Claude Monet into Russian'; and elsewhere Cocteau wrote: 'Russian French music or German French music cannot help being a bastard, even if it is inspired by a Mussorgsky, a Stravinsky, a Wagner or a Schœnberg. I want a French French music.'

Even Ravel, who was only forty in 1915, received a blow in passing: 'Nobody's scandalised by *La Mer* any more. It's attended by young girls who are now going into Durand's and buying Ravel's *Pavane pour une Infante défunte* instead of *La Prière d'une vierge*.'[19]

Fauré's music found a place easily enough in this new aesthetic, joining Satie and Chabrier among the corpus of 'French French music' which had stood out against Wagner and the Russians and the siren voices of Impressionism. On 11 May 1919, Félix Delgrange, one of the most active supporters of the 'nouveaux jeunes', put Fauré's Ballade beside *Parade* and *La Mer* on the programme of the concert he was conducting at the Salle Gaveau: Cocteau, in his review in *Paris-Midi*, slated Debussy's piece, but noted sympathetically that 'the audience which applauded that excellent composer Gabriel Fauré put up with the much reviled *Parade* without protest'.[20]

This general attitude of goodwill is a fairly clear reflection of the loving esteem in which the young members of the Groupe des Six held the work of their venerable predecessor, but it encompassed some important differences of nuance between them which should be brought out. Cocteau's opinions and musical ideas were, we know, closely based on those of the most literary-minded of the group, Georges Auric. Auric published a very sympathetic article in *La Revue musicale* on Fauré's death, in the number of 1 December 1924:

Other composers, naturally, whom we must admire, searched elsewhere for a vein that was more violent, or surprising or learned. Fauré's achievement was to invent musical forms which attracted our hearts and senses without debasing them. He offered a homage to Beauty in which there was not only faith, but a discreet yet irresistible passion ... I hope one day to expound my hopes for what the French will make of Stravinsky's compelling example, once they have assimilated it. But for the moment my grief, which must be shared by every heart that finds a place for a love of true art, brings me back to Fauré. I have no doubts but that, at the very time we think ourselves furthest from him, we shall turn again to this source of delight and wisdom ... The delicate precision of his architecture, the concision (without dryness) of his ideas will long guide us in our moments of anxiety. So will continue, for the youngest of us, the priceless lesson of a master who in his lifetime counted Ravel and Koechlin among his pupils.

At that time the young Poulenc was far from sharing this opinion, thanks to the mark left by childhood memories. In an unpublished letter to the poet Gabriel Faure (without the accent), he wrote:[21]

Alas, I have two nightmares, Fauré and the Capet Quartet. When my sister was studying with Raunay and Croiza and sang Schumann, Schubert and Debussy, I used to edge up to the piano which my mother played so marvellously and close my eyes with happiness – when it came to Fauré's turn, I would say 'Not Fauré.'

I hated Fauré until I was thirty and then I realised that he was a *very great composer*. So I made an effort with myself and began to admire him. It's an attitude I've maintained and built on, but physically it is for me an unbearable kind of music, what can I do about it?

I quoted earlier (pp. 240–1) on the passage from *La Bonne chanson* which Poulenc cites in his letter as an example of an 'unbearable' modulation. But Léon Vallas, in a brief article on 'Fauré and Poulenc', shows that Poulenc had second thoughts on the subject. In a review in 1928 of the recording of the A major sonata by Cortot and Thibaud, Poulenc wrote: 'Whether it's due to the perfection of the interpretation, the fact is that I have totally revised my opinion of this work. On reflection, I cannot think of a better violin sonata written in the last fifty years.'[22]

Poulenc's physical reaction is rather strange because, of all the members of Les Six, he is the nearest to Fauré: in the limpid clarity and singing quality of his writing, in his charm, in his penchant for sudden modulations, and in the length of his melodic lines, despite obvious differences of style and personality.

If the work of Louis Durey seems to look back to 'Debussysme', Germaine Tailleferre's harmonic finesse is not far from Fauré's. But most of all one turns to the opinion of Arthur Honegger who met Fauré more regularly than any of them. The young Zürich musician came to Fauré's notice during the war when, like Ravel and Milhaud before him, he came to work with André Gédalge at the Conservatoire. On Fauré's recommendation, Honegger joined other young musicians, such as the violinist Robert Krettly and the pianist Vlado Perlemuter, as recipients of a kind of study grant instituted by Fauré's friends the Maillots. The handsome young composer was invited to musical evenings in the rue de Talleyrand and did not fail to make an impact on Louise Maillot, the daughter of the house. In August 1923 Honegger was invited to Annecy-le-Vieux in Savoy, where the Maillots were spending the summer with Mme Hasselmans and Fauré. The enterprising M. Maillot had organised a performance in the village church of large extracts from Fauré's Requiem, and from *Le Roi David* which the composer was to conduct on 25 August. 'That evening there was a cold supper in the house for *fifty-eight people*(!)', wrote Fauré,[23] 'the garden illuminated, fireworks and dancing till two o'clock in the morning. But I was in bed by half past ten and remained undisturbed by all the racket down below: one of the advantages of being deaf!'

A charming photograph, taken in the garden, preserves for us this memorable meeting of two generations of composers (see p. 477). The success of the concert led to it being repeated a few months later at the Salle Gaveau in Paris, where Honegger's work was unknown, having been premièred in Switzerland. The names of Fauré and Honegger appeared together again the following year, on 3 May 1924, during the Eighth Olympic celebrations at the Champs-Elysées, with extracts from *Prométhée* and *Le Roi David*.

It is not really possible to say whether Honegger returned Fauré's affectionate concern. The score of *Le Roi David* that changed hands on this occasion bears an entirely neutral dedication: 'To Maître Gabriel Fauré, with my respectful admiration'. Honegger's 'conversion', like Poulenc's, was to be somewhat belated. In an article in 1943 he wrote:

I know that in many countries where music is loved and cultivated, Fauré's music is still not understood. Since I come from one of these countries, I am able to see dispassionately what the reasons are for this indifference; I must admit that I myself took a rather long time to penetrate the mystery and subtlety of his language. Like many other people, I regarded his admirable discretion as a lack of strength and the elegant ease of some of his melodic lines as smacking of facility, while his harmonic ambiguity assorted ill with that Beethovenian intransigence that formed the basis of my musical attitudes. Since then I have developed and all the magic virtues of this music have shone out for me.

They are, to a greater extent than in any other music, inexplicable through literary connections. I know of no other music which is more purely and uniquely music except, perhaps, that of Mozart or Schubert.

For Darius Milhaud, on the other hand, the clarity of Fauré's style had long proved a major attraction. In 1922 he wrote a 'Homage to Fauré'[24] which sounded almost like a manifesto:

He was unmoved by strident Wagnerian clamouring, the 'noble sentiments' of 'père Franck', the complete rethinking of technique brought about by Debussy, the compilation of detail in the music of the Impressionists, the unnecessary theories and discussions about polytonality and atonality. Fauré had only to let his heart sing, to give us the tenderest, most sincere music ever written. Nothing in his considerable output 'dates'. The discretion of the means he employs and the sense of balance in his lyricism ensure that his voice will never grow old.

Even if Milhaud was tolerably critical of Ravel, he placed Fauré beside Rameau, Berlioz, Chabrier, Gounod, Debussy and Satie in the pantheon of the 'true French tradition', which he defended all through his life in articles and lectures. It is no surprise to find, among the scores preserved in Fauré's library, La Brebis égarée, Milhaud's first opera, to a text by Francis Jammes, produced at the Opéra-Comique in 1923.

Fauré, meanwhile, had continued to follow fairly closely the development of several of his old pupils. In letters of 1923 and 1924[25] he writes to Roger Ducasse to say how much he has enjoyed two of his recent works, Epithalame and Madrigal, and an interview in 1922[26] gave him the opportunity to declare that 'Florent Schmitt's Psaume is a masterpiece.' Ravel, especially, remained much in his thoughts, and regularly sent Fauré copies of his latest works with affectionate dedications: we know that Fauré particularly liked Jeux d'eau, Daphnis et Chloé and the Piano Trio. He wrote to Ravel in October 1922[27] to thank him for his double participation in the Fauré number of La Revue musicale:

I am deeply touched by the delightful token of friendship you have offered, both in words and music, and I thank you from the bottom of my heart. I have followed the stages of your career since those days on the Faubourg Poissonière [the site of the Conservatoire until 1911] and you cannot imagine how happy I am to see the solid position you have acquired for yourself, and with such brilliance and speed. For your old teacher it is a cause of both joy and pride.

The reference to 'speed' touches on the astonishment, even the silent envy, Fauré felt at the noisy publicity surrounding some composers who were still little more than apprentices, and at the premature arrival of certain reputations; he himself, after all, had had to wait in effect for the première of *Prométhée*, when he was fifty-five, to gain a degree of notoriety. In the last letter he wrote to his wife he speaks bitterly of 'these hard times, but still shot through with *arrivisme*' which, in his view, ran clean against all notions of professional morality and were positively dangerous in instituting the cult of false values.

In this context the probity and immense technical command shown by Paul Dukas led Fauré to respect him profoundly and soon to find in him a close friend. He was overwhelmed with admiration for *Ariane et Barbe-Bleue* and it is significant that the last article Fauré wrote for *Le Figaro*[28] was devoted to a revival of Dukas' opera in 1921, the same year in which he dedicated his Second Quintet to him. On the purely musical front, Fauré deplored the fact that his successors were tending to succumb to the search for sonority *per se*, a dangerous search in his view since it could cover up technical inadequacies. When his son Emmanuel[29] had critical things to say about Ravel's *Rhapsodie espagnole* at its first performance, Fauré wrote back to him from London on 17 March 1908:

Your description of Ravel is to the point: that's the result of current, so-called 'musical', procedures. But I think you're unduly hard on Franck's *Variations*. The inspiration is lofty and really expressive, and it's one of his works I like the best ... It's indisputable that Ravel and his friends are unfailingly prodigal in their treatment of form, and the only result of this prodigality is to produce 'effects'!

As for the development of the more advanced musical languages, we may well imagine that, as a lover of style and beauty, he found them disturbing. He certainly heard *Le Sacre du printemps* at the famous 1913 performances at the Théâtre des Champs-Elysées, because it was played alternately with *Pénélope*, and Stravinsky later remembered meeting him there.[30] Even if Fauré's deafness can have allowed him only a very confused impression of the work, at least he was sufficiently intrigued by this landmark in twentieth-century music to borrow the score.[31] But I have not, unfortunately, found a reference to it in any of Fauré's correspondence that I have read so far.

Ten years later, his pupil Emile Vuillermoz had the unusual idea of showing him the score of Schœnberg's *Pierrot Lunaire*, which had recently had its first Paris performance at the concerts Jean Wiéner, conducted by Darius Milhaud. There was considerable uproar raised by these performances and long polemics in the press; Vuillermoz took Schœnberg's side, with open support from Ravel, Roussel and Roland Manuel, against bitter opposition (with anti-Semitic overtones) from the nationalist old guard, in the persons of Louis Vuillemin and Vincent d'Indy.[32]

Fauré humbly expressed his incomprehension in an outspoken letter to Vuillermoz: 'After reading through your *Pierrot Lunaire*, I must tell you in all honesty, I spent a miserable night!' Then, not wanting his old pupil to feel too disappointed, he justified himself by admitting his hearing was not what it was, before declaring, 'what I find so bewildering in the music of today – I'm not speaking of Les Six! – is the impression of ugliness I get from it'.[33]

This was an entirely private judgment. He would have felt it out of place to state such an opinion in public, and still more so to use it as any sort of basis for condemning his younger colleagues. One thinks of what Saint-Saëns said about *Le Jardin clos* when his old pupil sent him a copy:[34] 'Christ said, "It is not light that is lacking, it is your eye that is at fault." In all humility, I imagine the same applies in the present case.' Philippe Fauré-Fremiet, who saw much of his father during his final years, wrote:[35]

All his life he had attacked and been attacked. Should he attack the young because of what seemed to him 'excesses'? Was he perhaps lacking in perspicacity and foresight? These qualities had been so sorely lacking in his own critics! He held his peace; he did not want to lend his name to judgments, still less to condemnations, and he had work to do ... Of certain very modern works he used to say simply: 'I find that ugly.' The things he did unambiguously condemn were lack of passion, imaginative poverty and a taste for artifice ... He considered Honegger the only one of the young composers who had a truly *great* composing temperament.

The interior isolation Fauré felt as he grew older is in singular contrast with the honours and the expressions of admiration and sympathy which surrounded him during his final years. As someone who had been born under Louis Philippe, brought up in the starchy, moral atmosphere of the Second Empire and had seen Berlioz sitting on a jury at the Ecole Niedermeyer, he felt out of place in this post-war world, a world of reinforced concrete and furious new movements such as surrealism, bruitism, suprematism, atonalism, Dadaism, undermining the criteria of ordinary aesthetic judgment and apparently bent on relegating the very idea of the Beautiful to the ranks of obsolescence.

He wrote to the Beauniers in a letter of 1922,[36] '*Ubu Roi* is the sort of thing that makes my head spin! I'm of another era!' Fauré faced up to this feeling of disarray and unhesitatingly conquered it in his own world as a composer, where he had never doubted his own identity. His final works, which we shall now consider, belong to the three areas which had been his favourites for half a century: piano music, song and chamber music.

He composed his last two piano works, the Thirteenth Barcarolle and the Thirteenth Nocturne, at Nice in February and December 1921. It is worth noting that Fauré thus pursued these two great cycles in parallel – the pieces in each being not so much different in style as in temper and expression. A phrase from van Lerberghe's *La Chanson d'Eve* – 'How simple and clear thou art, living water' ('Que tu es simple et claire, eau vivante') – could serve as an epigraph to the final Barcarolle. This, like the song 'Eau vivante', is in C major, a key rare with Fauré who, as we know, preferred the shadows of the flat keys, like Chopin before him.

The naively singing theme in 6/8, which starts off as a descending line and then seems to lose itself in a modulation to G (bars 5–6), recalls the Twelfth Barcarolle of 1915 which immediately precedes it; it copies its development pattern too, going from extreme simplicity to extreme complexity through variations in harmony and rhythm and using the chromatic figurations and descents by whole tones (bars 31–40) characteristic of his late piano style. One is reminded particularly of the Ninth Barcarolle whose feeling of melancholy and whose mixture of repose and movement it recaptures, like a calm lagoon suddenly disturbed by an undertow of passion.

But the Thirteenth Nocturne is an infinitely greater work and, with the Sixth, incontestably the most moving and inspired of the series. He began it in Paris in the autumn of 1921, a year of fine works like the Second 'Cello Sonata and *L'Horizon chimérique*, and finished it in the Midi. 'You brought me good luck', he wrote to his wife on 2 January 1922,[37] 'when you said you embraced my manuscript paper; on the evening of the 31st I finished the Thirteenth Nocturne.'

The piece is in B minor, a key of seriousness in mature works of Liszt and Chopin like the Sonata and the Third Sonata respectively, and one Fauré chose for the pleading of the dead souls in the 'Offertory' of his Requiem. Immediately we find ourselves in the pure, almost rarefied atmosphere of the Andante of the Second Quintet, with the same tone of noble, gentle supplication, the imposing gravity and the rich, expressive four-part writing. The chromatic counterpoint and the dissonances caused by harmonic suspensions are of a daring that compares with the most astonishing of Bach's chorale preludes (see Ex. 85).

Ex. 85 Nocturne no. 13, first theme

Ex. 86 Nocturne no. 13, second theme

Ex. 87 Nocturne no. 13, rhythmic motif

The second theme, more vigorous and *cantabile* (bar 22) recalls the first in its outline of a descending third followed by four rising notes (Ex. 86), while the dotted motive with which it concludes is to be heard throughout the piece (Ex. 87).

A varied repeat of the opening counterpoint (bar 40) presents the tenor voice in chromatic diminution, while the *marcato* rhythmic motif I have just mentioned (bar 47) leads directly to the central Allegro, which is prepared by a brusque change from B minor to B major. A 'new' theme unfolds over a splendid series of arpeggios, recalling the passionate lyricism of *La Bonne chanson* or the Allegro section of the Sixth Nocturne; although on closer inspection it turns out to be derived from the opening idea. Soon the ever-insistent rhythmic motif returns clearly in the bass, in notional canon at the fifth with the right hand, the kind of formula that links this Nocturne with the chamber works of the same period. After an unusually impassioned build-up the initial notes of the opening idea return, alternating with the rhythmic motif and accompanied by brilliant scales. As in the Sixth Nocturne, two sweeping arcs in parallel sixths restore the peaceful, meditative atmosphere of the first section. In the coda the rhythmic motive is heard like a nostalgic voice amid the nocturnal calm – and with this beautiful passage Fauré's large, if not always consistent, piano output comes to an end.

Lyrical fervour and serenely soothed regret also mark the brief song cycle that Fauré wrote during the fertile autumn of 1921, between the Second 'Cello Sonata, finished on 10 November, and the Thirteenth Nocturne written in December.

This time Fauré chose poems by a young writer who died at the front in November 1914, Jean de la Ville de Mirmont; the volume of verses that he had left on his table had been written in 1912–13 and was published by Grasset in 1920. Fauré chose four poems from it, as well as the beautiful title, *L'Horizon chimérique*. As the composer of the seascape in the second Act of *Pénélope*, of 'La Chanson du pêcheur', 'Les Berceaux', 'Au Cimetière', 'La Fleur qui va sur l'eau', not to mention the Barcarolles, he was no doubt attracted by the seascape of this twenty-four-year-old poet from Bordeaux, and by his veiled romanticism and the strength of his inspiration.

No doubt he also appreciated the poet's utterly classical language, his firmly outlined forms and his evocative images: not one comma did he change.[38] The simple, immediate character of these poems inspired him to write four songs that are without digressions or ambiguities or needless complications. The flow of the poetry follows closely the inflections of heightened speech, and the melodic curves and the underlying harmonies come together so naturally that these thirteen pages of music seem as if born of a single creative instant, as if somewhere they were already in existence and Fauré had only to summon them complete from the innermost recesses of his creative imagination. There are no common motivic elements between the four songs; their unity springs simply from the words and the musical style. The two outer songs, 'La Mer est infinie' and 'Vaisseaux nous vous aurons aimés', are in D major, enclosing two songs in flat keys, 'Je me suis embarqué' in D flat major and 'Diane Séléné' in E flat major. Of these, it is notable that nos 1, 3 and 4 are through-composed and only 'Je me suis embarqué' adopts Fauré's favourite A B A form. In this second song, the evocation of the 'vessel that dances/And rolls from side to side and pitches and rights itself' ('vaisseau qui danse/Et roule bord sur bord et tangue et se balance') brings with it a somewhat heavy, bass motif with accents on the first and third beats of each bar. The manuscript reveals that the composer was a little undecided about this; the first

Ex. 88 *L'Horizon chimérique* (II) (MS)

version introduced an idea (A) recalling Ulysse's royal theme from *Péné-lope*, alternating regularly with the rhythm (B) (Ex. 88) which in the final version was to be heard throughout. Once again, images of reality proved troublesome for Fauré, enamoured as he was of dreams and pure emotions, and one might cite as proof of this the end of the song, 'Oh my pain, my pain, where have I left you?' ('O ma peine, ma peine, où vous ai-je laissée?'), where Fauré, unusually for him, achieves a tone of pathos.

In 'La Mer est infinie', on the other hand, the youthful sweep of the vocal line, the passionate, forceful declamation and the ever-changing colours in the broken chords of the accompaniment, all give this opening song a brightness and strength unique in the composer's output. This sunny seascape, echoing to the cries of seagulls and dashed with spray, contrasts with the moonlit calm of 'Diane Séléné', one of Fauré's most perfect evocations of night and the last of his peaceful dream-pictures which, with their slowly pulsing chords and intimate atmosphere, form a group of their own within his songs.

The fourth song is a powerful one, built over an accompaniment pattern that does not change throughout the piece. The tension in the vocal line is extreme and is resolved only with the great final climax, where the aging composer joins the young poet in the cry:

> Mais votre appel, au fond des soirs, me désespère,
> Car j'ai de grands départs inassouvis en moi.

> (But your summons, in the depth of the evening, calls me to despair,
> For I have in me a hunger for great journeys yet unsatisfied.)

L'Horizon chimérique is dedicated to the young baritone Charles Pan-zéra whose qualities of timbre and expression and whose clear and intelligent diction Fauré had noted during his years at the Conservatoire. He sent him the manuscript as proof of his satisfaction, with the dedication 'A souvenir of the happy evening of 13 May 1922 (first performance at the Société nationale)'.[39] At the same concert Gérard Hekking and Alfred Cortot gave the first performance of the Second 'Cello Sonata.

Panzéra sang the cycle again the following 10 June during the act of national homage at the Sorbonne, and at the end of 1924 recorded two of the songs (nos 2 and 3) for the Gramophone company. He sang the cycle all through his career and recorded it complete three times, on every occasion with his wife Madeleine Panzéra-Baillot at the piano. They were both dedicated performers of French songs and recorded a large number of songs by Duparc and Fauré on seventy-eights, including the first complete recording of *La Bonne chanson* in 1936.[40]

Roland Barthes, who was Panzéra's pupil for a time, has written several times of the importance he attached to his teacher's art:[41]

If I want to know what the French language is, it is to Panzéra's art that I turn: his enunciation of the language and his economy of means in this respect are the result of profound study. Whereas consonants are generally detached and emphasised in order, so we are told, to make the meaning clearer, Panzéra often skates over them, acknowledging the wear and tear this language has undergone in its many years of life and usage, making the consonant the launching pad for the admirable vowel and so manifesting the truth of the language which is superior to the truth of what it expresses ... Panzéra displayed this vocal radiance and power in everything he sang: in the action of the most subtle and delicate nuances, Panzéra always sings with his whole voice, his whole body, his whole heart. He is one of the rare ones who have offered us, without hysteria, and in an exact dosage, the extra physical dimension which organises, surpasses and overturns the whole cultural part of the art of music.

Fauré had also noted among the singing pupils at the Conservatoire the qualities, both vocal and physical, of a soprano called Madeleine Grey, introduced to him one day by her professor A. L. Hettich. Knowing her own abilities and being anxious to make a name for herself as soon as possible, Madeleine Grey showed from the start an unusual predilection for the music of her own time: on 12 June 1919 she gave a recital in Paris, including songs by a good composer now forgotten, Georges Hüe, whom she had asked to accompany her. Contact with living composers was important for her since she wanted to use her voice in the service of music – and not the other way round, as so often happens! One of the great regrets of her life was not to have been able to hear or meet Debussy, whom she glimpsed during the War at the end of a concert in which Ninon Vallin had taken part.

As far as Fauré was concerned, she quickly realised that his support was the key that would unlock the door to her career. On 30 May 1919 she took part in the fourth of the Fauré Galas organised under the auspices of the Université des Annales, singing *La Chanson d'Eve*, to the great satisfaction of the composer, who accompanied her. A month later she went to see Fauré at his home in the rue des Vignes and asked him to write for her a work with orchestra with which she could appear at the major Paris concerts. In an unpublished letter,[42] Fauré replied to her from Annecy-le-Vieux on 10 August 1919:

Here I too am looking out on a wide and splendid panorama, and as I'm 500 metres above the level of the Vicomté I'm enjoying the pure, revivifying air and working. I'm even working at something which you, in fact, will sing particularly well. Unfortunately it's not with orchestra. But on that score I've had an idea that you can put before Chevillard the Terrible – but not so terrible when he finds himself faced with a talented artist and with a piece of music he likes. I'm thinking of Gaia's aria from *Prométhée*, which Mlle Lapeyrette has sung at the Opéra under Chevillard's direction.[43] Write to him about it, mentioning that I suggested it ... My dear friend, my dear, enthusiastic artist, *You will get there*, don't have any doubts about that. But, even so, look around you and see how, for everyone, there has to be a large measure of *suffering* and *patience*! Let me have your news, with fond kisses from your old friend

Gabriel Fauré

I forbid you to be *depressed*!

Ten days after this letter Fauré finished the song cycle that he was writing for her. His friend Gabriel Hanotaux[44] had drawn his attention to the volume of poems by the Baronne Antoine de Brimont called *Mirages*, which had appeared some months earlier in a sumptuous edition with woodcuts by George Barbier. From this volume Fauré chose four poems. The poet, who had been born Renée de Bonninière and was very much more of a society lady than an author, wrote in free verse after the Symbolist manner that had been fashionable around 1890. No doubt Fauré was tired of leafing through endless books and slim volumes of unsuitable verse and was attracted by the flexibility of her writing and by the sensual, troubled, even ambiguous images it suggested; not that this inhibited him from making some fairly sizeable cuts, so as to limit the length of his songs and also to remove what was too blatant or too insistent for his taste. But it is to the credit of the poet, at least, that she inspired four such songs and that she acknowledged the immortality conferred on her unexceptionable poems by Fauré's music.[45]

The organisation of the cycle is, on several levels, covert to the point of easily escaping notice. It is clear that the keys of the first three songs form a progression to the flat side: F major for 'Cygne sur l'eau', B flat major for 'Reflets dans l'eau' and E flat major for 'Jardin nocturne'; while the last song, 'Danseuse', is in the relative of the first song, D minor. Less noticeable is the linking of all four songs by means of a melodic inflection – rather than a theme in the true sense – based on ascending stepwise motion

through the interval of a fourth: F to B flat. This motif is heard at the
beginning and end of 'Cygne sur l'eau', is lowered by a tone (E flat to A
flat) in 'Reflets dans l'eau', runs right through 'Jardin nocturne' and
reappears strikingly in the penultimate verse of 'Danseuse' (Ex. 89).

Ex. 89 *Mirages*

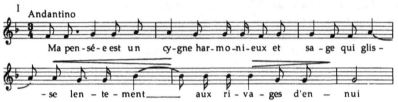

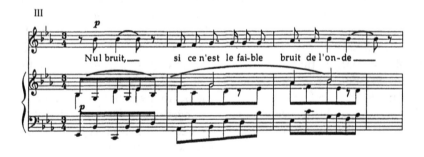

This unifying tetrachord, with its upper note oscillating between a perfect and an augmented fourth, is characteristic of the modal tendencies of Fauré's musical language. Vladimir Jankélévitch identified this motif some time ago as that of 'Lydia'[46] which, as we have seen, has already reappeared in *La Bonne chanson* and the chorus of the Océanides in the third act of *Prométhée*. It is further proof of the profound unity that marks Fauré's output.

This discreet use of a cyclic motif in *Mirages* recalls the same technique in the five Venice songs of thirty years before, and a further link between the two cycles is the care Fauré lavishes on setting to music the poetic images. We may remember how deftly Fauré evoked 'the dull rumbling of the pebbles' in 'C'est l'extase' and 'the golden note of the horn in the distant woods' in 'Une Sainte en son auréole'. Here too it is the accompaniment which carries the musical responses to the suggestions in the text: in 'Cygne sur l'eau', the image of the black swan cleaving its way through reeds and water lilies is conjured up by the continuous broken chords in semiquavers. While being a wholly appropriate texture for its context, it can be found earlier in the Eleventh Nocturne and appears regularly in the works that follow: the Andante of the Second 'Cello Sonata, *L'Horizon chimérique*, the coda of the Thirteenth Nocturne and the start of the Trio.

In the fourth and fifth verses of 'Cygne sur l'eau' the semiquavers turn into quavers, to match the disenchantment which stems the flow of the poet's happiness:

> Renoncez, beau cygne chimérique,
> À ce voyage lent vers de troubles destins;
> Nul miracle chinois, nulle étrange Amérique
> Ne vous accueilleront en des havre certains;
>
> (Think no more, beautiful swan of dreams,
> Of that slow journey towards a troubled fate;
> No Chinese miracle, no strange America
> Will receive you into its secure harbours.)

In the second song the broken chords in quavers fall an octave at the mention of the deep lake in which lie those 'things as pale as memories', so many vanished hopes and vain reflections. Once again the fourth and fifth verses form a digression, illustrating the 'supple, rhythmic step' of the nymphs and the 'galop of the aegypans' by the use of dotted crotchets in a passage of 3/2 time (Ex. 90).

Ex. 90 *Mirages* (II)

In the last verse the poet dreams for a moment of drowning her lassitude in the seductive waters of the lake:

> Si je glisse, les eaux feront
> Un rond fluide ... un autre rond ...
> Un autre à peine ...
>
> [If I slip, the waters will make
> A fluid circle ... another circle ...
> Barely another ...]

One thinks here of the scene of the ring in Debussy's *Pelléas* where a great calm overtakes the orchestra at Mélisande's words: 'There is now only a great circle in the water.' Fauré transfers the same image to the piano in a very different fashion, using a succession of triplets each time less densely textured and interspaced with long silences.

In the third song, 'Jardin nocturne', it is the 'faint sound of the wave' and the 'faint, magical sound' of the water dripping from the basin of the fountain which Fauré chooses to evoke by sporadically doubling the important notes of the vocal line in the right hand. Simple as this procedure may be, it is remarkably telling. Fauré's language is so unified, so free of all strivings for effect that the least underlining of any aspect of the score is enough to get across his intentions. The end of the central section, with its abrupt plunge into D flat at the words 'among the invisible palms' is one of the most moving harmonic inspirations in all Fauré's work.

I have to say that, beautiful though this song is, it suffers from following the first two, which are written in the same style and share the same atmosphere of discreetly troubled calm. The necessary change of tone comes, if a shade tardily, in the last song, 'Danseuse', which is one of the composer's most surprising pieces. It is based on a rhythmic ostinato which is barely altered for the final verse (Ex. 91).

Ex. 91 *Mirages* (IV)

Instead of the charming, exotic dancers of *Pénélope*, we find here an intense, almost abstract vision, like a bacchanale outlined in black figures against a red background on some Greek vase.

This new Parthenope, like an inspired priestess, circles around an unchanging dominant (A) as though hypnotised by the obsessive rhythm of the poet's flute. At the beginning of the third verse the cyclic idea momentarily returns, but then the basic rhythm reappears in the bass and again holds the dancer in its thrall.

Mirages occupies a very special place in Fauré's output. Certainly he never went further in the direction of 'le chant parlé'. The vocal lines of the first three songs can be seen as a recitation, or even as an example of psalmody, with its smooth melodic profile and reliance on intervals of the second, third and fourth; a number of words are sung to the same note and the verbal rhythms follow those of a sensitive reading of the text (see Example 89).

Seventeen years after *Pelléas* seems rather late for this to be the influence of Debussy. One might suggest rather that Fauré, probably unconsciously, was going back to the chanting of psalms as practised in the Catholic Church, and profiting from the suppleness of these incantations and, still more, from their private, devotional tone.

In November 1919, Madeleine Grey auditioned for Camille Chevillard on Fauré's recommendation, and was immediately engaged to sing as a soloist at the Lamoureux concert on 11 January 1920. She sang the aria 'When I am laid in earth' from Purcell's *Dido and Aeneas* and Gaia's aria from *Prométhée*, as suggested by Fauré. On 28 November 1919, she came to the Director's office at the Conservatoire to give a private first perform- ance of *Mirages* in the presence of the publisher Jacques Durand, the Baronne de Brimont and a few select friends. The first public performance was fixed for the following 27 December. Madeleine Grey was accompa- nied by the composer – his last appearance as a pianist at the Société nationale where he had performed regularly for nearly fifty years.

The performance was an outright success. Fauré wrote to Madeleine Grey on 31 December 1919:

Dear Lady of the Triumphs, I received yesterday, as well as your kind letter – in which with considerable modesty you talk of the success of the composer and say nothing about the success of the singer – a number of others which I am sorry I can't show you! You revealed, to an audience that is particularly difficult to satisfy, a voice, a talent and a feeling for music that were *absolutely* remarkable and quite unexpected! Well done! I cannot tell you how happy I am to have been the occasion of providing many of my friends with such a *startling* revelation, and how happy I am also to know that you will be singing in public more than once this winter.

With the performance of *Mirages* and the Chevillard concert that fol- lowed shortly afterwards, Madeleine Grey's career was well and truly launched. Ravel asked her to sing in the first performance of the orchestral version of his *Deux Mélodies hébraïques*, and was often to accompany her, notably for a Spanish tour in 1928. He also asked her to make the first recording of his *Chansons madécasses* and of the Hebrew melodies which he had harmonised.

Despite its successful reception, *Mirages* has never been as popular as *L'Horizon chimérique*. It does not fit the needs of the concert-going public; it lacks the expressive force which makes the previous cycle so convincing, at first hearing; and Mme de Brimont's poems are not of the same quality as those by Jean de la Ville de Mirmont. Nonetheless, *Mirages* retains the affection of those who love Fauré's music and gains, rather than loses, from being heard over a long period. Fauré would also not have been displeased at the notion, which I personally entertain, that it is better served by being sung in intimate surroundings rather than on the concert platform. But it had to wait until after the Second World War before it was appreciated, recorded and, more or less, rediscovered.[47]

19 Ultima verba

Fauré was never to experience again the creative outpouring of the years 1919–21. When he finished his Thirteenth Nocturne on 31 December 1921, he had less than three years to live during which his capacity for work noticeably diminished, due to age and a host of physical infirmities. On this subject his letters in 1922 express many regrets which he forced himself to season with humour: 'During these last four months I've aged almost as much as Wagner's little melodic turns', he wrote to Paul Dukas on 21 April 1922, citing a passage from *Tristan*.[1]

The tiredness that dogged him, sometimes for months at a time, made him regret particularly having devoted to the Conservatoire the years when his creative powers were at their height – and not so long ago. On 2 January 1922 he wrote to Fernand Bourgeat, his old secretary-general at the Conservatoire:[2]

I feel dreadfully the onset of old age and I regret not finding my freedom sooner . . . I've done good work even so. I've finished a Thirteenth Nocturne. But for my first work of the year I've embarked on an article on our dear Saint-Saëns which I've been asked to write by Henry Prunières' *Revue musicale*. A revue of a terrifying snobbishness! . . . It goes without saying that in spite of the arch avant-garde character of the *Revue musicale I shall make no concession* – rather the opposite!

This homage to his old teacher, who had recently died, was published in the number of February 1922.

During the first four months of 1922, Fauré was the guest of the Grémys in their handsome Villa Frya on the Promenade des Anglais in Nice. 'I'm ashamed to admit I'm living the life of a sloth!' he confided to his wife on 4 March.[3] 'I'm doing absolutely nothing and haven't thought of two notes worth writing down since I've been here. Have I come to the end of my resources? Is the climate really so depressing? I spend my days in the house without the least desire to go out or work, I just live peacefully and stupidly, but not without concern over this intellectual lassitude.'

449

He realised that his sight had got worse and that in the street he was now walking 'like a very old gentleman', and problems with his teeth were added to a deafness which every day isolated him further from the world of the living. As his son Philippe wrote:[4]

However much you love and admire someone, it is impossible to carry on a general conversation above a certain level. At table, as soon as you turned your attention from him in particular, you could see him becoming anxious. He would stare, trying to guess our thoughts from our facial expressions. This was tiring for him, but he did not like to impose himself. He would wait in silence for a speaker to come back to him.

His publisher Jacques Durand, knowing that he had reached a composing impasse, suggested in January 1922 that he might write a Trio for piano, violin and 'cello like the one Ravel had composed just before the war, but Fauré did not begin to sketch the new work until his return to Paris in April. When summer came, he wanted to see once again the mountains where he had been born.

In July 1922, as Philippe Fauré tells us:[5]

He spent a month at the Hôtel de France in Argelès, at the entrance of the lovely Luz and Cauterets valleys. He was enchanted by the countryside and was happy to stay there until the end of the season. As soon as he arrived, he asked me to look on his worktable in Paris and find some pages of manuscript which he had left behind. It was the sketch, not of the beginning, but of what became the central episode of the second movement of the Trio.

During this stay Fauré could hardly work at all and at the end of July he contracted bronchial pneumonia.

In August, he accepted the invitation of Louise and Fernand Maillot who were spending the summer in Savoy.

ANNECY-LE-VIEUX

The Trio and the String Quartet

The little village of Annecy-le-Vieux, between the lake and the mountains, was not unknown to Fauré: three years earlier, he had stayed there peacefully writing *Mirages*. 'Les Charmilles', the house rented from the Dunand family, is a large, comfortable house giving on to a tree-filled garden on one side, and on the other shaded by a portico from the square, not far from the fine Romanesque clock-tower which is all that is left of the church that once stood here. Fauré stayed in a beautiful room facing the garden, on the first floor. The spacious, peaceful setting was very much to his taste, and when the weather was fine he would spend hours looking at the lake sparkling in the distance. He himself had discovered the house on an outing from Evian in 1918,[6] noting its splendid position and then making enquiries through two young musicians, Victor and Jules Gentil, who used to spend their summers at Menthon-Saint-Bernard on the banks of Lake Annecy.

Fauré was delighted to return to Annecy-le-Vieux in the middle of August 1922. On 26 August, a Fauré festival was organised at the Annecy casino: 'Rather mediocre performances, but great enthusiasm all the same', he commented;[7] and was amused by the rivalry deliberately created by the Prefect and the Mayor, who intended this concert as a counterblow to the *Messe basse* put on the following day in the local church! 'The performance of the little Mass on Sunday was, on the other hand, excellent. The vicar collected two thousand francs for charity and you can imagine what a flood of blessings was let loose on me, my family and M. Maillot who organised it.'

In this friendly, peaceful atmosphere, Fauré at last felt strong enough to return to work. On 26 September 1922, he could write to his wife:[8] 'I've started a Trio for clarinet (or violin), 'cello and piano. An important section of the Trio was begun a month ago and is now *finished*. The trouble is that I can't work for long at a time. My worst tribulation is a *perpetual fatigue*.'

Fauré returned to Paris in October and decided to remain there for the winter. As he wrote on his arrival in Savoy, 'Despite my nomadic nature, I'm beginning to feel I'm past the age when long journeys seem quite simple. Provided I only go out in fine weather, I shall be better off in the house than anywhere. As for the winds in my beloved Mediterranean countries, the fact is that during the winter they don't do me any good. All I'll miss will be the clear skies!'[9] It was therefore in his secluded studio at 32, rue des Vignes that he wrote the first and last movements of the Trio. The work was finished in the middle of February 1923.

The opening Allegro ma non troppo, in 3/4 and in D minor, is remarkable for the clarity of both its texture and its form. Over gently pulsing quavers in the right hand of the piano, the 'cello and then the violin in turn sing an intensely lyrical idea, a graceful long-breathed melodic curve. Closer inspection reveals that it is constructed regularly, its twenty bars being divided, in accordance with Fauré's habits, into five groups of four.

A brief burst of light from the piano at bar 42 breaks the smooth, transparent surface of this opening and introduces a second, very simple idea in bar 51, a bell-like motif within the range of a minor third. These two linked ideas are in fact the constituents of a single theme, of the same length as the first (1 + 4 groups of four bars).

The development begins with a return of the opening theme in the dominant, *marcato e sostenuto* in the bass of the piano (bar 107). The second theme reappears on the violin, *cantando*, at bar 151 but is soon reduced to its second constituent. Its repeated notes now turn out to be less melodically rewarding, producing a rather dull development built up of eight-bar sections (bars 167–210). The reprise is unorthodox in producing a new exposition of the two themes both on the piano, the first in the left hand *fortissimo* (bar 211), the second in the right hand (bar 251). The coda at bar 291 blends the two in a lovely idea in which we can hear the ecstatic chiming of those bells whose echo remained in Fauré's memory from his childhood years.

The Andantino, in 4/4 in the relative key of F major, begins with one of the composer's most inspired passages (Ex. 92); a moment of beauty such as one finds in Mozart or Schubert.

The emotional tension created by this opening is so great that Fauré

Ex. 92 Piano Trio (II)

characteristically reacts by introducing a deliberately anodyne second idea, which interrupts the rarefied atmosphere. The same kind of break in tone can be found in the Sixth and Seventh Nocturnes, the *Elégie* and the slow movement of the First Piano Quartet – a sign above all of Fauré's *pudeur* and embarrassment at the intrusion of sublimity into his music.

Two movements from 1920–1, the Andante of the Second Quintet and that of the Second 'Cello Sonata, provide a precedent for the chorale style of the second theme, which appears straight away on the piano. It is worth noting that every year from 1906 to 1920 Fauré had had to provide a chorale theme for the counterpoint examinations at the Conservatoire: so that it almost seems as if he was now taking something which so far had been confined to his teaching programme into his own work.

The final Allegro vivo, in 3/8 and moving from D minor to D major, is a total success – not always the case, as we have seen, with Fauré's finales. The first theme is made up of two elements, stylistically wholly opposed but musically complementary. The first of these, powerfully enunciated by unison strings, is a dramatic call to attention in which some have seen a resemblance to Leoncavallo's 'Ridi, Pagliaccio' (much to Fauré's chagrin!). The second is a dance-like idea, firmly stressed by the piano (see Exx. 93a and b).

Ex. 93a Piano Trio (III)

Ex. 93b Leoncavallo

The long upward progression on the violin (bars 73–99), a sort of commentary on the first idea over a moving accompaniment on the piano, is not only beautiful but the result of strictly logical development. As in the first movement, a rhythmic motif casts a sudden shaft of light on to the argument (bar 100), followed by a sort of leaping counter-subject in the piano (bars 106–15). All the thematic and rhythmic elements are now in place and proceed to indulge in a joyful celebration, mixing that 'fantasy and reason' of which Verlaine, and Fauré, speak so persuasively at the end of *La Bonne chanson*. The 'scherzo' atmosphere of this movement goes even beyond that of the finale of the Second 'Cello Sonata in invention and mastery.

'If he lives to be a hundred, how far will he go?' his friends asked after the first performance of the Trio. The work had been tried out for them in April 1923, in the Maillot's salon in Paris. Thinking of the summer days spent in Annecy, Fauré turned with a smile to Mme Maillot and said, 'That's what your hospitality leads to.'[10]

At his request, the first public performance was given at the Société nationale by three ex-prizewinners from the Conservatoire: Robert Krettly, violin, Jacques Patté, 'cello, and Tatiana de Sanzévitch, piano, on 12 May 1923, Fauré's seventy-eighth birthday. The concert also included *La Bonne chanson* sung by Suzanne Balguerie, accompanied (from memory) by Roger Ducasse, but Fauré was confined to his room and could not attend.

But he was able to go at the end of June to the Ecole normale de musique, a private music school founded by Auguste Mangeot and Alfred Cortot in 1920. The famous Cortot–Thibaud–Casals trio rehearsed the work there in his presence and played it at a Paris concert on 29 June 1923 – the rehearsal eight days earlier was marked by a delightful photograph dedicated to the composer by his interpreters.[11] The score had recently been

published by Durand with the title *Trio for Piano, Violin and Violoncello*.
The idea Fauré had had after finishing the Andantino, of it being written
'with clarinet (or violin)', was suppressed for no reason that we are aware
of. Perhaps Jacques Durand, who had in a sense commissioned it, was
against this rather unusual grouping of forces which, in those days, would
have meant it being not so widely played; or perhaps it was tried and
proved disappointing. Even so, the idea is interesting and would have been
a new one for Fauré whose only wind music otherwise consists of two flute
pieces, written expressly for the Conservatoire.

It is unlikely that Fauré knew the trio with clarinet that Brahms wrote
before the Quintet and the two clarinet sonatas, since the German composer was unappreciated by the French for many a long year. But Fauré
certainly liked the veiled timbre of the clarinet, which he used in almost all
his scores, and had in his library an old French edition of Weber's *Grand
duo concertant*. It is probable though that he had in mind the fine sonata
that his teacher Saint-Saëns had just written, in 1921, and that he remembered hearing a performance of a trio with clarinet by his friend Vincent
d'Indy, which was a success at the Société nationale in 1888.

There is no real reason why the clarinet should not replace the violin in
the Fauré Trio, the only difficulty being the occasional double-stopping to
give the violin part more body. The solution is to take the top note in every
instance. This has been tried out several times in the last few years, and
from the point of view of variety and balance it works very well.

During the long internment to which his poor health condemned him
through the winter of 1922 and the following spring, Fauré had returned
to revising Schumann's piano works for his publisher, Jacques Durand.
This time he turned to the composer's neglected late works, especially the
Gesänge der Frühe, op. 133; these volumes were published in December.
But he also worked on his own piano pieces, which had been revised the
previous year by the faithful Roger Ducasse.

The original idea was to issue in volume form the pieces of the same title
which until then had appeared separately. It then proved necessary to
revise the musical texts since Fauré, particularly as a young man, had
obviously read his proofs somewhat carelessly. Together with Robert
Lortat, Roger Ducasse, himself an excellent pianist, had noted inconsistencies, omissions and a fairly large number of faulty pitches and rhythms.

Fauré had originally suggested regrouping the pieces published by
Hamelle into three volumes: 1, Nocturnes 1–8; 2, Barcarolles 1–6; 3,
Impromptus 1–3 together with the four *Valses-Caprices*.[12] Roger-

Ducasse's work was, by the French editorial standards of the time, of high quality. He wrote a general preface for the first eight Nocturnes, followed by specific notes for each of them on interpretation. Ducasse, who had a thorough knowledge of Chopin, goes so far as to say in his preface:

Since, in my opinion, Fauré's piano works are as important as Chopin's, it seemed sensible to issue an authorised revision of them and, both for pianists and in spite of them, to present an interpretation which they can follow, if they want to be true to the composer, and which they can ignore if they want to misrepresent him. In undertaking this task I have been able to take advantage of the composer's own suggestions.

Fauré, indeed, was personally involved in the editorial process. In February 1923, while he was finishing his Trio, he wrote to his one-time pupil:[13] 'Of the piano pieces, I've so far only revised the *Valses*. I've removed a large number of *pianissimi* and *accelerandi*. Enough of them will get added anyway!' And on 13 May: 'Just to remind myself, I've re-read your preface. I wonder whether you haven't been rather ferociously sardonic towards that creature known as "the pianist" and whether he won't have his revenge by treating us with disdain! ... Will we receive proofs of the *corrections*? I think it'll be extremely necessary.'

This undertaking, which Fauré had long set his heart on had, unfortunately, to overcome the reticence (to put it no more strongly) shown by Edgard Hamelle, who now took over the running of the small publishing house from his father Julien. Fauré wrote to Ducasse on 23 May 1923: 'Edgard said he was coming to see me, but that was a fortnight ago! I should like to know what he really feels about your work, but I'm giving up hope of doing so.'

Fauré's irony and mistrust were not unjustified, because he had too long suffered the immovable traditions of economy and lack of vision shown by this publishing house for him to have many illusions over the prospect of the new edition. Edgar Hamelle saw it merely as a source of complications and of quite unnecessary expense, since his Fauré editions were still selling, no matter what! Fauré wrote to Ducasse on 27 December 1922:[14] 'Edgard has been to see me. I told him that the large number of mistakes which you had corrected in my piano pieces would necessitate a new edition. I thought he was going to drop down dead!' Hamelle naturally refused to re-engrave and settled for correcting and re-correcting the plates which had done duty for thirty years and more.

In addition, it was now realised that most of the autographs of his early piano pieces could not be found, either in Fauré's collection or his publisher's. 'As for what Edgard told you about the manuscripts', Fauré wrote to Ducasse on 20 March 1923, 'it's very probably the truth. His father can't have attached much importance to them and – in those distant days – I confess I didn't either.' Some sixty-five years later, many of these manuscripts have still not been located and, until proof appears to the contrary, must be regarded as lost.

Matters dragged on endlessly. By the autumn of 1923, the volume of Eight Nocturnes had still not appeared. Fauré wrote to Ducasse:

Edgard told me a few days ago that the printing of your commentary was delaying publication of the *new* (!!!) edition and suggested we publish it straight away without the said commentary. I refused point blank. But it might be as well for you to go and see him! I told him it was absolutely imperative to change the last page of the Fifth Barcarolle, because of the crazy way the final bars are all squashed together.

The composer naturally hoped that his three successive publishers would co-operate and that his piano works could be brought out in three volumes: 1, Thirteen Nocturnes; 2, Thirteen Barcarolles; 3, Six Impromptus and Four *Valses-Caprices*, with notes by Roger-Ducasse for each volume.[15] Unfortunately, this overall scheme was never realised, although for some obscure reason Heugel handed over to Hamelle the Fourth and Fifth Impromptus and these alone were put into a volume with the first six Barcarolles.

The corrected edition of the Eight Nocturnes finally appeared in the summer of 1924. Fauré received a copy at the beginning of September and was not at all happy with it. 'I immediately wrote to Edgard', he told Ducasse,

to say that he is not to bring it out in its present condition. Even if we have to wait six months or a year, some emendations are absolutely indispensable. I'll say nothing about the mean-mindedness which is evident from the start: your Preface ought not to be presented like a chemist's advertisement, crammed on to a single page. Worse still is the page numbering of each Nocturne separately, so that your indications, referring to the old numbering, don't tally with the numbering in this edition. It's Edgard's job to realise that and warn you in advance. And there are some other small points which we can go over together in October. But we must stand firm and not let the volume out into the world in this condition.

Fauré's death, two months later, left Hamelle with a free hand, and the changes he wanted in the volume of Eight Nocturnes were never made. The Six Barcarolles in Hamelle's possession were combined with the Five Impromptus in 1926, and the Four *Valses-Caprices* with the *Mazurka* in 1930. These two volumes do not contain any of the commentaries Fauré wanted and, worse still, bear no indication that they were newly edited by Roger Ducasse and by the composer ...

At the beginning of July 1923, Fauré returned to Annecy-le-Vieux to stay with the Maillots for nearly three months: 'I don't think I have ever seen the scenery looking so beautiful and resplendent', the seventy-eight-year-old composer wrote to his wife on 6 August.[16] 'Every evening, about 6 o'clock, there's a profoundly moving effect of light over vast distances. Why do we have to live in towns, amid noise and, for a good third of the year, in gloom!'

There were times when he was able to shake off the lassitude of old age which he found so depressing. His son Philippe wrote:[17]

In 1923, Fauré could still surprise us by appearing really active. One day some friends had taken him out to dinner by the lake, at the Imperial Hotel, and he came back quite late in a mood of bravura, with his hat over one ear. A sparkling dining-room, bright dresses, a breath of society atmosphere, something lively and unexpected had been enough to lift his spirits and he declared himself *ready to go and paint the town red*!

In the local church on 25 August, Albert Bertelin, an old pupil of Fauré's, conducted long extracts from the Requiem and the *Tantum ergo* op. 55, with Rose Féart as the soprano soloist and Vlado Perlemuter playing the harmonium, and the Andante from the Second Violin Sonata played by the brothers Victor and Jules Gentil; the concert also included fragments of Honegger's *Le Roi David* conducted by the composer. 'Philippe came to hear the Requiem yesterday', Fauré wrote to his wife,[18] 'and was surprised, as I was, by the results. Coming out of church, I received my little ovation, complete with the little peasant girl offering me a bouquet ... just as they do for M. Poincaré!'

Two charming photographs taken as Fauré was leaving the church show him looking very sprightly and elegant, wearing a straw hat and tweed trousers, with a dark jacket and a cloak over his shoulders to keep out the cold. He is holding a stick and smiling, and looks almost dashing; he gives off an air of charm and extraordinary goodness. Another shot, taken a few moments earlier, shows him with Jules Gentil, coming out of the church carrying his violin bow, and Marguerite Hasselmans in a white hooded cape and a typically 1925 dress (see plate 59).

Fauré had been back at work since the middle of July. 'Every day I'm writing a little music, a very little it's true. *And as has so often been the case*, I don't yet know what these first fumblings will turn into.' On 9 September he finally confided to his wife:[19]

I've started a Quartet for strings, without *piano*. It's a medium in which Beethoven was particularly active, which is enough to give all those people who are not Beethoven the *jitters*! Saint-Saëns was always nervous about it and didn't try the medium until near the end of his life. He didn't succeed as he did in other areas of composition. So you can imagine that I'm nervous in my turn. I haven't told anyone, and shan't until I've nearly finished. If people ask, 'Are you writing anything?' I shall say bluntly 'No!' So keep this to yourself.

According to his son Philippe,[20] the movement that he finished a few days later, on 12 September, was the Andante of the String Quartet. The first movement was written in the rue des Vignes in Paris in the course of the autumn.

Fauré was now asked by Henry Prunières to contribute to the musical homage he was intending to publish on 1 May 1924 in the form of a special number of the *Revue musicale, Ronsard et la musique*. Renaissance poetry was then much in favour with composers. In 1898 Ravel had written two *Epigrammes de Clément Marot*, Debussy then composed songs, both accompanied and unaccompanied, on poems by Charles d'Orléans, Tristan L'Hermite and Francois Villon, and Saint-Saëns set Ronsard more than once, in 1908 and 1920. Less well known is Fauré's longstanding interest in the composers and poets of the French Renaissance whom he had studied as 'recreation' during his free time at the Niedermeyer School. In 1906 he collaborated briefly on Henry Expert's great publishing project *Les Maîtres musiciens de la Renaissance française*, editing three of his favourite songs: Costeley's *Mignonne allons voir si la rose*, on a celebrated poem by Ronsard, *Quand mon mary vient de dehors* and *Qui dort ici* by Lassus. He introduced this forgotten repertoire both to the Conservatoire and to the Société des concerts du Conservatoire, of which he was president. So it was that on 3 November 1923 he sent Prunières a favourable reply: 'Your idea is an excellent one. I shall be pleased to be associated with it, presuming that there will be no difficulties with my publisher Jacques Durand.' Fauré would be in excellent company too, the other contributors including Dukas, Ravel, Roussel, Louis Aubert (an old pupil of Fauré's), André Caplet, Arthur Honegger and two of Ravel's pupils, Maurice Delage and Roland-Manuel. He set to work, choosing the beautiful Ronsard poem in which the poet, thinking forward to his death, says farewell to his soul:

> Amelette Ronsardelette,
> Mignonelette, doucelette,
> Très chère hostesse de mon corps,
> Tu descends là-bas, foiblelette,

Pasle, maigrelette, seulette,
Dans le froid royaume des mors;
Toutesfois simple, sans remors
De meurtre, poison, et rancune,
Méprisant faveurs et trésors,
Tant enviez par la commune.
Passant, j'ay dit: suy ta fortune,
Ne trouble mon repos, je dors.

[Dear, gentle little soul of Ronsard, sweet denizen of my body, you go down there, feeble, pale, thin and alone, into the cold kingdom of the dead: ever simple, without remorse for any murder, poisoning or ill-will, despising favours and riches, envied by all around you. As you left, I said: good fortune, do not trouble my repose, I sleep.]

But it was not to be – by a great stroke of bad luck Ravel had, out of Ronsard's considerable body of work, chosen the same poem,[21] and his song was already finished (the manuscript is dated January 1924). Fauré's immediate reaction was to abandon his sketch and destroy it. As the critic Gustave Samazeuilh relates: 'When I told Ravel, he was not at all happy about it and offered to withdraw in his teacher's favour.'[22] The considerable beauty of Ravel's song is some compensation for the regret we must feel when we realise that Fauré surely saw this as his 'last will and testament' in the field of song. His choice of this funereal text can hardly have been fortuitous ...

The winter and spring of 1924, which he spent in Paris, were a gloomy time for him. The torpor of old age which engulfed him every afternoon made any continuous work impossible, and he was now obsessed by wondering whether he would ever have the strength to finish what he had begun in the summer. He was so superstitious that he continued to keep its existence secret, to the point of writing on the manuscripts of the first two movements the words 'Annecy-le-Vieux', to lead the inquisitive astray and avoid questions from visitors; only later did he add at the beginning the word 'Quatuor'. When he felt too weak to compose, he would turn to his voluminous correspondence. Those people who, as he put it, were 'thirsty for decorations' were forever writing to ask him to put in a word in official circles, and his promotion to the Grand Croix de la Légion d'honneur on 31 January 1923 (an exceptionally high rank for a composer) only encouraged such requests. This tiresome correspondence does at least show the importance attached to decorations in those days.

Fauré had always been interested in politics and, when work was impossible for him, he followed developments in this area with a mixture of interest and disquiet. He was fully aware of the tense political climate in these post-war years. A letter to his wife of 12 September 1917 shows that he was anxious about the Russian revolution and he was not happy either at the difficulties in Franco-German relations stemming from the question of war reparations, with the occupation of the Ruhr in 1923. A further problem was the increasingly worrying decline of the franc, deeply disturbing for those who had grown up with its almost total stability in the years before the war. Writing to Loeffler in 1921, Fauré complains that the engraving of his Second 'Cello Sonata is being delayed by the eight-hour day for manual workers, which went through the French parliament in 1919. Finally, in 1924, the forces of progress triumphed. In a move without precedent, the chamber elected on 11 May 1924 (*Le Cartel des gauches*) forced the president of the Republic, Alexandre Millerand, to resign. 'I don't know what M. Maillot thinks of current political events', Fauré wrote in an unpublished letter to Louis Maillot on 1 June.[23] 'I know that in France, however black things appear, they always sort themselves out in the end! But for the moment, I can't help feeling extremely nervous! Won't this battle against the President of the Republic weaken still further the respect for authority which is already ailing in this country?'; on 13 June 1924, Millerand was replaced by Gaston Doumergue.

In the same letter, Fauré goes on to say: 'Here we're thinking of leaving for Divonne in a fortnight. The inauguration of the monument to my father-in-law on 14 June is keeping me here longer than I would like.[24] But will the change of air do me any good? I really need to get my strength back and it's leaving me gradually day by day: I'm not worth *a franc*! And with the franc at its present level, that's not a great deal.'

On 20 June 1924, Fauré began a month's stay at the Grand Hôtel in Divonne, on the sunny slopes high above Geneva and the lake. The complete calm, the fresh air and the beauty of the Alps which he could admire from the terrace outside his room slowly revived him and restored his composing energy. His son Philippe, who went with him, wrote:[25]

On the fourth day he placed his manuscript paper on the table and quietly started on the finale of his String Quartet. He was no longer strong enough to walk. But he wanted to see Nyon again, where Niedermeyer was born, and had himself driven there, but he was unable to go on foot to his old teacher's monument. He was happy with his work and was full of a kind of inner energy which entirely revived him.

When the room in Divonne was no longer available, Fauré accepted M. Maillot's offer to come and collect him by car and take him, once again, to

Annecy-le-Vieux on 24 July. Despite the poor weather, the days seemed to pass in a flash. He worked every day and the finale of the Quartet slowly progressed. On 12 September he was able to write to his wife:[26] 'Yesterday evening I finished the *Finale*. So that's the *Quartet* finished, unless I have an idea for another short movement which could come between the first and the second. But as there's no real necessity for it, I won't exhaust myself searching for one, at least not for the moment.'

The first movement, an Allegro moderato in 2/2, is in the overall key of the work, E minor. This key belongs to many of Fauré's loftiest and most soberly meditative works, such as the Second Violin Sonata, the Tenth and Twelfth Nocturnes, the last of the Nine Préludes and 'Inscription sur le sable' which concludes *Le Jardin clos*. As in the finale of the Piano Trio, the first theme is made up of two contrasting elements: a questioning four-bar phrase on the viola, answered by a delicate arabesque on the first violin based on a modal scale of E. The two violins then take it in turn to present a beautiful melodic idea, a kind of secondary echo of the first motif (bars 19–26). This is followed immediately by the second main theme, a long phrase on the first violin which develops in the relative major with a passionate lyricism over the space of sixteen bars (bar 35, *cantando*; made up of four groups of four bars).

Philippe Fauré-Fremiet, in his biography of his father,[27] revealed that the two principal themes of the opening allegro were borrowed from the first movement of the Violin Concerto, which Fauré had written in 1878–9, but which he had left unfinished and unpublished. A comparison of the themes in the Quartet with their original models shows clearly the distance between the fumblings of the young composer and the creative control exercised by the mature master until the very end. I might add that the secondary idea joining these two themes also comes from the Concerto, where it fulfils the same function (see Ex. 58).

After a lyrical development, the reprise presents the thematic material in a more compact manner. The questioning phrase of the opening is almost completely ignored, while the harmonic thrust takes another direction with the secondary idea (bar 122), to introduce the second theme in the tonic according to the orthodox manner. In the coda, the opening viola motif appears in a calmer version in E major.

The Andante, in A minor and 4/4, was, as we have seen, the first movement to be composed and is without question the high point of the work, in the richness of its melodic inspiration, in its formal originality, in the density of its polyphonic texture and in its transparent quality, all of which place it among the finest movements in the history of the medium.

Ex. 94 String Quartet (II)

The first calm and dreamy idea (Ex. 94, A), played by the first violin, takes us irresistibly into an immaterial world, while the second (B) is one of those intensely expressive phrases that Fauré reserved for the veiled timbre of the viola (the instrument occupies a special place throughout the Quartet). The harmonies of the repeated quavers in the two violins emphasise its lyrical qualities by some startling dissonances. The intervals of a second which abound in this accompaniment (C against D, E against F, B against C) give a despairing edge to the sumptuous melodic curve.

In bar 24 a secondary idea appears on the first violin, a kind of echo of the first theme whose initial notes are clearly heard, this time by way of conclusion. Finally, in bar 48, a third theme is presented by the viola, a sort of lament, with the gentle obstinacy of a children's song (Ex. 94, C).

As in the opening Allegro, the reprise changes direction at the ninth bar to lead directly into the secondary idea and then the third theme, in bars 82 and 106. The second main theme is heard only now, in bar 116, and in the unexpected key of F minor. Fauré gives us no more than the beginning, a

kind of stretto moving up from the 'cello to the first violin. In the coda, the first theme and its melodic echo (the secondary idea) alternate in a tightly organised dialogue, moving easily through chromaticisms and harmonic progressions towards the final tonic.

The finale, an Allegro in E minor in 4/4, uses the form to which Fauré so often turned to finish his late chamber works, the sonata movement with two themes based on the rondo's alternation of couplet and refrain, all in the 'light and cheerful' mood of a scherzo (to give the composer's own description). The *pizzicato* octave idea which underlies it almost throughout looks back to the scherzo of the Second Quintet and, to go further, to the Piano Quartets and the First Violin Sonata. The principal (refrain) theme is given to the 'cello (Ex. 95), then to the viola and the first violin; it is like a popular dance, close in character to the motif emphasised by the piano in the Trio (see Ex. 93a). An intermezzo (first couplet) dominated by the first violin in due course reveals its importance as an extended variation of the theme–refrain which it mirrors all through the movement.

The second main theme in bar 21 is played by the 'cello in its higher

Ex. 95 String Quartet (III)

register, over a curiously jagged viola accompaniment: indeed, all the accompanying rhythms and lines in this finale are almost as important as the themes proper, as though the composer were affirming his adherence to contrapuntal principles.

Otherwise, the movement is organised according to the usual criteria of Fauré's late style: the development opens with a repeat of the opening theme in the tonic in bar 79, followed faithfully by its mirror—motif in bar 95. The reprise at bar 163 is abbreviated, the theme—refrain and its mirror being reduced to eight bars each to leave room for new developments (or new couplets, if we follow the rondo plan). As a result, the second theme is delayed until bar 234, where it appears varied and reduced to four bars.

The coda, based on the theme—refrain and its mirror, reaches a superb polyphonic climax, with the triplets in stretto singing like the morning birds in *La Bonne chanson*, and the work ends with a broad and powerful *fortissimo*.

*   *   *

So, after a year of interminable working and waiting, the String Quartet was finally finished. Fauré realised perfectly well what was at stake in attempting this medium, and in abandoning his beloved piano, for the first time in his life. During all these months he had lived in terror of seeing his faculties suddenly desert him, and for good. Robin C. Tait, in his excellent study of the extant sketches,[28] points out that at the end of the slow movement Fauré wrote a curious subtraction sum in the margin which turns out to produce the figure '77' – the age at which Haydn wrote the two central movements of his uncompleted quartet op. 103. At the period when Fauré was working on the Andante of his Quartet, in September 1923, he was seventy-eight ...

In order to get to the end of the Finale, Fauré had deliberately lengthened his working hours. His manuscript shows signs of a certain haste, which may also explain the rather repetitive nature of some of the harmonic progressions and some overworking of the triplets of the main theme. Work on the Quartet used up all Fauré's remaining strength, and after it he was exhausted. On 19 September double pneumonia was diagnosed and his elder son Emmanuel, taking over from Philippe, had to scour the countryside for oxygen containers which were now indispensable for the sick man.

By the middle of October, Fauré's life was out of danger but he realised that his eyesight had grown still worse and that his legs would no longer carry him. In his letters to his wife he constantly plays down the seriousness of his condition so as not to exacerbate her continual anxiety. Everything points to the fact that he faced death with serenity, seeing it as a passage towards that divine service which, despite his scepticism, he hoped for in his heart of hearts. 'That's how I see death', he had said of his Requiem, 'as a joyful deliverance, an aspiration towards a happiness beyond the grave, rather than as a painful experience.' In any case, why should he mind about death? His work remained, copious, not all of equal quality maybe, but at times coming close to those 'summits of perfection' of which he had always dreamed. His last letter to his wife, written from Annecy-le-Vieux on 14 October,[29] glows with satisfaction at having achieved his earthly task, the vast adventure of his creative labours. In turning to the past and rendering an account of his life, he tried to bring some comfort to the wife whom he had abandoned, and who was now prematurely aged, sad and embittered. Referring to the inauguration of the monument to her father, he wrote:

Look around you, and even beyond, and see whether any other woman has had such joy in her life? And if you will allow me to speak of myself in the same breath as your father – which you will, I'm sure – can you tell me what daughter and what wife has been able on the same day to hear of the pure beauty of her father's works and of his lofty and disinterested career, and of the pure beauty of her husband's works and of his no less lofty and disinterested career? Your life has been full of sorrow and perhaps your failure has been your inability to realise your wish to be someone yourself! But you still have this profound good fortune, to which you can add that of having brought up your sons. In these hard times, *but still shot through with arrivisme*, is that all nothing? I do hope you will understand me and that these lines will come over to you in all their sincerity! Do not read or look for anything in them which is not the plain, simple truth!

'On 18 October', wrote his son Philippe,[30]

he travelled in better weather. Through the car window he saw the sunlight streaming on Lake Bourget; it was the last sunshine he saw, because after that there were only grey, cloudy skies. He lived for another two weeks without regaining his strength or his appetite. Apart from his family he saw no-one except his doctor, Dr Emonet, who came from Ariège and was the son-in-law of his cousin Dominique ... On Sunday 2 November he was in great pain, had trouble with his memory and sudden spasms. Even so, he saw Roger Ducasse for a moment, but without being able to say more to him about the Quartet than: 'You see, you'll do it very well.'

The next morning he suddenly summoned my brother and myself and wanted to see us alone. He told us how tenderly he returned the feelings of all those who had loved him, then he was struck by the possibility of a hardship that we might have to bear: 'After I'm gone', he said to us, 'you'll hear people say "When all's said and done, that's all there is to it!" ... Supporters will fall away, maybe ... You mustn't be upset by this. It's fate, it happened with Saint-Saëns and with other composers ... They all go through a period of oblivion ... None of that is important. I did what I could ... now let God be my judge! ...'

And that was all; he did not speak again. It remained to alleviate his pain as he looked about him vaguely, without seeing anything. Gradually he closed his eyes. Then, at 11 o'clock in the evening, he suddenly opened them wide, as though to see the visible world for one last time. He breathed his last breath at 10 minutes to 2 in the early morning of 4 November, with his wife, his two sons and his doctor by his bedside.

The French government, in remorse at its lack of recognition, accorded him the full glory of a state funeral, little though this would have been to the taste of such a private man. There was a brief delay, too, in such a funeral being authorised. When the request was made by the composer's friends, the Arts minister, François Albert, replied: 'Fauré? Who's he?',[31] a *faux pas* that history has not forgotten ...

On 8 November 1924, Fauré's Requiem was sung in the church of the Madeleine, with black draperies hanging from a high canopy. The interpreters of this work, which had resounded so often beneath these neo-Byzantine cupolas, were the Opéra chorus and the orchestra of the Société des concerts du Conservatoire, conducted by Philippe Gaubert, with Fauré's successor, Henri Dallier, playing the organ and the solo parts taken by Jane Laval and Charles Panzéra. The orchestra also played the 'Nocturne' from *Shylock*, and the 'Molto adagio' from *Pelléas et Mélisande* which was lost amid the scraping of chairs as the procession left the church. Outside, there were numerous speeches, including those by Vincent d'Indy, Henri Rabaud and the minister François Albert, who was suddenly overcome with emotion, and Nadia Boulanger in deepest mourning paid her respects on behalf of Fauré's former pupils. All these high-sounding words were lost in the cold November wind and the crowd gathered in the rue Royale made no attempt to hear them. Passers-by were full of curiosity to know who was the man being buried with such a show of Swiss guards, plumed horses and carriages laden with flowers.[32]

Gabriel Fauré's body lies in Paris, not far from where he used to live, in the Passy cemetery (place du Trocadéro); his grave is near that in which his friend André Messager was soon to be buried, and also near those of Claude Debussy and of his second wife Emma, the inspiration behind so many songs ...

Fauré after Fauré

Even if Fauré's renown was slow in coming, it reached considerable proportions in the 1920s, when his music began to spread. The musical journals of the inter-war years show that his works were receiving an increasing number of performances, and this is confirmed by the sales figures of his scores; compared with the period before 1914, the average size of a printing doubled in the 1920s.

After the composer's death, there grew up a kind of Fauré cult. Marguerite Hasselmans was still young and could have played the high priestess, but her delicacy and reserve led her to limit her appearances to a few, distinguished concerts of chamber music in which she effaced herself totally before the music she loved. The rôle of high priestess was assumed with gusto by the other Marguerite, Madame Long, and such was the conviction she brought to it that she finally persuaded the spell-bound public that she, and she alone, held the secret of the musical inheritance, the interpretative tradition, the 'true' Fauré style.

A 'Société des Amis de Gabriel Fauré' was founded in 1935 by Mme Henry de Jouvenel,[33] and each year she organised an outstanding concert. In 1936 she awarded a prize to the fine recording of the Sixth Nocturne which Jean Doyen – a pupil of Mme Long – had brought out anonymously as one of the entrants in a competition, and in 1938 the Society had the excellent idea of supporting the publication of Vladimir Jankélévitch's book on Fauré's songs. But more than a few important people were alienated by Mme Long's excessive zeal. Philippe Fauré-Fremiet and E. de Stoecklin founded a 'Société fauréenne de musique de chambre' in 1938, at whose concerts Marguerite Hasselmans was surrounded by a faithful audience in the large studio at 32, rue des Vignes.[34]

The centenary of the composer's birth was marked in 1945 with some enthusiasm, though without the divisions being healed. 'Fauré has been mightily celebrated', wrote Roger-Ducasse,[35] 'but his sons and I, bearing in mind the source of these manifestations, stayed at home. It was all too clear to me that the name and the music of my old teacher were no more than an excuse to publicise certain performers who either had never known him or had quarrelled with him.'

At the Paris Conservatoire, the Fauré cult made unfortunate inroads, with his harmonic practice being held up as the *ne plus ultra* of modernity beyond which students should not go. A reaction was not only inevitable but salutary. The young composers born between the wars, who for the most part were among Messiaen's early pupils, violently rejected this superannuated legacy, turning with enthusiasm to Bartók, the Second Viennese School and the latest works of Stravinsky.

Marguerite Hasselmans died in 1947, Roger-Ducasse and Philippe Fauré-Fremiet in 1954. Books of memories by Emile Vuillermoz in 1960, and by Marguerite Long in 1963, did no more than revive briefly a flame that was going out. It was the period of discovering first Brahms, then Mahler, and to play Fauré at a concert was almost an act of audacity. It became obvious that his work was entering a kind of purgatory in which his reputation was at the mercy of contempt and sarcasm.

During the two decades between 1960 and 1980 a group of admirers organised various events which, though sometimes on a small scale, nonetheless encouraged talented young artists to discover a body of music which was very little played; they came together under the title 'Association des Amis de Gabriel Fauré', founded in 1963 by Mme Philippe Fauré-Fremiet who kept it going by her determination. Nadia Boulanger was the first president, followed by Vladimir Jankélévitch. The association died with Mme Fauré-Fremiet in 1983, but by that time Fauré's music no longer needed defending and had begun to reach an international audience. It is enough to note that his music is published both in Japan and in Eastern Germany, that the Requiem is recorded in London, Tokyo and Armenia and that eminent artists such as Seiji Ozawa, Carlo Maria

Giulini, Vladimir Horowitz and Jessye Norman are putting their favourite Fauré pieces on disc.

Now that a sizeable number of Fauré's works have passed the magic centenary marker, it looks as though his music has found its true place in the evolution of Western musical language. No one would claim that he occupies a place among the giants, the J. S. Bachs, the Mozarts or the Beethovens, and among the composers of his own time and place it may seem that Debussy's work is more radical, and certainly that Ravel's is more perfect. But Fauré's originality means that his output is more consistently rewarding than Saint-Saëns' or d'Indy's, and in the number of undoubtable successes it surpasses that of most of his elder contemporaries, as well as of most of his peers. In a European context, I would place the work of the young Fauré beside that of Brahms or Dvořák, and I would link him especially with Janáček, with whom he shares the same position in the evolution of musical language. Both of them chose to maintain a classical brand of harmony, not without its audacities nor indeed its original features, in music that exudes a powerful personality.

There is no call, though, for triumphalism. Apart from the Requiem, which can usually attract a good audience, Fauré's music is too subtle and reflective to appeal to the masses. 'I'm not used to drawing crowds', he commented to the pianist Robert Lortat in 1914. I would say this was because he never tried to. In his heart of hearts he was an aristocrat, happy with the approbation of a small number of musical friends. He felt that success, if success there were, was a bonus. We might even suspect him of deliberately sabotaging the public acceptance of many of his pieces. Both *Le Jardin clos* and *La Chanson d'Eve* finish in funereal gloom, while in the *Thème et variations* it is the penultimate variation which is the most brilliant one, the last being of a withdrawn nobility designed to curb an audience's enthusiasm. The same principle can be found in the Préludes and in many of the Nocturnes, where the virtuosic passages come in the middle of the piece.

It is easy to understand how this reserve has for years led interpreters to keep their distance. At a time when musical texts were treated whimsically and without respect, when pretty well everything (including music itself) was sacrificed to virtuosity, this pure, logical, severe style of writing was a source of bafflement.

Interpretation

Fauré was constantly concerned about the interpretation of his music and almost never satisfied with it. Like many composers, he felt for a long time that he was not understood, even betrayed by those who performed his works. Very few pianists found favour with him: 'the greater they are, the worse they play me', he said to Mimi Risler[36] in 1902. Virtuosity itself, he felt, often got in the way of an understanding of the deeper meaning of his music. He wrote to Robert Lortat, in an unpublished letter of 20 March 1919:[37]

> May I ask you – how tedious composers are! – to take the opening themes of each of the *Valses-Caprices* more slowly? The justification, as I see it, of the title *Valses-Caprices*, is *variety* of *tempo*. They're always played too fast and too *uniformly fast*. Oh pianists, pianists, pianists, when will you consent to hold back your *implacable* virtuosity!!!! (I am here, of course, addressing them in general!) Your nimble fingers go dizzy with speed!

From this we can see that Fauré's much-quoted desire for his music to be played quickly has to be treated with some reservation.

Very little is known of the earliest pianists to play his works. Marie Poitevin gave the first performance of Franck's *Prélude, choral et fugue*, which is dedicated to her; Marie Jaëll was a pupil and admirer of Liszt before taking up her own line of teaching; Marie Bordes-Pène gave the first performance with Ysaÿe of Franck's Violin Sonata. Records dating from 1904–6 show that Saint-Saëns, Raoul Pugno and Louis Diémer had a clean, clear, brilliant and rather dry style of playing, with sparkling runs. Risler, Cortot, Viñes and Blanche Selva brought more power, charm and colour to their playing, which often sounds orchestral in character. Marguerite Long's brilliant, 'perlé' style is not without panache, and her dovetailing of the hands still astonishes today. This kind of interpretation for a long time offered a charming but superficial view of Fauré's music. On the other hand, Jean Doyen's objective, retiring style lacked variety or warmth. But between the wars, the superb virtuosity of Robert Casadesus – a pupil of Diémer, whom Fauré approved of – the broad style of Yvonne Lefébure – a pupil of Marguerite Hasselmans – and the sobriety of Vlado Perlemuter – who played to Fauré around 1922 – all suggested new interpretative avenues which have been followed by the post-1945 generation. Among these, Jean-Philippe Collard deserves particular mention.

Fauré was no happier with his singers. As he wrote about his songs to Elisabeth Greffulhe:[38] 'I dream of hearing them performed by perfect singers, but I don't know of any among the professionals. It's the amateurs who understand and interpret me best.' And indeed the recording of 'Les Berceaux' made in 1902 by the celebrated Russian soprano Félia Litvinne (with Cortot at the piano) is stylistically fairly curious. Fauré preferred singers who were not involved in a professional career and appeared only in salons and at the occasional public concert, like the tenors Maurice Bagès and Reynaldo Hahn, the soprano Thérèse Roger, the contralto Emilie Girette and the pupils of Marie Trélat's singing course, like Pauline and Claudie Segond and Anita Eustis. None of these possessed great voices, so that the rumour soon went round (to Fauré's great annoyance) that you did not need a voice to sing his songs!

In the years 1910–14, singers such as Jane Bathori, Claire Croiza and Jeanne Raunay distinguished themselves by the musicality of their diction and style. During the last years of his life, Fauré was delighted by a number of young singers, such as Charles Panzéra, Germaine Lubin, Madeleine Grey and Suzanne Balguerie, who were at last doing justice to the output of songs that he had amassed with such patience. The refinement, intensity and purity of their singing was a basis for the major post-war interpreters like Camille Maurane and Gérard Souzay. But today one is bound to wonder whether this style of singing, based on extreme clarity of diction, is not on the road to oblivion. The international career and the wide spread of the disc have led, among other things, to a coarsening in the interpretation of a repertoire which is so closely linked with the proper speaking of French.

Of the conductors, Charles Münch, D. E. Inghelbrecht, Ernest Ansermet and André Cluytens among the older generation, and Seiji Ozawa and Carlo Maria Giulini among the present one have understood the unostentatious transparency of Fauré's music. But of all the areas that Fauré covered, his chamber music is the one that was understood and assimilated most rapidly. The violin sonatas have been splendidly played by Jacques Thibaud, Eugène Ysaÿe and Georges Enesco, all of them at various times accompanied by the composer, and after that by Zino Francescatti, and today by Pierre Amoyal and Schlomo Mintz. Among 'cellists, Maurice Maréchal, Pierre Fournier and Paul Tortelier have given legendary performances, as have the Calvet, Krettly and Pro Arte String Quartets.

Fauré himself used to grumble that his music was too often played 'in a half-light',[39] and interpreters like the artists above have been exemplary, in my opinion, because they give us the grandeur and sweep which are required, not excluding tenderness and charm, or indeed beauty and *fullness of tone*. The charm and breadth of Fauré's own performance of the early First Barcarolle, which he recorded on a piano roll, are very striking. As for the regularity of tempo, on which historic recordings and personal reminiscences all agree, it needs to be understood as a rhythmically supple movement based on a kind of internal tension.

Fauré's work is, like so much French music, all too dependent on its interpretation and often demands qualities that are contradictory: precision and rigour need to be tempered with a touch of fantasy and the occasional drop of mischief, an exquisitely delicate phrase may have to be developed to encompass passion and even violence; and one can never repeat often enough that dynamic markings, often sharply contrasted between one bar and the next, must be respected to the letter. Too often, the opposition of light and shade in this music is reduced to an insipid, boring level somewhere between *mezzo forte* and *mezzo piano*. There must be no rallentandos, no vulgar swooning, no holding back. Fauré's music needs to be grasped firmly, with a gentle violence and with the fervent intensity of true love.

56 Fauré at Saint-Raphaël, pension 'Le Gui', summer 1917, photo by Marguerite Hasselmans

57 Fauré and his younger son, Philippe, Evian, September 1918

58 Fauré at Tamaris-sur-mer, March 1920, photo by Marguerite Hasselmans, sent to Paul Dukas

59 Fauré leaving a concert, church of Annecy-le-Vieux (Haute-Savoie), 25 August 1923: left, Mme Hasselmans; centre, the violinist Victor Gentil

60 Fauré and Arthur Honegger, Annecy-le-Vieux, August 1923

61 A humorous wedding at the Maillot's house in Annecy-le-Vieux. From left to right: Louise Maillot, Veado Perlemuter (as a miller), Mlle X, Victor Gentil, Gabriel Fauré (as mayor, with a false beard), Jules Gentil, François and Paul Dubois-Taine, Mme Maillot (?)

62 Fauré in his room at Annecy-le-Vieux, summer 1924

63 Fauré's last letter to his wife, Annecy-le-Vieux, 14 October 1924

20 Inner voices

In his last letter to his wife, written in October 1924 (see opposite page),[1] Fauré ended by saying: 'When I get back to Paris I shall spend a little time each day giving you all my sketches and drafts and everything else of which I want *nothing to survive after me*, so that you can *burn* them. While I was ill, I realised this was something I really needed to do. You will help me to accomplish it.'

It is highly probable that this wish was carried out during the two weeks between the composer's return to Paris on 18 October and his death on 4 November: the large number of manuscripts that survive include very little in the way of drafts, sketches or unpublished items. We may conclude that during this period Fauré saw to the destruction – if they were not already destroyed – of the Andante and Finale of his Suite for orchestra op. 20 (Symphony in F), the complete manuscript of his Symphony in D minor, op. 40, the first version of the Finale of the First Piano Quartet, the Andante of his Violin Concerto, unfinished songs like 'Soirs II' on a poem by Albert Samain, or 'Dans le ciel clair' on a poem by Leconte de Lisle, and many other pieces of which we shall never know anything.

Given the current interest in preparatory sketches, especially of works that have an important place in musical history, this act of destruction is an irreparable loss. Fauré's motives were twofold: firstly, not to leave to posterity pages which he considered to fall short of his aspirations – like the symphonies and the concerto – and secondly, to preserve forever the veil of mystery with which his work was always surrounded, not so much out of coquetry as out of a mixture of pride and *pudeur*: in many of his autographs he crossed out, in very careful pen, passages, or whole pages indeed, which he had had to start again because of a mistake or a change of mind. In this we can see his unwillingness to be surprised by anyone in the most tormenting parts of his creative activity which, as we know, was a long round of hesitations, false starts and second attempts. 'As for the work I've been engaged on recently', he wrote as he was finishing the Andante of his String Quartet,[2] 'if I've said nothing about it, that's because all through my life, due to a sort of superstition, I have never liked revealing my projects before they had taken shape, and even before they were completely finished.'

We can nevertheless get a relatively precise picture of Fauré's compositional methods from allusions in his letters, from the evidence of his contemporaries and from some of the sketches that have survived.

The need to earn a living together with endless professional obligations took up perhaps four-fifths of his time right up until his retirement at the age of seventy-five. This sort of life did not fit in with the prolonged periods of concentration that any creative artist needs, and explains in part why he was particularly drawn to writing short works. When he was engaged on *Pénélope* he remarked, not without some envy and regret: 'Needless to say, these days when there is nothing to interrupt me are the only ones when I can really settle down to work. My brain gets going and produces results almost without an effort. That's how Saint-Saëns, Massenet and d'Indy live all the time.'[3] When people asked him why his opera had taken so long to finish, Fauré used to say that, if it had been six years in the writing (from 1907 to 1912), this was because he had only been able to work on it during the two months of the summer holidays.

As for the rather uncomfortable working conditions which always surrounded him, he had learnt to tolerate them from an early age: we may recall that the study room at the Niedermeyer School contained no less than fifteen pianos! It is hardly surprising, then, that the young Fauré should have taken refuge in the refectory where, as he recalled, he wrote 'Le Papillon et la fleur' 'amid the smells from the kitchen'. The concentration demanded of Niedermeyer's pupils was a useful lesson for Fauré to have learnt, and his creative activity made good use of his capacity for mental isolation. On journeys, on a tram, in the street, during a lesson, a meal or a party, musical ideas would come and formal difficulties or problems of continuation be solved. In a homage to her teacher,[4] Nadia Boulanger remembered the lunches she used to have with him at his house on the boulevard Malesherbes, 'during which sometimes he would not speak a word, then would disappear at the end of the meal and come back in some embarrassment, saying, "Forgive me, I've just been writing down what I composed during lunch."' Describing Fauré's weekly classes at the Conservatoire, Emile Vuillermoz wrote:[5]

His fingers were visibly magnetised by the keyboard. Instinctively, between trying out two of the exercises we had written, he would doodle on the keys, quietly trying out a scale or a group of chords which flitted into his imagination and which, as it passed, he caught and stored away in his memory until the time came to make use of it. It was no more than a flash, a brief, entirely private digression, a way of temporarily appeasing the thirst of creativity by which he was unceasingly tormented.

Philippe Fauré-Fremiet, who was a close observer of his father's final years, notes in his biography:[6]

He seemed calm and distant, kindly and inaccessible. But if real life called, whether it was the arrival of the postman or of lunch, he would leave his work without haste or regret, so certain was he of what had to come next and so clearly and ineradicably printed on his brain was the work that was then in progress. Only if he was grappling with an especially difficult passage would he ask to be excused *for five minutes*.

Unlike Debussy who, as we know, minded deeply about the beautiful flowers, the oriental carpets, the Japanese engravings and porcelain which were round him as he worked, Fauré was satisfied with very little. The room in which he worked on the boulevard Malesherbes was of no aesthetic interest, with its woodwork painted 1880 style, its large table piled with papers, its filing-cabinets of blackened wood and its bookcases overflowing with books. On the rue des Vignes, his studio decorated in red, black and gold suggested greater care on his part, but his work-table was small and unimpressive. His Erard piano, his work-table and the portrait painted by Sargent are now at the Musée du Conservatoire de Paris.[7]

During the many years he spent at the Madeleine, he tried to keep the afternoons free for composition – when, that is, a private lesson or a rehearsal did not summon him to the distant suburbs. 'All my life', he admitted,[8] 'I've woken up in a state of sluggishness which passes off only very slowly. I've never been up to working in the mornings, except for routine tasks like conducting the choir or playing the organ.' But really, as I have said, his professional activities in Paris left him little time for composing, and often he would merely sketch out works to be developed in detail during his summer break: many of his early works were written in the Normandy home of his friends the Clercs, his cycle of Verlaine poems was begun in Venice and, at Prunay, near Bougival, while staying with his parents-in-law, he wrote his finest works of the 1890s, including *La Bonne chanson*, the Sixth Nocturne and the Fifth Barcarolle.

From 1903 onwards, long stays in Switzerland and Italy were the favourite setting for weeks of intense hard work, interrupted by excursions, walks and photographic outings. Fauré was quite happy with the anonymity of hotel rooms, as long as he could see a panoramic view when he looked up from his little work-table, and he appreciated the total silence which allowed him to hear what he was writing (see plate 54). On the boulevard Malesherbes, the musical tastes of the Cantagrel family on the floor below were a torture for him: 'it's as though they're pulling the strings off the instrument,'[9] he used to say. In August 1906, he had to leave Pallanza for Stresa, on the banks of Lake Maggiore, because the bells and the noise of clogs in the car park underneath his window were preventing him from doing any work at all.

Often he would be allowed a piano in his hotel room, sent by his friend Blondel, the director of the firm of Erard. In fact, the piano was of more use to his companion, Marguerite Hasselmans, than to his work because, unlike Stravinsky or Poulenc, Fauré hardly used the piano when he was composing, at the most checking up on a complicated chord. Like his pupil Ravel, he used to work mostly in his head so that the final writing out took a relatively short time ... 'As my work never leaves my head while I'm walking around town', he wrote in 1904, 'it means that I don't stop composing as soon as I get up from my table. This time, I don't think I've used the piano to try out three notes of what I've written! It's so quiet here that I can hear it all clearly in my head.'[10] And in April 1898, while he was on a tour of inspection, he noted: 'All I know is that I'll really have to get down to *Mélisande* as soon as I get back. The whole score has to be written in a month and a half, though it's true some of it is already lying around in this old head of mine!'[11]

This ability to conceive music in the abstract is not uncommon in composers, but it was particularly valuable to Fauré when his hearing began to deteriorate. Trying out a work in progress soon became so painful that he had to give up the thought of hearing it. He could now close the piano lid, and content himself with a little ink, a pen and some manuscript paper.

He would sometimes fix a passing thought by writing it down on a cigarette packet, a matchbox or even his detachable sleeves![12] But usually he was careful to take a piece of manuscript paper with him. When he was settled in Zürich in 1904, he wrote to his wife:[13] 'Yesterday I went for a nice walk as far as a pretty clearing on the lake. But I was working too and scribbling from time to time with a frenzied pencil on a tiny scrap of manuscript paper. People must have thought I was walking along adding up my expenses.' These 'tiny scraps of manuscript paper' were taken from the sketchbooks which Fauré seems to have used habitually. Seven of them mysteriously survived the 1924 holocaust and were in the Fauré-Fremiet archives:[14] little manuscript books, oblong in shape, containing between ten and forty pages. Vladimir Jankélévitch was the first to study them and to identify the most important items in them. By relating them to Fauré's correspondence we can determine that the first three were used mainly between the second half of August 1887 and the end of that year. They give us an all-too rare opportunity to see the composer at work.

They are contemporary with a letter which Fauré sent to the Countess Greffulhe on 5 December 1887,[15] in which he says: 'I've only worked a little since returning to Paris. I'm engaged on several works in parallel, and slowly. All my dreams are, alas, of summits and perfections!'

Fauré was then occupied with at least six works: the Requiem, recognisable fragments of which appear in each of the notebooks; the Third *Valse-Caprice*, completed only in 1893 (1886, notebook 1); the motet *O Salutaris*,[16] written at the request of the well-known baritone, J. B. Faure (notebook 1); the *Pavane*, dedicated to Elizabeth Greffulhe (notebooks 1 and 3); the finale of the Second Piano Quartet (1886 notebook 3);[17] and the song 'Clair de lune'. The notebooks also contain unidentifiable material probably connected with another attempted symphony and a third piano quartet, two projects which haunted Fauré at this period, if we are to believe his letter to Mme Baugnies[18] dated 12 September 1887. There is also a connection between this quartet material and the F major theme, written down in 2/4 in notebook 1 (p. 21): transposed into D major, and written in 2/2, it was to become the refrain motif in the finale of the D minor Piano Quintet, completed in 1905. The same notebook also contains (on p. 19) a finished passage which has over it the cryptic indication 'Verlaine', suggesting a project that was abandoned.

These three notebooks covering the years 1886–7 give us an idea of the extreme complexity of Fauré's creative activity. Notebook 5 dating from the summer of 1902, contains the two songs op. 85, 'Dans la forêt de septembre' (final manuscript dated 2 September 1902) and 'La Fleur qui va sur l'eau' (final manuscript dated 23 September 1902), as well as important fragments of an unknown song, 'Dans le ciel clair', on one of Leconte de Lisle's *Poèmes tragiques*, which Fauré never finished. Notebook 6 is extremely mysterious: the rhythms outlined are of a sort of *Valse-Caprice* and further on there are sketches of a vocal work with orchestra – Robert Orledge sees it as a possible *Sanctus* although the text is clearly in French.[19]

Notebook 4 is in fact the latest one; Fauré very probably bought it from a shop run by the publisher Foetich on 14 August 1907, on a walk to Vevey during his long stay in Lausanne, while he was beginning *Pénélope*.[20] The stationer's name is printed on the manuscript paper, which shows Fauré searching for the themes of Ulysses and the Suitors. His letters to his wife mention with some precision this stage in his preparations, an essential one in the working method he had evolved:[21]

As for the Suitors, I've found a theme for them which I'm testing, as it doesn't satisfy me completely. I find it slightly Wagnerian ... And when I say I'm 'testing' this theme, it means I'm trying out all the combinations to which this theme might be subject according to the circumstances ... I'm also trying to see whether this theme can be combined with Pénélope's. I'm trying all possible ways of modifying it, of drawing various effects from it, both in its entirety and in fragments ... In a word, I'm compiling *record cards* to which I can refer as the work progresses or, if you prefer, I'm making *studies*, as one does for a picture.

The extreme ease with which Fauré is able to change, run together or superimpose the thematic ideas in his major chamber works suggests that he engaged in similar 'studies' before finally deciding on the shape or the rhythm of a basic theme: the first movement of the D minor Piano Quintet is a case in point.

Even so, it has to be said that Fauré did not always organise his composing so meticulously. He always preferred to work on a new piece in his head, and merely to back this up by writing out passages to confirm his judgment. It is remarkable that the above sketches for the Requiem, 'Clair de lune' and the Third *Valse-Caprice* show the music practically in its final form, with the important exception that at this stage the keys are curiously undecided: the whole of the opening of the Requiem seems to have been imagined not in D minor but in C minor; the Pie Jesu is in A minor and 'Clair de lune' in G minor – only later were they transposed into B flat major and B flat minor respectively. Sketches proliferate only where Fauré had particular difficulties. The phrase 'Au calme clair de lune', a vital point in the song of that name, appears in two different versions while the second verse of 'La Fleur qui va sur l'eau' appears in three.[22]

From these incomplete sketches Fauré moved to a first draft on the large sheets of manuscript paper which he used all his life.[23] Important fragments of what we might call 'developed sketches' have been preserved for works of his final years, notably the Second Quintet and the String Quartet. At this stage the overall physiognomy of the work was fixed, but further changes, and musically important ones, would still be made in the interests of clarity and logic, with particular attention being paid to the formal proportions and to Fauré's characteristic harmonic and melodic progressions.

The whole of his work of revision leading up to the final copy can be seen as a kind of polishing, to allow the music to flow as naturally and easily as possible. On finishing his reworking of the first movement of the D minor Quintet in 1904, Fauré wrote:[24] 'this labour of rewriting, reshaping and markedly improving the first movement has been very arduous. And now when I read it through and listen to it in my head, I find it sounds spontaneous – but how deceptively so!'

Finally, he would return to the same large sheets on which he had made the developed sketches to produce a fair copy for the printer. Nearly always at this stage certain passages would be further modified, with additions in the margin, scratchings out with a penknife and sometimes with changes pasted in. Bowing and dynamic markings were now added, often following the advice of some friendly performer, such as Alfred Cortot, Edouard Risler or Marguerite Long who had come to play the work through. All these additions were made with the greatest care, so that Fauré's manuscripts, like his compositional style, are remarkably legible and elegant. He would then take on the task of making one or more copies of this final version so as to have one for himself to keep and perhaps one or two to give away to some friend or interpreter.

The work would be tried out in private: in the salon of his apartment on the boulevard Malesherbes, later in his directorial office at the Conservatoire and finally, in the 1920s, at the home of the Maillots. A decision was then made about the first public performance, which was often given under the auspices of the Société nationale de musique. After that – and often some months after – Fauré would hand the manuscript over to his publisher, never being in a hurry to see his work in print so that he could improve still further some unsatisfactory 'corner', as he called it. 'And I always go *so slowly*', he wrote.[25] 'I have never been able to resist (and perhaps just as well) polishing and repolishing a piece and brooding over it endlessly!'

When the manuscript was finally handed over, it would have on it the opus number, the dedication and the metronome marks. Fauré always had great difficulty with these. In a letter of 1888[26] he notes ironically that his musical friends considered him as 'someone devoid of common sense when it comes to deciding on a speed'; this is why many of his autographs do not carry any precise indication or, if they do, why it has very often been corrected and recorrected. Fauré was usually unhappy with them or over-sensitive to some comment, so that he would change the figures on his own printed copies.[27] There are grounds therefore for not always following them, as some interpreters do who have more scruples than artistic sensibility: to them, one can only say 'let intuition be your guide'.

Once the work was engraved it was sent to the composer twice in proof form. Here again Fauré would touch up one or two details, often adding dynamic markings which had proved necessary at the early performances (see plate 55). Like many a composer, Fauré used to read his proofs somewhat carelessly, hearing the work in his head rather than reading what was actually on the page. Large publishing houses like Heugel or Durand had experienced readers on their staff who would correct the proofs both before and after the composer had seen them, but the same did not, apparently, apply in the case of Hamelle, so that their editions, particularly of the complex, polyphonic piano music, remain full of mistakes.

The publisher then authorised a first printing of a limited number of copies, as dictated by the primitive methods of the time. Most of Fauré's works published by Hamelle were initially printed in runs of two hundred, or of one hundred in the case of orchestral scores, those by Heugel in runs of three hundred and by Durand in runs of five hundred. Sometimes, if a work had a sudden success, the runs were larger and closer together. The well-known *Berceuse* for violin, of which Julien Hamelle published two hundred copies at the end of 1879, appeared in three separate runs in 1880, adding up to seven hundred copies in a year.[28] It is worth mentioning in this context that in those days the publisher took the whole risk of the enterprise on his own shoulders, as works were bought outright with no subsequent royalties on sales, whether these were large or small.

A work's gestation, from the first sketch to the first edition, was therefore a very long one and the date of that edition is often an unreliable guide to when that work was composed. Research on his manuscripts and letters gives us valuable and often surprising evidence on this front. 'Before the last fifteen years', Fauré said in an interview in 1922,[29] 'everything of mine that was published was done so seven or eight years after I wrote it.' So much for the 'facility' with which he has often been taxed. 'In any case, I've always gone for quality rather than quantity', he noted in 1903.[30]

His letters and his manuscripts together reveal that this 'charming improviser' was preoccupied with the formal equilibrium of his works and often with their mathematical proportions. We have seen how his themes tend to be built from the concatenation of carefully balanced elements. It was important to him that a piece should develop naturally, and he seems to have paid particular attention during his last years to the numbers of bars. On his manuscripts of this period, of works such as the two 'Cello Sonatas, the piano *Fantaisie*, the Trio and the String Quartet, he carefully marked the number of the last bar on each page.

Thus, despite the charges that have been made of easy-going seductiveness, Fauré's music is in fact highly disciplined, and the extent of his output, with its 120 opus numbers, each often containing two or three pieces, is due simply to his continuous labours over a period of sixty years. If we look at the chronological catalogue of his works (pp. 525–57) we can see that in some periods, like the years 1887–8, 1893–4 or 1917–21, he was extremely productive, while others, like the years 1890 or 1903, were apparently barren, no doubt because he was busy thinking or wrestling with some technical problem. These *rallentandi* in his creative cycle correspond in general with a change in his style. The desire to write things that were new was one of his main preoccupations. 'How difficult it is', he wrote in 1904,[31] 'to write good music which doesn't owe anything to anybody and which some people may find interesting. And, as Saint-Saëns says, the difficulty recurs with each new composition. And it is quite natural that one should always want a work to show some progress over its predecessors.' In an interview in 1922,[32] expressing his admiration for Gounod, he said 'he brought something new to music'. Around the time he was writing the Ballade, he defined it as a 'Fantasy rather outside the usual mould, at least I should like to think so.'[33] A similar desire can be detected in his remarks about the song 'C'est l'extase', which he sent to its dedicatee, Winnaretta Singer, with the words:

You'll see that, as in 'Clymène', I've tried out a form which I think is new, at least I don't know anything like it: trying something new is the least I can do when I'm writing for you, the one person in this world who is least like anybody else![34]

Such an attitude was remarkably courageous at a time when so many composers were happy to go along with the system; even if history has not looked kindly on them, at least during their lifetimes they were able to enjoy all the honours, the celebrity and the financial rewards that come with recognition by the Establishment. Fauré's almost obsessional interest in self-renewal gives him a place, if a discreet one, among the musical pioneers of the turn of the century (see chapter 13), and we may compare his attitude with that of Debussy, who declared in 1908 that 'the composer (or the artist of today) who has achieved widespread notoriety has now only one preoccupation: to produce works that bear his personal stamp, works which are as new as he can make them'.[35]

Certainly some of Fauré's music, and some of the best of it, seems to have sprung fully armed from his brain. He was really quite proud to have been able to conceive and finish a song as original as 'Le Don silencieux' in four days in August 1906, and during the summer of 1917 he astonished himself by writing the whole of the Finale of the First 'Cello Sonata in less than three weeks. This kind of speed was the result of continuous, daily work, a facility born of long experience of his craft and of its difficulties: 'It seems to me', he wrote in 1918,[36] 'that I work more quickly and easily the older I get.'

For all his self-discipline, Fauré was always prepared to accept the unexpected and to work some improvisational idea into the scheme of things. Paul Dukas used to say in his Conservatoire class that 'when Fauré starts a sonata he doesn't know what will be on the third page'. This is a true observation in the sense that it corresponds to the exterior impression given by Fauré's music, but it does not correspond with the interior reality. Any of his completed works is, in my view, the result of a precarious balance between improvisation and experience, between inspiration and technical expertise. The unalloyed freshness of so much of his music derives from the quality of his musical ideas, dictated in all their supple, lively prodigality by his inner voice – what one might call his inspiration. The bearing and solidity of his music (which is a paradox when his harmonies are so fluid) rest on the elaboration of these ideas and on the discreet skill with which they are treated, this playful ingeniousness making up what Roland Barthes calls a *text*. The definition of a 'great composer' could indeed consist in the happy marriage of the inspired artist and the proficient artisan.

The unconscious inspirational source is clear in Fauré's case: it can be reduced to the presence of singing at some level or other – a humming, an 'interior radio' in Barthes' terminology in which harmonies and melodies are as yet indistinguishable and no more than confused ideas which the composer must then try to translate, clarify and write down. Fauré would often talk of 'grabbing them by the hair'. This side of his 'inspiration' comes across clearly in his letters of August 1903, in which he says: 'If what I've started on goes well, I'd very much like to make something of it … I've put down a few vague thoughts and, *although I can't be sure*, I think that what's going through my head is a sonata for violin and piano'; and three days later: 'For several days now my head's been full of music: I can't yet say whether it's good music!'; and two days after that: 'I'm fairly happy with my work. I've got quite a lot done. It's like a sticking door that I've had to open and I've managed to do so at least halfway. I think, finally it will be the second movement of the [D minor] Quintet, whose first movement has been laid up for so long!'[37]

Fauré's uncertainty about the final form of his works may explain why he often began with the central idea of a movement. From the time of the Violin Concerto he joked about this habit of his: 'True to my fashion, I've started by finding the second theme of the first movement; but where's the first theme? If this is one of my special attributes, it is at least a curious one! The main thing is that it shouldn't seem too curious when everything's fitted together.'[38]

His letters show that the chamber works of his last years were not written in linear fashion, from start to finish, but that he would often work on several movements simultaneously,[39] as the muse took him. They show too that the difficulties he had were not so much a lack of ideas as the initial impossibility of organising them so that they flowed into each other logically and harmoniously. He would agonise over linking together two separately conceived passages to produce one of continuous, sustained interest. Above all he was wary of using his technical know-how to fill in bars that might be functional but which would be empty of thought. 'I've always avoided *padding* in my music. It's something I loathe', he wrote while largely rewriting the duet in the second act of *Pénélope*,[40] and occasionally his letters show him battling manfully with what he called 'the knot' or 'the wall of brass', 'that wall which rises up from time to time and which is so hard to break down'.[41]

His experience in dealing with such problems had the advantage at least of bringing with it a certain habitual functioning of his mental processes. He wrote to his wife in the summer of 1904:

A few days ago I was visited by a really weird phenomenon. While I was thinking about all sorts of unimportant things, a theme came into my head which was in the rhythm of a Spanish dance. And this theme jogged along without my paying the slightest attention to it. But the strangest thing is that, while I went on thinking about all these other things, the theme started to develop, to clothe itself in a variety of entertaining harmonies, to change and modulate etc … that's to say, to work away entirely on its own. Obviously it was only using material which my memory has stored away since the day I was born and which has become part of me. But isn't it strange, this duality of cerebral activity? This clear division between the two parts? If I'd written it down it would have had a perfect shape!

Some weeks earlier he noted that in a dream he had heard 'a work by Gounod and a work by Schumann, unknown ones that is, which were pure Gounod and pure Schumann'.[42]

Nonetheless he often complained of how hard it was to shut himself off from his professional worries (mostly to do with the administration of the Conservatoire) and regain the creative impetus of a work already begun.

He always needed a few days' rest at the start of the holidays to put himself in the mood; then, once his creative activity was set in motion, it took him over completely and ideas would keep him awake at night so that he had to get out of bed to write them down.

A further difficulty was Fauré's lifelong doubt about his own gifts. As he said to Henry Malherbe:[43]

What has been the saving of me is my conviction of not having much merit: I've always felt that any work I was finishing was a long way short of what I wanted it to be. I didn't think that what I wrote had any value or importance. Just once, maybe, I felt something resembling pride. I'd recently finished a song called 'Le Secret'. I played it to Henri Duparc who began to tremble with emotion. The composer of *La Vie antérieure* began to punch me with his fists, shouting, 'Savage! Brute!' I realised then that 'Le Secret' was something good.[44]

In his letters and critical writings Fauré never stopped playing down the importance of his works; he speaks of his 'little Requiem' or his 'little Trio' and describes *Le Jardin clos* as a collection of 'brief pages'. When he submitted a new work to any of his musical friends, his anxiety was that of a pupil showing his teacher an exercise: 'Tell Messager that showing him my new compositions makes me tremble', he wrote to Marguerite Baugnies around the time of the Requiem; 'that animal terrifies me almost more than Saint-Saëns does.'[45] When trying out his works he used to invite educated music-lovers like the lawyer Paul Poujaud, who was the friend and adviser of so many painters and musicians, Général de Lallemand, Mahler's great supporter in France, or the critic Camille Bellaigue. When he was seventy, Fauré wrote to his old pupil Charles Koechlin, 'you are one of the *rare* artists whose opinion I really value'. It is hardly credible that he should have asked for his String Quartet not to be performed until he had submitted it to his small group of loyal advisers: Paul Dukas, Pierre Lalo, Camille Bellaigue and Général de Lallemand. 'I have confidence in their judgment and I leave it to them to decide whether this Quartet should be published or destroyed.'[46]

Doubt was certainly the most faithful companion of Fauré's creative endeavours: 'I wake up in the night every now and then', he wrote in 1907, 'and in this unhappy state of sleeplessness I come to the conclusion that what I've so far completed of *Pénélope* is *absolutely mediocre*! I've had moments like that all through my life.'[47]

This doubt was compounded by his feeling of his own singularity, his status of outsider by comparison with those French composers of his own vintage whom he had to regard as colleagues. Modest he may have been,

but at least he knew that his work was as good as that of some people
whose meteoric and over-publicised success prompted him to temper his
self-doubt with jealousy. As a man of fifty and a mature artist, he did not
take kindly to being beaten twice for a seat in the Institut, by Théodore
Dubois and Charles Lenepveu, or to being passed over by the editor of *Le
Figaro* in favour of Alfred Bruneau when the post of music critic fell
vacant. We may well feel some astonishment when we read his correspondence in the summer of 1896 with Théodore Dubois, who was always
ahead of him on the official road: as organist of the Madeleine in 1877, as
a member of the Institut in 1894 and as director of the Conservatoire in
1896:

Fauré to Dubois [end of August 1896][48]

There is one last thing, my dear Dubois, which you can do for me. If you know of
any bias against me which promotes my exclusion from the official musical world,
as I was informed by your colleagues in the musical section of the Institut at the last
election (when the results were announced), or if you merely feel this to be the case,
tell me truthfully. Then I won't upset anyone any more, including myself, and I'll
stay in my corner perpetrating music which is probably detestable and certainly
inferior!

Dubois to Fauré, 3 September 1896

I am not aware of any bias against you which is promoting your exclusion from the
official musical world. The results of the Institut election mean nothing, as one can
see from the fact that Lenepveu, who belongs to this official world, was placed last
by his musical colleagues and was still elected. Since you ask me to be truthful, I had
the feeling that your music was found to be too vague, too modulatory, too
recondite. This is not to say, as you claim so modestly, that it is either detestable or
inferior. It is what you wish it to be, the music of an extremely talented artist who is
utterly sincere and an enemy of the banal. But you cannot insist that everyone
should like it nor hold a grudge against those who adopt a different aesthetic
attitude.

Fauré to Dubois, 5 September [1896]

Finally, on the personal front, I must thank you for reassuring me over what I was
afraid was an academic bias.
    I can certainly confirm that I do my best with what I write, but I do not confirm
that I expect to satisfy everybody. Even so, the faults people charge me with are
precisely those that I detest the most and the more clarity, correctness, precision,
even concision there is in a piece of music, the more it moves me. This merely shows
that for the most part we do not know ourselves very well!

Saint-Saëns was sad about Fauré's lack of ambition and was for ever urging him on. Fauré, for his part, was aware that his stature depended on his originality, marking him off from composers like Widor, Victorin Joncières and Théodore Dubois, whose success with the public needled his *amour propre*. He was always amazed that some of his works should meet with incomprehension or that his artistic creeds should be interpreted in a different way by himself and by his contemporaries, particularly his composing colleagues. He showed the song 'A Clymène' to Camille Benoît, a devoted disciple of César Franck, and reported his reaction with some irony to Winnaretta Singer:[49] 'I have to confess he told me, with a gloomy, severe expression, that I was becoming too *incoherent* and *nebulous*! Which left me very worried, as I've always thought I was too classical! Please don't spread this terrifying verdict around!'

Above all, Fauré was continually fighting against the limits which critics and colleagues repeatedly set on his talent; in an interview in 1922[50] he said of his songs: 'Yes, they've been sung a lot. Not enough to make my fortune, but too much all the same, because my colleagues claimed that as I'd been so successful in this field I ought to stick to it for good!' And further on: 'When I wrote *Prométhée*, my first attempt at composing for the theatre, everyone said, even before the score came out: "Fauré, writing on *Prometheus*! But his field is pure music, Prometheus is far too big a subject for him!" They said it so loudly, I might even have believed them!'

All these difficulties did not prevent Fauré from patiently pursuing his work, without letting himself be disturbed by the powerful and diverse aesthetic currents that surrounded him. This constant effort, this unremitting struggle against his own demons needs to be underlined; it explains why, occasionally, he allowed himself a brief moment of satisfaction – the outcome of lucidity or pride, but certainly not of vanity.

After the triumphant first performance of *Prométhée*, he exclaimed, almost naively: 'I'm finally satisfied with my work ... and it was done so *quickly*. What a pity I have other things to do except compose!' A few years later he wrote to his wife, when the first performance of the D minor Piano Quintet was taking place in Brussels:

Ysaÿe finds the style of the Quintet grander and more elevated than that of my Quartets, completely free of all attempts at effect: absolute music. I'm very happy he should have had this impression; all the more so because, for the moment, music has everything in its sights except remaining as music. Perhaps Ducasse won't approve of this work because it has no existence outside itself, but I'm not bothered about that. I'm perfectly well aware, in my heart of hearts, that my way of writing is not within the capabilities of *everybody*![51]

Coda

Unlike Debussy and, to a lesser extent Ravel, Fauré spent his whole life in the production of what is normally known as 'pure music'. Instinctively he kept clear of the programme music which Saint-Saëns had championed in France, following the symphonic poems of Liszt. It is true that he devoted much of his time to writing songs, an indisputably literary genre, but even here he was always careful not to be imprisoned by the text he had chosen and exercised a certain respectful boldness in making it his own, either by shortening it or by changing some detail as he thought fit.

Outside this particular field, his output yields nothing in the way of historical, philosophical or anecdotal references, whether in his piano, orchestral or chamber music. He never succumbed to the charms of 'Pièces pittoresques', 'Scènes alsaciennes' or 'Souvenirs d'Italie', and the exoticism which held such a longstanding attraction for Saint-Saëns was utterly alien to his favourite pupil. It is highly probable that, like Debussy, Fauré heard the Balinese *gamelan* at the Universal Exhibition in 1889, but we may be sure he regarded it as no more than a 'piquant curiosity', to use one of his own expressions. Even Spain, which is so close to Ariège, which fascinated so many of his contemporaries and which he enjoyed when recreated by Albéniz, Granados or Manuel de Falla, is almost entirely absent from his music: no *España*, no *Habanera*, *Iberia*, *Alborada* or *Rhapsodie espagnole*, just a 'Pas espagnol' (in *Dolly*), apparently inspired indirectly by one of his father-in-law's bronzes.

Fauré similarly remained on the fringes of the renaissance of French folksong to which Vincent d'Indy, Maurice Emmanuel and Maurice Ravel, among others, devoted their attention. There is no tender or humorous allusion to 'our old country songs' such as one finds in Debussy; Fauré had some regard for popular music, but as a source of inspiration it seemed to him too facile. In a letter from which I have already quoted[1] on the

495

Mazeppa project, he finds fault with Tchaikovsky, Brahms and Grieg for having successfully employed national airs. For him, folksong could never figure as an element of 'good style'.

This denial of local colour or of any extra-musical material should not be seen as stemming from any lack of technique. It was a considered position, but here and there we can find proof of his skill in this field: in the splendid Spanish colouring of the 'Pas espagnol' in *Dolly*, in the charming half-antique, half-oriental dances in *Pénélope* and in the refined pseudo-Chinese prints of the unpublished incidental music for *Le Voile du bonheur*. But these are notable exceptions in an output which aimed singlemindedly towards the final, total abstraction of the String Quartet.

Fauré's clear stance on this point should not lead us to assume he was at all dogmatic. The fact that he never adopted the form of the symphonic poem did not prevent him in the least from enjoying those by Saint-Saëns, which he liked playing with the composer on two pianos, and one of his most enthusiastic articles in *Le Figaro* was on Liszt's *Les Préludes*. Even if he never once used any of the songs from Ariège which, as a child, he used to be asked by Niedermeyer to sing at his parties, he appreciated the 'exquisite entertainment' of Saint-Saëns' *La Princesse jaune* and *Suite algérienne*, both of which he chose to transcribe for piano. It was merely that this way was not for him, and that his artistic ideals lay on a higher plane than 'evocations', however brilliant they might be. We know from his son Philippe[2] that the fairly abstract titles of Nocturnes, Barcarolles and Impromptus still seemed to him too suggestive: he would have preferred, like Schumann, the complete neutrality of 'Piano piece no....' (as in the German *Klavierstück*).

None of which has prevented critics from going seriously astray. The Ballade, for instance, has been included in the canon of 'Impressionist' music. If this seductive but dangerous epithet gives us a false idea of Debussy's music, it is particularly unsuited to describing Fauré's.

In 1922 Fauré mentioned 'having received congratulations on my *Ballade* which was taken to be one of my latest works. In fact it dates from 1881 ... And it was referring to this *Ballade* that a critic wrote that *I was imitating* Debussy quite obviously.' Music smacking of 'impressionism', in the work of Debussy's followers, irritated him considerably. In an unpublished letter of 1908 to his old friend Marguerite Baugnies (who had become Mme René de Saint-Marceaux), Fauré wrote:

I should like to thank your husband for sending me his appreciation of Paul Dubois. I have read it with *very real pleasure*. He has a good go at the insignificance of Impressionist art! There's a lot one could say in the same vein, about this unutterably vague music! Aren't you rather tired of all these vapours and approximations! *Aphrodite* would make me scream if I had to listen to it often!

Here Fauré is referring to the opera by Camille Erlanger, but almost certainly it is Debussy whom he has in mind in the preface he wrote to Georges Jean-Aubry's *Musique française d'aujourdhui*, published in 1916:

In the continuing safety of a prosperous peace which, it seemed, would never be brought to an end, a number of painters, burning with the fever of novelty, followed up impressionism with intentionism, cubism, etc., while various, less daring composers were trying in their works to suppress *sentiment* and to substitute *sensation*, forgetting that sensation is in fact, a necessary preliminary to sentiment.

In this, very French, discussion about sentiment and sensation, Fauré clearly states the case for a kind of decanting of sensation and, more generally, of everything which has to do with the real and the everyday, before it can rise to the dignity of Art (with a capital A). In the same text the composer cites Saint-Evremond: 'The love of pleasure and the avoidance of pain are the earliest and most natural impulses discernible in man.' And he comments: 'Art has therefore every right to be pleasurable. But one cannot forbid those who see life in more sombre colours to express it as they see it.'

The pleasurableness of art and the need to keep one's distance from it define quite well the essential poles of Fauré's art and bring him close to the committed attempts of Stéphane Mallarmé to render through articulate language what lies beyond language, to attain the Idea even before its shape becomes clear. Certain of Mallarmé's statements echo closely Fauré's distaste for any intrusion of realism into his art:

> Ainsi, le chœur des romances
> A la lèvre vole-t-il,
> *Exclus-en* si tu commences,
> Le réel, parce que vil.[3]

> [Thus, the chorus of romances flies to the lips,
> Exclude from it at the start what is real, because it is cheap.]

Just as Mallarmé commonly used fixed forms and the alexandrine, so Fauré stayed immutably bound by formal outlines and the overall frame of harmonic language inherited from the Romantic era. Both of them built their reputations on their treatment of classical elements, used with subtlety and discretion and always *from within*. With them innovation does not, as with Rimbaud or Debussy, take on radical, revolutionary forms; it prefers the narrow, perilous and somewhat perverse path of *diverted tradition*.

Mallarmé delights in escaping permanently, though effortfully, from the 'elementary employment of discourse'. He gives words back their primal meaning, twists the logical articulation of the sentence by cunning inversions of ideas and astonishingly bold interpolations, introducing sudden flights of images and meanings; Fauré similarly likes to divert harmonic functions by enharmonic volte-faces, to lose the captivated ear in the unexpected complications of some fleeting, graceful discourse and to blend the long-separated traditions of Tonality and Modality. In the field of prose, such virtuosity in holding a long line cannot be found anywhere except in the lofty, tortuous sentences of Proust.

Creation as the expression of the inexpressible, as a way of exploring the unknowable, the artist as medium, these are philosophical notions very representative of the thought of the greatest artists of the second half of the nineteenth century, from Baudelaire to Proust. We can find them expressed directly by Fauré in his well-known letter to Paul Poujaud about the *Mazeppa* project:[4]

It's not that I myself have the idea of turning *Mazeppa* into an essentially French opera: I may say that, in general I don't admit there are such subtleties in this art of music whose primary characteristic is to be a universal language or rather a language belonging to a country so far above all others that it is dragged down when it has to express feelings or individual traits that belong to any particular nation.

This letter is strangely prophetic of the famous passage in Proust's *La Prisonnière*, inspired by the Vinteuil Septet:[5]

Every artist thus appears as the citizen of an unknown homeland, which he himself has forgotten, different from that from which any other great artist will set out upon his journey to this earth ... Composers do not remember this lost homeland, but each of them remains unconsciously tuned in a kind of unison with it; he is delirious with joy when he sings in harmony with his homeland, he sometimes betrays it in the pursuit of fame, but in searching for fame he moves further away from it and it is only in disdaining fame that he finds it, when he intones that particular chant whose monotony – because whatever the subject it treats, it remains consistent with itself – confirms the stability of the elements that make up the composer's soul.

This aspiration towards the Ideal is the basis for the non-realism of the whole Symbolist aesthetic to which Fauré's work can be attached, and not only because around a half of his songs are on texts by Baudelaire, Verlaine, Maeterlinck and van Lerberghe.

The expression of the inexpressible, liberation from the tyranny of the word, avoidance of narrative, of convention, of dully realistic detail, disdain for effect, eschewal of local colour, of the big scene, of the cliché – these were the foundations of Fauré's aesthetic attitudes, ones which he shared with the imaginative poets and painters around 1890; one thinks of the best works of Puvis de Chavannes, of the disturbing portraits by Lévy-Dhurmer, of the gently perverse dream atmosphere of Burne-Jones' Perseus series.

Comparisons have sometimes been made between Fauré's music and the monochrome painting of Carrière. Personally, I would be inclined rather to suggest the pastels and lithographs of Fantin-Latour, because to me an analysis of this music seems desirable in terms, not of colour, but of values of light and intensity. Its penetrative gentleness, its sometimes severe *gravitas* and its velvety, dreamlike character are exactly the qualities of Fantin's pictures at their best. We have already seen that some time before 1877 the young Fauré had bought some of Fantin's lithographs on Wagnerian subjects (*Tannhäuser*, *The Ring*). Nearly thirty years later, an article by his friend the critic Arsène Alexandre in homage to Fantin-Latour gave Fauré the opportunity to define his aesthetic approach more precisely:[6]

What a delightful article you have written on Latour, and who but you could have written it? I've often been told that my music never extends to joy or sorrow. Might it possibly allow of that slightly veiled smile which is the only sensible attitude? If it's true that one unconsciously expresses oneself in one's art, I should be very flattered to think that I've seen life in the same way you do.

The charming surface of so much of Fauré's music and the 'pleasurableness' to which he long made obeisance have blinded many people to its underlying *gravitas*. His sense of discretion nearly always prevented him from expressing his tortured feelings directly: he is not given to loud cries, or outbursts of violence. In its most sombre moments, his music becomes the intimately murmured voice of that *spleen* so dear to Baudelaire and Verlaine. Often one has the feeling that for him creative work is a refuge, that music is a soothing balm, contained in the gently undulating arpeggios and in the frequent rocking rhythms one finds, either in the Barcarolles or in the Requiem, that 'lullaby of death'.

Taxed as he was with being snobbish and frivolous, Fauré was in fact particularly sensitive to the mystery that lies at the heart of music: 'Time and again', he wrote in 1903, 'it is impossible to define the point you have reached or the one you think you are going to. And how many times have I asked myself what music is for? What is it? What am I expressing? What feelings? What ideas? How can I express something which I myself can't analyse!'[7]

Five years later, his reflections on music have progressed to the point where he can make a real profession of faith in a letter to his younger son, Philippe:[8]

The art of imagination consists in trying to formulate all one's desires for the best, everything that goes beyond reality ... For me art, and music above all, consists in lifting us as far as possible above what is.

It is possible to accuse some of Fauré's music of lacking boldness, of staying within a limited scope and cultivating an unvaried reticence. These qualities probably stem from his sharp and painful awareness of the disproportion between the heights of his self-assigned goal ('to formulate all one's desires for the best') and the extreme narrowness of the path which he knew to be his: namely, to give form to that flexible, fleeting, immaterial, almost intangible language which is that of music, at a particularly crucial moment in its evolution – the end of the nineteenth century.

Fauré's art, like that of Proust or Mallarmé, is a product of high culture; it marks the culmination of a centuries-long evolution and, if it does not have the power belonging to ages of conquest and bold pioneering, it is nonetheless determinedly but prudently modern. Certainly we cannot ignore the limits imposed on him by his excessive modesty and by a certain artistic pusillanimity, but at least he should take the credit for having exploited the ambiguities of his character to the point of genius. Fauré's power always to charm and often to move us resides in this gentle melancholy of his, in the feeling of a poignant happiness irradiated by the blazing passion of a true artist.

Chronology

The information assembled here includes the major events of Fauré's life and the composition and first performance of his principal works (a full catalogue can be found on pp. 525–57). Numerous details have been taken from the composer's correspondence, from the programmes of concert societies, publishers' archives and paragraphs in the press. A thorough search of the newspapers between 1875 and 1924 would yield a lot of information about the concerts which the composer gave and about his works. Much remains to be done in this field, which would obviously need a team of researchers and a computer. Among much run-of-the-mill material, the newspapers contain information of the greatest interest, such as the notice of 1881 announcing that Fauré was finishing an opera called *Lizarda* on a libretto by Armand Silvestre and that it would receive its first performance at the Opéra-Comique in 1882. No trace of this score has been found so far.

I have indicated the hotels and villas where the composer stayed, because these details often provide a date for his letters.

1845
12 May: Born at Pamiers (17, rue Major) Gabriel-Urbain Fauré, son of Toussaint Fauré and of Marie-Antoinette de Lalène-Laprade

13 May: Baptised at Notre-Dame du Camp (Pamiers). The child is put out to a wet-nurse at Verniolle

1849
The Fauré family is installed at Montgauzy, near Foix. There Toussaint becomes head of the Ecole normale d'Instituteurs

c. 1850
The child improvises on the harmonium in the chapel; first music lessons with Bernard Delgay

1853
M. Dufaur de Saubiac recommends sending Gabriel to the School of Classical and Religious Music that Louis Niedermeyer is founding in Paris

1854
October: Toussaint Fauré takes Gabriel to Paris and entrusts him to Louis Niedermeyer

1857
Wins prizes in *solfège* and religious instruction

1858
Wins a prize in literary studies

1860
Wins a first prize for piano and a prize for harmony

1861
14 March: Niedermeyer dies. Camille Saint-Saëns is engaged to teach the piano: beginning of a sixty-year friendship with Fauré; Fauré wins an *accessit* for composition. Writes 'Le Papillon et la fleur' op. 1 no. 1, the first in a series of romances to words by Hugo

1862
Wins a *prix d'excellence* for piano and a prize for literary studies
August: Saint-Saëns visits Fauré's family in Tarbes

1863
Wins an *accessit* for organ. For the composition examination writes a *Super flumina* for choir and orchestra (unpublished) which receives an 'honourable mention'

1864
Wins a second prize for plainsong and a second prize for composition for a religious work that has not survived; makes friends with the Garnier family (the prefect of Tarbes)
Trois romances sans paroles, for piano (perhaps written earlier)
'La Chanson dans le jardin' (first version of the 'Berceuse' from *Dolly*)
Allegro de Symphonie for piano duet
May–August: the publisher Choudens negotiates with Victor Hugo over the publication of six romances written by Fauré to his poetry

1865
Wins a first prize for composition with the *Cantique de Jean Racine*
28 July: end of his studies at the Niedermeyer School
Autumn: the director of the school, Gustave Lefèvre, finds him a place as organist at St-Sauveur in Rennes

1866
January: moves to Rennes; lives at 4, rue de Nemours. Gives countless piano lessons
6 February: takes part in a concert at the Grand Théâtre, playing a *Fantaisie sur 'Faust'* by Saint-Saëns
4 August: St-Sauveur, has the *Cantique de Jean Racine* played with string and organ accompaniment (blessing of the St-Sauveur organ)
August: pilgrimage to Sainte-Anne-la-Palud (Brittany) with Saint-Saëns and Regnault. Saint-Saëns dedicates to him his *Trois rhapsodies sur des cantiques bretons* for organ

1868

8 February: Hôtel de Ville at Rennes; has an *Intermezzo pour orchestre* played

19 July: St-Sauveur, performance of a *Cantique à St Vincent de Paul* (now lost)

13 August: Casino at Saint-Malo; takes part in a concert in which he accompanies Mme Miolan-Carvalho; she sings 'Le Papillon et la fleur' which the composer dedicates to her

Takes part in a performance of Gounod's *Faust* at the Grand Théâtre in which he plays the harmonium

1869

16 February: concert with Saint-Saëns

6 March: first contract with Choudens: 'Le Papillon et la fleur', 'Dans les ruines d'une abbaye'

27 April: writes a cadenza for Beethoven's Third Piano Concerto

16 May: transcribes for piano a Gavotte written with a symphony in mind

June: Fugue in A minor for piano

November–December: Prelude and fugue in E minor for piano

1870

March: leaves Rennes for Paris where he becomes choir organist at Notre-Dame de Clignancourt; thanks to Saint-Saëns, meets César Franck, Edouard Lalo, Henri Duparc, Anton Rubinstein

19 July: Franco–Prussian War

16 August: joins the First Light Infantry Regiment of the Imperial Guard

Autumn: sees action at Champigny, Le Bourget, Créteil

1871

28 January: Armistice

25 February: takes part in the founding of the Société nationale de musique; lives at 45, rue des Missions with his brother Amand

9 March: demobilised, becomes organist of St-Honoré d'Eylau. The parish clergy flee the Commune, Fauré escapes to Rambouillet near one of his brothers

3 April: finishes 'L'Absent' (voice and piano)

28 June: goes to Cours-sous-Lausanne where the Niedermeyer School has taken refuge; teaches composition there during the summer; André Messager is his first pupil

20 August: first performance of an *Ave Maria* for men's choir and organ, sung by the choir of the School at the Hospice du Mont-Saint-Bernard

October: returns to Paris where he becomes choir organist at St-Sulpice (earning 80F a month)

17 November: first concert of the Société nationale de musique (SNM)

G. Hartmann publishes a volume of four songs: 'Lydia', 'Hymne', 'Mai' and 'Seule!'

1872

13 January and 23 March: SNM, plays the *Rouet d'Omphale* on two pianos with Saint-Saëns

9 March: SNM, plays an orchestral suite by Duparc on two pianos with Saint-Saëns

Saint-Saëns introduces him into Mme Viardot's salon where he meets Gounod, Renan, George Sand, Flaubert

Autumn: plays the harmonium in the orchestra for *L'Arlésienne* at the Vaudeville

1873

Moves to 19, rue Taranne (now 167, Bd St-Germain, 6ᵉ)

8 February: SNM, first performance of his Symphony in F on two pianos by Saint-Saëns and Fauré (only the first three movements); at the same concert, the first performance of the 'Chanson du pêcheur' by Mme Edouard Lalo

8 March: SNM, plays Saint-Saëns' *Trois rhapsodies bretonnes* on two pianos with the composer

End of the summer: first visit to Marie and Camille Clerc at Sainte-Adresse (le Havre)

19 October: finishes 'Barcarolle', a song dedicated to Pauline Viardot

13 December: SNM, plays *Phaéton* on two pianos with the composer

1874

January: hands over the choir organist's post at St-Sulpice to Messager in order to deputise for Saint-Saëns at the Madeleine during his concert tours

1 March: is upbraided by the committee of the SNM for his 'lamentably remiss behaviour'

21 March: SNM, plays Pauline Viardot's *Introduction et Polonaise* as a piano duet with the composer

16 May: SNM, Salle Herz, Colonne conducts the first orchestral performance of the Symphony in F (four movements)

July: moves to 7, rue de Parme (9ᵉ)

August: with the Clercs at Sainte-Adresse

Mid-September to 10 October: at Tarbes with his parents

1875

First Nocturne for piano

9 January: SNM, plays Saint-Saëns' Third Piano Concerto on two pianos with the composer

10 April: SNM, Claudie and Marianne Viardot give the first performance of the two duos op. 10 which Fauré dedicates to them

15 May: SNM, César Franck conducts the *Cantique de Jean Racine* (dedicated to him) in its orchestral version

August: long visit to the Clercs at Sainte-Adresse; works there on the First Violin Sonata with benefit of advice from the violinist Hubert Léonard

October: to Bagnères-de-Bigorre, then to Tarbes, with his parents

18 December: SNM, plays works by René Lenormand, Mme de Grandval and Saint-Saëns (Overture to *La Princesse jaune* on two pianos, eight hands, in Fauré's transcription)

1876

16 February: SNM, plays with Saint-Saëns his *Variations sur un thème de Beethoven*

21 February and 22 April: SNM, plays with d'Indy a *Suite de valses* for two pianos by Duparc

22 April: SNM, Pauline Viardot sings 'La Chanson du pêcheur' and 'Barcarolle' (both dedicated to her) and first performance of the chorus *Les Djinns* (with piano)

29 April: SNM, plays Saint-Saëns' *Marche héroïque* on two pianos with the composer

30 May: G. Hartmann hands over to Choudens his rights in the four songs he had published

August–September: long visit to the Clercs at Sainte-Adresse. Finishes the First Violin Sonata; begins the First Piano Quartet

October–November: at Tarbes with his parents; First Violin Sonata sent to Breitkopf who accepts it, thanks to the intervention of Camille Clerc

16 December: SNM, takes part in the performance on two pianos of a Suite for Orchestra by Saint-Saëns with Eugène Gigout, Jules Griset, d'Indy and the composer

F. Schoen publishes the *Cantique de Jean Racine*

31 December: first read-through of the First Violin Sonata before the SNM committee

1877

27 January: SNM, first public performance of the First Violin Sonata, Marie Tayau and Fauré; huge success

28 January: another performance of the Sonata at the house of Benjamin Godard

29 January: another performance at Saint-Saëns' Monday soirée

10 February: SNM, with Jules Griset plays three pieces for 'cello and piano by Paul Lacombe

24 February: SNM, plays Saint-Saëns' *Orient et Occident* with d'Indy, and with Théodore Dubois a *Scherzo* for two pianos by Th. Gouvy

End of February: First Violin Sonata published in Leipzig

24 March: SNM, another performance of the Sonata

7 April: the *Journal de Musique* publishes an article on the Sonata by Saint-Saëns

Mid-April: becomes choirmaster at the Madeleine on the recommendation of Saint-Saëns and Gounod. His salary (3,000F a year) makes it necessary for him to give numerous piano and harmony lessons and to accompany amateur choirs. Moves to 13, rue Mosnier in the Batignolles area

30 May: Marianne Viardot and her sister Claudie sing an *Ave Maria* by Fauré at the Madeleine

July: engaged to Pauline Viardot's daughter, Marianne

August: visits Cauterets to take the waters; writes there the *Romance* in B flat for violin

October: Marianne breaks off the engagement

December: journey to Weimar with Saint-Saëns for the first performance of *Samson et Dalila* (2 December)

Choudens publishes 'Lydia', 'Mai', 'Ici bas!', 'Barcarolle', 'Au bord de l'eau'

1878

5 January: SNM, takes part in the performance of a Piano Quartet by Charles Lefebvre, with the violinist Paul Viardot

6 January: performance of 'Après un rêve' before the SNM committee

19 January: SNM, another performance of the First Violin Sonata with Marie Tayau and first performance of 'Au bord de l'eau'; Fauré plays Saint-Saëns' Variations with Laure Donne

16 February: SNM, another performance of *Les Djinns*; with Messager gives the first performance of the *Valses* by Paul Lacombe

Writes 'Nell' (beginning of the second collection of songs) and *Poème d'un jour*; begins a violin concerto

27 June: Trocadéro, Edouard Colonne conducts *Les Djinns* in the version for choir and orchestra (500 performers) in a concert for the Universal Exhibition

5 July: plays the First Violin Sonata with Jean-Pierre Maurin (concerts for the Universal Exhibition)

August: to Villerville to stay with the Clercs; writes an *O Salutaris* and 'Automne'; returns to the Fugue in A minor for piano

28 December: SNM, first performance of the Andante from the Violin Concerto, Ovide Musin and André Messager (piano)

1879

January: Choudens publishes 'Hymne', 'Chant d'automne', 'L'Absent', 'Sérénade toscane'

11 February: Hippodrome, performance of *Les Djinns*

March: corresponds with Flaubert about operatic projects on *Faustine* and *Dolorès*, two plays by L. Bouilhet, librettist: L. Gallet

April: journey to Cologne with Messager to see *Das Rheingold* and *Die Walküre*; pilgrimage to Bonn: Beethoven's house and Schumann's grave

Spring: writes 'Les Berceaux'

July: considers an opera on *Manon Lescaut*; works on the finale of the Violin Concerto; quarrel with Choudens over the First Piano Quartet; Fauré offers it to Durand who turns it down

September: journey to Munich with Messager to see Wagner's *Ring*

Finishes the solo piano version of the Ballade

16 November: first contract with Julien Hamelle: First Piano Quartet, *Berceuse* for violin, three songs op. 18

December: Choudens publishes the first collection of twenty songs

1880

14 February: SNM, first performances of the First Piano Quartet and of the *Berceuse* for violin, with the composer at the piano. Ovide Musin plays the First Violin Sonata

12 April: SNM, Edouard Colonne conducts the first performance with orchestra of the Violin Concerto (Allegro and Andante), with Ovide Musin as soloist. The work was not completed and remained unpublished

24 April: SNM, first performance of the *Berceuse* with orchestra (Ovide Musin as soloist)

15 May: SNM, gives another performance of the First Piano Quartet

21 June: at Saint-Saëns' house, first performance of the *Elégie* for 'cello

15 July: contract with Hamelle for the Ballade (solo piano) and the *Trois Romances sans paroles* (1863–4)

18–20 July: second journey to Munich in the company of Théodore Dubois: hears *Die Meistersinger*, *Tannhäuser* and Goethe's *Egmont* with music by Beethoven

November: Durand publishes *Poème d'un jour* in a single volume

1881

Writes 'Le Secret'

29 January: SNM, Henriette Fuchs sings first performances of 'Nell' and 'Automne', M. Mazalbert does so for *Poème d'un jour*

21 February: SNM, plays Saint-Saëns' *Suite algérienne* with the composer in Fauré's piano duet transcription

16 March: first read-through of the orchestral version of the Ballade before the SNM committee

23 April: SNM, plays the solo part in the first performance of the orchestral version of the Ballade, conducted by Edouard Colonne

Works on *Lizarda*, an opéra-comique in three acts, libretto by Armand Silvestre, announced for the 1881–2 season at the Opéra-Comique

August: stays with the Clercs at Villerville

4 September: church at Villerville, first performance of the *Messe des pêcheurs de Villerville*, written in collaboration with Messager

21–26 September: third journey to Munich, with the Baugnies: *Lohengrin*, *Tristan*, *Die Meistersinger*

Conducts the choral society 'La Lyre', of which Marguerite Baugnies is patron

1882

14 January: SNM, first performance of *Le Ruisseau* by Pauline Roger's choral group

28 January: SNM, First Violin Sonata with Léon Heymann; plays the overture to Saint-Saëns' *La Princesse jaune* with E. Bernard, Marie Jaëll and Mme Ferrand

5–10 May: in London, with Messager and Camille Clerc, for *The Ring* sung by artists from Bayreuth

Beginning of July: journey to Zürich with Saint-Saëns; second meeting with Liszt; hears *La Légende de Sainte Elisabeth*

September: final stay Villerville with the Clercs

10 September: church at Villerville, performance of the *Messe des pêcheurs* with chamber orchestra

Mid-September: at Toulouse with his parents

Autumn: receives a commission from the Société chorale d'amateurs run by A. Guillot de Sainbris: *La Naissance de Vénus*, a 'scène mythologique' by Paul Collin

25 November: death of Camille Clerc

9 December: SNM, Saint-Saëns gives the first performance of the First Impromptu and of the First Barcarolle for piano

1883

8 March: the Société chorale d'amateurs gives the first performance of *La Naissance de Vénus* with Franck and Fauré at the piano

27 March: marries Marie Fremiet, daughter of the sculptor Emmanuel Fremiet

Spring: the Faurés move into 93, avenue Niel (17e)

May: writes Second Impromptu for piano

Summer: writes a new finale for First Piano Quartet

1 December: finishes the 'Madrigal' for four voices dedicated to Messager

15 December: SNM, first performance of the *Elégie* by Jules Loeb and Fauré

29 December: birth of his elder son, Emmanuel

1884

January: Hamelle publishes the first three Nocturnes for piano

9 February: SNM, plays Saint-Saëns' *La Jeunesse d'Hercule* with Messager

5 April: SNM, plays the First Piano Quartet (first performance with the new finale)

Summer: at Prunay (Louveciennes) with his parents-in-law the Fremiets

July: completes second *Valse-Caprice*; works at Symphony in D minor

13 December: SNM, Marguerite Mauvernay gives first performances of 'Aurore', 'Fleur jetée' (both written in May); performance by eight voices of *Madrigal*, op. 35

27 December: Thérèse Guyon gives first performance of 'Le Pays des rêves' and 'Les Roses d'Ispahan', written the same year

1885

10 January: SNM, Saint-Saëns gives first performance of Second and Third Impromptus

7 February: SNM, plays Chabrier's *España* with Messager

15 March: SNM, at the Châtelet, Colonne gives first performance of Symphony in D minor; rather cool reception

4 April: SNM, Henri Marsick and Saint-Saëns play First Violin Sonata

25 July: death of Toussaint Fauré in Toulouse

Early August: journey to Anvers (Universal Exhibition) to conduct Symphony in D minor; performance postponed until October

Mid-August: stays at the Hôtel de la promenade in Néris-les-Bains (Marie Fauré takes the waters)

Project for *Mazeppa* on a libretto by Ernest Dupuy

14 October: d'Indy conducts Symphony in D minor at Anvers (French festival)

Receives Prix Chartier from the Institut for his chamber music

1886

Writes 'Nocturne' (song), Fourth Barcarolle and finishes Second Piano Quartet

Makes acquaintance of Robert de Montesquiou who becomes his 'literary adviser'

3 April: SNM, plays Saint-Saëns' *Polonaise* for two pianos with the composer

June: meets Tchaikovsky in Paris; the Russian composer finds his First Piano Quartet 'excellent'

October: moves to 154, Bd Malesherbes (17ᵉ)

1887

22 January: SNM, first performance of Second Piano Quartet with Fauré playing piano part

16 April: SNM, plays Schumann's *Märchenbilder* with van Waefelghem

26 April: 'Audition de mélodies de Fauré' at the house of Robert de Montesquiou

August: brief stay in Dieppe with Elisabeth Greffulhe

Mid-August to November: stays at Le Vésinet: *Pavane*, 'Les Présents', 'Clair de lune' (first setting of Verlaine, to whose poetry Montesquiou introduced him)

15 September and 1 October: H. Imbert interviews Fauré and publishes the first study devoted to him in *L'Indépendance musicale et dramatique*

Mid-November: Jacques-Emile Blanche paints his portrait. Sketches for the Requiem

31 December: death of his mother, Hélène Fauré

1888

16 January: church of the Madeleine, conducts first performance of Requiem (still incomplete) for the funeral of the architect M. Lesoufaché

1 February: another performance of the Requiem at the Madeleine

4 February: SNM, plays Second Piano Quartet

3 March: first Brussels concert, by invitation of Octave Maus; plays First Violin Sonata and First Piano Quartet with Ysaÿe

15 March: second meeting with Tchaikovsky in Paris; gives him a score of Second Piano Quartet

28 April: SNM, first performance of orchestral version of *Clair de lune* by Maurice Bagès and of the choral version of the *Pavane*

4 May: first performance of Requiem outside liturgical context; brass added to string orchestra

8 and 15 May: at Winnaretta Singer's house, plays harmonium part in extracts from Chabrier's *Gwendoline*

End July: first pilgrimage to Bayreuth, with Messager: *Die Meistersinger*, *Parsifal*; meets Debussy and Pierre de Bréville there; is welcomed by Wagner's family

Summer: at Prunay

November: finishes 'Larmes', 'Au cimetière', 'Spleen' (Verlaine)

6 November: at the Odéon, revival of *Caligula* by Alexandre Dumas père, incidental music by Fauré for chorus and orchestra (thirty-four performances)

25 November: Charles Lamoureux conducts the *Pavane* with great success

1889

2 February: SNM, plays Second Piano Quartet

16 February: SNM, takes part in performance of Venusberg scene from *Tann-häuser* with Chevillard, d'Indy and Paul Vidal (two pianos eight hands)

25 February: in Brussels plays Second Piano Quartet with Ysaÿe quartet; d'Indy conducts 'Madrigal' and *Caligula*

6 April: SNM, first concert performance of *Caligula* in presence of Tchaikovsky, who finds it 'adorable'

23 May: Trocadéro, Lamoureux conducts Andante from Symphony in D minor (last hearing of this work before Fauré destroyed it)

10 June: Trocadéro, plays organ in performance of *Messiah* by Société philanthropique

John Singer Sargent paints his portrait; writes Offertorium (baritone solo) for Requiem; meets Glazunov, come to conduct his music in Paris (Universal Exhibition)

Summer: at Prunay, where younger son Philippe born, 28 July

Writes incidental music for Haraucourt's *Shylock*

End September: short stay with Comtesse Greffulhe at Bois-Boudran (Seine-et-Marne)

17 December: Odéon, conducts orchestra in première of *Shylock*

1890

Winnaretta Singer commissions an opera from him to inaugurate her music-room in rue Cortambert; she offers him 25,000F, allowing him to choose text

March: writes music for Haraucourt's *La Passion*; the Prelude with chorus, all that is written, conducted by d'Indy (SNM) 21 April

Summer: at Prunay with parents-in-law; completes 'La Rose', August

End July: to Munich; attends performance of Passion at Oberammergau

26 (or 28?) August: Aix-les-Bains, Colonne conducts recently orchestrated version of 'Les Roses d'Ispahan'

Autumn: Hamelle republishes first collection of *mélodies* in two versions (high voice, medium voice)

28 December: Colonne conducts orchestral version of *En prière*

1891

January: asks Verlaine for libretto for work commissioned by Winnaretta Singer
Works at Piano Quintet

15 March: *Caligula* at Société des concerts du Conservatoire

End May: stays with Winnaretta Singer in Palazzo Volkoff, Venice; writes 'Mandoline'

20 June: returns to Paris after stopping off in Florence and Genoa; finishes 'En sourdine'

21 July: evening party given by Comtesse de Greffulhe in Bois de Boulogne: the *Pavane* danced and sung

23 July: finishes 'Green'

August: writes 'A Clymène'

21 August: goes with family to Chatou

September: writes 'C'est l'extase', finishing set of 'Venice' songs on poems by Verlaine

26 December: SNM, plays Second Piano Quartet and, with d'Indy, Grieg's *Romance and Variations*

1892

Albert Samain writes for him a libretto commissioned by Winnaretta Singer: *La Tentation de Bouddha*

28 January: SNM, Church of St-Gervais, Louis Ballard sings in first performance of 'Libera me' added to Requiem

2 April: SNM, Maurice Bagès gives first performance of 'Venice' songs

30 April: SNM, orchestral concert under patronage of Winnaretta Singer: *Madrigal, Clair de lune, Pavane*

1 June: appointed inspector of musical instruction (until 1905)

Summer: candidature for Professor of Composition at Conservatoire blocked by Ambroise Thomas

At Prunay. Meets Emma Bardac

17 September: 'Une sainte en son auréole', first song of *La Bonne chanson*, Verlaine cycle inspired by Emma Bardac

27 November: Lamoureux conducts composer's orchestration of 'La Chanson du pêcheur'

1893

Receives Prix Chartier a second time for chamber music

21 January: church of the Madeleine, performance of Requiem

February–March: begins incidental music for *Le Bourgeois gentilhomme* (never staged)

April: plans *Lavallière* with Catulle Mendès, with support from Elisabeth Greffulhe

Summer: at Prunay, finishes Third *Valse-Caprice*, begins Fourth

May–December: continues work on *La Bonne chanson* (nos 2, 3, 8, 5)

27 September: at Madeleine, plays organ at Gounod's funeral (improvises on theme from Gounod's *Rédemption*)

1894

20 January: SNM, plays Second Piano Quartet

February: finishes *La Bonne chanson*

17 February: SNM, Edouard Risler plays Third Barcarolle, Second and Third Impromptus, *Romances sans paroles*, First *Valse-Caprice*

April: Hamelle publishes *La Bonne chanson*

12 April: Ecole des Beaux-Arts, first performance of the *Hymne à Apollon* discovered by Reinach at Delphi and harmonised by Fauré

25 April: first performance of *La Bonne chanson* at house of the Comte de Saussine (Bagès, Fauré)

17 May: Théâtre de la Bodinière, Eugène d'Harcourt conducts extracts from Requiem

19 May: Beaten by Théodore Dubois for seat in Institut (twenty votes for Dubois, four for Fauré)

Summer: to Prunay, returns to Piano Quintet

July: short stay with d'Eichthals, starts Sixth Nocturne, finished 3 August at Prunay

14 August: writes *Tantum ergo* op. 65 no. 2 for three voices

18 September: finishes Fifth Barcarolle at Prunay

17 October: La Madeleine, conducts Gounod's Requiem (second performance)

14 November: Fauré Festival at Geneva Conservatory, organised by Jaques-Dalcroze; plays First Piano Quartet, First Violin Sonata, first performance of *Romance* for 'cello, songs

22 November: London, concert at St James's Hall: First Piano Quartet, First Violin Sonata

Jean Thorel, helped by Adolphe Appia, writes for him a libretto on Lamotte Fouqué's *Ondine*, commissioned by Comtesse de Greffulhe

4 December: finishes 'Prison', last song on poem by Verlaine

17 December: finishes 'Soir', on poem by Samain

1895

February: orchestrates *Elégie* at request of Colonne

3 and 17 March: Colonne conducts *Shylock*

23 March: SNM, Gustave Doret conducts *Shylock*

12 May: Fauré's fiftieth birthday

Summer: stays in Paris to try and obtain post as music critic on *Le Figaro*; post goes to Alfred Bruneau

Spends two weeks at Dieppe

September: finishes *Thème et variations* for piano

Orchestrates *La Naissance de Vénus* at request of Colonne

End November: journey to London; discussions with publisher Metzler about propagation of his music in Great Britain; concert

1 December: Colonne conducts first orchestral performance of *La Naissance de Vénus*

29 December: Paris Opéra, *Pavane* danced as part of an evening of 'ancient dances'

1896

10 January: plays organ at Verlaine's funeral

15 January: contract with Metzler in London who publishes Sixth Barcarolle, March

21 April: finishes duet 'Pleurs d'or' (Samain)

End April: journey to London: 29 April, Sargent draws his portrait; 1 May, concert given by David Bispham and Camille Landi: first performance of *Pleurs d'or* which Fauré dedicates to them; plays First Piano Quartet

2 May: SNM, Léon Delafosse gives first performance of Fourth *Valse-Caprice*

and Fifth Barcarolle; another failure at Institut: Charles Lenepveu elected with nineteen votes against Fauré's four

Quarrels with Hamelle; Fromont publishes 'Prison' and 'Soir' in June

2 June: leaves post as choirmaster of Madeleine to become organist

4–13 August: second pilgrimage to Bayreuth, where he joins party of Princesse Edmond de Polignac (Winnaretta Singer); hears *The Ring*

15(?)–27 September: at Sainte-Lunaire (Brittany) with his English friends the Maddisons; finishes *Dolly* Suite for piano duet

1 October: succeeds Massenet as Professor of Composition at Conservatoire; teaches a number of composers, including Ravel, Schmitt, Koechlin, Enesco, Nadia Boulanger and Emile Vuillermoz

10 December: London (St James's Hall), Fauré Festival: plays Second Piano Quartet, Léon Delafosse gives first performance of *Thème et variations*; Fauré plays with him Second and Fourth *Valses-Caprices*, transcribed by Delafosse for two pianos

Metzler in London publishes six songs in English translations (including 'Pleurs d'or')

19 December: London (St James's Hall), plays First Violin Sonata with Johannes Wolf

1897

February: Hamelle publishes *Thème et variations*

March– December: Metzler in London publishes twelve songs in English translations as well as *Dolly* (March) and *Thème et variations* (August)

3 April: SNM, Edouard Risler gives first performance of Sixth Barcarolle and fourth *Valse-Caprice*, and Thérèse Roger of 'Prison' and 'Soir'

18 May: SNM, Thérèse Roger sings 'Les Roses d'Ispahan' with orchestra

June: Hamelle publishes second collection of songs

July: Andante in B flat for Violin and Piano (probably from the unpublished Concerto)

22 August: Paris, finishes 'Le Parfum impérissable' (Leconte de Lisle)

6 September: finishes 'Arpège' (Samain)

4 November: Emile Engel gives first performance of 'Le Parfum impérissable'

1898

January: Ravel enters his composition class at the Conservatoire

30 April: SNM, first performance of *Dolly* by Edouard Risler and Alfred Cortot

28 March–7 April: stays in London with Leo Frank Schuster; Mrs Patrick Campbell commissions him to write incidental music for Maeterlinck's *Pelléas et Mélisande*; 1 April at Schuster's house, first performance of *La Bonne chanson* with piano and string quintet (Maurice Bagès)

May–June: writes music for *Pelléas et Mélisande* in English translation by J. W. Mackail and has Koechlin orchestrate it for small orchestra

21 June: London, Prince of Wales Theatre, conducts orchestra for première of *Pelléas et Mélisande* (nine performances until 1 July; great success)

26 June: new portraits (charcoal) by Sargent

July: Saint-Saëns dedicates to him first of *Three Preludes and Fugues* op. 109 for organ

August: stays with Mrs George Swinton, Llandough Castle (Wales); finishes Seventh Nocturne for piano, dedicated to his English pupil and admirer, Adela Maddison

8 October: London (Lyceum), revival of *Pelléas et Mélisande*

1899

5 and 12 February: *La Naissance de Vénus* at the Société des concerts du Conservatoire

18 February: SNM, plays Second Piano Quartet and accompanies Bagès in *La Bonne chanson*

24 March: Salle d'horticulture, Jules Griset conducts Requiem (small orchestra)

27 and 29 August: Béziers, conducts revival of Saint-Saëns' *Déjanire* in amphitheatre; F. Castelbon de Beauxhostes, Béziers philanthropist, commissions a work from him for 1900

12 September: contract with Hamelle for Requiem, which has been rescored for full orchestra

24–26 September: stays with Mme de Saint-Marceaux (Marguerite Baugnies) at Cuy-Saint-Fiacre (Seine Maritime), in company with Adela Maddison

1900

February: Hamelle publishes vocal score of Requiem in reduction by Roger-Ducasse

6 February: Brussels, plays Second Piano Quartet and First Violin Sonata with Jacques Thibaud

24 February: SNM, plays First Violin Sonata with Jacques Thibaud

Spring: writes *Prométhée* for Béziers amphitheatre (libretto by Jean Lorrain and A. F. Hérold)

Maeterlinck suggests that he set a libretto *Sœur Béatrice*; works on it until 1902

6 May: Lille, a M. Maquez conducts the Requiem (170 performers)

12 July: Trocadéro (Universal Exhibition), first official performance of full orchestra version of Requiem, conducted by Paul Taffanel (250 performers)

6–31 August: at Béziers for première of *Prométhée* in amphitheatre

26 August: a storm postpones première of *Prométhée* until following day

27–28 August: *Prométhée* given before 15,000 enthusiastic spectators. Saint-Saëns says, 'you've buried the lot of us, me included'. Meets Marguerite Hasselmans who becomes his companion until the end of his life

Early September: rests at Bagnères-de-Bigorre with his brother Fernand

20 October: in Brussels where Ysaÿe conducts Requiem: a cool reception

November: receives Pinetti prize from Institut for *Prométhée*: 3,000F to be shared with Gustave Charpentier for *Louise*

Turns music for *Pelléas* into a suite and reworks it for full orchestra

1901

11 January: Salle Pleyel, Fauré Festival with the Parent Quartet: plays two piano quartets and accompanies various songs sung by Jane Arger

3 February: Chevillard conducts the orchestral suite *Pelléas et Mélisande*, first Paris performance (the 'Fileuse' is encored)

6 April: Société des concerts du Conservatoire, Paul Taffanel conducts Requiem: a revelatory performance

13 April: SNM, Ricardo Viñes plays First Barcarolle

25 April: Théâtre du Vaudeville, André Messager conducts *Pelléas* suite

26 April: SNM, Pablo Casals plays *Elégie*, conducted by composer

20 June: Neuilly, Pavillon des Muses, Robert de Montesquiou gives a reception in honour of Fauré who accompanies Maurice Bagès, Félia Litvinne and Victor Maurel

August: to Béziers for revival of *Prométhée* (25 and 27) – 11–13 August: returns briefly to Paris for funeral of Prince Edmond de Polignac (who leaves him 10,000F)

31 August–5 September: at Bagnères-de-Bigorre

September–October: stays with his family at Garches

September: Hamelle publishes orchestral score of Requiem; this same year scores come out of the *Elégie, Ballade, Pavane, Pelléas et Mélisande*

4 November: Théâtre Firmin Gémier, *Le Voile du bonheur*, play by Georges Clemenceau with 'Chinese' incidental music by Fauré

11 November: Ravel dedicates *Jeux d'eau* to him

1902

22 February: performance of *Prométhée* at the Girettes in Paris, accompanied on two pianos by Mme Girette and Fauré

2 March: Salle Erard, accompanies Emilie Girette in 'Aurore', 'Les Roses d'Is-pahan', 'Automne', 'Les Berceaux' as well as 'Gretchen am Spinnrade' (Schubert)

23 March: Angers, conducts *Pelléas* and *Pavane* at Société des concerts popu-laires

25 March: Fauré Festival at the Girettes: *Cantique de Jean Racine, Tantum ergo* op. 55, *Dolly* (Cortot and Fauré), *La Bonne chanson* (Bagès), Requiem (with organ)

28 March: finishes 'Accompagnement' (Samain), song written for Emilie Girette

April–May: goes to hear a number of performances of Debussy's *Pelléas* at Opéra-Comique

5 April: SNM, Ricardo Viñes plays *Thème et variations*

Mid–June: a 'Fête galante' sung and danced at Madeleine Lemaire's, with music by Fauré

13–21 August: at Béziers, première of Saint-Saëns' *Parysatis* (17 and 19)

4 September: finishes volume of *Huit pièces brèves* for piano

13 September: finishes 'La Fleur qui va sur l'eau' (Catulle Mendès)

29 September: finishes 'Dans la forêt de septembre' (Mendès)

Autumn: starts to rework *Prométhée* for normal symphony orchestra: plans to perform it at Théâtre Sarah Bernhardt under Cortot (Société des grandes auditions)

1903

18 January: Salle Humbert de Romans (Passy), conducts *Pelléas*, Ballade (Isidore Philipp), 'En prière' and 'Clair de lune' (Jane Arger), *Elégie* (Louis Hasselmans)

20 February: Angers, hears Casals play *Elégie* (Concerts populaires)

2 March: publishes first review in *Le Figaro*

5 April: made Officier de la Légion d'honneur

20 April: Fauré Festival at the 'five o'clock' concert of *Le Figaro*

Summer: first sign of hearing problems

1–6 August: Aix-les-Bains; 5: conducts *Pelléas*, *Pavane*, 'Clair de lune', 'En prière' at Le Cercle

7–8 August: Thonon-les-Bains

9 August–3 September: first summer holiday at Lausanne; returns to work on quintet with piano sketched out between 1890 and 1894

Ravel dedicates String Quartet to him

1904

1 March: Angers, goes to hear *Pelléas* suite

July: writes a sight-reading piece for Conservatoire and Impromptu for harp. London, revival of Maeterlinck's *Pelléas* with Sarah Bernhardt as Pelléas. Debussy goes to a performance with Mary Garden

10–11 August: Aix-les-Bains, conducts *Caligula*, *Les Djinns*, 'Madrigal'

12 August–4 October: Zürich (Pension Sternwarte), works at length on First Quintet

1905

7 January: SNM, Micheline Kahn gives first performance of Impromptu for harp; Marguerite Long plays three piano pieces

9–11 January: Cologne, 10: First Violin Sonata and First Piano Quartet

12–16 January: Frankfurt, 13: concert; 15: visits Frau Somanhof, Schumann's daughter

17–18 January: Strasbourg

Writes Fourth Impromptu

12 May: Fauré's sixtieth birthday

15 June: appointed Director of Conservatoire with effect from 1 October at annual salary of 12,000F

11 July: contract with Heugel with effect from 1 January 1906

6 August–19 September: stays in Zürich (Pension Sternwarte); writes Seventh Barcarolle and works on First Quintet; strikes up friendship with Albéniz family

7 August: Amphitheatre, Orange, Colonne conducts *Jules César*, incidental music (based on *Caligula*) for Shakespeare's tragedy

1 October: plays for last time on organ of the Madeleine; succeeded by Henri Dallier

1906

January: finishes First Quintet

28 January: orchestral version of *Cantique de Jean Racine* at Société des concerts du Conservatoire

3 February: Salle Erard, Arnold Reitlinger gives first performance of Seventh Barcarolle

2 March: Cercle musical: Fauré Festival, plays in First Violin Sonata, First Piano Quartet, *Elégie* and six songs (Mme Mellot Joubert)

19–23 March: Brussels, 20: at Octave Maus's: *Dolly* (with Blanche Selva), both Piano Quartets, songs; that evening, at Anna Boch's: Requiem, 'Madrigal'; 23: first performance of First Quintet with Ysaÿe and his quartet (the work is dedicated to him); Albert Mockel introduces him to *La Chanson d'Eve* by Charles van Lerberghe

24–25 March: at Conservatoire in Gand

30 April: Salle Pleyel, first Paris performance of First Quintet with Ysaÿe Quartet

15 May: SNM, Fauré Festival: First Quintet, *Thème et variations*, Sixth Nocturne, Third Barcarolle (Marguerite Long), *La Bonne chanson* (Jane Bathori, Fauré), First Violin Sonata (Lucien Capet, Fauré)

4 June: finishes 'Crépuscule', first song to be written of cycle *La Chanson d'Eve*

Early August: brief stay in Lucerne

7–26 August: stays at Vitznau, Lac des Quatre cantons (Hôtel Vitznauerhof), writes duet *Ave Maria* and 'Le Don silencieux' (Jean Dominique)

27–30 August: Pallanza, 30: meets Giordano by Lake Maggiore

31 August–23 September: Stresa (Hôtel des Iles Borromées), works on *La Chanson d'Eve*: 8 September, finishes 'Paradis'

24 September–3 October: ill, stays in Lausanne (Hôtel Beausite); 28 September: finishes 'Prima verba'

December: revises *Messe des pêcheurs de Villerville* and publishes extracts with Heugel under title *Messe basse*

1907

First Quintet published by Schirmer in New York

12 January: SNM, Edouard Risler gives first performance of Fourth Impromptu and Eighth Barcarolle; at same concert, performance of First Quintet, after the, riotously received, first performance of Ravel's *Histoires naturelles*, sung by Jane Bathori

20 January: concert at house of Princesse de Polignac

February: in Monte Carlo, Lucienne Bréval asks him to write opera for her on subject of Penelope, in collaboration with René Fauchois: Raoul Gunsbourg promises to put opera on at Monte Carlo

12 March: Brussels, Jane Bathori sings 'Le Don silencieux' for first time

1 July: Proust gives dinner at Ritz in honour of Fauré, who is ill and does not attend: Risler plays a Nocturne, Mme Hasselmans accompanies Maurice Hayot in First Violin Sonata and *Berceuse*

26 July–6 October: Lausanne (Hôtel Mont Fleuri), begins *Pénélope*; end of August, visit from Paul Dukas who becomes a friend; 25 September, hears *Pelléas* suite in Lausanne

December: Castelbon de Beauxhostes organises two performances of *Prométhée* in Paris, at Hippodrome (5) and at Opéra (15)

1908

19 January: Marguerite Long plays Ballade at Société des concerts du Conservatoire

February: concert in Milan

14–23 March: in London, with Leo Schuster; 17: Bechstein Hall, Ballade on two pianos, songs sung by Jeanne Raunay, including *La Bonne chanson* and three songs from *La Chanson d'Eve*; 20: accompanies Jeanne Raunay before Prince and Princess of Wales; 22: at Schuster's, plays Second Piano Quartet with Lucien Capet, and Risler plays some Nocturnes; 23: accompanies Susan Metcalfe for Queen Alexandra at Buckingham Palace

June: finishes 'Roses ardentes' and 'L'Aube blanche' (*La Chanson d'Eve*); Hamelle publishes third collection of songs

31 July–4 October: Lausanne (Hôtel Cecil); 9–11 August: takes his son Emmanuel to Argentière for a stay in the mountains; 24–26 August: to Lucerne to conduct *Pelléas*; 15 September: finishes Tenth Nocturne; works at Act I of *Pénélope*, sketches Act II

21–27 November: concerts in Berlin: Second Piano Quartet, songs

28 November–5 December: in Great Britain; 30 November, Manchester: First Piano Quartet, First Violin Sonata, songs; 1 December, London: Ballade, First Piano Quartet on two pianos; 5 December, London, accompanies Mrs Swinton in his songs

December: Albéniz procures for him the Order of Isabella the Catholic

1909

1 January: new contract with Heugel for three following years; separate contract for *Pénélope*

March: concerts in Barcelona, 11: *Shylock*, *Caligula*, Requiem; 14: Ballade (Mme Long), Requiem, piano pieces, songs

13 March: elected to Institut

30 March: Salle Erard, Marguerite Long gives Fauré recital: first performance of Ninth Barcarolle and Fifth Impromptu; Fauré accompanies Ballade

18 May: death of Albéniz at Cambo; Fauré's Requiem played at his funeral

26 May: Salle Erard, accompanies Jeanne Raunay in seven songs from *La Chanson d'Eve*

19 July–early October: Lugano (Hôtel Métropole et Monopole), writes final songs of *La Chanson d'Eve*; works on Act II of *Pénélope*; concerts at M. Lombard's in Trevano; visits Milan, Vicenza, Verona, meets D'Annunzio

Autumn: writes first three Preludes for piano

His old pupils found Société musicale indépendante, in opposition to Société nationale de musique. Fauré is elected president of SMI

1910

January: 'O Mort poussière d'étoiles' (final song of *La Chanson d'Eve*)

End March: at Portofino

4–9 April: to Monte Carlo where (7) he conducts *Pelléas* and *Shylock*

24 March: Société des concerts du Conservatoire, Messager conducts Requiem

April: *La Chanson d'Eve* published by Heugel in single volume

10 April: first concert of SMI, accompanies Jeanne Raunay in *La Chanson
d'Eve* (first complete performance)

17 May: SMI, Marguerite Long gives first performance of Preludes 1 to 3

20 July: directorship of Conservatoire renewed for five years

17 July–8 September: Lugano (Hôtel Métropole), 9–25 August: takes waters
for his hearing at Bad Ems (Königl Hotel); writes Preludes 4–7

11 September: death of father-in-law, Emmanuel Fremiet

12–13 November: concerts in St Petersburg: conducts *Shylock*, plays First
Quintet with Capet Quartet, songs sung by Maria Kousnezoff. Glazunov organises
a triumphant reception for him at Conservatory

16 November: concert in Helsinki: First Violin Sonata, Second Piano Quartet,
First Quintet

18 and 19 November: concerts in Moscow: First Violin Sonata with Ysaÿe,
Second Piano Quartet with members of Capet Quartet; conducts *Pelléas*

23 November: returns to Paris

29 December: made Commandeur de la Légion d'honneur

1911

Hamelle publishes volume of Fauré's *Musique religieuse*

April: moves to 32 rue des Vignes (16ᵉ)

21 July–4 October: Lugano (Hôtel Métropole), recasts Act II and finishes Act I
of *Pénélope*

1912

18 February: in Marseilles conducts *Pelléas*, Ballade, three songs sung by G.
Sanderson

9 March: SNM, accompanies Jeanne Raunay in *La Chanson d'Eve* and Venice
songs

2–24 April: Hyères, works on Act III of *Pénélope*

Spring: corrects proofs of Acts I and II of vocal score of *Pénélope*

8 May: Brussels, conducts *Pelléas* as part of homage to Maeterlinck

24 July–17 October: Lugano, finishes composition of *Pénélope* on 31 August;
begins orchestration of Act I; end September, visit from Lucienne Bréval who reads
through her part accompanied by Cortot

17 November: read-through of *Pénélope* in apartment of Mme Hasselmans

1 December: Société des concerts, Messager conducts *Pelléas*, now including
Sicilienne

19 December–12 January: Monte Carlo, finishes orchestration of *Pénélope* with
help of Fernand Pécoud

1913

Early January: Monte Carlo, first orchestral read-through of Act I of *Pénélope*

9 January: Théâtre des Arts, Paris, première of ballet on *Dolly Suite*, orchestrated by Henri Rabaud, scenario by Louis Laloy

9 February: read-through of *Pénélope* in Fauré's office at Conservatoire with
Cortot at piano

18 February–6 March: Monte Carlo (Hôtel du Helder)

4 March: Théâtre de Monte Carlo, première of *Pénélope* with Lucienne Bréval, Charles Rousselière, conducted by Léon Jehin

10 May: Théâtre des Champs-Elysées, triumphant Paris première of *Pénélope* with Lucienne Bréval, Lucien Muratore, sets by Ker-Xavier Roussel

26 June: 11th and final performance of *Pénélope* (end of Astruc's season)

26 June: contract with Jacques Durand

Mid-July: at Ouchy

25 July–11 September: Lugano, begins Tenth Barcarolle, reads van Lerberghe's *Entrevisions*

September: Heugel publishes orchestral score of *Pénélope*

12–21(?) September: Lausanne (Hôtel Beau Site)

2 October: reopening of Théâtre des Champs-Elysées with *Pénélope* (6 performances)

6 November: closure of Théâtre des Champs-Elysées (Astruc bankrupt)

Autumn: makes five piano rolls in Paris for Welte Mignon

1 December: Brussels, première of *Pénélope* at Théâtre de la Monnaie, with Claire Croiza

1914

February: Louis Vuillemin publishes first biography of Fauré

March: asks Roger-Ducasse to arrange *Prométhée* for full symphony orchestra

Negotiations with Gheusi for revival of *Pénélope* at Opéra-Comique

Paris, 29 April, 6, 13, 20 May, then 16, 19, 22 June: London, Aeolian Hall, takes part in performances of complete piano works by Robert Lortat

21–30 July: to Ems to take waters again, writes opening songs of *Le Jardin clos* (Charles van Lerberghe)

2 August: start of First World War; his younger son Philippe joins up (Verdun, Salonica)

31 July, 1, 2 August: difficult crossing of German frontier with Switzerland (St-Louis, Basle)

Early August: to Geneva (Pension Sutterlin), then returns to Paris

October: stays at Pau (Grand Hôtel du Palais), where brother Fernand lives

Autumn: finishes *Le Jardin clos*

Re-opening of Conservatoire

1915

28 January: Concerts Casella, accompanies Croiza in first performance of *Le Jardin clos* published in May by Durand

12 May: Fauré's seventieth birthday

30 July–19 September: first summer holiday in Midi, at St-Raphaël (pension 'le Gui'); writes Twelfth Nocturne and Twelfth Barcarolle; revises Schumann's piano works for Durand (thirty-seven volumes up to 1924)

21 September: his duties as Director of Conservatoire extended 'for the duration of the war'

Durand publishes an edition of Bach's 48 made by Fauré, with fingerings by Marguerite Long

1916

Works with Joseph Bonnet and Eugène Gigout on a revised edition of Bach's organ works for Durand (thirteen volumes up to 1920)

9 August–end September: Evian (Villa Saffrettes), writes two outer movements of Second Violin Sonata; 19 August, concert for Red Cross at Casino (First Violin Sonata, songs)

21 August: Ballets russes give première at San Sebastian of *Las Meninas*, Massine's ballet on *Pavane*, conducted by Ansermet

23 November: Concerts Jacques Durand, Louis Diémer gives first performance of Twelfth Nocturne and Twelfth Barcarolle (which is dedicated to him)

17 December: unsuccessful attempt to bring together rival societies of Société nationale and SMI

1917

Elected President of Société nationale de musique

February: stays at Nice

15 March: publishes in *Le Courrier musical* an 'Appel aux musiciens français' asking them to come together

May: finishes Second Violin Sonata

17 May: Paris Opéra, *Prométhée* in Roger-Ducasse's reorchestration (three performances); begins 'Cello Sonata

25 and 26 May: Ballets russes perform *Las Meninas* at Châtelet

19 July–mid-September: St-Raphaël (Pension 'le Gui'), finishes First 'Cello Sonata; revises orchestration of *Pénélope*

10 November: concerts for reopening of SNM, Lucien Capet and Alfred Cortot give first performance of Second Violin Sonata

9 December: Société des concerts, Messager conducts Prelude from *Pénélope*

1918

19 January: SNM, André Hekking and Cortot give first performance of First 'Cello Sonata

Mid-February–8 April: stays at Nice to recover from severe bronchitis

28 February: death of brother Fernand at Pau

9–10 April: Toulon, charity concert

12–18 April: Toulouse: 14: concert; then pilgrimage to Gailhac-Toulza and Pamiers

19 April: rejoins wife at Châteauroux, then returns to Paris

Early July–27 September: Evian (Villa Beaurivage); writes *Fantaisie* for piano and orchestra

Early September: visit of son Philippe on leave; Albert I of Monaco commissions him to write a stage work for the theatre at Monte Carlo

28 September: returns to Paris, stays at Hôtel Windsor (Marie Fauré is in Ariège)

October: death of his brother Amand

20 October: Albert Carré comes to ask his permission for *Pénélope* to be revived at the Opéra-Comique

3 November: SNM, Micheline Kahn gives first performance of *Une Châtelaine en sa tour*

11 November: armistice

1919

20 January: revival of *Pénélope* at Opéra-Comique, with Germaine Lubin and Lucien Muratore: sixty-three performances up until 1931

6 February: concert in Bordeaux

7 February: concert in Pau

9 February: concert in Toulouse

Mid-February–20 March: Menton (Hôtel Balmoral), writes *Masques et bergamasques*

21 March–mid-April: Monte Carlo (Hôtel de la Terrasse); 10 April: première in Monte Carlo of *Masques et bergamasques* (great success); 12: unofficial first performance of *Fantaisie* for piano and orchestra, soloist Mme Hasselmans, conductor Léon Jehin

14 May: SNM Salle Gaveau, first performance of *Fantaisie* by dedicatee, Alfred Cortot, conductor d'Indy

Mid-July–mid-September: first stay at Annecy-le-Vieux (Villa Dunand: 'les Charmilles') in company with Maillots; writes *Mirages* (Renée de Brimont); begins Second Piano Quintet

26 September: his directorship of Conservatoire extended by one year

October: Durand publishes orchestral score of *Fantaisie*

28 November: first private performance of *Mirages* in Fauré's office at Conservatoire

December: Monte Carlo (Hôtel de la Terrasse)

27 December: SNM, accompanies Madeleine Grey in first performance of *Mirages*

End December: returns to Monte Carlo

1920

January: Monte Carlo, seriously ill with influenza

February: Monte Carlo, works at Second Quintet

23 February–7 April: stays at Tamaris (Grand Hôtel)

4 March: Paris première of *Masques et bergamasques* at Opéra-Comique

20 March: SNM, Georges Enesco and Marcel Ciampi play Second Violin Sonata

8–26 April: Nice (Palace Hôtel)

26 April: made Grand Officier de la Légion d'honneur

End July–early September: Veyrier-du-lac (Château de Fésigny, lac d'Annecy) with Maillots and Lortats; finishes second and third movements of Second Quintet

Mid-September: stay in Venice (Hôtel Savoia) with Lortats

1 October: retires from Conservatoire

November: to Brussels where Claire Croiza sings in revival of *Pénélope*

1921

17 January–28 March: Nice–Cimiez (Villa Mercedes), finishes Second Quintet,

writes Thirteenth Barcarolle, *Chant funéraire* for Napoleon (state commission); begins Second 'Cello Sonata

21 March: Cannes, attends performance of Requiem

5 May: Hôtel des Invalides, G. Balay conducts *Chant funéraire* (centenary of Napoleon I's death)

19 May: rehearsal of Second Quintet at Maillots in Paris

21 May: SNM, first performance of Second Quintet: outstanding success

July: Durand publishes score of Second Quintet, dedicated to Dukas

Early July–mid-September: Ax-les-Thermes (Villa Rose-Marguerite); works on Second 'Cello Sonata; long interruption through illness; abandons idea of staying at Annecy-le-Vieux

10 November: finishes Second 'Cello Sonata

10 December: first private performance at Maillots with Gérard Hekking and Marguerite Hasselmans

Autumn: writes *l'Horizon chimérique* (La Ville de Mirmont)

16 December: death of Saint-Saëns

21 December–end April: Nice (Hôtel de l'Europe; then Villa Frya with the Gremys)

31 December: finishes Thirteenth Nocturne; end of prolific creative period

1922

January: Nice, writes article on Saint-Saëns for *La Revue musicale*; Jacques Durand suggests he write a trio with piano

Mid-April: Durand publishes *L'Horizon chimérique*

End April: returns to Paris

12 May: Fauré's seventy-seventh birthday

13 May: SNM, Charles Panzéra gives first performance of *L'Horizon chimérique* which is dedicated to him; Gérard Hekking and Cortot give first performance of Second 'Cello Sonata

20 June: National Act of Homage at Sorbonne: huge concert of his works with Croiza, Panzéra, Jeanne Raunay, Cortot, Lortat, Casals, d'Indy, Messager

Summer: revises piano works, new edition of which Roger-Ducasse is preparing for Hamelle

5 July–8 August: Argelès (Hôtel du Parc); ill with bronchial pneumonia

9 August–early October: second stay at Annecy-le-Vieux (Villa Dunand); writes article 'Souvenirs' of Niedermeyer School for *La Revue musicale*

26 August: Fauré Festival at Annecy Casino

27 August: performance of *Messe basse* in Annecy-le-Vieux church

September: begins Andante of Trio

28 September: Mengelberg conducts Requiem in Amsterdam with Claire Croiza

1 October: *La Revue musicale* publishes special Fauré number

13 December: SMI, first performance of musical homage on name of Fauré written by his old pupils for supplement of *La Revue musicale*

Winter in Paris: works on Trio

1923

31 January: made Grand croix de la Légion d'honneur

27 February: Strasbourg, production of *Pénélope*, conducted by Guy Ropartz

16 April: Opéra-Comique, Lucienne Bréval and Lucien Muratore return to rôles they created in *Pénélope* (tenth anniversary of première)

28 April: SNM, Blanche Selva gives first performance of Thirteenth Barcarolle and Thirteenth Nocturne

12 May: Fauré's seventy-eighth birthday; SNM, first performance of Trio; Suzanne Balguerie sings *La Bonne chanson*, accompanied by Roger-Ducasse; Fauré, not being able to leave the house, does not attend the concert

21 June: Ecole normale de musique, attends rehearsal of Trio by Thibaud, Casals and Cortot who play it in Paris on 29 June

25 June–20 September: third stay at Annecy-le-Vieux (Villa Dunand); begins Andante of String Quartet in utmost secrecy; meets Honegger, come to conduct extracts from *Le Roi David*, given with Requiem in Annecy-le-Vieux on 25 August

30 July: *Pénélope* is given in amphitheatre at Orange

Autumn: Henri Prunières asks him to write song for supplement to Ronsard number of *Revue musicale*; tears up sketch on learning that Ravel has finished song on same poem

1924

15 March: Anvers, première of *Pénélope* in Flemish

3 May: Théâtre des Champs-Elysées, Ruhlmann conducts substantial passages from *Prométhée* with Jacques Copeau as reciter

12 May: Fauré enters eightieth year

21 May: Mengelberg conducts Requiem at Théâtre des Champs-Elysées; Fauré is ill and cannot attend

20 June–24 July: Divonne (Nouvel Hôtel), works on String Quartet

July: Hamelle publishes volume of Nocturnes nos 1–8, revised by Ducasse and Fauré

24 July–17 October: fourth stay at Annecy-le-Vieux (Villa Dunand)

11 September: finishes String Quartet

Mid-September: seriously ill with bronchial pneumonia

18 October: returns to Paris, very weak

4 November: dies at his Paris home, 32, rue des Vignes

8 November: state funeral at Madeleine: Requiem played; buried in Passy cemetery

1925

12 June: SNM Salle du Conservatoire, first performance of String Quartet

1926

13 March: death of Marie Fauré

Chronological catalogue of Fauré's works

This catalogue follows the chronological order of composition of Fauré's works; it differs considerably from the order of the opus numbers, which is based on that of publication. The delay of 'seven or eight years' mentioned by Fauré himself (*Excelsior*, 12 June 1922) between the dates of composition and publication justifies my choice, if justification were needed.

In any case, the Fauré catalogue was not really begun until 1875–6, when the publication was being envisaged of three fairly long works: two choruses with orchestra, the *Cantique de Jean Racine* and *Les Djinns*, and especially the First Violin Sonata. Fauré gave them the opus numbers 11, 12 and 13, leaving only ten numbers for his earlier works of which there were around twenty. This shows how little importance he attached to his earliest *romances* and *mélodies*.

Hamelle, who took Fauré on in 1879, then Heugel in 1906 and finally Durand in 1913 continued the opus numbers in the order of publication, though with some inconsistencies. Nos. 9, 53, 60, 64 and 100 were not allotted and, what is more, some works which in the end remained unpublished, notably some of his transcriptions, were given a number of their own while about a dozen works, including such important ones as *Pénélope*, never had one at all.

The first collection of twenty *mélodies* and *romances*, published initially by Choudens in 1879, bore no opus numbers and neither did any of the songs when published separately; and the same was true of the successive new editions brought about by Hamelle from 1887 . . . until the present day, because these Choudens plates have served for about a hundred years. The question of matching these early songs with the opus numbers 1 to 10, left vacant in 1875, came up only in 1896 when Fauré was canvassing for a seat in the Institut and asked Hamelle to print a list of his works. This list appears on the back of the Fauré scores printed around this time and contains the earliest mention of the first ten opus numbers. Unfortunately, the numbering did not follow the order of composition, which, by now, Fauré had probably forgotten, nor the order of publication, which would have been something, but the order of the songs inside the first volume. These early opus numbers therefore bring into close proximity songs composed ten or fifteen years apart.

525

A revised list was therefore necessary, especially as my researches into Fauré's unpublished correspondence and into publishers' archives allowed me very often to change and to bring a greater certainty to the chronologies presented by Octave Séré (*Musiciens français d'aujourd'hui*, 1911 and 1922), in *La Revue musicale* (October 1922, special Fauré no.) and by Philippe Fauré-Fremiet (*G. Fauré*, 2/1957). The present catalogue served as the basis for the list by genres which I published in the Fauré article of *The New Grove Dictionary* (London, 1980) as well as for the list in Robert Orledge's book *Gabriel Fauré* (London, 1979 and 1983).

This catalogue does not claim to put an end to uncertainties about the chronology of Fauré's work. This can be explained partly by the changes that have come about in scholarly method and in modern musicology's demands for greater precision, but also by Fauré's own regal indifference to such matters: until he was sixty he dated his letters only rarely, and not always his manuscripts, which he also allowed to be dispersed. In spite of everything, there remains some margin of uncertainty, as there does in all similar catalogues, even the Mozart one which Köchel began to compile over a century ago. But, as I have said, the early works are the hardest to date because of the lack of precise documentary evidence.

Each entry contains: the title of the work, the author of the words (for vocal works), the original key and tessitura: l.v. = low voice, m.v. = medium voice, h.v. = high voice; the opus number; the dedicatee; the publisher; the date of first publication; then, for the songs, the reference to the three Hamelle collections; finally the date and performers of the first public performance (SNM = Société nationale de musique), in Paris unless otherwise indicated. The dates of composition in inverted commas are those which I have taken from the autographs. I have given the type of voice which the first performers of his *mélodies* had, when this was known: s = soprano; t = tenor; mez = mezzo-soprano; bar = baritone; al = alto; bs = bass. I have included transcriptions when they were the work of Fauré's friends or close colleagues.

1861

'Le Papillon et la fleur' (Victor Hugo), D♭ maj.?, first publ. in C maj., m.v., op. 1 no. 1.

Ded. Mme Miolan-Carvalho. – Choudens, 1869. Hamelle, 1887; first coll. (no. 1).

First perf. Casino de Saint-Malo, 13 August 1868 – Caroline Miolan-Carvalho (s), Fauré.

1862?

'Mai' (Victor Hugo), F maj., m.v., op. 1 no. 2.

Ded. Mme Henri Garnier. – G. Hartmann, 1871. Choudens, 1877. Hamelle, 1887; first coll. (no. 2).

First perf. SNM, 22 March 1873 – Félix Lévy (t).

1862?

'Rêve d'amour' ('S'il est un charmant gazon') (Victor Hugo), E♭ maj., l.v., op. 5, no. 2. Ded. Mme C. de Gomiecourt. – Choudens, 1875. Hamelle, 1887; first coll. (no. 10).

First perf. SNM, 12 December 1874 – Mlle Marguerite Baron.

1862?

'L'Aube naît' (Victor Hugo), no op. no.
Unpub. and lost.

'8 December 1862'

'Puisque j'ai mis' (Victor Hugo), C maj., h.v., no op. no.
Unpub.

c. 1862

Fugue à 3 parties, F, no op. no. Unpub. (see '30 June 1869').

1863?

Trois Romances sans paroles, for piano, op. 17. no. 1, A♭ maj. Ded. Mme Félix Lévy. no. 2, A min. Ded. Mlle Laure de Leyritz. no. 3, A♭ maj. Ded. Mme Florent Saglio. – Hamelle, 1880.

First perf. nos. 1 and 2, SNM, 25 February 1881 – Pauline Roger. no. 3, SNM, 19 January 1889 – Mlle Kasa Chatteleger.

Transcription for violin or 'cello and piano by Jules Delsart. Hamelle, 1896.

No. 1 transcribed by Fauré for four hands, unpublished ms. dated 'Tarbes, 10 August 1864'.

'14 July 1863'

Super flumina, 'Psalmus CXXVI', for mixed choir and full orchestra, no op. no. (Honourable mention in the composition competition at the Ecole Niedermeyer.) Unpub.

'12 January 1864'

La Chanson dans le jardin, for piano duet, no op. no.
Ded. Mlle Suzanne Garnier. Published with minor changes as 'Berceuse' in *Dolly Suite* (1894).

c. 1865

'Tristesse d'Olympio' (Victor Hugo), E min., no op. no.
Ded. 'A mon ami Adam Laussel'.
Unpub.

c. 1865

'Dans les ruines d'une abbaye' (Victor Hugo), A maj., h.v., op. 2 no. 1.
Ded. Mme Henriette Escalier. – Choudens, 1869. Hamelle, 1887; first coll. (no. 3).
First perf. SNM, 12 February 1876 – Léonce Waldec.

1865

Cantique de Jean Racine, four-part choir and organ, op. 11.
First prize in the composition competition at the Ecole Niedermeyer.
Ded. César Franck. – F. Schoen, 1876. Hamelle, 1893.
– with harmonium and string quintet accompaniment, 1866. Unpub.
First perf. Church of St-Sauveur de Rennes, 4 August 1866. SNM, 15 May 1875, cond. César Franck.
– with orchestral accompaniment, 1905. Hamelle.
First perf. Société des concerts du Conservatoire, 28 January 1906, cond. Georges Marty.

1868

Cantique à St-Vincent-de-Paul, for voice and organ, no op. no.
First perf. Church of St-Sauveur de Rennes, 19 July 1868.
Unpub. and lost.

'30 March 1869'

Intermède symphonique for piano duet, F maj., no op. no.
Ded. Valentine and Laure de Leyritz.
Unpub. (re-used as finale (?) of the Symphony in F, op. 20 and as overture of *Masques et bergamasques*, op. 112).
Orchestral version played under the title *Intermezzo de Symphonie*, Rennes, 8 February 1868. A piano duet ms. dedicated 'A Mme Brun' with the title *Allegro de Symphonie* could be dated 1864.

'27 April 1869'

Cadenza for the Concerto in A minor by Beethoven, op. posthum.
[Ded. Laure de Leyritz]. – Magasin musical P. Schneider, 1927.

'16 May 1869'

Gavotte for piano, C# min., no op. no.
Unpub.
First perf. Paris, Maison de la Radio, 15 November 1974 – Louis-Claude Thirion.
(Re-used in the Gavotte of the Symphony op. 20 and in *Masques et bergamasques*, op. 112.)

'30 June 1869'

Petite fugue for piano, A min., op. 84 no. 3.

Ded. Laure de Leyritz.

Published in the collection of *Pièces brèves*, op. 84. Hamelle, 1902.

(Probably composed as Fugue on a free subject for the composition competition at the Ecole Niedermeyer *c.* 1863.)

'30 November 1869'

Fugue for piano, E min., op. 84 no. 6.

Ded. Valentine de Leyritz.

Published in the *Pièces brèves*, op. 84. Hamelle, 1902.

(See comments on the preceding fugue.)

'31 December 1869'

Prelude for piano, E min., no op. no.

Ded. Valentine de Leyritz.

Unpub.

First perf. Paris, Maison de la Radio, 15 November 1974 – Louis-Claude Thirion.

c. 1870

'L'Aurore' (Victor Hugo), A♭ maj., h.v., op. posthum.

Ded. Mlle Anne Dufresne.

Pub. *in*: Fritz Noske: *La Mélodie française de Berlioz à Duparc*, 1954 and *Das ausserdeutsche Sololied*, 1500–1900 (*Das Musikwerk* vol. 16), 1958.

c. 1870

'Les Matelots' (Théophile Gautier), E♭ maj., m.v., op. 2 no. 2.

Ded. Mme Edouard Lalo. – Choudens, 1876. Hamelle, 1887; first coll. (no. 4).

First perf. SNM, 8 February 1873 – Mme Edouard Lalo (al).

c. 1870

'Lydia' (Leconte de Lisle), F maj., m.v., op. 4 no. 2.

Ded. Mme Marie Trélat. – G. Hartmann, 1871. Choudens, 1877. Hamelle, 1887; first coll. (no. 8).

First perf. SNM, 18 May 1872 – Marie Trélat (me'z.).

1870?

'Hymne' (Charles Baudelaire), G maj., h.v., op. 7 no. 2.

Ded. M. Félix Lévy. – G. Hartmann, 1871. Choudens, 1879. Hamelle, 1887; first coll. (no. 16).

First perf. SNM, 22 March 1873 – Félix Lévy (t).

'1871'

'Seule!' (Théophile Gautier), E min., l.v., op. 3 no. 4.

Ded. M. E. Fernier. – G. Hartmann, 1871. Choudens, 1877. Hamelle, 1887; first coll. (no. 5).

First perf. SNM, 18 May 1872 – Marie Trélat (me'z).

'3 April 1871'

'L'Absent' ('Sentiers ou l'herbe se balance') (Victor Hugo), A min., m.v., op. 5 no. 3.

Ded. M. Romain Bussine (bar). – Choudens, 1879. Hamelle, 1887; first coll. (no. 11).

1871?

'La Rançon' (Charles Baudelaire), C min., m.v., op. 8 no. 2.

Ded. Mme Henri Duparc – Choudens, 1879. Hamelle, 1887; first coll. (no. 19, then no. 18).

c. 1871

'Chant d'automne' (Charles Baudelaire), A min., m.v., op. 5 no. 1.

Ded. Mme Camille Clerc. – Choudens, 1879. Hamelle, 1887; first coll. (no. 9).

First perf. SNM, 6 January 1883 – André Quirot (bs).

'August 1871'

Ave Maria, for three-part male choir and organ, op. posthum.

'Hommage au Grand Saint-Bernard.' – Heugel, 1957.

First perf. Chapelle de l'Hospice du Mont Saint-Bernard (Switz.) – choir of the Ecole Niedermeyer, 20 August 1871.

c. 1872

Tu es Petrus, for baritone solo, four-part choir and organ, no op. no.

Durand, 1884. Hamelle, coll. of *Musique religieuse* by Fauré, 1911.

1872?

'Chanson du pêcheur' (Lamento) (Théophile Gautier), F min., m.v., op. 4 no. 1.

Ded. Mme Pauline Viardot. – Choudens, 1877. Hamelle, 1887; first coll. (no. 7) London, Metzler, 1896.

First perf. SNM, 8 February 1873 – Mme Edouard Lalo (al).

– with orchestral accompaniment arr. Fauré, 1891? Hamelle, 1896.

First perf. (?) Concerts Lamoureux, 27 November 1892 – Marcella Pregi, cond. Charles Lamoureux.

c. 1873

'Tristesse' (Théophile Gautier), C min., m.v., op. 6 no. 2.

Ded. Mme Edouard Lalo (al). – Choudens, 1876. Hamelle, 1887; first coll. (no. 13).

c. 1873

'Aubade' (Louis Pomey), F maj., m.v., op. 6 no. 1.

Ded. Mme Amélie Duez. – Choudens, 1879. Hamelle, 1887; first coll. (no. 12).

1866–73

Suite for orchestra or Symphony in F. Allegro. Andante. Gavotte. Finale. Op. 20. Unpub.

First perf. (except Finale) SNM, 8 February 1873 – C. Saint-Saëns and G. Fauré, two pianos. Complete with orchestra, SNM, 16 May 1874, cond. Edouard Colonne.

The Allegro, transcribed for piano duet by Léon Boëllmann, appeared under the title *Allegro symphonique* op. 68. – Hamelle, 1895.

The Gavotte, using the Gavotte for piano of 1869, is re-used in 1919 in *Masques et bergamasques* op. 112.

c. 1863–73

'Puisqu'ici bas' (Victor Hugo), duet for two sopranos and piano, op. 10 no. 1.

Ded. Mme Claudie Chamerot and Mlle Marianne Viardot. – Choudens, 1879. Hamelle, 1887.

First perf. SNM, 10 April 1875 – Claudie Chamerot and Marianne Viardot (s). (Partly uses an early work of 1864.)

c. 1873

'Tarentelle' (Marc Monnier), duet for two sopranos and piano, op. 10 no. 2.

Ded. Mme Claudie Chamerot and Mlle Marianne Viardot. – Choudens, 1879. Hamelle, 1887.

First perf. SNM, 10 April 1875 – Claudie Chamerot and Marianne Viardot. – with orchestral accompaniment by A. Messsager.

Unpub.

'19 October 1873'

'Barcarolle' (Marc Monnier), G min., h.v., op. 7 no. 3.

Ded. Mme Pauline Viardot. – Choudens, 1877. Hamelle, 1887; first coll. (no. 17), then second coll. (no. 20)*.

First perf. SNM, 20 March 1875 – Mme de Grandval.

---

* In 1908 Hamelle carried out certain modifications to the deployment of Fauré's *mélodies* gathered together in the three collections. The first edition of the second collection comprised twenty-five *mélodies*. When in 1908 he considered making up a third volume of the remaining *mélodies*, already published separately, he only found fourteen (op. 57, 58, 76, 85, 87). Fauré would have happily kept to this number but such was not the opinion of his editor who wanted to equalise each of the three collections at twenty *mélodies*. The reduction of the second collection from twenty-five to twenty *mélodies* could not be carried out easily (the op. 51 would have been divided between the second and third collections) and Hamelle took an unfortunate step in the transfer from one volume to another. The op. 51, together with 'Prison' and 'Soir', were moved from the second to the third collection; the second collection being thus reduced to nineteen *mélodies*, 'Barcarolle', op. 7 no. 3, was borrowed from the first collection where this piece was more at home than after 'Clair de lune'; the first collection now being itself incomplete as a result of this borrowing, 'Noël', op. 43, which is a carol, not a *mélodie*, was inserted, paralleling 'En Prière' in the third collection.

1874?

'Ici bas!' (Sully Prudhomme), F♯ min., m.v., op. 8 no. 3.

Ded. Mme G. Lecoq, née Mac Brid. – Choudens, 1877. Hamelle, 1887; first coll. (no. 20, then no. 19).

First perf. SNM, 12 December 1874 – Mlle Marguerite Baron.

c. 1875

Cadenza for the Concerto no. 1 by Mozart, K.37, no op. no.

Unpub.

1875?

Les Djinns (Victor Hugo), four-part choir and orchestra, or piano, op. 12.

[Ded. Louise Héritte Viardot]. – Hamelle, 1890.

First perf. SNM, 22 April 1876, with piano. Trocadéro, 27 June 1878, with orchestra, cond. Edouard Colonne.

'August 1875'

'Au bord de l'eau' (Sully Prudhomme), C♯ min., h.v., op. 8 no. 1.

Ded. Mme Claudie Chamerot. – Choudens, 1877. Hamelle, 1887; first coll. (no. 18, then no. 17).

First perf. SNM, 19 January 1878 – Mlle Miramont-Tréogate.

1875–6

Sonata for violin and piano [no. 1], in A maj., op. 13.

Ded. Paul Viardot. – Leipzig, Breitkopf & Härtel, 1877.

First perf. SNM, 27 January 1877 – Marie Tayau, vl., G. Fauré, p.

c. 1875?

Mazurka for piano, B♭ maj., op. 32.

Ded. Mlle Adèle Bohomoletz. – Hamelle, 1883; coll. 1930 (with the *Valses-Caprices*, nos 1–4).

First perf. SNM, 23 January 1886, Mme Bordes-Pène.

c. 1875

Nocturne no. 1 for piano, E♭ min., op. 33 no. 1.

Ded. Mme Marguerite Baugnies. – Hamelle, 1883; 2nd edn. 1924 as collection (nos 1–8).

First perf. SNM, 21 February 1885 – Marie Jaëll.

1876–9

Quartet no. 1 for piano, violin, viola and 'cello, in C min., op. 15.

Ded. Hubert Léonard. – Hamelle, 1884.

First perf. SNM, 14 February 1880 – G. Fauré, p., Ovide Musin, vl., Louis van Waefelghem, vla, Ermanno Mariotti, vlc.

The Finale was re-written in 1883.

First perf. with new Finale, SNM, 5 April 1884 – G. Fauré, p., Lucien Lefort, vl., Bernier, vla, Ermanno Mariotti, vlc.

1877

Romance, for violin and piano, B♭ maj., op. 28.

Ded. Mlle Arma Harkness. – Hamelle, 1883.

First perf. SNM, 9 February 1883–Arma Harkness, vl.

– with orchestral accompaniment by Philippe Gaubert, 1919. Hamelle, 1920.

First perf. Concerts Lamoureux, 11 January 1920 – Lydie Demyrgian, vl., cond. Camille Chevillard.

1877

Ave Maria, for two sopranos and organ, no op. no.

Unpub.

First perf. Church of the Madeleine, 30 May 1877 – Claudie Chamerot and Marianne Viardot (s).

Used in *Ave Maria*, op. 92, in 1906.

1877

Libera me for baritone and organ, no op. no.

Unpub.

Used in the Requiem op. 48.

1877

'Après un rêve' ('Levati sol que la luna è levata') (anon., adapt. Romain Bussine), C min., m.v., op. 7 no. 1.

Ded. Mme Marguerite Baugnies. – Choudens, 1878. Hamelle, 1887; first coll. (no. 15).

First perf. SNM, 11 January 1879 – Henriette Fuchs (s).

1878?

'Sérénade toscane', ('O tu che dormie riposata stai') (anon., adapt. Romain Bussine), B♭ min., m.v., op. 3 no. 2.

Ded. Mme la baronne de Montagnac, née de Rosalès. – Choudens, 1879. Hamelle, 1887; first coll. (no. 6).

1878

O Salutaris for voice and organ, no op. no.

Unpub.

First perf. Eglise d'Arromanches, summer 1878.

Probably used in the *O Salutaris* op. 47 no. 1, 1887.

1878

'Sylvie' (Paul de Choudens), F maj., m.v., op. 6 no. 3.

Ded. Mme la vicomtesse de Gironde. – Choudens, 1879. Hamelle, 1887; first coll. (no. 14).

First perf. SNM, 11 January 1879 – Henriette Fuchs (s).

1878

Poème d'un jour (Charles Grandmougin), h.v., op. 21.

1. 'Rencontre', D♭ maj. 2. 'Toujours', F♯ min. 3. 'Adieu', G♭ maj.

Ded. Mme la comtesse de Gauville. – Durand, 1880. Hamelle, 1897; second coll. (nos 4, 5, 6). London, Metzler, 1897.

First perf. SNM, 22 January 1881 – M. Mazalbert (t).

The manuscript bears the opus no. 17. The first edition for m.v. transposed into B maj., E min., and E maj. The edition for h.v. (1902–3) does not keep to the keys in the manuscript for nos 2 and 3 which are transposed into F min. and F maj.

1878

'Nell' (Leconte de Lisle), G♭ maj., h.v., op. 18 no. 1.

Ded. Mme Camille Saint-Saëns. – Hamelle, 1880; second coll. (no. 1). London, Metzler, 1896.

First perf. SNM, 29 January 1881 – Henriette Fuchs (s).

1878?

'Le Voyageur' (Armand Silvestre), A min., h.v., op. 18 no. 2.

Ded. M. Emmanuel Jadin. – Hamelle, 1880; second coll. (no. 2).

1878

'Automne' (Armand Silvestre), B min., m.v., op. 18 no. 3.

Ded. Mlle Alice Boissonnet. – Hamelle, 1880; second coll. (no. 3).

First perf. SNM, 29 January 1881 – Henriette Fuchs (s).

1878–9

Berceuse for violin and piano, op. 16.

Ded. Mme Hélène Depret. – Hamelle, 1880.

First perf. SNM, 14 February 1880 – Ovide Musin, vl., G. Fauré, p.

– with orchestra, 1880. Hamelle, 1898. First perf. SNM, 24 April 1880 – Ovide Musin, cond. Edouard Colonne.

1878–9

Concerto for violin and orchestra, op. 14. Allegro. Andante. Finale.

Unpub.

First perf. Allegro and Andante, SNM, 12 April 1880 – Ovide Musin, vl., cond. Edouard Colonne.

The Andante had already been performed with piano acc., SNM, 27 December 1878, by Ovide Musin and André Messager.

The Finale, sketched in 1879, was abandoned. The themes of the Allegro were used in the initial Allegro of the String Quartet op. 121 (1923–4); those of the Andante seem to figure in the Andante for violin op. 75 (1897). Only the Allegro survives in manuscript.

1879

Ballade for piano, in F$^\sharp$ maj., op. 19.

Ded. Camille Saint-Saëns. – Hamelle, 1880.

– with orchestral accompaniment by the composer, 'April 1881'. Hamelle, 1902.

First perf. SNM, 23 April 1881 – G. Fauré, p., cond. Edouard Colonne.

1879

'Les Berceaux' (Sully Prudhomme), B$^\flat$ min., m.v., op. 23 no. 1.

Ded. Mlle Alice Boissonnet. – Hamelle, 1881; second coll. (no. 7).

First perf. SNM, 9 December 1882 – Jane Huré.

c. 1879

'Notre amour' (Armand Silvestre), E maj., h.v., op. 23 no. 2.

Ded. Mme C. Castillon. – Hamelle, 1882; second coll. (no. 8). London, Metzler, 1897. Supplement no. 8 *La Musique des Annales*, 1922.

1880–1

'Le Secret' (Armand Silvestre), D$^\flat$ maj., m.v., op. 23 no. 3.

Ded. Mlle Alice Boissonnet. – Hamelle, 1881; second coll. (no. 9). London, Metzler, 1897.

First perf. SNM, 6 January 1883 – André Quirot (bs).

1880

Elégie for 'cello and piano, op. 24.

Ded. M. Jules Loëb. – Hamelle, 1883.

First perf. SNM, 15 December 1883 – Jules Loëb, vlc.

– with orchestral accompaniment by the composer, 1895. Hamelle, 1901.

First perf. SNM, 26 April 1901 – Pablo Casals, cond. Fauré.

c. 1880

Benedictus for four-part mixed choir, organ and double bass, B$^\flat$ maj., no op. no. Unpub.

1881

Messe des pêcheurs de Villerville for three-part women's choir, with soloists, no op. no. First version, with harmonium acc. and violin solo, in collaboration with Messager.

1 Kyrie (Messager) 2 Gloria (Fauré) 3 Sanctus (Fauré) 4 O Salutaris (Messager) 5 Agnus Dei (Fauré).

Unpub.

First perf. Church of Villerville (Calvados), 4 September 1881.

1882

Second version, with accompaniment of small orchestra. Nos 1–4 orchestrated by Messager, no. 5 by Fauré.

Unpub.

First perf. Church of Villerville, 10 September 1882.

'30 December 1906'

Third version, under the title *Messe basse*, with organ, without the pieces by Messager and with a Kyrie by Fauré. 1 Kyrie 2 Sanctus 3 Benedictus (on the 'Qui tollis' of the unpub. Gloria) 4 Agnus Dei.

Ded. Mme Camille Clerc (on the ms.). – Heugel, 1907.

***c*. 1881**

c. Nocturne no. 2 for piano, B maj., op. 33 no. 2.

Ded. Mme Louise Guyon. – Hamelle, 1883; 2nd edn. 1924, collected (nos 1–8).

1881

Impromptu no. 1 for piano, E♭ maj., op. 25.

Ded. Mme Emmanuela Potocka. – Hamelle, 1881, 2nd edn. 1926, collected (nos 1–5).

First perf. SNM, 9 December 1882 – Camille Saint-Saëns.

1881?

Barcarolle no. 1 for piano, A min., op. 26.

Ded. Mme Montigny-Rémaury. – Hamelle, 1881, 2nd edn. 1926, collected (nos 1–6).

First perf. SNM, 9 December 1882 – Camille Saint-Saëns.

1881?

'Le Ruisseau' (anon.), two-part female choir and piano, op. 22.

Ded. Mme Pauline Roger. – Hamelle, 1881.

First perf. SNM, 14 January 1882–Pauline Roger choir.

– with accompaniment of two flutes and string quintet, by the composer?

First perf. SNM, 2 April 1887.

Unpub. and lost.

1882

'Chanson d'amour' (Armand Silvestre), F maj., m.v., op. 27 no. 1.

Ded. Mlle Jane Huré. – Hamelle, 1882; second coll. (no. 10).

First perf. SNM, 9 December 1882 – Jane Huré.

1882

'La Fée aux chansons' (Armand Silvestre), F maj., h.v., op. 27 no. 2.

Ded. Mme Edmond Fuchs. – Hamelle, 1883; second coll. (no. 11).

First perf. SNM, 12 May 1888 – Maurice Bagès de Trigny (t).

'Villerville, 16 September 1882'

La Naissance de Vénus (Paul Collin), mythological scene for soloists, choirs and orchestra, op. 29.

Ded. M. Antonin Guillot de Sainbris. – Hamelle, 1883.

First perf. Paris, 8 March 1883 – Choir of the Société chorale d'amateurs. André Quirot (bs); G. Fauré, César Franck, M. Maton, pianos, cond. A. Guillot de Sainbris.

Second perf. SNM, 3 April 1886 – Choir Guillot de Sainbris, soloists Mmes Castillon and Storm, MM. Auguez and Dupas.

– with orchestra by the composer, 1895. Hamelle. First perf. 1 December 1895 – Eléonore Blanc, Louise Planes, Numa Auguez, M. Gandubert, cond. Edouard Colonne.

Later ded. M. Sigismond Bardac. English version by Adela Maddison, 1898.

1882?

Valse-Caprice no. 1, for piano, A maj., op. 30.

Ded. Mlle Alex. Milochevitch. – Hamelle, 1883, 2nd edn. 1930, collected (nos 1–4).

'May 1883'

Impromptu no. 2, for piano, F min., op. 31.

Ded. Mlle Sacha de Regina. – Hamelle, 1883, 2nd edn. 1926, collected (nos 1–5).

First perf. SNM, 10 January 1885 – Camille Saint-Saëns.

1883

Nocturne no. 3, for piano, A♭ maj., op. 33 no. 3.

Ded. Mme Bohomoletz. – Hamelle, 1883, 2nd edn. 1924, collected (nos 1–8).

First perf. SNM, 23 January 1886 – Mme Bordes-Pène.

1883

Impromptu no. 3, for piano, A♭ maj., op. 34.

Ded. Mme Eugène Brun. – Hamelle, 1883, 2nd edn. 1926, collected (nos 1–5).

First perf. SNM, 10 January 1885 – Camille Saint-Saëns.

'1 December 1883'

Madrigal (Armand Silvestre), vocal quartet or choir, with piano accompaniment, or orchestra, op. 35.

Ded. M. André Messager. – Hamelle, 1884.

First perf. SNM, 12 January 1884 – Choir of the Société nationale.

– with orchestra, SNM, 30 April 1892 – soloists and orch. of the Société nationale, cond. G. Fauré.

1884

Nocturne no. 4, for piano, E maj., op. 36.

Ded. Mme la comtesse de Mercy-Argenteau. – Hamelle, 1885, 2nd edn. 1924, collected (nos 1–8).

1884

Nocturne no. 5, for piano, B♭ maj., op. 37.

Ded. Mme Marie P. Christofle. – Hamelle, 1885, 2nd edn. 1924, collected (nos 1–8).

'20 May 1884'

'Aurore' (Armand Silvestre), G maj., h.v., op. 39 no. 1.

Ded. Mme Henriette Roger-Jourdain. – Hamelle, 1885; second coll. (no. 12).

First perf. SNM, 13 December 1884 – Marguerite Mauvernay.

Appeared in the Album of the journal *Le Gaulois*, 1885.

'25 May 1884'

'Fleur jetée' (Armand Silvestre), F min., h.v., op. 39 no. 2.

Ded. Mme Jules Gouin – Hamelle, 1885; second coll. (no. 13).

First perf. SNM, 13 December 1884 – Marguerite Mauvernay.

'30 May 1884'

'Le Pays des rêves' (Armand Silvestre), A♭ maj., h.v., op. 39 no. 3.

Ded. Mlle Thérèse Guyon. – Hamelle, 1885; second coll. (no. 14).

First perf. SNM, 27 December 1884 – Thérèse Guyon.

June ? 1884

'Les Roses d'Ispahan' (Leconte de Lisle), D maj., m.v., op. 39 no. 4.

Ded. Mlle Louise Collinet. – Hamelle, 1885; second coll. (no. 15).

First perf. SNM, 27 December 1884 – Thérèse Guyon.

– with orchestra, by the composer, 1891.

First perf. Aix-les-Bains, 26 or 28 August 1891, cond. Edouard Colonne.

'July 1884'

Valse-Caprice no. 2, for piano, D♭ maj., op. 38.

Ded. Mme André Messager. – Hamelle, 1884, 2nd edn. 1930 (collected nos 1–4).
First perf. SNM, 16 February 1889 – Mme Bordes-Pène.

1884
Papillon, piece for 'cello and piano, op. 77. Hamelle, 1898.

1884
Symphony in D min.: Allegro deciso. Andante. Finale. Op. 40.
Unpub. and destroyed.
First perf. SNM, 15 March 1885 – Orchestra of the Concerts Colonne, cond. Edouard Colonne.
Second perf. Anvers, 14 October 1885, cond. Vincent d'Indy.
Andante only, 23 May 1889, Concerts Lamoureux, cond. Charles Lamoureux (in the series of concerts of the Exposition universelle, at Trocadéro).
(Themes of nos 1 and 2 re-used in the violin and 'cello sonata of 1916–17.)

'August 1885'
Barcarolle no. 2, for piano, G maj., op. 41.
Ded. Mlle Marie Poitevin. – Hamelle, 1886, 2nd edn. 1926, collected (nos 1–6).
First perf. SNM, 19 February 1887 – Marie Poitevin.

1885
Barcarolle no. 3, for piano, G$^{\flat}$ maj., op. 42.
Ded. Mme Henriette Roger-Jourdain. – Hamelle, 1886, 2nd edn. 1926, collected (nos 1–6).

1885
'Noël' (Victor Wilder), A$^{\flat}$ maj., h.v., one voice, piano and harmonium *ad lib.*, op. 43 no. 1.
Ded. 'A mon ami A. Talazac'. – Hamelle, 1886; first coll. (no. 20).

1886
'Nocturne' (Villiers de l'Isle Adam), E$^{\flat}$ maj., l.v., op. 43 no. 2.
Ded. Mme Henriette Roger-Jourdain. – Hamelle, 1886; first coll. (no. 17).

1886
Barcarolle no. 4, for piano, A$^{\flat}$ maj., op. 44.
Ded. Mme Ernest Chausson. – Hamelle, 1887, 2nd edn. 1926, collected (nos 1–6).

1885–6
Quartet no. 2, for piano, violin, viola and 'cello in G min., op. 45.
Ded. Hans von Bülow. – Hamelle, 1887.
First perf. SNM, 22 January 1887 – G. Fauré, p., Guillaume Rémy, vl., Louis van Waefelghem, vla, Jules Delsart, vlc.

1887

'Les Présents' (Villiers de l'Isle Adam), F maj., h.v., op. 46 no. 1.

Ded. M. le comte Robert de Montesquiou-Fezensac. – Hamelle, 1888; second coll. (no. 18).

1887

'Clair de lune' (Paul Verlaine), B♭ min., m.v., op. 46 no. 2.

Ded. M. Emmanuel Jadin. – Hamelle, 1888; second coll. (no. 19). London, Metzler, 1897.

– with orchestra, by the composer 1888.

First perf. SNM, 28 April 1888 – Maurice Bagès (t) (with orchestra).

1877–87

O *Salutaris*, for baritone and organ, B maj., op. 47 no. 1.

Ded. Jean-Baptiste Faure. – Hamelle, 1888.

First perf. Church of the Madeleine, 21 November 1887 – Jean-Baptiste Faure.

– with accompaniment of two horns, harp and string quintet, by the composer (in B♭ maj.). Hamelle.

1887

Pavane for orchestra and chorus *ad lib.* (Robert de Montesquiou), in F♯ min., op. 50.

First perf. Concerts Lamoureux, 25 November 1888, cond. Charles Lamoureux.

– with chorus, SNM, 28 April 1888.

1887–99

Requiem, for soprano and baritone solo, mixed chorus, organ and orchestra, in D min., op. 48.

Hamelle, 1900 (voice and piano), 1901 (orchestra). 1 Introit and Kyrie, 1887, 2 Offertorium, 1889–91, 3 Sanctus, '8 Jan. 1888', 4 Pie Jesu, 1887, 5 Agnus Dei, '6 Jan 1888', 6 Libera me, 1877, 1890?, 7 In Paradisum, 1887.

First perf. nos 1, 3, 4, 5, 7 with string orchestra (one single violin, solo in the Sanctus), harp, timpani and organ, Church of the Madeleine, 16 January 1888, cond. Fauré.

First perf. with additional two horns and two trumpets, the Madeleine, 4 May 1888, cond. Fauré.

First complete perf. in the original orchestration, the Madeleine, 21 January 1893, cond. Fauré.

First complete perf. with full orchestra (new orchestration augmented by wind and violins), Trocadéro, 12 July 1900 – Mlle Torrès (s), M. Vallier (bs), Eugène Gigout, organ, orch. and choir of the Société des concerts du Conservatoire, cond. Paul Taffanel.

The *Libera me*, planned in 1877 for voice and organ, was given a separate first performance, in its definitive version for baritone, chorus, organ and orchestra at the Société nationale de musique, Church of St-Gervais, 28 January 1892 – solo Louis Ballard (bar).

'1 March 1888'

'Maria Mater gratiae', duo for tenor and baritone with organ, op. 47 no. 2.

Hamelle, 1888, collected, 1911.

1888?

Souvenirs de Bayreuth, 'fantasie in the form of a quadrille on favourite themes from the *Ring* by Wagner', for piano duet (in collaboration with A. Messager), op. posth.

Costallat, 1930.

c. 1888

Petite pièce for 'cello and piano in G maj., op. 49.

Unpub. and lost.

1888

Caligula, incidental music for the tragedy by Alexandre Dumas *père*. Female chorus and orchestra, op. 52.

Ded. Ernest Dupuy. – Hamelle, 1888 (voice and piano), 1890 (orchestra).

First perf. (with small orchestra) Théâtre de l'Odéon, 8 November 1888, cond. Fauré.

First concert perf. of the full orchestral version, SNM, 6 April 1889, cond. Gabriel Marie.

I Prologue: (a) fanfare (b) marche (c) chœur des Heures.
II Act 5: (a) chœur 'L'Hiver s'enfuit' (b) Air de danse (c) Mélodrame et chœur 'De roses vermeilles' (d) chœur final: 'César a fermé la paupière'.

The later editions bear a dedication to Paul Porel.

1888

'Larmes' (Jean Richepin), C min., h.v., op. 51 no. 1.

Ded. Mme la princesse Edmond de Polignac. – Hamelle, 1888; second coll. (no. 20), then third coll. (no. 1).

1888

'Au cimetière' (Jean Richepin), E min., h.v., op. 51 no. 2.

Ded. Mme Maurice Sulzbach. – Hamelle, 1888; second coll. (no. 21), then third coll. (no. 2).

First perf. SNM, 2 February 1889 – Maurice Bagès (t).

1888

'Spleen' (Paul Verlaine), D min., m.v., op. 51 no. 3.

Ded. Mme Henri Cochin. – Hamelle, 1888; second coll. (no. 22), then third coll. (no. 3).

'23 December 1888'

Il est né le divin enfant, harmonised carol, for children's choir in unison with acc. of organ, harp, oboe, 'cellos and double-basses, in B♭ maj., no op. no. Hamelle, 1920.

First perf. Church of the Madeleine, 25 December 1888.

1889

Shylock, incidental music for the play by Edmond Haraucourt, based on Shakespeare, for tenor solo and orchestra, op. 57.

Ded. M. Paul Porel. – Hamelle, 1897.

First perf. (with small orchestra) at the Théâtre de l'Odéon, 17 December 1889, cond. G. Fauré. In concert (full orchestra), SNM, 17 May 1890 – M. Leprestre (t), cond. Gabriel Marie.

The two serenades *Chanson* (B♭ maj.) and *Madrigal* (F maj.) appear, with piano acc., in the third coll. (nos 5 and 6). *Madrigal*, London, Metzler, 1897.

'March' [1889]

Ecce fidelis servus, trio for soprano, tenor and baritone, with organ, op. 54.

For the feast-day of St Joseph (19 March). – Hamelle, 1893; collected, 1911.

c. 1890

Noël d'enfants (Les Anges dans nos campagnes), harmonisation for unison children's choir and organ, no op. no.

Hamelle, 1921.

1890

En prière (Stephan Bordèse), canticle for voice and organ, E♭ maj., m.v., no op. no.

Ded. Mme Leroux-Ribeyre. – Durand, 1890 (*in* collected edition: *Les Contes mystiques*). Hamelle; second coll. (no. 16). London, Metzler, 1897 and in *La Musique des Annales*, no. 37, 7 December 1924.

– with orchestra, by the composer, 1890.

Hamelle, 1923.

First perf. Concert Colonne, 28 December 1890 – Mlle B. de Montalant, cond. E. Colonne.

'August 1890'

'La Rose' (Leconte de Lisle), F maj., h.v., op. 51 no. 4.

Ded. M. Maurice Bagès. – Hamelle, 1890; second coll. (no. 23), then third coll. (no. 4).

before 1891

Tantum ergo for tenor solo, mixed chorus with harp and organ acc., op. 55.

Ded. M. l'abbé J. Panis. – Hamelle, 1893; collected, 1911.

First perf. SNM, St-Gervais, 22 January 1891 – M. Warmbrodt (t), M. Frank, harp.

– with string quintet accompaniment.

Unpub.

1890

La Passion, prologue for the play by Edmond Haraucourt, for mixed chorus and orchestra, no op. no.

Unpub.

First perf. SNM, 21 April 1890, cond. Vincent d'Indy.

Originally written for a concert of sacred music 4 April 1890, at the Cirque d'hiver; the choir was not able to perform this as the orchestration was not finished.

1891

Cinq Mélodies, 'Venice' songs (Paul Verlaine), h.v., op. 58.

Ded. Mme la princesse Edmond de Polignac. – Hamelle, 1891; third coll. (nos 7–11).

First perf. SNM, 2 April 1892 – Maurice Bagès (t).

1 'Mandoline', G maj., 'Venice 7 June 1891'.
2 'En sourdine', E♭ maj., Venice, Paris '20 June 1891'.
3 'Green', G♭ maj., Paris, '23 July' 1891.
4 'A Clymène', E min., Paris, July–Aug. 1891.
5 'C'est l'extase', D♭ maj., Paris, Aug.–Sept. 1891.

– no. 1 with orchestra, by Florent Schmitt.

'Mandoline' appeared in *Le Figaro musical* of November 1891 and in London, Metzler, 1896.

'Monday 27 February' 1893

Sérénade du bourgeois gentilhomme (Molière), F min., m.v., op. posth.

Heugel, 1957.

'March 1893'

Sicilienne, written on four staves with a view to orchestration for the music of the *Bourgeois gentilhomme*?

– transcribed for 'cello and piano, by the composer, 1898 (see below, p. 548).

– for chamber orchestra by Charles Koechlin (see incidental music for *Pelléas et Mélisande*, 1898); version inserted into the orchestral suite of *Pelléas et Mélisande* op. 80, in 1909.

Hamelle, 1909.

First perf. in concert (with the *Pelléas* suite), Société des concerts du Conservatoire, 1 December 1912, cond. André Messager.

1893?

Menuet, for small orchestra, in F, no op. no.

Unpub.

For *Le Bourgeois gentilhomme?*

1892–4

La Bonne chanson (Paul Verlaine), h.v., op. 61.

Ded. Mme Sigismond Bardac. – Hamelle, 1894.

First perf. 25 April 1894 – Maurice Bagès (t) (private concert at the house of the Comtesse Henri de Saussine). SNM, 20 April 1895 – Jeanne Remacle (s).

1 'Une Sainte en son auréole', A♭ maj., '17 September 92'.
2 'Puisque l'aube grandit', G maj., 1893.
3 'La Lune blanche', F♯ maj., '20 July 1893'.
4 'J'allais par des chemins perfides', F♯ min., 1892.
5 'J'ai presque peur, en vérité', E min., '4 December 1893'.
6 'Avant que tu ne t'en ailles', D♭ maj., 1892.
7 'Donc, ce sera par un clair jour d'été', B♭ maj., '9 August 92'.
8 'N'est-ce pas?', G maj., '25 May 1893'.
9 'L'Hiver a cessé', B♭ maj., 'February 1894'.

– with string quintet and piano accompaniment, by the composer, 1898.

Unpub.

First perf. London, 1 April 1898 (private concert at the house of Frank Schuster) – Maurice Bagès (t).

– with orchestra by Maurice Le Boucher, 1933. Hamelle.

1887–93

Valse-Caprice no. 3, for piano, G♭, op. 59.

Ded. Mme Philippe Dieterlen. – Hamelle, 1893, 2nd edn. 1930, collected (nos 1–4).

1893–4

Valse-Caprice no. 4, for piano, A♭, op. 62.

Ded. Mme Max Lyon. – Hamelle, 1894, 2nd edn. 1930, collected (nos 1–4).

First perf. SNM, 2 May 1896 – Léon Delafosse.

– for two pianos by Isidore Philipp. Hamelle, 1902.

1894

Hymne à Apollon, Greek song of the second century BC, reconstructed by Théodore Reinach, accompaniment by G. Fauré, for voice, harp, flute and two clarinets in B♭, op. 63a bis.

Ded. M. Théodore Homole. – Paris, O. Bornemann, 1894; 2nd edn. revised and corrected, 1914.

First perf. Ecole des Beaux-Arts, 12 April 1894 – Jeanne Remacle (s), M. Frank, harp, G. Fauré, harmonium.

1894

Romance for 'cello and piano, A maj., op. 69.

Ded. M. Jules Griset. – Hamelle, 1895.

First perf. Geneva, 14 November 1894 – Adolf Rehberg, Fauré.

(The manuscript bears the title *Andante* and is numbered op. 63.)

'Prunay, 3 August 1894'

Nocturne no. 6 for piano, D♭ maj., op. 63.

Ded. M. Eugène d'Eichthal. – Hamelle, 1894, 2nd edn. 1924, collected (nos 1–8).

1894

Ave verum, two-part female choir with organ, op. 65 no. 1.

Hamelle, 1894; collected, 1911.

'Bas Prunay, 14 August 1894'

Tantum ergo, three-part female choir, with soloists, and organ, in E maj., op. 65 no. 2.

Hamelle, 1894; collected, 1911.

1894

Sancta Mater, for tenor solo, mixed chorus and organ, no op. no.

Hamelle, 1922.

1894?

Ave Maria for tenor, baritone and organ, in F maj., no op. no.

Unpub.

'Bas Prunay, 18 September 1894'

Barcarolle no. 5 for piano, F♯ min., op. 66.

Ded. Mme Vincent d'Indy. – Hamelle, 1894, 2nd edn. 1926, collected (nos 1–6).

First perf. SNM, 2 May 1896 – Léon Delafosse.

'4 December 1894'

'Prison' (Paul Verlaine), E♭ min., m.v., op. 83 no. 1.

Paris, E. Fromont, 1896 (with no. op. 51 no. 1). London, Metzler, 1897 (with no. op. 68 no. 1). Hamelle, 1897 *in*: second coll. (numbered op. 73 no. 1), then (1908) third coll. (numbered op. 83 no. 1).

– with orchestra, by Florent Schmitt. – Hamelle.

'17 December 1894'

'Soir' (Albert Samain), D♭ maj., m.v. op. 83 no. 2.

Paris, E. Fromont, 1896 (numbered op. 68 no. 2). London, Metzler, 1896 (numbered op. 68 no. 2). Hamelle, 1897 *in*: second coll. (numbered op. 73 no. 2), then (1908) third coll. (numbered op. 83 no. 2).

Also published in the supplement of *L'Illustration*, no. 2773, 18 April 1896, no op. no.

– with orchestra, by Louis Aubert.

'25 March 1895'

Salve Regina, for soprano and organ, op. 67 no. 1.

Ded. Mme Sigismond Bardac. – Hamelle, 1895; collected, 1911.

In musical supplement of *L'Illustration*, 4 May 1895.

1894–5

Ave Maria, for mezzo soprano and organ, op. 67 no. 2.

Ded. Mme Adèle Bohomoletz. – Hamelle, 1895; collected, 1911.

1895

Thème et variations, for piano, C♯ min., op. 73.

Ded. Mlle Thérèse Roger. – Hamelle, 1897, London, Metzler, 1897.

First perf. London, 10 December 1896 – Léon Delafosse.

1895?

Barcarolle no. 6 for piano, E♭ maj., op. 70.

Ded. M. Edouard Risler. – Hamelle, 1896, 2nd edn 1926, collected (nos 1–6). London, Metzler, 1896.

First perf. SNM, 3 April 1897 – Edouard Risler.

'21 April 1896'

Pleurs d'or, duo for mezzo and baritone with piano, E♭ maj., op. 72.

Ded. Mlle Camille Landi and M. David Bispham. – London, Metzler, 1896. Paris, Hamelle, 1896.

First perf. London, 1 May 1896 – Camille Landi, David Bispham, Fauré.

1893–6

Dolly, six pieces for piano duet, op. 56.

Ded. Mlle Hélène Bardac (Dolly). – Hamelle, 1894 (no. 1), 1897 (nos 1–6) London, Metzler, 1897.

First perf. SNM, 30 April 1898 – Edouard Risler and Alfred Cortot.

1. 'Berceuse', '12 January 1864' (first version).

2. 'Mi-a-ou', 'for 20 June 1894'.
3. 'Le Jardin de Dolly', '1 January 1895'.
4. 'Kitty valse', '20 June 1896'.
5. 'Tendresse', Sept.–Oct. 1896.
6. 'Le Pas espagnol', 1896.

(20 June is Dolly's birthday. The original titles of nos 2 and 4 are 'Messieu Aoul!' (=M. Raoul, Dolly's brother), and 'Ketty Valse'.)

– for orchestra, by Henri Rabaud. – Hamelle, 1906.

First perf. Monte Carlo, 6 December 1906, cond. Léon Jehin.

Staged as a ballet, libretto by Louis Laloy, Théâtre des Arts, 9 January 1913, cond. Gabriel Grovlez.

1897

Prelude for piano in C maj., for the volume *Etudes d'octaves* by Isidore Philipp. Durand, 1897 (sixteen bars).

1897

Sight-reading piece for 'cello (with second 'cello acc.).

Unpub.

First perf. Concours du Conservatoire, July 1897.

'July 1897' [1878–97]

Andante for violin and piano in B♭ maj., op. 75.

Ded. Johannès Wolff. – Hamelle, 1897. London, Metzler, 1897.

First perf. SNM, 22 January 1898 – Armand Parent, vl., Germaine Polack, p.

(Probably re-using the themes of the Andante from the Concerto for Violin, op. 14.)

'22 August 1897'

'Le Parfum impérissable' (Leconte de Lisle), E maj., m.v., op. 76 no. 1.

Ded. Paolo Tosti. – London, Metzler, 1897. Hamelle, 1897; third coll. (no. 12).

First perf. Paris, 4 November 1897 – Emile Engel.

'6 September 1897'

'Arpège' (Albert Samain), E min., m.v., op. 76 no. 2.

Ded. Mme Charles Dettelbach. – London, Metzler, 1897. Hamelle, 1897; third coll. (no. 13).

First perf. SNM, 30 April 1898 – Thérèse Roger (s).

Appeared in the musical supplement of *Le Figaro*, 16 October 1897.

'16 April 1898'

Sicilienne for 'cello and piano, op. 78.

Ded. M. W. H. Squire. – London, Metzler, 1898. Paris, Hamelle, 1898. (See under 'March 1893' and below, *Pelléas et Mélisande*, May–June 1898.)

May–June 1898

Pelléas et Mélisande, incidental music for the play by Maurice Maeterlinck, English transl. by J. W. Mackail, op. 80.

– London version with unpub. interludes. Orchestration for reduced instrumental group by Charles Koechlin.

First perf. London, Prince of Wales Theatre, 21 June 1898, cond. G. Fauré. Unpub.

– orchestral suite: 1 Prélude 2 Fileuse 3 Sicilienne 4 Molto adagio (Death of Mélisande). Orchestration for full orchestra by G. Fauré, based on the orchestration of Charles Koechlin, 1898.

Ded. Mme la princesse Edmond de Polignac. – Hamelle, 1901.

First perf. Concert Lamoureux, 3 February 1901, cond. Camille Chevillard.

'31 May 1898'

Mélisande's song from *Pelléas et Mélisande*, (Maurice Maeterlinck, trans. J. W. Mackail), Act III, sc. 1, D min., m.v., voice and piano, op. posth.

Hamelle, 1937.

Reorchestrated version by Charles Koechlin, 1936; first perf. Paris, 21 December 1936.

Appears in the London original version, with small orchestra.

June–July 1898

Fantaisie for flute and piano, op. 79.

Ded. M. Paul Taffanel. – Hamelle, 1898.

First perf. Paris, Concours du Conservatoire, 28 July 1898 (winner of competition: Gaston Blanquart).

– with orchestra, by Louis Aubert (1957). Hamelle, 1958.

First perf. Salle Gaveau, 24 February 1957 – Jean-Pierre Rampal, fl., cond. Fernand Oubradous.

14 July 1898

Sight-reading piece for flute and piano, no op. no.

First perf. Paris, Conservatoire competition, 28 July 1898.

Edited and arranged by Anabel Hulme Brieff, New York, Bourne, 1977.

August 1898

Nocturne no. 7 for piano, C♯ min., op. 74.

Ded. Mme Adela Maddison. – Hamelle, 1899, 2nd edn. 1924, collected (nos 1–8).

First perf. SNM, 20 March 1901 – Alfred Cortot.

February–July 1900

Prométhée, tragédie lyrique by Jean Lorrain and André-Ferdinand Hérold, op. 82.

Ded. M. Fernand Castelbon de Beauxhostes. – Hamelle, 1900 (voice and piano).

– Original orchestration (1900), for wind band by Charles Eustace, and string orchestra by G. Fauré.

Unpub.

Performances: Arènes de Béziers, 27 and 28 August 1900, 25 and 27 August 1901, cond. G. Fauré. Paris, Hippodrome, 5 December 1907, Opéra, 15 December 1907, Cond. G. Fauré. Repeated: Nice, Arènes de Cimiez, August 1939.

– Orchestration for symphonic orchestra (1914–17) by Roger Ducasse. – Hamelle. Opéra de Paris, 17 May 1917 (three performances), cond. C. Chevillard.

Repeated: Paris: 1924, 1931, 1936, 1938, 1939, 1949, 1960, 1961, 1973. Aix-les-Bains: 1925. Nantes: 1925. Angers: 1925. Strasbourg: 1928. Lyon: 1928, 1930, 1934, 1972. Vaison-la-Romaine; 1973.

Autumn 1901

Le Voile du bonheur, incidental music for the play by Georges Clemenceau, op. 88.

Unpub.

First perf. Théâtre de la Renaissance, 4 November 1901, cond. Emile Vuillermoz.

(Chinese music for small instrumental ensemble: flute, oboe, clarinet, trumpet, string quartet, gong, tubophone, orchestration by E. Vuillermoz.)

'28 March 1902'

'Accompagnement' (Albert Samain), G♭, m.v., op. 85 no. 3.

Ded. Mme Edouard Risler. – Hamelle, 1902; third coll. (no. 20).

'15 April 1902'

Cadenza for Concerto in C min. by Mozart (no. 24, K. 491).

Op. posth.

Paris, Magasin musical Pierre Schneider, 1927. Edited and fingered by Marguerite Hasselmans.

First perf. Paris, Concerts Hasselmans, 15 April 1902 – Marguerite Hasselmans, piano, cond. Louis Hasselmans.

1869–1902

Huit Pièces brèves, for piano, op. 84.

1 in E♭, July 1899
2 in A♭, 1902?
3 in A min., '30 June 1869'
4 in E min., '27 August 1902'
5 in C♯ min., '9 July 1901'
6 in E min., '30 November 1869'
7 in C maj., '2 August 1902'
8 in D♭, '4 September 1902'

Ded. Mme Jean Léonard-Koechlin. – Hamelle, 1902.

First perf. nos 2, 4, 7, 8, SNM, 18 April 1903 – Ricardo Viñes.

The first piece was written for the competition at the Conservatoire (22 July 1899) and appeared in *Le Figaro* of 29 July 1899. The version published in the *Pièces brèves* is longer than that for the Conservatoire. The definitive version was also published in *L'Illustration*, 1 July 1905.

Piece no. 5 was, similarly, written for the Conservatoire competition of 19 July 1901 and appeared in *Le Monde musical* of 30 August 1901.

In a later printing (1903), Hamelle thought good to give individual titles to each of these pieces, against the wishes of the composer: 1 Capriccio 2 Fantaisie 3 Fugue 4 Adagietto 5 Improvisation 6 Fugue 7 Allégresse 8 Nocturne no. 8.

'13 September 1902'

'La Fleur qui va sur l'eau' (Catulle Mendès), B min., m.v., op. 85 no. 2.
Ded. Mlle Pauline Segond. – Hamelle, 1902; third coll. (no. 19).

'29 September 1902'

'Dans la forêt de septembre' (Catulle Mendès), G♭, m.v., op. 85 no. 1.
Ded. Mlle Lydia Eustis. – Hamelle, 1902; third coll. (no. 18).

Autumn 1902

'Dans le ciel clair' (Leconte de Lisle), E min., m.v., no op. no.
Unpub. and unfinished (sketches preserved).

July 1903

Sight-reading piece for violin and piano, no op. no.
For the Conservatoire competition, 24 July 1903.
Le Monde musical, 30 August 1903.

July 1904

Sight-reading piece for harp, no op. no.
For the Conservatoire competition, 25 July 1904.
Unpub.

July 1904

Impromptu for harp, op. 86.

Ded. Mme Alphonse Hasselmans. – Durand, 1904.

For the Conservatoire competition, 25 July 1904.

First perf. Conservatoire, July 1904 – Mlle Charlotte Landrin (Mme Jacques Lerolle).

— SNM, 7 January 1905 – Micheline Kahn.

– Transcription for piano (by Alfred Cortot) under the title Impromptu no. 6, op. 86 bis. Durand, 1913.

1904

'Le Plus doux chemin' (Armand Silvestre), F min., m.v., op. 87 no. 1.

Ded. Mme Edouard Risler. – Hamelle, 1907; third coll. (no. 16).

1904

'Le Ramier' (Armand Silvestre), E min., m.v., op. 87 no. 2.

Ded. Mlle Claudie Segond. – Milan, The Gramophone comp., 1904. Hamelle; third coll. (no. 17).

'8 November 1904'

Tantum ergo, for soprano solo and mixed four-part chorus, with organ, in G♭, no op. no.

'Pour la Messe de mariage de Mlle Greffulhe'. – Durand, 1905. Hamelle, collection of religious music by Fauré, 1911.

First perf. Church of the Madeleine, 14 November 1904.

– with string quintet accompaniment.

Unpub. (The original key of the ms. is F major.)

1905

Piece for two double-basses (twenty-five bars).

For the collection *Déchiffrage du manuscrit* (facsimiles).

Lemoine, 1905.

1905

Jules César, incidental music, based on *Caligula*, for the play by Shakespeare (trans. François-Victor Hugo), op. 52 bis.

First perf. Théâtre antique d'Orange, 7 August 1905, cond. Edouard Colonne.

Unpub.

1890–4
1903–5
Quintet no. 1 for piano, two violins, viola and 'cello, in D min., op. 89.
Ded. Eugène Ysaÿe. – New York, Schirmer, 1907.
First perf. Brussels, Cercle artistique, 23 March 1906 and Paris, Salle Pleyel, 30 April 1906, G. Fauré and the Ysaÿe Quartet (Eugène Ysaÿe, Edouard Deru, Léon Van Hout, Joseph Jacob).

11–14 August 1905
Barcarolle no. 7 for piano, in D min., op. 90.
Ded. Mme Isidore Philipp. – Heugel, 1906.
First perf. Salle Erard, 3 February 1906 – Arnold Reitlinger.
Initially, Ms published in facsimile in the Christmas no., 1905, of *Le Figaro illustré*, then in *Le Ménestrel* of 18 February 1906.

1905
Impromptu no. 4 for piano, in D♭, op. 91.
Ded. Mme de Marliave (Marguerite Long). – Heugel, 1906, 2nd edn.: Hamelle, 1926, collected.
First perf. SNM, 12 January 1907 – Edouard Risler.

'10 August 1906'
Ave Maria for two sopranos and organ, in B min., op. 93.
Ded. Mme Georges Kinen (Anita Eustis). – Heugel, 1906.
(Uses elements of unpublished *Ave Maria* of 1877.)

'20 August 1906'
'Le Don silencieux' (Jean Dominique), E maj., m.v., op. 92.
Ded. Mme Octave Maus. – Heugel, 1906.
First perf. Brussels, La Libre esthétique, 12 March 1907 – Jane Bathori (mez), Fauré.

1906
'Chanson' (Henri de Régnier), E min., m.v., op. 94.
Heugel, 1907.

1906
Barcarolle no. 8 for piano, in D♭, op. 96.
Ded. Mlle Suzanne Alfred-Bruneau. – Heugel, 1908.
First perf. SNM, 12 January 1907 – Edouard Risler.

1906

'Vocalise-Etude' (singing exercise), for high voice with piano acc., E min., no op. no.

Leduc, 1907.

(No. 1 in the collection of singing exercises by A.-L. Hettich.)

Transcription for flute or oboe or violin, and piano, by Th. Doney, under the title of *Pièce*. – Leduc, 1920.

1906–10

La Chanson d'Eve (Charles van Lerberghe), m.v., op. 95.

Ded. Mme Jeanne Raunay. – Heugel, 1906–10; collected, 1911.

First performances, incomplete (nos 1, 2, 9), Salle des Agriculteurs, 3 February 1908 and London, Bechstein Hall, 18 March 1908 – Jeanne Raunay, Fauré; (nos 1, 2, 3, 5, 4, 6, 9), Salle Erard, 26 May 1909 – Jeanne Raunay, Fauré.

First complete perf. SMI, 20 April 1910 – Jeanne Raunay, Fauré.

1   'Paradis', E min., '8 September 1906'. Heugel, 1907.
2   'Prima verba', G♭ maj., '28 September 1906'. Heugel, 1907.
3   'Roses ardentes', E maj., June 1908. Heugel, 1909.
4   'Comme Dieu rayonne', C min., 1909. Heugel, 1909.
5   'l'Aube blanche', D♭ maj., June 1908. Heugel, 1908.
6   'Eau vivante', C maj., 1909. Heugel, 1909.
7   'Veilles-tu ma senteur de soleil?', D maj., January 1910. Heugel, 1910.
8   'Dans un parfum de roses blanches', G maj., 1909. Heugel, 1909.
9   'Crépuscule', D min., '4 June 1906'. Heugel, 1906.
10 'Ô Mort poussière d'étoiles', D♭ maj., January 1910. Heugel, 1910.

1908?

Nocturne no. 9, in B min., op. 97.

Ded. Mme Alfred Cortot. – Heugel, 1908.

1908?

Sérénade, for 'cello and piano in B min., op. 98.

Ded. Pablo Casals. – Heugel, 1908.

'November 1908'

Nocturne no. 10 for piano, in B min., op. 99.

Ded. Mme Brunet Lecomte. – Heugel, 1909.

1908–9

Barcarolle no. 9 for piano, in A min., op. 101.

Ded. Mme Charles Neff. – Heugel, 1909.

First perf. Salle Erard, 30 March 1909 – Marguerite Long.

1908 – 9

Impromptu no. 5 for piano, in F# min., op. 102.

Ded. Mlle Cella Delavrancea. – Heugel, 1909. 2nd edn.: Hamelle, 1926, collected.

First perf. Salle Erard, 30 March 1909 – Marguerite Long.

1909–10

Nine Preludes for piano, op. 103.

1 D♭ maj., 2 C# min., 3 G min., 4 F maj., 5 D min., 6 E♭ min., 7 A maj., 8 C min., 9 E min.

Ded. Mlle Elisabeth de Lallemand.

Nos 1–3: finished early January 1910. Heugel, 1910.

First perf. SMI, 17 May 1910 – Marguerite Long.

Nos 4–9: summer–autumn 1910. Heugel, 1911.

The Nine Preludes, collected. Heugel, 1923.

1907–12

Pénélope, lyric drama in three acts, libretto by René Fauchois, no op. no.

Ded. Camille Saint-Saëns. – Heugel, 1912 and 1913 (vocal score 2 diff. ed.), 1913 (orchestral score).

Monte Carlo: 4, 11 and 15 March 1913 – Lucienne Bréval, Charles Rousselière, cond. Léon Jehin.

Paris, Théâtre des Champs-Elysées (17 performances), first: 10 May 1913 – Lucienne Bréval, Lucien Muratore, dir. Louis Hasselmans.

Paris, Opéra-Comique (sixty-three performances), first: 20 January 1919 – Germain Lubin, Lucien Muratore, cond. François Ruhlmann.

Repeats in 1922, 1923, 1924, 1927, 1931.

Pénélope – Medelaine Mathieu, Lucienne Bréval, Claire Croiza, Suzanne Balguerie.

Ulysse – Charles Fontaine, René Lapelletrie, Maurice Oger, Lucien Muratore.

Paris, Théâtre national de l'Opéra (27 performances), 1943 and 1949, first: 14 March 1943–Germaine Lubin, Georges Jouatte, cond. François Ruhlmann; 18 February 1949 – Marysa Ferrer, Georges Jouatte, cond. Désiré-Emile Inghelbrecht.

Abroad: Brussels, 1 December 1913 (Claire Croiza, ten performances) and 1920; Anvers (trans. Flemish Maurits Sabbe), 15 March 1924; Liège (1951); Buenos Aires (1962); Lisbon (1966).

In the provinces: Rouen (1913), Orange (1923), Strasbourg (1923), Nice (1924), Lyon (1927, 1943 and 1957), Bordeaux (1927, 1943 and 1969), Angers (1931), Toulouse (1957 and 1964), Marseille (1957), Vichy (1958).

Concert performances in Paris (RTF), cond. Désiré-Emile Inghelbrecht (1948, 1951, 1956, 1963) and Paul Paray (1974); Amsterdam (Concertgebouw), dir. Jean Fournet (1963); London (BBC), cond. David Lloyd-Jones (1973). *Pénélope* – Régine Crespin, Joséphine Veasey, Liliane Guitton. *Ulysse* – Guy Chauvet, Georges Jouatte, Raoul Jobin, André Turp.

1913
Nocturne no. 11 for piano, in F# min., op. 104 no. 1.
In memory of Noémi Lalo. – Durand, 1913.

'October 1913'
Barcarolle no. 10 for piano, in A min., op. 104 no. 2.
Ded. Mme Léon Blum. – Durand, 1913.

1913–14
Barcarolle no. 11 for piano, in G min., op. 105.
Ded. Mlle Laura Albéniz. – Durand, 1914.

July–November 1914
Le Jardin clos (Charles van Lerberghe), h.v. and m.v., op. 106.
Durand, 1915.
First perf. Concerts Casella, 28 January 1915 – Claire Croiza (mez), Fauré.
1 'Exaucement', A maj., ded. Mme Albert Mockel.
2 'Quand tu plonges tes yeux dans mes yeux', F maj., ded. Mlle Germaine Sanderson.
3 'La Messagère', G maj., ded. Mlle Gabrielle Gills.
4 'Je me poserai sur ton cœur', E♭ maj., ded. Mme Louis Vuillemin.
5 'Dans la Nymphée', D♭ maj., ded. Mme Claire Croiza.
6 'Dans la pénombre', E maj., ded. Mme Houben-Kufferath.
7 'Il m'est cher, Amour, le bandeau', F maj., ded. Mme Faliero-Dalcroze.
8 'Inscription sur le sable', E min., ded. Mme Durand-Texte.

August–September 1915
Nocturne no. 12 for piano, in E min., op. 107.
Ded. Robert Lortat. – Durand, 1916.
First perf. Concerts Jacques Durand, 23 November 1916 – Louis Diémer.

'September 1915'
Barcarolle no. 12 for piano, in E♭ maj., op. 106 bis.
Ded. Louis Diémer. – Durand, 1916.
First perf. Concerts Jacques Durand, 23 November 1916 – Louis Diémer.

August 1916–May 1917

Sonata no. 2 for violin and piano, in E min., op. 108.

Ded. Her Majesty Elisabeth, Queen of the Belgians. – Durand, 1917.

First perf. SNM, 10 November 1917 – Lucien Capet, Alfred Cortot.

1917

Sonata no. 1 for 'cello and piano, in D min., op. 109.

Ded. Louis Hasselmans. – Durand, 1918.

First perf. SNM, 19 January 1918 – André Hekking, Alfred Cortot.

1918

Une Châtelaine en sa tour, for harp, op. 110.

Ded. Mme Micheline Kahn. – Durand, 1918.

First perf. SNM, 30 November 1918 – Micheline Kahn.

1918

Fantaisie for piano and orchestra in G maj., op. 111.

Ded. Alfred Cortot. – Durand, 1919. (Orchestration by Marcel Samuel-Rousseau.)

First performances: Monte Carlo, 12 April 1919 – Marguerite Hasselmans, cond. Léon Jehin; Paris, SNM, 14 May 1919 – Alfred Cortot, cond. Vincent d'Indy.

1919

Masques et bergamasques, musical comedy in one act, words by René Fauchois.

Ded. 'to my great-great nieces Nicole and Huguette Réveillac'. – Durand, 1919.

Theatrical version:

1 *Ouverture* (based on the *Intermède symphonique* 1864–9).

2 *Pastorale* (1919).

3 *Madrigal* op. 35 (with orchestra by the composer, 1883).

4 *Le Plus doux chemin*, op. 87 no. 1 (in F min., 1904, with orchestration by Marcel Samuel-Rousseau).

5 *Menuet* (c. 1869 ?).

6 *Clair de lune* op. 46 no. 2 (in C min., with orchestration by the composer, 1888).

7 *Gavotte* (based on the *Gavotte* for piano, 1869 and that of the Symphony op. 20). Orchestration by Marcel Samuel-Rousseau.

8 *Pavane* op. 50 with chorus (1887).

First performances: Monte Carlo, 10 April 1919, cond. Léon Jehin; Paris, Opéra-Comique, 4 March 1920, cond. Fernand Masson (105 performances up to 1952).

– Orchestral suite op. 112.

Ouverture, Menuet, Gavotte, Pastorale. – Durand, 1920.

First perf. Société des Concerts du Conservatoire, 16 November 1919, cond. Philippe Gaubert.

– This suite for piano duet by the composer. Durand, 1919.

summer 1919

Mirages (Renée de Brimont), m.v. and h.v., op. 113.

Ded. Mme Gabriel Hanotaux. – Durand, 1919.

First perf. SNM, 27 December 1919 – Madeleine Grey (s), Fauré.

1 'Cygne sur l'eau', F maj.
2 'Reflets dans l'eau', B♭ maj.
3 'Jardin nocturne', E♭ maj.
4 'Danseuse', D min.

'8 December 1919'

'C'est la paix' (Georgette Debladis), A maj., h.v., op. 114.

Durand, 1920 and *Le Figaro* of 10 October 1920.

(Work written to the winning poem in an open competition in *Le Figaro* on the theme of peace.)

September 1919–March 1921

Quintet no. 2 for piano, two violins, viola and 'cello, op. 115.

Ded. M. Paul Dukas. – Durand, 1921.

First perf. SNM, 21 May 1921 – Robert Lortat, p. André Tourret and Victor Gentil, vl., Maurice Vieux, vla, Gérard Hekking, vlc.

February 1921

Barcarolle no. 13 for piano, in C maj., op. 116.

Ded. Mme Soon-Gumaelius. – Durand, 1921.

First perf. SNM, 28 April 1923 – Blanche Selva.

February–March 1921

Chant funéraire for the centenary of the death of Napoleon I, no op. no.

Orchestration for military band by Guillaume Balay.

Durand, 1932.

First perf. Hôtel des Invalides, 5 May 1921 – Orchestra of the Garde Républicaine, cond. Guillaume Balay.

(Transcribed by Fauré as the Andante of the Sonata no. 2 for 'cello.)

10 November 1921

Sonata no. 2 for 'cello and piano, in G min., op. 117.

Ded. Charles-Martin Loeffler. – Durand, 1922.

First perf. SNM, 13 May 1922 – Gérard Hekking, Alfred Cortot.

1921

L'Horizon chimérique (Jean de la Ville de Mirmont), m.v., op. 118.

Ded. M. Charles Panzéra. – Durand, 1922.

First perf. SNM, 13 May 1922 – Charles Panzéra and Madeleine Panzéra-Baillot.
1 'La mer est infinie', D maj.
2 'Je me suis embarqué', D♭ maj.
3 'Diane Séléné, E♭ maj.
4 'Vaisseaux, nous vous aurons aimés', D maj.

'31 December 1921'

Nocturne no. 13 for piano, in B min., op. 119.

Ded. Mme Fernand Maillot. – Durand, 1922.

First perf. SNM, 28 April 1923 – Blanche Selva.

1922–3

Trio for piano, violin and 'cello, in D min., op. 120.

Ded. Mme Maurice Rouvier. – Durand, 1923.

First perf. SNM, 12 May 1923 – Tatiana de Sanzévitch, p., Robert Krettly, vl., Jacques Patté, vlc.

Second perf. Paris, 29 June 1923 – Alfred Cortot, Jacques Thibaud, Pablo Casals.

August 1923–11 September 1924

String Quartet, in E min., op. 121.

Ded. Camille Bellaigue. – Durand, 1925.

First perf. SNM, Salle du Conservatoire, 12 June 1925 – Jacques Thibaud and Robert Krettly, vl., Maurice Vieux, vla, André Hekking, vlc.

Facsimile of autograph manuscript. Durand, 1925.

– for piano duet by Alfred Cortot (the Andante by G. Fauré). Durand, 1925.

Notes

Note Quotations from G. Fauré *Correspondance*, ed. J.-M. Nectoux (Paris, Flammarion, 1980) have all been newly translated for this volume. References to the English edition, *Gabriel Fauré, His Life through his Letters*, trans. John Underwood (London, New York, Marion Boyars, 1984) use the abbreviated form *LTL*. Readers should note that both French and English editions bear the same numbering for the letters.

I GRADUS AD PARNASSUM

1 See the typed document *La famille Fauré à travers les siècles* prepared in 1906 by a Paris genealogist, E. Nierendorf, at the request of the composer's brother Albert Fauré who had, in 1880, inquired about the name (de Lalène Laprade) of their mother who was terminally ill.

2 See Toussaint Nigoul: 'Gabriel Fauré', *L'Ariège pittoresque*, 29 May 1913, pp. 1–3. Emmanuel Fauré-Fremiet passed on to me a family tree to which I have made certain additions.

3 Transcribed by Jean Nohain, alias Jabunne, in 'Les grands hommes lorsqu'ils étaient petits', an unidentified newspaper article dated 8 May 1924, reprinted in a book (same title) published *c.* 1925 by Flammarion in Paris.

4 *Lettres intimes*, ed. Philippe Fauré-Fremiet (Paris, La Colombe; later Grasset, 1951). This volume of Fauré's letters to his wife is a book of central importance to which I shall frequently refer under the heading *Lettres intimes*.

5 *Gabriel Fauré* (Paris, Rieder, 1929; rev. Paris, Albin Michel, 1957), p. 28. In the early chapters of the book, Fauré's younger son tells a number of stories about his father's childhood, some of which had been handed down in the family. The frequent references to this book are to the revised edition.

6 *Ibid.*, p. 19.

7 *Revue éolienne* (Béziers), 1 September 1900, p. 439.

8 According to the *Dictionnaire des familles françaises* by Chaix-d'Est-Ange, Vol. XVII, p. 74, and the *Almanach impérial pour 1855*; and not the deputy for Ariège, as I wrote in 1972 following information from Philippe Fauré-Fremiet. M.-L. Boëllmann, in his article on the Niedermeyer School, suggests that it was

Niedermeyer himself who discovered the young Fauré's talent. The only documentary evidence we have (letters from T. H. Fauré to M. de Saubiac, published in Philippe Fauré-Fremiet's biography) indicates clearly the crucial rôle played by M. de Saubiac.

9 On this point see the remarks of Dr Charles Burney made in the last third of the eighteenth century (*The Present State of Music . . .*) and the reports of Mendelssohn in his early letters.

10 Archives Nationales (Paris), F. 3947.

11 These details of Fauré's school career are taken from Niedermeyer's report, which I have already quoted, on the prize lists published by *La Maîtrise*, the Niedermeyer School's magazine; and from the article by M.-L. Boëllmann (actually written by Jacqueline Gachet) which appears in the bibliography.

12 'Gabriel Fauré à l'Ecole Niedermeyer', *Le Courrier musical*, 15 November 1924, pp. 540–1. I quote at some length from this eye-witness account which is not found in any bibliography.

13 *Le Ménestrel* of 4 August 1901 (p. 247) likewise announces the appointment of Fauré as professor of composition at the Niedermeyer School, but it seems he soon gave in his notice, to judge by an undated letter to Gustave Lefèvre (coll. E. Labeyrie).

14 'Souvenirs', *Revue musicale*, special number, *G. Fauré*, October 1922.

15 *La Maîtrise*, 15 March 1858, pp. 178–9.

16 'Souvenirs'.

17 BN (Mus. Dept); a notebook dated 1859. Fauré is classified as 'satisfactory', 'mediocre' or 'hopeless' on a daily basis.

18 Paris, Société française de musicologie, 1973.

19 *Lettres intimes*, p. 282.

20 *La Maîtrise*, 15 August 1858, p. 70.

21 Reply to the questionnaire: 'Sous la musique que faut-il mettre?', *Musica*, no. 101, February 1911, p. 38.

2 SCENES FROM PROVINCIAL LIFE

1 *Excelsior*, 12 June 1922, p. 2.

2 I would like to acknowledge in this field the kind help of Mme M.-Cl. Mussat-Lemoigne of the University of Rennes, all the more gratefully received because the Breton press collection for this period in the Bibliothèque Nationale is far from complete.

3 'Festival Fauré', *Journal de l'Université des Annales*, 10 June 1908, pp. 430–2.

4 See Julien Torchet, 'Les Hommes du jour', quoted by Toussaint Nigoul in 'Gabriel Fauré', *L'Ariège pittoresque*, 29 May 1913, pp. 2–3.

5 This was probably the adaptation of Tamino's first aria in *The Magic Flute* (K. Anh. B zu 620).

6 29 June 1867, p. 515.

7 *Ibid.*, 11 August 1866, pp. 523–5.

8 This cadenza was published in 1927 by Alfred Cortot at the Magasin musical Pierre Schneider, Paris.

9 See the advertisement in the *Journal d'Ille et Vilaine (breton)*, 30 January 1866, pp. 2–3.

10 A favourable review appeared in the *Journal d'Ille et Vilaine* of 11 February 1868, p. 3.

11 See the reference in the *Journal de Rennes* of 26 August 1868.

12 *Le Petit Parisien*, 20 April 1922, p. 1.

13 See G. Fauré and C. Saint-Saëns, *Correspondance. Soixante ans d'amitié (1862–1921)*, ed. J.-M. Nectoux, no. VII. (See Bibliography.)

14 18 July 1868, p. 592.

15 The story was recounted by Alfred Cortot who said he got it from Fauré himself (see the introduction and addendum to the Fauré and Saint-Saëns *Correspondance*).

16 See the ironic letter in which Fauré gives an account, worthy of Balzac, of the salons in Rennes under the Second Empire, in G. Fauré: *Correspondance*, pp. 23–4; *LTL*, p. 22. (See p. 559 for note on this title.)

17 *La Vie et les Œuvres de Gabriel Fauré* (Paris, Fasquelle, 1925), p. 19.

18 *La Semaine religieuse du diocèse de Rennes* mentions someone by the name of Gortebeck as organist of St-Sauveur in its edition of 5 February 1870.

19 *La Vie et les Œuvres de Gabriel Fauré*, pp. 19–20.

20 Information given by Philippe Fauré-Fremiet in a talk on Radio Lausanne around 1956 and passed on by M. Alex van Amerongen.

21 These details from the files of the Land Registry kept in the *Archives du département de la Seine* in Paris.

22 In *Comoedia illustré*, 1 April 1909, p. 202.

23 Archives of the *Société nationale de musique* in the Music Department of the Bibliothèque Nationale.

24 Fauré, *Correspondance/LTL*, no. 5.

3 FRIENDS AND LOVERS

1 Numerous details of Fauré's friendship with the Clerc family can be found in the introduction to chapter 2 of my volume of Fauré's correspondence.

2 See the Princess' memoirs published in *Horizon*, August 1945, p. 118.

3 See the collection of documents referring to this episode in G. Fauré, *Correspondance/LTL*, letter 9.

4 Baedeker informs visitors in the early years of this century: 'Fashionable society tends to go to Mass at midday and at 1 o'clock. The departure from these services at the principal churches is one of the sights of Paris, and at the Madeleine in particular' (1907 edition, p. 57).

5 Saint-Saëns, Fauré, *Correspondance*, letter 26.

6 This information comes from the parish accounts and from Félicien Grétry's article, 'La maîtrise de la Madeleine', *Musica*, January 1903, p. 62.

7　Eugène Labiche (1815–88), playwright, whose farcical comedies include *The Italian Straw Hat*.

8　It covered the First Piano Quartet op. 15, the *Berceuse* for violin, and the three songs op. 18. See p. 86 for further details of the agreement.

9　Ed. Calmann Lévy, *c.* 1890, pp. 174–5.

10　See Fauré, *Correspondance/LTL*, letter 16 and the article by Jean Mongrédien in *Cahiers I. Tourgueniev, P. Viardot, M. Malibran*, no. 2, 1978, pp. 39–45.

11　Letter to a lady by the name of Nerozat, headed 'Bougival, 8 September, Maison Halgan', dating probably from 1873 or 1874. Kindly made available by Thierry Bodin.

12　Dated 17 September 1877. See G. Fauré, *Correspondance/LTL*, letter 24.

13　The story appears in a letter from Romain Bussine to Marie Clerc. See J.-M. Nectoux, *Fauré* (Paris, ed. du Seuil, 1986), p. 26.

14　Fauré, *Correspondance/LTL*, letter 21.

15　These letters were published, with cuts, by Camille Bellaigue in the *Revue des deux mondes*, 15 August 1928, pp. 910–43. Marianne had returned them after the engagement was broken off and they are now in the Bibliothèque Nationale (Music Dept).

16　This letter has been kept in the Clerc family papers and is now in the Bibliothèque Nationale (Music Dept).

17　Text made available by M. Alexandre Zviguilski.

18　*G. Fauré*, 2nd ed., p. 58; see also Fauré, *Correspondance/LTL*, letters 25 and 26.

19　*Ibid.*, letter 34.

20　The manuscript in fact bears the opus no. 17, which puts the work before 'Automne', written during the summer of 1878. *Poème d'un jour* was finally published by Durand as op. 21.

21　*Gabriel Fauré* (Paris, Laurens, 1930), p. 31.

22　See also J.-M. Nectoux, 'Musique, symbolisme et Art nouveau, notes pour une esthétique de la musique française fin-de-siècle', in a volume in honour of Willi Schuh, edited by Jürg Stenzl: *Art nouveau, Jugendstil und Musik* (Zürich, Atlantis, 1980).

23　On Proust and Fauré see chapter 6 of G. Fauré, *Correspondance/LTL*.

24　See J.-M. Nectoux, 'Debussy et Fauré', *Cahiers Debussy*, nouvelle série, no. 3, 1979, pp. 13–30.

25　See chapters 8 and 9.

26　*Excelsior*, 12 June 1922.

27　See chapter 3 in Fauré, *Correspondance/LTL* and Chronology in the present volume.

28　Published by Albert Vander Linden in *Octave Maus et la vie musicale belge (1875–1914)*, (Brussels, 1950), p. 44.

29　Fauré, *Correspondance/LTL*, letter 72.

4 'EN BLANC ET NOIR'

1 On the organ teaching at the Niedermeyer School, see the method by Jacques Lemmens, *École d'orgue* (Brussels, 1862), and Walter Corten's excellent unpublished study, 'Le procès de canonisation de Sébastien Bach en France au XIXe, siècle' (Université libre de Bruxelles, 1977–8).

2 Quoted by Bernard Gavoty, *Louis Vierne* (Paris, 1943), p. 280.

3 'Les hommes du jour', 'M. Gabriel Fauré', *L'Eclair*, 23 January 1893.

4 Entry for 6 April 1902. I have transcribed her references to Fauré in *Etudes fauréennes*, no. 18, 1981, pp. 3–25.

5 See J.-M. Nectoux, 'Albéniz et Fauré', including their letters to each other, in *Travaux de l'Institut d'Etudes Ibériques et Latino-Américaines de Strasbourg*, 1977, p. 169. The music example in the Fauré letter has been reproduced inaccurately.

6 *Memoirs* (see chapter 3, n. 2), p. 119.

7 Preface to *Œuvres complètes pour orgue de J. S. Bach* (Paris, Durand, 1917).

8 Abbot Hazé 'of the diocese of Rouen' announced in 1884 that a piece by Fauré would be included in the second volume of his *Album d'auteurs modernes, pièces inédites pour orgue et harmonium*. This volume was apparently never published. See also Fauré's letter to Saint-Saëns of 14 July 1898.

9 *G. Fauré*, p. 76.

10 See the photographs in the *Bulletin SIM*, February 1911, pp. 5–6, illustrating an article by P. Jobbé Duval: 'Leurs mains'.

11 See Jean-Jacques Eigeldinger, *Chopin vu par ses élèves* (Neuchâtel, La Baconnière, 3rd ed., 1988); trans. as *Chopin: Pianist and Teacher – as seen by his pupils* (Cambridge, CUP, 3rd ed., 1986).

12 *Vie de J. S. Bach*, ed. Walter Dürr (Paris, Flammarion, 1981), p. 72.

13 See the observations of Walter Corten (Corten, 1977–8), p. 83.

14 In a letter of 1875 to J. Koszul (*Correspondance/LTL*, letter 6) he says he charges ten francs a lesson. Writing to Mme Baugnies in the summer of 1887 (*ibid.*, letter 58) he complains, 'and my pupils are at Versailles (twice a week), Ville d'Avray (likewise), Saint-Germain and Louveciennes!'

15 *Au piano avec G. Fauré* (Paris, Julliard, 1963), p. 102.

16 *Gabriel Fauré* (Paris, Laurens, 1930), p. 31.

17 A list is given as an appendix on pp. 623–4.

18 *Etudes fauréennes*, no. 18, 1981, p. 11.

19 *Alfred Cortot* (Paris, Buchet et Chastel, 1977), p. 76.

20 *G. Fauré*, p. 139.

21 *Lettres intimes*, 2 August, 1910, p. 186.

22 *Revue des deux Mondes*, 15 August 1928, p. 936.

23 Fauré, *Correspondance/LTL*, letter 45.

24 *Au piano avec G. Fauré*, p. 55.

25 Letter to the musicologist Edouard Ganche, dated 23 December 1929 (Bibliothèque Nationale, Music Dept). The piece in question was probably the

'cello and piano version of Liszt's *First Elegy* (Raabe 471). Liszt had set a light-hearted trap for Planté, having originally asked him to come and play the Chopin 'Cello Sonata! For an account of the occasion, see *Le Ménestrel*, 4 April 1886, p. 143.

26 Liszt's advice, in short, was for Fauré to do what he himself had done to Schubert's *Wanderer Fantasy*. This conversation is given, both in Fauré's letter to Marie Clerc and by his son Philippe in the second edition of his biography (p. 52), as having taken place in 1882 in Zürich. But Alfred Cortot in his lecture given on 10 February 1938 ('Le Dialogue du piano et de la symphonie', *Conférencia*, 1 June 1938) and Philippe Fauré-Fremiet in the first edition of his book (Paris, Rieder, 1929, p. 37) claimed it was in Weimar, that is to say in December 1877. This second suggestion is not impossible. In another letter to Mme Clerc (17 September 1879, *Correspondance/LTL*, letter 37) Fauré says about the Ballade that he has managed to build a unified structure out of three pieces which were originally separate, and this early three-part version could have been more or less complete by December 1877. What is more, Liszt's advice to orchestrate it belongs more naturally to 1877 than to 1882 as Fauré finished the orchestral score in April 1881. Even so by 1882 only the piano solo version had been published and there is no reason why it should not have been shown to Liszt at this later date. His suggestion to orchestrate it because it was so complex could have been made in ignorance that this had already been done. In any case the orchestral score was not published until after his death and it is the piano solo version which is to be found in his library. In 1877 Saint-Saëns was busy with rehearsals for *Samson et Dalila* and might well have had no time to introduce Fauré to Liszt; and in Fauré's letter of July 1882 he speaks of an 'introduction' and says in so many words that next day he will be 'on the piano-stool'. In my opinion he played the piano solo version of the Ballade on 10 July 1882 in Zürich.

27 The list is given in Fauré, *Correspondance*, p. 69; *LTL*, p. 68.

28 Saint-Saëns, Fauré, *Correspondance*, no. 124.

29 Fauré, *Correspondance/LTL*, letter 114.

30 *Ibid.*, letter 117.

31 On Thérèse Roger, see *LTL*, index of correspondents, pp. 357–8.

32 'Œuvres de Gabriel Fauré publiées chez J. Hamelle', a list printed in April 1896, in support of Fauré's candidature for the Institut. It appeared on the back of Hamelle's editions and was revised when new works appeared. One of the earliest copies is in the archives of the Institut de France (5 E 67).

33 On the relationship between Fauré and Chabrier, see the two Fauré letters to Chabrier published in *Association des amis de Gabriel Fauré, Bulletin*, no. 13 (1976), pp. 17–18.

34 M. Long, *Au piano avec G. Fauré*, p. 155. Was it *Le Muletier espagnol*, dating from 1879? See the list of works in Philippe Fauré-Fremiet's book on his grandfather: *Fremiet* (Paris, Plon, 1934), p. 143.

35 M. Ravel, 'Au Théâtre des Arts', *Comoedia illustré*, 5 February 1913, pp. 418–19. Laloy's scenario has remained unpublished (Archives Laloy).

1 For example, the songs 'Seule!' (1871) and 'Sérénade toscane' (1878?) were both allotted to opus 3, while 'Rêve d'amour' (1862?) appeared under opus 5.

2 See my volume of Fauré's correspondence, chapter 1 and especially pp. 19–20 and 26; *LTL*, pp. 17–19 and 24–5. A chronological list complete with dates of composition, first performance and publication can be found in the booklet accompanying the complete EMI recording of Fauré's songs.

3 Georges Servières has pointed to a similarity between Fauré's 'Dans les ruines d'une abbaye' and Saint-Saëns' *L'Enlèvement*, written in 1865. This link provides a possible dating for Fauré's work.

4 Fauré, *Correspondance/LTL*, letter 5.

5 *L'Obvie et L'Obtus*, 1982, p. 248.

6 'Le Grain de la voix', in *ibid.*, p. 240.

7 According to his friend Fernand Gregh. See Fauré, *Correspondance*, pp. 204–5; *LTL*, p. 207.

8 Mme Beltrando-Patier suggests in her thesis on Fauré's songs (see bibliography) that the beginning of 'La Rançon' owes something to the end of *Frauenliebe und -leben*. Schumann's influence is felt generally throughout the songs of this period in the instrumental preludes and postludes.

9 Recalled by Fauré in a letter to his wife, *Lettres intimes*, 26 August 1907, p. 147.

10 It would be interesting to hear the orchestral version by André Messager. The MS score, which has never been published, was given to the Bibliothèque Nationale by the Fauré-Fremiet family.

11 Related by his son Philippe in his biography (p. 59).

12 Fauré, *Correspondance/LTL*, letter 29.

13 *Ibid.*, letter 35.

1 Fauré, *Correspondance/LTL*, letter 8.

2 *Ibid.*, letter 13.

3 *Journal de musique*, 7 April 1877.

4 Fauré, *Correspondance/LTL*, letter 13.

5 *Ibid.*, letter 11.

6 *Ibid.*, letter 24.

7 In an unpublished letter of November 1898 to the Director of the Geneva Conservatoire, Fauré expresses his chagrin that his editor should have lost the score (probably autograph) and the parts of his chorus *Les Djinns*, and says he intends to rewrite them (Archives of the Geneva Conservatoire; made available by M. Horneffer).

8 That is to say, for less than Choudens was offering at the same period. To put this sum in perspective, we should record that Fauré's monthly salary at the

Madeleine was a very modest 250 francs; that his equally modest apartment at 13, rue Mosnier cost him 63 francs a month; and that for music lessons he received a maximum of 20 francs each.

9 See Fauré, *Correspondance/LTL*, letter 39.
10 *Paris-Comoedia*, 3–9 March 1954, pp. 1, 6.
11 Mentioned by Fauré in a letter to Hugues Imbert, *Correspondance/LTL*, letter 57.
12 Compare bars 19–20 in the violin part in the Adagio with bars 5–6 in this same part in the opening Allegro.
13 *Le Figaro*, 2 March 1903; reprinted in G. Fauré, *Opinions musicales* (Paris, Rieder, 1930), p. 46.
14 Fauré, *Correspondance/LTL*, letter 58.
15 *G. Fauré*, p. 74.
16 Fauré, *Correspondance/LTL*, letter 113.
17 *Association des amis de G. Fauré. Bulletin* no. 9 (1972), p. 13.
18 Fauré, *Correspondance/LTL*, letter 83.
19 *Lettres intimes*, p. 89.
20 *Ibid.*, p. 110.
21 *Ibid.*, pp. 75 and 77.
22 *G. Fauré*, p. 85.
23 *La Prisonnière* (ed. de la Pleiade, Gallimard, 1954), p. 161.
24 *Lettres intimes*, p. 118.

7 CHORAL MUSIC

1 Fauré, *Correspondance/LTL*, letter 28.
2 See Anatole de Ségur, *Portrait d'âme. Henri de Lassus Saint Geniès* (Paris, Retaux, 1901). Alice Boissonnet was also the dedicatee of one of Duparc's songs, *Testament*. See Nancy van der Elst, *Henri Duparc: l'homme et l'œuvre*. Thesis published by the Service central de reproduction de Lille, 1972.
3 See his letter to Pierre Lalo, Fauré, *Correspondance/LTL*, letter 149.
4 See *ibid.*, his letter to the Countess Greffulhe, no. 123.
5 See *ibid.*, letter 122.
6 *Gabriel Fauré* (Paris, Alcan, 1927; second ed., Paris, Plon, 1949); p. 50 of the second edition.
7 On the genesis of this work, see Fauré, *Correspondance/LTL*, letters 58–63.
8 See M. D. Calvocoressi, *Musicians Gallery* (London, Faber, 1933), p. 136.
9 *Dolly*, orchestrated by Henry Rabaud for the Théâtre des Arts (1912); *Thème et variations*, orchestrated by D.-E. Inghelbrecht for the Paris Opéra, given in 1928 under the title *Rayon de Lune*. Extracts from *Pelléas et Mélisande* and *Shylock* in George Balanchine's *Jewels* (1967); and even the Requiem, choreographed by Joseph Russillo (1980) and others.
10 Interview with Louis Aguettant, *Paris-Comoedia*, 3–9 March 1954, pp. 1–6.

11 Fauré, *Correspondance/LTL*, letter 113.

12 See plates 52–3, p. 377.

13 *Lettres intimes*, p. 99.

14 *Ibid.*, pp. 279–80.

15 *G. Fauré*, p. 137.

16 *En ce temps là* (Paris, Le Bateau ivre, 1946), pp. 237–8.

17 François Crucy, 'Les Grandes figures contemporaines', *Le Petit Parisien*, 28 April 1922.

18 Fauré, *Correspondance/LTL*, letter 150.

19 *Ibid.*, letter 145.

20 *Ibid.*, p. 49, n. 3; p. 16, n. 2.

21 *Ibid.*, letter 64.

22 *Ibid.*, letter 48.

23 The autograph of *Ecce fidelis servus* op. 54 bears an adaptation of the words *Mulierem fortem* in Fauré's hand. There also exists his arrangement of the well-known 'Air d'église de Stradella' to the words of the Pie Jesu.

24 Fauré, *Correspondance/LTL*, letter 47.

25 Archives Ceillier/Maspéro, Paris, now at the Bibliothèque Nationale.

26 Also dating from around 1880 is a Benedictus for four-part choir and soloists with organ accompaniment, the parts of which have been discovered at the Madeleine. The sketch for a Kyrie, now held by the University of Texas, is probably earlier still.

27 The validity of this original version has been proved in two trial performances, one at Saint-Saëns' church in Normandy, conducted by Henri Farge (9 June 1980), the other in Strasbourg, conducted by Roger Delage (22 March 1984). It was recorded in Paris in September 1988 by Philippe Herreweghe for Harmonia Mundi.

28 Jean-Baptiste Moreau (1656–1733) was a well known song composer and singing master. His setting of Racine's *Esther* was made for the famous academy for young ladies at Saint-Cyr.

29 Fauré, *Correspondance/LTL*, letter 67.

30 'La Musique sacrée en France depuis la Révolution', a contribution to the *Congrès international de musique sacrée* (Paris, Desclée de Brouwer, 1937), pp. 147–53.

31 'La Messe de Requiem de Gabriel Fauré', *Le Guide musical*, 9–16 August 1888, pp. 195–7.

32 Bussine wrote in a hitherto unpublished letter of June 1877 to Marie Clerc:
    He came to see me yesterday evening and played me a *Libera me* for a Mass for the Dead. It's extremely charming, not profound enough maybe, but full of hope and tenderness and with some delicious melodic surprises.
    (Archives Ceillier/Maspéro: now at the Bibliothèque Nationale)

33 Fauré, *Correspondance/LTL*, letter 75.

34 The chorus 'O Domine' could have been written for the incomplete performance of the *Requiem* in Paris on the 17 May 1894 at the Concerts d'Harcourt. On 3 May Fauré sent a note to Mme de Saint-Marceaux: 'I've still got corrections to make to the *Requiem*, and . . . the copyist is bullying me!'

35 The vocal score, which appeared at the beginning of 1900, was probably made after the reorchestration was finished. In general it corresponds closely with the orchestral score in tempi, dynamics etc.

36 Letters to Ysaÿe in Fauré, *Correspondance/LTL*, letters 132 and 129.

37 Unpublished letter-card to Paul Taffanel, 6 July 1900 (Samaran Archives).

38 For the Sanctus, of which the most complete material survives even if there may be items lacking, the parts are for: two horns, two trumpets, timpani, two harps, one violin solo, three first violas, two second violas, one first 'cello, one second 'cello, three double basses and organ. The viola and 'cello parts were probably doubled, with two players to each desk. It is possible that there were three second violas and that there were more 'cellos. The autographs of the orchestral score (of nos. 1, 3, 5 and 7, which were the only ones Fauré kept) were given by his family to the Conservatoire in 1925 and are now in the Bibliothèque Nationale.

39 I am pleased to record the help and advice I have received in this difficult work of reconstruction from Roger Delage, who has brought to the task his skills as both scholar and conductor.

40 Fauré, *Correspondance/LTL*, letter 128.

41 Unpublished letter in Croiza archives, now in Bibliothèque Nationale (Music Dept). The composer Louis Aubert (1877–1968) was later a pupil of Fauré in his composition class at the Paris Conservatoire.

42 The irregularities in the text include a single invocation of the final 'Kyrie eleison', instead of the triple one laid down in the rite. In the orchestral score published by Hamelle this single repeat of the word 'Kyrie' is mistakenly replaced by a further 'eleison'.

43 Saint-Saëns, Fauré, *Correspondance*, 12 October 1862, no. 5.

8 THE THEATRE I: OPERATIC PROJECTS AND INCIDENTAL MUSIC

1 See Fauré's interview in *Le Petit Parisien*, 20 April 1922, p. 1.

2 See Fauré, *Correspondance/LTL*, letter 34.

3 Letter from Fauré to d'Indy, *ibid.*, p. 119.

4 Georges Courteline (alias Georges Moinaux, 1858–1929), writer, author of famous satiric comedies.

5 On his relationship with Gallet, see my article 'Flaubert, Gallet, Fauré ou le démon du théâtre', *Bulletin du bibliophile*, 1976, no. 1, pp. 33–47.

6 *Le Journal de musique*, 12 April 1881 (information provided by Roger Delage).

7 *Le Courrier musical*, 15 March 1929, pp. 179–80.

8 Fauré, *Correspondance/LTL*, letter 55.

9 *Le Figaro*, 1 March 1907, p. 6 on the subject of Alfred Bruneau's music for Zola's *La Faute de l'abbé Mouret*.

10 Fauré, *Correspondance/LTL*, letter 180.

11 See his letter to Hugues Imbert, *ibid*., letter 57.

12 *Ibid*., letter 77.

13 *Ibid*., letter 78.

14 See *Le Guide musical*, 6 April 1890, p. 107.

15 Saint-Saëns, Fauré, *Correspondance*, no. 16.

16 E. Vuillermoz, *Gabriel Fauré* (Paris, Flammarion, 1960), pp. 185–6.

17 Georgette Leblanc (1875–1941) was a singer and actress and for many years Maeterlinck's companion. Debussy's refusal to allow her to sing the rôle of Mélisande in his opera led to a break between the two men.

18 See the anonymous review in *The Athenaeum*, 30 March 1895, pp. 417–18.

19 This translation remains unpublished. I have unearthed a typed copy in the Bibliothèque royale Albert Ier in Brussels (Dept of Manuscripts, MSS III, 322) which seems to relate to a London revival in 1911.

20 *My Life and Some Letters* (London, Hutchinson, *c*. 1922), pp. 126–42.

21 Alan Dent, *Mrs Patrick Campbell* (London, Museum Press, 1961), p. 148.

22 *My Life and Some Letters*, p. 127.

23 *Correspondance de Claude Debussy et Pierre Louÿs*, ed. Henri Borgeaud (Paris, J. Corti, 1945), p. 65. No source is given for the attributed date; the postmark perhaps?

24 Debussy, *Lettres 1884–1918* ed. François Lesure (Paris, Hermann, 1980), pp. 92–3, trans. Roger Nichols, *Debussy Letters* (London, 1987), pp. 99–100. Letter of 9 August 1898. On the difficult relationship between Fauré and Debussy, see my article 'Fauré et Debussy', *Cahiers Debussy*, Nouvelle série, no. 3 (1979).

25 *My Life and Some Letters*, p. 127.

26 *Lettres intimes*, pp. 31–2.

27 The notebooks and the traveller's journal kept by Koechlin, together with the letters he received from Fauré, were kindly made available to me by the Koechlin family and by M. Pierre Renaudin. The various musical manuscripts referred to are in the Bibliothèque Nationale.

28 This letter is reproduced in the actress's memoirs already quoted, pp. 131–4.

29 Bibliothèque royale Albert Ier. Musée de la littérature. Text quoted by Hubert Juin in *Ch. van Lerberghe* (Paris, Seghers, 1969), p. 57.

30 The Theatre Museum, however, possesses a photograph of Mrs Patrick Campbell as Mélisande, published in 1901 when she took the play over to the USA (see pl. 23). The already mentioned dossier in the Bibliothèque Albert Ier in Brussels contains a photograph of Martin Harvey as Pelléas (see pl. 24) and a reproduction of George Dobson's scenery for the revival at the London Lyceum in July 1911 (see plate 22). It is not known whether this is the scenery for the 1898 production.

31 Quoted in the article by Fernand Séverin: 'Maeterlinck et van Lerberghe (documents inédits)', *Gand Artistique*, 1 March 1923, p. 52.

32 See the article signed 'The Tramp' in *The Weekly Dispatch*, 26 June 1898, p. 2.

33 *The Times*, 22 June 1898, p. 12, and *The Athenaeum*, 25 June 1898, p. 832 (anonymous article).

34 *L'Œuvre de Fauré* (Paris, Janin, 1945), pl. XI and XII, p. 128.

35 *Les Cinq chansons de Mélisande*, printed separately, from the magazine *Le Livre et L'Estampe*, nos 57–8 (1969), 9 pp.

36 *Gabriel Fauré* (Paris, Plon, 2/1949), p. 87 n.

37 Articles in *Le Figaro*, 9, 16 and 23 February 1939, reprinted in his book *Thèmes variés* (Paris, Janin 1946), pp. 139–48.

38 *Ibid.*, p. 147.

39 Pp. 14–15 in the Hamelle edition; p. 12 of the *Prélude* in the London conducting score.

40 With the titles: *Prélude, 2e Entr'acte (Fileuse), 4e Entr'acte (Mort de Mélisande)*.

41 *Lettres intimes*, p. 135.

42 Mr Paul Shore informs me that there is a printed Hamelle full score of the Suite op. 80, with a dedication and various corrections by Koechlin, in the Eda Kuhn Loeb Music library, Harvard College, Cambridge, Massachusetts (Mus. 676.2.251). I have in my own possession another copy with the same corrections by Koechlin, who seems to have used the work for teaching his pupils.

43 Letter from Fauré to E. Hamelle, 27 August 1920 (Hamelle archives).

44 'Fauré's Pelléas et Mélisande', *Music and Letters*, April 1975, pp. 178–9. This interesting article is based on a rather rapid consultation of the microfilm of the London conducting score – the original score has come into the possession of the Bibliothèque Nationale since that time. This explains some mistakes and confusions between the different layers of annotation.

45 For the 1939 performance at the Odéon, the conductor André Cadou took it upon himself to supplement the incidental music with the Epithalame and Nocturne from *Shylock* (the first both before and after the scene with the wounded Golaud II.2, the second after the death of *Pelléas*, end of Act IV). These additions were not well received by the public and led Maeterlinck to say, when interviewed on the evening of the première: 'there's too much music' (see Yves Jandet: 'Pelléas 40 ans après', *Les Nouvelles littéraires*, 4 February 1939, p. 10). For this occasion Cadou composed a new *Chanson de Mélisande* and copied a new orchestral score for the whole of the incidental music, now in the Hamelle archives.

46 *Le Figaro*, 12 August 1910, p. 1.

47 See *The Sketch*, 7 September 1910.

48 See the articles by Georges Bourdon in *Le Figaro*, 12 and 31 August 1910, p. 1 and a companion article in the same paper, 30 November 1915, p. 3.

49 Brussels, Bibliothèque Albert Ier, Mss III, 322.

50 R. Hahn, *Thèmes variés*, p. 148. This new conducting score is in the possession of the publishers Hamelle.

51 Letter to Gabriel Astruc, 6 July 1931. Bibliothèque Nationale (Music Dept).

52 *Essais de musicologie et autres fantaisies* (Paris, Le Sycomore, 1980), in particular chapter 10, pp. 224–9.

53 *L'Envers du décor (Souvenir d'une grande cantatrice)* (Paris, Editions de Paris, 1952), p. 101. Quoted from A. Schaeffner, p. 233.

9 THE VERLAINE YEARS: SONG CYCLES AND FURTHER OPERATIC PROJECTS

1 For Fauré's relationships with Winnaretta Singer (Princesse Edmond de Polignac), see 'Une Châtelaine en sa tour', the introduction to Chapter 5 of Fauré, *Correspondance/LTL*, containing eighteen of his letters to her.

2 See *ibid.*, p. 164, a portrait by Fauré of Verlaine in his hospital bed.

3 *Horizons*, August 1945, pp. 120–1.

4 See the article by Georges Jean-Aubry, of interest despite some errors and confusions: 'G. Fauré, P. Verlaine et A. Samain ou les tribulations de "Bouddha"', in: *Le centenaire de Gabriel Fauré* (Paris, Editions de la Revue Musicale, 1945), p. 46.

5 A. Samain (1858–1900), a Symbolist poet in a delicate vein, owed his fame to his collection *Au Jardin de l'Infante* (1893).

6 Bibliothèque Nationale, Musique and Coll. Mouquet Derville (Paris).

7 Fauré, *Correspondance/LTL*, letter 101.

8 Unpublished letters (draft of the Princess's letter to Fauré and his reply), coll. Alain Ollivier.

9 Unpublished letter to Fanny Lépine, kindly communicated by M. Thierry Bodin.

10 See Léon Vallas, *Claude Debussy et son temps* (Paris, Albin Michel, 1958), pp. 137–9, and Robert Orledge, *Debussy and the Theatre* (Cambridge, Cambridge University Press, 1982), pp. 17–35.

11 A project which probably staged the loves of Louise de Lavallière (1644–1710) who preceded Mme de Montespan in the affections of King Louis XIV.

12 Unpublished letter to the Countess Greffulhe. Bibliothèque Nationale (Music Dept), L.a. Fauré 21.

13 The *Revue wagnérienne*, a monthly revue founded by Edouard Dujardin at the height of Wagner's popularity in France (1885–8); among its contributors were J. K. Huysmans, Catulle Mendès, Paul Verlaine, Villiers de l'Isle Adam, Stéphane Mallarmé, as well as Fantin-Latour and Odilon Redon.

14 André Antoine (1858–1943), founder of the Théâtre libre (1887) which revolutionised dramatic art with the introduction of realist and naturalist tendencies, both in production matters and in the scenery and costumes.

15 Aurélien-François-Marie Lugné, known as Lugné-Poe (1869–1940), an actor

and director and founder of the Théâtre de l'Oeuvre which, from 1893 to 1914, staged works by Jarry, Ibsen, Strindberg, Gorky and Maeterlinck, among others.

16 Adolphe Appia (1862–1928), a Swiss director, fierce opponent of historical realism in the theatre, defender of a more abstract conception of presentation and a great Wagnerian who influenced avant-garde theatre aesthetic both before and after the Second World War.

17 See Fauré, *Correspondance/LTL*, letter 115.

18 Unpublished letter, archives of the Duc de Gramont.

19 The Greffulhe archives contain a letter from Fauré, probably to Paul Poujaud, in which he accepts an invitation from the Viscountess Greffulhe. Although this document is not dated, it can be ascribed to the 1885–6 season because of the black-bordered paper Fauré was using after his father's death on 25 July 1885. Elisabeth Greffulhe became a Countess in 1888.

20 Fauré, *Correspondance/LTL*, chapter 6: 'Music, Salons 1900: Proust, Montesquiou and Fauré.'

21 Department of Manuscripts (Nouvelles acquisitions françaises), inventory by Florence Callu.

22 *Les Pas effacés* (Paris, E. Paul, 1923), II, p. 231.

23 Reply to the questionnaire 'Sous la musique que faut-il mettre?' *Musica*, no. 101, February 1911, p. 38.

24 'Les roses étaient toutes rouges/Et les lierres étaient tout noirs'; Debussy set this poem, under its original title, in his collection *Ariettes oubliées* which he finished in 1887.

25 Fauré, *Correspondance/LTL*, letter 73.

26 With all due respect to the Hamelle edition which announces the transposition into D minor as being the 'original key', both the manuscript and the first edition of the song as a separate entity are notated a tone higher. The publisher no doubt succeeded thereby in attracting some of the numerous amateur singers of the time who might have found the top G in the central section 'bothersome'.

27 I give here the keys in the original manuscript (for tenor or soprano). The first edition, by Durand, published nos 2 and 3 a semitone lower, in F minor and F major, presumably for commercial reasons. When Hamelle published them in their second collection in 1897, the note 'ton original' was mistakenly attached to the transposed version, for baritone or mezzo-soprano (B major, E minor and E major).

28 Published in Fauré, *Correspondance/LTL*, letter 90.

29 *Ibid.*, letter 96.

30 'Ne le déchirez pas avec vos deux mains blanches!'; the third line of the first stanza of 'Green'.

31 Quoted by Philippe Fauré-Fremiet, *Gabriel Fauré*, p. 71; I give here the original text.

32 Fauré, *Correspondance/LTL*, letter 98.

33 *Ibid.*, letter 99.
34 'O le frêle et frais murmure' refers back to 'J'arrive tout couvert encore de rosée.'
35 'Cette âme qui se lamente' refers back to 'Ferme tes yeux à-demi'.
36 See n. 49 below.
37 V. Jankélévitch, *Fauré et l'inexprimable* (Paris, Plon, 1974), p. 112.
38 Pp. 2, 12, 22 and 36 in the Hamelle edition.
39 *Livres et autographes, succession de Mme Agnès van Parys*, sale at the Hôtel Drouot, 7 and 8 March 1979, no. 400 in the catalogue.
40 *Ravel par quelques-uns de ses familiers* (Paris, Le Tambourinaire, 1939), p. 134. Tristan Klingsor, alias Léon Leclère, was the author of the Shéhérézade poems and a friend of Ravel.
41 Letter of 18 July 1921 to Henry Prunières. I have already published it in 'H. Prunières, Fauré et la Revue musicale', *Etudes fauréennes*, no. 17, 1980.
42 Letter of 17 May 1923, Fauré, *Correspondance/LTL*, letter 204.
43 Quoted by Robert Pitrou, *De Gounod à Debussy* (Paris, A. Michel, 1957), p. 96. The changes are limited to two bars in the conclusion of this song.
44 The complete manuscript of the original tenor version is in the Bibliothèque François Lang, Royaumont; nos. 1, 4 and 9 are in the Bibliothèque Nationale (Music Dept., donated by Fauré-Fremiet); nos 3 and 7, transposed into F major and A major, in the Sisley Music Library, Eastman School of Music, University of Rochester, New York.
45 Saint-Saëns, Fauré, *Correspondance*, letter 20. The letter to Paul Poujaud is unpublished.
46 Michel Soulard has devoted an excellent thesis to it ('Mémoire de Maîtrise', University of Poitiers, Faculty of Letters, 1975).
47 *Lettres intimes*, pp. 27–8.
48 *Correspondance de Marcel Proust*, ed. Philipp Kolb (Paris, Plon, 1970), p. 338.
49 Letter of 12 July 1902, published for the first time complete in *Etudes fauréennes*, no. 19, 1982; text made available by J. Lonchampt.
50 A more likely candidate is Lydia Eustis, a pupil of Marie Trélat's to whom Fauré dedicated 'Dans la forêt de septembre' in 1902, the date of the interview with Aguettant.
51 H. René Lenormand, *Confessions d'un auteur dramatique* (Paris, A. Michel, 1949), vol. I, pp. 43–4
52 *Albert Samain à sa sœur, 1877–1900*, with introduction and notes by Jules Mouquet (Paris, Emile-Paul, ?c. 1950), pp. 168–9. I am grateful to M. and Mme Philippe Derville for making available this volume which never went beyond the proof stage. The original of this letter was sold at a public sale at the Hôtel Drouot on 3 June 1977 (Collection Alfred Dupont), no. 171 in the catalogue.
53 'The two endings of Fauré's "Soir"', *Music and Letters*, July 1979.
54 See n. 52 above.

10 THE THEATRE II: *PROMÉTHÉE*

1 Fauré's harmonisation was published in 1894 by Borneman in two versions: voice and piano, and voice with flute, two clarinets and harp. A revised version came out in 1914. A second hymn, less complete than the first, was discovered in 1894. Fauré refused the offer of harmonising it and the job was undertaken by Léon Boëllmann.

2 Archives Castelbon de Beauxhostes, Boujan/Libron (Hérault).

3 Max d' Ollone (1875–1959) was a pupil of Massenet and later a critic. Déodat de Séverac (1873–1921) studied with d' Indy at the Schola Cantorum. Like Fauré, he was a native of Southern France. Henri Rabaud (1873–1949) was a pupil of Massenet who became Director of the Paris Conservatoire in 1920. His best known work is his opera *Mârouf*, first given at the Paris Opéra in 1914.

4 Archives of the Hérold family, Paris.

5 *Gabriel Fauré*, p. 77.

6 The text was published by the *Mercure de France* in May 1900 but did not take account of the changes Fauré made on the vocal parts.

7 Francis Vielé-Griffin (1863–1937) was an American-born Symbolist poet and editor of the review *Entretiens littéraires et politiques*.

8 Page references are to the Hamelle vocal score.

9 25 August 1900, p. 6.

10 Lamoureux Concert on 11 January 1920, conducted by Camille Chevillard.

11 Letter of May 1900 to F. Castelbon.

12 Referring to a performance of his Requiem in Brussels; letter of 21 March 1906 (*Lettres intimes*, p. 117).

13 See my article: 'Charles Koechlin et Henri Büsser témoins du *Prométhée* de Fauré aux arènes de Béziers', *Association des Amis de G. Fauré, Bulletin* no. 16 (1979), pp. 7–19. For Saint-Saëns' opinion, see the introduction to his correspondence with Fauré, *Correspondance*, pp. 17–18.

14 *Ibid.*

15 Article of 26 August 1900, reprinted in his *Poussière de Paris* (Paris, Ollendorf, 1902), vol. II, p. 350.

16 11 November 1924, p. 1. 'Gabriel Fauré et de Max, Prométhée aux arènes de Béziers'.

17 26 August 1901, *Lettres intimes*, p. 60. These three artists sang their rôles again in the 1901 revival. Of the other rôles, Aenoë was sung by Mlle Torrès (1900), Mlle Armande Bourgeois (1901); Kratos in both years by Charles Rousselière, who was to be the first Ulysse in *Pénélope*; Gaia by Rose Feldy (1900), Mlle Flahaut (1901). Edouard de Max was Prométhée in both years while Pandore was taken by Cora Laparcerie (1900) and then Berthe Bady (1901).

18 J.-M. Nectoux: 'Ravel, Fauré et les débuts de la Société musicale indépendante', *Revue de Musicologie*, 1975, no. 2, p. 299.

19 *Revue musicale*, no. spécial *Gabriel Fauré*, October 1922, pp. 35–6.
20 These important fragments are in the possession of the Bibliothèque Nationale.
21 'Considérations sur la musique en plein air', *Gil Blas*, 19 January 1903, in *Monsieur Croche et autres écrits*, edited by F. Lesure (Paris, Gallimard, 1987), p. 76; trans. Richard Langham Smith as *Debussy on Music* (London, 1977), pp. 93–4.

11 WORKS AND DAYS

1 *Gabriel Fauré*, p. 70.
2 Fauré, *Correspondance/LTL*, letters 58 and 64 dating from 1887.
3 Marcel Girette was employed in the Finance Ministry and was a friend of Léon Bourgeois.
4 *Fauré*, p. 17.
5 Private collection, Paris. Text made available to me by Mme A. Risler.
6 Indre et Loire, a *département* of central France. Chabrier owned a house in La Mambrolle.
7 Théodore Lack, virtuoso pianist and prolific composer of salon pieces for his instrument.
8 *Etudes fauréennes*, no. 19, 1982, p. 4. Text made available to me by M. Jacques Lonchampt.
9 1 July 1901, see *Debussy on Music* (translated by Richard Langham Smith: London, 1977), p. 48.
10 Debussy, *Lettres 1884–1918*, ed. F. Lesure (Paris, Hermann, 1980), p. 93, trans. R. Nichols, *Debussy Letters* (London, 1987), pp. 99–100. I have traced the delicate relationship between Debussy and Fauré in *Cahiers Debussy*, nouvelle série, no. 3, 1979, pp. 13–30.
11 Paris, Richard Masse, 1971, *Revue musicale*, nos 272–3.
12 *Traité théorique et pratique de l'accompagnement du plain-chant*, in collaboration with Joseph d'Ortigue, 1857.
13 See the scales mentioned by F. Gervais, *Etude comparée des langages harmoniques de Fauré et Debussy*, vol. I, p. 41 and bottom of p. 45.
14 See the extracts from the diary kept by this favourite interpreter of Fauré's in *Etudes fauréennes*, no. 18, 1981, p. 13.
15 Fauré, *Correspondance/LTL*, letter 144.
16 'Combat de Ceste – Pas des lutteurs', *Les Troyens*, Act I no. 5.
17 'How I have developed' (1948) in *Style and Idea*, ed. Stein.
18 'Hommage à Gabriel Fauré' (1924), in *Notes sur la musique, essais et chroniques*, ed. Jeremy Drake (Paris, Flammarion, 1982), p. 115.
19 Saint-Saëns, Fauré, *Correspondance* (Paris, Société française de musicologie, 1973), pp. 21–2.
20 *Ibid.*, p. 107.
21 Pierre Lalo (1886–1943) was for many years the music critic of *Le Temps*. He was the son of the composer Edouard Lalo.

22 Hector Guimard (1867–1934), architect; one of the principle creators of 'Art Nouveau' in France.

23 Saint-Saëns, Fauré, *Correspondance*, p. 41. Letter of 12 October 1862.

24 Unpublished letter to the poet Gabriel Faure, written from 'Noizay, 11 June' (*c.* 1945?); made available to me by M. Maurice Chattelin.

25 Letter of 2 October 1893 to Saint-Saëns, *Correspondance*, p. 53.

26 Quoted in Henri-René Lenormand, *Les Confessions d'un auteur dramatique* (Paris, A. Michel, 1949), vol. I, pp. 43–4.

27 Quoted by André Schaeffner in his article on Rhythm in the Fasquelle *Encyclopédie de la Musique* (Paris, 1961), vol. III, p. 606.

28 *Fauré et l'inexprimable* (Paris, Plon, 1974), p. 264.

29 *Les mélodies de G. Fauré* (Lille, Service de reproduction des thèses, 1981), p. 297.

30 The themes from the Allegro of the Violin Concerto are used again in the first movement of the String Quartet (see music example no. 58); the Andante from the Concerto was probably reworked in the Andante in B flat op. 75 for violin and piano, published in 1897. The Allegro of the F major Symphony was published in 1895 under the title *Allegro symphonique* op. 68, in a piano duet transcription by Léon Boëllmann; the 'Gavotte' from this symphony found a place in *Masques et bergamasques*. The first theme of the D minor Symphony (1884) was the inspiration for the opening of the First 'Cello Sonata, while the main theme of the Andante reappears in the Andante of the Second Violin Sonata.

31 Only two of these four symphonies were published in his lifetime.

32 Fauré, *Correspondance/LTL*, letter 59.

33 *Lettres intimes*, p. 77.

34 *Ibid.*, p. 209.

35 *Ibid.*, p. 208.

36 24 May 1874, p. 198.

37 According to a long letter to Colonne, of which a resumé appeared in the Coulet et Faure sale catalogue (Paris), no. 120, item no. 673.

38 *Les Annales du Théâtre et de la Musique*, the year 1885. (Paris, 1886), p. 550.

39 5 January 1879, p. 7.

40 *Lettres intimes*, p. 254.

41 Debussy turned to André Caplet, Roger Ducasse and Charles Koechlin; Saint-Saëns to André Messager, Liszt to various pupils . . .

42 Ch. Koechlin, *Gabriel Fauré* (Paris, Plon, 1949), pp. 57 and 58.

43 Unpublished letter (Koechlin family archive).

44 In: *Gabriel Fauré*, special no. of *La Revue musicale*, October 1922, p. 65.

45 'I'm thinking of that orchestral colour which seems to be lit from behind, which there are such wonderful examples of in *Parsifal*' (Debussy to André Caplet, 25 August 1912) in: Debussy, *Lettres*, ed. F. Lesure (Paris, Hermann, 1980), p. 229; Eng. trans., *Debussy Letters*, ed. F. Lesure and R. Nichols (London, Faber, 1987), p. 262.

46 'L'orchestre de Fauré', in *Comoedia*, 20 March 1943; on a revival of *Pénélope* in Bordeaux. On Fauré and Poulenc, see chapter 18.

47 Letter of 19 April 1922, *Lettres intimes*, p. 281.

48 Letter of 14 April 1919, *ibid.*, p. 256.

49 See from six bars before letter K in the Hamelle orchestral score.

50 *Le Figaro*, 9 May 1907, in: G. Fauré, *Opinions musicales* (Paris, Rieder, 1930), p. 140.

51 In: *Gabriel Fauré* (Paris, Publications techniques et artistiques, 1946), p. 21.

52 Of 25 January 1904, in: *Opinions musicales*, p. 21. Fauré's failure to appreciate Berlioz drew a lively reaction from Saint-Saëns; see their *Correspondance*, letter 49 of 24 November 1904.

53 *Le Figaro*, 4 June 1913, in: *Opinions musicales*, p. 29.

54 See n. 50 above.

55 See n. 51 above.

12 POMP AND CIRCUMSTANCE

1 Saint-Saëns, Fauré, *Correspondance*, pp. 51–2.

2 Roger-Ducasse, 'L'Enseignement de Gabriel Fauré', in: *Gabriel Fauré* (Paris, les Publications techniques et artistiques, 1946), p. 16.

3 'Portrait. Maurice Ravel', *Gringoire*, 22 July 1932, quoted by Marguerite Long, 'G. Fauré, M. Ravel, le maître et l'élève', *Les Annales, Conférencia*, 10 October 1950, pp. 434–5.

4 'Hommage à Nadia Boulanger', *Etudes fauréennes*, 1980, p. 4.

5 *Gabriel Fauré*, pp. 19–20.

6 Archives nationales, AJ37 296 (13 June 1899) and 297 (16 June 1900).

7 *Ravel* (Paris, Gallimard, 1967), p. 31 and M. Long, 'G. Fauré, M. Ravel', p. 435.

8 Louis Guitard, 'Entretien avec Louis Aubert', *La Table ronde*, October 1961, p. 144.

9 E. Vuillermoz, *Gabriel Fauré* (Paris, Flammarion, 1960), p. 29.

10 *Ravel*, p. 30.

11 Fauré, *Correspondance/LTL*, letter 131.

12 According to Roland-Manuel, *Ravel*, p. 44, Fauré had serious reservations about the finale of the Quartet, finding it too short and unsatisfying. Marguerite Long recalls, 'G. Fauré, M. Ravel', p. 435: 'Ravel used to tell me jokingly that when he saw how surprised Fauré was by some of the passages in the Quartet he decided to try and escape criticism by asking him to accept the dedication.' On the relations between Ravel and Fauré see my article: 'Ravel, Fauré et les débuts de la Société musicale indépendante', *Revue de Musicologie*, 1975, no. 2, pp. 295–318.

13 This dedication, the composition dates 1900–9, and the rubric for the finale on the name of Fauré are printed on Durand's 1909 edition of Roger Ducasse's First Quartet in D minor.

14 In the number for 14 November 1920. It is clear from this phrase that the article is based on Fauré's own testimony – the composer had in fact come to the Théâtre de la Monnaie for a revival of *Pénélope*. He also describes the work as a 'sonata for four instruments'. Paule Ladmirault, the composer's daughter, informs me that the work was a string quartet and that her father wrote the slow movement during the summer holidays. As she remembers, the project was never completed. For further details see my article: 'Fauré, Henry Prunières et la Revue musicale', *Etudes fauréennes*, no. 17, 1980, pp. 17–24.

15 For information on 'L'Affaire Ravel' and its consequences, read Julien Torchet's article 'Gabriel Fauré, directeur du Conservatoire de Paris', *Le Guide musical*, 25 June–2 July 1905, pp. 475–8; Romain Rolland's letter to Paul Léon reproduced in the special Ravel number of *La Revue musicale* (December 1938), pp. 173–4; Arbie Orenstein's book *Ravel, Man and Musician* (New York, 1975) and the article by Sophie Bres 'Le Scandale Ravel de 1905', *Revue internationale de musique française*, no. 14, June 1984, pp. 41–50.

16 Saint-Saëns, Fauré, *Correspondance*, letter dated 29 September 1905.

17 See 'Les réformes du Conservatoire' in *Musica*, November 1905, p. 166.

18 See *L'Echo de Paris*, 7 October 1905; *Le Temps*, 8 October 1905; *La Liberté*, 10 November 1905.

19 Saint-Saëns, Fauré, *Correspondance*, 31 July 1920.

20 See *Lettres intimes*, pp. 202–3, and Fauré, *Correspondance/L TL*, letters 149 and 159.

21 *Lettres intimes*, p. 120.

22 See my article 'Albéniz et Fauré', *Travaux de l'Institut d'Etudes Ibériques et Latino-Américaines*, Université de Strasbourg, 1976–7, pp. 160–86.

23 Fauré, *Correspondance/L TL*, letter 152.

24 M. Long, *Au piano avec Gabriel Fauré* (Paris, Julliard, 1963), p. 89.

25 *Albéniz et Granados* (Paris, Plon, 1926), pp. 57–8.

26 They are preserved in the Biblioteca central de Cataluña in Barcelona (shelf no. M. 986), together with Fauré's letters to the Albéniz family.

27 A letter from Fauré to their common publisher, Heugel, dated 28 September 1906, shows the keen interest he took in Dukas's opera. He wrote two enthusiastic articles about it in *Le Figaro* (11 May 1907 and 4 May 1921).

28 See plate XLV of the first edition of Philippe Fauré-Fremiet's biography (Paris, Rieder, 1929). The preceding plate reproduces Fauré's manuscript of the Maeterlinck pastiche 'La Ballade du Roi sourd'. An autograph copy of this by Dukas is in Barcelona.

29 See Fauré, *Correspondance/L TL*, letter 16 and *Lettres intimes*, p. 121.

30 *Lettres intimes*, p. 174.

31 Fauré, *Correspondance/L TL*, letter 135.

32 See the well documented but occasionally rather superficial article by General H. Chevalier, 'Gabriel Fauré à Bruxelles (1888–1912)', *Synthèses*, no. 230–1, July–August 1965.

33 *Etudes fauréennes*, no. 18, 1981, p. 21.
34 I have here made use of the excellent article by Serge Siguitov, 'La musique de
    Fauré en Russie', *Association des Amis de Gabriel Fauré, Bulletin* no. 14,
    1977. Siguitov is the author of the first Russian biography of Fauré, published
    in Moscow in 1982.
35 This must refer to the First Piano Quartet, which was given with the Marsick
    Quartet on 7 June at the house of Adèle Bohomoletz, an old friend of Fauré's.
    See Tchaikovsky, Taneyev, *Letters* (Moscow, 1957) quoted by S. Siguitov in
    the above-mentioned article (n. 34), p. 6; also Vladimir Fedorov, 'Tchaïkovski
    et la France', *Revue de musicologie*, 1968, no. 1.
36 Quoted, rather strangely, by Edward Lockspeiser in *Debussy, his life and
    mind*, vol. I (Cambridge, Cambridge University Press, 1978), p. 52, n. 2. He
    also quotes, though without the source, the inscription on the First Quartet:
    'To Tchaikovsky, in homage and as a token of my warmest admiration.
    Gabriel Fauré'. Fauré had been a keen attender at the Russian concerts given as
    part of the Paris Universal Exhibition in September 1878.
37 Fauré, *Correspondance/LTL*, letter 75.
38 See *ibid.*, letter 38.
39 'Fauré en Angleterre', *Association des Amis de G. Fauré, Bulletin* no. 13, 1976,
    p. 11.
40 Fauré, *Correspondance/LTL*, letter 118.
41 *Ibid.*, letter 122.
42 R. Orledge, 'Fauré en Angleterre', p. 14.
43 Philippe Fauré-Fremiet, *Gabriel Fauré*, 2/1957, pp. 147–65. Pierre Auclert,
    'La Ballade op. 19 de Fauré', *Association des Amis de G. Fauré*, Bulletin no. 15,
    1978 and errata, no. 16, 1979.
44 These details are taken from Adela Maddison's will, consulted by Robert
    Orledge at Somerset House, London (1929, no. 2132). Adela had two chil-
    dren, Diana Marion Adela Aird, who in turn had a daughter Jacqueline, and a
    son, Noel Cecil Guy Maddison. Mr Albi Rosenthal informs me that he bought
    the manuscript of Fauré's Seventh Nocturne from Adela Maddison's daughter
    in Oxford after the Second World War. At that time the first page was missing,
    and the incomplete manuscript was bought by Alfred Cortot. Some years later
    Rosenthal found the missing page in a bookseller's in Nice and passed it on to
    Cortot. After Cortot's death the manuscript was acquired by Robert Owen
    Lehman who gave it to Nadia Boulanger as an eightieth birthday present. She
    left it, with all her papers, to the Bibliothèque Nationale in 1978.
45 Vladimir Jankélévitch, *Gabriel Fauré, ses mélodies, son esthétique* (Paris, Plon,
    1951), Preface, p. II.

13 TOWARDS THE TWENTIETH CENTURY

1 *Lettres intimes*, pp. 72–3.
2 *Ibid.*, p. 79.

3 *Ibid.*, p. 185.

4 *Ibid.*, p. 254.

5 Bibliothèque Nationale, Music Dept.

6 *Lettres intimes*, pp. 195–6.

7 Philippe Fauré-Fremiet, *Gabriel Fauré* (Paris, Albin Michel, 1957), pp. 95–6.

8 Hélène Abraham, *Un art de l'interprétation, Claire Croiza* (Paris, Office de centralisation d'ouvrages, 1954), p. 199.

9 *Gabriel Fauré*, pp. 118–19.

10 Fauré special number, October 1922, p. 55.

11 *Revue de musicologie*, 1973, no. 2, pp. 136–7.

12 Fauré's stage projects during the years 1877–85 have already been discussed at the beginning of chapter 8.

13 See Arbie Orenstein, *Ravel, Man and Musician* (New York, Columbia University Press, 1975), p. 243.

14 Unpublished letter of 28 August 1899, Brussels, Bibliothèque royale Albert Ier, Manuscrits, Mss II, 70004.

15 See Robert Guiette, *La légende de la sacristine, Étude de littérature comparée* (Paris, H. Champion, 1927), pp. 346–50. G. Fabre set to music Mélisande's song, 'The Three Blind Sisters', for the première of Maeterlinck's play in Paris in 1893. His other settings of Maeterlinck include *Trois chansons de Mélisande* (Enoch, 1898) and *Huit chansons de Mélisande* (Heugel, 1905).

16 Unpublished diary of Marguerite Baugnies (later Mme René de Saint-Marceaux), entry for 1 June 1900.

17 See Madeleine Maus, *Trente années de lutte pour l'art, (1884–1914)*, and Albert van der Linden, *Octave Maus et la Vie musicale belge (1875–1914)* (Brussels, Palais des académies, 1950).

18 Brussels, Bibliothèque royale Albert Ier, Manuscrits, Mss II, 70004.

19 Communicated by M. Thierry Bodin. The complete text is printed in my article 'Debussy et Fauré', *Cahiers Debussy*, nouvelle série, no. 3, 1979, p. 24.

20 Letter to his wife, 3 August 1903, *Lettres intimes*, p. 72.

21 'Les débuts du théâtre nouveau chez Maeterlinck', *Annales de la Fondation Maeterlinck*, vol. III, 1957, pp. 45–8. This article, though well documented in other respects, does not mention that the libretto passed from Gabriel Fabre to Gabriel Fauré.

22 The text of *Sœur Béatrice* was published first in 1900 in the German translation by Bronikovski, then in the original French in volume III of Maeterlinck's stage works (Brussels, Lacomblez, 1902).

23 *Etudes fauréennes*, no. 18, 1981, p. 12.

24 Antinoüs' recitative '... Et désigne l'époux qui sèchera tes larmes': p. 217 in the first edition of the vocal score (1912, 267 pp.), and p. 221 in the 2nd edition (1913, 274 pp.).

25 *Etudes fauréennes*, no. 18, 1981, p. 15.

26 *Lettres intimes*, p. 72, 3 August 1903.

27 *Ibid.*, pp. 89–90.

28 See the catalogue of the firm Il Grammofono, Milan, 1912.

29 Antoine Boesset (c. 1586–1643), Pierre Guédron (c. 1570–c. 1620), Michel Lambert (c. 1610–96), famous composers of the French vocal genre 'airs de cour'.

30 *Lettres intimes*, p. 121, 17 August 1906.

31 Fauré's predecessor as Director of the Conservatoire.

32 *Lettres intimes*, 22 August 1906.

33 Letter reproduced in Madeleine Maus, *Trente années de lutte pour l'art (1884–1914)* (Brussels, l'Oiseau bleu, 1927), pp. 379–80.

34 I shall have more to say about this cycle in Chapter 15.

35 *Au piano avec Gabriel Fauré* (Paris, Julliard, 1963), pl. 3. (Not included in English translation.)

36 *At the Piano with Fauré* (London, Kahn and Averill, 1980), p. 14.

37 *Ibid.*, p. 65.

38 *Ibid.*, pp. 34 and 54.

39 *Ibid.*, p. 15.

40 *Gabriel Fauré*, p. 148.

41 See his remarkable *Etudes musicales* (Paris, Alcan, 1917).

42 In the collection of Dr Vacher, Paris.

43 Camille Chevillard (1869–1923), French conductor.

44 Lucien Capet (1873–1928), French violinist and leader of the Capet Quartet.

45 *Lettres intimes*, p. 138.

46 M. Long, *At the Piano with Fauré*, p. 3.

47 *Ibid.*, p. 113.

14 THE THEATRE III: *PÉNÉLOPE, MASQUES ET BERGAMASQUES*

1 Article in *Le Figaro*, 9 May 1907, reprinted in G. Fauré, *Opinions musicales* (Paris, Rieder, 1930), pp. 140–1.

2 I refer here to the second edition of the vocal score (Heugel, 1913) which contains 274 pages. The first edition, printed at the end of 1912, has only 267. Between the première in Monte Carlo and the performances in Paris Fauré made some important changes in the duet in Act II (four pages inserted between the pause and pedal point on p. 145 and the marking 'crotchet = 80' on the new p. 149), in the scene of the bow in Act III (eight bars inserted in the orchestra on p. 245 in the second edition) and at the very end of the opera (two bars added, pp. 266–7 in the first edition; pp. 272–4 in the second).

3 *Lettres intimes*, p. 142.

4 *Ibid.*, p. 144.

5 *Ibid.*, p. 207.

6 *Ibid.*, p. 216.

7 Saint-Saëns, Fauré, *Correspondance* (Paris, Société française de musicologie, 1973), p. 98 (text kindly communicated by Yves Gérard).

8 *Lettres intimes*, p. 216.

9 Saint-Saëns, Fauré, *Correspondance*, p. 100.

10 Extract published in a sale catalogue of N. Rauch, Zürich, 1958, no. 1044.

11 Review in *SIM*, 15 May 1913.

12 *L'Aiglon*, a historical drama by Edmond Rostand (1868–1918) which enjoyed considerable success from its first performance in Paris in 1900 with Sarah Bernhardt in the rôle of the Duke of Reichstadt, the son of Napoleon I.

13 *Lettres intimes*, p. 153.

14 Fauré, *Correspondance/LTL*, letter 151.

15 See *ibid.*, letter 158.

16 *Lettres intimes*, p. 196.

17 *Ibid.*, pp. 153 and 182.

18 *Ibid.*, pp. 206 and 208–9.

19 *Gabriel Fauré* (Paris, Plon, 2/1949), p. 23.

20 *Mercure de France*, 16 June 1913, p. 851.

21 *Gazette des Beaux-Arts*, July 1913, p. 80.

22 Text communicated by Mme Li-Koechlin.

23 In: D. E. Inghelbrecht, *Le Chef d'orchestre parle au public* (Paris, Julliard, 1957), pp. 33–42.

24 Saint-Saëns, Fauré, *Correspondance*, pp. 21–2.

25 *Lettres intimes*, p. 217.

26 Fauré, *Correspondance/LTL*, letter 165.

27 *Ibid.*, letter 176.

28 Unpublished diary of Marguerite Baugnies, entry for 16 June 1902.

29 The Pavillon des muses, a private mansion in Neuilly, thus named by Robert de Montesquiou who held famous parties there at the turn of the century.

30 I refer to Fauré's reduction for piano duet of the suite op. 112 (Paris, Durand, 1919), as being the only version currently available.

31 Fauré, *Correspondance/LTL*, letter 188.

32 *Ibid.*, letter 187.

15 WORDS AND MUSIC. THE VAN LERBERGHE YEARS

1 *Etudes fauréennes*, no. 18, 1981, p. 6.

2 See the alliteration in '*s*' in the second verse of Renée de Brimont's 'Cygne sur l'eau' (*Mirages*, I) or the triple repetition of the word *pleurer* at the end of Hugo's *Puisqu'ici bas toute âme*.

3 Unpublished letter, dated Nice, 11 March 1921.

4 See Fauré, *Correspondance/LTL*, chapter 5.

5 See the letters to Albert Mockel and Fernand Séverin quoted in my article 'Le "Pelléas" de Fauré', *Revue de musicologie*, 1981, no. 2, p. 174.

6 *Etudes fauréennes*, no. 18, 1981, p. 12.

7 Once in the possession of Emma Bardac's daughter, Dolly de Tinan, and now in the music section of the Bibliothèque Nationale (Vmd. 3211).

8 Now in the music section of the Bibliothèque Nationale (Ms 17787 (1) and (5)).
9 *Revue de musicologie*, 1976, no. 2, pp. 257–74.
10 *Ibid.*, pp. 264 and 265.
11 *'La Bonne chanson': du poème à la mélodie (Verlaine-Fauré)*. 'Mémoire de maîtrise', Faculty of Letters, Poitiers University, 1975, p. 102.
12 See the article by Mimi Segal Daitz, 'Les manuscrits et les premières éditions des mélodies de Fauré: Etude préliminaire', *Etudes fauréennes*, no. 20–1 (1983–4), which gives (pp. 24–5) the variants in 'Rêve d'amour'.
13 *'La Bonne chanson': du poème à la mélodie*, p. 112.
14 Hélène Abraham, *Un art de l'interprétation. Claire Croiza* (Paris, Office de centralisation d'ouvrages, 1954), p. 143.
15 *Lettres intimes*, p. 127.
16 The cover of the manuscript of 'Roses ardentes' (Bibliothèque Nationale, Music Dept) has the following autograph annotations: 'Paradis' 1 – 'Prima verba' 2 – 'Roses ardentes' 3 – 'L'Aube blanche' 4 – 'Crépuscule' 5. This numbering was printed on the cover of the original editions of 'Roses ardentes' and of 'L'Aube blanche' in July 1908 ('Crépuscule' was, however, left without a number). This order was retained for the first, incomplete performance on 28 May 1909 when 'Crépuscule' was placed seventh and last, giving way to the two songs recently composed: 'Comme Dieu rayonne' (no. 5) and 'Eau vivante' (no. 6). At this stage, Fauré was quite clear in his mind that the cycle would contain ten songs: the cover of the original edition of the three songs published in 1909 leaves two numbers (8 and 9) to be filled in. We may also note that a still different order is to be found on the autograph cover of 'Comme Dieu rayonne' and on the original edition of the two songs published in 1910 ('Veilles-tu' and 'O mort'). The final order was fixed only when the whole cycle was published together in March 1910.
17 Author's collection.
18 The cuts are as follows: the end of 'Paradis' (p. 19), the last verse of 'L'Aube blanche' (p. 39), the seventh verse of 'Dans un parfum de roses blanches' (p. 66), the fifth verse of 'Crépuscule' (p. 190) and the last two lines in both the fourth and fifth verses of 'O mort, poussière d'étoiles'. For that text, Fauré has indicated that two paragraphs beginning with the word 'viens' should be changed round and this was in fact done. Such exchanges were made easier by van Lerberghe's use of free verse, without fixed rhymes.
19 *Lettres intimes*, pp. 130 and 129.
20 A fine letter from Ravel to Fauré gives a glimpse of the atmosphere of that memorable evening: see Fauré, *Correspondance/LTL*, letter 157.
21 Saint-Saëns, Fauré: *Correspondance*, 12 October 1905.
22 A letter from Lausanne (2 August 1908), printed in my article 'Deux interprètes de Fauré: Emilie et Edouard Risler', *Etudes fauréennes*, no. 18, 1981, p. 23.

23 *Lettres intimes*, p. 185. Being a civil servant, Fauré was bound by a rule of discretion (*l'obligation de réserve*) and so could not speak out freely in the press about his duties.

24 *Ibid.*, pp. 222–3.

25 Fauré, *Correspondance/LTL*, letter 172 (15 February 1915).

16 'POUR LE PIANO'

1 M. Long, *At the Piano with Fauré* (London, Kahn and Averill, 1980), p. 75.

2 This recording has still not appeared! The Ninth Nocturne is dedicated to Mme Alfred Cortot (Clotilde Bréal), while the *Fantaisie* was written specially for the great pianist (see the end of this chapter). The Seventh Barcarolle is dedicated to Isidor Philipp's wife and the Sixth Barcarolle to Edouard Risler, one of Fauré's most devoted interpreters.

3 I. J. Paderewski, *The Paderewski Memoirs* (London, Collins, 1939), p. 153. He calls Fauré a 'great song composer' but regrets the lack of depth in his chamber music and says nothing about his piano music whatever.

4 J.-M. Nectoux, 'Deux interprètes de Fauré: Emilie et Edouard Risler', *Etudes fauréennes*, no. 18, 1981, pp. 3–25.

5 *Lettres intimes*, p. 220.

6 *Ibid.*, p. 186.

7 *Ibid.*, p. 185.

8 On relations between Fauré and Albéniz, see J.-M. Nectoux, 'Albéniz et Fauré. (Correspondance inédite)'. *Travaux de l'Institut d'Etudes ibériques et latino-américaines* (TILAS, University of Strasbourg), 16–17, 1977, pp. 159–86.

9 *Lettres intimes*, p. 164.

10 M. Long, *At the Piano with Fauré*, pp. 92–3.

11 D. Milhaud, 'Hommage à Gabriel Fauré' in D. Milhaud, *Etudes* (Paris, C. Aveline, 1927) and in *Notes sur la musique. Essais et chroniques*, ed. J. Drake (Paris, Flammarion, 1982), p. 115.

12 Long, *At the Piano with Fauré*, see n. 10.

13 Milhaud, 'Hommage à Gabriel Fauré', pp. 115–16, see n. 11.

14 This expression is found in his writings in 1876, see Fauré, *Correspondance/LTL*, letter 10.

15 *Lettres intimes*, p. 220 (1 August 1913).

16 *Ibid.* (5 August 1913).

17 It eventually turns into an amplification of the descending octave idea that accompanies the first theme.

18 R. Lortat, 'Dans le souvenir de Gabriel Fauré', *Les Nouvelles musicales*, 1 June 1933; text largely repeated from a lecture of 3 March 1929, published in *Conférencia*, 20 August 1929.

19 To be precise, by 1912 there were ten Nocturnes and nine Barcarolles; but this hardly takes anything away from Lortat's achievement . . .

20 See *Journal de l'Université des Annales*, 15 July 1914, pp. 118–19, with an

introduction by Reynaldo Hahn (pp. 115–18). Fauré himself accompanied the Ballade, some songs, the First Violin Sonata, the *Elégie, Sicilienne, Papillon* (Mme Caponsachi) and the two Piano Quartets (M. Hayot, M. Denayer, J. Salmon).

21 Especially the First Violin Sonata, played by Lady Speyer. The other works are not mentioned in the reviews in the *Athenaeum*, 13 and 20 June 1914, pp. 835, 862–3.

22 Fauré, *Correspondance/LTL*, letter 170.

23 See n. 18 above.

24 See the review by Florent Schmitt in *Le Courrier musical*, 1 December 1919. He calls the performer an 'intelligent and sensitive pianist' but deplores a certain 'languor', particularly in 'the second bar from the beginning and its *con suono* repeats'.

25 Impromptu no. 2 (Duo Art no. 5923, made in 1917), *Valse-Caprice* no. 1 (Duo Art no. 6069, made in 1922).

26 *Lettres intimes*, 1 and 9 August, 16 September 1915, pp. 226–8.

27 Saint-Saëns, Fauré, *Correspondance*, nos 104, 105, 107–11.

28 Archives of M. Kahn, Paris.

29 Fauré, *Correspondance/LTL*, letter 174.

30 *Ibid.*, letter 176.

31 *Lettres intimes*, pp. 244–5.

32 *Ibid.*, pp. 253–4.

33 Bibliothèque Nationale, Music Dept.

34 *Ibid.*

35 Fauré, *Correspondance/LTL*, letter 179.

36 *La Revue musicale*, special Fauré number, October 1922: reprinted in A. Cortot, *La Musique française de piano*, vol. I (Paris, 1930; 2/1981), pp. 167–9.

17 LIGHT AND SHADE: CHAMBER MUSIC II

1 Fauré, *Correspondance/LTL*, letter 172.

2 This information is taken from a letter of Fauré to Jeanne Raunay (Mme A. Beaunier), written from St Raphaël on 2 September (1917), and made available by Thierry Bodin. Philippe Fauré-Fremiet's wartime letters to his parents are preserved in the Music Dept of the Bibliothèque Nationale.

3 *Lettres intimes*, p. 242.

4 *D'Indy, Duparc, Roussel, lettres à Auguste Serieyx* (Lausanne, Editions du Cervin, 1961), pp. 24–5.

5 The autograph of this document, in Fauré's hand, is in the Pierpont Morgan Library in New York.

6 On these episodes, see further documentation in J.-M. Nectoux, 'Ravel/Fauré et les débuts de la Société musicale indépendante', *Revue de musicologie*, 61 (2) 1975, pp. 308–10.

7 *Lettres intimes*, p. 260.

8 Articles in the *Revue de Paris*, collected in a posthumous volume: *Etudes musicales* (Paris, Alcan, 1917).

9 See J.-M. Nectoux, 'Deux interprètes de Fauré: Emilie et Edouard Risler', *Etudes fauréennes*, no. 18, 1981.

10 We know of this difficult period from the daily letters Fauré wrote to Louise Maillot (coll. Hayet, Paris).

11 See his letter to Marie Fauré, Lausanne, 20 August 1903, in *Lettres intimes*, p. 75.

12 *Gabriel Fauré*, p. 117.

13 These parts are preserved in the Music Dept of the Bibliothèque Nationale.

14 H. Jourdan-Morhange, *Mes amis musiciens* (Paris, Les éditeurs français réunis, 1955), p. 29.

15 See *Lettres intimes* (2 August 1917) and the letter Fauré wrote to the Queen, now in Brussels, and made available by Ludovic de San.

16 *Gabriel Fauré*, p. 157.

17 See *Lettres intimes*, p. 234. The sonata in question is the first of Saint-Saëns' two 'cello sonatas (op. 32, 1873), which is indeed a fine work.

18 V. Jankélévitch, *Fauré et l'inexprimable* (Paris, Plon, 1974), p. 321.

19 *Lettres intimes*, p. 258.

20 *Ibid.*, p. 264.

21 For example Webern (1906), Florent Schmitt (1908), Elgar (1918), Pierné (1919) and d'Indy (1924). Saint-Saëns' Piano Quintet, though of interest, belongs to quite another era (1856).

22 *Gabriel Fauré*, p. 122.

23 *Lettres intimes*, p. 269.

24 *Ibid.*, p. 267.

25 *Ibid.*, p. 269.

26 *Ibid.*

27 *Ibid.*, p. 272 for all three of these extracts.

28 Fauré, *Correspondance/LTL*, letter 189.

29 *Ibid.*, letter 193.

30 Recalled by Philippe Fauré-Fremiet, *Gabriel Fauré*, p. 122.

18 FAURÉ 'MODERN STYLE'

1 See J.-M. Nectoux, 'Chemins de la musique française', in *20ᵉ siècle. Images de la musique française* (Paris, Papiers, 1986).

2 Philippe Fauré-Fremiet, *G. Fauré*, p. 111.

3 *Lettres intimes*, pp. 256 and 261.

4 *Ibid.*, p. 261.

5 His pension was initially fixed at 8,225 francs a year, based on his director's salary which had been raised from 12,500 francs in 1914 to 18,000 francs on 1 July 1919. The 'indemnity for infirmity', fixed at 3,000 francs, was doubled by

a decree of 15 November 1920. See Archives nationale, F17 22528 and F21, 5158; I gratefully acknowledge the research undertaken on this question by Mlle Dunan.

6 Information from Mr David McKibbin. Contrary to what I wrote in my edition of Fauré's correspondence (p. 317, n. 2), the manuscripts given to Loeffler have in fact been preserved; they were given next to one of Loeffler's pupils, Miss Gertrude Marshall Wit, and then to the violinist Louis Krasner (Brookline, Boston). The manuscript of the Second Quintet was given by Sargent to the Harvard Library as soon as he received it.

7 Marguerite Long, *At the Piano with Fauré* (London, Kahn and Averill, 1980), p. 26.

8 *Lettres intimes*, p. 270.

9 On the history of this Fauré number, see my article, 'Fauré, Henry Prunières et la Revue musicale', *Etudes fauréennes*, no. 17, 1980, pp. 17–24.

10 Gustave Bret conducted the Requiem in March 1920 in Paris, in the presence of the composer's wife; he made the first complete recording of the work in April 1931, for the Gramophone company.

11 The Mengelberg archives (Gemeente Museum, The Hague) contains several notes written by Fauré and Mme Loudon to the conductor. Lydia Eustis had been a pupil of Marie Trélat; Fauré dedicated 'Dans la forêt de septembre' to her in 1902.

12 Programme in the Claire Croiza papers in the Bibliothèque Nationale (Music Dept). See J.-M. Nectoux, *Hommage à Claire Croiza*, Exhibition (BN, 1983).

13 On this work, see chapter 14.

14 See the letter from Fauré to Fauchois of 17 June 1921, in Fauré, *Correspondance/L T L*, letter 188.

15 An anecdote related by D. E. Inghelbrecht: *Le Chef d'orchestre parle au public* (Paris, Julliard, 1957), p. 40.

16 See the account by Gabriel Faure: *Gabriel Fauré* (Paris, Artaud, 1945), pp. 86–90. Even so the performance was mediocre, we are told, despite the presence of Germaine Lubin and Lucien Muratore.

17 See the article by Henry Malherbe, 'Deux Maîtres que j'ai connus' [Fauré et Debussy], *Candide*, 9 December 1937, p. 19.

18 *G. Fauré*, pp. 113–15.

19 Passages taken from *Le Rappel à l'ordre* (Paris, Stock, 1948), pp. 28, 26, 101. *La Prière d'une vierge* is a piano piece by Tekla Badarzewska which had an enormous success, from its publication in Paris in 1858 up until the 1930s.

20 *Ibid.*, p. 103, review of 19 May 1919.

21 Letter communicated by Mme Faure and M. Maurice Chattellin; although not dated, it can be placed around 1945.

22 *Nouvelle Revue musicale*, no. 1, November 1928, p. 14, quoting the record review *Arts phoniques* of the same year. This change in attitude was only partial. In a violent article on 'L'Orchestration de Fauré', prompted by a revival of *Pénélope*, (*Comoedia*, 20 March 1943), Poulenc wrote: 'If I love the

work of a Debussy or a Ravel without restriction, the same does not go, I confess it humbly, for that of Fauré. Many pages by this master, especially of his piano music, pass me by totally. The truth of what I say can be judged by the fact that *Pénélope* moves me to tears.' But Poulenc disputed the orchestration of *Pénélope*, which he thought was the work of a third party, and he asked Koechlin to redo it.

23 *Lettres intimes*, p. 288.

24 This homage appeared first in *Entretiens* in January 1923, then in a more complete form in Milhaud's book *Etudes* (Paris, Cl. Aveline, 1927). It can be found in his *Notes sur la musique. Essais et chroniques*, ed. Jeremy Drake (Paris, Flammarion, 1982); I have already quoted from it the passages referring to the Fourth Prélude and the Fifth Impromptu (see pp. 236 and 383).

25 See Fauré, *Correspondance/LTL*, letter 200, and also an unpublished letter (archives Réglade, Pichebouc).

26 *Le Petit parisien*, 28 April 1922.

27 See J.-M. Nectoux, 'Ravel/Fauré et les débuts de la SMI', *Revue de musicologie*, 1975, no. 2, pp. 310–11. The following Ravel scores were in Fauré's library (the inscribed copies are marked*): *Introduction et Allegro, D'Anne qui me jecta de la neige*, *Jeux d'eau*, *Menuet antique, Pavane*, *l'Heure espagnole*, *Miroirs*, *Daphnis et Chloé* (piano two hands and extracts for piano duet), *Gaspard de la nuit*, *la Valse* (two hands), *Sonate pour violon et violoncelle*.

28 This appears in G. Fauré, *Opinions musicales* (Paris, Rieder, 1930), pp. 42–3, together with the earlier review he wrote of the première in 1907 (*ibid.*, pp. 39–41).

29 J.-M. Nectoux, ed. 'Cinq lettres de Gabriel Fauré à son fils Emmanuel', *Association des Amis de Gabriel Fauré*, *Bulletin* no. 9, 1972, p. 6.

30 I. Stravinsky and R. Craft, *Expositions and Developments* (London, Faber, 1962), p. 60: 'I met Fauré, too, at the time of his *Pénélope*, which I heard in May 1913, shortly before the première of *Le Sacre*. Ravel introduced me to him at a concert in the Salle Gaveau. I saw a white-haired, deaf, very kind-faced old man – indeed, he was compared for gentleness and simplicity to Bruckner.'

31 The piano duet reduction, which was the only format available until 1921. The copy preserved by Fauré carries the bookplate of Raymond Petit. According to the 1914 edition of *Bottin mondain*, there was a doctor called Raymond Petit living in Paris. The score now belongs to M. Henri Six (Boulogne-Billancourt).

32 See the articles printed in Jean Wiéner's memoirs: *Allegro appassionato* (Paris, Belfond, 1978), pp. 58–71. Vuillemin headed his diatribe of 1 January 1923 'Concerts métèques' ('Dago concerts').

33 The only letter from Fauré still held by the Vuillermoz family. I quote from memory, as Mme Vuillermoz would not allow me to take a copy of it. The other letters of the composer to Vuillermoz were sold to the library of Texas University.

34 Saint-Saëns, Fauré, *Correspondance*, pp. 106 and 107.

35 *G. Fauré*, pp. 114 and 123.
36 Letter made available by the Librairie François Loliée in Paris.
37 *Lettres intimes*, p. 275.
38 In fact, he did omit the last verse of 'Je me suis embarqué', which is rather anecdotal.
39 The manuscript was given by Panzéra's family to the Bibliothèque Nationale in 1985.
40 Details can be found in my *Phonographie, Gabriel Fauré* (Paris, Bibliothèque Nationale, 1979). These discs have been reissued a number of times. Panzéra included some notes on interpreting this cycle in his book: *L'Art vocal, 30 leçons de chant* (Paris, Librairie théâtrale, 1959), pp. 109–22.
41 This appears as a preface to the double album reissue I prepared for EMI Pathé–Marconi: *Charles Panzéra. Mélodies et Airs* (2c 151–73084/85, Series reference). See also the well known appreciation by Barthes in *Musique en jeu* no. 9, 1972, reprinted in the volume *L'Obvie et l'Obtu* (Paris, le Seuil, 1986).
42 Letter made available by Madeleine Grey; many of the details published here were given to me by her in the early 1970s.
43 An allusion to the performances at the Paris Opéra in May 1917.
44 The work is dedicated to Mme Gabriel Hanotaux.
45 Testimony direct from Mme Philippe Fauré-Fremiet. The composer cut four verses in no. 1, three in no. 2 and two in no. 4. No. 3, the shortest, is complete.
46 *Fauré et l'inexprimable* (Paris, Plon, 1974), p. 216; it appeared first in 1938 in *Gabriel Fauré et ses mélodies*.
47 I refer particularly to the versions by Camille Maurane (1959), Gérard Souzay (1964) and Bernard Kruysen (1973).

19 ULTIMA VERBA

1 Sold at Sotheby's, London, 21–2 May 1987, catalogue no. 394.
2 Sold at Hôtel Drouot, Paris, 26 June 1987, catalogue no. 20.
3 *Lettres intimes*, p. 278.
4 *Gabriel Fauré*, p. 125.
5 *Lettres intimes*, p. 274 (in the commentary).
6 Letter to Mme F. Maillot of 17 March 1919, in G. Fauré, *Correspondance/LTL*, letter 178.
7 *Lettres intimes*, pp. 283–4.
8 *Ibid.*, p. 284.
9 *Lettres intimes*, 11 and 25 August 1922, pp. 282–3.
10 Quoted by Philippe Fauré-Fremiet: *G. Fauré*, pp. 120–1.
11 Reproduced in J.-M. Nectoux, *Fauré* (Paris, Le Seuil, 1986), p. 165.
12 See letter to Roger-Ducasse, 23 July 1922 in Fauré, *Correspondance/LTL*, letter 196.
13 *Ibid.*: for his work on this edition see letters 196, 200, 202, 203, 205, 211.
14 Archives Réglade, Pichebouc (le Taillan, Médoc).

15 Letter from Fauré to E. Hamelle, 4 November 1923, Fauré, *Correspondance/LTL*, letter 206.
16 *Lettres intimes*, p. 287.
17 *Gabriel Fauré*, p. 125.
18 *Lettres intimes*, p. 288.
19 *Ibid.*, p. 288.
20 *Ibid.*, p. 285.
21 This poem appeared in the collection *Derniers vers*, published on the day of the poet's funeral (24 February 1586).
22 G. Samazeuilh, *Musiciens de mon temps* (Paris, M. Daubin, 1947), p. 430. See also the article mentioned in chapter 18, n. 9.
23 Archives Hayet, Paris.
24 This was a statue of Fremiet at work by Greber, erected in the Jardin des Plantes, not far from the small building where Fremiet for a long time taught drawing. See the article by Félicien Pascal in *Le Gaulois* of 15 June 1924, p. 3 and the one signed 'E.G.' in *Le Figaro* of the same day, p. 2.
25 *G. Fauré*, pp. 124–5.
26 *Lettres intimes*, p. 293.
27 *G. Fauré*, p. 118.
28 Sketches preserved in the Bibliothèque Nationale (Music Dept), analysed by Robin C. Tait in *Etudes fauréennes*, nos 20–1, 1983–4, pp. 37–47.
29 *Lettres intimes*, pp. 294–5.
30 *G. Fauré*, pp. 129–30.
31 Quoted by Charles Koechlin, *Gabriel Fauré* (Paris, Plon, 2nd edn, 1949), p. 33.
32 See the description and the photographs published in *Le Temps*, *Excelsior* and *Comoedia* of 9 November 1924. Koechlin says that François Albert's speech, reproduced in several newspapers, was written by the critic Robert Brussel.
33 Marguerite Long was the vice-president; see her memories in *At the Piano with Gabriel Fauré* (London, Kahn and Averill, 1980), pp. 58–61.
34 Vladimir Jankélévitch, *Gabriel Fauré, ses mélodies, son esthétique* (Paris, Plon, 1951), p. III.
35 Original in the Bibliothèque Nationale (Music Dept); communicated by Dr Depaulis (Bordeaux).
36 *Association des Amis de Gabriel Fauré*, Bulletin no. 18, 1981, p. 11.
37 Communicated by Mme la baronne de Labeau.
38 Fauré, *Correspondance/LTL*, letter 135.
39 According to Marguerite Long, *At the Piano with Fauré*, p. 65.

20 INNER VOICES

1 *Lettres intimes*, p. 295.
2 *Ibid.*, p. 289; 20 September 1923.
3 *Ibid.*, p. 166; Lausanne, 28 August 1908.
4 *Association des Amis de G. Fauré*, Bulletin no. 10, 1973, p. 5.
5 *Gabriel Fauré* (Paris, Flammarion, 1960), pp. 23–4.

6   *Gabriel Fauré*, pp. 112–13.
7   Bequest of Blanche Fauré-Fremiet in 1983.
8   To his wife, 1 April 1919, *Lettres intimes*, p. 254.
9   A remark recorded by his son Emmanuel. *Association des Amis de G. Fauré, Bulletin* no. 9, 1972, p. 13.
10 Zürich, 21 September 1904. *Lettres intimes*, p. 96.
11 *Lettres intimes*, pp. 31–2.
12 Witnessed by Hélène Jourdan-Morhange, *Mes amis musiciens* (Paris, Les éditeurs français réunis, 1954), p. 27.
13 1 September 1904, *Lettres intimes*, p. 90.
14 Together with all Fauré's manuscripts, these were deposited in the Bibliothèque Nationale in 1978 (gift of Mme Philippe Fauré-Fremiet); Music Dept., Ms 17787.
15 Fauré, *Correspondance/LTL*, letter 64.
16 Based on an unpublished motet to the same text, written in 1878; see Fauré, *Correspondance/LTL*, letters 28 and 64.
17 This suggests that notebook 3 is earlier than the first two, since the first performance of the Second Piano Quartet took place on 22 January 1887. But I have kept to the numbering of the notebooks as established by Vladimir Jankélévitch.
18 Fauré, *Correspondance/LTL*, letter 58.
19 *Gabriel Fauré* (London, Eulenburg, 2nd edn, 1983), p. 206.
20 See Fauré's letter to his wife, 15 August 1907, *Lettres intimes*, p. 143.
21 16 August 1907, *Lettres intimes*, p. 144. A sketch for the Suitors' theme appears in facsimile in my *Fauré* (Paris, Le Seuil, 2nd edn, 1986), p. 143 and in the book by Robert Orledge (London, Eulenburg, 2nd edn, 1983), pl. 18.
22 Notebooks 1 and 5.
23 This manuscript was normally in a format 35 × 27 cm, containing a variable number of staves depending on the type used but always with the stamp of Lard Esnault, 25 rue Feydeau, Paris, who supplied almost all the composers in the capital at this period; from 1897 onwards the stamp reads 'Lard Esnault, Ed. Bellamy successeur'.
24 31 August 1904, *Lettres intimes*, p. 82.
25 20 August 1903, *Lettres intimes*, p. 75.
26 Fauré, *Correspondance/LTL*, letter 72.
27 In his article on the Ballade (see bibliography), Pierre Auclert passes on the indications given him by Marguerite Hasselmans. Philippe Fauré-Fremiet noted the indications marked on a copy of the First Violin Sonata, corrected by Fauré for the use of Mme de Saint-Marceaux. They were used by Alex van Amerongen in his edition of the Sonata, published by Peters (Leipzig) in 1982 (see p. 130). See also the letter to Durand in Fauré, *Correspondance/LTL*, letter 209, about the Second Quintet.
28 The figures I quote are taken from the archives of the three publishers concerned, to whom I offer my thanks. The Choudens archives are inaccessible for the time being.

29 *Excelsior*, 12 June 1922.
30 30 August 1903, *Lettres intimes*, p. 72.
31 *Ibid.*, p. 85.
32 See n. 29 above.
33 To Marie Clerc, 17 September 1879, Fauré, *Correspondance/LTL*, letter 38.
34 September 1891, *ibid.*, letter 99.
35 *L'Eclair*, February 1908, in: *M. Croche et autres écrits* (Paris, Gallimard, 1987), p. 281.
36 8 September 1918, *Lettres intimes*, p. 244.
37 *Lettres intimes*, pp. 75–7.
38 Fauré, *Correspondance/LTL*, letter 35.
39 For the Second Violin Sonata, the order of composition was: movements I and III simultaneously, then II; for the Second Quintet, II, III and I simultaneously, then IV. Philippe Fauré-Fremiet says that the earliest sketches for the Trio were of the central episode of the slow movement, that is the exact centre of the work (*Lettres intimes*, p. 274). For the String Quartet, like the Second 'Cello Sonata, he began with the slow movement, in the order II, I, III.
40 *Lettres intimes*, p. 197.
41 *Ibid.*, pp. 197 and 90.
42 *Ibid.*, pp. 96 and 84.
43 'Gabriel Fauré', *Le Temps*, 6 November 1924.
44 In L. Rohozinski, ed. *Cinquante ans de musique française* (Paris, Librairie de France, 1925), vol. II, p. 367, Henry Prunières tells the same story and describes Duparc's reaction as ' "Go on with you, you old devil", he said, with tears in his eyes.' This version sounds more likely, but Prunières does not give the title of the song.
45 *Gabriel Fauré*, p. 121.
46 *Ibid.*, p. 127.
47 *Lettres intimes*, p. 150.
48 Unpublished letters, private collection.
49 Fauré, *Correspondance/LTL*, letter 98.
50 *Le Petit Parisien*, 28 April 1922, p. 1.
51 *Lettres intimes*, pp. 52 and 118.

CODA

1 Fauré, *Correspondance/LTL*, letter 55.
2 *Gabriel Fauré*, p. 139.
3 Stéphane Mallarmé, *Œuvres complètes* (Paris, Gallimard, 1945), p. 73.
4 See n. 1 above.
5 *A la recherche du temps perdu* (Paris, Gallimard, 1954), vol. III, p. 257.
6 Unpublished letter to Arsène Alexandre, Zürich, *c.* 3 September 1904; previously in the collection of Dr G. H. Robert.
7 *Lettres intimes*, p. 78.
8 Fauré, *Correspondance/LTL*, letter 153.

Bibliography

There is a considerable body of written work about Fauré and any inventory aiming at completeness would run to several hundred entries. It is hard to know what limits to set here, especially to the collecting of articles from reviews and newspapers: in Fauré's time, the Parisian press alone contained several dozen daily papers. I have therefore made as large a selection as possible using as a basis the lists drawn up by Octave Séré (*Musiciens d'aujourd hui*, 1911 and 1921), by Philippe Fauré-Fremiet (*G. Fauré*, 2/1957) and by Robert Orledge (*G. Fauré*, 1979). My own research has enabled me to add several dozen new entries, both old and recent. I have paid particular attention to the stage works which, to a far greater degree than the chamber works, the piano pieces or the songs, have given rise to studies and reviews of some length. Future bibliographers, whose arrival is devoutly to be wished, will be able to add still more from the press's inexhaustible store.

HEADINGS

  I Bibliographies, discographies, lists of works, principal articles in dictionaries and encyclopaedias
  II Fauré's writings, interviews and letters
  III Fauré in his own time: contemporary writings and accounts
  IV Fauré since his death: critical writings
  v Literary sources for Fauré's work

I Bibliographies, discographies, lists of works, principal articles in dictionaries and encyclopaedias

Bernard, Robert: 'Fauré et ses élèves' in *Histoire de la Musique* (Paris, F. Nathan, 1962), vol. II, chapter 11, pp. 782–804.
'Bibliografia delle composizioni di Gabriel Fauré', *Bolletino bibliografico musicale* (Milan), 5 March 1930, pp. 9–17.
'Bibliographie de l'œuvre de Gabriel Fauré par numéro d'œuvre' in 'Gabriel Fauré', special issue of *La Revue musicale*, 4, 11 October 1922, pp. 112–16.
'Chronological List of Compositions by Gabriel Fauré', *Franco–American Musical Society Quarterly* (New York), March 1925, pp. 8–10.

Dumesnil, Robert: 'Gabriel Fauré' in *Histoire de la musique*, vol. IV, 'L'Aube du XXᵉ siècle' (Paris, A. Colin, 1958), pp. 110–52 (bibliography).

Fauré-Fremiet, Philippe: 'Fauré' in *Die Musik in Geschichte und Gegenwart* (Kassel, B. Bärenreiter, 1954), vol. 3, col. 1867–79 (list of works, bibliography).

Haraszti, Emile: 'Gabriel Fauré' in *Enciclopedia dello spettacolo* (Rome, Le Maschere, 1954), vol. V, pp. 75–9 (bibliography).

Honegger, Marc: 'Fauré' in *Dictionnaire de la musique* (Paris, Bordas), vol. I, 1/1970; 2/1979 (list of works, bibliography), pp. 333–7 (2nd edn).

Nectoux, Jean-Michel: *Phonographies. I Gabriel Fauré, 1900–1977* (Paris, Bibliothèque Nationale, 1979).

'Fauré' in *The New Grove Dictionary of Music and Musicians* (London, Macmillan, 1980), vol. VI, pp. 417–28 (list of works, bibliography); rev. edn in *The New Grove Twentieth-Century French Masters* (London, Macmillan, 1986), pp. 1–37.

Schmitt, Florent: 'Gabriel Fauré' in *Cobbett's Cyclopedic Survey of Chamber Music* (London, Oxford University Press, 1929), vol. I, pp. 386–92.

Séré, Octave [alias Jean Poueigh], 'Gabriel Fauré' in *Musiciens français d'aujourd'hui* (Paris, Mercure de France), 1/1911, pp. 181–98; 2/1921 with a supplement, pp. 428–30 (list of works and important bibliography).

Smolian, Steven: 'Discography' in Vuillermoz, Emile: *G. Fauré* (Philadelphia, Chilton, 1969), pp. 173–259.

Thomson, Kenneth: 'Gabriel Fauré' in *A Dictionary of Twentieth-Century Composers (1911–1971)* (London, Faber and Faber, 1973), pp. 167–81 (list of works and important bibliography).

II Fauré's writings, interviews and letters

A Writings

Opinions musicales (selection of critical articles from *Le Figaro*, 1903–21), ed. P. B. Gheusi ((Paris, Rieder, 1930).

'L'Ancêtre, drame lyrique de Saint-Saëns', *Le Figaro*, 25 February 1906, p. 4 (not reprinted in *Opinions musicales*).

'Un grand interprète de Mozart, Joachim', *Musica*, no. 43, April 1906, p. 63.

'La faute de l'aabbé Mouret de A. Bruneau', *Le Figaro*, 1 March 1907, p. 6 (not reprinted in *Opinions musicales*).

'Lucienne Bréval', *Musica*, no. 64, January 1908, p. 3.

'Jeanne Raunay', *Musica*, no. 64, January 1908, p. 10.

'Edouard Lalo', *Le Courrier musical*, 15 April 1908, pp. 245–7.

'André Messager', *Musica*, no. 72, September 1908, pp. 131–2.

'M. Charles-Marie Widor', *Comoedia illustré*, 1 April 1909, pp. 202–3.

'Reprise d'Henry VIII de Saint-Saëns', *Le Figaro*, 19 June 1909, p. 4 (not reprinted in *Opinions musicales*).

Preface to: Huré, Jean: *Dogmes musicaux* (Paris, Editions du Monde musical, 1909).

Preface to: Bach, Johann Sebastian: *Inventions à deux et trois voix revues par Bruno Mugellini* (Paris, Ricordi, c. 1910).

Preface to: Philipp, Isidore, ed.: *Nouvelle édition des œuvres classiques pour piano* (Paris, Ricordi, c. 1910).

Preface to: Auriol, Henri: *Décentralisation musicale* (Paris, E. Figuière, 1912) (also appeared in *Comoedia*, 26 December 1912).

Preface to: Bach, Johann Sebastian: *Le Clavecin bien tempéré* (Paris, Durand, 1915).

Preface to: Jean-Aubry, Georges: *La Musique française d'aujourd'hui* (Paris, Perrin, 1916). English transl. Edwin Evans: *French Music of Today* (London, K. Paul, Trench, Trubner and Co., 1919).

'Appel aux musiciens français', *Le Courrier musical*, 19, 15 March 1917, p. 133.

Preface to: Bach, Johann Sebastian: *Œuvres complètes pour orgue* (Paris, Durand, 1917).

'Camille Saint-Saëns', *La Revue musicale*, 1 February 1922, pp. 97–100. Italian transl. by Stefano Bianchi, in: *All'ombra delle Fanciulle in Fiore. La Musica in Francia nell' Età de Proust*, ed. Carlo de Incontrera (Monfalcone, Teatro communale, 1987), pp. 214–17.

'Souvenirs' [of the Ecole Niedermeyer], *Revue musicale*, 4 (11), special no. *Gabriel Fauré*, October 1922, pp. 3–9. Italian transl. as above, pp. 201–6.

Hommage à Eugène Gigout (Paris, Floury, 1923) [in collaboration with Marie-Louise Boëllmann, from the autograph].

Preface to: Vuillermoz, Emile: *Musiques d'aujourd'hui* (Paris, G. Crès, 1923).

Preface to: Marliave, Joseph de: *Les Quatuors de Beethoven* (Paris, Alcan, 1925; 2nd edn. Julliard, 1960).

B Interviews, responses to articles

'Le compositeur de 'Prométhée' à Montpellier', *Le Petit Méridional*, 21 March 1900.

'La réforme de la musique religieuse. Opinions de MM. C. Saint-Saëns, Gabriel Fauré . . .', *Le Monde musical*, 15 February 1904, p. 35.

Response to an article on music criticism by F. Duquesnel, *Le Gaulois*, 30 October 1904, p. 3. Leading article reprinted in the collection *Opinions musicales*.

'Le nouveau directeur du Conservatoire', by André Nede, *Le Figaro*, 14 June 1905.

Response to an article on modern Italian music by L. Borgex, *Comoedia*, no. 854, 31 January 1910, p. 1.

'En l'absence du directeur du Conservatoire, M. Gabriel Fauré nous parle de la SMI', by Louis Vuillemin, *Comoedia*, 20 April 1910, pp. 1–2.

Response to an article 'La musique étrangère et les compositeurs français', *Le Gaulois*, 10 January 1911, p. 4.

Response to an article 'Sous la musique que faut-il mettre: de beaux vers, de mauvais, des vers libres, de la prose?' *Musica*, no. 101, February 1911, p. 38.

'Les Célébrités artistiques à Monte Carlo. Une interview de M. Gabriel Fauré', by Sébastien Jaspard, *Monaco Revue*, 5 January 1913, pp. 154–6.

'Le Théâtre de Monte Carlo . . . Indiscrétions sur *Pénélope*', by Jules Méry, *Revue de la Riviera*, 2 March 1913.

'A l'Opéra de Monte Carlo. Avant *Pénélope*. Interview de M. Gabriel Fauré', by Louis Schneider, March 1913 (unidentified press cutting. Bibliothèque de l'Arsenal, Paris, Rf 18384).

'Les Grandes figures contemporaines. Gabriel Fauré', by François Crucy, *Le Petit Parisien*, 28, 1922, pp. 1–2.

'Entretien avec M. Gabriel Fauré', by Roger Valbelle, *Excelsior*, 12 June 1922, p. 2, ed. J.-M. Nectoux in: *Association des Amis de G. Fauré, Bulletin*, no. 12, 1975, pp. 7–9.

'Chronique musicale. Gabriel Fauré', by Henri Malherbe, *Le Temps*, 6 November 1924, p. 3.

'Souvenirs sur *Pénélope*', by Jean Grandrey-Réty, *Comoedia*, 10 November 1924, p. 4.

C *Correspondence**

'Autour de *Pénélope*' [open letters to Albert Carré], *Comoedia*, 9 November 1912, p. 2.

'Lettres à une fiancée' [Marianne Viardot], ed. Camille Bellaigue, *Revue des Deux Mondes*, 98, 15 August 1928, pp. 910–43.

'Trois lettres de Gabriel Fauré' [to Thérèse Roger], ed. André-Charles Coppier, *Candide*, 24 October 1929, p. 13.

'Gabriel Fauré, Paul Verlaine et Albert Samain ou les Tribulations de "Bouddha" ', unedited letters presented by Georges Jean-Aubry in *Le Centenaire de Gabriel Fauré* (Paris, Editions de la Revue musicale, 1945), pp. 39–58.

Lettres intimes [selection of letters to his wife, 1885–1924], ed. Philippe Fauré-Fremiet (Paris, La Colombe, later Grasset, 1951). Anthology of these letters, trans. Edward Lockspeiser in *The Literary Clef* (London, Calder, 1958), pp. 140–59.

'L'Amitié de Gabriel Fauré et de Vincent d'Indy', by Gustave Samazeuilh, *Mercure de France*, August 1956, pp. 755–9.

'Deux lettres de Gabriel Fauré à C. Debussy (1910–1917)', in *Claude Debussy. Textes et documents inédits*, ed. F. Lesure, *Revue de musicologie*, 48, 1962, pp. 75–6.

G. Fauré et C. Saint-Saëns: '*Correspondance. Soixante ans d'amitié* (1862–1921)', ed. J.-M. Nectoux, Paris, 1/1971 (duplicated by the Association des Amis de

---

* In the volume G. Fauré, *Correspondance/LTL*, there is the most complete bibliography possible of the manuscript and printed correspondence of the composer. Here we give the principal examples.

G. Fauré); 2/1972 in *Revue de musicologie*, 58, 1972, no. 1, pp. 65–89, no. 2, pp. 190–252. Edited in one volume (Société française de musicologie, 1973).

'Cinq lettres de Gabriel Fauré à son fils Emmanuel', ed. J.-M. Nectoux, *Association des Amis de Gabriel Fauré. Bulletin*, no. 9, 1972, pp. 6–11.

'Autour de quelques lettres inédites de Robert de Montesquiou, Charles Koechlin et Gabriel Fauré', ed. J.-M. Nectoux, *Association des Amis de Gabriel Fauré. Bulletin*, no. 11, 1974, pp. 7–11.

'Albéniz et Fauré, correspondance inédite', ed. J.-M. Nectoux, *Travaux de l'Institut d'Etudes Ibériques et Latino-américaines*, 16–17, 1976–7, pp. 159–86.

'Inédits. Deux lettres de Gabriel Fauré à Emmanuel Chabrier', ed. J.-M. Nectoux, *Association des Amis de Gabriel Fauré. Bulletin*, no. 13, 1976, pp. 17–18.

Gabriel Fauré: *Correspondance* [1862–1924] texts compiled and annotated by J.-M. Nectoux (Paris, Flammarion, 1980). Rev. edn., trans. J. A. Underwood: *Gabriel Fauré, his Life Through his Letters* (London, New York, Marion Boyars, 1984).

NB The book of Gabriel Faure (1945), the articles by Philippe Fauré-Fremiet 'La Genèse de Pénélope' (1945), as well as those of J.-M. Nectoux: 'Ravel et Fauré' (1975), 'Flaubert, Gallet et Fauré' (1976), 'Debussy et Fauré' (1979) cited below also contain numerous letters by the composer.

III Fauré in his own time: contemporary writings and accounts

Abraham, Hélène: *Un Art de l'interprétation. Claire Croiza, les cahiers d'une auditrice* (Paris, Office de centralisation d'ouvrages, 1954).

Aguettant, Louis: 'Rencontres avec Gabriel Fauré' [1902], ed. J.-M. Nectoux, in *Etudes fauréennes*, no. 19, 1982, pp. 3–7 (partly published in *Paris-Comoedia*, 3–9 March 1954, pp. 1 and 6).

'Les Mélodies de Gabriel Fauré', *Le Courrier musical*, 6, no. 3, 1 February 1903.

'Le Génie de Gabriel Fauré, conférence', Lyon, 17 October 1924 (Lyon, Aux deux collines, 1924).

'Gabriel Fauré', *La Vie intellectuelle*, November 1949, pp. 388–97.

La Musique de piano des origines à Ravel (Paris, A. Michel, 1955), pp. 387–405.

Amiel, André: 'Prométhée, la première aux Arènes de Béziers', *Revue éolienne*, no. 17, September 1900, pp. 440–8.

Aubert, Louis: 'G. Fauré. Son œuvre', *Le Courrier musical*, no. 18, 15 November 1924, pp. 538–40.

'Quelques souvenirs' in Rohozinski, Ladislas: *Cinquante ans de musique française*, II, pp. 382–5.

'Gabriel Fauré et ses mélodies de Vl. Jankélévitch', *Radio Magazine*, 16, no. 762, 22 May 1938, p. 2.

'Fauré 1845–1924' in *Les Musiciens célèbres* (Geneva, L. Mazenod, 1946), pp. 274–7.

'Entretiens avec Louis Aubert à propos du "Gabriel Fauré" d'Emile Vuillermoz' by Louis Guitard, in *La Table ronde*, no. 165, October 1961, pp. 141–5.

Auclert, Pierre: 'A propos de deux malentendus: Brahms et Fauré', *Association des Amis de G. Fauré, Bulletin*, no. 10, 1973, pp. 15–17.

'La Ballade op. 19 de Fauré', *Association des Amis de Gabriel Fauré, Bulletin*, no. 15, 1978, pp. 3–11 (and errata *Bulletin*, no. 16, 1979, p. 19).

Bathori, Jane: 'Les Musiciens que j'ai connus', *Journal of the British Institute of Recorded Sound*, 1, no. 5, 1961–2, pp. 146–7.

Beaunier, André: 'Festival Gabriel Fauré', conference, Paris, 16 December 1911. *Journal de l'Université des Annales*, 15 February 1912, pp. 284–90.

Beerhom, Max: 'Pelléas and Mélisande', *Saturday Review*, 18 June 1898, pp. 843–6.

Bellaigue, Camille: 'Revue musicale: La Bonne chanson', *Revue des Deux Mondes*, 15 October 1897, pp. 933–6.

'Le "Requiem" de M. Gabriel Fauré', *Etudes musicales*, 3rd series, Paris, Delagrave, 1907, pp. 217–20.

'Revue musicale. Pénélope', *Revue des Deux Mondes*, 1 July 1913, pp. 217–24. Reprinted in the collection *Notes brèves*, 2nd series, Paris, Delagrave, 1914, pp. 259–70. The same author has published two other articles on *Pénélope* in the same journal: no. of 15 February 1919, pp. 921–9 and no. of 15 May 1923.

'Gabriel Fauré', conference, Paris, 20 February 1925, *La Revue hebdomadaire*, 34, no. 10, 7 March 1925.

'Pénélope', *Revue universelle*, 15 December 1928, pp. 699–707.

Benoit, Camille: 'La Messe de Requiem de Gabriel Fauré', *Le Guide musical*, 34, nos 32–3, 9–16 August 1888, pp. 195–7 (Paris, Schott, 1888).

Berteaux, Eugène: *En ce temps là (souvenirs)* (Paris, Le Bateau ivre, 1946).

Bertelin, Albert: 'Quelques souvenirs sur Gabriel Fauré', *La Musique et le Théâtre*, 1 April 1925, p. 14.

Bidou, Henry: 'La Musique. Masques et bergamasques', *L'Opinion*, 13 March 1920, pp. 297–8.

'L'opus 118 et l'opus 119 de Gabriel Fauré' [*L'Horizon chimérique*, Nocturne no. 13], *L'Opinion*, 29 September 1922, pp. 1117–22.

Boschot, Adolphe: 'Dolly', *L'Echo de Paris*, 11 January 1913.

Chez les musiciens du XVIIIe siècle à nos jours (Paris, Plon, 1922). [Articles appeared in *L'Echo de Paris*]. 1st series, pp. 159–71: *Pénélope*, Second Quintet; 2nd series, pp. 148–52: works for piano; 3rd series, pp. 137–40 and 146: Death of G. Fauré. 'Fauré et le sens de la beauté'.

Portraits de musiciens I (Paris, Plon, 1946), pp. 118–25.

Boulanger, Nadia: 'Opéra de Monte Carlo. Pénélope, *Le Ménestrel*, 15 March 1913, pp. 82–3.

'La Musique religieuse' in *La Revue musicale*, 4, no. 11, October 1922, special no., *Gabriel Fauré*, pp. 104–11.

[Souvenirs de G. Fauré]. Interview with J.-M. Nectoux, *Etudes fauréennes*, no. 17, 1980, pp. 3–5.

Bourgeat, Fernand: 'Festival Fauré, conférence du 4 avril 1908', *Journal de l'Université des Annales*, 10 June 1908, pp. 416–33.

Bruneau, Alfred: 'Au Théâtre des Champs-Elysées . . . Pénélope', *Le Matin*, 10 May 1913.

'La Vie et les œuvres de Gabriel Fauré. Notice lue par l'auteur à l'Académie des Beaux-Arts' (Paris, Fasquelle, 1925).

Brussel, Robert: 'Prométhée à Paris' and 'La Représentation de Prométhée', *Le Figaro*, 4 December 1907, pp. 5 and 6 December 1907, p. 4.

'Les "Lieder" de Fauré', *Musica*, no. 77, February 1909 (special no. G. *Fauré*), pp. 21–2.

Bruyr, José: 'En parlant de Gabriel Fauré avec son fils' [Philippe Fauré-Fremiet], *Le Guide du concert*, 24, no. 23, 4 March 1938, pp. 615–17.

A.C.: 'Opéra flamand. Pénélope', *Le Courrier d'Anvers*, 21 March 1924.

Calvocoressi, Michel Dimitri: 'Les grandes premières à l'Opéra de Monte Carlo. Pénélope', *Comoedia illustré*, 20 March 1913, pp. 559–60.

'Modern French Composers 1. How they are encouraged', *The Musical Times*, 62, no. 938, 1921, pp. 238–40.

Musician's Gallery (London, Faber, 1933).

Carraud, Gaston: 'Prométhée', *La Liberté*, 7 December 1907, p. 3.

'L'Ame harmonique de Gabriel Fauré', *Musica*, no. 77, February 1909 (special no. G. *Fauré*), pp. 19–20.

'Pénélope', *La Liberté*, 12 May 1913, p. 2.

'Gabriel Fauré', *Le Ménestrel*, 82, no. 15, 1920, pp. 149–51.

Castelbon de Beauxhostes, Fernand, et Saint-Saëns, Camille: 'Les Arènes de Béziers', *Musica*, October 1912, pp. 194–5.

Le Centenaire de Gabriel Fauré (Paris, Editions de la Revue musicale, 1945). Articles by Ph. Fauré-Fremiet, R. Dumesnil, G. Jean-Aubry.

Chalupt, René: 'Gabriel Fauré et les poètes', *La Revue musicale*, 4, no. 11, October 1922, special no. Gabriel *Fauré*, pp. 28–33.

Chantavoine, Jean: 'A l'Opéra de Monte Carlo. Pénélope', *Excelsior*, 4 March 1913, p. 2.

Charpentier, Raymond: 'A l'Opéra-Comique. Masques et bergamasques', *Comoedia*, 5 March 1920, p. 1.

Chaumont, Gaby: 'Récit de Mme Chaumont, de Cancale', *Elle*, 29 May 1964, pp. 152–3 (information from the composer's god-daughter, with letters received from him).

Collet, Henri: 'Œuvres nouvelles de M. Gabriel Fauré', *Comoedia*, 26 December 1919.

'A propos de *Pénélope* et *Masques et Bergamasques*', *Comoedia*, 19 March 1920, p. 2.

'Le Cas Gabriel Fauré', *Comoedia*, 31 December 1920.

Cools, Eugène: 'Le Quatuor à cordes, de Gabriel Fauré', *Le Monde musical*, no. 11–12, June 1925, pp. 228–30 (ill.).

Cortot, Alfred: 'La Musique de piano', *La Revue musicale*, 4, no. 11, October 1922, special no. Gabriel *Fauré*, pp. 80–103.

La Musique française de piano (first series, Paris, Rieder, 1930).

'Gabriel Fauré', pp. 133–69. New edn. Paris, Presses Universitaires de France, 1948 and 1981 (complete version of the article which appeared in the special no. *Gabriel Fauré* of *La Revue musicale*, 4, no. 11, October 1922, pp. 80–103. English translation by Hilda Andrews: *French Piano Music. Series 1* (London, Oxford University Press, 1932), pp. 109–39.

'La Dialogue du piano et de la symphonie', *Conférencia*, 12, 1 June 1938, pp. 698–700 [on the Ballade op. 19].

'Gabriel Fauré et la Suisse', *Feuilles musicales* (Lausanne), 7, nos. 4–5, May–June 1954, pp. 73–9.

Croiza, Claire: 'A Gabriel Fauré', *Le Journal*, 16 June 1922.

'Le Chant. Cours d'interprétation: *Pénélope* de G. Fauré', *Le Monde musical*, 30 June 1934, pp. 183–5.

Croiza, Claire: see also under Abraham, Hélène.

Cruppi, Louise: *Avant l'heure* (Paris, P. Ollendorff, 1905) [novel taking Fauré as model].

Curzon, Henri: 'Le *Prométhée* de M. G. Fauré', *Le Guide musical*, 15 December 1907, pp. 779–80.

Pénélope au Théâtre de Monte Carlo', *Comoedia*, 9 March 1913.

'*Pénélope* de Gabriel Fauré', *Le Guide musical*, 9 March 1913, p. 198–9.

Dandelot, Arthur: 'Prométhée à Béziers', *Le Monde musical*, 15 September 1900, p. 266.

Dardenne, Roger: 'Du Cirque d'Hiver à la Comédie-Française. Histoire d'une pièce', *Le Figaro*, 18 June 1927, p. 1 [on *La Passion* by E. Haraucourt, article containing an interview with the dramaturg].

Dauphin, Léopold: 'Gabriel Fauré et le *Prométhée*', *La Vogue*, 15 October 1900, pp. 59–65.

Debussy, Claude: *M. Croche et autres écrits*, ed. F. Lesure (Paris, Gallimard, 1971; 2nd edn. 1987); trans. Richard Langham Smith: *Debussy on Music* (London, Secker and Warburg, 1977).

Deymier, Georges: 'A propos de la reprise de *Caligula*', *Revue d'art dramatique*, 15 November 1888, pp. 243–8.

Doret, Gustave: *Temps et contretemps, souvenirs d'un musicien* (Fribourg, Librairie de l'Université, 1942), pp. 258–60.

Dukas, Paul: 'Chronique musicale, *Prométhée*', *Revue hebdomadaire*, 6 October 1900, pp. 131–40; reprinted in *Les Ecrits de Paul Dukas sur la musique* (Paris, Société d'éditions françaises et internationales, 1948), pp. 505–10.

'Adieu à Gabriel Fauré', *La Revue musicale*, 6, 1 December 1924, pp. 97–9.

Durand, Jacques: *Quelques souvenirs d'un éditeur de musique* (2nd series, Paris, Durand, 1925).

Fabre, Joseph, ed.: *Prométhée*, special nos. of the journal *L'Hérault*, August 1900 and August 1901.

Faure, Gabriel: *Ames et décors romanesques* (Paris, Charpentier, 1925). 'Le dernier enchanteur: Gabriel Fauré', pp. 33–41.

'Gabriel Fauré', *France Illustration*, no. 5192, September 1942, pp. 183–4 (with a letter from Fauré to R. Fauchois).

Mes Alyscamps. Maîtres et amis disparus (Paris, J. Haumont, 1942), pp. 149–59.

'Naissance de *Pénélope* de Gabriel Fauré', *Comoedia*, 6 March 1943, p. 154.

Gabriel Fauré (Grenoble, Paris, B. Artaud, 1945).

'Quelques souvenirs sur Gabriel Fauré', *Revue historique et littéraire du Languedoc* (Albi), no. 6, June 1945, pp. 111–22.

Fauré-Fremiet, Emmanuel: 'Entretien avec Emmanuel Fauré-Fremiet', ed. J.-M. Nectoux (14 January and 11 February 1971), *Scherzo*, 1, no. 8, December 1971, pp. 14–15, complete version in *Association des Amis de Gabriel Fauré. Bulletin*, no. 9, 1972, pp. 7–10.

'Gabriel Fauré my father', trans. Judith Alstadter, *Triangle* (Campbell, California), 66, 1972, pp. 9–11.

Fauré-Fremiet, Philippe: *Gabriel Fauré* (Paris, Rieder, 1929 (ill. edn.); 2nd edn. Paris, Albin Michel, 1957). (2nd edn. expanded to include 'Réflexions sur la confiance fauréenne', 'Notes sur l'interprétation', 'Liste des œuvres', 'Discographie', 'Bibliographie', without ills.). Japanese trans. Yataka Fujiwara, Tokyo, Ongaku-no-tomo, 1972.

'La Genèse de Pénélope', *La Revue musicale*, 10, May–June 1929, pp. 53–8 (extract from above title). Expanded version in *Le Centenaire de Gabriel Fauré* (Paris, Editions de la Revue musicale, 1945), pp. 8–26. Reprinted in *Association des Amis de Gabriel Fauré. Bulletin*, no. 11, 1974, pp. 13–24.

'La Pensée fauréenne', in *Gabriel Fauré* (Paris, Publications techniques et artistiques, 1946), pp. 8–14.

'La Chanson d'Eve de Van Lerberghe-Fauré', *Synthèses* (Brussels), no. 196–7, September–October 1962, pp. 261–72; extracts re-edited in *Association des Amis de Gabriel Fauré. Bulletin*, no. 10, 1973, pp. 7–14.

Fauré-Fremiet, Philippe, editor of Fauré, Gabriel: *Lettres intimes* (Paris, La Colombe, then Grasset, 1951).

Fouquier, Marcel: 'Drame et comédie' [review of *Shylock* by E. Haraucourt], *La Nouvelle Revue*, January 1890, pp. 209–16.

Gabriel Fauré, special no. of *Musica*, no. 77, February 1909. (Articles by G. Carraud, R. Brussel, E. Vuillermoz, J. Saint-Jean (R. de Marliave), G. Pioch, J. Torchet).

Gabriel Fauré, special no. of *La Revue musicale*, 4, no. 44, October 1922. (Articles by E. Vuillermoz, M. Ravel, R. Chalupt, Ch. Koechlin, Fl. Schmitt, R.-Ducasse, A. Cortot, N. Boulanger. Musical supplement on the name of Fauré by L. Aubert, G. Enesco, Ch. Koechlin, P. Ladmirault, M. Ravel, R.-Ducasse).

Gabriel Fauré, special no., *Le Monde musical*, nos. 21–2, November 1924. (Contributions from A. Mangeot, E. Cools, N. Boulanger, E. Vuillermoz, P. Dukas, A. Roussel, L. Aubert, not listed individually in this bibliography on account of their brevity).

Gabriel Fauré (Paris, Les Publications techniques et artistiques, 1946). (Articles by H. Malherbe, Ph. Fauré-Fremiet, R.-Ducasse, J. Thibaud, L. Beydts, G. Pioch.)

Gabriel Fauré, special no. of *Feuilles musicales* (Lausanne), 7, nos. 4–5, May–June 1954. (Articles by A. Cortot, H. Jourdan-Morhange, M. Perrin, M. Favre).

Gabriel Fauré, special no. of *Journal musical français*, 10 October 1964 (brief articles and information from E. Vuillermoz, B. Gavoty, M. Long, L. Aubert, E. Bondeville, P. Descaves, D. Lesur, L. Martini, A. Maurois, D. Milhaud, A. Obey, J. Romains, M. Rosenthal, M. Tagliaferro, L. Aguettant, J. Lonchampt).

Galerne, Maurice: 'L'Ecole Niedermeyer: sa création, son but, son développement' (Paris, Margueritat, 1928).

Gallet, Mme Maurice: *Schubert et le Lied* (Paris, Perrin, 1907), pp. 157–65.

Garden, Mary: *L'Envers du décor. Souvenirs d'une grande cantatrice* (Paris, Editions de Paris, 1952).

Garnier, Paul-Louis: 'Prométhée à Béziers', *La Revue blanche*, 15 September 1900, pp. 141–3.

Gauthier-Villars, Henry (Willy): 'M. Gabriel Fauré', *Revue éolienne*, no. 17, September 1900, pp. 437–9.

'Revue musicale' [Prométhée], *Revue encyclopédique Larousse*, 17 November 1900, pp. 141–3.

Garçon l'audition (Paris, H. Simon-Empis, 1900).

Gheusi, Pierre Barthélemy: *Guerre et Théâtre (1914–1918)* (Paris, Berger-Levrault, 1919).

Gheusi, P. B., ed. Fauré, Gabriel: *Opinions musicales* (Paris, Rieder, 1930).

Gigout, Eugène: 'Gabriel Fauré à l'Ecole Niedermeyer', *Le Courrier musical*, 15 November 1924, pp. 540–1.

Gounod, Charles: *Mémoires d'un artiste* (Paris, Calmann Lévy, c. 1890).

Grétry, Félicien: 'La Maîtrise de la Madeleine', *Musica*, January 1903, p. 62.

Guichard, Léon: *La Musique et les Lettres au temps du wagnérisme* (Paris, Presses Universitaires de France, 1963).

Hahn, Reynaldo: 'Pénélope', *Le Journal*, 11 May 1913, p. 4.

'Préambule pour un festival', conference of 29 April 1914, *Journal de l'Université des Annales*, 15 July 1914, pp. 115–18.

'A l'Odéon' [*Pelléas et Mélisande* by Maeterlinck], *Le Figaro*, 9, 16 et 23 February 1939, p. 5. Reprinted in *Thèmes variés* (Paris, J. B. Janin, 1946), pp. 139–41.

Du chant (Paris, Gallimard, 1957), pp. 57–65: 'Le Parfum impérissable'.

Haraucourt, Edmond: 'Comment fut rétabli en France le droit de représenter la Passion', *Le Journal*, 3 April 1930, p. 1.

Mémoires. Des jours et des gens (Paris, Flammarion, 1946).

Henderson, Archibald Martin: 'Church and Organ Music. Memories of some distinguished French organists', *The Musical Times*, 78, 1937, pp. 817–19.

'Personal Memories of Fauré', *Musical Opinion*, 80, October 1956, pp. 39–40.

Hermant, Pierre: 'Musique de chambre et de piano' in Rohozinski, Ladislas, ed.: *Cinquante ans de musique française*, II, pp. 87–96.

Hill, Edward Burlingame: 'Gabriel Fauré's Piano music', *The Musician* (Boston), 16, no. 8, 1911, pp. 511 and 561.

Modern French Music (Boston, Houghton Mifflin, 1924).

Hippeau, Edmond: 'Musiciens contemporains: Gabriel Fauré', *La Musique des familles*, 25 August 1888, pp. 357–8.

Honegger, Arthur: 'Pénélope. Un Chef-d'œuvre', *Comoedia*, 20 March 1943.

Huré, Jean: *Musiciens contemporains* (Paris, M. Sénart, 1923).

Huvelin, Paul: 'Impressionnistes et symbolistes', in *Pour la musique française* (Paris, Crès, 1917), pp. 299–328.

Imbert, Hugues: 'Profils de musiciens. Gabriel Fauré', *L'Indépendance musicale et dramatique*, nos. 14 and 15, 15 September and 1 October 1887, pp. 393–401 and 425–39. Reprinted in the volume by the same author *Profils de musiciens* (Paris, Fischbacher, 1888).

'Les Nouveaux professeurs de composition au Conservatoire. Ch. M. Widor, Gabriel Fauré', *Le Guide musical*, 8 November 1896, pp. 725–6.

d'Indy, Vincent: 'Gabriel Fauré', *Tablettes de la Schola*, 24, no. 1, November 1924, pp. 2–3 [d'Indy's speech at Fauré's funeral].

d'Indy, Vincent; Duparc, Henri; Roussel, Albert: *Lettres à Auguste Sérieyx*, ed. Marie-Louise Sérieyx (Lausanne, le Milieu du Monde, Paris, Ploix, 1961).

Inghelbrecht, Désiré-Emile: *Mouvement contraire. Souvenirs d'un musicien* (Paris, Domat, 1947).

Le Chef d'orchestre parle au public (Paris, Julliard, 1957) [*Pénélope*, pp. 33–42].

Jaques-Dalcroze, Emile: 'Gabriel Fauré', *La Semaine littéraire*, 10 November 1894, pp. 532–3.

'La Bonne chanson', *Gazette musicale de la Suisse romande*, no. 18, 1 November 1894, pp. 207–11.

Jean-Aubry, Georges: *La Musique française d'aujourd'hui* (Paris, Perrin, 1916), pp. VII–XII: Preface by G. Fauré; pp. 72–81: 'Gabriel Fauré'; pp. 236–52: 'Paul Verlaine et les musiciens'.

Jobbé-Duval, P.: 'Leurs mains. Gabriel Fauré' (ill.), *Bulletin SIM*, February 1911, pp. 5–6.

Jourdan-Morhange, Hélène: 'Gabriel Fauré intime', *Feuilles musicales*, 7, nos. 4–5, May–June 1954, pp. 78–81. Text reprinted, slightly expanded, in the volume by the same author *Mes Amis musiciens* (Paris, Editeurs français réunis, 1955), pp. 22–30.

Jullien, Adolphe: 'Pénélope', *Journal des débats*, 10 May 1913, pp. 1–2.

'A l'Opéra: Prométhée de M. Fauré', *Journal des débats*, 26 May 1917, p. 3.

Klingsor, Tristan: 'Les Musiciens et les poètes contemporains', *Le Mercure de France*, 142, November 1900.

Koechlin, Charles: 'Charles Koechlin et Henri Busser témoins du Prométhée de Fauré aux arènes de Béziers' (Letter from Busser to Koechlin and diary of Ch. Koechlin 'Huit jours à Béziers', 1901, ed. J.-M. Nectoux), *Association des Amis de Gabriel Fauré, Bulletin*, no. 16, 1979, pp. 7–19.

'Représentations de Béziers' [*Prométhée*], *Le Mercure de France*, 143, November 1901, pp. 550–3.

'Pénélope', *Gazette des Beaux-Arts*, July 1913, pp. 77–81.

'Gabriel Fauré', *Le Ménestrel*, 83, nos. 21 and 22, 27 May and 3 June 1921, pp. 221–3 and 233–5 (conference at the Concerts historiques Pasdeloup, Paris, Opéra, 17 March 1921).

'Le Théâtre', special no. *Gabriel Fauré* of *La Revue musicale*, 4, no. 11, October 1922, pp. 34–49.

'La Mélodie' in Rohozinski, Ladislas, ed.: *Cinquante ans de musique française*, II, pp. 23–31.

'Souvenirs' in Rohozinski, Ladislas, ed.: *Cinquante ans de musique française*, II, pp. 378–95.

Gabriel Fauré (Paris, Alcan, 1927, 2nd edn, corrected, Plon, 1949). English translation by Leslie Orrey (London, D. Dobson, 1945). (List of works, bibliography).

'Les Tendances de la musique moderne française' and 'Evolution de l'harmonie; période contemporaine, depuis Bizet et C. Franck jusqu'à nos jours' in Lavignac, Albert, ed.: *Encyclopédie de la musique* (Paris, Delagrave, 1930), vol. I, pp. 56–145 and 591–760.

'Gabriel Fauré musicien dramatique', *La Musique française*, Revue de la SIAMF, 2, no. 3, July 1933.

Ladmirault, Paul: 'La Bonne Chanson', *Le Courrier musical*, 3, no. 13, 31 March and 7 April 1900.

Lalo, Pierre: 'La Musique. A Béziers, Prométhée', *Le Temps*, 30 October 1900, p. 1.

'Les réformes du Conservatoire', *Le Temps*, 22 August 1905 [on this subject, see also articles from 9 and 13 August 1910, same journal].

'Le Quintette nouveau de M. Gabriel Fauré' [op. 89], *Le Temps*, 13 July 1906.

'A l'Hippodrome: première représentation à Paris de *Prométhée*', *Le Temps*, 10 December 1907, p. 1.

'Dolly', *Le Temps*, 28 January 1913.

'Pénélope', *Le Temps*, 15 April 1913, p. 3.

'Prométhée', *Le Temps*, 28 May and 11 June 1917, p. 3.

'Les deux sonates de M. Gabriel Fauré' [opp., 108 and 109], *Le Temps*, 18 February 1918.

'Le Théâtre lyrique de G. Fauré' in *De Rameau à Ravel* (Paris, A. Michel, 1947), pp. 350–61. (Article appeared in *Le Temps*, 5 October 1900 and 15 April 1913).

Laloy, Louis: 'Gabriel Fauré', *Music Lovers' Calendar* (Urbana), vol. II, 1906, pp. 77–80.

'Prométhée', *Le Pays*, 2 June 1917, p. 2.

Larroumet, Gustave: 'Chronique théâtrale' [*Prométhée*], *Le Temps*, 3 September 1900, pp. 1–2.

Lassus, Jean de: 'Pénélope au Théâtre d'Orange', *Le Monde musical*, March 1924, pp. 89–90.

Lefèvre, Gustave: *Traité d'harmonie à l'usage des cours de l'Ecole de musique classique fondée par L. Niedermeyer* (Paris, Ecole Niedermeyer, 1889).

Lefèvre, Gustave and Heurtel, Mme Henri: 'L'Ecole de musique classique Nieder-

meyer' in Lavignac, Albert, ed.: *Encyclopédie de la Musique* (Paris, Delag-
    rave, 1925), vol. II, pp. 3617–21.
Lenormand, Henri-René: *Confession d'un auteur dramatique* (Paris, A. Michel,
    1949).
Lenormand, René: *Etude sur l'harmonie moderne* (Paris, M. Eschig, 1913).
Leroux, Xavier: 'La Musique au théâtre. Pénélope', *Musica*, July 1913, p. 142.
Long, Marguerite: 'Gabriel Fauré–Maurice Ravel, le maître et l'élève, conférence',
    Les Annales Conférencia, 39, no. 10, 10 October 1950, pp. 430–9.
Au piano avec Gabriel Fauré (Paris, Julliard, 1963). (Appendix by Joseph de
    Marliave on *Pénélope*.) Trans. as *At the Piano with Fauré* (London, Kahn and
    Averill, 1980).
Lorrain, Jean: *Poussière de Paris* (Paris, Ollendorf, 1902) [article on *Prométhée*].
Lortat, Robert: 'Gabriel Fauré. Conférence, 23 Février 1929', *Conférencia*, nos.
    16 and 17, 5 and 20 August 1929, pp. 188–98 and 252–64. Text partially
    reprinted in 'Dans le souvenir de Gabriel Fauré', *Les Nouvelles musicales*, 1
    June 1933.
Maeterlinck, Maurice: *Le Temple enseveli* (Paris, Fasquelle, 1902).
'La Chanson d'Eve de Ch. van Lerberghe', *Le Figaro*, 14 March 1904,
    p. 1.
Malherbe, Henry: 'Dolly', *Musica*, no. 140, May 1914, p. 95.
'Pénélope', *Le Temps*, 25 April 1923, p. 3.
'Gabriel Fauré', *Le Temps*, 6 November 1924 [different ideas of the musician].
'L'Opéra-Comique' in Rohozinski, Ladislas: *Cinquante ans de musique fran-
    çaise*, I, pp. 178–83.
'Deux maîtres que j'ai connus' [Fauré et Debussy], *Candide*, 9 December 1937,
    p. 19.
'Le Génie de Gabriel Fauré', in *Gabriel Fauré* (Paris, Publications techniques et
    artistiques, 1946), pp. 3–7.
Mangeot, André: 'A Béziers' [Prométhée], *Le Monde musical*, 15 September 1901,
    pp. 262–5.
'Prométhée et le Roi David', *Le Monde musical*, 8 May 1924, p. 170.
'Gabriel Fauré', *Le Monde musical*, 35, November 1924, pp. 359–62.
Marcel, Gabriel: 'Gabriel Fauré, *L'Europe nouvelle*, 8 November 1924, p. 1501.
Marliave, Joseph de (alias: J. M. Saint-Jean): 'M. Gabriel Fauré', *La Nouvelle
    Revue*, July 1905, pp. 102–4.
'Prométhée', *La Nouvelle Revue*, 1 January 1908, pp. 140–1.
'La Musique de piano de Gabriel Fauré by E. Saint-Jean, *Musica*, no. 77,
    February 1908 (special no. G. *Fauré*), p. 24.
'Pénélope', *La Nouvelle Revue*, 7, 15 June 1913, pp. 513–23; same review
    revised, 1 February 1919, pp. 241–55 and in the book by Marguerite Long
    cited above.
Etudes musicales (Paris, F. Alcan, 1917) I, 'Un musicien français: Gabriel Fauré',
    A. 'Sa musique de piano', pp. 1–34; B. 'Pénélope', pp. 35–60.
Marnold, Jean: *Musique d'autrefois et d'aujourd'hui* (Paris, Dorbon, 1911).
'Pénélope', *Mercure de France*, 16 June 1913, pp. 849–53.

Maus, Madeleine: *Trente années de lutte pout l'art, 1884–1914* (Brussels, L'Oiseau bleu, 1926).

Maus, Octave: 'Pénélope', *L'Art moderne*, 25 May 1913.

Mendès, Catulle: 'A l'Hippodrome. Prométhée', *Le Journal*, 6 December 1907, p. 2.

Méraly, Jean: 'G. Fauré, l'homme et le musicien. La Bonne chanson', *Revue musicale*, no. 16, 15 November 1903, pp. 622–30.

Méry, Jules: 'Opéra de Monte Carlo: Pénélope de M. Gabriel Fauré' [Interview, unidentified press cutting dated 2 March 1913. Bibliothèque de l'Arsenal, Paris, Rf. 58384].

'Le Théâtre à Monte Carlo. L'Art du décor à Monte Carlo' [création de *Pénélope*], *Revue de la Riviera*, 23 March 1913.

'A l'Opéra de Monte Carlo. Les premières *Pénélope* et de *Venise*' [by R. Gunsbourg]. *Musica*, April 1913, p. 74.

Mesnil, François de: 'Nos grands organistes', *Musica*, 1, no. 4, January 1903, p. 58.

Messager, André: 'Gabriel Fauré', *Le Figaro*, 7 June 1922.

Milhaud, Darius: 'Hommage à Gabriel Fauré', *Intentions*, 2, no. 11, January 1923. Reprinted and completed in the volume by the same author, *Etudes* (Paris, Cl.Aveline, 1927). New version in D. Milhaud: *Notes sur la musique, essais et chroniques*, ed. Jeremy Drake (Paris, Flammarion, 1982), pp. 114–16.

Mischa-Léon: 'Opera in Paris. Gabriel Fauré's *Pénélope*. A Master of French Music', *The Morning Post*, 14 April 1923.

Montesquiou, Robert de: *Les Pas effacés* (mémoires). (Paris, E. Paul, 1923).

Morlot, Emile: 'Odéon, Caligula', *Revue d'art dramatique*, 15 November 1888, pp. 231–2.

Niedermeyer, Louis: 'Ecole de musique religieuse de Paris – Rapport annuel', *La Maîtrise*, 1, no. 12, 15 mars 1858, pp. 178–9.

Niedermeyer, Louis and d'Ortigue, Joseph: *Traité théorique et pratique de l'accompagnement du plain-chant* (Paris, E. Repos, 1858; 2nd edn. Paris, Heugel, 1878).

Niedermeyer, Louis-Alfred: *Vie d'un compositeur moderne* [L. Niedermeyer] (Paris, Fischbacher, 1893) (Preface by C. Saint-Saëns).

Nierendorf, E.: 'La Famille Fauré à travers les âges', typescript, 1906.

Nigoul, Toussaint: 'Gabriel Fauré', *L'Ariège pittoresque*, 2, no. 50, 29 May 1913, pp. 1–3.

Panzéra, Charles: 'Clair de lune', *Musica*, no. 29, August 1956, pp. 18–20.

'L'Horizon chimérique', in *L'Art vocal, 30 leçons de chant* (Paris, Librairie théâtrale, 1959), pp. 109–22.

Patrick Campbell, Beatrice Stella Cornwallis-West, Mrs: *My life and some letters* (London, Hutchinson, c. 1922), pp. 126–42, on *Pelléas et Mélisande*.

Pioch, Georges: 'Gabriel Fauré et Prométhée', *Musica*, February 1908, pp. 24–5.

'L'Oeuvre dramatique de Gabriel Fauré', *Musica*, no. 77, February 1909 (special no. *Gabriel Fauré*), pp. 25–6.

'Gabriel Fauré', *Conservatoires et théâtres*, 1, 1 December 1910.

'Une lecture de Pénélope', *Gil Blas*, 7 November 1912, p. 1.

'Pénélope', *Gil Blas*, 10 May 1913, p. 4.

'L'homme', in *Gabriel Fauré* (Paris, Publications techniques et artistiques, 1946), pp. 38–41.

Polignac, Winaretta Singer, princess Edmond de: 'The Memoirs of the Late Princess of Polignac', *Horizons*, no. 68, August 1945, pp. 110–41. Extracts trans. by Hélène de Wendel in *Revue de Paris*, August–September 1964, pp. 97–105.

Poueigh, Jean: 'Prométhée à l'Opéra', *La Rampe*, 24 May 1917.

Pougin, Arthur: 'Théâtre des Champs-Elysées' [*Pénélope*], *Le Ménestrel*, 17 May 1913, pp. 154–6.

Poulenc, Francis: 'L'Orchestration de Fauré' [in *Pénélope*], *Comoedia*, 20 March 1943, p. 4.

[Anonymous]: 'Prince of Wales' Theatre' [*Pelléas et Mélisande*], *The Times*, 22 June 1898, p. 12.

Prométhée. Album officiel, Preface by Fernand Castelbon de Beauxhostes. Text by Henri Gauthier-Villars (Béziers, 1900).

Prométhée, special no. of journal *Le Titan*, Béziers, 25 August 1901 (Articles by Ernest Gaubert, Henry Rigal, Marius Labarre, Pierre Hortala, Marc Varenne, Jean Poueigh).

Prunières, Henry: 'Portraits et médaillons de musiciens . . . Gabriel Fauré', in Rohozinski, Ladislas, ed.: *Cinquante ans de musique française*, II, pp. 367–8.

Quittard, Henri: 'Pénélope', *Le Figaro*, 6 March 1913, pp. 5–6.

Ravel, Maurice: 'Au Théâtre des Arts' [*Dolly*, ballet], *Comoedia illustré*, 5 February 1913, pp. 418–19.

[in collaboration with Roland-Manuel]: 'Les Mélodies de Gabriel Fauré', *La Revue musicale*, special no. *Gabriel Fauré*, 4, no. 11, October 1922, pp. 22–7.

Reinach, Théodore: 'A propos de l'Hymne d'Apollon', *Revue de métrique et de versification*, 1, no. 1, July 1894, pp. 10–16.

La Musique grecque et l'hymne à Apollon. Conférence (Paris, E. Leroux, 1894; taken from the *Revue des Etudes grecques*, June 1894).

'La Musique des hymnes de Delphe', *Bulletin de correspondance hellénique*, 17, August–December 1893, pp. 584–610.

'Une page de musique grecque', *Revue de Paris*, 1, no. 10, 15 June 1894, p. 204–24.

Risler, Emilie: 'Deux interprètes de Fauré: Emilie et Edouard Risler', texts edited by J.-M. Nectoux, *Etudes fauréennes*, no. 18, 1981, pp. 3–25 [Diary of Emilie Risler and letters received from Fauré by Emilie and Edouard Risler].

Roger-Ducasse, Jean: 'La Musique de chambre', *La Revue musicale*, special no. *Gabriel Fauré*, 4, no. 11, October 1922, pp. 60–79.

Preface to Fauré, Gabriel: *Huit Nocturnes* (new rev. edn., Paris, J. Hamelle, 1924).

'L'Enseignement de Gabriel Fauré' in *Gabriel Fauré* (Paris, Publications techniques et artistiques, 1946), pp. 15–22.

Rohozinski, Ladislas, ed.: *Cinquante ans de musique française, de 1874 à 1925* (Paris, Librairie de France, 1925 [2 vols.]).

Saint-Saëns, Camille: 'Une Sonate' [First Sonata for violin], *Journal de Musique*, no. 45, 7 April 1877, p. 3. Re-edited in *Au courant de la vie* (Paris, Dorbon, 1914) and in *Saint-Saëns. Regards sur mes contemporains*, ed. Yves Gérard (Arles, B. Coutaz, 1990).

   'Les Hommes du jour. Gabriel Fauré', *L'Eclair*, 23 January 1893.

   'Louis Niedermeyer', *La Nouvelle Maîtrise*, no. 19, 12 June 1902.

Samazeuilh, Gustave, 'La leçon de l'art de G. Fauré', in *Musiciens de mon temps* (Paris, M. Daubin, 1947), pp. 56–9.

Sarcey, Francisque: 'Chronique théâtrale' [*Shylock*], *Le Temps*, 23 December 1889, pp. 1–2.

Schmitt, Florent: 'Les Oeuvres d'orchestre', in *La Revue musicale*, special no. *Gabriel Fauré*, 4, no. 11, October 1922, pp. 50–9.

   'Gabriel Fauré', *The Chesterian*, 6, no. 43, December 1924, pp. 73–8.

   'Sur Gabriel Fauré', *La Revue de France*, 5, January 1925, pp. 158–65.

   'Gabriel Fauré', *Le Temps*, 21 November 1931.

Schneider, Louis: 'Pénélope', *Les Annales*, 9 March 1913, pp. 208–10.

   'Pénélope', *Le Théâtre*, June 1913, pp. 12–17.

Servières, Georges: 'Lieder français. V: 2ᵉ Recueil et mélodies récentes de Gabriel Fauré', *Le Guide musical*, 44, no. 4, 23 January 1898, pp. 71–4.

   'Gabriel Fauré', *Revue pour les jeunes filles*, 5 April 1898, pp. 270–82.

   'Lieder français, Gabriel Fauré', *Le Guide musical*, 3 and 10 August 1913.

   Gabriel Fauré (Paris, H. Laurens, 1930).

   'Prométhée de Gabriel Fauré aux Arènes de Cimiez', *Le Temps*, 16 August 1939, p. 5.

Séverin, Fernand: 'Maeterlinck et Van Lerberghe, documents inédits', *Gand artistique*, 1 March 1923, pp. 49–54.

Sivry, A. de: 'Gabriel Fauré', *Le Monde Musical* 17, no. 12, 20 June 1905.

Souday, Paul: 'Les Premières. Hippodrome. Prométhée', *L'Eclair*, 6 December 1907, p. 2.

Thibaud, Jacques: 'La Musique de chambre', in *Gabriel Fauré* (Paris, Publications techniques et artistiques, 1946), pp. 23–30.

Tiersot, Julien: 'Gabriel Fauré', *Zeitschrift der Internationalen Musikgesellschaft*, 7, 1905, pp. 45–52.

   Un demi-siècle de musique française. Entre les deux guerres (1870–1917) (Paris, F. Alcan, 1918), pp. 165–72.

Tinan, Hélène, called Dolly de: 'Memoirs of Debussy and his circle', *Journal of the British Institute of Recorded Sound*, nos. 50–1, April–June 1973, pp. 158–63.

Torchet, Julien: 'Gabriel Fauré, directeur du Conservatoire de Paris', *Le Guide musical*, 25 June–2 July 1905, pp. 475–8.

   'La vie de Gabriel Fauré', *Musica*, special no. *Gabriel Fauré*. February 1909, pp. 27–8.

   'Gabriel Fauré', *Les Hommes du jour*, 12 April 1913.

Udine, Jean d': 'Théâtre national de l'Odéon, Pelléas et Mélisande', *Le Courrier musical*. 15 March 1918, pp. 125–8.

Vallas, Léon: 'Pénélope aux Champs-Elysées', *Revue française de musique*, May 1913, pp. 557–60.

Claude Debussy et son temps (Paris, A. Michel, 1958).

Van Lerberghe, Charles: *Lettres à Fernand Séverin* (Brussells, La Renaissance du livre, 1924).

Pelléas et Mélisande. Notes critiques (Liège, Dynamo, 1962).

Véran, Jules: 'Gabriel Fauré et de Max. Prométhée aux arènes de Béziers', *Comoedia*, 11 November 1924, p. 1.

Vierne, Louis: 'Concerts Ysaÿe-Pugno' [First Quintet], *Le Monde musical*, 15 May 1906.

'Silhouettes d'artistes. Gabriel Fauré', *L'Echo musical*, vol. 1, no. 12, 5 December 1912, pp. 1–3.

Vinteuil, Roger: 'Théâtre de l'Odéon. Pelléas et Mélisande de Maurice Maeterlinck', *Le Ménestrel*, 10 February 1939, pp. 34–5.

Vitu, Auguste: 'Premières représentations. Odéon . . . Shylock', *Le Figaro*, 18 December 1889, p. 6.

Vuillemin, Louis: 'Pénélope et les Prétendants', *Comoedia*, 8 November 1912, p. 3.

'Dolly', *Comoedia*, 10 January 1913.

'Trois motets de Gabriel Fauré', *Comoedia*, 5 May 1913.

'Pénélope', *Comoedia*, 10 May 1913.

Gabriel Fauré et son œuvre (Paris, Durand, 1914).

Vuillermoz, Emile: 'Gabriel Fauré', *Le Courrier musical*, 8, no. 13, 1 July 1905.

'Gabriel Fauré', *La Revue illustrée*, 20, no. 14, 1 July 1905.

'La Musique de chambre de Gabriel Fauré', *Musica*, special no. *Gabriel Fauré*, no. 77, February 1909, p. 23.

'Pénélope', *Bulletin SIM*, May 1913, pp. 59–61.

'Opéra. Prométhée', *Le Théâtre et la musique*, May 1917.

'Gabriel Fauré', *Le Théâtre et la musique*, 2, no. 7, August–September 1917, p. 14.

'Pénélope', five reviews: *L'Eclair*, 19 January 1919, p. 3; *Le Théâtre et la musique*, 1 March 1919, pp. 4–6; *Excelsior*, 17 April 1922, p. 4; 16 April 1923, p. 5; 15 December 1924, p. 3.

'Gabriel Fauré', *La Revue musicale*, special no. *Gabriel Fauré*, 4, no. 11, October 1922, pp. 10–21.

Musiques d'aujourd'hui (Paris, G. Crès, 1923) [pp. vii–viii: Preface by Gabriel Fauré; pp. 1–20: 'Gabriel Fauré': articles on *Mirages* and the second Quintet appeared in *Le Temps*, 20 October 1920 and 2 December 1921].

'Le "Pelléas" de Fauré', *Candide*, 11 January 1939, p. 15.

Gabriel Fauré (Paris, Flammarion, 1960. Trans. Kenneth Schapin, discography by Steven Smolian (Philadelphia, Chilton Book Co., 1969).

'Gabriel Fauré, mon maître. Première rencontre, Le professeur. Le critique musical', extracts from preceding book, *La Revue des Deux Mondes*, 1 June 1960, pp. 481–90.

Weil, Henri: 'Inscriptions de Delphe, II. Nouveaux fragments d'hymne accompag-
    nés de notes de musique', *Bulletin de correspondance hellénique*, 17, August–
    December 1893, pp. 569–83.
Wiéner, Jean: *Allegro appassionato* [memories] (Paris, P. Belfond, 1978).

IV Fauré since his death: critical writings

For American theses the reference number is given (where it exists) for the 'Uni-
    versity Microfilm' reproduction service at Ann Arbor and London.
Alexandrescu, Romeo: *Gabriel Fauré* (Bucharest, ed. musicales de l'Union des
    compositeurs de la République socialiste roumaine, 1968 [list of works,
    critical bibliography]).
Almeida, Vieira de: 'La Chanson d'Eve', *Gazeta Musical e de todas Artes* (Lisbon),
    9, July–August 1959, pp. 333–4.
Alstadter, Judith: 'The Life and Works of Gabriel Fauré', Master's Degree, Yale
    University, 1966.
    'Recollections of Gabriel Fauré', *Music Clubs Magazine* (Chicago), 49, 1969–
    70, pp. 12–13.
    'Fauré: the Man and Music', *Music Journal* (New York), 29, 1971.
Aprahamian, Felix: 'Rare Fauré', *Opera*, autumn 1970, pp. 85–6.
Auric, Georges: 'Gabriel Fauré', *La Revue musicale*, 6, 1 December 1924,
    pp. 100–3.
    'La Musique' [Pénélope], *Les Nouvelles littéraires*, 10 January 1925, p. 7.
Austin, William W.: 'Tonalität und Form in den Préludes op. 103 von Gabriel
    Fauré' in *Bericht über den internationalen musikwissenschaftlichen Kongress*
    (Berlin, 1974, Kassel, Bärenreiter, 1980), pp. 399–401.
Barraqué, Jean: 'Ballade op. 19 de Gabriel Fauré', in *Larousse de la Musique*
    (Paris, Larousse, 1957), I, pp. 598–9.
Barthes, Roland: 'L'Art vocal bourgeois' in *Mythologies* (Paris, le Seuil, 1957).
    'Le Grain de la voix', *Musique en jeu*, no. 9, November 1972. Re-edited in the
    collection *L'Obvie et l'Obtus* (Paris, le Seuil, 1982).
    'La Musique, la voix, la langue', conference, Rome, 20 May 1977, in the
    collection *L'Obvie et l'Obtus* (Paris, le Seuil, 1982). In Italian in the *Nuova
    Rivista italiana di musicologia*, 12, no. 3, July–September 1978, pp. 362–6.
Baust, Laurel Joane: 'The great Requiems of Fauré, Mozart and Verdi', SMM
    Thesis, Union Theological Seminary, 1954.
Beltrando-Patier, Marie-Claire: 'Les Mélodies de G. Fauré', state thesis, University
    of Strasbourg II, 1978 (Lille, Service de reproduction des thèses, 1981).
Benevides, Walter: *Compositores surdos: Beethoven, Smetana, Fauré* (Rio de
    Janeiro, Laemment, 1970).
Berger, Jean: 'On Accompanying Fauré', *Bulletin of the National Association of
    Teachers of Singing* (Chicago), 26, no. 4, 1970, pp. 18–21.
Berger-Levrault, Mathilde: 'Les musiciens-compositeurs vus à travers leur écriture.
    Gabriel Fauré', *Musica*, no. 82, January 1961, pp. 50–1.

Bernac, Pierre: *The Interpretation of French Song* (New York, V. Gollancs, Toronto, G. J. Macleod, 1970). Revised, New York, London, W. W. Norton, 1978.

Bernard, Robert: 'Fauré vu de l'étranger', *Revue française de musique*, 4, no. 1, January 1935.

Bertschinger, Walter: 'Gabriel Fauré', *Schweizerische Musikzeitung*, 94, 1 October 1954, pp. 363–6.

Beydts, Louis: 'Les Mélodies' in *Gabriel Fauré* (Paris, Publications techniques at artistiques, 1946), pp. 31–7.

Bland, Stephen F. 'The Songs of Gabriel Fauré', Ph.D. thesis. Florida State University, 1976 (UM 76–28597) 108 pp.

Boëllmann-Gigout [et Ginot Gachet, Jacqueline]: 'L'Ecole de Musique classique et religieuse. Ses maîtres, ses élèves' in Roland-Manuel, ed.: *Encyclopédie de la Musique* (Paris, Gallimard, 1963), II, pp. 841–86.

Borgman, Jean Pawley: 'The Fauré Requiem', Master of Music Thesis, Rochester, Eastman School of Music, 1948.

Bowman, Robin: 'Eight late Songs of Fauré [op. 113 and 118]; an approach to analysis', *Musical Analysis* 1, no. 1, 1972, pp. 3–5.

Boyd, Malcolm: 'Fauré's Requiem; a reappraisal', *The Musical Times*, 104, no. 1444, June 1963, pp. 408–9.

Bres, Sophie: 'Le Scandale Ravel de 1905', *Revue internationale de musique française*, no. 14, June 1984, pp. 41–50.

Bruyr, José: 'Les Mélodies qu'il faut savoir chanter: "Clair de lune"', *Musica*, no. 84, March 1961, pp. 33–7.

'Les grands Requiem et leur message', *Musica*, no. 116, November 1963, pp. 4–10.

Carter, Elliott: 'Gabriel Fauré', *Listen*, 6, no. 1, May 1945.

Chailley, Jacques: 'La Renaissance de la modalité dans la musique française avant 1890' in *Bericht über den internationalen musikwissenschaftlichen Kongress*, Vienna, 1956. Cologne, Ed. Graz, 1958.

Chandler, Theodore: 'Gabriel Fauré, a reappraisal', *Modern Music*, 22, no. 3, 1945, pp. 165–9.

Cheiner, Sophie: 'Ravel–Fauré–Glazunov', *Heterofonia*, 12, no. 3, 17, pp. 8–12 (in Spanish).

Chevalier, général H.: 'Gabriel Fauré à Bruxelles (1888 à 1912)', *Synthèses*, 20, nos. 230–1, July–August 1965, pp. 251–4.

Cobb, Margaret: *The poetic Debussy, a collection of his Song Texts and selected Letters* (Boston, Northeastern University Press, 1982).

Cocteau, Jean: *Le Rappel à l'ordre* (Paris, Stock, 1948).

Cœuroy, André: 'La Musique religieuse', in Rohozinski, Ladislas: *Cinquante ans de musique française*, II, pp. 158–9.

La Musique française moderne (Paris, Delagrave, 1922), pp. 23–9.

Cooper, Martin: 'Some Aspects of Fauré's Technique', *Monthly Musical Record*, 75, May 1945, pp. 75–9.

'The Operas of Gabriel Fauré', *The Monthly Musical Record*, February 1947, pp. 32–6.

French Music from the death of Berlioz to the death of Fauré (London, Oxford University Press, 1951).

Copland, Aaron: 'Gabriel Fauré, a neglected Master', *The Musical Quarterly*, 10, no. 4, October 1924, pp. 573–86.

Corten, Walter: *Le procès de canonisation de Sébastien Bach en France au 19e siècle* (Mémoire de Musicologie, Université libre de Bruxelles, 1977–8).

Cossart, Michael de: *The Food of love. Princesse Edmond de Polignac (1865–1943) and her Salon* (London, Hamish Hamilton, 1978). Translated into French as *Une Américaine à Paris* (!) (Paris, Plon, 1979).

Crouch, Richard Henry: 'The Nocturnes and Barcarolles for solo piano of Gabriel Fauré', Ph.D. Thesis, The Catholic University of America, 1980.

Daitz, Mimi Segal: 'Pierre de Bréville (1861–1949)' *19th Century Music*, 5, no. 1, summer 1981, pp. 24–37.

'Les Manuscrits et les premières éditions des mélodies de Fauré. Etude préliminaire', *Etudes fauréennes*, nos. 20–1, 1983–4, pp. 1–28.

Davies, Laurence: *The Gallic Muse* (London, J. M. Dent, 1967).

Della Corte, Andrea: 'Le Vacanze di Fauré', *La Scala*, no. 89, April 1957, pp. 24–5.

Demuth, Norman: 'Gabriel Fauré', *Musical Opinion*, 71, no. 845, February 1948, pp. 165–6.

Musical trends in the 20th Century (London, Rockliff, 1952).

French piano Music: a Survey with Notes on its Performance (London, Museum Press, 1959).

Dent, Alan: *Mrs Patrick Campbell* (London, Museum Press, 1961).

Desbruères, Michel: 'Le "Prométhée" de Jean Lorrain et André-Ferdinand Hérold', *Etudes fauréennes*, nos. 20–1, 1983–4, pp. 7–17.

Dommel-Diény, Amy: *Trois analyses complètes . . . G. Fauré, 'les Berceaux'* (Neuchâtel, Delachaux et Niestlé, 1963) (supplement to *L'Harmonie vivante*, vol. II), pp. 15–25.

L'Analyse harmonique en exemples, de J. S. Bach à Debussy, vol. XII (Paris, Centre de Documentation Universitaire, Ploix, 1967) (*Thème et variations, Nocturnes*, nos. 1, 6, 13); vol. XIII (Neuchâtel, Delachaux et Niestlé, 1967) ('Prison', 'les Roses d'Ispahan', 'Le Secret', 'Au Cimetière', 'L'Horizon chimérique').

De l'Analyse harmonique à l'interprétation. (2nd edn. Paris, 1980), pp. 86–90: *La Bonne chanson*, no. 4; pp. 98–106: *Thème et variations*, pp. 121–31: 'Les Berceaux'.

Douglas, Wilfred: *Maurice Maeterlinck. A Study of his Life and Thought* (Oxford, Clarendon Press, 1960).

Dumesnil, René: 'L'Enseignement', in Rohozinski, Ladislas: *Cinquante ans de musique française*, II, pp. 209–12 [on the Ecole Niedermeyer].

La Musique contemporaine en France (Paris, A. Colin, 1930; 2nd edn 1949), vol. I, pp. 105–12; vol. II, pp. 130–8 (ed. 1949).

Portraits de musiciens français (Paris, Plon, 1938), pp. 77–98.

'Le Centenaire de Gabriel Fauré', in *Le Centenaire de Gabriel Fauré* (Paris, Editions de la Revue musicale, 1945), pp. 29–35.

'Le Génie de Gabriel Fauré', *Le Monde*, 18 November 1954.

Eigeldinger, Jean-Jacques: *Chopin vu par ses élèves*, 3rd edn. (Neuchâtel, La Baconnière, 1988), trans. as *Chopin: Pianist and Teacher – as seen by his pupils* (Cambridge, CUP, 3rd edn., 1986).

Fabre, Michel: 'Gabriel Fauré dans les Pyrénées', *Revue régionaliste des Pyrénées*, nos. 191–2, July–December 1971.

Faure, Michel: 'La Nostalgie, du 18e siècle chez Fauré, Debussy et Ravel', Thèse de doctorat de 3e cycle, University of Paris IV, 1974.

'L'époque 1900 et la résurgence du mythe de Cythère . . . Fauré et Debussy', *Mouvement social*, no. 109, October–December 1979, pp. 15–34.

Musique et société, du Second Empire aux années vingt. Autour de Saint-Saëns, Fauré, Debussy et Ravel (Paris, Flammarion, 1985).

Favre, Georges: *Ecrits sur la musique et l'éducation musicale* (Paris, Durand, 1966) ['Gabriel Fauré et le théâtre lyrique' pp. 88–92].

Favre, Max: *Gabriel Fauré's Kammermusik. Dissertation der Universität Bern*, Fakultät für Philosophie, 22 February 1947 (Zürich, Max Niehans, 1948).

'L'Evolution du style de Fauré dans les œuvres de musique de chambre', *Feuilles musicales*, 7, nos. 4–5, May–June 1954, pp. 85–8.

Ferguson, David Milton: 'A Study Analysis and Recital of the Piano Quartets of Gabriel Fauré', Educational Dissertation, Columbia University, New York, 1969.

Fortassier, Pierre: 'Rythme musical et rythme verbal à propos de la prosodie de G. Fauré' in *Mélanges d'histoire et d'esthétique musicale offerts à Paul-Marie Masson* (Paris, Richard-Masse, 1955), I, pp. 29–37.

'Verlaine, la musique et les musiciens', *Cahiers de l'Association internationale des études françaises*, 12, 1960, pp. 29–37.

'Le Rythme dans les mélodies de Gabriel Fauré', *Revue de musicologie*, 62, no. 2, 1976, pp. 257–74.

Gavoty, Bernard: *Alfred Cortot* (Paris, Buchet et Chastel, 1977).

Gervais, Françoise: 'Etude comparée des langages harmoniques de Fauré et Debussy'. Thèse de doctorat d'Université. Paris, Sorbonne, 1954. (Paris, Editions de la Revue musicale, 1971 [nos. 272–3]).

'Gabriel Fauré, traditionnaliste et novateur', *Association des Amis de Gabriel Fauré. Bulletin*, no. 15, 1978, pp. 12–17.

'Le Rythme harmonique de Gabriel Fauré', *Association des Amis de Gabriel Fauré. Bulletin*, no. 17, 1980, pp. 25–33.

Gilson, Paul: '*Pénélope*. Première représentation au Théâtre de la Monnaie', *Le Soir* (Brussels), 3 December 1913.

Ginot-Gachet, Jacqueline: *L'Ecole de musique classique et religieuse et Gabriel Fauré*, Mémoire d'Histoire de la Musique, Conservatoire de Paris, 1959 [see above, Boëllmann-Gigout, Marie-Louise].

'Les Représentations lyriques aux Arènes de Béziers, de 1898 à 1911'. Thèse de Doctorat de 3e cycle, Université de Paris IV, 1976.

Golovatchoff, Dika: 'Suites by Debussy, Fauré and Ravel for Piano duet', Doctor-ate of Musical Arts Degree, Indiana University, 1974.

anonymous: *Les Grandes orgues de la Madeleine et ses organistes* (Paris, Alsa-tia, 1958).

Guiette, Robert: *La Légende de la sacristine, étude de littérature comparée* [Sœur Béatrice] (Paris, H. Champion, 1927).

Halls, Wilfred Douglas, 'Les débuts du Théâtre nouveau chez Maeterlinck', *Fondation Maurice Maeterlinck. Annales*, vol. III, 1957, pp. 45–58.

Maurice Maeterlinck. A Study of his Life and Thought (Oxford, Clarendon Press, 1960).

Hermans, Dr G.: 'Les Cinq Chansons de Mélisande', *Le Livre et l'estampe*, nos. 57–8, 1969.

Hertrich, Charles: *Le Génie poétique de Gabriel Fauré* (Saint-Etienne, Edition des Flambeaux, 1945).

Hilson Woldu, Gail: 'Gabriel Fauré as Director of the Conservatoire national de musique et de déclamation, 1905–1920', Ph.D. thesis, Yale University, 1983.

'Gabriel Fauré directeur du Conservatoire: les réformes de 1905', *Revue de Musicologie*, 70, 1984, pp. 199–228.

'L'Enseignement de Gabriel Fauré au Conservatoire', *Etudes fauréennes*, nos. 20–1, 1983–4, pp. 29–35.

Hirsbrunner, Theo: 'Gabriel Fauré und Claude Debussy, oder das Ende der Salon-musik', *Schweizerische Musikzeitung*, 115, no. 2, 1975, pp. 66–71.

'Musik und Sprache bei Gabriel Fauré und Claude Debussy', *Melos*, 42, no. 5, September–October 1975, pp. 365–72 [*C'est l'extase* in the versions by Fauré and Debussy].

'Zum Liedschaffen von Gabriel Fauré und Claude Debussy' in Haselauer, Elisabeth, ed.: *Wort–Ton–Verhältnis* (Cologne, Graz, Böhlau, 1981), pp. 101–8.

Howat, Roy: *Debussy in proportion: a Musical Analysis* (Cambridge, Cambridge University Press, 1983) [chapter on *Mirages*].

Imberty, Michel: *Entendre la musique; sémantique psychologique de la musique* (Paris, Dunod, 1979) [on several *mélodies* by Fauré].

Jandet, Yves: 'Pelléas 40 ans après', *Les Nouvelles littéraires*. 4 February 1939, p. 10.

Jankélévitch, Vladimir: *Gabriel Fauré et ses mélodies* (Paris, Plon, 1938) 2nd edn., expanded: *Gabriel Fauré, ses mélodies et son esthétique* (Paris, Plon, 1951). New edn., expanded: *Gabriel Fauré et l'inexprimable* (Paris, Plon, 1974; new edn. Presse Pocket, 1988).

'Pelléas et Pénélope', *Revue historique et littéraire du Languedoc* (Albi), no. 6, June 1945, pp. 123–30.

Le Nocturne: Fauré, Chopin et la Nuit; Satie et le Matin (Paris, A. Michel, 1957).

La Musique et l'ineffable (Paris, A. Colin, 1961).

Jarocínsky, Stefan: *Debussy, impressionnisme et symbolisme*. Preface by V. Janké-lévitch (Paris, le Seuil, 1970).

'Fauré en Pologne', *Association des Amis de Gabriel Fauré. Bulletin*, no. 14, 1977, pp. 12–13.

Jones, John Barrie: 'The Piano and Chamber works of Gabriel Fauré', Ph.D. thesis, University of Cambridge, England, 1974.

Juin, Hubert: *Charles van Lerberghe* (Paris, Seghers, 1969).

Kidd, James Charles: 'Louis Niedermeyer's System for Gregorian Chant Accompaniment as a Compositional Source for Gabriel Fauré', Ph.D. thesis, University of Chicago, 1974 (UM 74–10279).

Kimpara, Reiko: *Gabriel Fauré et ses poètes*. Edition with commentaries on the poetry used by the composer; French and Japanese text with revisions and variants:

1   'Fauré et Verlaine', *Cahier des études françaises* (Tokyo), no. 3, November 1974, pp. 77–96.

2   'Gabriel Fauré et ses rencontres avec les poètes: Hugo, Gautier et Leconte de Lisle', *Gengobunka Ronshu* (Studies in Languages and Cultures, Tokyo. University of Tsukuba Ibaraki-Ken), no. 13, October 1982, pp. 47–82.

3   'Gabriel Fauré et ses poètes: Baudelaire, Sully Prudhomme et Romain Bussine', *Gengobunka Ronshu* (Studies in Languages and Cultures) no. 14, March 1983, pp. 63–86.

4   'Gabriel Fauré et Van Lerberghe, *Le Jardin clos*', *Gengobunka Ronshu*, no. 15, September 1983, pp. 235–52.

5   'Gabriel Fauré et ses poètes. La poésie d'Armand Silvestre', *Gengobunka Ronshu*, no. 16, September 1984, pp. 99–126.

6   'Gabriel Fauré et *La Chanson d'Eve* de Charles Van Lerberghe', *Faculty Bulletin* (Tokyo, Toho Gakuen School of Music), no. 10, November 1984, pp. 59–83.

7   'Gabriel Fauré et ses poètes symbolistes. I', *Gengobunka Ronshu*, no. 17, March 1985, pp. 119–39.

8   'Gabriel Fauré et ses poètes symbolistes. II', *Gengobunka Ronshu*, no. 18, September 1985, pp. 97–122.

9   'Sur les Mélodies de Gabriel Fauré: autour de ses *Mirages*', *Faculty Bulletin* (Tokyo, Toho Gakuen School of Music), no. 11, November 1985, pp. 21–47.

10   'Gabriel Fauré et les poètes inconnus (Louis Pomey, Marc Monnier, Charles Grandmougin, Victor Wilder et Stéphan Bordèse)', *Gengobunka Ronshu*, no. 19, March 1986, pp. 129–46.

11   'Gabriel Fauré et Jean de la Ville de Mirmont. Sur *L'Horizon chimérique*' (in Press).

Kinsinger, Dan Howard: 'The Seven Song Collections of Gabriel Fauré', Dissertation, Musical Art, University of Illinois at Urbana-Champaign, 1971 (UM 72–12246).

Knox, Roger Martin: 'Counterpoint in Gabriel Fauré String Quartet op. 121', Master of Art Dissertation. Indiana University, 1978.

Kurtz James Lawrence: 'Problems of Tonal Structure in Songs of Gabriel Fauré', Ph.D. thesis, Brandeis University, 1970 (UM 70–24645).

Lafagette, Roger: 'Promenade au pays de Gabriel Fauré', *Revue historique et littéraire du Languedoc* (Albi), no. 6, June 1945, pp. 131–41.

Landormy, Paul: 'Gabriel Fauré (1845–1924)', *The Musical Quarterly*, 17, no. 3, July 1931, pp. 293–301 (trans. M. D. Herter Norton).

La Musique française de Franck à Debussy (Paris, Gallimard, 1943), pp. 174–95.

Landowska, Wanda Alice L.: *Frédéric Chopin et Gabriel Fauré* (Paris, Richard-Masse, 1946).

Lefébure, Yvonne: 'Métier de Pénélope et fil d'Ariane', *Contrepoint*, January 1946, pp. 75–91.

Lesure, François: *Gabriel Fauré* [exhibition catalogue], (Paris, Bibliothèque Nationale, 1963).

Lockspeiser, Edward: 'The French Song in the 19th Century', *Musical Quarterly*, 26, 1940, pp. 192–9.

'Fauré and the song', *The Monthly Musical Record*, 75, May 1945, pp. 79–84.

Lombardi-Giordano, Clara: 'Gabriel Fauré, essai historique et analytique', Conférence, Rome, 10 April 1954, (Messine, Florence, G. D'Anna, 1959).

Loppert, M.: 'Fauré *Pénélope*', *Opera*, 33, March 1982, pp. 250–4.

Lot, Ferdinand: 'Naissance d'un chef-d'œuvre [*Pénélope*]. René Fauchois et Gabriel Fauré', *Gavroche*, 17 May 1945.

Lubin, Ernest: *The Piano Duet, a Guide for Pianists* (New York, Grossman, 1970), pp. 148–51.

Mare, Jeanne de: 'Gabriel Fauré', *Pro Musica* (the Franco–American Musicological Society Quarterly Bulletin), March 1925, pp. 6–10.

Mariotti, G.: *Gabriel Fauré* (Florence, 1930).

Martino, Pierre: *Parnasse et Symbolisme* (Paris, A. Colin, 1967).

Matter, Jean: 'Brahms et Fauré', *Schweizerische Musikzeitung*, 99, no. 2, February 1959, pp. 58–9.

McKay, James: 'Le Trio op. 120 de Fauré: une esquisse inconnue du troisième mouvement', *Etudes fauréennes*, no. 19, 1982, pp. 8–17.

Meister, Barbara: *Nineteenth-Century French Song. Fauré, Chausson, Duparc and Debussy* (Bloomington and London, Indiana University Press, 1980), pp. 1–177 [texts of poems in French and English].

Mellers, Wilfrid: 'The Later Work of Gabriel Fauré' in *Studies in Contemporary Music*, no. 3 (London, D. Dobson, 1947), pp. 56–72. First version in 'The Composer and Civilization', *Scrutiny* (Cambridge), 6, 1938, pp. 386–401.

Meunier-Thouret, Marc: 'L'âme de la musique de chambre: Vivaldi et Haendel', *Les Annales*, 78, no. 253, November 1971, pp. 13–22 [Fauré at the Conservatoire, memoirs of Jules Boucherit].

Nectoux, Jean-Michel: 'Proust et Fauré', *Bulletin des Amis de Marcel Proust*, no. 21, 1971, pp. 1101–20. Revised and expanded in 'Musique, salons 1900', chap. 6 of G. Fauré: *Correspondance*, pp. 194–219, *LTL*, pp. 195–222.

Fauré (Paris, le Seuil, 1972). Revised edition 1986 [list of works, illustrations].

'Gabriel Fauré ou les contraires réconciliés', *Scherzo*, no. 17, November 1972, pp. 7–10.

'Shylock', *Association des Amis de Gabriel Fauré. Bulletin*, no. 10, 1973, pp. 19–27.

Gabriel Fauré, 1845–1924 [travelling exhibition] (Paris, Bibliothèque Nationale, 1974). Portuguese translation (Lisbon, C. Gulbenkian Foundation, 1974).

'Gabriel Fauré. Mélodies'. Texte de présentation de l'enregistrement intégral (Paris, E M I Pathé Marconi, 1974). American translation (Connoisseur Society, 1977).

'Fauré le novateur', *Musique de tous les temps*, no. 18, September–October 1974, pp. 7–11. Reprinted in G. Fauré: *Correspondance*, pp. 337–44, *L T L*, pp. 341–9 and in *L'Auditorium* (Lyon), no. 24, February 1978, pp. 29–30.

'L'œuvre de Fauré et le disque', *Diapason*, no. 191, November 1974, pp. 12–15.

'Ravel/Fauré et les débuts de la Société Musicale Indépendante', *Revue de musicologie*, 61, no. 2, 1975, pp. 295–318 [contains the correspondence between the two composers]. Italian translation by Stefano Bianchi in *All'ombra delle Fanciulle in Fiore. La Musica in Francia nell' Età di Proust*, ed. Carlo de Incontrera (Monfalcone, Teatro comunale, 1987), pp. 158–79.

'Les Orchestrations de Gabriel Fauré: Légende et vérité', *Revue musicale suisse*, 115, no. 5, September–October 1975, pp. 243–9.

'Flaubert, Gallet, Fauré ou le démon du théâtre', *Bulletin du bibliophile*, 1976, no. 1, pp. 33–47 [contains the exchange of letters between the two writers and the composer].

'Works Renounced, Themes Rediscovered: Eléments pour une thématique fauréenne'. Trans. K. and B. Holoman, *19th Century Music*, 2, no. 3, March 1979, pp. 231–44.

'Debussy et Fauré', *Cahiers Debussy*, nouvelle série, no. 3, 1979, pp. 13–30 [contains the letters exchanged between the two composers].

'Manuscrits de Gabriel Fauré au Département de la Musique', *Bulletin de la Bibliothèque Nationale*, 4, no. 1, March 1979, pp. 3–7.

'Fauré et le théâtre, de la musique de scène au drame lyrique', thesis for a Doctorat d'Etat. University of Paris IV – Sorbonne, 1980.

'Fauré, Henry Prunières et la Revue musicale', *Etudes fauréennes*, no. 17, 1980, pp. 17–24 [contains the letters of Fauré and Ravel].

'Musique, symbolisme et Art Nouveau. Notes pour une esthétique de la musique française fin-de-siècle' in *Art Nouveau, Jugendstil und Musik*, ed. Jürg Stenzl (Zürich, Atlantis, 1980). Italian translation by Stefano Bianchi in *All'ombra delle Fanciulle in Fiore. La Musica in Francia nell' Età di Proust*, a cura du Carlo de Incontrera (Monfalcone, Teatro comunale, 1987), pp. 110–31.

'Gabriel Fauré et l'esthétique de son œuvre théâtral', *Revue musicale de suisse romande*, 33, May 1980, pp. 50–9 [extract from 'Fauré et le théâtre', thesis].

'Le "Pelléas" de Fauré', *Revue de musicologie*, 67, no. 2, 1981, pp. 169–90 [extract from 'Fauré et le théâtre', thesis].

See also above, II: *Correspondence*.

Nicolodi, Fiamma: 'Parigi e l'opera verista: dibatti, riflessioni, polemiche', *Nuova*

Rivista musicale italiana, 15, no. 4, October–December 1981, pp. 577–623.

Northcott, Bayan: 'Fauré our Contemporary', *Music and Musicians*, 18, no. 8, April 1970, pp. 32–6 and 38–40.

Noske, Fritz Rudolf: 'La Mélodie française de Berlioz à Duparc. Essai de critique historique', Doctoral thesis, University of Amsterdam, 1954 (Amsterdam, North Holland Publishing Company, 1954 and Presses Universitaires de France). [Study of the first collection of Fauré, pp. 226–41. Edition of the *mélodie* 'L'Aurore' in facsimile, pp. 277–79]. Rev. and trans. Rita Benton (New York, Dover, 1970).

Orledge, Robert: 'Fauré's Pelléas et Mélisande', *Music and Letters*, 56, no. 2, April 1975, pp. 170–9.

'Fauré en Angleterre', *Association des Amis de Gabriel Fauré. Bulletin*, no. 13, 1976, pp. 10–16.

Gabriel Fauré (London, Eulenburg, 1979 [list of works, bibliography], 2nd edn. 1983).

'The two endings of Fauré's "Soir"', *Music and Letters*, July 1979.

Orrey, Leslie: 'Gabriel Fauré, 1845–1924', *The Musical Times*, 86, May 1945, pp. 137–9.

'The Songs of Gabriel Fauré', *Musical Review*, 6, no. 2, May 1945, pp. 72–84.

'Gabriel Fauré: 1845–1924. 1 The Songs; 2 The Chamber Music', *Musical Opinion*, 68, April 1945, pp. 197–8; May 1945, pp. 229–30.

Owyang, Lily Siao: 'The Solo Pianoforte Works of Gabriel Fauré', Doctorate of Musical Arts, Boston University, 1973 (UM–73–23641).

Paap, Wouter: 'En sourdine van Paul Verlaine, Fauré, Debussy, Dipenbrock', *Mens en Melodie*, 1946, pp. 144–92.

Parigi, Luigi: 'Del "lied" contemporaneo in Francia. 1. Gabriel Fauré', *Rivista musicale italiana*, 21, no. 4, 1914, pp. 127–49.

Parker, D. C. 'Gabriel Fauré. A Contemporary Study', *The Monthly Musical Record*, 48, no. 574, October 1918, pp. 225–6.

Patier, Marie-Claire: 'Fauré et le wagnérisme', *Association des Amis de Gabriel Fauré. Bulletin*, no. 13, 1976, pp. 5–9. See also: Beltrando-Patier.

Pennington, Kenneth D.: 'A Historical and Stylistic Study of the Melodies of Gabriel Fauré', Dissertation, Doctor of Music, Indiana University, Bloomington, 1961 (UM–62–1076).

Perrin, Maurice: 'Notes sur Gabriel Fauré', *Feuilles musicales* (Lausanne), 7, nos. 4–5, May–June 1954, pp. 81–4.

Pési, Jacques: *Le Concept de musique pure d'après l'œuvre de musique de chambre de Fauré. Mémoire de maîtrise en esthétique* (Université de Paris I, 1977).

Pitrou, Robert: *De Gounod à Debussy* (Paris, A. Michel, 1957), pp. 79–110.

Pontalba, M.: 'Le Centenaire de Gabriel Fauré', *Canada français*, September 1945, pp. 26–38.

Poulenc, Francis: 'L'Orchestration de Fauré' [à propos of *Pénélope*], *Comoedia*, 20 March 1943.

Rebber Dodge, Mary Lee: 'The Piano Style of Gabriel Fauré', Master of Music Thesis. University of California, 1953.

Riessauw, Anne-Marie: 'Musico-literaire verhoudingen in de Verlaine-liederen van Fauré en Debussy en commentaar bij een catalogus van vocale werken van Europese componisten op gedichten van Verlaine', *Revue belge de Musicologie*, 32–33, 1978–9, pp. 188–97.

Roland-Manuel: 'L'Héritage de Gabriel Fauré', *Revue Pleyel*, November 1924, pp. 20–1.

'La Reprise de "Pénélope" à l'Opéra-Comique', *L'Eclair*, 23 December 1924, p. 2.

Plaisir de la musique, vol. III: *De Beethoven à nos jours* (Paris, le Seuil, 1951), pp. 156–72.

'L'Evolution de l'harmonie en France et le renouveau de 1880' in *Encyclopédie de la Pléiade. Histoire de la Musique*, vol. II (Paris, Gallimard, 1963), pp. 867–79.

Rorick, William C: 'The A major sonatas of Fauré and Franck: a stylistic comparison', *Musical Review*, 42, no. 1, February 1981, pp. 46–55.

Rostand, Claude: *L'Oeuvre de Gabriel Fauré* (Paris, J. B. Janin, 1945). German translation (Lindau, Werk Verlag, 1950).

Rouet de Journel, J.: 'Un Maître de la mélodie: Gabriel Fauré', *Etudes*, 181, 1924, pp. 705–9.

Rowley, Alec: 'The Pianoforte Music of Gabriel Fauré', *The Chesterian*, 12, no. 96, July 1931, pp. 224–7.

Ryelandt, Baron: 'Gabriel Fauré et l'évolution musicale', *Académie royale des sciences, des lettres et des beaux-arts* (Brussels), 23, 1941, pp. 90–5.

Schouten, Hennie: *Drie Franse Liederencomponisten. Duparc, Fauré, Debussy* (Amsterdam, Ulteversmaatschappi, 1950).

Schumacher, Gerhard: 'Fauré und Bach', *Musik und Kirche*, 39, no. 5, 1969, pp. 235–6.

Scott, Earl Keithley Jr.: 'The Requiem by Gabriel Fauré: a conductor's analysis for performance', Doctoral thesis, Indiana, University of Bloomington, 1980.

Shattuck, Roger: *The Banquet Years: the Arts in France, 1885–1918* (New York, Doubleday, 1961).

Sievers, Gerd: '"Pelléas et Mélisande": Sibelius, Debussy, Schoenberg, Fauré', *Musica* (Kassel), 115, April 1961, pp. 171–4.

Siguitov, Serge: 'La Musique de Fauré en Russie', *Association des Amis de Gabriel Fauré. Bulletin*, no. 14, 1977, pp. 5–11.

Gabriel Fauré (Moscow, Edition of Soviet Composers, 1982 [in Russian]).

Solliers, Jean de: 'Les neuf Préludes op. 103', *Association des Amis de Gabriel Fauré. Bulletin*, no. 12, 1975, pp. 5–8.

'Fauré et le piano', *Etudes fauréennes*, no. 17, 1980, pp. 11–16.

Sommers, Paul Bartholin: 'Fauré and his Songs: the Relationship of text, melody and accompaniment', Doctoral dissertation, University of Illinois, 1969 (UM–70–13495).

Soulard, Michel: *'La Bonne chanson', du poème à la mélodie (Verlaine-Fauré)*. Mémoire de Maîtrise de Lettres, University of Poitiers, 1975.

Steinbauer, Robert Anders: 'A Discussion of the Fauré Ballade for Piano and Orchestra, op. 19, 1877', Doctoral dissertation, University of Indiana, 1957.

Stonequist, Elisabeth: 'The Musical entente cordiale: 1905–1916', Ph.D. Thesis, University of Colorado, 1, 1972.

Stricker, Rémy: La Musique française, du Romantisme à nos jours (Paris, La Documentation française, 1966), pp. 32–43.

Suckling, Norman: 'Homage to Gabriel Fauré', The Monthly Musical Record, 74, July–August 1944, pp. 121–8.

'The Songs of Fauré', The Listener, 33, no. 844, 15 March 1945, p. 305.

'The Unknown Fauré', The Monthly Musical Record, 75, May 1945, pp. 84–7.

'Gabriel Fauré, classic of modern times', The Music Review, 6, no. 2, May 1945, pp. 65–71.

Fauré (London, New York, J. M. Dent, 1946).

Suffran, Michel: Jean de la Ville de Mirmont, preface by François Mauriac (Paris, Seghers, 1968).

Swann, Linda: 'The Fauré Requiem', SMM Thesis, Union Theological Seminary, 1958.

Tait, Robin C.: 'Le Quatuor à cordes de Fauré', Etudes fauréennes, nos. 20–1, 1983–4, pp. 37–47.

'The Musical Language of Gabriel Fauré', Ph.D. Thesis, University of St Andrews, 1984.

Tammaro, Ferrucio: 'Mélisande dai quattro volti', Nuova rivista italiana di musicologia, 15, no. 1, January–March 1981, pp. 95–119.

Valicenti, Joseph Antony: 'The thirteen Nocturnes of Gabriel Fauré', Master of Arts Dissertation, University of Miami, 1980.

Van Ackere, Jules Emile: De Kammermusiek en het lied van Corelli tot Debussy (Hosselt, Uitgeven, Heideland, 1967) [in German].

Van Amerongen, Alex: 'Gabriel Fauré's laatste scheppingsperiode', Mens en Melodie (Utrecht), 3, no. 7, July 1948, pp. 204–7.

'Brieven van Gabriel Fauré' [à propos of the collection Lettres intimes], Mens en Melodie, 6, April 1951, pp. 115–18.

'Gabriel Fauré et les Pays-Bas', Association des Amis de Gabriel Fauré. Bulletin, no. 14, 1977, pp. 14–19.

Van Den Linden, Albert: Octave Maus et la vie musicale belge (1875–1914) (Brussels, Palais des Académies, 1950).

Van Der Elst, Nancy: 'Twee Lied Componisten. Fauré en Brahms', Mens en Melodie, October 1949, pp. 308–10.

'Henry Duparc: l'homme et l'œuvre', Thesis (Lille, Service central de reproduction des thèses, 1972).

Van Nuffel, Robert O. J.: 'Charles Van Lerberghe et la musique' in Regards sur les lettres françaises de Belgique, studies dedicated to the memory of Gustave Vanwelkenhuyzen (Brussels, A. de Rache, 1976, pp. 125–43).

Vuiallat, Jean: Gabriel Fauré, musicien français (Lyon, E. Vitte, 1974).

Wegren, Thomas: 'The Solo Piano Music of Gabriel Fauré', Doctoral Thesis, Ohio State University, 1973 (UM–74–11067).

Winter, James H.: 'Gabriel Fauré', Master of Music Thesis, Northwestern University, 1947.

Wirsta, Aristide: 'Un autographe inédit de Gabriel Fauré' in Huglo, Michel, ed.: *Les Sources en musicologie* (Paris, Centre National de la Recherche Scientifique, 1981), pp. 165–7 [on a copy of the Sonata op. 13 with a dedication from Fauré to H. Léonard].

Wiseman, Daniel: 'Gabriel Fauré and the French Musical Renaissance', *Contemporary Review*, 127, 1927, pp. 333–40.

Wright, Craig: 'Rare music manuscripts at Harvard', *Current Musicology*, 10, 1970, pp. 25–33 (à propos of the Second Quintet].

V Literary sources for Fauré's work

The poems, prose texts and dramatic works set to music by Fauré are indicated in the editions which, from their dates of publication, are likely to be the ones he used.

Appia, Adolphe and Thorel, Jean: *Ondine* (libretto) in Appia, Adolphe: *Oeuvres complètes* (Lausanne, l'Age d'automne, 1985).

Baudelaire, Charles: *Les Fleurs du mal*, in *Oeuvres complètes*, I (Paris, M. Lévy, 1869).

Bouilhet, Louis: *Faustine* (Paris, M. Lévy, 1864). – *Dolorès* (Paris, M. Lévy, 1862).

Brimont, baronne Renée de: *Mirages* (Paris, E. Paul, 1919).

Clemenceau, Georges: *Le Voile du bonheur*, play in one act (Paris, Fasquelle, 1901).

Collin, Paul: 'La Naissance de Vénus' in *Poèmes musicaux* (Paris, Tresse et Stock, 1876).

Dominique, Jean (Marie Closset): *L'Anémone des mers* (Paris, Mercure de France, 1906).

Dumas, Alexandre, père: *Caligula*, in *Théâtre complet*, VI (Paris, Calmann-Lévy, 1886).

Fauchois, René: *Pénélope*, lyric poem in three acts (Paris, Heugel, 1913).
    Masques et bergamasques (Paris, Librairie théâtrale, 1920).

Gautier, Théophile: *Poésies nouvelles. Poésies diverses* in *Poésies complètes* (Paris, Charpentier, 1858).

Haraucourt, Edmond: *Shylock*, play in three acts after Shakespeare (Paris, G. Charpentier, 1890).
    La Passion, mystery play in two acts and six scenes (Paris, G. Charpentier, 1890).

Hugo, Victor: *Les Rayons et les ombres* (Paris, L. Hachette, 1857).
    Les Chants du crépuscule (Paris, L. Hachette, 1857).
    Les Voix intérieures (Paris, L. Hachete, 1857).
    Les Chansons des rues et des bois (Paris, Librairie internationale, 1866).
    Les Châtiments (Paris, J. Hetzel, 1870).

La Ville de Mirmont, Jean de: *L'Horizon chimérique* (Paris, Société littéraire de France, 1920).

Leconte de Lisle, Charles-Marie Leconte, called: *Poèmes antiques* (Paris, Poulet Malasis et de Broise, 1858).

Poèmes tragiques (Paris, A. Lemerre, 1884).

Lorrain, Jean et Hérold, André-Ferdinand: *Prométhée*, lyric tragedy in three acts (Paris, Mercure de France, 1900).

Maeterlinck, Maurice: *Pelléas et Mélisande* (Brussels, Lacomblez, 1892).

Sœur Béatrice in *Théâtre*, III (Brussels, Lacomblez, 1902).

Molière, Jean-Baptiste Poquelin, called: *Le Bourgeois gentilhomme* in *Oeuvres complètes* VIII (Paris, Hachette, 1883).

Monnier, Marc: *Poésies* (Geneva, S. Jolimay-Desrogis; Paris, A. Lemerre, 1872).

Régnier, Henri de: *La Sandale ailée* (Paris, Mercure de France, 1906).

Richepin, Jean: *La Mer* (Paris, M. Dreyfous, 1886).

Samain, Albert: *Au Jardin de l'Infante* (Paris, Mercure de France, 1894).

Silvestre, Armand: *La Chanson des heures* (Paris, G. Charpentier, 1878).

Les Ailes d'or, poésies nouvelles 1878–1880 (Paris, G. Charpentier, 1880).

Le Pays des roses, poésies nouvelles, 1880–1882 (Paris, G. Charpentier, 1882).

Sully Prudhomme, René A. Fr. Prudhomme, called: *Poésies. Stances et poèmes, 1865–1866* (Paris, A. Lemerre, 1872).

Poésie, 1872–1878 (Paris, A. Lemerre, 1879).

Van Lerberghe, Charles: *La Chanson d'Eve* (Paris, Mercure de France, 1904).

Entrevisions (Brussels, Lacomblez, 1898).

Verlaine, Paul: *Romances sans paroles* (Sens, Impr. M. L.'Hermitte, 1874).

Fêtes galantes (Paris, L. Vanier, 1891).

La Bonne chanson (Paris, L. Vanier, 1891).

Sagesse (Paris, L. Vanier, 1893).

Villiers de L'Isle-Adam, Mathias Auguste: *Contes cruels* (Paris, Calmann-Lévy, 1883).

Discography

Having published in 1979 a *Phonographie* of Gabriel Fauré listing all the known recordings of his works from 1900 to 1977 (that is, 260 pages of references), I do not think it necessary to give discographical details here, except for the list of piano rolls recorded by Fauré himself in two separate series; not all of these have been re-issued on disc, despite being of such great interest.

A critical selection of recordings is to be found in the two editions of my first book on Fauré (Editions du Seuil, 1972 and 1986).

FAURÉ BY FAURÉ

Barcarolle No. 1 op. 26
Welte Mignon 2773 (1913)
re-issued on long-playing record (microgroove): Columbia USA ML 421 (1950); Telefunken GMA 91 and HT 38; Book of the Month Club (USA) SWV 6033; Recorded Treasures (USA) Welte 678 (1970, with the Pavane); His Master's Voice 153 12845–6 (Fauré historical album) (1975)

Barcarolle No. 3 op. 42
Aeolian Metrostyle 65841 (*c.* 1905)

Berceuse op. 16
Hupfeld Triergon 53081 (1908?)

Nocturne No. 3 op. 33
Hupfeld Triergon 53082 (1908?)
Second version, Welte 2775 (1913)

Pavane op. 50
Aeolian Metrostyle 65303 (*c.* 1905)
re-issued on Blüthner roll 55912 (1928)
Second version, Welte 2772 (1913); re-issued on long-playing record (microgroove): Recorded Treasures 678 (USA) (1970) (with Barcarolle No. 1)

Prélude No. 3 op. 103
Welte 2774 (1913); re-issued on long-playing record (microgroove): His Master's
Voice 153 12845–6 (Fauré historical album) (1975)

Romance sans paroles op. 17 no. 3
Hupfeld Triergon 53083 (1908?)
Ampico 66531
re-issued on Blüthner roll 53083 (1926)
re-issued on long-playing record (microgroove): Allegro 39 (1950); 1573 (1954);
LEG 9021 (1964) and ALL 761 – BBC 28259

Sicilienne op. 78
Welte 2777 (1913)
re-issued on Blüthner roll 55916 (1928)

Thème et Variations op. 73
Hupfeld Triergon 55917–18 (2 rolls) (1908?)
Aeolian Metrostyle 63546

Valse-Caprice No. 1 op. 30
Hupfeld Triergon 55919 (1908?)
Aeolian Metrostyle 64203
re-issued on Blüthner roll 55915 (1926)

Valse-Caprice No. 2 op. 38
Hupfeld Triergon 55920 (1908?)

Valse-Caprice No. 3 op. 59
Hupfeld Triergon 53084 (1908?)
Aeolian Metrostyle 64893
re-issued on Blüthner roll 53084 (1927)

Valse-Caprice No. 4 op. 62
Aeolian Metrostyle 66531 (1905?)

Index of names

Fremiet, Emmanuel (F's father-in-law) 36, 38, 62, 384, 466–7, 508, 519

Fremiet, Marie Ernestine (F's mother-in-law) 38, 404

Freud, Sigmund 311

Friedrich, Gustav 23

Fromont, Eugène, publishers 190, 513, 545

Fuchs, Henriette (Mme Edmond) 21, 27, 67, 114, 225, 507, 533–4, 537

Gabrieli, Andrea 105

Gailhac-Toulza 2, 521

Gallet, Louis 29, 136–8, 173, 192–4, 356, 506

Ganderax, M. and Mme Louis 129

Gandubert, M. 537

Gap 3

Garcia, Manuel 28, 29

Garden, Mary 160, 161, 516

Garnier, Mme Henri 526

Garnier, Suzanne 62, 527

Gaubert, Philippe 85, 260, 425, 428, 468, 533, 557

Gautier, Théophile 18, 20, 64–5, 68–9, 173, 348–55, 529–30

Gauville, Countess de 225, 534

Gaveau 389

Gavoty, Bernard 45, 148

Gédalge, André 264, 266, 434

Gémier, Firmin 311

Geneva 371–2

Gentil, Jules 451, 458, 478

Gentil, Victor 419, 451, 458, 477, 478, 557

Gérard, Yves xx, 295

Gervais, Françoise 227, 229, 236

Gesualdo, Carlo 227

Gheusi, Pierre-Barthélemy 520

Gibert (singer) 129

Gide, André 213

Gieseking, Walter 46

Gigout, Eugène 7–8, 16, 43, 270, 505, 521, 540

Gills, Gabrielle 373, 555

Giordano, Umberto 273, 302, 517

Girette, Emilie (Mimi) (Mme Edouard Risler), 42, 45, 70, 226, 232, 299–302, 347–8, 357, 379–80, 404, 471–2, 515, 549, 551

Girette, Jean 225

Girette, Marcel 147, 223, 224

Gironde, Vicountess de 534

Giulini, Carlo Maria 469–70, 472

Glazunov, Alexander 279, 510, 519

Gluck, Christoph Willibald 135, 315–16

Godard, Benjamin 226, 505

Gomiecourt, Mme C. de 527

Gouin, Mme Jules 538

Gounod, Charles 5, 12–31, 51, 138, 489, 504–5; *Ave Maria* 14; choral music 105; church music 110, 112; *Faust* 8, 15, 503; funeral 511–12; *Gallia* 17; *Lamento* 18; *Redemption* 27; Requiem 25; *Sapho* 136; *Sérénade* 67; songs 64, 66, 76, 354

Gouvy, Théodore 505

Granados, Enrique 495

Grandmougin, Charles 32, 173, 356

Grandval, Vicountess de (Marie-Clémence de Reiset) 504, 531

Greffulhe, Countess Henri (Elisabeth de Caraman Chimay) 34–5, 38–9, 108–9, 131, 145, 169, 172–6, 224–5, 280, 412, 471, 485, 509–12

Grémy, M. and Mme 449, 523

Grey, Madeleine 203, 428, 430, 442–3, 448, 472, 522, 557

Grieg, Edvard 138, 496, 511

Griffith, David Wark 311

Griset, Jules 225, 505, 514, 545

Gropius, Walter 311

Grovlez, Gabriel 403, 547

Grovlez, Madeleine 427

Guédron, Pierre 302

Guichard 14

Guillot de Sainbris, Antonin 27, 107, 508, 537

Guilmant, Alexandre 110, 270

Guimard, Hector 240

Guiraud, Ernest 224, 263

Guitton, Liliane 555

Gunsbourg, Raoul 326–7, 517

Guyon, Louise 536

Guyon, Thérèse 508, 538

Habeneck, François-Antoine 20

Hahn, Reynaldo 76, 151, 156–7, 161, 179, 219, 297, 472

Halévy, Ludovic 19, 79, 269

Halls, W. D. 297

Hamelle, Edgard 112, 394, 456–7

Hamelle, Julien (*Père*) 26–7, 85–9, 95, 117–19, 183, 273–4, 275, 305, 394, 456, 488, 506–7

Index of works by Gabriel Fauré

Page numbers in italics refer to main references; those in bold relate to music examples, and those with an asterisk relate to illustrations.

Printed in the USA
CPSIA information can be obtained
at www.ICGtesting.com
JSHW010929151223
53753JS00031B/68

9 780521 616959